杨东平 许 进 刘 洋 主编

2025 年绿色发展报告
2025 GREEN DEVELOPMENT REPORT

（中文版）

**"绿水青山就是金山银山"的
中国实践、中国创新与中国方案**

Chinese practice, Chinese innovation, and Chinese solutions of
"Lucid Waters and Lush Mountains Are Invaluable Assets"

社会科学文献出版社
SOCIAL SCIENCES ACADEMIC PRESS (CHINA)

图书在版编目（CIP）数据

2025 年绿色发展报告：汉文、英文／杨东平，许进，
刘洋主编 . --北京：社会科学文献出版社，2025.8.
ISBN 978-7-5228-5432-8

Ⅰ . F124.5

中国国家版本馆 CIP 数据核字第 2025FN4958 号

2025 年绿色发展报告（中英双语版）

主　　编／杨东平　许　进　刘　洋

出 版 人／冀祥德
责任编辑／陈凤玲　武广汉
责任印制／岳　阳

出　　版／社会科学文献出版社
　　　　　地址：北京市北三环中路甲 29 号院华龙大厦　邮编：100029
　　　　　网址：www.ssap.com.cn
发　　行／社会科学文献出版社（010）59367028
印　　装／三河市东方印刷有限公司

规　　格／开　本：787mm×1092mm　1/16
　　　　　印　张：44.5　插　页：2.5　字　数：755 千字
版　　次／2025 年 8 月第 1 版　2025 年 8 月第 1 次印刷
书　　号／ISBN 978-7-5228-5432-8
定　　价／198.00 元（全二册）

读者服务电话：4008918866

编　委　会

＊ 本书英文版由吴金华、林世宋、林世宾、凡玉、刘立翔、爱莎翻译。

"绿水青山就是金山银山"重要理念提出二十周年绿色发展成就展

浙江省湖州市安吉县余村："绿水青山就是金山银山"理念的发源地

供图：丝路国际智库曹震、黄文亚

经过生态修复的永定河：全年全线有水，又见水清岸绿

供图：北京市门头沟区文化和旅游局

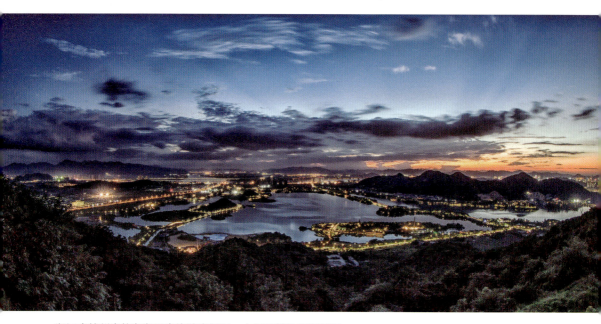

浙江省杭州市的湘湖国家旅游度假区：中国最美生态湖景区

供图：方晨光

白洋淀：全域还清，打造水城共融、城淀相依的绿色发展"雄安样板"

雄安媒体中心王伟倩　摄

湖北省武汉市东湖绿道：中国首条城区内 AAAAA 级旅游景区绿道

供图：田春雨

华洪运河：湖南省"美丽河湖"

供图：岳阳市君山区融媒体中心

贵州省铜仁市梵净山：列入世界自然遗产名录和世界自然保护联盟绿色名录

供图：杨向阳、戴成

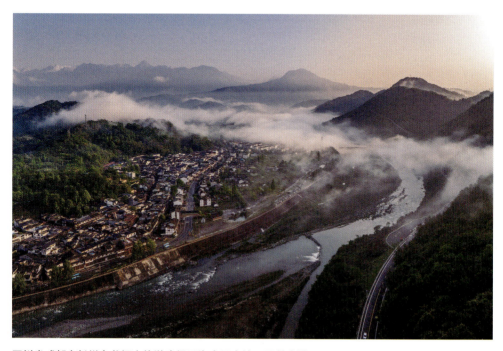

四川省成都市彭州市龙门山旅游度假区海窝子古镇：最美古镇

供图：彭州市人民政府办公室

江西省宜春市武功山明月山旅游区：国家级风景名胜区

供图：郑德华

兴安岭南麓乌兰毛都草原

内蒙古自治区兴安盟融媒体中心毕力格　摄

河北省塞罕坝机械林场：全球环境治理的"中国榜样"

供图：林新民

内蒙古自治区达拉特旗光伏发电应用领跑基地：库布齐沙漠光伏治沙典型案例

供图：鄂尔多斯市林业和草原局、达拉特旗融媒体中心

京东方能源苏尼特右旗"20 万千瓦牧光储 + 治沙综合示范项目"

供图：内蒙古自治区锡林郭勒盟融媒体中心张士霖

内蒙古自治区鄂尔多斯市乌审旗乌兰降勒盖治沙站：毛乌素沙地歼灭战典型案例

供图：乌审旗萨拉乌素文旅开发有限公司

大连金石滩黄金海岸：辽宁省美丽海湾

供图：田大伟

辽宁省营口市美丽海湾：鸟飞湿地的生物多样性保护壮观景象

张配仁　摄

北海市滨海国家湿地公园（冯家江流域）水环境治理工程项目：入选中国特色生态修复十大典型案例

供图：广西壮族自治区生态环境厅韦善康

南京市溧水区晶桥镇曹庄村：江苏省美丽乡村

溧水区融媒体中心朱红生　摄

石家庄市鹿泉区白鹿泉乡东土门村：河北省美丽乡村精品村

供图：《石家庄日报》张晓峰

如诗如画的云南省临沧市临翔区南美拉祜族乡多依村

供图：临沧高新技术产业开发区管委会

云南省昭通市昭阳区永丰镇美丽乡村

供图：柴峻峰

四川省泸州市纳溪区（入选全国"五好两宜"和美乡村试点试验区）护国镇德红村红岩子茶园

马光焱 摄

简阳：城山相映、人水共生的公园城市

供图：四川省简阳市委宣传部

绿色能源供应的北京冬奥村和国家雪车雪橇中心"雪游龙"

供图：北京市延庆区文化和旅游局

充分应用可再生能源的北京城市副中心 · 城市绿心公园

供图：首都图书馆

苏州工业园区：绿色低碳发展"园区样本"

供图：成玉干

长寿经济技术开发区：入选中国"无废园区"典型案例

供图：重庆市长寿经济技术开发区管委会

"太湖之星"：世界首创、具有中国完全自主知识产权的生态清淤智能平台船

供图：吕枫

应用中国绿色技术、设备、标准的埃及新行政首都中央商务区项目

供图：中建八局

"蓝海益路"青年志愿者团队：在马来西亚开展"点亮山区"绿色公益活动

供图：中建马来西亚有限公司

丝路青年论坛·马中合作会议（绿色发展　共创未来）

供图：丝路国际智库

"'一带一路'十年筑　丝路青年添新树"共建丝路青年友谊林活动

供图：丝路国际智库

绿水青山也是金山银山[*]

（2005 年 8 月 24 日）

我们追求人与自然的和谐，经济与社会的和谐，通俗地讲，就是既要绿水青山，又要金山银山。

我省"七山一水两分田"，许多地方"绿水逶迤去，青山相向开"，拥有良好的生态优势。如果能够把这些生态环境优势转化为生态农业、生态工业、生态旅游等生态经济的优势，那么绿水青山也就变成了金山银山。绿水青山可带来金山银山，但金山银山却买不到绿水青山。绿水青山与金山银山既会产生矛盾，又可辩证统一。在鱼和熊掌不可兼得的情况下，我们必须懂得机会成本，善于选择，学会扬弃，做到有所为、有所不为，坚定不移地落实科学发展观，建设人与自然和谐相处的资源节约型、环境友好型社会。在选择之中，找准方向，创造条件，让绿水青山源源不断地带来金山银山。

---

* 2005 年 8 月 24 日，时任浙江省委书记的习近平同志在《浙江日报》"之江新语"专栏发表短论《绿水青山也是金山银山》，后被收录于浙江人民出版社 2007 年出版的《之江新语》。

习近平关于"绿水青山就是金山银山"理念的部分重要论述

绿水青山就是金山银山，我们过去讲，既要绿水青山，又要金山银山，实际上绿水青山就是金山银山。

——2005 年 8 月，时任浙江省委书记习近平在浙江省湖州市安吉县余村调研时提出

中国明确把生态环境保护摆在更加突出的位置。我们既要绿水青山，也要金山银山。宁要绿水青山，不要金山银山，而且绿水青山就是金山银山。我们绝不能以牺牲生态环境为代价换取经济的一时发展。我们提出了建设生态文明、建设美丽中国的战略任务，给子孙留下天蓝、地绿、水净的美好家园。

——2013 年 9 月，习近平主席在哈萨克斯坦纳扎尔巴耶夫大学演讲时的答问

绿水青山和金山银山决不是对立的，关键在人，关键在思路。

——2014 年 3 月，习近平总书记在参加十二届全国人大二次会议贵州代表团审议时强调

必须贯彻创新、协调、绿色、开放、共享的发展理念，加快形成节约资源和保护环境的空间格局、产业结构、生产方式、生活方式，把经

济活动、人的行为限制在自然资源和生态环境能够承受的限度内，给自然生态留下休养生息的时间和空间。

——2018 年 5 月，习近平总书记在全国生态环境保护大会上的重要讲话

绿水青山就是金山银山，改善生态环境就是发展生产力。良好生态本身蕴含着无穷的经济价值，能够源源不断创造综合效益，实现经济社会可持续发展。

——2019 年 4 月，习近平主席在 2019 年中国北京世界园艺博览会开幕式上的重要讲话

绿水青山就是金山银山。保护生态环境就是保护生产力，改善生态环境就是发展生产力，这是朴素的真理。我们要摒弃损害甚至破坏生态环境的发展模式，摒弃以牺牲环境换取一时发展的短视做法。

——2021 年 4 月，习近平主席在"领导人气候峰会"上的重要讲话

大自然是人类赖以生存发展的基本条件。尊重自然、顺应自然、保护自然，是全面建设社会主义现代化国家的内在要求。必须牢固树立和践行绿水青山就是金山银山的理念，站在人与自然和谐共生的高度谋划发展。

——2022 年 10 月，习近平总书记在中国共产党第二十次全国代表大会上的报告

我们讲绿水青山就是金山银山，生态搞不好就不是"金山银山"，反而成了亏钱买卖。

——2023 年 3 月，习近平总书记在参加全国两会江苏代表团审议时强调

让我们积极行动起来，从种树开始，种出属于大家的绿水青山和金

山银山，绘出美丽中国的更新画卷。

——2023 年 4 月，习近平总书记在参加首都义务植树活动时强调

今后 5 年是美丽中国建设的重要时期，要深入贯彻新时代中国特色社会主义生态文明思想，坚持以人民为中心，牢固树立和践行绿水青山就是金山银山的理念，把建设美丽中国摆在强国建设、民族复兴的突出位置，推动城乡人居环境明显改善、美丽中国建设取得显著成效，以高品质生态环境支撑高质量发展。

——2023 年 7 月，习近平总书记在全国生态环境保护大会上强调

中国坚持绿水青山就是金山银山的理念，坚定不移走生产发展、生活富裕、生态良好的文明发展道路，美丽中国建设取得举世瞩目的巨大成就。

——2024 年 7 月，习近平主席向上海合作组织国家绿色发展论坛致贺信

目 录

主　报　告

专题报告

序一
绿水青山就是金山银山：
共建地球生命共同体和清洁美丽世界

顾秀莲

2005 年 8 月 15 日，时任浙江省委书记的习近平在浙江省湖州市安吉县余村调研时，首次提出"绿水青山就是金山银山"的重要理念和科学论断。这一理念将环境保护从"成本负担"升华为"战略资产"，深刻揭示生态保护与经济发展的辩证关系，形成坚定不移走生态优先、绿色发展之路，促进经济社会发展全面绿色转型，加快推进人与自然和谐共生的现代化的绿色发展观，成为习近平生态文明思想的经典论断。

"绿水青山就是金山银山"，这代表着一个国家发展理念和方式的深刻转变，更是中国共产党人对人类文明发展规律、自然规律和经济社会发展规律的深刻洞见，引领着中国发展迈向新境界。同时，这一理念也跨越了西方"先污染后治理"的传统发展道路，得到了国际社会的广泛认同和支持。2013 年 2 月，联合国环境规划署第 27 次理事会通过了推广中国生态文明理念的决定草案，并于 2016 年发布《绿水青山就是金山银山：中国生态文明战略与行动》报告。

党的十八大以来，在习近平新时代中国特色社会主义思想指引下，中国坚持"绿水青山就是金山银山"的理念，创造了举世瞩目的生态奇迹和绿色发展奇迹，美丽中国建设迈出重大步伐。2012 年 11 月，党的十八大将生态文明建设纳入中国特色社会主义事业"五位一体"总体布局，中国共产党成为世界上第一个将生态文明建设纳入行动纲领的执政党。2017 年 10 月，党的十九大通过关于《中国共产党章程（修正案）》的决议，把"增强绿水青山就是金山银山的意识"写入党章，并在大会报告中明确指出，"建设生态文明是中华民族永续发展的千年大计"，"必须树立和践行绿水青山就是金山银山的理念"。党的二十大报告在阐述过去五年的工作和新时代十年的伟大变革时指出，"坚持绿水青山就是金山银山的理念，坚持山水林田湖草沙一体化保护和系统治理，全方位、全地域、全过程加强生态环境保护……生态环境保护发生历史性、转折性、全局性变化，我们的祖国天更蓝、山更绿、水更清"。

2024 年 1~12 月，中国生态环境质量持续改善，地级及以上城市 PM2.5 平均浓度为 29.3 微克/米^3，同比下降 2.7%，连续 5 年稳定达标，空气质量优良天数比例达到 87.2%，同比上升 1.7 个百分点；优良水质断面比例达到 90.4%，首次超过 90%，同比上升 1 个百分点，近岸海域水质优良比例为 83.7%，提前达到"十四五"规划目标，长江干流连续 5 年、黄河干流连续 3 年全线水质稳定保持在 Ⅱ 类；天然气、水电、核电、风电、太阳能发电等清洁能源消费量占能源消费总量的比重为 28.6%，上升 2.2 个百分点，全国万元国内生产总值能耗比上年下降 3.8%；全国碳排放权交易市场碳排放配额成交量 1.89 亿吨，成交额 181.1 亿元。

实践证明，习近平生态文明思想是在世情、国情、社情发生复杂深刻变化的百年未有之大变局历史背景下，对生态文明建设的时代之问、世界之问、人民之问做出的科学解答，为人类可持续绿色发展提供思想启迪和发展路径。因此，深入学习和阐释习近平生态文明思想的时代背景、核心要义、丰富内涵和世界贡献，系统梳理总结"绿水青山就是金山银山"的创新实践，有助于我们深刻理解社会主义生态文明建设的本质特征和基本规律，有助于我们准确领会这一重要思想的深刻内涵与精髓要义，从而更加自觉地走人与自然和谐共生的中国式现代化道路，更加坚定地在习近平生态文明思想指引下努力绘就美丽中国新画卷，共建地球生命共同体和清洁美丽世界。

《2025 年绿色发展报告》（中英双语版）以"'绿水青山就是金山银山'的中国实践、中国创新与中国方案"为主题，由丝路国际智库联合有关机构共同组建编委会编写出版，全面阐释"绿水青山就是金山银山"重要理念提出 20 年来的理论创新、制度创新、机制创新和实践创新，为尊重自然、顺应自然、保护自然，促进经济发展与生态保护协调统一，共建繁荣、清洁、美丽的世界，提供立意新颖、体例完整、逻辑缜密、可读可查的高质量智库成果。

绿水丰涟漪，青山多绣绮。期待更多组织、读者和公众弘扬"绿水青山就是金山银山"理念，争做绿色发展的传播者和践行者！希望有更多的国内外研究机构、智库组织和学者将绿色发展作为研究对象，推出更多实效智库成果，为生态文明建设与绿色高质量发展提供决策参考和理论依据。

序二
绿水青山就是金山银山：
绿色发展的中国实践与全球价值

凌　文

绿水青山是人民幸福生活的重要内容。良好的生态环境是最公平的公共产品，是最普惠的民生福祉。进入新时代新征程，中国生态环境保护依然存在结构性、根源性、趋势性压力，压力叠加、负重前行仍是中国生态文明建设关键期的特征，因而更要确保"绿水青山就是金山银山"理念的科学践行，并培育发展新质生产力来赋能绿色高质量发展。

习近平总书记对生态环境工作历来看得很重，无论是在中央还是在地方工作，都把生态文明建设作为一项重大工作来抓，身体力行推动生态环境治理和绿色发展。早在40多年前，在河北省正定县工作期间他就强调，宁肯不要钱，也不要污染，严格防止污染搬家、污染下乡。在福建、浙江工作期间，他对生态环境保护进行了系统的实践探索和理论思考，提出"生态兴则文明兴""绿水青山就是金山银山"等前瞻性论断，领导厦门市筼筜湖综合治理和福建创建生态省，打造"绿色浙江"，深入推进"千村示范、万村整治"工程。

党的十八大以来，以习近平同志为核心的党中央把生态文明建设作为关系中华民族永续发展的根本大计，统筹推进"五位一体"总体布局、协调推进"四个全面"战略布局，大力推进生态文明理论创新、实践创新、制度创新，污染防治攻坚战持续推进，中央生态环保督察全面开展，长江、黄河大保护深入实施，对山水林田湖草沙实施一体化保护和系统治理，自然保护地体系加快建设，中国生态文明建设发生历史性、转折性、全局性变化，节约资源和保护环境的空间格局、产业结构、生产方式、生活方式正在逐步形成，为 2035 年生态环境根本好转、美丽中国建设目标基本实现奠定坚实基础。

伟大思想引领伟大实践。进入新时代以来，作为世界上最大的发展中国家，中国生态文明建设取得举世瞩目的重大成就，根本在于以习近平同志为核心的党中央坚强领导，根本在于习近平生态文明思想的科学指引。习近平生态文明思想继承发展马克思主义生态观蕴含的唯物的、辩证的、实践的生态哲学思维和方法，汲取中华优秀传统文化中的生态智慧，借鉴西方工业化进程中的经验教训，系统阐释和科学谋划了生态文明建设的战略定位、目标任务、总体思路、重大原则、制度保障等，为新时代美丽中国建设提供了根本遵循和行动指南。

进一步看，绿色低碳发展是国际潮流所向、大势所趋，习近平生态文明思想为中国带来一场"绿水青山就是金山银山"的变革性实践，取得举世瞩目的突破性进展和标志性成就并惠及全球，凝结了对发展人类文明和清洁美丽世界的睿智思考和深刻洞见。中国倡议国际社会要追求人与自然和谐共生、追求绿色发展繁荣、追求热爱自然情怀、追求科学治理精神、追求携手合作应对，这是构建人类命运共同体理念在生态文明领域的体现，为人类文明可持续发展提供经典案例与重要指引。

当前，国内外学术界将绿色发展作为重要研究主题，中国绿色发展实践是其中的研究热点，但围绕习近平生态文明思想的研究和阐释，尤其是关于中国绿色发展的智库报告仍需要进一步丰富丰满，促进更多读者系统了解中国生态文明建设和绿色发展的实践经验及最新成效。丝路国际智库联合有关机构组建编委会，编写出版《2025 年绿色发展报告》（中英双语版），在整合丝路国际智库关于绿色丝绸之路建设和绿色国际合作的智库成果基础上，总结中国在生态环境保护、构建绿色发展空间、绿色低碳转型、绿色国际合作等领域的主要成效和创新举措，深度分析有关部门重点推荐、编委会专题调研、在国内外具有一定影响力的 200 多个绿色发展典型案例，阐述青年群体参与绿色国际合作的创新实践，向广大读者呈现中国共产党领导下的中国新时代绿色发展波澜壮阔的奋斗诗篇，用智库成果诠释人与自然和谐共生的中国方案，为推进中国式现代化和共建人类命运共同体提供决策参考和理论依据。

习近平总书记指出，"唯有携手合作，我们才能有效应对气候变化、海洋污染、生物保护等全球性环境问题"，"只有并肩同行，才能让绿色发展理念深入人心、全球生态文明之路行稳致远"。期待更多国内外研究机构、专家学者将中国绿色发展作为研究对象，将中国生态文明建设和绿色发展的成熟经验推广到世界各地，促进全球环境治理体系变革和发展方式绿色转型，展现可信、可爱、可敬的中国形象，让国际社会更好地读懂中国、理解中国。

序三
绿水青山"生金" 美丽中国可期

杜祥琬

2025 年是"绿水青山就是金山银山"理念提出 20 周年。作为植根中国大地、符合中国实际、具有中国气派的原创理论,"绿水青山就是金山银山"理念科学阐释了经济社会绿色高质量发展和生态环境高水平保护的共生关系,深刻揭示了保护生态环境就是保护生产力、改善生态环境就是发展生产力的硬道理,系统重构工业革命以来人类生产力增长与生态危机加剧这一失衡关系,有效破解发展与保护的"二元悖论"。尤其是党的十八大以来,以习近平同志为核心的党中央把生态文明建设作为关系中华民族永续发展的根本大计,开展了一系列开创性工作,决心之大、力度之大、成效之大前所未有,中国绿色发展成就举世瞩目,成为新时代党和国家事业取得历史性成就、发生历史性变革的显著标志。

传承马克思主义发展观和中华优秀传统文化

"绿水青山就是金山银山"理念的孕育、实践、形成和发展,经历了地方经验提炼、哲学概念提出、理论思想升华的发展历程。

习近平同志对绿色发展历来非常重视,在正定、厦门、宁德、福建、浙江、上海等地工作期间,都把相关工作作为重大事项来抓。1997 年 4 月,习近平同志在福建省三明市常口村调研时就提出:"青山绿水是无价之宝,山区要画好'山水画',做好山水田文章。"2002 年,习近平同志在福建省担任省长时就提出福建要建设中国首个生态省。2004 年 7 月,时任浙江省委书记的习近平同志在浙江省"千村示范、万村整治"工作现场会上指出,"千村示范、万村整治"作为一项"生态工程",是推动生态省建设的有效载体,既保护了"绿水青山",又带来了"金山银山"。

2005 年 8 月 15 日，习近平同志到浙江省湖州市安吉县余村考察调研，以充满前瞻性的战略眼光，首次提出"绿水青山就是金山银山"理念，这一理念表达了中国人对优美自然的理解、热爱和敬畏，是传承马克思主义基本原理、凝聚中国传统文化精髓的精神财富，蕴含着思想伟力和磅礴生命力。

进入新时代以来，"绿水青山就是金山银山"理念的内涵和实践不断深化。党的十九大将"必须树立和践行绿水青山就是金山银山的理念"写入大会报告，将其作为新时代坚持和发展中国特色社会主义的基本方略之一。党的十九大通过的《中国共产党章程（修正案）》，把"增强绿水青山就是金山银山的意识"写入党章，鲜明展示了中国共产党领导全国各族人民绿色发展的坚定决心。2021 年 11 月，"必须坚持绿水青山就是金山银山的理念"写入《中共中央关于党的百年奋斗重大成就和历史经验的决议》，成为向着全面建成社会主义现代化强国的第二个百年奋斗目标迈进的重要指导思想。

进一步看，以"绿水青山就是金山银山"理念为核心的习近平生态文明思想指导中国昂首阔步于绿色发展的现代化之路，绿水青山既是自然财富、生态财富，又是社会财富、经济财富，保护生态环境就是保护自然价值、增值自然资本和培育新质生产力，有效破解"先污染后治理"传统发展模式的路径依赖，将生态环境保护从"成本支出"转化为"发展红利"，为中国和全球可持续发展提供了理论遵循和实践路径。

智库成果阐释绿色发展中国方案

在以习近平同志为核心的党中央坚强领导下，中国各地区各部门各行业统筹产业结构调整、污染治理、生态保护，应对气候变化，积极稳妥推进碳达峰碳中和，绿色低碳转型展现新气象，高质量发展底色更加鲜明。2025 年第一季度，中国绿色发展继续稳中向好，"绿水青山就是金山银山"理念形成更加广泛的共识和行动，风电、光伏发电合计新增装机容量 7433 万千瓦，占新增发电装机总容量的比重达 86.7%，风电、光伏发电合计装机容量达 14.8 亿千瓦，历史性超过火电装机规模；绿色低碳产业销售总收入同比增长 13.6%，较 2024 年平均水平高出 11.5 个百分点，绿色低碳产业新办企业户数同比增长 19.3%，较上年同期提高 12.3

个百分点；企业购进环保治理服务总金额同比增长 11%，其中，制造业购进金额同比增长 16.5%，节能、环保等绿色技术推广服务销售收入同比分别增长 28.9% 和 17.6%，绿色治理投入继续呈快速增长态势。

在"绿水青山就是金山银山"理念提出 20 年之际，丝路国际智库联合有关机构组建编委会，编写出版《2025 年绿色发展报告》（中英双语版），既是对过去中国各地践行习近平生态文明思想的成效经验总结的"承前"，也是传播习近平生态文明思想，建构中国绿色发展知识体系，建言美丽中国和美丽世界建设的"启后"，具有较强的学术价值和社会价值。2025 年 5 月 20 日，《2025 年绿色发展报告》（中英双语版）在北京国家会议中心预发布，得到国内外政产学研投媒各界人士与公众的广泛关注和认可，编委会吸纳各方意见，形成目前正式出版的中英文报告，进一步丰富研究和阐释习近平生态文明思想的智库成果体系。

知行合一，贵在行动。做好美丽中国这篇大文章需要持之以恒，久久为功，发挥人民群众主体作用，深化习近平生态文明思想大众化传播，始终把绿色发展作为解决生态环境问题的治本之策，同步实现百姓富、生态美。期待更多专业机构将绿色发展作为研究对象，推出更多实效智库成果，做"绿水青山就是金山银山"理念的积极传播者和模范践行者。

序四

"绿水青山就是金山银山"理念提出 20 年：新时代美丽中国建设的 理论创新与行动指南

杨东平　　刘　洋

　　人类进入工业文明时代以来，在创造巨大物质财富的同时，也加速了对自然资源的攫取，打破了地球生态系统平衡，人与自然深层次矛盾日益显现。近年来，气候变化、生物多样性丧失、荒漠化加剧、极端气候事件频发，给人类生存和发展带来严峻挑战。浙江省湖州市安吉县余村是"绿水青山就是金山银山"理念的发源地。2005 年，时任浙江省委书记的习近平在余村首次提出"绿水青山就是金山银山"理念，既为余村从"石头经济"向"绿色经济"蜕变指明方向，也为中国生态文明建设提供理论支撑。20 年来，余村大力发展生态农业、乡村旅游、文创产业、民宿经济，走出生态环境保护和特色产业培育并行不悖的绿色发展范式，获得全国文明村、中国美丽休闲乡村、全国乡村旅游重点村、联合国世界旅游组织"最佳旅游乡村"等荣誉，成为乡村振兴的样本，向世人昭示：绿水青山与金山银山可以相互贯通、相得益彰。

　　建设生态文明，关系人民福祉，关乎民族未来。新中国成立以来，中国不断深化对生态文明建设的规律性认识和行动。特别是党的十八大以来，以习近平同志为核心的党中央把生态文明建设作为关系中华民族永续发展的根本大计，谋划开展一系列具有根本性、开创性、长远性的工作，生态文明之路越走越笃定、越走越宽广，在中华大地上不断书写新的绿色奇迹，绿色成为新时代中国的鲜明底色，绿色发展成为中国式现代化的显著特征。

完善生态文明制度机制，形成绿色发展中国方案

制度机制是守护绿水青山和实现金山银山的重要力量。党的十八大以来，中国印发实施《关于加快推进生态文明建设的意见》《生态文明体制改革总体方案》及几十项具体改革方案，逐步建立起生态环境保护、自然资源资产产权、国土空间开发保护、空间规划体系、资源总量管理和全面节约、资源有偿使用和生态补偿、生态文明绩效评价考核和责任追究等基础制度，中国特色社会主义生态文明建设的"四梁八柱"制度体系基本形成，全面深化生态文明领域改革实现由局部探索、破冰突围向系统集成、全面深化转变，生态环境治理体系和治理能力现代化水平明显提高。

经过数十年的探索，中国务实管用、严格严密的生态环境保护法律体系基本形成。从 1978 年首次将"国家保护环境和自然资源，防治污染和其他公害"写入《中华人民共和国宪法》，到 1989 年《中华人民共和国环境保护法》通过，生态环境保护工作逐步进入法治化轨道。21 世纪以来，中国颁布一系列生态环境保护领域的法律法规、部门规章和规范性文件、地方性法规和规章等。进入新时代以来，党中央要求用最严格制度和最严密法治保护生态环境，党委领导、政府主导、企业主体、社会组织和公众共同参与的生态环境保护体系更加严密健全，全党全国推进生态文明建设的自觉性主动性不断增强。中国现行有效的生态环境类法律 30 余部、行政法规 100 多件、地方性法规 1000 余件，涵盖大气、水、土壤、噪声等污染防治领域以及长江、湿地、黑土地等重要生态系统和要素。

生态环境保护筑就美丽中国

1973 年 8 月，国务院召开第一次全国环境保护会议，生态环境保护摆上国家重要议事日程。改革开放激发发展活力，但在中国经济高速发展取得巨大成就的同时，也积累了一些生态环境问题。从确立保护环境为基本国策，到实施可持续发展战略，再到建设资源节约型和环境友好型社会，生态环境保护的战略地位不断提升。比如，应对生态环境挑战，中国投入大量资金、科研力量和社会资源，重点治理太湖、巢湖、滇池三大湖泊，大力治理酸雨等污染问题。

党的十八大以来，在党中央的领导下，中国将解决突出生态环境问题作为民生优先领域，打响史无前例、规模巨大的污染防治攻坚战，形成精准、科学、依法治污的方法经验，生态环境质量得到明显改善，人民群众的获得感、幸福感和安全感不断增强。2023 年，中国环境污染治理投资总额为 8723.4 亿元，占国内生产总值的 0.7%，占全社会固定资产投资总额的 1.7%。进一步看，中国是全球第一个大规模开展 PM2.5 治理的发展中国家，也是全球空气质量改善速度最快的国家；河湖面貌实现根本性改善，地表水优良水质断面比例接近发达国家水平；土壤环境风险得到有效管控，城乡生活垃圾分类和集中收集处理能力不断提升，化肥农药使用量持续减少，如期实现固体废物"零进口"目标。

生态保护修复和国土空间治理筑牢生态安全屏障

新中国成立之初，全国森林覆盖率仅 8.6%，人民群众饱受风沙肆虐、水土流失之苦。20 世纪 50 年代以来，党中央号召"绿化祖国"，启动生态保护修复事业。1978 年，党中央、国务院做出在西北、华北、东北风沙危害和水土流失重点地区建设大型防护林的战略决策，至今已在祖国北方建起一道绵亘万里的绿色长城，重点治理区实现由"沙进人退"到"绿进沙退"的历史性转变。同时，天然林保护工程、退耕还林还草工程等，让荒山披锦绣，沙漠变绿洲。正如习近平总书记指出的，"人的命脉在田，田的命脉在水，水的命脉在山，山的命脉在土，土的命脉在林和草，这个生命共同体是人类生存发展的物质基础"。

进入新时代以来，中国从生态系统整体性出发，科学划定生态保护红线，建立以国家公园为主体的自然保护地体系，加强大江大河和重要湖泊湿地及海岸带生态保护，统筹山水林田湖草沙一体化保护和系统治理，实施重要生态系统保护和修复重大工程，定期开展全国生态状况调查评估，科学开展大规模国土绿化行动，国土空间生态保护修复逐步实现由单一要素向系统治理、由工程措施为主向自然恢复为主、由末端治理向全链条管理、由依靠财政支持向多元化投入的转变，从山顶到海洋、从高原到平原、从国家到地方的生态保护修复"大蓝图"基本形成。

绿色低碳转型稳步推进碳达峰碳中和

新质生产力即绿色生产力，推动经济社会发展绿色化、低碳化是实现高质量发展的关键环节。在习近平生态文明思想的指引下，中国全方位、全领域、全地域构建覆盖生产、分配、流通、消费各个环节的绿色生产生活方式，以创新驱动为引领塑造经济发展新动能新优势，以资源环境刚性约束推动产业结构深度调整，在"共抓大保护、不搞大开发"理念引领下推动长江经济带、黄河流域、京津冀地区、长三角地区、粤港澳大湾区、成渝地区双城经济圈等重点区域率先建设绿色发展高地，将碳达峰碳中和纳入生态文明建设整体布局和经济社会发展全局，建设全国碳排放权交易市场和全国温室气体自愿减排交易市场，探索生态产品价值实现路径，协同推进降碳、减污、扩绿、增长，加快构建绿色低碳循环发展的现代化经济体系。

2013～2023年，中国以年均3.3%左右的能源消费增速支撑年均6.1%的经济增长，能耗强度累计下降超过26.1%，成为全球能耗强度降低最快的国家之一。2024年，中国非化石能源消费占能源消费总量的比重比上年提高1.8个百分点，水电、核电、风电和太阳能发电占比提高到32.6%；推动大规模设备更新和消费品以旧换新，更多绿色低碳节能设备、产品便利群众生产生活；国家层面累计培育6430家绿色工厂，带动地方累计培育省市层面绿色工厂1.6万余家，绿色制造体系不断完善；国家层面累计培育491家绿色工业园区，单位工业增加值能耗为全国平均水平的2/3，万元工业增加值用水量为全国平均水平的1/4，平均工业固废处置利用率超过95%，成为绿色低碳发展的示范样板。

共建清洁美丽世界和绿色丝绸之路

"人类生活在同一个地球村里，生活在历史和现实交汇的同一个时空里，越来越成为你中有我、我中有你的命运共同体。"习近平主席以宏阔的全球视野和深厚的人文情怀，提出全球发展倡议、全球安全倡议、全球文明倡议，着重强调"完善全球环境治理，积极应对气候变化，构建人与自然生命共同体"，为全球共同营造和谐宜居的人类家园提供坚实支撑。作为负责任的发展中大国，中国与世界携手同行，推进全球环境与气候治理，共同落实联合国2030年可持续发展议程，维护公平合理、合作共赢的全球环境治理体系。中国广泛开展绿色国际合作，共享绿色技术、经验和资源，加强绿色标准与合格评定国际合作，提高境外项目环境可持续性，鼓励绿色低碳产品进出口，为全球绿色低碳转型注入澎湃动力。中国引领全面平衡有效执行"昆蒙框架"，支持发展中国家生物多样性保护事业。中国开展生态环境保护多层面交流合作，共建上海合作组织环保信息共享平台等载体，拓展双多边对话合作渠道和机制，将合作共识转化为全球绿色发展的务实行动和积极成效。

作为最受欢迎的国际公共产品和最大规模的国际合作平台，"一带一路"既是一条开放发展之路，也是一条绿色发展之路。2017 年 5 月，习近平主席在第一届"一带一路"国际合作高峰论坛上指出："要践行绿色发展的新理念，倡导绿色、低碳、循环、可持续的生产生活方式，加强生态环保合作，建设生态文明，共同实现 2030 年可持续发展目标。"中国积极推动建设绿色丝绸之路，与联合国环境规划署签署《关于建设绿色"一带一路"的谅解备忘录》，与 31 个共建国家共同发起"一带一路"绿色发展伙伴关系倡议，与 32 个共建国家共同建立"一带一路"能源合作伙伴关系，落实"一带一路"绿色投资原则，深化绿色基建、绿色能源、绿色交通等领域合作，加大对"一带一路"绿色发展国际联盟的支持，举办"一带一路"绿色创新大会，建设光伏产业对话交流机制和绿色低碳专家网络，积极帮助共建国家探索最符合其国家利益所需的绿色发展模式。

智库成果诠释"绿水青山就是金山银山"

阔步绿色发展新征程，丝路国际智库联合有关机构共同组建编委会，编撰出版《2025 年绿色发展报告》（中英双语版），阐释以"绿水青山就是金山银山"理念为核心的中国绿色发展的理论创新、制度创新、机制创新和实践创新。总的来看，本报告的编撰出版具有如下价值和意义。

1. 廿年回顾，成果总结

"绿水青山就是金山银山"理念提出 20 年以来，中国将"美丽中国"纳入强国目标、"生态文明"纳入"五位一体"总体布局、"人与自然和谐共生"纳入现代化方略、"绿色"纳入新发展理念、"污染防治"纳入三大攻坚战，坚定走绿色发展之路，并为发展中国家平衡经济发展和生态保护提供具有借鉴性、可操作性的中国方案。本报告以习近平生态文明思想引领构建人类命运共同体为指引，通过数据分析、现状总结、挑战梳理、对策建议等实证研究，形成以20年为研究视角且兼顾最新成效及战略目标的绿色发展智库成果，进一步丰富国内外有关智库成果体系。

2. 引领示范，创新成果

在距离2035年基本实现社会主义现代化仅有十年的冲刺阶段，"十四五"规划即将收官、"十五五"规划正在谋划的关键时期，"绿水青山就是金山银山"理念提出和践行20年的全新起点，结合党的二十届三中全会提出的"聚焦建设美丽中国，加快经济社会发展全面绿色转型，健全生态环境治理体系，推进生态优先、节约集约、绿色低碳发展，促进人与自然和谐共生"的战略部署，本报告总结"绿水青山就是金山银山"的中国实践、中国创新与中国方案，提出对策建议和未来展望，为国内外政产学研投媒各界及广大读者提供绿色高质量发展的路径指南、决策参考和理论依据。

3. 决策参考，谋划未来

面对百年未有之大变局，本报告充分把握绿色发展的全球趋势，结合问题导向、战略导向、需求导向、创新导向，围绕制度机制建设、生态环境保护、国土空间治理、绿色低碳转型、绿色国际合作等五大领域和若干热点专题，开创性开展中国绿色发展的顶层设计、实践创新、典型案例等实证研究，打磨、推出一批高质量、具有国际影响力智库成果，为中国绿色发展鼓劲发声，讲好绿色发展中国故事，围绕成果编撰、出版、发布、传播、研讨、活动、项目等系列工作推进，进而打造绿色发展的"全球智库+产学研用合作平台"。

绿水逶迤去，青山相向开。在习近平生态文明思想的科学引领下，中国走出一条绿色发展的光明之路，天蓝、地绿、水净、人与自然和谐共生的美丽中国梦想正一步一步成为现实。在新时代新征程上，中国坚定不移走绿色、低碳、可持续发展之路，以中国智慧、中国担当、中国方案、中国行动推动世界走向生态文明新时代，必将为保护地球家园做出新的更大贡献。

丝路国际智库、丝路青年论坛是专注服务"一带一路"建设的国际交流平台，以"团结、友谊、进步"为宗旨，每年举办年会及主题论坛、圆桌对话会，组织丝路青年论坛·马中合作会议（绿色发展　共创未来）、中美生态文明建设国际研讨会、"'一带一路'十年筑，丝路青年添新树"共建丝路青年友谊林活动等系列绿色发展主题的交流活动，开展"绿水青山就是金山银山"课题研究，发起《保护地球　守望未来　丝路青年双碳行动倡议书》，向国内外各界人士、丝路青年传播中国故事和中国方案。截至目前，中国全国人大常委会副委员长、全国政协副主席，以及尼泊尔副总理、尼泊尔驻华大使、多米尼克驻华大使、塞拉利昂驻华大使、牙买加驻华大使、白俄罗斯驻华公使、科摩罗驻华大使等 100 多位领导作为嘉宾出席相关活动和项目。我们期待与更多政府部门、国际组织、企事业单位等加强绿色发展交流合作，为推进中国式现代化贡献更多高质量的智库研究、科技创新、产融合作等实效成果，向广大发展中国家、丝路青年广泛宣传中国绿色发展的新实践、新成效和新经验，助力共建人类命运共同体与世界现代化进程。

主 报 告

第1章
人与自然和谐共生：绿色发展的中国方案

习近平总书记深刻指出："我们要站在对人类文明负责的高度，尊重自然、顺应自然、保护自然，探索人与自然和谐共生之路，促进经济发展与生态保护协调统一，共建繁荣、清洁、美丽的世界。"党的二十大报告明确指出："中国式现代化是人与自然和谐共生的现代化"；"坚定不移走生产发展、生活富裕、生态良好的文明发展道路，实现中华民族永续发展"。自习近平总书记提出"绿水青山就是金山银山"理念，到明确"双碳"目标，中国将生态文明建设提升到前所未有的战略高度，实现从理念到行动的跨越，从被动到主动的蜕变，为全球生态文明建设做出重要贡献。新时代的中国用实际行动证明，绿色发展不是负担而是机遇，不是权宜之计而是长远之策。

第1节　绿色发展的时代背景和现实需求

一　世界各国尤其是发展中国家面临如何协调环境保护和经济发展的巨大挑战

1. 全球生态环境面临严峻挑战

近年来，人类赖以生存的地球面临气候变化、生物多样性丧失和污染废物三重危机。2024年以来，暴雨、热浪和干旱等极端天气气候事件在全球多地频发，给人类可持续发展带来严峻挑战。联合国政府间气候变化专门委员会第六次评估报告指出，最近 50 年全球变暖正以过去 2000 年以来前所未有的速度发生。持续变暖加剧气候系统的不稳定性，导致极端天气事件增多、增强，且影响范围更大。随着各国经济社会的发展，关于自然资源的约束日益明显，加之各种自然资源全球分布不均衡，加剧资源争夺造成的社会动荡。一些国家对自然资源过度开发利用，水、土壤、空气、噪声等污染恶化，给人类健康和可持续发展带来巨大风险，生物栖息地破坏或改变，生物种群数量下降。

2. 全球环境治理和绿色发展尚未形成广泛共识及清晰路径

各国政府认识到生态环境问题对人类带来的不利影响，为此不懈努力，但是全球环境治理是一项复杂的系统工程，需要各国通力合作。各国基于自身利益和发展阶段，在环境治理上往往有不同的优先级和立场，使得全球性的环境协议或措施难以在短时间内形成广泛共识和有效执行。全球环境治理需要大量资金投入，但资金筹措渠道单一，主要依靠各国政府承诺和投入，或者跨国协议中的资金安排，而市场投资的力量还远远不够。

二 中国生态文明建设仍然处于压力叠加、负重前行的关键期

回顾历史，中华民族之所以能够生生不息和繁衍发展，良好生态环境是重要保障，倡导"天人合一"的生态观是中华文明的鲜明特色。改革开放以来，中国把节约资源和保护环境确立为基本国策，把可持续发展确立为国家战略，大力推进社会主义生态文明建设。进入新时代以来，在习近平新时代中国特色社会主义思想指引下，全党全国各族人民坚持"绿水青山就是金山银山"理念，坚定不移走生态优先、绿色发展之路，促进经济社会发展全面绿色转型，创造举世瞩目的生态奇迹和绿色发展奇迹，美丽中国建设迈出重大步伐。同时，中国绿色发展依然处于负重前行的关键攻坚期、压力叠加的破题窗口期、增进福祉的质效提升期、突破瓶颈的变革攻坚期，环境容量有限，生态系统脆弱，生态环境保护结构性、根源性、趋势性压力尚未根本缓解，人民群众对优美生态环境、

优质生态产品的期望值更高，对生态环境问题的容忍度更低。

第一，绿色发展目标任务叠加，工作难度进一步增大。绿色发展由原来的坚决打赢污染防治攻坚战向加强污染防治、绿色低碳转型、国土空间生态保护、碳达峰碳中和、守牢美丽中国安全底线、绿色国际合作等更高标准和长效机制全面发力，工作任务的全面性、系统性、复杂性、艰巨性都发生巨大变化，绿色发展进入攻坚克难的深水区。

第二，统筹经济发展和环境保护的压力不断增大，深层次矛盾更加凸显。当前，全球贸易增速放缓，经济复苏缓慢，国际货币基金组织发布的《2025 年全球经济展望报告》预测，2025 年全球经济增速保持在2.8%，与 2024 年持平，仍低于新冠疫情前 3.2%的平均水平。外部环境的复杂性、严峻性、不确定性上升，加剧中国国内有效需求仍显不足、部分行业产能过剩、社会预期偏弱、风险隐患仍然较多、国内大循环存在堵点等深层次矛盾。在现实压力下，甚至出现生态环境保护力度应有所放松、为经济发展让路的论调。

第三，生态环境改善和产业结构调整压力加大，绿色转型任务更为艰巨。比如，受厄尔尼诺现象影响，极端天气事件增多。2024 年春季，中国气候总体呈现暖湿特征，平均气温为历史同期最高，遭遇 14 次区域暴雨过程袭击，南方强对流天气频发，西南地区、黄淮江淮地区等出现冬春旱情；生产和消耗大量钢铁、水泥、电解铝等原材料，但部分资源、能源利用效率相对较低；能源需求仍保持刚性增长，煤炭消费占能源消费总量的半数以上；全国有超过 700 万家公路货运承运单位，公路货运量占比长期维持在 70%左右，污染排放压力大。

第四，国际生态环境治理形势复杂严峻，全球生态危机传导风险进一步加剧。在世界新的动荡变革期，全球环境治理风险挑战和博弈压力加大，气候变化和生物多样性等公约谈判斗争激烈。一些西方国家将生态环境保护政治化和纳入地缘政治，甚至以保护生态为名抢夺资源、转移污染、限制他国发展权，更执行"双标"对中国施压，打气候牌，妄图消解中国绿色发展成果。

第 2 节　"绿水青山就是金山银山"理念提出 20 年回顾：以浙江省绿色发展为样本

改革开放以来，浙江省经济社会快速发展，21 世纪初全省人均 GDP 接近 3000 美元，但存在缺水、缺电、缺地现象，生态环境破坏事件时有发生，资源环境约束越发趋紧，面临着"成长的烦恼"。2003 年，时任浙江省委书记习近平在浙江省委十一届四次全会上做出"发挥八个方面的优势""推进八个方面的举措"的决策部署（以下简称"八八战略"），成为指引浙江改革发展和全面小康建设的总方略。"发挥浙江的生态优势，创建生态省，打造'绿色浙江'"则是其中一项战略部署。2005 年，习近平同志考察湖州市安吉县余村时，创造性、前瞻性地做出"绿水青山就是金山银山"的重要论断，强调"不要以环境为代价，去推动经济增长，因为这样的增长不是发展"。

20 年来，浙江历届省委、省政府坚持一张蓝图绘到底，持续推动美丽生态、美丽经济、美好生活有机融合，实现从"绿色浙江"到"生态浙江"再到"美丽浙江"的跃升。2023 年，浙江以占全国 1%的土地、3%的用水量、4.7%的人口、5%的能源消耗量，创造全国 6.5%的国内生产总值，经济总量、质量稳居全国第一方阵，生态环境"高颜值"和经济发展"高质量"协同并进的完美答卷铺展在广袤的之江大地上。

案例 1-1　　小山村惊艳大世界：余村从"卖石头"到"卖风景"的绿色蝶变

余村隶属浙江省湖州市安吉县，因地处天目山余脉的余岭而得名，全域面积仅有 4.86 平方千米。村子虽然小，名气却不小。作为"绿水青山就是金山银山"理念的发源地，余村用 20 年走出一条生态美、产业兴、百姓富的乡村生态振兴之路。2024 年，余村接待游客 122 万人次，实现村集体经济收入 2205 万元，村民人均收入达 7.4 万元，远高于全省和全国平均水平。

20 世纪八九十年代，余村依靠炸山开矿和经营水泥厂，一度成为富裕村，集体年收入最高时达到 300 万元。"卖石头"虽给余村带来短暂的经济繁荣，但留下满目疮痍的环境问题。1998 年，安吉县被国家环保部门列为太湖水污染治理重点区域，余村作为重要源头村落，生态环境治理逐渐加码。2003 年，浙江省启动"千村示范、万村整治"工程，余村毅然停止发展"矿山经济"，开展垃圾清理、厂区拆迁、河道整治等环境治理，但在接续产业尚未产生效益的情况下，村集体经济出现收支倒挂，村民收入锐减。如何在发展经济和保护环境中"鱼与熊掌兼得"，成为当时余村的必答题。

2005 年 8 月 15 日，时任浙江省委书记习近平到安吉县调研时来到余村。按计划，习近平同志在村里停留 20 分钟，只听汇报，不作讲话。但当他得知余村通过民主决策关停矿山和污染企业时，便当即为余村的发展把脉，对大家说："生态资源是你们最宝贵的资源，搞经济、抓发展，不能见什么好都要，更不能以牺牲环境为代价，要有所为有所不为，不能迷恋过去的那种发展模式""过去我们讲既要绿水青山，又要金山银山，其实绿水青山就是金山银山，本身，它有含金量"。这是习近平同志首次提出"绿水青山就是金山银山"的科学论断。9 天后，他在《浙江日报》"之江新语"专栏发表《绿水青山也是金山银山》一文，指出"绿水青山可带来金山银山，但金山银山却买不到绿水青山。绿水青山与金山银山既会产生矛盾，又可辩证统一"。

"绿水青山就是金山银山"理念打开余村村民的眼界，他们真正认识到保护生态环境就是保护生产力。从此，余村破除"等、靠、要"的观望心态，坚持不懈地对矿山复垦复绿，加强生态保护与修复，持续改善人居环境，将废弃矿山和水泥厂改造为观光产业区，将毛竹、白茶和旅游业叠加为农旅融合业态，将村民住房改造为农家乐和民宿，走上绿色发展之路。2020 年 3 月，习近平总书记再访余村，看到村里的变化，他说："余村现在取得的成绩证明，绿色发展的路子是正确的，路子选对了就要坚持走下去。"

而后，余村继续探索绿色发展升级版。一是提升环境品质，打造如画余村。编制村庄规划，"微改精提"水环境，构建"横向到边、纵向到底"的山洪灾害防御和防汛防台体系，打造未来乡村数字孪生空间，实现全村人居环境全闭环数字化管理。

二是加速业态创新，打造共富余村。余村联合周边 4 村共同成立"五子联兴"公司，抱团发展，打造差异化旅游产品，形成游客畅游的乡村旅游精品线路。"余村云村民"小程序是余村发起的"城乡破圈计划"，通过云认养、云畅游、云共创、云过节、云社交等社群服务，打造与城市青年云端互动体验和消费的场景。

三是打造乡村赋能新载体，培育品牌余村。引导域内机构统一使用"余村研学"品牌开展服务，推出"余村研学"小程序，打造生态文明、青年入乡、文旅体验等研学产品矩阵。依托"余村"品牌影响力，发起"全球合伙人"招募计划，联合周边 24 个村，整合 10 万平方米创业空间、2 万余平方米厂房、近 6 万亩竹林和农田，设立 1 亿元"余村产业基金"，聚焦研学教育、乡村旅游、文化创意、农林产业、数字经济、绿色金融、零碳科技、健康医疗等绿色产业，广邀全球英才共建未来乡村新业态。

四是推动低碳循环发展，建设零碳余村。编制中国首个零碳乡村规划——《中国余村零碳乡村建设规划（2022～2035）》，提出力争在 2027 年前实现村域范围碳中和的发展目标。余村印象青年图书馆由老旧厂房改造而成，利用光伏发电进行碳抵消。余村开展"绿电绿证"交易，购买来自宁夏、黑龙江、安徽等地的光伏和风力电，实现绿电全村覆盖。余村设置监测步行、骑行数据的智能设备，将游客的绿色出行情况折换成碳积分，抵扣景区消费。

一　生态变"绿"：污染防治一脉相承

20 年来，浙江省接续推进"811"环境污染整治、"五水共治"①、蓝天保卫战、"无废城市"、美丽海湾等污染防治工作，生态环境公众满意

---

① 五水共治：治污水、防洪水、排涝水、保供水、抓节水。

度连续 13 年提升，生态环境治理效能保持全国领先水平。比如，2002 ～ 2024 年，浙江省控以上断面达到或优于 Ⅲ 类水质标准比例从 66.4% 上升至 98.6%，全面消除劣 Ⅴ 类断面；设区城市 PM2.5 平均浓度从 61 微克/米^3 降到 26.3 微克/米^3；2023 年，浙江省重点建设用地安全利用率保持 100%，近岸海域优良水质海水面积平均比例为 56.3%，设区市功能区声环境监测昼夜达标率分别为 96.6%、88.5%。

针对群众反映强烈的污水、异味等问题，浙江省补齐人居环境基础设施短板，建成超过 2000 个 "污水零直排区" 城镇生活小区，完成 1000 余个生活垃圾中转站改造提升，在全国率先实现餐厨垃圾处理设施 "县县全覆盖"、原生垃圾 "零填埋"。同时，浙江省大力传播生态文化，率先开展生态文明教育基地和绿色学校等绿色细胞创建，形成全社会绿色新风尚。

2004 年，浙江省启动实施首轮 "811" 环境污染整治行动，针对全省环境污染和生态破坏趋势踩下急刹车，其中 "8" 指浙江的八大水系，"11" 既指浙江 11 个设区市，也指当时浙江省政府划定的 11 个省级环保重点监管区。2008 年，"811" 环境保护第二轮 3 年行动启动，此时的 "8" 演化成环保工作 8 个方面的目标和 8 个方面的主要任务，"11" 既指当年提出的 11 个方面的政策措施，也指浙江省政府确定的 11 个重点环境问题。2011 年和 2016 年，浙江分别启动第三轮 "811" 生态文明建设行动、第四轮 "811" 美丽浙江建设行动，生态文明先行示范的路径进一步清晰。2023 年，围绕打造生态文明高地和美丽中国省域先行地的目标，浙江启动实施第五轮 "811" 生态文明先行示范行动，开展国土空间治理现代化、绿色低碳赋能、优美环境品质提升、生物多样性友好、美丽城乡全域提质、生态富民惠民、生态文明治理提效、全民生态自觉培育等 8 大专项行动，要求 11 个设区市打造各自的生态文明先行品牌，形成更多具有浙江辨识度、示范推广性、战略引领力的标志性成果。生态治理 "永远在路上"，每一轮浙江 "811" 行动尽管有不同主题和内涵，但工作内容一脉相承、层层推进。

二 追"新"逐"绿"：打造减污降碳转型标杆

20 年来，浙江省制定节能环保产业、绿色经济、绿色低碳循环发展经济体系等政策，实施四轮循环经济"991"行动计划，坚持"腾笼换鸟、凤凰涅槃"，持续淘汰"散乱污"、培育"高精尖"，探索中国首个跨省流域生态补偿机制，率先推行排污权、用水权、用能权等环境权益交易，出台中国首部省级生态系统生产总值（GEP）核算标准，推进生态产业化、产业生态化，在新旧动能转换中提升发展质量，国家循环经济试点省和减污降碳协同示范区建设取得突破性进展。打造风、光、水、核等清洁能源供应体系，高质量建成国家清洁能源示范省，新能源装机占比超过煤电。同时，以示范试点带动全面低碳转型，通过企业培大育强、创新能力提级、市场应用提档、产业集群打造等举措，形成具有规模化、高端化、智能化的新能源制造基地，光伏产业规模、光伏辅材企业数量和规模位居全国前列，新能源汽车产业年总营收突破万亿元。

三 变"绿"为"金"：完善生态产品价值实现机制

2021 年 5 月，中共中央、国务院发布《关于支持浙江高质量发展建设共同富裕示范区的意见》，明确要求浙江"拓宽绿水青山就是金山银山转化通道，建立健全生态产品价值实现机制，探索完善具有浙江特点的生态系统生产总值（GEP）核算应用体系"。《浙江省生态环境保护条例》专设"生态产品价值实现"一章，构建生态产品价值实现的基本法治框架。进而，浙江省以生态保护、修复、提升为工作基础，以产权构建、资产配置、运营管护为主要手段，形成一系列自然资源领域生态产品价值实现创新路径，促进"资源—资产—资本"有序转化。

比如，湖州市构建"生态系统生产总值（GEP）+ 特定地域单元生态产品价值（VEP）"核算机制。通过自然资源确权登记和生态产品总值试点核算，掌握市域生态资产分布与总量，对重点生态型乡镇进行 GEP 核算，将 GEP 核算结果纳入基层政府绩效考核和领导干部自然资源资产离任（任中）审计。湖州市金融机构开发 GEP 项目贷、VEP 绿色贷、VEP 绿企贷、VEP 惠农贷等绿色金融产品，通过核算项目建设前的生态价值基准值与建设运营后的最终值，以未来生态收益量为抵押物，为相关企业、农户提供低息授信贷款，将生态增值收益专项用于生态保护或回馈给对生态保护有贡献的主体。

另外，浙江省将零碎的山、水、林、田、湖、房等闲置低效生态资源"打包"，借助 40 多家市县乡三级两山合作社，深化社会资本与村集体、农户之间的利益联结，累计开发项目 200 余个、总投资 560 亿元，带动村集体超 2000 个、村集体增收超 6.7 亿元，辐射农户 8 万家，创出安吉"两入股三收益"①、衢州乡村资产储蓄分红②等新模式，实现生态富民惠民。21 世纪以来浙江省绿色发展的首创经验见表 1-1。

表 1-1　21 世纪以来浙江省绿色发展的首创经验

序号	绿色发展首创经验	具体情况
1	首提"绿水青山就是金山银山"理念	2005 年 8 月 15 日，时任浙江省委书记习近平到湖州市安吉县余村调研，首次提出"绿水青山就是金山银山"的科学论断
2	"绿水青山就是金山银山"实践创新基地数量全国最多	截至 2023 年末，浙江已创成 49 个国家生态文明建设示范市县和 14 个"绿水青山就是金山银山"实践创新基地
3	全国第一个"生态日"	2003 年安吉县"两会"期间，有政协委员提出设立"生态日"。2003 年 9 月，安吉县人大常委会通过决议，从 2004 年起，每年的 3 月 25 日为"生态日"
4	发布中国首个"河长制"任命文件	2003 年，长兴县发布"河长制"任命文件，建起"县—乡镇—村社"三级"河长制"体系。2017 年 7 月，浙江省第十二届人大常委会表决通过《浙江省河长制规定》，这是中国首个专门规范河长制的地方性法规
5	率先开展"千万工程"	2003 年，浙江省启动"千万工程"，将环境脏乱差、发展滞后的村庄变成生态宜居、富裕文明的绿色家园，惠及数千万农民

① "两入股三收益"：农民以乡村资产资源入股，实现拿租金、挣薪金、分股金三种收益。
② 乡村资产储蓄分红：两山合作社和村委会签订整村经营合作开发协议，收储闲置农用地、闲置农房、林地、山塘、水库等乡村资产，吸引村集体、农户参与整村经营，农民获得资产储蓄、资产转让、项目运营等收益分红。

续表

序号	绿色发展首创经验	概述
6	全国首个跨省流域生态补偿机制试点	2011 年，跨省流域生态补偿机制试点在新安江启动，此后，新安江流域水质明显改善
7	全国首个省域美丽建设中长期规划	2020 年 8 月，浙江省发布《深化生态文明示范创建　高水平建设新时代美丽浙江规划纲要（2020~2035 年）》
8	绿色发展指数表现优良	2018 年 4 月，中国人民大学发布《绿色之路——中国经济绿色发展报告 2018》，对省（区、市）绿色发展进行测度，浙江省绿色发展指数较高
9	首批国家生态县	2006 年 6 月，安吉县入选国家环保总局发布的生态县名单
10	全国率先出台省级层面的生态补偿办法	2005 年 9 月，浙江省出台《关于进一步完善生态补偿机制的若干意见》
11	全球首个大型"无废"赛事	2023 年杭州亚运会制定《"无废亚运"实施指南（试行）》，推动杭州亚运会期间固体废物能减尽减、办会物资可用尽用
12	全国首个生物多样性友好乡镇试点项目	2022 年 6 月，生态环境部宣教中心为宁波市海曙区龙观乡"生物多样性友好乡镇"项目授牌。龙观乡位于"浙东绿肺"四明山东麓，森林覆盖率达 86%，是华东地区生物多样性的"绿色宝库"
13	率先实现"绿色标尺"省市县三级全覆盖	2021 年，浙江省省、市、县三级"三线一单"① 生态环境分区管控方案全部发布

案例 1-2　　"千村示范、万村整治"工程：绘就"绿富美"的乡村振兴画卷

2003 年 6 月，时任浙江省委书记习近平在广泛深入调查研究的基础上，立足省情、农情和发展阶段特征，做出实施"千村示范、万村整治"（以下简称"千万工程"）的战略决策，提出从全省近 4 万个村庄中选择 1 万个左右行政村进行全面整治，把其中 1000 个左右中心村建成全面小康示范村。在浙江工作期间，习近平同志亲自制定"千万工程"目标要求、实施原则、投入办法，建立"四个一工作机制"，即实行"一把手"负总责，落实分级负责责任制；成立一个"千万工程"工作协调小组，由省委副书记任组长；每年召开一次"千万工程"工作现场会，省委、

---

① 三线一单：生态保护红线、环境质量底线、资源利用上线和生态环境准入清单。

省政府主要领导到会并部署工作；定期表彰一批"千万工程"的先进集体和个人。

20 年来，浙江历届省委、省政府按照习近平同志的战略擘画和重要指示要求，持续深化"千万工程"，整治范围不断延伸，从最初的 1 万个左右行政村，推广到全省所有行政村；内涵不断丰富，从"千村示范、万村整治"引领起步，到"千村精品、万村美丽"深化提升，再到"千村未来、万村共富"迭代升级，形成"千村向未来、万村奔共富、城乡促融合、全域创和美"的生动局面。

习近平同志在浙江工作期间强调，要将村庄整治与绿色生态家园建设紧密结合起来，同步推进环境整治和生态建设；打好"生态牌"，走生态立村、生态致富的路子。浙江把这些重要理念和要求贯穿实施"千万工程"全过程各阶段，以整治环境"脏乱差"为先手棋，推进农村环境"三大革命"①，开展农业面源污染治理，建设"无废乡村"，整治重污染、高耗能行业，关停"小散乱"企业，培育"美丽乡村＋"新产业，持续打通"绿水青山就是金山银山"价值转化通道，城乡居民收入比从 2003 年的 2.43 缩小到 2024 年的 1.83，"城市促乡村更美好、乡村让城市更向往"成为浙江城乡融合发展的生动写照。

习近平同志始终牵挂着"千万工程"，担任总书记以来多次做出重要指示批示，各地纷纷学习借鉴浙江的"千万工程"经验，农村人居环境整治和乡村建设取得显著成效。"千万工程"在国际上得到认可，2018 年 9 月荣获联合国"地球卫士奖"，为营造和谐宜居的人类家园贡献了中国方案。中共中央、国务院 2024 年 1 月出台的《关于学习运用"千村示范、万村整治"工程经验有力有效推进乡村全面振兴的意见》进一步强调，"千万工程"从农村环境整治入手，由点及面、迭代升级，20 年持续努力造就了万千美丽乡村，造福了万千农民群众，创造了推进乡村全面振兴的成功经验和实践范例。

---

① 农村环境"三大革命"：厕所革命、垃圾革命、污水革命。

第3节　中国绿色发展的体制改革、机制建设和法治保障

一　系统性重塑生态文明制度体系

进入新时代以来，以习近平同志为核心的党中央将制度建设贯穿于生态文明建设全过程各领域，坚持全方位布局、系统化构建、多层次推进，将"中国共产党领导人民建设社会主义生态文明""增强绿水青山就是金山银山的意识"写入党章，2018 年 3 月通过的宪法修正案将生态文明写入《中华人民共和国宪法》，实现党的主张、国家意志、人民意愿的高度统一，充分彰显生态文明建设在党和国家事业中的重要地位，表明中国共产党加强生态文明建设的坚定意志和坚强决心。

中国先后印发实施《关于加快推进生态文明建设的意见》《生态文明体制改革总体方案》及几十项具体改革方案，源头严防、过程严管、损害赔偿、后果严惩等生态文明基础性制度框架初步建立。值得关注的是，新时代生态文明制度建设更加注重系统集成和协同高效，既覆盖自然资源管理、生态环境监管等生态文明建设的各个方面，也覆盖各重点区域、各环境要素，不仅关注各环境要素之间的相互关系，也关注各制度之间的协调配合。比如，中国出台《大气污染防治行动计划》《水污染防治行动计划》《土壤污染防治行动计划》，集中攻坚解决突出生态环境问题，同时，制定实施支持绿色低碳发展的财税、金融、投资、价格政策和标准体系，建设新型能源体系，发展绿色低碳产业，健全绿色消费激励机制，科学引导绿色低碳转型，体现出在生态环境保护上算大账、算长远账、算整体账、算综合账，不因小失大、顾此失彼、寅吃卯粮、急功近利。

与此同时，在党中央、国务院统一部署下，支持各地区因地制宜，大胆探索，大胆试验生态文明体制机制创新。中共中央办公厅、国务院

办公厅 2016 年印发《关于设立统一规范的国家生态文明试验区的意见》，福建、江西、贵州和海南四省相继获批开展试验区建设，陆续形成一批具有复制推广价值的制度成果，将改革经验"由点到面"进行推广。

2012 年，党的十八大报告把"绿色发展、循环发展、低碳发展"作为生态文明建设的重要途径。2017 年，党的十九大报告正式提出建立健全绿色低碳循环发展的经济体系。2021 年 2 月，国务院印发《关于加快建立健全绿色低碳循环发展经济体系的指导意见》，提出要全方位全过程推行绿色规划、绿色设计、绿色投资、绿色建设、绿色生产、绿色流通、绿色生活、绿色消费，使发展建立在高效利用资源、严格保护生态环境、有效控制温室气体排放的基础上。

党的二十大报告将"推动绿色发展，促进人与自然和谐共生"作为专章，提出必须牢固树立和践行绿水青山就是金山银山的理念……推进生态优先、节约集约、绿色低碳发展。《中共中央关于进一步全面深化改革、推进中国式现代化的决定》有 14 处提及"绿色"，设"深化生态文明体制改革"专章，要求完善生态文明制度体系，协同推进降碳、减污、扩绿、增长，积极应对气候变化，加快完善落实绿水青山就是金山银山理念的体制机制。

2024 年 8 月，中共中央、国务院印发《关于加快经济社会发展全面绿色转型的意见》，这是国家层面首次对全面绿色转型进行系统部署，涵盖区域发展、产业结构、能源、交通运输、城乡建设等不同领域，通过实施"五大领域、三大环节"重点任务①，力争到 2035 年基本建立绿色

---

① "五大领域、三大环节"重点任务："五大领域"分别是构建绿色低碳高质量发展空间格局，优化国土空间开发保护格局，打造绿色发展高地；加快产业结构绿色低碳转型，推动传统产业绿色低碳改造升级，大力发展绿色低碳产业，加快数字化绿色化协同转型发展；稳妥推进能源绿色低碳转型，加强化石能源清洁高效利用，大力发展非化石能源，加快构建新型电力系统；推进交通运输绿色转型，优化交通运输结构，建设绿色交通基础设施，推广低碳交通运输工具；推进城乡建设发展绿色转型，推行绿色规划建设方式，大力发展绿色低碳建筑，推动农业农村绿色发展。"三大环节"分别是实施全面节约战略，大力推进节能降碳增效，加强资源节约集约利用，大力发展循环经济；推动消费模式绿色转型，推广绿色生活方式，加大绿色产品供给，积极扩大绿色消费；发挥科技创新支撑作用，强化应用基础研究，加快关键技术研发，开展创新示范推广。

低碳循环发展经济体系。

案例1-3　　　福建：深化国家生态文明试验区建设，构建
从山顶到海洋的保护治理大格局

福建省是习近平生态文明思想的重要孕育地和实践地。在福建工作期间，习近平同志提出一系列生态文明建设的创新理念，亲自部署、亲自参与、亲自推动生态文明建设重大实践，为福建省生态文明建设走在全国前列奠定坚实基础。截至2024年，福建省森林覆盖率连续46年保持全国第一，在水、大气等生态环境质量稳定优良并持续居全国前列的同时，以约占全国1.3%的土地、3%的能耗创造全国4.3%的经济总量。

福建省龙岩市长汀县曾是中国南方红壤区水土流失最为严重的地区之一，"山光、水浊、田瘦、人穷"。1999年11月，时任福建省委副书记、代省长习近平同志来到长汀县了解水土流失情况，他说："要锲而不舍、统筹规划，用八到十年时间，争取国家、省、市支持，完成国土整治，造福百姓。"次年，时任福建省省长习近平同志将"开展以长汀严重水土流失区为重点的水土流失综合治理"列为全省15件为民办实事项目之一。25年来，长汀县实施封山育林、改良植被、补贴烧煤、发展绿色产业、转移农村剩余劳动力、生态移民搬迁等措施，水土流失率从1985年的31.5%降至2023年的6.44%，远低于发达国家水平，森林覆盖率提高到79.55%，水土流失治理取得决定性胜利。生态环境改善带动长汀县生态产业振兴，2024年共接待游客1044.87万人次，实现旅游收入91.81亿元，多次入选福建省县域经济发展"十佳县"。

长汀县是福建省绿色发展的缩影。早在2000年，时任福建省省长习近平同志就极具前瞻性地提出建设生态省的战略构想。2001年，他亲任福建省生态省建设领导小组组长。2002年，习近平同志在省政府工作报告中正式提出建设生态省战略目标。2004年，福建省出台《福建生态省建设总体规划纲要》，成为全国首批生态省试点省份。2016年，福建省获批全国首个国家生态文明试验区，绿色发展从局部探索、试点突围，延伸到创新试验、全面深化。

2000 年以来，福建省落实污染防治"一盘棋"，深入实施蓝天、碧水、碧海、净土"四大工程"，建立分区分类分层的海漂垃圾治理机制，上线覆盖省市县三级的生态云平台，率先探索按流域设置环境监管和执法机构；系统构建沿海产业节约高效集聚、山区生态重点保护、山海协同联动的发展格局，2024 年林业年总产值约 8000 亿元，海洋产业年总产值超 1.2 万亿元，生物医药、新材料、新能源等领域培育形成 4 个国家级、17 个省级战略性新兴产业集群；建成全国首个海洋、农业碳汇交易平台，率先出台陆海统筹、适用全省的生态产品总值核算技术指南，建立综合性绿色价值转化体系。

2014 年，习近平总书记在福建考察时深情寄语，要努力建设"机制活、产业优、百姓富、生态美"的新福建。2024 年 7 月，福建省出台《关于更高起点建设生态强省谱写美丽中国建设福建篇章的实施方案》。2024 年 10 月，习近平总书记在福建考察时指出："深化国家生态文明试验区建设，构建从山顶到海洋的保护治理大格局，加强重点领域、重点流域、重点海域综合治理，扩大生态环境容量。"总的来看，福建省接续推进实施生态省战略，高水平建设国家生态文明试验区，向绿、向美、向未来，福建目标明确、路径清晰、步履坚定。

二　为美丽中国建设提供坚强法治保障

进入新时代以来，在习近平生态文明思想和习近平法治思想的科学指引下，中国绿色发展法治建设进入立法力度最大、监管执法尺度最严、法律制度实施效果最为显著的时期。2020 年 5 月通过的《中华人民共和国民法典》第九条规定：民事主体从事民事活动，应当有利于节约资源，保护生态环境；用专章对环境污染和生态破坏责任做出规定，并确立生态环境损害赔偿制度。至今，中国生态环境领域形成由 1 部基础性、综合性的环境保护法，若干部涉及大气、水、固体废物、土壤、噪声、海洋、湿地、草原、森林、沙漠等的专门法律，长江保护法、黄河保护法、黑土地保护法、青藏高原生态保护法等 4 部特殊区域法律组成的"1+N+4"法律制度体系。

2014 年修订的《中华人民共和国环境保护法》将生态文明建设和绿色发展必须遵循的基本理念、基本原则、基本制度以法律形式确立下来。2014 年《中华人民共和国环境保护法》加强对各级人民政府履行环境保护职责的监督，规定各级人民政府对所辖行政区域环境质量负责，实行环境保护目标责任制和考核评价制度，增加查封、扣押等强制措施，对拒不改正的违法者规定按照原处罚数额按日连续处罚等严厉的行政处罚制度，被称为"史上最严"的环保法律。中国建成全球唯一的从最高人民法院、最高人民检察院到覆盖各级司法机关的环境司法体系，办理系列具有世界典范意义的生态环境案件，联合国环境规划署网站开辟中国环境资源审判专栏，向各国推广中国经验。中国施行检察公益诉讼制度，检察机关办理的公益诉讼案件中，环保公益诉讼占到一半以上。2014 年《中华人民共和国环境保护法》专门增加信息公开和公众参与一章，环保公益组织和志愿者越来越多并发挥积极作用。

《中共中央关于进一步全面深化改革、推进中国式现代化的决定》提出编纂生态环境法典，表明生态环境立法的立法方式从"成熟一个制定一个"转向协同共进，从以创制为主转向统筹创制和清理、编纂和解释，更加注重增强法治的可持续发展能力。

令在必信，法在必行。进入新时代以来，中国突出生态环境领域依法行政、依法执法，推进机构、职能、权限、程序、责任的法治化，把全部执法活动纳入法治轨道，建立生态环境保护综合行政执法机关、公安机关、检察机关、审判机关信息共享、案情通报、案件移送制度，强化生态环境行政执法与刑事司法的衔接，形成对破坏生态环境违法犯罪行为的查处侦办工作合力，一批生态环境保护领域的违法违规问题被严厉查处，有效遏制同类环境违法行为的发生。

三　不断完善生态环境治理体系

在责任层面，加强党的全面领导，实施生态文明建设目标评价考核、污染防治攻坚战成效考核、领导干部自然资源资产离任审计、河湖长制、林长制、生态环境损害责任终身追究、生态环境损害赔偿等制度，严格落实生态环境保护"党政同责"、"一岗双责"和"管发展必须管环保、管生产必须管环保、管行业必须管环保"要求，全党全国推进生态文明建设和绿色发展的自觉性主动性不断增强。自 2015 年建立中央生态环境保护督察制度以来，实现对 31 个省（区、市）和新疆生产建设兵团的两轮督察全覆盖，第二轮督察还把国务院 2 个部门和 6 家中央企业纳入督察范围。在中央生态环境保护督察有力推动下，甘肃祁连山国家级自然保护区生态破坏、陕西秦岭北麓西安境内违建别墅、青海木里矿区非法开采、吉林长白山违建高尔夫球场及别墅等问题得到解决。

在管理层面，中国组建自然资源部，统一行使所有国土空间用途管制和生态保护修复职责；组建生态环境部，统一行使各类污染排放监管与行政执法职责。2018 年国务院机构改革，把原来六个部委与环境行政处罚相关的事项进行整合，成立专门的环境执法监督机构，集中行使环境执法权。实施省（区、市）以下生态环境机构监测监察执法垂直管理制度和生态环境保护综合行政执法改革，加强生态环境监测、监察、执法的独立性、统一性、权威性。

四　探索优化生态资源市场调节机制

进入新时代以来，中国不断健全资源环境要素市场化配置体系，创新节水节能、污水处理、垃圾处理、大气污染治理等重点领域的价格形成机制，实施 50 余项税费优惠政策，把碳排放权、用能权、用水权、排污权等纳入要素市场化配置改革总盘子。建立统一的自然资源确权登记和有偿使用制度，完善自然资源价格形成机制。健全生态保护补偿制度，政府调动各方力量以资金支付、产业合作等为纽带对生态保护者予以激励性补偿。截至 2024 年 11 月，全国累计已有 24 个省（区、市）建立 28 个跨省（区、市）流域生态保护补偿机制，中央层面生态保护补偿资金已由年均几十亿元增长到近 2000 亿元，地方补偿资金达到近千亿元的规模。

近年来，中国绿色金融体系建设取得明显成效，形成绿色贷款、绿色债券、绿色保险、绿色基金、绿色信托等多层次绿色金融产品和市场体系，为服务实体经济绿色低碳发展提供强大动力。截至 2024 年末，中国本外币绿色贷款余额 36.6 万亿元，同比增长 21.7%，投向具有直接和间接碳减排效益项目的贷款合计占绿色贷款的 67.5%。在绿色金融支持下，中国新能源、电动车、电池产业已占全球最大市场份额，污水和固废处理能力居全球前列。此外，中国还提出倡议和发起多个绿色金融国际合作机制，在形成可持续金融全球共识、提高绿色金融标准的兼容性、为发展中国家提供能力建设支持等方面发挥引领性作用。

第 4 节　党的十八大以来中国绿色
发展的经验和启示

实践和成效证明，习近平生态文明思想系统回答了为什么建设生态文明、建设什么样的生态文明、怎样建设生态文明等重大理论和实践问题，中国绿色发展的经验启示集中体现在"四个重大转变"[①]、"五个重大关系"[②]、"十个坚持"[③]。

一　坚持以人民为中心的发展思想

以人民为中心是中国共产党的执政理念，良好生态环境是最公平的公共产品、最普惠的民生福祉。随着中国式现代化建设不断推进和人民生活水平的不断提高，人民对优美生态环境的需要更加迫切，生态环境在人民生活幸福指数中的地位不断凸显。中国顺应人民日益增长的优美

[①]　四个重大转变：由重点整治到系统治理的重大转变、由被动应对到主动作为的重大转变、由全球环境治理参与者到引领者的重大转变、由实践探索到科学理论指导的重大转变。

[②]　五个重大关系：高质量发展和高水平保护的关系、重点攻坚和协同治理的关系、自然恢复和人工修复的关系、外部约束和内生动力的关系、"双碳承诺"和自主行动的关系。

[③]　十个坚持：坚持党对生态文明建设的全面领导，坚持生态兴则文明兴，坚持人与自然和谐共生，坚持绿水青山就是金山银山，坚持良好生态环境是最普惠的民生福祉，坚持绿色发展是发展观的深刻革命，坚持统筹山水林田湖草沙系统治理，坚持用最严格制度最严密法治保护生态环境，坚持把建设美丽中国转化为全体人民自觉行动，坚持共谋全球生态文明建设之路。

生态环境需要，坚持生态惠民、生态利民、生态为民，大力推行绿色生产生活方式，重点解决损害群众健康的突出环境问题，持续改善生态环境质量，提供更多优质生态产品，让人民在优美生态环境中有更多的获得感、幸福感、安全感。

二　着眼中华民族永续发展

生态兴则文明兴，生态衰则文明衰。大自然是人类赖以生存发展的基本条件，只有尊重自然、顺应自然、保护自然，才能实现可持续发展。中国立足环境容量有限、生态系统脆弱的现实国情，既为当代发展谋，也为子孙万代计，把生态文明建设作为关系中华民族永续发展的根本大计，推动绿水青山转化为金山银山，让自然财富、生态财富源源不断带来经济财富、社会财富，实现经济效益、生态效益、社会效益同步提升，建设人与自然和谐共生的现代化。

三　坚持系统观念统筹推进

绿色发展是对生产方式、生活方式、思维方式和价值观念的全方位、革命性变革。中国把系统观念贯穿经济社会发展和生态环境保护全过程，正确处理发展和保护、全局和局部、当前和长远等一系列关系，构建科学适度有序的国土空间布局体系、绿色低碳循环发展的经济体系、约束和激励并举的生态文明制度体系，统筹产业结构调整、污染治理、生态保护、应对气候变化，协同推进降碳、减污、扩绿、增长，推进生态优先、绿色发展，形成节约资源和保护环境的空间格局、产业结构、生产方式、生活方式。

四　共谋全球可持续发展

保护生态环境、应对气候变化，是全人类的共同责任。只有世界各国团结合作、共同努力，携手推进绿色可持续发展，才能维持地球生态整体平衡，守护好全人类赖以生存的唯一家园。中国站在对人类文明负责的高度，积极参与全球环境治理，向世界承诺力争于 2030 年前实现碳达峰、努力争取 2060 年前实现碳中和，以"碳达峰碳中和"目标牵引绿色转型，以更加积极的姿态开展绿色发展双多边国际合作，推动构建公平合理、合作共赢的全球环境治理体系，为全球可持续发展贡献智慧和力量。

案例1-4　　成渝地区双城经济圈共筑长江上游生态屏障：跨区域绿色协同发展的样本

2020 年 1 月 3 日，习近平总书记在中央财经委员会第六次会议上提出，要推动成渝地区双城经济圈建设，在西部形成高质量发展的重要增长极。作为中国经济发展最活跃、开放程度最高、创新能力最强的区域，地处西南腹地的成渝地区双城经济圈，承东启西，连接南北，在国家区域协调发展战略大局中具有重要地位。据《成渝地区双城经济圈建设规划纲要》，成渝地区双城经济圈的空间范围包括重庆的 29 个区县和四川的 15 个市，总面积 18.5 万平方千米，2023 年常住人口 9853.58 万人，2024 年地区生产总值 8.6 万亿元，分别占全国的 1.9%、7.0%、6.5%。

夜发清溪向三峡，思君不见下渝州。成渝地区双城经济圈是自然资源、水能资源、矿产资源丰富的生态沃土，同处长江上游，山同脉、水同源，大气、水、土壤环境相互影响，尤其是两地水系发达，河流湖泊相连相通，流域面积为 50 平方千米以上的跨界河流多达 81 条，长度合计超过 1 万公里，是休戚与共的生态共同体，在长江流域的生态安全中占有重要战略地位。同时，长江在该地区流经山地生态脆弱区、城镇人口稠密区和工业集聚区，各类生态环境风险叠加交织，生态治理点散、面广、量大。五年来，成渝地区双城经济圈坚持"绿水青山就是金山银山"理念，坚持"共抓大保护、不搞大开发"，携手筑牢长江上游生态屏障，探索绿色转型发展新路径，在西部地区生态环境保护中发挥示范作用。

生态环境共保联治

五年来，川渝坚持统一环保标准和一张负面清单管两地，累计签订合作协议 120 余项，共同印发工作方案、重点任务，建立专项工作组、联席会议、联合执法等协作机制，形成区域生态共建、污染共治、政策共商、发展共促的美丽成渝建设路径。

2020 年 9 月，中国首个跨省市设立的联合河长办——川渝河长制联合推进办公室正式完成组建。联合河长办主任由川渝省级河长办副主任兼任，一年一轮值，双方每年各派工作人员集中办公，研究解决跨区域、流域、部门的重点难点问题，建立省级河长联席会议、联合巡查、联合督查、跨省界河流环境污染联防联控、流域生态环境事故协商处置等制度，绘制川渝跨界河流水系图和"一河一策"方案，开展污水"三排"（偷排、直排、乱排）专项整治和"清四乱"（乱占、乱采、乱堆、乱建），共建跨界流域横向生态保护补偿机制，促进水环境治理由"分段治"变"全域治"。

嘉陵江是长江上游的最大支流，在重庆市和四川省的流域面积合计为 11.2 万平方千米，占嘉陵江流域总面积的 70%。2021 年 11 月 25 日，重庆市第五届人大常委会第二十九次会议表决通过《重庆市人民代表大会常务委员会关于加强嘉陵江流域水生态环境协同保护的决定》。同日，四川省第十三届人大常委会第三十一次会议表决通过《四川省嘉陵江流域生态环境保护条例》。该《决定》和《条例》均自 2022 年 1 月 1 日起施行，川渝从信息共享、生态保护补偿协同、专项规划编制协同、水污染治理协同、水生态修复协同、水资源保护协同、标准协同、监测协同、河湖长协同、应急协同、执法协同、司法协同、人大监督协同 13 个方面，实现"五个统一"（统一规划、统一标准、统一监测、统一责任、统一防治措施）。同时，川渝生态环境部门联合印发琼江、铜钵河、南溪河等嘉陵江重要支流水环境联合治理方案，进而形成"条例+决定+联合治理方案"的法规政策库。

川渝生态环境部门建立大气环境信息共享、预警预报、环评会商、联合执法等工作机制，协同修订重污染天气应急预案，开展毗邻地区大气污染联防联控专项行动，共同编制发布水泥、陶瓷、玻璃工业大气污染物排放标准，突出臭氧、PM2.5 污染协同防控和交通、工业、扬尘、生活污染协同治理。川渝毗邻地区空气站点基本档案信息、空气自动监测数据（小时报）纳入川渝首批跨界共享的政务数据资源。川渝经信、生态环境部门要求两地所有水泥熟料生产线实行错峰生产，缩短水泥熟料装置运转时间，压减过剩产能，每条水泥熟料生产线年度错峰生产基准天数为 140 天+X 天（X 为根据环保、能耗、减碳、环境敏感时期等因素实时调整的停窑天数）。

川渝协同开展"无废城市"建设，出台中国首个跨省域的"无废城市细胞"评价标准，在高竹新区（四川省广安区和重庆市渝北区共建）实行固废跨省转移省市内审批试点，建立中国首个跨省域的固危废、新污染物治理联防联控机制。川渝生态环境部门建立危险废物跨省市转移"白名单"合作机制，每年 12 月，川渝生态环境部门在确保环境风险可控的条件下，分别提出下年度危险废物经营单位、相应接收的危险废物类别和数量等"白名单"，经双方协商确认并正式函告对方后，便可依据"白名单"直接审批，双方生态环境部门不再函商确定。该做法大幅减少双方的函商程序，审批时间从之前的一个月左右缩短到 5 个工作日。

共建碳达峰碳中和示范区

川渝共同出台碳达峰碳中和联合行动方案，在产业、清洁能源、交通、建筑、科技、农林、金融等领域，携手减排、协同治污、共同增绿。

一是共建中国重要的清洁能源基地。川渝在水电、页岩气、储气库、天然气管道、能源设施等领域加强合作，能源互保能力不断提升。例如，四川水电每年送重庆电量达 200 亿千瓦时左右，枯水期重庆火电送四川电量 5 亿~8 亿千瓦时。川渝氢能资源丰富，集聚氢气"制、储、运、加、用"数百家上下游企业及科研院所。2021 年 11 月，"成渝氢走廊"正式贯通，超过 900 辆氢燃料电池汽车每天穿梭于成都、重庆及周边城市，带动沿线城市共建立足成渝、辐射西部的氢能及燃料电池产业高地。

二是碳金融改革稳步推进。两江新区上线重庆气候投融资对接平台，编制气候友好型项目重点支持清单、汽车及电子信息行业碳中和供应链标准，以区内控排企业"碳账户"为基础，构建"碳减排—碳核算—碳认证—碳融资"的碳金融生态链。川渝共同打造"碳中和服务平台"，作为集自愿减排量合作、碳中和服务、绿色机制研究、碳市场能力建设等功能于一体的公共服务载体。重庆形成中国唯一全面推动工业减排的地方碳市场，纳入碳市场的控排工业企业碳排放量占全市总量的 87%，覆盖全部 7 种中国规定管控的温室气体。

第2章
美丽中国建设：中国生态环境保护的举措、成效、经验和建议

习近平总书记强调："生态环境没有替代品，用之不觉，失之难存。在生态环境保护建设上，一定要树立大局观、长远观、整体观，坚持保护优先，坚持节约资源和保护环境的基本国策，像保护眼睛一样保护生态环境，像对待生命一样对待生态环境，推动形成绿色发展方式和生活方式。"党的十九大报告将污染防治作为决胜全面建成小康社会的三大攻坚战之一，为全面建成小康社会增添绿色动力。2018年、2021年，《中共中央 国务院关于全面加强生态环境保护 坚决打好污染防治攻坚战的意见》《中共中央 国务院关于深入打好污染防治攻坚战的意见》相继印发。在党中央领导下，中国将解决突出生态环境问题作为民生优先领域，打响史无前例、规模巨大的污染防治攻坚战，形成精准、科学、依法治污的方法经验，生态环境质量明显改善。

第1节 中国"打好蓝天保卫战"的创新举措、主要成效和典型案例

一 环境空气治理的创新举措

空气质量是污染防治攻坚战最直接、最普惠的指标。产业结构偏重、能源结构偏煤、交通运输偏公路等状况，决定中国大气环境问题的

长期性、复杂性、艰巨性，蓝天保卫战是污染防治攻坚战的重中之重。国务院 2013 年发布《大气污染防治行动计划》、2018 年发布《打赢蓝天保卫战三年行动计划》、2023 年发布《空气质量持续改善行动计划》，党的十八大以来中国接续出台三个"大气十条"，持续用力，久久为功。

进入新时代以来，中国全面加强重污染天气应对和区域联防联控，编制应急预案，推动应急减排清单涉气企业全覆盖，实施秋冬季长时间、大范围重污染天气分阶段差异化管控，开展重点区域空气质量改善监督帮扶；有序推进北方地区清洁取暖改造，完成约 4100 万户散煤治理；淘汰高排放车辆近 5000 万辆，新能源公交车占比 2024 年提高到的 70% 以上，大宗货物清洁运输水平持续提升。

中国综合运用金融、价格、财税、环保等差异化管理政策，激发市场主体参与大气污染治理的内生动力，建成世界上规模最大的清洁煤电体系和清洁钢铁生产体系，越来越多企业绿色转型和利润增长实现同频共振。例如，出台燃煤电厂超低排放电价政策，以及钢铁、水泥等行业超低排放差别化的电价、水价，中央和地方大气污染防治资金对改造项目予以支持，完成改造的企业享受环境税、购置税等减免优惠政策，落实超低排放和环保绩效 A 级企业重污染天气预警期间不停产、不限产，环保检查"无事不扰"，保障绿色、优质产能尽量发挥。至今，中国累计淘汰落后煤炭产能 10 亿吨、钢铁产能 3 亿吨、水泥产能 4 亿吨；95% 以上的煤电机组和 45% 以上的粗钢产能完成超低排放改造，燃煤锅炉从近 50 万台减少到不足 10 万台；完成超低排放改造企业的利润率比其他企业高出 1.7 个百分点。

案例 2-1　　"北京蓝"：超大城市大气污染治理的成功路径

北京大气污染治理要比历史上不少发达国家城市更加复杂与艰巨，其既有煤炭污染特征，也有机动车污染特征。北京通过借鉴发达国家的治污经验，根据本地复合型污染特征，从煤烟型污染治理到工业、机动车、扬尘等综合防治，连续实施 16 个阶段大气污染控制措施、清洁空气五年行动计划、打赢蓝天保卫战三年行动计划和"一微克"行动，各项措施"压茬"推进，环境效益逐步释放。

北京建立城市空气质量预测预报体系，为开展精细化治污提供技术支撑，协助民众绿色出行。当空气污染即将到来时，北京可提前开展污染应对，实现削峰降速，精准管控。北京从 2013 年以来开展三轮 PM2.5 源解析，量化分析 PM2.5 来源组成和区域传输影响，为针对性治霾提供指导。北京开发大气环境监测大模型——"三监"大模型，利用大数据、人工智能等技术，实现"监管部门统筹调度、监测部门智慧感知、监察执法部门精准执法"的联动工作机制。

2013 年，北京开始执行国家环境质量标准《环境空气质量标准》，开展环境空气中 PM2.5 和臭氧监测。经过多年与津冀及周边省市联防联控，各项大气污染物浓度明显下降，2021 年，北京市空气质量首次全面达标，PM2.5 年均浓度较 2013 年下降 63.1%，平均每年下降 7.9%，远超发达国家城市同期下降幅度。2024 年，北京市 PM2.5 浓度为 30.5 微克/米^3，同比下降 6.2%，连续 4 年稳定达到国家二级标准；优良天数达 290 天，同比增加 19 天。在地区生产总值、常住人口、机动车保有量、能源消耗持续增加的背景下，北京从十余年前深受雾霾困扰，到如今天清气朗的"北京蓝"成为大国首都的靓丽底色。联合国环境规划署发布的《北京二十年大气污染治理历程与展望》评估报告认为，北京在大气环境质量改善方面取得令人瞩目的成效，世界上没有其他城市或者区域能够在这么短的时间内取得这样好的成绩，其中有很多值得学习和借鉴的经验、做法。

案例 2-2　　　广东：协同互通打好湾区蓝天保卫战，探索生态保护"湾区标准"

三面环山、三江汇聚，漫长的海岸线、优良的港口群、广阔的海域面、繁茂的红树林，共同交织绘就粤港澳大湾区"山海连城、和谐共生"的生态画卷。共建国际一流美丽湾区是广东省建设美丽中国先行区的重要内容。广东省围绕"开展六大行动、完善两个体系、强化一个保障"①，率先试行与国际接轨的生态环境管理体系、标准体系和合作模式，建立区域内产品碳足迹管理与低碳产品认证制度，在大气污染联防联控、海洋环境保护、应对气候变化、固体废物处置等重点领域深化与香港、澳门的规则衔接、机制对接，实现高水平互利共赢。

在系统治污方面，广东省以 PM2.5 治理为主线，坚持"控车、降尘、少油气"工作思路，实施大气污染防治重点任务清单、冬春季节大气污染区域联防联控强化方案、国Ⅲ柴油货车限行措施、高污染燃料禁燃区通告等；开展涉挥发性有机物含量产品限值抽查，深化储罐综合治理、企业简易低效污染治理设施升级改造，督促钢铁、水泥、玻璃等行业重点企业超低排放深度治理；开展柴油车遥感监测、道路抽检及用车大户入户检查，细化检查机动车排放检验机构，防治移动源污染。2024 年，广东省大气六项主要污染物浓度连续 10 年全面达标，优良天数比例为 95.8%，同比改善 1 个百分点，重度及以上污染天数为 0，PM2.5 浓度为 21 微克/米³，较"十三五"时期同比下降 30%，空气质量保持总体优良。

2024 年 11 月，广东印发《广东省空气质量持续改善行动方案》，强调持续打好蓝天保卫战的路径为"深入推进产业结构、能源结构、交通结构优化调整，强化多污染物协同减排、面源污染防治，加强大气污染联防联控，提升大气环境管理能力"。粤港澳大湾区空气质量改善先行示范区有望在 3~5 年全面建成。

二 环境空气治理的主要成效

2024 年，中国重点城市 PM2.5 的平均浓度为 29.3 微克/米³，同比下降 2.7%，重度及以上污染天数比例为 0.9%，同比下降 0.7 个百分点，优良天数比例连续 5 年达到 86% 以上，蓝天白云成为人民群众日常生活中的常态，中国成为全球空气质量改善速度最快的国家。京津冀地区、天山北坡城市

---

① "六大行动"为产业绿色低碳转型行动、能源清洁低碳高效发展行动、绿色低碳交通运输体系建设行动、提质增效降低排放强度行动、精细化综合治理行动、大气污染区域协同行动；"两个体系"为法规标准体系、大气环境管理体系；"一个保障"为加大措施落实保障。

群、成渝地区、汾渭平原、长江中游城市群、长三角地区 PM2.5 浓度同比分别下降 3.4%、13.4%、10.8%、4.8%、4.4%、0.9%，上述六大区域人口数量、土地面积和经济总量累计分别占全国的 52%、39% 和 57%，在稳增长任务十分繁重的形势下，改善局面来之不易。PM 2.5 和臭氧协同控制取得初步成效，与 2019 年相比，中国 PM2.5 浓度下降 19.4%；臭氧浓度下降 2.7%，且连续 3 年稳定在 144~145 微克/米^3，2015 年以来臭氧连续上升的趋势得到初步控制。

案例 2-3　　南京钢铁集团：建绿色美丽钢厂，做全球绿色钢铁先行者

在 2025 年 2 月召开的生态环境部新闻发布会上，生态环境部大气环境司负责人介绍持续深入打好蓝天保卫战工作进展情况，以南京钢铁集团为例，阐述企业在绿色转型中实现环保与利润双赢的成果。南京钢铁集团将绿色低碳循环发展作为核心战略，优先使用清洁能源，采用资源利用率高、污染物排放量少、废弃物综合利用的先进工艺和设备，实现厂容整洁、环境优美、产城融合，获评绿色发展标杆企业、绿色工厂、清洁生产环境友好型企业等荣誉称号。

超低排放，添"绿"增"效"

南京钢铁集团建成 100 多个具有国际先进水平的节能降耗、环境治理项目，陆续增加 11 套脱硫脱硝装置，完成 112 套除尘器升级改造，通过"有组织超低排放""无组织超低排放""清洁物流"三个方面组合拳，实现"用矿不见矿、用煤不见煤、运料不见料、出铁不见铁、绿叶不见尘"的环保目标。

在"有组织超低排放"方面，南京钢铁集团采用先进的"三干技术"（干法除尘、干法脱硫、干熄焦），大幅减少废气排放。在"无组织超低排放"改造方面，南京钢铁集团建成铁矿粉、煤炭堆场全封闭大棚和煤筒仓、焦炭仓，增设除尘装置，实现出铁沟盖板严丝合缝、出铁厂房一尘不染。在清洁物流方面，南京钢铁集团建设管式皮带，将高炉水渣密闭输送至超细粉加工厂，物流车辆全部更换为"国六"标准，物资运输普遍使用电动重卡和电动机车。

数智赋能，智慧监管

随着大量环保投入，为掌握数量众多的环保设施实时数据，解决"有没有、用没用、好不好"的复合型管理问题，南京钢铁集团建成智慧运营中心，上线搭载多个大模型的"智慧环保管控平台"，实现"一屏看全域、一键知指标、一网管环保"的实时精准管控，提升环保设施动态管理和达标预警水平。

工厂花园，"绿色明珠"

南京钢铁集团对厂区环境全面规划和提档升级，对厂区绿化、美化、净化、亮化改造，形成三季有花、四季常青、色彩丰富、层次分明的景观效果。打造南京钢铁博物馆、南钢党建陈列馆、文体公园、未来钢铁智造馆等 20 余个工业旅游景点，荣获国家工业旅游示范基地、文化和旅游数字化创新示范十佳案例等荣誉。

第 2 节　中国"打好碧水保卫战"的创新举措、主要成效和典型案例

水是生存之本、文明之源。胸怀祖国江河山川，习近平总书记一直关心水，他到地方考察调研时，都把察看水生态环境保护情况作为行程安排的重要内容，深入一线指导相关工作。党的十八大以来，以习近平同志为核心的党中央把解决突出水生态环境问题作为民生优先领域，以最坚定的决心和最有力的举措开展水污染防治行动，碧水保卫战取得显著成效，水环境质量处于有监测记录以来历史最高水平。2024 年，全国优良水质断面比例达到 90.4%，首次超过 90%，同比上升 1 个百分点，接近发达国家水平，较 2012 年改善 28.8 个百分点；近岸海域水质优良比例为 83.7%，提前达到"十四五"规划目标；长江干流连续 5 年、黄河干流连续 3 年全线水质稳定保持在 II 类。一幅河湖安澜、秀水长清的壮丽画卷，舒展在中华大地上。

一　水生态环境治理体制机制进一步完善

2019 年，生态环境部挂牌成立七大流域海域生态环境监督管理局[①]，主要负责流域生态环境监管和行政执法，解决长期以来流域海域生态环境监管职责交叉重复、多头管理等问题。中国在所有江河湖泊全面建立以党政领导负责制为核心的河湖长制，31 个省（区、市）党委和政府主要领导担任省级总河长，120 余万"省、市、县、乡、村"五级河湖长上岗履职，全面负责河湖的水资源保护、水域岸线管理、水污染防治、水环境治理、水生态修复等工作。长江、黄河、淮河、海河、珠江、松花江辽河、太湖等七大流域全部建立省级河湖长联席会议机制，定期协商议事，部署联合行动。南水北调、引江济淮等 110 个大型引调水工程推行河湖长制。各地建立河湖长履职、监督检查、考核问责、正向激励等制度，以及"河湖长+警长""河湖长+检察长"等协调机制。推动河湖长制进企业、进校园、进社区、进农村，全民关爱河湖意识显著增强。

案例 2-4　　　　河湖长制能效提级：城湖共生的巢湖治理答卷

巢湖东临长江，西接大别山，与淮河沟通，是中国五大淡水湖之一。2011 年 7 月，国务院同意安徽省撤销地级巢湖市及部分行政区划调整，巢湖成为合肥市的内湖。2012 年 3 月，安徽专设治理巢湖的管理机构——安徽省巢湖管理局。进入新时代以来，安徽省、合肥市共同设立环巢湖生态保护治理资金池、项目库和智库，巢湖治理走上流域共治、生态修复的治源之路，开启一座城与一片湖的共生发展新局。2020 年 8 月，习近平总书记在安徽考察时指出："巢湖是安徽人民的宝贝，是合肥最美丽动人的地方。一定要把巢湖治理好，把生态湿地保护好，让巢湖

---

①　生态环境部七大流域海域生态环境监督管理局包括长江流域生态环境监督管理局、黄河流域生态环境监督管理局、淮河流域生态环境监督管理局、海河流域北海海域生态环境监督管理局、珠江流域南海海域生态环境监督管理局、松辽流域生态环境监督管理局、太湖流域东海海域生态环境监督管理局。

成为合肥最好的名片。"

合肥市一共有 39 条一级支流从四面八方汇入巢湖，支流污染与否，直接关系巢湖的水质。合肥市实施"碧水、安澜、富民"三大工程，构建全流域水污染防治体系：城市污水提质增效破解点源污染，重点河流治理攻坚线源污染，大数据管控应对农业面源污染，控磷行动遏制内源污染。同时，合肥市以科技创新培育新兴产业，从新型显示到集成电路，从人工智能到新能源汽车，发展以"芯屏汽合""集终生智"为代表的现代化绿色产业体系。2024 年，巢湖全湖水质稳定保持 Ⅳ 类，蓝藻水华面积十年来最小，居民退居、渔业退养、生态修复为特色的十八联圩湿地修复入选联合国生态恢复行动优秀案例。

合肥市做深做实巢湖河湖长制，扩大巢湖市委常委担任河长的比例，由分管市领导担任河长办主任，划片设立"片区总河长"，开展河长交叉巡河"三看三比"① 活动、河长参与的河道环境月考核和奖补。巢湖市委党校、市河长办联合成立安徽省首个河湖长教育培训基地——河长行政学校，定期对各级河湖长开展业务授课，通过学分制考核颁发结业证书。建设河湖长制水文化科普基地，培育以水域、湿地、公园、科普为特色的研学旅游线路。设立巢湖"河湖长日"，上线"全民护水"小程序，建设可通过河湖管护积分兑换商品的"河湖长制积分超市"，引导社会各界主动参与巡河、护河。

进入新时代以来，中国构建以排污许可制为核心的固定污染源监管制度，基本实现固定污染源排污许可全覆盖。全面开展长江、渤海和黄河入河入海排污口排查整治，织就空中、地面、水下一体化的监测网络。中国建立水资源刚性约束制度，坚持以水定城、以水定地、以水定人、以水定产，实施国家节水行动，严格水资源论证和取水许可，推动农业节水增效、工业节水减排、城镇节水降损，积极发展节水产业，推广合同节水管理。建立覆盖省、市、县的用水总量和强度"双控"指标体系，基本完成重要跨省（区、市）江河流域水量分配。2014 年以

---

① 三看三比：看面貌、比环境，看指标、比水质，看管理、比内业。

来，在中国国内生产总值增长近一倍的情况下，用水总量总体稳定在6100 亿立方米以内；2024 年万元国内生产总值用水量、万元工业增加值用水量同比分别下降 4.4%、5.6%；全国耕地灌溉亩均用水量下降至350 立方米以下，在农业用水保持稳定的情况下，实现灌溉面积和粮食产量稳步增加。

案例 2-5　　跨省流域生态补偿：构建责任共担、发展成果和优质生态产品共享的流域保护长效机制

习近平总书记指出："全面建立生态补偿制度。要健全区际利益补偿机制，形成受益者付费、保护者得到合理补偿的良性局面。要健全纵向生态补偿机制，加大对森林、草原、湿地和重点生态功能区的转移支付力度。要推广新安江水环境补偿试点经验，鼓励流域上下游之间开展资金、产业、人才等多种补偿。要建立健全市场化、多元化生态补偿机制，在长江流域开展生态产品价值实现机制试点。"

进入新时代以来，中国已有 18 个省份、13 个流域（河段）探索开展跨省流域上下游横向生态保护补偿，中央财政投入引导资金累计超过 200亿元。相关省份建立水污染防治协作小组、水污染突发环境事件联防联控机制，编制流域生态环境共同保护规划，开展联合监测和跨界水环境联合排查。除 2021 年新签订跨省补偿协议的 3 个流域（河段）刚起步外，其他 10 个流域（河段）涉及的 23 个考核断面水质均能稳定达到或优于协议目标要求，部分考核断面特征污染物浓度较政策实施前显著下降。同时，31 个省份全部开展省内流域生态补偿机制建设，其中浙江、重庆、山东、天津等 14 个省份实现省内流域生态补偿全覆盖。

源头活水出新安，百转千回下钱塘。新安江发源于安徽省黄山市，自西向东流入杭州市新安江水库，再向东北汇入钱塘江，干流长 373 公里，流域面积 1.1 万多平方千米。新安江水库是杭州第二水源，库区60% 的水来自上游新安江补给，著名旅游景点千岛湖位于此，生态价值、经济价值非常重要。2007 年，新安江流域被国家列为跨省流域生态补偿机制建设试点。2012 年，浙江省与安徽省签订《新安江流域水环境补偿协议》。经过前三轮试点，浙皖两省建立以 P 值（由高锰酸盐指数、氨氮、总氮、总磷 4 项指标，以及水质稳定系数、指标权重系数组成）为主要内容的补偿考核体系，形成全流域生态环境共同保护的"新安江模式"，安徽每年向千岛湖输送近 70 亿立方米干净水。据生态环境部环境规划院评估，新安江生态系统服务价值总计 246.5 亿元，水生态服务价值总量 64.5 亿元，实现青山有"价"、绿水含"金"。2023 年，新安江流域启动第四轮生态补偿，前三轮单方补偿、单方受偿的模式转变为双方共同出资和共同分配，以"浙皖合作十件事"强化两地的产业、人才等对接合作，共建新安江-千岛湖生态环境共同保护合作区。新安江流域四轮流域横向生态补偿方案关键点见表 2-1。

表 2-1　新安江流域四轮流域横向生态补偿方案关键点

试点期限	第一轮（2012~2014 年）	第二轮（2015~2017 年）	第三轮（2018~2020 年）	第四轮（2023~2027 年）
基本原则	保护优先，合理补偿；保持水质，力争改善；地方为主，中央监管；监测为据，以补促治。			
补偿资金	以财政转移支付为主，由中央财政和浙皖两省共同设立新安江流域水环境补偿基金。		以财政转移支付为主，由浙皖两省设立新安江流域水环境补偿基金。	
试点资金	中央财政每年出资 3 亿元，浙皖两省每年各出资 1 亿元。	中央财政按第一年 4 亿元、第二年 3 亿元、第三年 2 亿元退坡方式补助。浙皖两省每年各出资 2 亿元。	浙皖两省每年各出资 2 亿元。	2023 年，浙皖两省共同出资 10 亿元。从 2024 年起，参照两省年度经济增速，建立逐年增长机制。若 P ≤ 0.95，浙江出资 60%、安徽出资 40%。若 0.95<P ≤ 1，浙江与安徽各出资 50%。若 P>1 或新安江流域安徽界内出现重大水污染事故，浙江出资 40%、安徽出资 60%。
考核依据	根据浙皖两省交界断面联合水质监测数据（高锰酸盐指数、氨氮、总磷、总氮 4 项指标，以及水质稳定系数、指标权重系数），综合测算补偿指数 P 值。			在保持前三轮 P 值考核的基础上，引入产业、人才补偿指数 M 值。

试点期限	第一轮 （2012~2014 年）	第二轮 （2015~2017 年）	第三轮 （2018~2020 年）	第四轮 （2023~2027 年）
考核方式	浙皖两省联合监测，中国环境监测总站核定，并向国家有关部门报送。			
补偿方式	若 P≤1，浙江资金拨付给安徽；若 P>1，安徽资金拨付给浙江。中央财政资金全部拨付给安徽。	若 P≤1，浙江拨付 1 亿元给安徽；若 P>1，安徽拨付 1 亿元给浙江；若 P≤0.95，浙江再拨付 1 亿元给安徽。中央财政资金全部拨付给安徽。	当年水质达到考核标准，浙江拨付 2 亿元给安徽；水质达不到考核标准，安徽拨付 2 亿元给浙江。	若 M>1.25，浙皖两省补偿资金分配比例为 0.25：0.75；若 1<M≤1.25，浙皖两省补偿资金分配比例为 0.2：0.8；若 M≤1，浙皖两省补偿资金分配比例为 0.15：0.85。

二　江河湖泊保护治理取得积极进展

中国坚持以流域为单元、河湖水系为脉络，以"河安湖晏、水清鱼跃、岸绿景美、宜居宜业、人水和谐"为目标，统筹流域上下游、左右岸、干支流、地上地下，共同抓好水灾害防治、水资源节约、水生态修复、水环境治理，将经济社会发展与河湖保护治理深度融合，建立河湖生态产品价值实现机制，推动河湖生态优势、资源优势向发展优势、经济优势转化，累计建成各具特色的幸福河湖 3200 多条（个），完成 10000 余条（个）河湖的健康评价，逐河逐湖建立健康档案，滚动编制实施"一河（湖）一策"方案。强化河湖水域岸线空间管控，全国 123 万千米河道、1996 个湖泊明确管控边界，开展河湖"清四乱（乱占、乱采、乱堆、乱建）"行动。实施母亲河复苏行动，强化河湖生态流量管理，开展河湖水系连通和生态补水，断流百年的京杭大运河连续四年全线水流贯通，断流干涸 26 年的永定河实现全年全线有水，华北地下水超采区的地下水水位显著回升。

长江、黄河是中华民族的母亲河，把长江、黄河打造成为造福人民的幸福河，是中国江河战略的出发点和落脚点。中国出台《长江保护法》，加强长江岸线、非法码头、非法采砂和污染治理，开展小水电清理，实施河湖湿地保护修复、长江十年禁渔等。出台《黄河保护法》，完善流域水沙调控和防洪减灾体系，强化水资源节约集约利用，开展水生态保护修复，加强水土流失治理等。长江和黄河的治理保护取得历史性成就，发生历史性变化，水之害得到有效防范。

中国实施集中式饮用水水源地环境保护专项行动，按照"一个水源地、一套方案、一抓到底"的要求，实施生活面源污染、工业企业排污、农业面源污染、旅游餐饮污染、交通穿越等问题清单管理制度，依法清理饮用水水源保护区内违法建设项目。2023 年，全国地级及以上城市饮用水水源达标断面（点位）为 96.5%，县级城镇为 94.8%，保持较高水平，南水北调水源地及沿线生态环境质量明显改善，群众饮水安全得到可靠保障。

案例 2-6　　　湖岸同治、流域共治：唱响新时代"太湖美"

湖泊治理是公认的世界性难题，太湖治理尤甚。太湖流域位于长三角核心区域，是中国经济最具活力、人口密度最高、城镇最为密集的区域之一。过去在粗放型经济发展模式下，各类污水排入太湖，酿成 2007 年太湖蓝藻暴发的恶果。太湖治理是习近平总书记念兹在兹、反复强调的"国之大者"，2023 年全国两会期间，习近平总书记在参加江苏代表团审议时问起太湖治理情况，语重心长地说："我们讲绿水青山就是金山银山，生态搞不好就不是'金山银山'，反而成了亏钱买卖。"

多举措发力，再现碧波荡漾

污染在水里，病根在岸上。在全面落实《太湖流域水环境综合治理总体方案》的基础上，江苏省 2023 年出台《推进新一轮太湖综合治理行动方案》，对辖内 40 条河流"一河一策"编制水质达标提升方案，开展污染源、蓝藻种源"双源齐溯"。以控源截污和减磷控氮为主攻方向，开展涉磷企业、农村生活污水、主要入湖河流等综合整治，高强度实施污水处理厂及管网建设、底泥疏浚、蓝藻打捞等治理工程。内源减负，健全"挡、引、捞、控"并举的蓝藻应急防控体系，"引江济太"，增加流域水资源供给，推进流域生态修复，构建环太湖生态湿地圈。

在无锡太湖近岸 142 公里岸线上，分布着 83 个蓝藻打捞平台、13 座藻水分离站，应用"围隔挡藻导流+深井加压控藻"集成配套技术，构建科学化监测、专业化队伍、机械化打捞、管网化运输、工厂化处理、无害化处置、信息化管理的蓝藻打捞处置利用模式。2024 年 3 月，中国自主设计研发的生态清淤智能一体化平台船"太湖之星"投入使用，开创水上大规模河湖清淤与底泥就地固化的新路径。2007~2024 年，无锡累计打捞蓝藻 2256 万吨，占全太湖打捞量的 90% 以上，相当于直接从湖体中捞走 6023 吨总氮和 1511 吨总磷等污染物质。

腾笼换鸟，培育新质生产力

江苏省太湖区域占全省土地面积的 20%，承载 30% 以上的人口和 40% 以上的经济总量。近年来，深化工业污染防治，太湖一级保护区内 230 家化工企业全部清零，削减粗钢产量 461.9 万吨，关停"散乱污"企业数万家，完成 2 万余家涉磷企业整治，累计削减原料磷使用 4000 余吨。出台太湖流域禁止和限制的产业产品目录、传统产业和未来产业高质量发展实施意见，建设苏州、常州两个国家级战略性新兴产业集群，累计建成国家级绿色工业园区 24 个、绿色工厂 200 家、绿色供应链管理企业 56 家。推进化肥农药减量增效，太湖一、二级保护区内具备条件的田块全面取消直播稻，主要入湖河道两侧秸秆全部离田处置，开展渔业生态健康养殖，促进农渔业绿色转型。发展"河湖+文体旅"新业态，繁荣帆船、赛艇等水上运动，主客共享的幸福河湖效应得以具象化体现。

一湖碧波映天际，江湖万里水云阔。2024 年，太湖水质总体达到 Ⅲ 类，创 30 年来最高水平，首次全年达到国家良好湖泊标准；蓝藻发生强度持续减轻，上半年首次未监测到蓝藻水华，太湖连续 17 年实现安全度夏；流域生态系统更加健康，太湖水生生物多样性指数首次提高到"优秀"等级。

案例 2-7　　白洋淀生态之变：城与淀相互辉映、美美与共

白洋淀是华北平原最大的淡水湖泊，流域面积 3 万多平方千米，涉及 30 多个县（市、区），143 个淀泊星罗棋布，3700 多条沟壕纵横交错，

对维护华北地区生态安全具有重大意义。20 世纪 70 年代后，由于气候干旱、上游来水减少、工农业用水量增加等原因，纵然处于"九河下梢"，白洋淀也面临水位下降、污染等困境。2017 年 2 月，习近平总书记实地考察雄安新区建设规划时专程前往白洋淀并强调，建设雄安新区，一定要把白洋淀修复好、保护好。2017 年 4 月，中共中央、国务院决定设立河北雄安新区，这是千年大计、国家大事，白洋淀由此迎来有史以来最大规模的系统性生态治理。2018 年 4 月公布的《河北雄安新区规划纲要》明确，加强白洋淀生态环境治理和保护，逐步恢复白洋淀"华北之肾"功能。

至 2021 年，白洋淀全域还清，水质提升至地表水 Ⅲ 类标准，并连续三年保持该水平，打造水城共融、城淀相依的绿色发展"雄安样板"，即：坚持流域"控源—截污—治河"系统治理，实施入淀河流水质目标管理，全面治理工业污染源，强化城乡污水收集处理，有效治理农业面源污染，打造良好河湖生态环境，确保入淀河流水质达标。

探索多水源生态补水机制

从 20 世纪 90 年代末开始，为维持白洋淀不干涸，有关部门先后十余次引水济淀，但在长期资源性缺水状态下，白洋淀水危机并未得到根本解决。雄安新区设立以来，开展入淀河道综合整治，潴龙河、孝义河、唐河、府河、漕河、萍河、瀑河和白沟引河等白洋淀周边河流基本贯通。实施"引黄济淀"和"引江入淀"等重点工程，使用黄河水、南水北调中线工程途经的多条河流、上游水库水、再生水等为白洋淀生态补水，白洋淀水位保持在 7 米左右，达到《白洋淀生态环境治理和保护规划（2018~2035 年）》要求的目标水位，淀区面积恢复至 300 平方千米左右，并向下游河道（赵王新河）放水 1 亿米³ 以上，有效改善白洋淀的水动力和水循环。

探索内外源治理新路径

2017 年以来，白洋淀全流域排查取缔污染企业，完成流域内 37 个省级以上工业园区的污水集中处理设施建设，雄安新区水产养殖和规上畜禽养殖场全部退出。2020 年 6 月，白洋淀流域生态环境监测中心挂牌成立，在全流域设置 61 个考核监测断面，建设 42 座水质自动监测站，上游各市对流域内全部入淀排口及 852 家重点涉水企业安装污水在线监控设施，织密流域监测网络。

污水处理能力持续提标扩容，保定市日污水处理能力超 175 万吨，比 2015 年增加近 50%。日处理能力 10 万吨的保定鲁岗二期污水处理厂是白洋淀流域规模最大的全地埋式污水处理设施，采用"地上绿地休闲场所+地下治污"模式，除了传统污水处理单元外，雨污调蓄系统兼具城市排涝、流量调节与污水应急处理功能，地下箱体内部设有环境教育基地展厅，成为公众了解污水处理流程和环保知识的窗口。

以前白洋淀一些淀区围堤围埝养鱼、种藕，还有一些淀区变为耕地，水面被分割得支离破碎，导致底泥堆积，水面减少，水流无法畅通，水质随之变差。2019 年以来，雄安新区实施百淀连通、清淤疏浚、退耕还淀等生态工程，对清淤后的区域实施自然修复，栽种沉水植物，增殖放流底栖性水上动物。新建成的府河、孝义河湿地采用近自然生态治污模式，即：上游入淀河水进入湿地后，首先经过前置沉淀生态塘，降低进水悬浮物浓度，随后进入潜流湿地，通过三级床体中的"基质—微生物—植物"共同作用，强化污染物净化，最后经过水生植物塘，对水质进行再次提升。

案例 2-8　　　　云南："一湖一策"开展高原湖泊精准治污

云南省地处中国西南边陲，是长江上游重要的生态安全屏障和水源涵养地，锚定"生态文明建设排头兵"目标，在立法、政策、技术、资金、监管等方面加强协调配合，推进治污水、治农业面源污染、治垃圾、改善水生态"三治一改善"，九大高原湖泊[①]水质总体向好，主要出境、跨界河流断面水质达标率为 100%，六大水系[②]出境跨界断面水质均为 Ⅱ 类及以上，实现"一江清水出云南"。

护好洱海清波

作为云南第二大高原淡水湖，洱海一直是习近平总书记牵挂的地方。

---

① 云南九大高原湖泊：滇池、洱海、抚仙湖、程海、泸沽湖、杞麓湖、异龙湖、星云湖、阳宗海。
② 云南六大水系：长江（金沙江）、珠江（南盘江）、红河（元江）、澜沧江（湄公河）、怒江（萨尔温江）、伊洛瓦底江（大盈江）。

2015 年 1 月和 2020 年 1 月，他两次考察云南都对洱海治理保护做出重要指示，强调"一定要把洱海保护好"。10 年来，大理州 5 次修订《洱海保护管理条例》，把科学立法、严格执法、公正司法、全民守法贯穿于洱海保护治理全过程；通过截污治污、提升入湖水质、"三禁四推"① 防治农业面源污染、修复生态等，统筹推进洱海流域山水林田湖草沙一体化保护；成立洱海保护与流域生态文明建设促进会，把每月第一个星期六设为"洱海保护日"，定期组织群众开展科普教育和志愿服务……洱海水质连续多年保持优良水平，湖体透明度提升至 2.29 米，27 条主要入湖河流水质优良率达 100%，一度消失 20 多年被称为"水质指示生物"的海菜花环湖开放。

依托洱海湖泊生态系统国家野外科学观测研究站、洱海"科技小院"和专家工作站等平台，大理州建立科研统筹和专家会商工作机制，持续开展洱海治理重点难点科技攻关。"数字洱海监管服务平台"涵盖智能感知、数据中心、决策支持、协同管理、信息服务、业务应用六大功能模块，实时收集水质、雨量、气象、污染治理设施运行等监测数据，定量分析洱海未来 7 天的水质发展趋势，适时预警响应，实现监测数据、专家意见与行政决策、工作措施的互联互通、深度融合。

滇池清水还复来

滇池是云南最大的淡水湖，素有"高原明珠"美誉。20 世纪中期，受多种因素影响，滇池水质出现恶化，到 90 年代部分水质下降为劣 V 类。2020 年 1 月，习近平总书记来到昆明滇池星海半岛生态湿地，了解滇池保护治理和水质改善情况，他指出，滇池是镶嵌在昆明的一颗宝石，要拿出咬定青山不放松的劲头，按照山水林田湖草是一个生命共同体的理念，加强综合治理、系统治理、源头治理，再接再厉，把滇池治理工作做得更好。近年来，昆明市秉持"滇池是用来保护的，不是用来开发的"理念，采取"退、减、调、治、管"等措施，2008～2024 年均保持全湖水质 Ⅳ 类。

---

① 三禁四推：禁止销售使用含氮磷化肥和高毒高残留农药，禁止种植大水大肥农作物；推行有机肥替代化肥、病虫害绿色防控、绿色生态种植和畜禽标准化养殖。

补水截污是解决滇池水资源匮乏、环境压力大、湖体自净能力弱的关键举措，昆明建成多个域外调水工程、29 座水质净化厂、7864 千米的市政排水管网，日处理污水超过 250 万立方米，截至 2024 年 5 月，仅牛栏江-滇池补水工程累计向滇池补水 45.53 亿立方米，提供城市应急供水 6.05 亿立方米。按照"人工干预最小化、自然恢复最大化"原则，建成以湿地为主的滇池环湖生态带 6.29 万亩，滇池湖滨建成平均宽度约 200 米的闭合生态带，进一步缓冲污水入湖并净化水质。

科技赋能是破解滇池生态修复之困的重要工具。龙门藻水分离站是中国第一座专门用于湖库蓝藻水华的处理站，经过"藻水打捞—物理过滤—加压沉淀—高效气浮—尾水利用—藻泥脱水—环保处置"工序，将富藻水处理为地表Ⅲ类水，藻泥加工后"变废为宝"，成为有机肥。昆明市滇池高原湖泊研究院开发的"生境改善—水草恢复—浊清转换"等成套生态修复技术体系在滇池大泊口水域示范应用，大泊口水域总体水质基本可达Ⅲ类，沉水植物分布面积从 2015 年不足 10% 增加到 2022 年的 50% 以上，海菜花、水鸟越来越多。

三　其他领域的水环境治理成效显著

中国持续实施城乡黑臭水体整治环境保护专项行动，开展黑臭水体动态排查，将其中面积较大、群众反映强烈的水体纳入监管清单，优先采用资源化、生态化治理措施，实行"拉条挂账，逐一销号"。强化监测抽查，建立"返黑返臭"防范机制，综合运用卫星遥感、水质监测等方式开展跟踪监管。目前，全国地级及以上城市建成区黑臭水体基本消除，较大面积农村黑臭水体治理完成超过 3000 个，国家监管的农村黑臭水体治理率达 82.3%，已完成治理水体的水质监测抽样合格率达 97% 以上，往日的"一沟黑水"变身为一池绿水、一湾清水，有力促进城乡融合发展。

水利部会同相关部门和省份推进南水北调东中线一期工程受水区、华北地区及其他重点区域地下水超采综合治理，形成"一减一增"系统治理模式。通过科学划定地下水超采区、强化重点领域节水、严控开发规模和强度、多渠道增加水源补给、实施河湖地下水回补、严格地下水利用管控等综合施策，中国地下水超采量、超采程度持续缓解，与 2015 年相比，2024 年地下水超采区面积减少 1.95 万平方千米、减少 6.8%，严重超采区面积减少 8.83 万平方千米、减少 51%，超采量减少 50 亿立方米、减少 31.9%。

第 3 节　中国海洋生态环境保护的创新举措、主要成效和典型案例

中国是海洋生态环境保护的坚定推动者和积极行动者。进入新时代以来，习近平总书记对海洋生态环境保护做出一系列重要论述，强调"要像对待生命一样关爱海洋"。中国把海洋生态环境保护纳入国家生态环境保护体系，建立陆海统筹的海洋生态环境治理体系，海洋生态环境质量总体改善，局部海域生态系统服务功能显著提升，海洋资源有序开发利用，碧海银滩向金山银山转化的路径越走越宽。

案例 2-9　　　厦门"山水海城"相融共生：打造新时代美丽中国建设的窗口

筼筜湖综合治理是习近平生态文明思想的重要发端，厦门市是习近平生态文明思想的重要孕育地和先行实践地。习近平总书记在厦门工作期间亲自谋划、亲自部署、亲自推动筼筜湖综合治理，以前瞻性的战略眼光创造性提出"依法治湖、截污处理、清淤筑岸、搞活水体、美化环境"20 字方针，指出一条人与海洋和谐共生的高质量发展道路。

以筼筜湖综合治理为发端，厦门市锚定建设美丽厦门目标，强化目标协同、部门协同、政策协同、区域协同、治理协同，坚持陆海统筹、河海联动、系统治理，深入打好近岸海域污染防治攻坚战，全方位、全地域、全要素开展城乡国土空间生态修复，有效破解海湾型城市资源约束紧、污染排放高、人海矛盾多等难题。

进一步看，厦门市将海漂垃圾综合治理列入为民办实事项目，纳入党政领导生态环保目标责任考核，建立制度化责任落实机制、常态化海上环卫机制、系统化综合治理机制、信息化预测预报机制的海漂垃圾"四化"治理机制，实现垃圾海上收集、陆上处置，被国家发展改革委纳入国家生态文明试验区改革举措和经验做法清单。市、区财政每年投入近 1 亿元，用于船舶车辆维护、人员支出及保洁船舶委外服务，确保海域、沙滩清扫保洁和垃圾转运有效运行。上线海漂垃圾监测预警预报系统，运用无人机航拍巡查重点岸段，精准预测入海垃圾漂移轨迹及分布区域，发现问题及时通报整改。通过综合施策，厦门市近岸海域的国省控点位水质优良比例从 2019 年的 50% 提升至 2024 年的 95% 以上，2024 年海水浴场水质优良率 100%，均创历史最高水平。

作为中国首批 14 个海洋经济发展示范区之一，厦门市发挥涉海资源优势，串联政务服务、产业布局、环境保护、区域协同、要素支持等海洋经济政策，建设海洋高新技术产业园，培育海洋科研创新载体和人才高地，发展"龙头企业作引领＋专精特新树品牌＋科技型中小企业培育壮大"为特色的海洋新兴产业。2020 年以来，厦门市海洋战略性新兴产业增加值年均增速 11.3%，超过 GDP 年均增速。截至 2024 年 9 月，厦门市拥有涉海企业超过万家，其中国家高新技术企业 28 家、产业链龙头企业 30 家、上市企业 13 家。

一　多部门协同、中央地方联动的海洋生态环境保护工作机制基本建成

2018 年，国务院机构改革将海洋环境保护职责整合到生态环境部门，海洋保护修复和开发利用职责整合到自然资源部门，交通运输、海事、渔业、林草、海警、军队等部门依照各自职能共同参与海洋生态环境保护，增强了陆海污染防治协同性和生态环境保护整体性。在海河流域北海海域、珠江流域南海海域、太湖流域东海海域设置生态环境监管机构。沿海各省（区、市）承担近岸海域生态环境保护的具体责任。同时，中国逐步建立刑事、民事和行政诉讼"三合一"的海洋环境保护司法体系，

以及具有中国特色的海洋环境公益诉讼制度，筑牢海洋生态环境保护司法防线。

二　重点海域综合治理取得重大进展

渤海是中国的半封闭型内海，海水交换能力和自净能力不足。自2018 年起，中国连续开展两轮渤海综合治理攻坚，以环渤海 "1+12" 城市①为重点，建立近岸海域跨地区、跨部门的协同治理、会商通报、联防联控等机制，加强入海河流总氮治理，做实入海排污口查测溯治，开展滨海湿地和生态岸线保护修复，实现 "流域－河口－近岸海域" 一体化的陆海统筹污染治理。2023 年，渤海近岸海域水质优良比例达 83.5%，比2018 年增长 18.1 个百分点，环渤海 49 条入海河流国控断面全面消除劣V 类水质，渤海生态环境质量持续向好。

浙江省发布《杭州湾海域生态修复提升行动方案》，建立中国首个入海河流上下游协同治理考核体系，省市县三级协同管好干支流重点控制断面，设立入海河流水质财政奖惩、流域横向生态保护补偿等制度，对钱塘江、曹娥江、甬江等入海河流开展全流域共治。值得关注的是，全流域管控范围 "严上加严"，即使在距离入海口约 180 公里的钱塘江四级支流东阳市南江，也设置重点控制断面，足见浙江管好每滴水的精度和决心。

广东省海域面积达 42 万平方千米，是陆地面积的 3 倍，海岸线蜿蜒曲折，绵延 4084 千米。广东省完成珠江口海域入海排污口的 "查、测、溯" 工作，开发重点入海排污口监管系统，在科学测算环境总容量的基础上，对化学需氧量、氨氮、总磷排放物等进行总量削减控制。同时，遵循 "一湾一策" 的原则，针对不同类型的海湾采取差异化的保护和修复措施，打造出各具特色的美丽海湾。

---

① 　环渤海 "1+12" 城市："1" 为天津市，"12" 为大连市、营口市、盘锦市、锦州市、葫芦岛市、秦皇岛市、唐山市、沧州市、滨州市、东营市、潍坊市、烟台市。

案例 2-10　　　**营造海洋生态和美空间：上海书写**
现代海洋城市新篇章

上海市依海而生、因海而兴，"加强海洋生态保护，强化近岸海域污染治理和海洋生态修复……构建陆海统筹、江海联动的一体化保护修复格局，提升海洋安全韧性"是建设现代海洋强市和海洋强国建设示范基地的关键。2022 年 10 月，上海市委、市政府提出上海建设现代海洋城市的宏伟蓝图，组建以市政府主要领导为组长的上海市建设现代海洋城市工作领导小组；2023 年 1 月，上海市出台《关于加强本市长江河口海域重叠区域管理工作的实施意见》，要求"实施长江河口海域、海岸线生态保护修复"；2024 年 3 月，上海市政府召开建设现代海洋城市工作领导小组会议，要求系统推进长江口-杭州湾海洋生态保护修复；2024 年 5 月，上海市出台《关于全面推进美丽上海建设　打造人与自然和谐共生现代化国际大都市的实施意见》，要求"分阶段推进杭州湾北岸临港、奉贤、金山海岸线和长江口海洋生态保护修复"；2024 年 7 月，上海市出台《关于贯彻落实党的二十届三中全会精神，进一步全面深化改革、在推进中国式现代化中充分发挥龙头带动和示范引领作用的决定》，提出下一阶段海洋生态环境保护的重点改革任务……随着一件件政策的出台，上海市向"海"图强步履坚定。

近年来，上海市巧做陆海统筹的生态环境保护"加减法"。例如，对一度遭受污染之困的苏州河、黄浦江进行截污纳管、河道疏浚、生态修复，水质明显改善；位于长江与黄浦江汇流之处的上海吴淞口古炮台经历生态恢复与文化重建，由杂乱丛生的"钢渣堆场"变身具备水质净化功能的湿地公园；对标"最高标准、最高水平"，率先建成长江禁捕智能管控系统，实现智能发现、智能警告、综合研判、指挥调度、属地监管、及时查处和信息共享的监管闭环。

崇明岛被誉为"长江门户、东海瀛洲"，地处长江入海处，被上海市政府定位为"世界级生态岛"。近年来，崇明岛开展滩涂自然湿地生态修复，有效控制外来入侵物种（互花米草）的扩张，逐步恢复芦苇、海三棱藨草等本土物种，推动新旧动能转换，督促违规企业还滩于民、还水于民，全面消除黑臭和劣 V 类水体，地表水环境功能区达标率 100%，空气优良率 91.9%，森林覆盖率为全市平均水平的两倍，江海相连、水天一色、万鸟翔集成为"新常态"。崇明区以碳中和示范区建设为抓手，统筹减排、控源、固碳、增汇，在滩涂、海洋、森林、河湖、农田、城镇等 6 类生态系统开展特色生态产品调研、登记、确权、核算和精细化管理，开发渔光互补、陆上风电等新能源，可再生能源发电量占全区用电总量的 32%，聚力发展都市现代绿色农业和海洋装备两个主导产业，配套引育高品质旅游业、特色体育产业、健康服务业三个优势产业，加快构建绿色低碳的生态产业体系，"世界级生态岛"因"双碳"目标而焕然一新。

三 联动治理陆源污染

1. 加强入海河流污染防治

中国持续提升城镇污水处理质效，建设雨污分流管网，加强污水处理行业监管，降低城镇生产生活污水对入海河流水质的影响。截至 2023 年末，全国城市排水管道长度 95.25 万千米，同比增长 4.27%；污水处理厂处理能力达 2.27 亿米³/日，同比增长 4.84%；污水处理率 98.69%，比上年增加 0.58 个百分点；生活污水集中收集率 73.63%，比上年增加 3.57 个百分点；沿海地级及以上城市污水处理厂基本完成一级 A 提标改造。同时，开展农村环境整治。2021~2024 年，沿海省份完成超过 1.7 万个行政村环境综合整治，编制 170 个畜牧大县畜禽养殖污染防治规划，农村生活污水治理率超过 45%。

河长、湾长协调联动，海洋、海警、海事等部门开展常态化执法，利用无人机开展海湾全覆盖巡查，加强对涉海工程项目监督监管，将总氮削减作为跨区域入海河流补偿协议中的重要指标，实施入海河流"一河一策"治理。2023 年，中国国控河流入海断面总氮平均浓度同比下降 12.2%，近岸海域水质优良比例达 85%，同比增长 3.1 个百分点，实现自 2018 年以来的"六连增"，劣 V 类断面基本消除。

2. 守住沿岸污染入海的关键闸口

中国统筹推进入海排污口排查、监测、溯源、整治，建立近岸水体、入海排污口、排污管线、污染源全链条治理体系，实现"受纳水体—排污口—排污通道—排污单位"全过程监督管理。按照"有口皆查、应查尽查"要求，摸清各类入海排污口的数量、分布及排放特征、责任主体等信息，累计排查入海排污口 5.3 万余个，完成入海排污口整治 1.6 万余个。建设统一的入海排污口信息平台，规范入海排污口的设置与管理，严格禁止在自然保护地、重要渔业水域、海水浴场、生态保护红线等区域新设排污口。

案例 2-11　　　江苏：以入海排污口整治为切入点，谱写海洋生态治理的"江苏样本"

江苏省沿海地区（南通市、连云港市、盐城市）地处黄海海域，拥有954 千米海岸线，海域面积 3.75 万平方千米，沿海陆域面积 3.59 万平方千米。2019 年，江苏省启动入海排污口"拉网式排查"，通过"无人机航空摄影+卫星遥感+人工勘察"组合拳，对每处疑似排污口采取县、市、省三级复核模式，成为环渤海省外最早完成入海排污口全面排查的省份。同时，江苏省坚持监溯同步、有口皆溯的原则，详细记录入海排污口关键信息，切实查清入海排污口"谁在排、排什么"及废水"从哪里来、到哪里去"。

江苏省建立入海排污口设置、登记备案、整治销号、监测监督检查全流程闭环监管机制。其一，按照"依法取缔一批、清理合并一批、规范整治一批"要求，"一口一策"整治入海排污口。例如，在超标排污口较为集中的区域，通过雨水管末端建设观察井、增加排放前水质监控、安装即时控污截污设施等方式，提高排污风险防范处置能力；结合海水养殖池塘生态化改造，开展海水养殖排污口分类整治，清理合并散排污口，统一收集处理养殖尾水，严防直排入河入海；将陆海排污口整治与入海河流整治结合，纳入城乡基础设施建设、环境综合治理等。其二，建立省级入海排污口信息管理平台，对每个入海排污口建立电子档案，实现入海排污口监测、溯源、整治信息全过程管理。

3. 系统开展海洋垃圾清理整治

中国建立海洋垃圾监测、拦截、收集、打捞、运输、处理体系，持续开展海洋垃圾和微塑料监测调查，统筹规划建设陆域接收、转运、处理海洋垃圾设施，实施 11 个重点海湾专项清漂行动和沿海城市海洋垃圾清理行动，各沿海城市通过"海上环卫"等制度，多环节多举措遏制海洋垃圾入海，全国近岸海域海洋垃圾和近海微塑料的平均密度总体处于中低水平。

案例 2-12　　　　福建：海漂垃圾综合治理引领美丽海湾建设

福建是海洋大省，海岸线长达 3752 千米。多年来，福建持续深化生态省建设，连续 5 年将海漂垃圾治理作为为民办实事项目，从海漂垃圾治理的方案、机制、项目、模式、队伍、标准和平台 7 个方面持续发力，强化海漂垃圾源头管控，建立海漂垃圾智慧监管系统，岸上遏制源头产生量、流域拦截垃圾入海量、海面削减垃圾存量，走出一条"岸上管、水域拦、海面清"的海漂垃圾全链条治理之路。沿海县区全部建成专业化海上环卫队伍，实现大陆岸线及有居民海岛海漂垃圾清理范围全覆盖。截至 2023 年末，福建省共清理海漂垃圾约 47 万吨，重点岸段海漂垃圾分布密度比整治前（2020 年）下降超过 60%，滩净海碧的美丽海湾建设成效显现。

宁德市有海岸线 1046 千米、海域面积 4.45 万平方千米，约占福建省的 1/3，海上养殖历史悠久，是沿海群众脱贫致富的"当家产业"。宁德市推进海上养殖综合整治，将传统"木质+白色泡沫浮球"渔排改造为可回收再利用的环保型高密度塑胶渔排，定点设置垃圾集中回收设施和垃圾转运堆场。实施沿海乡村垃圾处理与海漂垃圾保洁陆海统筹，交付宁德市城建集团成立的二级子公司专事负责。建设覆盖渔排、渔船、渔港、执法部门等责任主体的"智慧海洋"大数据系统，实现"海漂垃圾第一时间发现—调度人员第一时间预警—环卫力量第一时间清理"的高效管理模式。

四　精准防治海上污染

1. 严控海洋工程倾废

从源头入手，中国不断优化涉海工程环评管理，将海洋工程依法纳入排污许可管理，严格管控围填海、海砂开采等项目。加强海洋油气勘探开发污染防治，由国家生态环境部门统一行使环评审批与污染物排放监管事权。按照科学、合理、经济、安全的原则选划设立倾倒区，科学、精细评价倾倒区运行状况，保障倾倒区生态环境与通航水深安全。严格实施倾倒许可制度，综合运用船舶自动识别系统、海洋倾倒在线监控等手段开展非现场监管，最大限度降低废弃物倾倒对海洋生态环境的影响。

2. 系统开展海水养殖污染治理

作为全球水产养殖第一大国，通过制定排放标准、强化环评管理、推动排污口分类整治和尾水监测等，中国不断强化海水养殖环境监管。沿海各地按照"取缔一批、合并一批、规范一批"要求，清理整治非法和设置不合理的养殖尾水排污口，推进池塘养殖、工厂化养殖、网箱等环保升级改造，净化养殖环境。沿海省市县全部发布养殖水域滩涂规划，科学划定海水养殖禁养区、限养区和养殖区。开展防治船舶水污染专项整治活动，实施船舶水污染物转移处置联合监管，沿海各省（区、市）基本完成港口船舶污染物接收、转运、处置设施建设。持续开展船舶燃油质量监督检查，加强靠泊船舶岸电设施配备及使用情况监管。

五　倾力打造美丽海湾

《中华人民共和国国民经济和社会发展第十四个五年规划和二〇三五年远景目标纲要》明确要求推进美丽海湾保护与建设。《关于全面推进美丽中国建设的意见》将美丽海湾纳入美丽中国建设全局。《"十四五"海洋生态环境保护规划》《"十四五"海洋生态环境保护规划》提出，"聚焦建设美丽海湾的主线""健全陆海统筹的生态环境治理制度体系"。由此，中国以海湾为基本单元，以打造"水清滩净、鱼鸥翔集、人海和谐"的美丽海湾为建设目标，制定美丽海湾建设基本标准，建立美丽海湾建设管理平台，鼓励经营主体、社会资本参与，"一湾一策"推进近岸海域污染防治、生态保护修复和岸滩环境整治。2023 年，全国 283 个海湾中有 126 个海湾水质与前三年均值相比得到改善，24 个典型海洋生态系统连续三年保持"不健康"状态清零。

案例 2-13　　　　深圳：以海湾综合治理为抓手建全球海洋中心城市

深圳市地处广东省南部、珠江口东岸，毗邻香港，海域面积 2297 平方千米，海岸线长 311.4 千米（含深汕特别合作区）。海域范围受香港九龙半岛分割，分为东、西两部分，东有大亚湾、大鹏湾以及深汕特别合作区的红海湾，西为珠江口和深圳湾，各海湾自然禀赋各异、海洋生物资源丰富，分布有红树林、盐沼、珊瑚礁等多样且重要的滨海湿地，拥有全国唯一位于城市腹地的自然保护区——福田红树林自然保护区，是东半球国际候鸟重要的栖息地和南北迁徙通道上重要的"中转站"。近年来，深圳市"一湾一策"严格控制陆源污染入海，在西部海域持续削减污染物入海总量，在东部海域设置污染物总量排放限值，在入海排放口分类管理、陆海联动监测、联合执法等方面取得实效成果。

其一，深圳市将"美丽海湾"指标与治污保洁工程、污染防治任务融合，纳入市、区两级生态文明考核。建设"固定路线巡航+指点飞行详察"的无人机 24 小时远程调度巡查系统和中国首个区县级全要素生态环境动态监测平台，构建海洋监测浮标、地波雷达、卫星遥感"海-陆-空"立体观测网，建立政府部门、街道、社区、社会组织、志愿者等多方参与，人力、物力、财力有效保障的海岸线和海洋垃圾综合治理机制，形成以水质监测数据为导向的近岸海域基本覆盖、海岸线全部监管、常态化巡查快捷高效、突发事件跟踪处置的陆海统筹环境监管格局。

其二，深圳市高标准打造集休闲娱乐、健身运动、观光旅游、体验自然等功能于一体的滨海休闲带，不同主题的公园、长廊互联互通，实现亲海空间岸线全贯通。成立中国首家民间发起的红树林基金会，开展"山海林河"自然教育活动，动员市民积极参与生物多样性保护。

案例 2-14　　海南美丽海湾：创环境之优、生态之美、治理之效的"蓝色名片"

海南岛拥有 1900 多千米形态各异、风光旖旎的海岸线，拥有丰富的生态、旅游、文化等绿色资源。2023 年初，海南省出台《关于加强美丽海湾保护与建设的意见》，明确"分批次、分类型，梯次推进全省美丽海湾建设"的任务措施。在国家美丽海湾建设 5 项指标（海湾水质优良比例、海湾洁净状况、海洋生物保护情况、滨海湿地和岸线保护情况、海水浴场和滨海旅游度假区环境状况）的基础上，增设公众满意度、入海河流劣 V 类消除情况、入海排污口规范化管理、属地环境及相关部门工作情况、国内外影响力提升、重大战略落实情况 6 项海南特色指标，"一湾一策"推进全省美丽海湾创建。

海口市按照"各美其美、梯次推进"建设思路，聚焦农业农村污染、海水养殖、海漂垃圾等重点环境问题，强化陆海统筹、流域海域协同治理，实施分区管控生态修复，同步提升海岸的生态景观功能和灾害防御功能，打造渔旅融合湿地，实施渔船打捞垃圾行动，形成"生态保育型"美丽海湾名片，海口湾入选全国美丽海湾优秀案例，铺前湾（海口段）、澄迈湾（海口段）入选全省美丽海湾名单，成为海南省首个全域美丽海湾城市。

三亚湾位于三亚市主城区南部，海域面积 75 平方千米，岸线长 35.7千米。三亚市建立综合执法、公安、海洋、环卫、生态环境等多部门协调机制，实现"区域全覆盖、过程全覆盖、人员不间断"的美丽海湾建设机制。以"日保洁"作为海滩和海上垃圾治理基本模式，将"美丽海湾建设"和"无废城市建设"串联实施，严控垃圾入河入海，加强海洋生物多样性保护，大面积开展湾区内珊瑚礁生态修复和增殖放流活动，建成沿湾 15 千米长的滨海公园，延伸"生态+旅游+经济"价值链，还景于民、还绿于民，将三亚湾打造成帆船、游艇、潜水等海上运动项目和滨海旅游度假的理想场所。

第4节　中国固体废物与化学品环境治理的创新举措、主要成效和典型案例

一　"无废城市"建设纵深推进

自 2018 年 12 月国务院办公厅印发《"无废城市"建设试点工作方案》以来，各地累计出台 400 余项"无废城市"政策。例如，上海颁布"无废城市"建设条例，山东等 6 个省份将"无废城市"建设写入地方性法规，江苏等出台省级"无废城市"建设奖励办法。浙江、吉林、重庆等 19 个省份推进全域"无废城市"建设，粤港澳大湾区、长三角地区、成渝地区双城经济圈等推进区域"无废城市"共建。各地以机关、企业、学校为对象，累计建设 2.5 万余个"无废细胞"，形成全社会"无废"文化传播链。"十四五"期间，全国 113 个地级及以上城市和 8 个特殊地区计划建设 3700 余项"无废城市"建设项目，投资超过 1 万亿元。在源头减量方面，2023 年，参与"无废城市"建设的 109 个地级市工业固体废物产生强度平均为 2.03 吨/万元，较 2020 年下降 6.8%。在资源化利用方面，贵州形成磷石膏建材利用、生态修复等消纳成熟途径，综合利用率达到 91.8%；重庆利用建筑弃土回用回填，完成历史遗留矿山和关闭矿山的生态修复面积达 241 公顷。

案例 2-15　　河北：打造绿意盎然的"无废城市"新场景

"十四五"期间，河北省在石家庄、唐山、保定、衡水、雄安新区纳入全国"113+8""无废城市"建设名单基础上，全部地市一并启动建设"无废城市"。在中国率先开展重金属排污权确权，发布重金属交易基准价格，开展多批次重金属排污权交易，支持钢铁高炉除尘灰等固废综合利用项目，消耗利用固废 780 万吨/年。发布"无废小区""无废乡村""无废医院""无废商场""无废工地""无废机关""无废学校""无废景区" 8 类"无废细胞"建设指南，累计建设各类"无废细胞"近千个。

河北各地依托当地经济社会发展基础，因地制宜建设各具特色的"无废城市"。例如，雄安新区投运中国首个隐藏式半地下邻利型垃圾处理设施，创建白洋淀"无废淀泊"示范；石家庄市以"可循环包装"和"智慧系统"为引导，打造物流园区固废治理试点；张家口市延伸风电产业循环链，开展新能源固废资源化利用；承德市以国家工业固废综合利用基地为平台，打造环京绿色砂石骨料循环利用基地；邯郸市以国家大宗固体废弃物综合利用示范基地建设为引领，不断提升粉煤灰、冶炼渣等利用效率。

锅炉渣、工业污泥、脱硫灰、粉煤灰、除尘灰、钢渣、水渣等工业固废处理是钢铁企业的传统难题。唐山首钢京唐公司结合工业固废的特点和用途，以"依法合规、全量处置、效益最大"为目标，构建固体废物梯级全量处置、利用和消纳体系，每年消纳固废 100 余万吨，入选工信部和生态环境部评定的"无废企业"典型案例（全省唯一入选的钢铁企业）。作为重要的钢铁生产基地，唐山面向市内钢铁企业推广"固废不出厂"模式，工业固废利用处置能力达 1157.7 万吨/年。

衡水市安平县是国家级畜牧大县，年产生养殖废弃物 102 万吨、各类农作物秸秆约 40 万吨，农作物秸秆就地焚烧、畜禽粪便露天存放等固废污染问题曾是困扰全县的难题。安平县裕丰京安养殖有限公司走出一条新路，即在猪舍下预埋管道，粪便不出栏，直接输送到沼气发电厂，生猪粪经过厌氧发酵后产生沼气，沼气发电或提纯为生物天然气，沼液再次发酵转化为液态有机肥，沼渣转化为固态有机肥，实现废水废物零排放的"气、电、热、肥"联产循环农业模式。裕丰京安公司进而承担全县畜禽粪污集中处理和资源化开发任务，每年消耗粪污 10 万吨、秸秆 7 万吨，生产沼气 1800 万立方米，实现发电并网 1512 万千瓦时，提纯生物天然气 636 万立方米，生产有机肥 25 万吨，绿色发展成为企业新的收益增长点。

案例 2-16　　南京市栖霞区餐厨垃圾收运处一体化项目：集成式减污降碳协同增效

近年来，栖霞区全方位联动探索废弃物减量化、资源化、无害化新路径，推进再生资源回收网与垃圾分类回收网"两网融合"，建立"专业+职业"回收渠道，实施"区中转+中心集中收集"转运形式，形成以再生资源交易市场为龙头、分拣加工中心为载体、城乡回收网点为终端的"链条式作业、闭环型管理"运营体系。

以前，栖霞区餐厨垃圾大部分依靠区外末端设施处置，58.6%的餐厨垃圾送往生活垃圾焚烧厂处置，34.2%的餐厨垃圾送往垃圾转运站，7.2%的餐厨垃圾送往肥料厂利用处置。但是，餐厨垃圾具备有机质含量高、含水量高、易腐等特点，在处理过程中容易产生异味、废水、杂物和残渣。栖霞区餐厨垃圾收运处一体化项目由政企合作共建，建立覆盖全区9个街道800多处餐厨垃圾产生点的收运网和餐厨废弃物集中处置厂，采用"机械预处理+湿式厌氧消化技术"处理，即餐厨垃圾经收集后首先送至预处理车间，分离油脂、残渣后，经过均质罐、消化罐，再进入厌氧发酵罐，分离出的油脂提纯后制取生物柴油、航空煤油等，液相及固相混合后用于生产沼气进行发电，废水进入后端污水处理系统后达标排放，沼渣外运焚烧。

该项目通过构建高效的集中收运体系、实施精细化的预处理和分类、采用先进的资源化处置技术以及建立闭环管理机制，将栖霞区餐厨垃圾处理由零散式向集中式转型，不仅解决餐厨垃圾量大、难处理的难题，还创造出高价值的工业原料、有机肥料和清洁能源，实现生态环境保护与经济社会发展双赢，被巴塞尔公约亚太区域中心评为2023年中国"无废城市"减污降碳协同增效典型案例，是南京市唯一上榜案例和江苏省生活垃圾领域唯一入选案例。

二 危险废物监管和处置能力短板不断补齐

近年来，中国修订发布《固体废物鉴别标准通则》《危险废物转移管理办法》《国家危险废物名录》《危险废物排除管理清单》等政策，提升危险废物监管信息化水平，开展危险废物"1+6+20"（1个危险废物国家技术中心、6个区域技术中心、20个区域性特殊危险废物集中处置中心）重点工程建设，明确危险废物跨省转移审批程序、时限和简化审批条件，优化废铅蓄电池等跨省转移管理试点工作，全国危险废物集中利用处置能力超 2 亿吨/年，较 2020 年增长 50%，与产废情况总体匹配；超 78 万家企业纳入国家固废信息系统管理，较信息系统启动时的 2018 年增加近 15 倍。

　　中国实施危险废物跨省利用许可证豁免管理制度，实现危险废物利用处置能力共享和优势互补。开展"无废集团"建设，支持试点企业实行危险废物"点对点"定向利用豁免管理、集团范围内危险废物利用处置设施共享等政策，提升集团内危险废物资源化利用水平。例如，徐州市建成危险废物智慧监管平台，打造危险废物"来源可查、去向可追、全程留痕"的完整信息链和可追溯、可视化智慧监管机制，徐州危废处置中心通过危废智慧监管平台，将产废方信息、处置方案等数据整合，给每包待处置的危废贴上"数字身份证"，采用高温回转窑危险废物熔渣焚烧技术，将危险废物分解和转化。

三　大宗固废规模化利用取得突破

　　进入新时代以来，中国统筹推进大宗固废综合利用处置，成立中国资源循环集团有限公司，突破相关技术瓶颈，带动形成一批循环经济领域精深加工产业集群，拓宽大宗固废规模化利用渠道，提升复杂难用大宗固废综合利用水平。2023 年，中国典型大宗工业固废综合利用量达 22.58 亿吨，综合利用率达 53.32%，较 2012 年提高 10.52 个百分点。

　　鄂尔多斯出台中国地级市首部《绿色矿山建设管理条例》，发布《鄂尔多斯市绿色矿山建设评价指标（试行）》等政策文件，"一矿一策"建设绿色矿山示范区、整山整沟治理典范矿、集中连片治理区，每年综合利用超 6000 万吨煤矸石对煤矿采空区、沉陷区等进行生态修复和土地复垦，促进伴生高岭土、硫铁矿等资源回收和深度利用，开发煤矸石制备的化工、水泥、改良土壤、肥料、纤维材料等高新利用产品，形成规模化生态治理与高值化综合利用的煤矸石综合利用产业链。

　　作为磷化工产业大省，云南每年磷石膏产生量约为 2300 万吨，推行"以渣定产"模式，实施磷石膏废弃矿坑生态修复利用、磷石膏建筑材料推广、磷石膏路基材料应用三大工程，磷石膏综合利用率提升至 50% 以上，超过全国平均水平。昆明成立由市政府负责人担任组长的专门领导小组，市政府与磷石膏产地区县政府签署《磷石膏三年攻坚行动目标责任书》，与当地磷化工企业建立项目合作、生态补偿机制，搭建磷石膏环境统计信息平台，每年有 1400 万吨磷石膏实现多方参与的综合处置利用。

案例 2-17　　　浙江"蓝色循环"：探索海洋塑料废弃物
综合治理新模式

联合国环境规划署发布的报告显示，塑料制品是海洋垃圾中占比最大、最有害和最持久的部分，至少占海洋垃圾总量的 85%。联合国将预防和大幅减少海洋垃圾列为可持续发展的一项指标。浙江省的海域面积 26 万平方千米，有海岛 4350 个，治理海洋塑料污染任务重、压力大。

2019 年，浙江省台州市椒江区推出"海洋云仓"智慧治污模式，在中心渔港和大陈渔港铺设智能设施，回收船舶产生的含油洗舱水、机舱舱底污水、含油压载水等污染物。2021 年，椒江区利用数字化平台"渔省心"，扩大船舶污染物处理种类。2022 年，椒江区作为全省唯一试点，率先实施升级版"蓝色循环"模式，即通过"政府引导＋市场运作"，结合海洋垃圾的产生和分布特点，建立数字化管理平台和实体化收集网络，吸纳群众参与海洋塑料废弃物收集，专业公司将回收的海洋塑料加工成高值原料并出售，设立"蓝色联盟共富基金"进行价值二次分配，实现生态保护与增收富民。"蓝色循环"模式用"高收益"解决"无人收"的问题，用"高信用"解决"价值低"的问题，用"高回馈"解决"可持续"的问题，在浙江全部沿海县（市、区）和中国沿海省份复制推广，获得 2023 年联合国"地球卫士奖"。

不少制造企业积极履行保护海洋生态环境的社会责任，愿意采购价格更高的再生海洋塑料粒子替代原生塑料粒子，但难点在于如何解决海洋塑料溯源、材料再生认证等问题。浙江省构建"市场化垃圾收集—国际化认证增值—高值化资源利用"新型治理机制，运用区块链和物联网等技术，保障海洋塑料废弃物收集、再生、再制造、再销售等全环节可视化追溯，进行碳标签、碳足迹标定，经过国际权威认证机构认证，实现塑料废弃物回收利用的高溢价、高收益，提高群众参与海洋垃圾收集的积极性。为防止非海洋塑料废弃物混入"蓝色循环"，浙江为一线收集者配备视频记录仪，记录塑料废弃物来源地。

浙江省在沿海城市建立"小蓝之家"海洋塑料废弃物收集储存站点，对海洋塑料废弃物预处理，大幅降低后续运输处置成本。台州市围绕一线收集人员历史守信记录、日常管理、垃圾收集作业管理、环保培训记录等，构建信用评价体系，持续从事海洋塑料废弃物收集并且信用评价为"优良"的人员，可获得经费补贴、意外保险、大病医保、绿色贷款等回报。

四 重金属和尾矿库治理不断强化

近年来，中国持续加强铅、汞、镉、铬、砷、铊、锑等重金属污染物减排分类管理，推行企业重金属污染物排放总量控制制度，探索重金属污染物排放总量替代管理豁免，严格重有色金属矿采选、重有色金属冶炼、铅蓄电池制造、电镀、化学原料及化学制品制造、皮革鞣制加工等重点行业企业准入管理，依法推动落后产能退出，加强企业清洁生产改造。2021~2024 年，中国累计实施重金属行业淘汰落后产能项目 730 多个，完成重金属深度治理项目 240 余个，纳入重金属重点行业监管清单的企业达 11345 家。

中国尾矿库数量多，长江经济带、黄河流域尾矿库的数量占到 43%，总体情况复杂。近年来，中国明确尾矿库运管单位主体责任和生态环境部门监管责任，细化尾矿库全过程污染防治。按照环境风险高低，将尾矿库分为三个等级，建立尾矿库环境风险分级清单和差异化监管机制，将 7820 座尾矿库纳入环境监管系统，每年开展汛期尾矿库环境风险隐患排查整治，推动重点地区尾矿库"一库一策"污染治理，尾矿库环境安全水平明显提升。

五　新污染物治理迈出重要步伐

2022 年国务院办公厅印发《新污染物治理行动方案》后，中国成立由生态环境部牵头、15 部门组成的新污染物治理部际协调小组，组建新污染物治理专家委员会，各省份印发新污染物治理工作方案，在修订产业结构调整指导目录、推行清洁生产、印发绿色产品评价标准等工作中，纳入新污染物治理要求，初步形成国家统筹、省（区、市）负总责、市县落实的工作机制。2021～2024 年，中国已完成 122 个行业、7 万余家企业、4000 余种具有高危害、高环境检出的化学物质生产使用情况摸底调查，初步掌握潜在新污染物分布情况。针对 14 种类具有突出环境与健康风险的新污染物，实施禁止、限制、限排等全生命周期环境风险管控措施，共批准登记 2 万余种新化学物质，提出 3200 多项环境风险控制措施。

第 5 节　中国其他领域生态环境保护的创新举措、主要成效和典型案例

一　持续深入打好净土保卫战

土壤是"生命之基、万物之母"，与大气、水污染相比，土壤污染具有隐蔽性、滞后性和复杂性。党的十八大以来，中国扎实推进净土保卫战，开展第二次全国污染源普查、土壤污染状况详查、重点行业企业用地土壤污染状况调查等，查明农用地土壤污染面积、分布及其对农产品质量的影响，筛选排查 10 多万个存在潜在污染的场地，基本掌握重点行业企业用地土壤与地下水污染状况及环境风险。各地区加强土壤污染防治，全面禁止洋垃圾入境，累计减少固体废物进口约 1 亿吨，全国受污染耕地安全利用率和污染地块安全利用率均超 90%，土壤污染加重趋势得到遏制。中国将 1.6 万余家企业纳入土壤污染重点监管单位名录，实施

124 个土壤污染源头管控项目，带动数千家重点监管单位实施绿色化改造。建立优先监管地块制度，将近万个潜在高风险地块纳入土壤污染风险管控或者修复名录。

二　声环境质量总体向好

中国城市建设快速发展，人口密度逐步增大，机动车保有量日益增加，工业、商业、建筑施工等活动越来越频繁，导致噪声源不断增多。2023 年，在全国生态环境信访投诉举报管理平台接到的投诉举报中，噪声扰民问题占 61.3%，在各环境污染要素中占比最大。中国建成 3800 多个噪声自动监测站点并联网，依法划分声环境功能区和噪声敏感建筑物集中区域，建立"规划—环评—设计—施工—验收—运维"全流程噪声管控机制，综合整治工业、建筑施工、交通运输、社会生活等领域噪声，加强对涉声产品质量监督和认证监管，共建"消除杂音、睡得安心"的宁静小区，严格处理噪声污染违法案件，噪声污染治理取得积极进展。目前，各地将工业噪声纳入排污许可的企业约 11.9 万家，建成 2132 个宁静小区，声环境功能区昼间达标率由 2020 年的 94.6% 上升至 2024 年的95.8%，夜间达标率由 2020 年的 80.1% 上升至 2024 年的 88.2%。

第 6 节　降污减排：中国生态环境保护的经验及对发展中国家的启示

一　坚持环保为民，为满足人民群众优美生态环境不懈奋斗

从 1972 年北京官厅水库发生水污染事件后实施中国第一项治污工程，到 20 世纪 90 年代全面开展"三河""三湖"水污染防治，到 21 世纪初大力推进主要污染物总量减排，中国污染防治力度持续加大，努力为人民群众创造良好生产生活环境。特别是党的十八大以来，全党全国各族人民坚持"绿水青山就是金山银山"理念，坚决向污染宣战，推进蓝天、

碧水、净土保卫战，解决一大批关系民生的突出环境问题，人民群众生态环境获得感、幸福感、安全感持续增强，厚植中国式现代化的绿色底色和质量成色。不断完善生态环境保护制度体系，建立覆盖所有固定污染源的企业排放许可制，加强环境立法、环境司法、环境执法等依法治污，用最严格制度和最严密法治保护生态环境。建立系统完整、责权清晰、监管有效的生态环境管理格局，严格落实"党政同责、一岗双责"，落实生态环境保护修复主体责任，深化污染治理跨区域合作，构建齐抓共管、联防联控联治的新格局。

二 坚持系统治理、分区施策、精准治污

中国坚持山水林田湖草沙一体化生态保护和修复，强化从源头到末端的全链条治理，加强环境基础设施和专业队伍建设，实施分区分类差异化精细管控，污染治理不再聚焦减排量、排放标准等孤立指标，而是以环境质量、改善成效和长效机制为核心的综合性考核指标，下决心要以看得见的成效回应人民群众对生态环境的关切。

在打赢蓝天保卫战方面，中国以改善空气质量为核心，减少重污染天气和解决人民群众身边的突出大气环境问题为重点，降低细颗粒物（PM2.5）浓度为主线，推动氮氧化物和挥发性有机物减排，强化面源大气污染治理，开展区域联防联治。在打赢净水保卫战方面，中国全面统筹左右岸、上下游、陆上水上、地表地下、河流海洋、水生态水资源、污染防治与生态保护，以流域为单元综合治理，从治理污水向水环境综合整治转变，"治差水"挥别黑臭，"保好水"提升品质。在海洋生态环境保护方面，中国健全海洋生态监测、预警和监管体系，全面开展入海排污口排查整治，严控和削减陆源污染物，加强海上污染分类整治，推进海洋塑料垃圾治理，保护海洋生态系统和生物多样性，推动海洋生态环境质量持续改善和美丽海湾示范引领。在固体废物治理方面，中国深入推进"无废城市"建设和大宗固废综合利用，严守"一废一库一重"①

---

① "一废"指危险废物，"一库"指尾矿库，"一重"指重金属。

生态环境风险防控底线，提升生活垃圾分类处置实效，强化固废源头减量和高效利用，提升危废、医废、建筑垃圾等处置能力，推进新污染物协同治理，解决固废产生量大、利用不畅、非法转移倾倒、处置设施选址难等问题。

案例 2-18　　　　长三角地区：生态环境共保联治，

绘就绿色发展"同心圆"

2020 年 8 月，在安徽合肥召开的扎实推进长三角一体化发展座谈会上，习近平总书记指出，长三角地区是长江经济带的龙头，不仅要在经济发展上走在前列，也要在生态保护和建设上带好头。2023 年 11 月，习近平总书记在深入推进长三角一体化发展座谈会中强调："长三角区域要加强生态环境共保联治。"而后，通过组建区域生态环境保护协作小组，规划一张图，环保一把尺，沪苏浙皖三省一市生态环境保护从"独奏"变"交响"，迈向绿色发展快车道。自 2024 年 5 月 1 日起，上海、江苏、浙江两省一市人大常委会分别表决通过的《促进长三角生态绿色一体化发展示范区高质量发展条例》在三地同步施行，形成"不破行政隶属，打破行政边界"的生态环境共保联治长效机制。

跨界水体联保共治

上海市青浦区、江苏省苏州市吴江区、浙江省嘉兴市嘉善县相互毗邻，河道纵横交错，湖泊星罗棋布，被誉为"最江南的江南"。2019 年 11 月，三地共同成立长三角生态绿色一体化发展示范区。经过共保联治，长三角生态绿色一体化发展示范区地表水优Ⅲ类断面比例从 2019 年的 75%上升到 96.2%，"一河三湖"（太浦河、淀山湖、元荡湖、汾湖）重点跨界水体水环境质量提前达到或优于 2025 年目标。

元荡湖岸线的 73%属吴江区，27%属青浦区，过去因行政归属不同，两地在元荡湖治理上存在责任划分不明晰问题。如今，两地共同实施元荡湖生态岸线贯通工程，对元荡湖及其周边支流采取水系连通、河道清障、岸坡整治等治理措施，打通省际"断头路"（元荡桥），将两地通行时间从 40 分钟缩短至 5 分钟，给两地居民带来桥上慢行、"跨域无感"

的舒适体验。

作为太湖流域最大的人工河道，太浦河是上游吴江区的泄洪通道、青浦区和嘉善县的饮用水源，过去因为功能定位、治水标准不同，分段治理带来环境风险。2019 年，三地建立联合河长制，共定水质联合监测、水污染治理联合执法、河长联合巡查等"一套标准"，形成共同决策、联合保护和一体管控机制。

携手打赢蓝天保卫战

2018 年，长三角区域环境气象一体化业务平台上线，涵盖大气污染精准治理、重污染天气预报预警、大气环境中长期调控三大功能，三省一市环境气象部门不仅共享相关数据，而且通过污染物输送通道分析，了解域内外的空气污染源。2022 年，长三角区域空气质量预测预报结果图上线，"一图"发布未来 7 天三省一市的空气质量预测数据，这是中国首次由地方层面共同公开发布的跨省级行政区空气质量预报结果。如今，在三省一市生态环境部门微信公众号和其他新媒体平台上，这份数字可视化报告持续更新，为重污染天气联合应对和协同治污提供精准依据。2024 年，长三角地区 31 个城市 PM2.5 平均浓度为 33 微克/米³，同比下降 0.9%，连续五年达到国家二级标准；臭氧平均浓度为 161 微克/米³，同比下降 1.2%；平均优良天数比例为 82.1%，未出现重度及以上污染天。

第 7 节 中国式现代化视域下进一步推进高水平生态环境保护的对策建议

一 接续打好蓝天保卫战

1. 强化多污染物减排和面源污染治理

继续推进钢铁、水泥、焦化、玻璃、石灰、矿棉、有色等重点行业及燃煤锅炉超低排放改造，确保工业企业全面稳定达标排放。持续开展餐饮油烟、恶臭异味专项治理和第三方运维。普及规模化畜禽养殖场粪污输送、存储及处理封闭管理，稳步推进大气氨污染防控。强化挥发性有机物全流程、全环节综合治理。深化扬尘污染综合治理，推广装配式绿色建筑，对城镇较大规模的公共裸地、干散货码头物料堆场等排查建档并采取防尘措施。推进矿山生态环境综合整治，普遍建设绿色矿山。健全秸秆收储运服务和资源化利用体系，加强秸秆焚烧网格化监管。

2. 加速能源、交通领域清洁低碳发展

在保障能源安全供应的前提下，重点区域继续实施煤炭消费总量控制和减量替代，将燃煤锅炉及茶水炉、经营性炉灶、储粮烘干设备、农产品加工等燃煤设施替代项目纳入设备设施更新计划。以"以供定改"为导向推进工业炉窑以电代煤、以气代煤。综合利用补贴、税费、运价、运力调配、用地用海保障等杠杆，引导大宗货物中长距离运输优先采用铁路、水路运输，短距离运输优先采用封闭式皮带廊道或新能源车船。加强铁路专用线和联运转运接驳设施建设，推广公铁水联运等"外集内配"物流方式。普及公交、出租、城市物流配送、环卫等车辆的新能源替代，培育清洁运输企业和零排放货运车队。严厉打击非标油品的非法销售行为，保障民营加油站的成品油质量。

3. 完善大气环境监管执法体系

督促空气质量未达标的县区编制大气环境质量限期达标方案，并向社会公开。继续推进 PM2.5 和臭氧协同控制。完善京津冀地区、长三角地区、粤港澳大湾区、成渝地区双城经济圈、长江中游城市群、东北地区、汾渭平原、天山北坡城市群等重点区域和省级行政区域内的大气污染联防联控机制，在跨省毗邻地区建立空气治理改善先行示范区，常态化开展联合交叉执法。健全省市县三级重污染天气应急管理体系，清单式开展涉气企业清洁转型和应急减排。一体化健全城市、重点镇及机场、港口、铁路货场、物流园、工业园、公路等重点区域的空气质量监测网络，加强数据联网、共享和发布。科学评估各地沙尘量及固沙滞沙成效，强化沙源区及沙尘路径区气象、空气质量等监测网络建设和干预

措施联动。定期更新、公告大气环境重点排污单位名录，倒逼企业承担治污主体责任。稳定运行污染源智能监测设备，加强基于数据支撑的监督执法。

二 接续打好碧水保卫战

1. 加强水污染治理能力建设

统筹好上下游、左右岸、干支流、城市和乡村，强化溯源整治和截污控源，充分发挥河（湖）长制作用，加强入河（湖）排污口整治，严控城镇、工业、农业等废水直排，系统推进城乡和园区污水收集、处理设施补短板及升级改造，优化污水、污泥资源化利用，在有条件的地方推进雨污分流，提级实施污染较重河流综合治理，建立防止返黑返臭的长效机制。强化地表水与地下水协同防治。因地制宜开展水体内源污染治理和生态修复，增强河湖自净功能。以场景应用为导向，创新突破制约水生态环境持续改善的瓶颈技术。

2. 推动江河湖泊综合治理

实施"一河一策"，严格落实水资源用途管制、水资源论证、取水许可监管、承载能力评价、超载治理等硬措施，构建河湖良好连通性，加强岸线保护利用，强化流域污染跨区域联防联治，实现江河功能永续利用。加快坡耕地治理和生态清洁小流域建设，促进流域水土提质增效。普及排污权、碳排放权、水权交易，健全横向流域生态保护补偿和生态产品价值实现机制。打好长江保护修复攻坚战，加强三峡库区及上游、沱江、乌江等为重点的总磷污染防治，加强汉江、乌江、嘉陵江、赣江等支流和鄱阳湖、洞庭湖等湖泊为重点的农业面源污染防治，推进长江岸线生态修复，实施好长江流域重点水域十年禁渔，有效恢复长江水生生物多样性。打好黄河生态保护治理攻坚战，开展黄河流域"清废行动"，推进干流及主要支流水质较差河段、二三级支流等"毛细血管"水环境综合治理，加强中下游水土流失治理，实施黄河三角洲湿地保护修复，开展深度节水控水行动，通过以草定畜、定牧来维护上游水源涵养功能。整治和清理以房地产、旅游、康养等为名目打"擦边球"搞沿湖贴线开发的行为。因地制宜开展湖泊水资源利用、水污染防治、水生态修复、水生生物保护等，建立覆盖重要湖泊流域的取用水总量控制体系，坚决遏制"造湖大跃进"。

三　健全陆海统筹、多方共治的海洋生态环境治理体系

1. 深化涉海重点领域污染分类整治

以沿海乡镇为单元持续开展入海排污口"查、测、溯、治"，实现地理分布、排放特征、责任主体、排污许可"一张图"，构建"近岸水体—入海排污口—排污管线—污染源"全链条治理体系。打好重点海域综合治理攻坚战，建立沿海、流域、海域协同一体的综合治理体系，强化沿海城乡污水收集处理设施补短板，实施滨海地区人工湿地净化和生态扩容工程，实现入海河流与重点海域生态环境同步改善。提升船舶、渔港等污染物收集和转运设施的运营效能，与城市相关公共设施衔接，及时收集、清理、转运并处置渔港及到港渔船产生的垃圾。严格海水养殖环评准入和审查，补齐海水养殖环保设施，推动海水养殖由近海向深远海布局，推广生态健康养殖模式。建设数据共享的涉海工程项目和海洋倾废监督系统。实施海湾、河口、岸滩等区域塑料垃圾专项清理行动。

2. 扎实推进美丽海湾建设

"一湾一策"梯次推进生态环境综合治理，以沿海大中城市毗邻海湾海滩为重点，常态化排查整治海水浴场、滨海旅游度假区周边入海污染源，坚决取缔非法和设置不合理的排污口。实施岸滩和海漂垃圾长效监管，推进海湾水体和岸滩环境质量同步改善。加强海水浴场环境质量监测预报和信息发布，加大海洋环保宣传力度，提升公众临海、亲海、护海的获得感和幸福感。将美丽海湾纳入沿海美丽城市总体规划布局，探索各具特色的美丽海湾建设路径。

四 纵深推进"无废城市"建设

1. 健全固体废弃物精细管理体系

将"无废城市"建设纳入乡镇（街道）、村（社区）的污染防治攻坚战考核内容。依法依规将固体废物产生、利用、处置纳入企业信用评价体系。将小微企业和社会源的危险废物纳入统计体系，形成主要类别固体废物管理"一本账"。推动工业固体废物源头减量和资源化利用，普及建设绿色工厂、绿色园区、绿色矿山，培育"无废企业"。全面摸底排查历史遗留固体废弃物堆存场，实施分级分类整改。推广绿色建材和建筑垃圾再生利用产品，普遍应用装配式、智能化的新型建造方式。建立农户广泛参与农业农村废弃物治理激励机制，加强废旧农用物资回收。推动生活垃圾分类网点与废旧物资回收网点"两网融合"。深入推进危险废物环境监管"五全"体系①建设。

2. 提高废弃物资源化和再利用水平

在符合环境质量标准和要求的前提下，拓宽大宗固体废弃物综合利用产品在建筑领域的应用。发展废钢铁、废有色金属、废纸、废塑料等再生资源精深加工产业链，支持汽车零部件、工程机械、机床、文化办公设备等高频消耗品再制造产业发展，探索盾构机、航空发动机、工业机器人、发电设备等高端装备再制造。补齐县域生活垃圾焚烧处理能力短板，合理规划建设厨余垃圾、农林生物质等处理设施。推广企业内、园区内、产业间能源梯级利用、水资源循环利用、固体废弃物综合利用等循环经济新模式。以财政奖补、绿色金融等为杠杆，加强低值可回收物循环利用。探索退役后的风电设备、光伏设备、数据中心、通信基站等新型废弃物循环利用路径。

---

① "五全"：全域排查、全面清理、全量处置、全过程监管、全方位提升。

第3章
筑牢生态安全屏障：中国构建绿色发展空间格局的举措、成效、经验和建议

  人与自然是生命共同体。习近平总书记指出，我们要把自然恢复和人工修复有机统一起来，因地因时制宜、分区分类施策，努力找到生态保护修复的最佳解决方案。新时代以来，中国坚持系统观念，从生态系统整体性出发，推进山水林田湖草沙一体化保护和修复，从山顶到海洋、从高原到平原、从国家到地方的生态保护修复"蓝图"基本形成。同时，中国积极健全国土空间体系，加强生产、生活、生态空间用途统筹和协调管控，加大生态系统保护修复力度，有效扩大生态环境容量，推动自然财富、生态财富快速积累，为经济社会持续健康发展提供有力支撑。

第1节　中国优化国土空间保护开发格局的创新举措、主要成效和典型案例

一　实现国土空间规划"多规合一"

  国土是绿色发展的空间载体，国土空间规划是国家空间发展的指南、可持续发展的空间蓝图，是各类开发保护建设活动的基本依据。2018年，党中央、国务院做出改革部署，将原分属不同部门的主体功能区规划、土地利用规划、城乡规划、海洋功能区划等空间规划职责统一整合到自然资源部，由其负责建立国土空间规划体系并监督实施，实现"多规合

一"。而后，"五级三类"国土空间规划①编制实施，"多规合一"的规划编制审批体系、实施监督体系、法规政策体系和技术标准体系逐步建立，初步形成全国国土空间开发保护"一张图"，在支撑新型城镇化发展和乡村振兴、促进国土空间合理利用和有效保护方面发挥积极作用。

2022 年以来，中国首部"多规合一"的国家级国土空间规划——《全国国土空间规划纲要（2021~2035 年)》印发，地方各级总体规划、详细规划和专项规划编制统筹推进。至今，省级国土空间规划均获得国务院批复，80%以上的市县国土空间总体规划获得批准实施，长江经济带（长江流域）、京津冀、成渝地区双城经济圈、黄河流域、海岸带及近岸海域等重点区域、流域的国土空间规划正加快编制，完善城镇开发边界内外的建设开发规则，推进有条件、有需求的村庄编制村庄规划。规划引领，纲举目张，各地政府加强规划与土地政策融合，实现规划用地"多审合一、多证合一"，提升审批效能和监管服务水平，并按照"统一数据、统一标准、统一技术流程"的原则，叠加人口、用地、产权、产业等信息，因地制宜优化经济社会发展空间布局。

案例 3-1　　南京：以"多规合一"推进国土空间治理体系和治理能力现代化

2023 年 1 月，南京开始实施《南京市国土空间规划条例》，将国土空间规划编制、实施、监督全链条纳入法治轨道，从源头解决因编制理念、方法、控制手段方面的差异而导致的规划之间重叠、矛盾的问题。基于行政事权，南京市全域划定"总体规划-详细规划-专项规划"单元，建立以行政管理逻辑为主体、以功能组织逻辑为支撑、行政与功能相互融合、自上而下和自下而上相结合的国土空间规划体系。以"助力项目审批、服务项目企业、优化营商环境"为目标，构建"系统合一、流程合一、人员合一"的涉企服务融合办理模式，推进土地供应与规划许可深度融合。南京市国土空间总体规划、专项规划、详细规划的衔接传导关

---

① "五级三类"国土空间规划："五级"为国家级、省级、市级、县级、乡镇级的国土空间规划；"三类"指总体规划、详细规划、相关的专项规划。

系可见图 3-1。

坚持"古都彰显、中心（城区）升级、副城集聚、新城支撑"的发展模式，南京市规划中心城区和外围城镇组团式、内涵式发展，农业生产向粮食生产功能区、重要农产品生产保护区集聚，促进耕地集中连片，并设计以水为脉、生态空间与城市空间相连通、与农业空间相融合的生态功能片区与绿色廊道体系。

南京市将国土空间规划与历史文化名城保护结合，坚持"保护第一、应保尽保、活化利用、以用促保、远近结合、融合发展"的原则，按照"严管、控高、留白、更新"的思路，完善古都格局和风貌、历史地段、古镇古村、文物古迹、非物质文化遗产等保护框架。同时，将国土空间规划与城市更新融合，以"小规模、渐进式、微更新"模式策划一批城市更新示范项目，共谋、共建、共享以人为本、特色鲜明、开放多元的特色公共服务新空间。

二　统筹优化国土空间布局

中国高标准划定"三区三线"[①]，科学布局城镇、农业、生态等功能空间，优化农产品主产区、重点生态功能区、城市化地区三大空间格局。统筹划定城镇开发边界、耕地和永久基本农田、生态保护红线等空间管控边界以及各类海域保护线，筑牢国家安全发展的空间基础，努力实现生产空间集约高效、生活空间宜居适度、生态空间山清水秀，即：全国划定不低于 18.65 亿亩的耕地和 15.46 亿亩的永久基本农田；完成陆域生态保护红线约 304 万平方千米划定，初步划定约 15 万平方千米海洋生态保护红线；城镇开发边界扩展倍数控制在基于 2020 年城镇建设用地规模的 1.3 倍以内。

---

① 　三区三线：城镇空间、农业空间、生态空间三种类型空间所对应的区域，以及分别对应划定的城镇开发边界、耕地和永久基本农田、生态保护红线三条控制线。

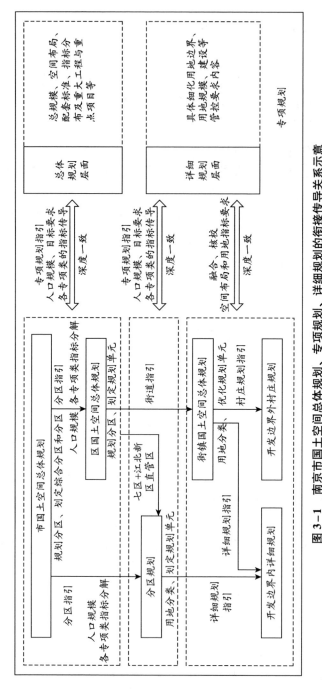

图 3-1 南京市国土空间总体规划、专项规划、详细规划的衔接传导关系示意

资料来源：南京市规划和自然资源局。

三　加强重点生态功能区管理

中国将承担水源涵养、水土保持、防风固沙、生物多样性保护、固碳释氧、海岸防护等重要生态系统服务功能的县级行政区确定为重点生态功能区，以保护生态环境、提供生态产品为重点，限制大规模、高强度的工业化、城镇化开发，推动其自然生态系统总体稳定向好、生态服务功能逐步增强、生态产品供给水平持续提升。2013~2023年，国家重点生态功能区转移支付资金由423亿元增加到1091亿元，累计投入7900亿元，覆盖全国31个省份的800多个县域。

案例3-2　　　湖南省岳阳市君山区：绿色发展"守护好一江碧水"

2024年10月，生态环境部联合财政部通报2023年度国家重点生态功能区县域生态环境质量监测与评价结果，湖南省岳阳市君山区成为六个评估结果为"明显变好"的县域之一。2018年4月，习近平总书记在岳阳视察，留下"守护好一江碧水"的殷殷嘱托。君山区严格落实河（湖）长、林长制，大力开展"夏季攻势""洞庭清波"等专项污染治理行动，创新开展湿地生态修复，以"君山之为"贡献"长江之治"。

君山区湿地面积占全区国土总面积的34.79%，利用紧靠洞庭湖和长江的地理优势，通过取缔非法码头、清理欧美黑杨、复绿长江岸线、种植护堤林等举措，累计修复湿地近6万亩。2022年7月，湖南省君山农垦集团在君山区人民政府授权下，完成君山淡水湿地碳汇调研、注册、审定、核证、签发和交易等流程，成为全球首个达到国际核证减排计划标准、挂牌公示的淡水湿地修复项目，预计带来4600万元以上的40年总收益，带动项目区周边25个村庄、约1.2万户家庭和4万名居民增收。2024年8月，君山区政府与中国科技大学地球和空间科学学院共建的君山湿地生态碳汇研究中心揭牌，这是中国首个淡水湿地生态碳汇研究平台，推动将"君山经验"复制到洞庭湖及长江中下游地区。

君山区政府将域内4.6万亩的14个湖泊统一转交给区属生态渔业集

团经营，改变过去养殖分散、管理粗放的低效局面，"一湖一策"实施投苗和养殖，新建现代化的陆基和水基设施渔业基地，上线集实时视频、远程诊断、信息交流、病害防治、项目管理等功能于一体的数字渔业大数据平台，创建国家级水产良种中心和华中地区最大的渔业种业基地，实现"以渔养水、以水护渔"，渔业年产值达数亿元，"江湖君山产好鱼"品牌影响力越来越大。聚焦"休闲渔业+"，君山区融合发展国际湿地景区、城市野生垂钓基地、湿地文化研学基地、候鸟栖息保护和服务基地，以特色湖鲜美食和高品质生态环境带动高价值乡村旅游。

案例 3-3　　广西壮族自治区梧州市蒙山县：以"甜蜜经济"引领多元化生态产品价值实现路径

作为国家级生态示范区和国家重点生态功能区，蒙山县以绿色农业、新型工业、康养旅游、精品城镇、民生福祉为发展思路，开展城镇污水处理和村庄环境综合整治，空气质量优良天数占比在 99% 以上，地表水考核断面水质均达到或优于 I 类标准，在 2022 年国家重点生态功能区县域生态环境质量考核中，名列广西第一，湄江流域生态带正加快建成。

蒙山县以国土空间规划为统领，构建"茧丝绸、林产业、长寿食品"三个主导产业和"特色农业、康养旅游"两个特色产业的"3+2"绿色经济体系。其中，凭借 82.87% 的森林覆盖率、90 多种植物蜜源与良好的气候条件，蒙山县成为养殖蜜蜂的天然基地，养蜂量居广西首位。当地政府采取以奖代补、先建后补、企业赊销、合作社托养分红、跟班学习等方式精准帮扶养蜂户，采取"资源变资产、资金变股金、农民变股东"机制，引导农户将蜜源植物生态保护林入股村集体经济组织，专业公司利用集体资产、集体场地建立蜂蜜加工生产线，将生态资源折股量化并发放股权证书给农户，实现"一乡一业""一村一品"产业化经营，农户通过"订单收购+分红"模式获得收益。

进一步看，通过"政府扶持+企业运营+农户参与+供销系统+数字赋能"，蒙山县构建集养殖、加工、生产、研发、销售及生态旅游于一体的蜂产业链，年产值超过 1 亿元。蒙山县推进"蜂+N"融合发展，建设蜂业深加工园区，与中国农科院合作研发"智慧蜂场"，发放蜂产品上市溯源码，打造区域公共品牌，发展蜂王浆、蜂面膜、蜂胶囊等绿色食品和医疗保健品，建设蜜意小村、蜜蜂科技馆、蜂情小镇等乡村旅游载体，促进蜂产业提档升级。

四　全域土地综合整治稳妥有序

中国开展全域土地综合整治试点，保护农耕肌理，修复生态基底，改善人居环境，助力乡村振兴，在25个省实施356个以乡镇为单元的试点，以及探索浙江宁波、广州从化、福建泉州、广西崇爱高速公路沿线和浙江跨乡镇等不同尺度试点。此外，各地自行开展892个以乡镇为单元的试点。截至2023年末，试点地区共完成土地综合整治378万亩，实现新增耕地47万亩、减少建设用地12万亩。

浙江省台州温岭市横峰街道民营经济发达，但土地资源紧张，秉持"全域整、全域富、全域新"的理念，构建城郊融合型土地综合整治模式。打破村界限制，盘活农村老旧宅基地等闲置建设用地，补齐乡村基础设施短板，统一规划住宅安置区、产业升级区、生态修复区，推动23%的农村用地腾出变为产业空间。推出"公寓式住宅+工业厂房"安置模式，安置村民身兼"房东+股东"双重身份，按3∶2的比例分配住宅和厂房，厂房入股有分红，住宅出租有租金。通过完善教育、商业等配套设施，优化水系和路网布局，打造生态绿廊，提升居民生活质量。

广州市从化区按照"先易后难、分类实施、循序渐进"的原则，一体化实施"田块归并、河道修复、村庄提升、产业提振"全域土地综合整治行动，盘活利用、腾挪优化闲置宅基地和"空心村"，实施流溪河流域综合治理、矿山复绿、林相修复等工程，串联艾米稻香农业园、风云岭湿地公园、华南国家植物园迁地保护示范区等自然禀赋，探索"留用地入股"模式，村集体以土地和物业作价入股，以出租形式流转至企业开发建设，打造生态设计小镇、流溪温泉广场等特色园区，发展滨水休闲、水上运动、河湖游艇等"秀水"新业态，为村集体带来每年10%、每5年递增10%的利润分红，形成"土地增值-集体增收-村民受益"的

"森林下的山水城市"生态经济模式。

江苏省苏州昆山市张浦镇是工业重镇、农业强镇，也是昆山传统村落数量最多的城镇，构建"城乡融合、全域焕新"存量土地综合整治模式，2024 年地区生产总值超 320 亿元，集聚 800 多家外资企业和 2000 多家民营企业，综合实力居全国千强镇前列。昆山市成立由 12 个市直部门参与的张浦镇全域土地综合整治试点项目领导小组，镇级层面细化成立工作小组，汇总形成一张规划布局图、一个项目计划包、一张时间安排表，一体实施河道生态环境整治、农村闲置资源资产盘活、基础设施完善、历史文化保护与风貌提升等项目，依托"龙头企业+强村公司+农业基地+专业农户"的合作模式，将腾出的土地指标用于产业园区建设，促进一二三产业融合，拓宽富民增收渠道。

第 2 节　中国生态系统保护修复的创新举措、主要成效和典型案例

一　定期开展全国生态状况调查评估

21 世纪以来，中国连续完成 4 次全国生态状况调查评估，其中第 4 次调查评估结果显示，全国生态状况总体稳中向好，生态系统格局整体稳定，生态系统质量持续改善，生态系统服务功能不断增强，生物多样性保护水平逐步提高。2024 年，中国启动为期两年的第 5 次调查评估工作。从历次生态状况调查评估看，调查不同时期中国生态状况及其变化趋势、时空分布特征，包括全国生态系统格局、质量和功能的变化，长江经济带、黄河流域、京津冀、粤港澳大湾区、长三角地区等国家重大战略区域的生态状况及变化情况，为生态保护红线划定、推动形成主体功能区战略、重大生态保护修复工程布局等发挥重要支撑作用。

二　科学划定生态保护红线

中国将生态功能极重要、生态极脆弱以及具有潜在重要生态价值的

区域以及整合优化后的自然保护地划入生态保护红线，实现一条红线管控重要生态空间。至今，中国陆域生态保护红线面积占陆域国土面积比例超 30%。通过划定生态保护红线和编制生态保护修复规划，巩固以青藏高原生态屏障区、黄河重点生态区（含黄土高原生态屏障）、长江重点生态区（含川滇生态屏障）、东北森林带、北方防沙带、南方丘陵山地带、海岸带等为依托的"三区四带"生态安全格局。进一步看，中国实施的生态保护红线制度为全球首创，被国际社会评价为应对全球气候变化的实质性创举。

三　以国家公园为主体的新型自然保护地体系初步建立

中国加快构建以国家公园①为主体、自然保护区为基础、各类自然公园为补充的自然保护地体系，已建立各级各类自然保护地近万处，占陆域国土面积的 17% 以上，90% 的陆地自然生态系统类型和 74% 的国家重点保护野生动植物物种得到有效保护。另外，在北京和广州设立两个国家植物园，再遴选 14 个国家植物园候选园，纳入国家植物园体系布局，形成以国家植物园为主体的植物迁地保护体系。

2021 年 10 月，习近平主席在《生物多样性公约》第十五次缔约方大会上宣布，中国正式设立三江源、大熊猫、东北虎豹、海南热带雨林、武夷山 5 个首批国家公园。在首批 5 个国家公园的基础上，中国设立 44 个国家公园候选区，涉及 700 多个现有自然保护地，总面积约 110 万平方千米。中国出台《建立国家公园体制总体方案》《国家公园空间布局方案》等，制定国家公园创建设立、监测评估、资金项目等制度、办法和标准，初步建立中央直管和中央委托省级人民政府代管两种国家公园管理体制，以及主体明确、责任清晰、密切配合的央地、部门、园地协同联动机制。

如今，国家公园的旗舰物种数量持续增长，比如，藏羚羊增长至 7

---

①　以现有自然保护地为基础，在自然生态系统中最重要、自然景观最独特、自然遗产最精华、生物多样性最富集，最具全球价值、国家象征和国民认同度高的区域，整合划建保护范围大、生态过程完整的国家公园。

万多头，雪豹恢复到 1200 多只，东北虎、东北豹数量分别从试点之初的 27 只、42 只增长到 70 只、80 只左右，海南长臂猿野外种群数量从 40 年前的仅存 2 群、不到 10 只增长到 7 群 42 只；生态系统多样性、稳定性、持续性稳步提升，比如，长江、黄河、澜沧江源头实现整体保护，保护 70% 以上的野生大熊猫栖息地，连通 13 个大熊猫局域种群生态廊道；民生持续改善，国家公园所在地实施野生动物损害保险、生态搬迁、入口社区和示范村屯建设、黄牛集中养殖等民生项目，近 5 万名社区居民被聘为生态管护员，人均获得工资性年收入 1 万~2 万元。

地跨福建、江西两省的武夷山国家公园是唯一一个既是世界生物圈保护区，又是世界文化与自然"双遗产"的国家公园，拥有地球同纬度地带最完整、最典型、面积最大的中亚热带原生性森林生态系统。武夷山国家公园设立"管理局、管理站"两级管理体系，建立"林长+警长"、检察监督协作、"负面清单"等网格化精细管理制度。两省分别出台武夷山国家公园条例，武夷山市法院设立中国首家以"国家公园"命名的人民法庭，加强对武夷山国家公园专门化、专业化司法保护。作为乌龙茶和红茶的发源地，武夷山国家公园探索"茶-林""茶-草"等模式，免费向茶农提供苗木，鼓励套种楠木、红豆杉、银杏等珍贵树种，根据不同季节见缝插针地套种紫云英、大豆、油菜花等绿肥，辅以污染防控技术，维护茶园生态平衡，提高茶叶品质。武夷山打造 251 公里的国家公园 1 号风景道，串起多个景区，成为游客探寻"武夷文化"的索引图，2023 年旅游接待人数和收入分别达 1550 万人次、216 亿元。

海南热带雨林国家公园是中国分布最集中、类型最多样、保存最完好、连片面积最大的大陆性岛屿型热带雨林，成立国家公园研究院，建设省级智慧管理中心、智慧雨林大数据中心、长臂猿监测平台、智慧游客服务中心等系统，搭建"森林动态监测大样地、卫星样地、随机样地、公里网格样地"四位一体的热带雨林监测体系。2021~2024 年，海南省连续四年开展热带雨林国家公园 GEP 核算，成为中国首个完成 GEP 核算的国家公园，形成"自然资源确权-GEP 核算-碳汇交易-智慧管护"生态保护机制。2024 年 7 月，海南省林业局举办热带雨林碳汇交易暨项目合作签约仪式，这是中国首例国家公园碳汇交易活动。

案例 3-4　　　三江源国家公园：守护"中华水塔"的绿色答卷

三江源地处青藏高原腹地，孕育长江、黄河和澜沧江等大江大河，被誉为"中华水塔""江河之源"。三江源国家公园是首个国家公园体制试点，也是现有中国最大、海拔最高且生物多样性高度富集的国家公园，完整纳入黄河、长江源头。2024 年 6 月，习近平总书记在青海考察时强调："重中之重是把三江源这个'中华水塔'守护好，保护生物多样性，提升水源涵养能力。加强以国家公园为主体的自然保护地体系建设，打造具有国家代表性和世界影响力的自然保护地典范。"

机制创新破解保护发展瓶颈

2016 年 3 月，《三江源国家公园体制试点方案》发布。同年 4 月，青海省成立由省委书记、省长任双组长的体制试点领导小组，印发《实施〈三江源国家公园体制试点方案〉的部署意见》，一场关乎三江源地区自然生灵万物乃至下游数亿人口的深刻变革就此启动。针对体制试点范围内 6 类 15 个保护地条块管理的弊端，青海省将分散在林业、国土、环保、住建、水利、农牧等部门的生态保护管理职责划归三江源国家公园管理局，完成国家公园"一块牌子管到底"的历史性变革。编制《三江源国家公园总体规划》以及生态保护规划、生态体验和环境教育规划、产业发展和特许经营规划、社区发展和基础设施建设规划、管理规划"1+5"规划体系，配套出台系列管理办法，搭建"一把尺子量到底"的制度体系，形成"九个一"①的三江源生态保护模式。

山水林田湖草沙冰一体化管理保护

以"整体恢复、全面好转、生态健康、功能稳定"为目标，三江源国家公园累计投入超 300 亿元，提升草地生态系统，修复荒漠生态系统，保护湖河、雪山冰川、湿地生态系统，地表水资源较多年平均值增加 33.7%，水体与湿地生态系统面积净增 309 平方千米，水源涵养量平均增

---

① 　九个一：一面旗帜引领、一个部门管理、一种类型整合、一套制度治理、一户一岗管护、一体系统监测、一支队伍执法、一众力量推动、一种精神支撑。

幅在 6% 以上，每年向中下游稳定输送近千亿立方米 I 类及以上的优质水，草地覆盖率、产草量分别比 10 年前提高 11%、30% 以上，野生动物种群明显增多，重点生态建设工程区生态环境状况持续好转。

科技智绘生态蓝图

三江源国家公园管理局与中国航天科技集团等合作，构建覆盖重点生态区域的"天空地"一体化监测网络体系，实现"远距离、大范围、非接触、全方位"的近地实时监测，已完成野生动植物资源本底调查，首次形成陆生脊椎动物物种名录，精细绘制优势兽类和鸟类物种分布图。可可西里卓乃湖 5G 基站开通运行，中国面积最大、海拔最高的世界自然遗产地中心区域通过 5G 网络连接全球。索南达杰保护站实现周边近 600 平方千米"可见光+热成像"24 小时全方位视频远程监控数据稳定传输，为动态了解野生动物种群现状、变化和栖息的情况提供技术支撑。为 1.5 万余名生态管护员安装"生态管护员"App，实时网络传输巡护情况。

生态保护与民生改善相协调

三江源国家公园管理局为当地牧户设立生态管护员岗位，开展专业技能培训，提供人均 2 万元/年的经费补贴。2.3 万名放下牧鞭的牧民持证上岗，在遇到未知动物时，及时拍摄视频或照片传回后方大数据中心。园区组建乡镇管护站、村级管护队和管护小分队，推进山水林草湖冰的组织化管护和网格化巡护。引导牧民通过投资入股、合作经营、提供劳务等多种方式，参与家庭旅馆、牧家乐、民族文化演艺等特色经营项目。出台野生动物与家畜争食草场损失补偿管理制度，缓解人、畜、野生动物之间的冲突。如今，当地群众走上生态路、吃上生态饭，一幅三江源各族人民与山水相融、与生灵共处、与草木共生的大美画卷徐徐展开。

案例 3-5　　　大熊猫国家公园：全民参与提级保护国宝家园

自 20 世纪 60 年代以来，中国陆续建立以大熊猫及其栖息地为主要保护对象的自然保护区 67 个，大熊猫野外种群数量从 20 世纪 80 年代的约 1100 只增长到全国第四次大熊猫调查时的近 1900 只，大熊猫受威胁程度由"濒危"降为"易危"。2021年10月，中国在川陕甘三省的大熊猫主要栖息地设立大熊猫国家公园，区划总面积2.2万平方千米，打造大熊猫保护升级版（生物多样性保护示范区、生态价值实现先行区和世界生态教育样板）。

协同开展生态保护修复

国家林草局与川陕甘三省政府建立局省联席会议协调推进机制，成都专员办履行协调机制办公室职责。三省共同编制《大熊猫国家公园总体规划（2023~2030年）》，三省人大常委会同步出台《关于加强大熊猫国家公园协同保护管理的决定》，三省高级人民法院共同发布《关于加强大熊猫国家公园司法协同保护的意见》，毗邻地区的公安机关、大熊猫国家公园管理机构常态化开展跨区域警园协作。四川片区在核心保护区、一般控制区和毗邻的特定区域及外围关联区采取差异化的分类动态管控措施，并在中国首次利用局域网结合超短波传输和大熊猫"猫脸"识别技术，实现野外监测实况无线传输野生大熊猫图像和视频。甘肃片区制定"一矿一策""一站一策"处置方案，完成相关矿区、水电站的关停拆除、修复验收、赔偿注销。

发展当地居民深度参与的绿色产业

陕西省汉中市佛坪县打造"大熊猫"IP，开发国宝探秘之旅等旅游线路，推出文创雪糕、智慧积木等"熊小馨"品牌文创产品，上线"佛坪熊猫之旅"网游平台，沉浸式展示大熊猫文化和秦岭生态文化；四川唐家河国家级自然保护区与当地的青溪镇政府、落衣沟村两委、社会组织等共同成立唐家河-落衣沟共建共管委员会，取缔零星养殖业，发展对野生动物危害程度低的生态种植、林下养殖等友好型产业，开展原生态产品认定备案上市，奖补参与调整产业结构的农户，适度发展生态旅游、康养旅游……共管共建、协同发展的绿色产业正在大熊猫国家公园得到广泛探索。

自然教育活动蓬勃发展

甘肃陇南市李子坝村属于大熊猫国家公园白水江分局管辖范围。2023年，在白水江自然保护区管理局和文县政府的支持下，当地组建中国首支农民义务森林巡护队，驱逐非法盗伐、盗猎人员。李子坝村与农户签订《森林资源保护承诺书》，建设清洁能源示范村，成立茶叶合作社，发放生态保护奖金。而后，李子坝村组建自然教育团队，建立自然教育中心，以自身实践为教材，向村民、游客普及环保知识。李子坝村生态保护案例入选《生物多样性公约》第十五次缔约方大会非政府组织平行论坛公布的"生物多样性100+全球典型案例"。

其他地区也在努力开发有地域特色的自然教育课程，成为研学旅游的亮点。比如，龙溪-虹口国家级自然保护区位于成都都江堰市，是离特大型城市最近的国家级自然保护区，推出"熊猫课堂"品牌，组建熊猫志愿者、熊猫讲师队伍，推进教材开发、课程设置、文创研发、基地建设，开展自然科普进校区、进景区、进社区、进街区、进山区，成为自然教育IP；阿坝州汶川县开发自然教育线路，编写《汶川生物多样性图鉴》《大熊猫国家公园汶川自然教育手册》，上线大熊猫国家公园自然教育汶川片区访客预约平台，打造高水平学术交流平台、高层次宣传平台、高质量访客目的地。

案例 3-6　　　　　东北虎豹国家公园：青山更青虎豹归

东北虎豹国家公园地处吉林、黑龙江两省交界的老爷岭南部区域，东与俄罗斯豹地国家公园毗邻，南隔图们江与朝鲜相望，是中国唯一承担跨境保护合作任务的国家公园。这里曾经"众山皆有虎"，但在一个世纪前，野生东北虎远走他乡，数量急速萎缩。实现东北虎豹种群的长期稳定繁衍，既需要大面积的连通栖息地和完整的森林景观，又需要健康的植被结构、丰富的生物多样性资源和完整的食物链，以及不受干扰的繁衍环境。2021 年 12 月，东北虎豹国家公园正式设立。

东北虎豹国家公园建立"管理局—管理分局—管护中心—保护站"四级网格化管护体系，与吉林和黑龙江两省法院、检察院、森林公安局等建立司法协作机制，常态化开展清山清套、打击偷盗猎、"绿卫"、"绿盾"等专项行动。落实生态管护员"一户一岗"政策，从园区居民中选聘村屯生态管护员，每户每年兑现专项补贴 1 万元。把国家公园内发生的人身财产损失、吉林和黑龙江两省全域发生的野生虎豹造成的人身伤害、生态管护员在工作期间受到的意外伤害、非重点保护野生动物造成的损失全部纳入理赔范围，扩大农作物受损的理赔种类。围绕旗舰物种、生态系统、人为活动三大监测内容，开发专业监测平台，实现对虎豹等野生动物活动节律、时空分布趋势、种群活跃趋势、分布热力图等数据的实时监测和分析。

通过综合施策，东北虎豹国家公园创造野生东北虎豹"数量翻倍"、园区居民"生态共富"的绿色发展奇迹，成为中国生物链最完整的地区之一以及欧亚大陆同纬度地区原始状态保存最好、生物多样性最丰富的物种基因库。

四 海洋生态修复有序开展

中国将海洋生态系统作为整体考量，有针对性地采取保护保育、自然恢复、辅助再生、生态重建等模式。2016 年以来，中央财政支持沿海城市实施"蓝色海湾"整治行动、渤海综合治理攻坚战生态修复、海岸带保护修复工程、红树林保护修复等海洋生态保护修复重大项目。截至2023 年末，累计投入中央财政资金252.58 亿元，带动全国累计整治修复海岸线近 1680 公里、滨海湿地超过 75 万亩。

山东东营市黄河口湾区滨海湿地是全球暖温带保存最完整、最年轻的湿地生态系统，当地政府坚持"刈割+围淹""刈割+翻耕"系统施治与长效管护相结合，科学保障湿地用水，长效呵护物种栖息，引活水、修湿地、筑家园，建立外来入侵物种预防、监测、预警、处置机制。如今，湾区优良水质面积比例较"十三五"期间平均增长超过 30%，黄河入海断面水质稳定达到Ⅱ类，每年数百万只候鸟在此停歇和繁殖。

过去由于海平面上升、风暴潮、入海泥沙减少等原因，北戴河岸滩遭遇侵蚀后退。秦皇岛出台《秦皇岛市海岸线保护条例》《秦皇岛市海水浴场管理条例》，将海洋生态修复纳入法治机制。建立"覆植沙丘-滩肩补沙-人工沙坝-离岸潜堤"的海滩静态平衡修复模式，解决传统人工养滩模式后期维护难、海滩自我修复能力弱等问题。采用高消能、强渗透卵石分层技术，保护基岩海蚀地貌，提高区域防灾减灾能力。在沙滩修复基础上，以"封闭保护保育为主、生物资源修复为辅"策略，筛选投放抗盐碱、耐海风的乡土植物构建生态廊道，改善湿地生物种群结构，提升海岸带生物多样性及生态景观价值。

青岛西海岸新区是以海洋经济为特色的国家级新区，309 公里海岸线绵延勾勒，23 处港湾纵横交错，42 个岛屿星罗棋布，2129 平方千米陆域和 5000 平方千米海域交相渲染。围绕拆违建、清岸线、调项目、修慢道、植绿化、保文化六大任务，青岛西海岸新区实施"蓝色海湾"整治行动。比如，实施灵山岛海洋生态保护修复项目，开展植被群落修复、岛体稳定性防护、岸线保护修复、牡蛎礁修复、入海污染物治理和建设生态保护修复管理平台"5+1"工程，灵山岛省级自然保护区碳排放核算结果获得中国质量认证中心认证，成为中国首个得到权威部门认证的自主负碳区域。

老市村是海南省儋州市海头镇珠碧江入海口的小村庄。该村清除养殖区域废弃物，疏浚河道和沟渠，恢复水系连通和水体交换条件，采用生态滤坝加固沟渠岸坡和河道边坡，沿河道种植乡土植物，强化水土保持功能，将虾塘传统养殖模式向生态塘及盐田综合利用方式转换，将清退养殖区微改造为红树林湿地和以沙生植被为特色的滨海湿地，建设市民、游客亲水的生态小岛，入选自然资源部发布的海洋生态保护修复典型案例名单。

案例 3-7　　　　福建省莆田市涵江区："蓝碳增汇+生态修复"
织密"海上森林"

促淤保滩、防风消浪、降解污染、调节气候，红树林素有"海洋绿肺""海岸卫士"的美誉，是生物多样性最丰富的生态系统之一。截至 2023 年底，中国已营造红树林约 7000 公顷，修复现有红树林约 5600 公顷，红树林地面积增至 3.62 万公顷，比本世纪初增加约 1.4 万公顷，成为世界上少数几个红树林面积净增长的国家之一。

2023 年起，涵江区人民法院、检察院、公安分局等单位，在木兰溪入海口设置"木兰溪口湿地红树林保护区"，优化木兰溪流域生态司法保护。针对部分无法进行原地生态修复的生态环境资源破坏类案件，涵江区法院引导当事人委托第三方企业在保护区补植红树，以"造林增汇"蓝碳替代性修复方式履行生态环境修复义务。为让红树林幼苗能在泥泞中"站稳脚跟"，涵江区法院在上述案件执行程序中引入"生态技术调查官"机制，邀请农林专家介入执行环节，提供生态环境鉴定、评估、修复等专业意见，填补执行法官在生态技术领域的"知识盲区"，督促第三方企业提升人工定植修复的红树林成活率。另外，针对在冬季执行的生态环境资源破坏类案件，面对并非补种植绿、替代修复的适宜季节，涵江区法院将案件的生态修复费用用于除治保护区内的外来入侵物种，构建"减量型"生态司法修复模式，得到最高人民法院推广。

值得关注的是，木兰溪治理是习近平总书记在福建工作期间亲自擘画、全程推动治水工作的先行探索。在习近平总书记治理木兰溪的重要理念的指引下，莆田市各级党委、政府出台系列政策措施，率先对单条流域开展专项巡察，首创流域双河长、企业河长、委员河长、网络河长，实施"木兰溪流域+饮用水源"双补偿机制，治理城市污源，疏通扩宽河道，实施绿化民心工程，恢复自然植被，修建河堤护栏，铺设沿河林荫小径，布置亲水景观和场馆等，一跃成为中国"十大最美家乡河"，成功打造绿色发展的木兰溪样本。

涵江区法院的实践说明，人民法院环境资源审判既要依法惩治环境资源犯罪，又要秉持生态恢复的司法理念，探索多元修复方式，积极引导被告人修复受损生态环境，让破坏者成为守护者。

五　重要生态保护修复重大工程稳步推进

1. 山水林田湖草沙一体化保护修复重点工程成效明显

中国以国家重点生态功能区、生态保护红线、自然保护地等为重点，陆续实施三北、长江等防护林和天然林保护修复、退耕还林还草、矿山生态修复、"蓝色海湾"整治行动、海岸带保护修复、渤海综合治理攻坚战、红树林保护修复等具有重要生态影响的生态环境修复治理工程，推动森林、草原、湿地、河流、湖泊面积持续增加，森林覆盖率和森林蓄积量连续 30 多年保持"双增长"，是全球森林资源增长最多和人工造林面积最大的国家，自 2000 年以来，中国始终是全球"增绿"的主力军，全球新增绿化面积中约 1/4 来自中国，在世界范围内率先实现土地退化"零增长"，荒漠化土地和沙化土地面积"双减少"。

围绕国土空间规划、生态保护修复规划等确定的生态安全屏障重点地区，或者具有全球意义的生态关键区，中国持续推进 52 个山水林田湖草沙一体化保护和修复工程（中国山水工程），截至 2023 年末，完成修复治理面积超过 6.7 万平方千米。江苏、浙江、河北等 10 余个省份启动省级山水工程项目，整体提升相关地区的生态系统质量。

内蒙古巴彦淖尔市乌梁素海是中国北方防沙带的关键核心区、黄河流域生物多样性保护的重要区域、世界鸟类迁徙通道在中国迁徙路线的重要节点。乌梁素海山水工程围绕"修山—保水—扩林—护草—调田—治湖—固沙"的路径，修复流域生态系统结构和治理功能受损、退化趋势等问题。乌梁素海的芦苇属一年生植物，如果不能及时处理，就会腐烂在湖里，产生二氧化碳，加剧水体富营养化，而水生植物资源化综合处理项目由专业公司按照市场价收购清理收割的湖区芦苇，制成年产值数千万元的无醛环保板材，替代森林采伐的木材，带动当地交通、包装、材料、服务等行业发展。

铜仁市梵净山是武陵山脉最高峰，97% 的区域被林地覆盖，是贵州省首屈一指的旅游胜地，保存着 7925 种古老孑遗、珍稀濒危和特有物种，被誉为地球同纬度"唯一绿洲"，列入世界自然遗产名录和世界自然保护联盟绿色名录。梵净山生物多样性保护和修复项目针对野生动植物生境压缩、外来物种入侵、耕地生态系统退化等问题，实施生态系统保育、生态功能提升、河道水环境综合整治、农田生态功能提升、矿山生态修复、人类活动区缓冲带建设六个工程。铜仁出台《铜仁市梵净山保护条例》，建立梵净山生态执法协作和资源管理联动机制，设立梵净山警务区、生态法庭，保留当地少数民族村寨的民风民俗，深化文体农旅等融合发展，建设"生态领先"的世界级康养旅居目的地。

湖北省宜昌市枝江金湖国家湿地公园是长江中游地区最大的天然浅水型湖泊，实施源头减污、退渔还湖、水系连通等措施，系统治理排放端的外源污染和湖泊养殖的内源污染。以恢复湖滨生态系统结构与功能、增强生态产品供给能力为重点，对沿湖岸线重新整理和修复，划定金湖周边的陆域保护红线，每月市河长办通报水质监测结果，市政府根据年度水质达标率，对乡（镇）政府和金湖湿地管理处兑现奖惩资金。

2. 历史遗留废弃矿山生态修复稳步推进

中国出台矿山生态修复激励措施，在长江经济带、黄河流域、京津冀周边、汾渭平原、青藏高原等重点流域和区域，带动地方政府和社会投入，加快推进矿山修复。2022 年起，累计实施 49 个历史遗留矿山修复示范工程，完成历史遗留废弃矿山治理面积超过 480 万亩，有效改善矿区生态状况和周边人居环境，促进自然资源节约集约循环利用，提升采矿废弃土地利用价值，在产业导入和促进资源型城市转型发展中起到引领作用。

中煤平朔矿区是国家确立的亿吨级煤炭生产基地，下属安太堡露天矿是改革开放以后中国第一个中外合作项目。平朔集团实施"剥-运-排-造-复"工艺，将"少占地、造好地、快复垦、利用好"的理念落实到矿区土地复垦，将露天煤矿表土排弃位置和数量纳入采矿生产计划，土地复垦成为露天采煤的最后一个环节，创出黄土高原大型露天煤矿"边开采、边修复"的矿山生态修复"平朔模式"。同时，平朔集团建设近千亩苗圃，将自用以外的树苗推向市场；在平整的土地上种植紫花苜蓿，为当地养殖业提供优质牧草；建成 300 个日光温室、1.6 万平方米智能温室的生态园，年产蔬菜 600 万斤，培养花卉 30 余万株，出栏肉羔羊 4000 余只。

鞍钢矿业大孤山铁矿是新中国第一座恢复生产的铁矿山，经过连年开采，形成垂深 400 多米、体积 2.92 亿米^3 的深凹采坑，被称为亚洲最深露天铁矿。鞍钢矿业采用尾矿砂加入胶剂回填露天采坑，建立尾矿分矿、料浆制备、料浆输送、露天坑排水等系统，将生态修复形成的农林用地打造为生态园，设置科普展示区、水果采摘区、蔬菜种植区、苗木培植区等 4 个功能区，实现两季结果、三季观花、四季常绿，形成采场复垦修复及时化、矿区建设绿色化、生态破坏风险最小化、废水利用共享化为特色的生态修复模式。

安徽淮南矿区属多煤层重复开采，累计采厚达 30 米，最大沉陷深度达 22 米，累计形成沉陷区 41.15 万亩，沉陷区具有下沉深度大、沉陷范围广、稳沉时间长、地下水位浅、积水占比高等特点。淮南矿区按照"三色图引领"①"三规划融合"②"三类型治理"③ 的总体思路，坚持政校企合作、产学研融合，推进治理模式、工艺和技术创新，实现资源开采与沉陷防治同步、综合治理与合理利用结合，建成 6 个生态公园，复垦土地超 6000 公顷，建成装机 60 万千瓦水面光伏发电项目，蹚出永久安全区根本性治理、10 年及以上稳沉区系统性治理、10 年以下非稳沉区动态治理的矿山生态修复新路径。

东方希望重庆铜矿山水泥灰岩矿地处三峡库区腹地，创新"石电共生""采复并举"模式，采用露天台阶式分层开采技术，构建"先覆后采"土地循环、"截流蓄灌"水循环等系统，将剥离表土、溶洞填充土和边坡夹层土用于工厂绿化、边坡复绿，实现区域 100% 生态修复，年减碳 307 万吨。针对矿山修复面临的植被存活率低问题，东方希望水泥公司采取"三年轮种法"，第一年种高粱，第二年种草本和灌木，第三年再栽树，改善土壤环境，植被存活率大幅提升，修复后的效果和周边未开采的效果基本一致。

---

① "三色图引领"：针对 10 年以下非稳沉区，将动态维护作为治理修复主要手段，恢复土地可供利用状态，在深部积水区发展光伏，在浅部积水区试种浮床水稻，对未积水区进行动态恢复，形成立体化系统修复利用模式。

② "三规划融合"：针对 10 年及以上阶段稳沉区，根据采场接替规划、沉陷治理规划与国土空间总体规划，统筹修复利用与乡村环境品质提升，实施道路硬化、岸基复绿、土地复垦、景观建设，改善生产生活环境。

③ "三类型治理"：对于城市规划范围内的全部稳沉永久安全区，发展文化旅游，为居民提供休闲空间。对于城乡接合部全部稳沉永久安全区，加强设施修复与景观提升，延伸城市辐射范围。对于远离城镇的全部稳沉永久安全区，开展基础设施维护与土地整治，恢复土地耕种功能。

第3节　中国科学开展大规模国土绿化行动的
创新举措、主要成效和典型案例

一　全民义务植树全面开展

习近平总书记强调，全国人民坚持植树造林，荒山披锦绣，沙漠变绿洲，成就举世瞩目。绿化祖国要扩绿、兴绿、护绿并举，推动森林"水库、钱库、粮库、碳库"更好联动。增绿就是增优势，植树就是植未来，要人人尽责，畅通群众参与渠道、创新尽责形式，发挥好林长制作用，把各方面力量调动起来，推动全民义务植树不断走深走实。2013年4月，习近平同志参加了当选中共中央总书记后的首次首都义务植树活动。此后，每年春天，习近平总书记都会身体力行，拿起铁锹和群众一起参加义务植树活动，这是以实际行动示范引领，更是表达坚持绿色发展的决心。全国人大、全国政协、中央军委领导同志分别集体参加义务植树活动。中央和国家机关推进节约型绿化美化单位建设，2024年，137名部级领导履"植"尽责，9.3万名干部职工完成义务植树38.5万株。31个省份及新疆生产建设兵团组织开展省级领导集体义务植树活动，400余个地级市组织开展市级领导集体义务植树活动。建成"互联网＋全民义务植树"基地2600余个，为适龄公民就近、适时、多样尽责提供服务。

自开展全民义务植树以来，北京已有1.1亿余人次通过各种形式履行义务，累计植树2.2亿株，森林覆盖率由1980年的12.83%提高至2024年的44.95%。结合花园城市建设，北京推动义务植树多样化、常态化、全年化，从一季植树到全年尽责，形成"春植、夏认、秋抚、冬防"等组织形式，市民可全年线上预约、线下劳动，也可通过认种认养、捐资捐物等方式参与，随时、随地、随愿履行植树义务。引导市民在自家庭院、屋顶、墙体、阳台等打造"一米花园""半米阳台"等家庭园艺场景，且均可折算义务植树株数，实现"不出家门尽义务，方寸之间添新绿"。

广东省实施"绿美广东"生态建设行动，倡导"有喜事来种树"，呼吁"我为家乡种棵树"，建设青年林、先锋林、巾帼林等主题林，2024 年组织开展义务植树活动超 2.45 万场次，植树场次居全国首位。以高速公路、国省道、铁路等为载体，将古村落、历史遗迹、自然公园、绿美示范点等串珠成链，构建互连互通的绿美生态网络。广东连续 17 年提高省级及以上公益林补偿标准，优化公益林差异化补偿，对森林质量高、林相好的区域额外安排每年每亩 4 元的激励性补偿，推行公益林管护奖惩和生态产品价值实现激励机制，政策性森林保险参保率达 66%，碳普惠核证减排备案累计签发 247 万吨。

由于地形限制，湖南省难以在各市州找到大面积的平整地块稳定作为义务植树活动基地，难以满足市民全部通过现场栽种方式履行义务植树责任的需求。为此，湖南省强化其他履行责任方式，比如，市民参与树木抚育管护劳动、野生动物栖息地保护、荒漠化防治、退耕还林（草）、退耕还湿、山体或废弃地生态修复、认养和保护古树名木、修建绿色廊道、捐赠资金用于国土绿化、国土绿化公益活动等，均可折算完成一定量的植树任务。部分湿地公园、景区、林场对义务植树尽责证书持有人提供门票优惠及生态教育、自然体验、森林康养等优先服务。

二 "三北"工程攻坚战迈出坚实步伐

1978 年，党中央作出在西北、华北、东北风沙危害和水土流失重点地区建设大型防护林的战略决策。"三北"工程区涵盖北方防沙带、东北森林带等中国生态安全重要区域，全长 4480 千米，分布着中国 84% 的沙化土地和八大沙漠、四大沙地和广袤戈壁，是中国自然条件最恶劣、生态最脆弱的地区。与之对应，"三北"工程区面积占中国陆域国土的近一半，分布有东北平原、河套灌区、河西走廊、新疆绿洲等农产品主产区，也是"向森林要食物、向草原要食物"和开发利用太阳能、风能等资源的重要基地。

在国务院"三北"工程协调机制的统一指挥下，各地区各部门、央企民企在"黄沙遮天日，飞鸟无栖树"的荒漠沙地上，锁黄沙、造绿林，让祖国北疆大地由黄到绿、由绿生金。新时代以来，习近平总书记对加强"三北"工程建设作出一系列重要指示批示，亲自谋划、亲自部署、亲自推动黄河"几字弯"攻坚战、科尔沁和浑善达克两大沙地歼灭战、河西走廊-塔克拉玛干沙漠边缘阻击战三大标志性战役，将"三北"工程作为党委政府的"一把手"工程，"三北"各地相继发布关于打好"三北"攻坚战的总林长令，统筹封禁保护、造林种草、荒漠植被修复、生态输水、风电光伏等措施，发展林下经济、中药材、经济林果、沙漠旅游等绿色产业。至今，累计完成治理面积7600多万亩，工程区森林覆盖率由5.05%提高到13.84%，61%的水土流失面积得到有效控制，45%以上可治理沙化土地得到初步治理，有效庇护农田4.5亿亩，1500多万人依靠特色林果业实现稳定脱贫，从根本上实现从"沙进人退"到"绿进沙退"的历史性转变，祖国北疆筑起抵御风沙的"绿色长城"。"三北"工程打造防沙治沙的中国标杆，中国成为全球荒漠化防治事业的重要推动者、引领者。《联合国防治荒漠化公约》秘书处称赞，"世界荒漠化防治看中国"。

案例3-8　　黄河"几字弯"攻坚战：增厚黄河流域高质量发展的"绿色家底"

黄河"几字弯"区域地跨中国华北、西北地区，是黄河流经甘肃、宁夏、内蒙古、陕西和山西5个省（自治区）所形成的"几"字形生态区域，分布着库布齐、乌兰布和、腾格里、毛乌素等沙漠沙地，是黄河中下游泥沙的主要来源地以及影响京津和东部地区沙尘暴的重要沙源区和路径区。1978年以来，黄河"几字弯"区域实施"三北"、退耕还林还草和京津风沙源治理等林业生态工程，控制黄土丘陵沟壑区水土流失，黄河流域年均土壤侵蚀模数由每平方千米8000~12000吨下降至2000~5000吨，年均入黄泥沙量由16亿吨减至2.42亿吨，实现区域森林覆盖率和草原植被盖度"双提高"，荒漠化和沙化土地面积"双减少"。

而后，中国实施黄河"几字弯"攻坚战。针对沙患问题，以固沙滞尘、阻沙入黄为重点，区分不同沙漠、沙地对症下药。针对水患问题，控制黄河岸线流沙入黄，推进小流域系统治理。针对盐渍化问题，培育、推广耐盐碱的林草种质资源，加强盐碱化土地综合治理。针对草原超载过牧问题，把"三化"（退化、沙化、盐碱化）草原作为修复重点，加大禁牧力度。针对河湖湿地保护问题，确保沿黄重要湿地面积不萎缩，严控新增湿地数量和规模。

2020 年 5 月，习近平总书记在山西考察调研时指出，要牢固树立绿水青山就是金山银山的理念，发扬"右玉精神"。山西省朔州市右玉县地处毛乌素沙地边缘，属晋西北高寒冷凉干旱区，"一年一场风，从春刮到冬，白天点油灯，黑夜土堵门，风起黄沙飞，十年九不收"，短短几句民谣道出过去右玉县的脆弱生态和发展困境。按照山上治本、身边增绿、生态致富、综合保护的思路，右玉县把造林绿化、改善生态作为打基础、利长远的事情，作为全县人民的生命工程和发展工程，一任接着一任干，造林绿化 70 多年来从未间断，总结出"消一层、挖一层"冻土造林法、"挖坑换黏土"种苗法，破解"冻土层制约造林工程进度"的难题，绿化率从不足 3% 攀升至 57%，成功把"不适宜人类生存的地区"发展为国家级生态示范区。

进一步看，毛乌素沙地横跨蒙陕宁甘四省区，总面积 4.72 万平方千米，至今八成染绿，展现中国荒漠化防治理念和技术途径迭代升级、引领世界荒漠化防治的最新成果。在《联合国防治荒漠化公约》第十三次缔约方大会上，毛乌素沙地治理被称为"中国乃至世界治沙史上的奇迹"。联合国治理荒漠化组织总干事对此评价说："毛乌素沙漠的治理实践，让世界向中国致敬。"内蒙古鄂尔多斯市乌审旗全境处于毛乌素沙地腹部，国土总面积约占毛乌素沙地总面积的 25%。70 多年来，乌审旗将毛乌素治沙作为中心任务，形成划区轮牧、封沙育林禁休牧、飞播造林、小流域治理、家庭草牧场、造林大户、生态移民、龙头企业治理、农业综合开发草原建设等九种防沙、治沙、用沙模式。近年来，乌审旗全力推进毛乌素沙地歼灭战，科学划定"五区治理"（东西阻隔锁边、东部保护修复、南部产业振兴、西部精准治理、北部沙地歼灭），打造裸露沙地治理、退化林修复、荒漠化草原改良、林沙产业和灌木加工利用、生态红线巩固提升等五类生态基地，推广"以工代赈"方式，带动农村低收入人口治沙增收，森林覆盖率和植被覆盖度提升至 32.92% 和 80%，沙化土地大面积缩减。

内蒙古巴彦淖尔市河套灌区拥有总干渠、干渠、分干渠、支渠、斗渠、农渠、毛渠七级灌排渠（沟）道 10.36 万条、6.4 万千米，是中国三个特大型灌区之一，也是重要的商品粮油基地。为更好发挥农田防护林效益，巴彦淖尔市探索出"渠林路"造林模式，把树栽在渠和路之间，林带间距 500 米，主副林带垂直，林网闭合，林带宽度 2~3 米，株距 2~3 米，树种主要选用新疆杨、小美旱杨等乡土树种，有效解决农民惜地、林木胁地的矛盾。目前，巴彦淖尔市农田防护林面积 36 万亩，控制农田面积 1000 余万亩，基本形成"田成方、林成网、路相通、渠相连、旱能灌、涝能排"的综合效益格局。

宁夏中卫市沙坡头区是腾格里沙漠直接入黄的沙头之一，过去环境恶劣，气候干旱，风力强的时候风沙流直接入黄河。沙坡头区采取草方格治沙法，在沙漠布置网绳式草方格沙障，利用植物根系固定沙土，减少风沙流动，建立"五带一体"铁路治沙体系（砾石防火带、灌溉造林带、草障植物带、前沿阻沙带、封沙育草带），在治沙区发展光伏绿能，运用"林光互补""农光互补"技术，恢复和增加植被，探索出"以固为主、固阻结合"绿色治沙新模式。

案例 3-9　　河北省塞罕坝机械林场：人工修复伟大工程缔造绿色发展奇迹

地处河北省最北部的塞罕坝曾是一处天然名苑，水草丰美、森林茂密，是清朝皇家猎苑"木兰围场"的重要组成部分。由于清朝末年的开围放垦、连年战争和山火，塞罕坝原始自然生态遭到严重破坏，到新中国成立前夕，原始森林荡然无存，变成风沙漫天、草木凋敝的茫茫荒原。

1962 年，林业部批准建立河北省塞罕坝机械林场，靠着三代人努力，建起世界上面积最大的人工林，林场内石质荒山全部实现绿化，林地面积由 24 万亩增加到 115.1 万亩，林木蓄积量由 33.6 万米³ 增加到 1036.8 万立方米，森林覆盖率由 11.4% 提高到 82%，单位面积的林木蓄积量达到中国人工林平均水平的 2.76 倍，植树近 5 亿棵，如果把塞罕坝林场的树按一米株距排开，可绕地球赤道 12 圈，生物多样性得到恢复，为滦河、辽河下游地区涵养水源、净化淡水 2.84 亿米³/年，减少土壤流失量 513.55 万吨/年，固定二氧化碳 86.03 万吨/年，释放氧气 59.84 万吨/年，成为华北地区的风沙屏障和水源卫士，荣获联合国环保最高荣誉"地球卫士奖"和防治荒漠化领域最高荣誉"土地生命奖"，成为全球环境治理的"中国榜样"。

塞罕坝人摸索总结出高寒地区全光育苗技术，培育优质壮苗，凝练客土回填、覆膜保水、幼苗保墒、防寒越冬等整套造林技术规范，构建多树种、多层次、复合式的森林结构，营造针阔混交、色彩层次丰富的异龄复层混交林，逐步使林分达到近自然状态。另外，塞罕坝机械林场建立"天空地"一体化监测预警体系，实现卫星、直升机、无人机、探火雷达、视频监控、高山瞭望、地面巡护有机结合，并开展落叶松高效培育技术、遥感技术监测、森林湿地资源价值评估、林业有害生物技术防治等领域科技攻关和成果应用。

2021 年 9 月，经中共中央批准，以"牢记使命、艰苦创业、绿色发展"为核心的塞罕坝精神成为首批被纳入中国共产党人精神谱系的伟大精神之一。塞罕坝精神的价值在于：一是为国植绿山川的神圣使命，"革命理想高于天"的精神力量激励塞罕坝人坚韧不拔，坚持不懈，让荒芜之地重披绿装；二是防风沙、蓄水源的为民情怀，保持水土、阻风断沙、改良环境是中国共产党"一切为了人民"的鲜活体现，塞罕坝机械林场应党和人民的呼唤而上马，吹响"向荒山要树，还我森林"号角；三是迎难而上、勇于担当的创业精神，塞罕坝植树造林坚持科学求实和积极探索，以革命乐观主义精神开展技术攻关、标准编制、规程设置，把"造林保护"和"生态利用"结合，每年产出物质产品和生态服务总价值为 145.8 亿元（中国科学院评估数据），带动当地居民增收脱贫，获得"全国脱贫攻坚楷模"荣誉称号。

案例 3-10　　河西走廊－塔克拉玛干沙漠边缘阻击战：打造
"一带一路"干旱区荒漠化防治示范样板

河西走廊－塔克拉玛干沙漠边缘阻击战片区涉及内蒙古、甘肃、青海、新疆四省区，沙漠、戈壁广布，流动沙丘约占 70%，分布有塔克拉玛干、巴丹吉林、腾格里、古尔班通古特等沙漠和中国 2/3 的风沙口，是中国北方风沙活动最为频繁、灾害最为严重的沙尘源区，也是古代丝绸之路和新亚欧大陆桥经济走廊的咽喉通道，具有特殊的地理位置和生态地位。

河西走廊－塔克拉玛干沙漠边缘阻击战以"防风、阻沙、控尘"为关键目标，通过识别区域风口、大风作用强度和通道、流沙外侵方式和绿洲风沙防护缺口，将塔克拉玛干沙漠、腾格里沙漠、巴丹吉林沙漠边缘绿洲之间的防护林缺口作为治理的重点区域。通过粉尘释放源区划定和传输路径跟踪，重点控制主要尘源地的风蚀，即：在重点区域部署重点项目，层层设防，步步为营，构筑起点线面结合、多廊多屏交织、防治用全链条阻击的主体框架。

塔克拉玛干是世界第二大流动沙漠，1978 年以来，数十万人在其边缘日夜搏斗沙海，堪称当代"愚公移山"。2024 年 11 月，3046 公里的塔克拉玛干绿色阻沙防护带工程实现全面锁边"合龙"，这是世界上最长的环沙漠绿色生态屏障，有效阻止沙漠继续向外移动，防护沙漠周边的农田、牧场和人居环境，减轻京津冀沙尘暴发生频率和强度，为荒漠地区野生动物创造良好的生存繁育和迁徙条件。

塔克拉玛干沙漠治理取得显著成效的关键在于分类施策、科学治沙。工程治沙方面，当地利用麦草、稻草、芦苇、树枝、石头、棉花秆、尼龙网等材料制作草方格，在流动沙丘上扎出方格状的沙障，通过增加地面粗糙度起到削减风力、阻挡沙粒作用。生物治沙方面，当地在绿洲外围沙漠边缘育草覆绿，绿洲前沿地带种植乔灌木结合的防沙林带，绿洲内部地带建设农田防护林网。光伏治沙方面，打造"林草＋光伏"立体治沙模式，解决抽取地下水浇灌沙生植物的用电问题，利用光伏发电板降低风速、减弱气流、阻风挡沙，改善沙地表层土壤水分条件，抑制沙尘暴发生。智能治沙方面，国产智能机器人实现按照预设路线，在沙漠穿梭、挖坑、播种、覆土，每台机器人每天能完成数十亩沙地植绿任务，是传统人工种植的数十倍。

治沙致富双赢也在徐徐延伸。从硕果累累的阿克苏苹果林，到遍地花开的于田县玫瑰花基地，再到新疆杨、红柳、西梅交错而立的麦盖提县生态林，特色沙产业越来越红火。沙漠、戈壁、荒漠地区成为清洁能源发展重镇，陆续招引龙头企业集中连片、合理布局光伏治沙项目。

三 城乡绿化美化水平持续提升

1. 人与自然和谐共生的美丽城市建设稳步推进

中国把保护城市生态环境摆在突出位置，推进以人为核心的新型城镇化，依托现有山水脉络等独特风光推进城市建设，打造宜居城市、韧性城市、智慧城市，创建国家园林城市、国家森林城市，建设城市公园体系和绿道网络，大力实施城市绿化，让城市融入大自然，让居民望得见山、看得见水、记得住乡愁。2012~2024 年，中国城市建成区绿化覆盖率由 39.22% 提高到 43.32%，人均公园绿地面积由 11.8 平方米提高到 15.65 平方米。

案例 3-11　　成都：建设践行新发展理念的公园城市示范区

在中国式现代化之路上，城市现代化是"主战场"。2018 年 2 月，习近平总书记在天府新区考察时指出，要突出公园城市特点，把生态价值考虑进去。2022 年，国家发展改革委等部门联合印发《成都建设践行新发展理念的公园城市示范区总体方案》，赋予成都"两新"使命（探索山水人城和谐相融新实践和超大特大城市转型发展新路径）、"三高"要求（实现高质量发展、高品质生活、高效能治理相结合）、"三示范"发展定位（城市践行绿水青山就是金山银山理念、城市人民宜居宜业、城市治理现代化的示范区）。

"公园城市"首次在成都提出，核心理念是将城市建成一个大公园，强调生态与生产、生活的和谐统一。七年多来，成都制定"总体规划+专项规划+技术指引"公园城市规划体系，通过立法固定公园城市建设的目标和措施，形成"园中建城、城中有园、城园相融、人城和谐"的生态美境，成为中国第1个常住人口突破2100万人、第3个经济总量突破2万亿元的副省级城市，连续16年获得"最具幸福感城市"。

千园融城，宜居宜人

成都市以林长制为抓手，实施"五绿润城"生态示范工程，突出打造大熊猫国家公园成都片区"生态绿肺"、龙泉山城市森林公园"城市绿心"、天府绿道"活力绿脉"、环城生态公园"超级绿环"、锦江公园"精品绿轴"，夯实城市绿色生态本底。

龙泉山城市森林公园累计增绿增景35万亩，区域森林覆盖率从54%提升至60%以上，年均固定二氧化碳超120万吨、释放氧气超90万吨，成为市民家门口的"天然氧吧"，获得2024年世界绿色城市大奖。

成都规划建设总长16930公里的天府绿道体系（全球最长绿道），串联市域绿地、水系、森林、湖泊、河流和田园，累计建成各类公园1500余个、天府绿道超9000公里，配套植入3500多个文旅体科设施，打造一园一主题、一园一特色、一园一故事的独特景观，为市民提供丰富多样的休憩与娱乐空间。同时，成都上线"碳惠天府"绿色公益平台，将绿色出行、垃圾分类、光盘行动打卡、低碳阅读等绿色场景纳入平台积分激励，引导市民践行绿色生活方式。

生态导向，宜业宜商

走进天府新区核心区，最吸引眼球的却是水鸟翩飞、鱼翔浅底的兴隆湖，8.84公里的环湖绿道串连起公园、社区、商圈和产业园区。在公园城市理念指引下，天府新区压缩生产用地规模，提高生态空间占比，保存80%以上原生地貌，沿河、沿绿布局产业空间，集聚26家国家级科研机构、1000多家高新技术企业。进一步看，公园城市示范区加速成都制造强市建设，通过实施"优化提质、特色立园，赋能增效、企业满园"行动，淘汰低端产业，培育生物医药、航空航天、轨道交通、人工智能、机器人、低空经济、氢能、文创、旅游、康养等绿色主导产业，重塑这座西部中心城市的可持续发展优势。

2. 绿色生态宜居的和美乡村蓬勃涌现

中国将绿色发展作为推进乡村振兴的新引擎，加强生态保护与修复，持续改善农村人居环境，全面推进乡村绿化，加强传统村落保护利用，传承优秀传统文化，积极发展生态农业、农村电商、休闲农业、乡村旅游、康养产业等新业态，提高乡村基础设施完备度、公共服务便利度、人居环境舒适度、乡风文明美誉度，广大农村呈现山清水秀、天蓝地绿、村美人和的美丽画卷。

福建省泉州市建立田园风光建设工作协调机制，由市委农办牵头抓总，联合农业农村、水利、资规、住建、发改、文旅、林业、交通等部门协同推进，强化区域统筹、工作统筹、资金统筹"三个统筹"，突出连片建设、融合发展、立体推进"三个突出"，建立"指挥部牵头+国企承建+政策性融资+财政补助"生态保护设施建设运营机制，开展美丽河道、美丽田园、美丽村庄、美丽经济"四美"建设，设立河道综合治理长度完成率、高标准农田覆盖率、裸房整治完成率、村集体经营性收入增长率等晾晒比拼考核机制，将"山、水、路、人居"的生态底色转变为特色农旅风景线。

云南省腾冲市曲石镇清河社区下表院村处于世界生物圈保护区（高黎贡山）和国家级火山自然保护区内，村党支部组织党员群众协商确定"自主设计、就地取材、变废为宝、乡土气息"的绿色村庄发展思路，农民画家在现有墙体、皂角树、烟囱等创作乡村特色画，用田间地头的石材、木材、植物建设崖边生态观光走廊和村内农旅休闲走廊，引导村民将废弃的猪槽、簸箕、风车、石磨、瓦罐等改造为景观小品，村民自发捐出 3000 多盆盆景，营造拥党爱党的浓厚氛围和美丽清新的村寨环境，成功创建 AAA 景区和绿美乡村。

广东省清远市佛冈县开展"四旁"（宅旁、村旁、路旁、水旁）植绿活动，提升"五边"（山边、水边、路边、镇村边、景区边）绿化美化品质，充分利用"三清三拆三整治"① 等手段建设美丽庭院，增加村庄绿化总量。"和美"以"宜游"为基，佛冈县石角镇打造"山水画龙"乡村

---

① 三清三拆三整治："三清"为清理村巷道及生产工具、建筑材料乱堆乱放，清理房前屋后和村巷道杂草杂物、积存垃圾，清理沟渠池塘溪河淤泥、漂浮物和障碍物；"三拆"为拆除危旧房、废弃猪牛栏及露天厕所茅房，拆除乱搭乱建的违章建筑，拆除违法商业广告的招牌；"三整治"为整治垃圾乱扔乱放，整治污水乱排乱倒，整治水体污染。

振兴示范带，串联现代农业基地、"田野绿世界"景点、绿化景观和民宿等配套服务设施，打造集运动休闲、文化体验、农事体验、农耕观光于一体的田园综合体。

河北省石家庄市鹿泉区白鹿泉乡东土门村开展"大清扫"和"搬家式"环境卫生大清理专项行动，清理大街小巷的陈年垃圾，美丽庭院户数占比达 85％以上，获评河北省美丽乡村精品村。落实党员网格化管理、环境卫生门前三包和建房保证金制度，维护和美乡村建设成果。引导村民以土地入股，引入社会资本打造土门关驿道小镇，建设村民自主创业经营区，发展"旅游+"新业态，带动 350 余名村民稳定就业，村集体经济收入稳步增长，获评河北省旅游特色乡村。

广西百色市田东县朔良镇坚持党建引领、党员示范、全民参与，形成"四力驱动、五曲齐奏、六治并举"[①] 的统筹、共商、共建、共享、共管"456 模式"，所有行政村均制定《村规民约》，建立修缮垃圾转运池，聘请保洁员网格化开展清洁乡村行动，通过"六个一点"[②] 汇聚各方资源参与人居环境维护，将村内空地、废弃场地和破旧房屋重新设计利用，变废为宝，见空植绿，勾勒出村庄景色宜人、百姓生活富足、产业蓬勃发展、生态环境宜人的和美乡村新画卷。

第 4 节　中国促进生态产品价值实现的创新举措、主要成效和典型案例

一　生态产品价值实现机制试点创新推进

2021 年以来，自然资源部在江苏、福建、山东、河南、广东、重庆 6 省份选择 10 个市县，开展自然资源领域生态产品价值实现机制试点。

---

① "四力"为支部引领力、党员先行力、党群联动力、乡贤助力，"五曲"为规、清、集、美、护，"六治"为德治、法治、自治、智治、廉治。

② "六个一点"：争取财政投入一点、社会资本注入一点、集体经济筹集一点、群众投工投劳一点、后援单位支持一点、比武打擂争取一点。

2024 年 5 月，国家发展改革委确定首批国家生态产品价值实现机制试点①，推动试点地区利用三年时间探索政府主导、企业和社会各界参与、市场化运作、可持续的生态产品价值实现路径。至今，试点地区形成外溢共享型、赋能增值型、配额交易型 3 类生态产品价值实现典型路径②。

2024 年 12 月，北京市延庆区完成全市首例 2000 万元的 GEP 补偿奖励资金兑现。2016 年，延庆区成立生态文明体制改革专项小组，与中国工程院团队合作开展 GEP 数据核算，而后参考北京市在全国率先出台的生态系统调节服务价值（GEP-R）核算方法，将 2023 年的 GEP 总额最终核算为 498.6 亿元，在全市生态涵养区中增幅第一。四海镇地处延庆深山区，2022 年初还有近 40% 的集体经济薄弱村，推出"绿水青山使用费"生态权益交易模式，辖内每处民宿向村集体交 1 万元/年使用费，让村民们精心保护的山林、溪流、经济作物都有价。按照村村组团、镇村联合、村民入股、企业投资的模式，打造花海夜市、"小溪嘟嘟"农文旅综合体，集体经济薄弱村全部摘帽，50% 的村年集体收入超过 50 万元。

黑龙江省大兴安岭地区森林覆盖率达 86.26%，是中国北方重要的生态屏障和绿色基因库，中国林科院专家团队对大兴安岭森林、湿地、草地生态产品价值核算结果高达 8021.44 亿元/年。2021 年以来，大兴安岭地区加速探索寒温带类型地区生态产品价值实现路径，开展自然资源确权调查、生态产品目录清单编制、森林碳储量和碳变化量测算、GEP 核算地方标准制定、生态产品总值试算，布局林下经济、特色文旅、新能源等生态主导型产业。打造大兴安岭生态产品区域公共品牌，建立生态产品追溯体系，将纳入生态产品目录清单、符合生态产品认证标准的生

---

① 首批国家生态产品价值实现机制试点包括北京市延庆区、河北省承德市、黑龙江省大兴安岭地区、浙江省湖州市、浙江省丽水市、安徽省黄山市、福建省南平市、江西省抚州市、山东省烟台市、湖南省怀化市、广西壮族自治区桂林市、陕西省商洛市 12 个市区。

② 外溢共享型是针对难以分割确权的生态产品，由政府通过转移支付、财政补贴等方式进行购买或补偿。赋能增值型是针对能够明确（或扩展）自然资源产权或权能的生态产品，通过市场交易体现生态价值对资源产品的赋能增值。配额交易型是针对需要开展利用或保护等总量控制的生态产品，通过法律或行政手段将非标准化的生态系统服务转化为标准化的配额（或指标），通过市场交易配额以实现其价值。

态产品溢价销售，百亿级林下产业集群正在形成。

陕西省商洛市地处秦岭腹地，是"中国气候康养之都"，将生态资产存量与生态产品流量同步评估、生态产品供给与利用同步考量，推动"生态资产-生态产品供给-生态产品利用-生态产品价值"同步关联，以群众增收入、企业增效益、政府有收益作为标准，构建"五个四"生态产品价值实现体系①，建成气候生态监测中心和大数据展示平台，开发生态价值评估、山岳型景区高影响天气预警、生态环境动态监测、生态康养等业务系统，实现秦岭气候生态大数据"一张图"展示，发展"气象+旅游""气象+康养""气象+研学"等绿色产业。

案例 3-12　　　　浙江省丽水市：生态产品价值实现机制改革让绿水青山"生金淌银"

中国第一个乡镇和村级 GEP 核算、第一宗包含 GEP 增值的土地出让、第一笔公共机构大型活动碳中和交易、第一批"生态信用贷""生态抵质押贷"等绿色金融创新产品……这是丽水市生态产品价值实现机制改革的成绩单。

制度创新，量化价值

2019 年 8 月，丽水市出台生态产品价值核算技术办法，形成生态产品功能量和价值量核算的技术流程、指标体系与核算方法。而后，丽水市成立生态产品价值实现机制改革工作领导小组，建立市、县、乡（镇）、村四级 GDP 和 GEP 双核算、双评估、双考核机制，编制自然资源资产负债表，推行与生态产品质量和价值相挂钩的财政奖补机制，拓展GEP 进规划、进决策、进交易、进考核、进监测、进项目、进金融、进司法、进生态损害赔偿等"九进"应用场景。

---

① "五个四"生态产品价值实现体系："四个关键点"为生态产品、价值、实现、机制，"四大属性"为物质供给、文化服务、调节服务、金融，"四类表现形式"为农特产品等物质供给类产品价值依靠市场实现、旅游康养和公共服务类产品价值分别依靠市场和政府购买实现、完全公共产品和准公共产品价值分别依靠政府补偿和政策性交易市场实现、基于担保物权的金融属性价值依靠金融市场实现，"四个难题"为核算难、交易难、变现难、抵押难，"四类长效机制"为顶层设计、机制建设、典型案例、工作成效。

基于 GEP 核算，丽水市建立生态产品政府采购和市场化交易机制。依托市、县国企组建"两山合作社"，在乡镇（街道）组建"生态强村公司"，成为收储分散生态资源的经营主体。按照生态产品收储、交易、招商、服务"四统一"原则，建立全省首个区域性生态产品交易中心，构建生态资源资产开发经营服务平台和生态产品市场化交易平台，累计完成各类生态资源、生态产品、绿色产权等交易超过 58 亿元。由此，通过建立生态产品价值核算和交易机制，明晰生态产品价格，形成丽水市绿色发展"一本账"。

生态信用，价值变现

丽水市在中国首创生态信用制度，从生态保护、生态经营、绿色生活、生态文化、社会责任 5 个维度，编制生态信用行为正负面清单，设置生态信用积分兑换生活物品、守信激励等应用场景，开展与生态信用相挂钩的"生态信用贷"服务，辖内金融机构对生态信用良好的借款人在贷款额度、利率、办贷流程等方面给予优惠政策，推出 GEP 未来收益权、国家公园林地地役权收益、公益林补偿收益权、林权、取水权等"生态抵质押贷"产品，实现生态信用作抵押、生态资源变资产、生态资产变资金。截至 2024 年 6 月末，"生态抵质押贷"余额达 325.55 亿元。

案例 3-13　　福建省南平市："森林生态银行"实现生态产品价值

福建省南平市建立"森林生态银行·四个一"林业股份合作经营模式，形成"水美经济"新业态培育、"武夷山水"品牌价值力提升、林业碳汇产品交易、土地综合开发等生态产品价值实现路径，森林覆盖率提高至 78.89%，主要流域和小流域Ⅱ类以上优质水比例提高至 100%，空气质量保持全国前列，主要污染物排放总量、碳排放强度等持续下降，绿色动能越来越强。

南平市搭建村级森林资源运营平台，形象地比喻为"森林生态银行"，把分散在单家独户的无林地、有林地集中收储到"森林生态银行"，整合打包成集中连片的资源包，依托国有林场（林业企业）技术、管理等优势，实行规模化管理、专业化经营。"森林生态银行"核算无林地、有林地股份合作经营的保底收益总额度，以一家一户为单位，为每户林农办理股权证，林农手中的股权相当于储存到"森林生态银行"的固定"存款"，可按照合作约定获得"储蓄利息"。"森林生态银行"采取"保底收益+一年一分红+主伐再分红"的收益分配模式，解决林业生产周期长、林农短期收益少问题，效益比林农个体经营提高30%以上。

各县（市、区）建设县级林地林木资源数据库，实现森林资源的立地质量、林分状况、资源权属、林下空间、经营收益等关键数据"一键查"，为市场化投资经营林业提供支撑。以邵武市为例，对符合发展林下经济条件且有流转意愿的林下空间进行存储登记，录入"森林生态银行"，建立林下空间资源数据库，参照林权发证模式，在不动产系统内增设"林下空间经营权证"子目录，发放"林下空间经营权证"，推出"福林·林下经营权贷"，破解"非林权证持有者的林下经济经营主体难以获得信贷支持"的问题。

二 拓宽全民所有自然资源资产转化路径

中国以土地、矿产、海洋、森林、草原、湿地、水、国家公园8类全民所有自然资源资产（含自然生态空间）所有权委托代理机制试点为切入点，引导各地探索自然资源资产多要素配置路径和方法，推进"土地+""水域+"等资源资产用益物权组合配置，促进自然资源资产高效利用和增值增效。

宁夏回族自治区构建"资源+资产""实物量+价值量""专项报告+报表体系"为核心内容的自然资源资产报告框架体系，建成专门管理信息系统，编制覆盖全域的全民所有自然资源资产清查、核算和平衡表，为自然资源资产转化提供实物属性、价值属性、价值量等数据支撑。贺兰县"稻渔空间"一二三产业融合项目通过土地整治、以渔治碱、循环种养、统防统治等措施，完成从传统种植到稻、鱼、蟹、鸭立体种植养殖，再到一二三产业融合发展的迭代升级。宁夏政府部门委托专业评估机构对宁夏农垦集团使用的国有农用地按照现行土地价格重新进行地价评估，通过作价出资评估增资，宁夏农垦集团资本结构进一步优化，资产负债率明显下降，资产总额持续增长。

江西省九江市探索"确权登记—赋予职责—全要素储备与赋能—整体评估—市场机制—绿色金融—创新分配—保护修复"的自然资源资产组合供应路径。编制九江市政府代理履行全民所有自然资源资产所有者职责的自然资源清单，明晰自然资源资产"谁来管、管什么"。纳入国土空间规划"一张图"管理，明晰自然资源资产"有什么"、"有多少"。建立自然资源资产确权信息数据库，明晰自然资源资产"在哪里"。将有市场需求的经营性自然资源资产打包形成优质"资产包"，破解自然资源资产"如何配置"难题。成立自然资源资产保护和价值转换中心，通过征收、赎买、租用等方式，将自然资源"资产包"各项权利集中到单一主体，破解自然资源资产"多头储备"难题。建成全民所有自然资源资产交易系统，实现自然资源资产多门类、一站式、全流程网上交易。

第 5 节　长治久安：中国构建绿色发展空间格局的经验及对发展中国家的启示

一　优化国土空间开发保护格局

中国首部"多规合一"的国家级国土空间规划《全国国土空间规划纲要（2021~2035 年）》印发实施，地方各级总体规划、详细规划和专项规划编制统筹推进，"五级三类"国土空间规划取得决定性进展，全国统一、责权清晰、科学高效的国土空间规划"一张图"总体形成。尤其是"三区三线"作为国土空间规划的核心内容和重要组成部分，是保障和维护国家粮食安全、生态安全和城镇化健康发展的空间底线，为其他国家处理好人与自然、发展与保护的关系贡献"中国方案"。中国创新全域土地综合整治、城镇低效用地再开发、城乡建设用地增减挂钩、集体经营性建设用地入市等政策手段，严控总量、盘活存量、优化结构、提高效率，推进土地、矿产、海洋等资源节约集约利用，学习运用"千万工程"经验，提升人居环境品质，保护传承传统文化，形成"资源—资产—资本—资金—保护修复"全流程闭环，构建从山顶到海洋的国土空间保护、修复、治理大格局。

二 山水林田湖草沙一体化保护修复

中国遵循山水林田湖草沙生命共同体理念，构建跨部门、跨区域、跨流域的生态保护修复体系，实现由单一要素向系统治理转变，由工程措施为主向自然恢复为主转变，由末端治理向全链条管理转变，由依靠财政向多元化投入转变。中国建立以国家公园为主体的自然保护地体系，对跨行政区域、大尺度的自然空间进行有效的规划、建设、管理、监督、保护和修复。国家公园实行分区管控，核心保护区严格管理，在一般控制区开展适宜的绿色产业开发，让当代人享受天蓝地绿水净、鸟语花香的美好家园，给子孙后代留下宝贵自然遗产。中国扩绿、兴绿、护绿并举，强化植树造林全国动员、全民动手、全社会共同参与，国土绿化从"数量增长"向"质量提升"转变。

从"三北"工程经验看，一是以水定绿、以绿调水，构建水资源与大规模、高密度人工造林的动态平衡，重构干旱区"降水—地表水—地下水—生态用水"的健康循环网络；二是空间优化，探索土地资源复合利用，为生态建设预留充足空间，通过林田镶嵌等方法实现空间增效；三是天人协同，把握人工干预与自然恢复的平衡点，建立"短期人工干预筑基、长期自然恢复增效"的良性机制。

三 生态产品价值实现拓宽"绿水青山就是金山银山"转化路径

草木植成，国之富也。中国因地制宜构建生态产品价值核算体系、生态产品价格体系、生态产品交易体系，增强生态产品供给能力，将绿水青山蕴含的生态产品和服务转化为现实环境生产力。建立区域性自然资源调查监测系统，摸清资源底数，开展自然资源确权登记和设权赋能。按照公益性、经营性等特征，统筹谋划自然资源资产储备、配置、价值实现、收益管理等事宜。形成主体明确、边界清晰的组合标的和整体配置机制，推动自然资源资产组合供应和价值变现，推进效率效益更优的生态产业化和产业生态化。

第6节　中国式现代化视域下进一步优化绿色发展空间格局的对策建议

一　构建以自然资源合理利用为导向的国土空间保护开发新格局

1. 优化国土空间规划、保护和开发

持续开展数量、质量、生态"三位一体"的自然资源调查、监测和预警，提高识别、应对重点地区生态状况的能力。健全县、乡镇等生态修复规划体系，系统谋划"十五五"山水治理、矿山修复、海洋修复、红树林保护修复等专项行动计划。开展国土空间规划实施监测评估，落实自然生态空间用途管制制度，维护"三区三线"划定成果的严肃性。依据资源环境承载能力和国土空间开发适宜性，落实主体功能区战略。深入实施"藏粮于地、藏粮于技"战略，确保现状耕地应划尽划、应保尽保，坚决遏制耕地"非农化"，严格管控"非粮化"。引导都市圈和城市群等重点区域形成多中心、组团式的城市空间形态，推动中小城市紧凑布局，防止城镇无序蔓延。将目前基本没有人类活动、具有潜在重要生态价值的区域列为战略留白空间，审慎开发，应对未来不确定性。

2. 稳妥推进全域土地综合整治

依据国土空间规划，以县（市、区）为统筹单元，以乡镇为基本实施单元，科学合理确定全域土地综合整治区域和推进路线，同步改善农村生态、生产、生活环境，促进农村一二三产业融合发展，建设宜居宜业和美乡村。重点对布局散乱、配套设施不完善、耕种不便的地块进行微调，实现耕地数量不减少、质量有提升、生态有改善。对已划入生态

保护红线范围的耕地、被生态保护红线围合的永久基本农田、原有零星建设用地，按照程序实施增补平衡和调出优化。积极盘活"空心村"、农村闲置宅基地、工矿废弃地等零散、低效、闲置的建设用地，将小块存量用地整治归并为大块宗地。加强古镇、古街等保护修复，留住乡愁乡韵，强化农文旅等绿色产业导入。

二　统筹推进山水林田湖草沙海一体化保护修复

1. 做亮"中国山水"工程品牌

坚持以自然恢复为主、人工修复为辅，科学部署、持续实施山水工程，因地因时制宜，分区分类施策，源头治理、系统治理、科学治理和规范治理，构建科学合理的城乡生态格局。综合评估已完成的"中国山水"工程，总结和推广成熟经验。分类有序建设绿色矿山，完善清单式动态管理监督机制，加强绿色低碳技术工艺装备升级改造，严格第三方评估管理，推进边生产、边治理。以"陆海统筹+江海联动+一湾（岛）一策"推进美丽海湾建设与和美海岛创建，加强河口、海湾、海岛等综合生态系统和盐沼等典型生态系统的保护修复，维护海洋生态系统多样性、稳定性、持续性。健全生物多样性调查、监测、评估和保护体系，加强外来入侵物种防治。

2. 构建国家公园生态保护修复"中国方案"

制定国家公园法，确定国家公园主管部门及其职责，规定国家公园创建、设立、规划、建设、管理的制度机制，加强多部门和多区域的协调合作。加快国家公园创建设立步伐。建立"天空地"一体化生态监测预警系统"一本账"，实现各类自然保护地的数据共享和统一管理。构建"园地联动、共建共享、生态补偿"的治理格局，提升社区及居民参与成效。分区分类建立商品林赎买、地役权管理补偿、生态管护岗位、野生动物致害补偿与保险理赔等生态补偿机制，创新生态产品价值转化途径。

3. 稳步推进"三北"工程攻坚战走深走实

持续开展三大标志性战役区等重点区域联防联控联治，实现治沙、治水、治山全要素治理。推广行之有效的治沙模式，建立重点项目跨部门联合审查机制，实行项目储备、开工建设和监测评估全过程闭环管理。构建以各级政府投入为主，国企、国有林场和社会机构广泛参与的多元化建设运营机制。实施"揭榜挂帅"机制，引导国内外科技力量参与"三北"工程，共同破解"荒漠变绿洲"的科技密码。坚持治沙效果和节约水资源统筹谋划，推广沙障治沙、光伏治沙、覆膜保水、灌木截秆等先进技术。大力宣传弘扬"三北精神"、塞罕坝精神，以榜样力量带动更多力量参与，讲好防沙治沙中国故事。

三 整体性构筑生态产品价值实现长效机制

建立县域生态资源数据库和生态产品清单，以权责统一导向确定自然资源资产配置的时序、方式、规模、用途等，探索收储、租赁、置换和入股等方式，引导自然资源资产确权登记、设权赋能、布局合理和配置高效。健全生态产品价值核算国家标准体系，量化各类生态产品的经济价值及其时空分布特征。布局专业交易市场和线上交易平台，创新自然资源权益交易、生态产品抵押贷款、生态保护补偿、自然资源资产损害赔偿、自然资源资产账户、绿色产品期货期权、绿色保险等价值实现路径，让保护绿水青山获得合理回报。构建生态产品产业化经营开发机制，科学开发利用海洋可再生能源、地质遗迹、地热、矿泉水等自然资源。建立风险防范机制，管控生态产品交易存在的自然风险、市场风险、政策风险等。

第4章
高质量发展：中国绿色低碳转型的举措、成效、经验和建议

2020年9月，习近平主席在第75届联合国大会一般性辩论上做出中国二氧化碳排放力争于2030年前达到峰值、努力争取2060年前实现碳中和的重大宣示。党中央将碳达峰碳中和纳入生态文明建设整体布局和经济社会发展全局。2024年1月，习近平总书记在二十届中央政治局第十一次集体学习时发表讲话强调："绿色发展是高质量发展的底色，新质生产力本身就是绿色生产力。"推动经济社会发展绿色化、低碳化是实现高质量发展的关键环节。中国在把握高质量发展和高水平保护的辩证统一关系中，坚持创新、协调、绿色、开放、共享的新发展理念，以资源环境刚性约束推动产业结构深度调整，以强化区域协作持续优化产业空间布局，改变传统的"大量生产、大量消耗、大量排放"的生产和消费模式，在绿色转型中推动发展实现质的有效提升和量的合理增长。

第1节　中国能源绿色低碳转型的创新
举措、主要成效和典型案例

一　能源供给新体系加快构建

在"四个革命、一个合作"① 能源安全新战略指引下，中国坚持先立

---

① 　四个革命、一个合作："四个革命"指能源消费革命、能源供给革命、能源技术革命、能源体制革命，"一个合作"指能源合作。

后破、通盘谋划，在不断增强能源供应保障能力的基础上，加快构建新型能源体系，走出一条符合国情、适应时代要求的能源转型之路。2024年，中国清洁能源消费占比达 28.6%，较 2013 年提高 13.3 个百分点，煤炭消费占比累计下降 14.5 个百分点；发电总装机容量达 33.5 亿千瓦，非化石能源发电装机容量占总装机容量的比重为 58.2%。十年来，新增清洁能源发电量占全社会用电增量一半以上，中国能源"含绿量"不断提升。

在化石能源清洁高效利用方面，中国以促进煤电清洁低碳发展为目标，建设安全智能绿色现代化煤矿，开展煤电节能改造，新增煤电机组执行更严格节能标准，发电效率、污染物排放控制达到世界领先水平，煤电平均供电煤耗降至 303 克标准煤/千瓦时，先进机组的二氧化硫、氮氧化物排放水平与天然气发电机组限值相当；在终端用能上，推行天然气、电力和可再生能源等替代煤炭，积极推进北方地区冬季清洁取暖；在城镇燃气、工业燃料、燃气发电、交通运输等领域有序推进天然气高效利用，发展天然气热电冷联供；建设绿色油气田，推进石油炼化产业转型升级，实施成品油质量升级专项行动，实现从国Ⅲ到国Ⅵ的"三连升"，用不到 10 年时间走完发达国家 30 多年成品油质量升级之路。

案例 4-1　齐鲁石化碳捕捉[①]技术创新：实现石油增产和碳减排双赢

大部分石油藏在岩石的孔隙和缝隙中，过去多靠水驱动将其开采出来，但低渗油的岩石十分紧密，水无法进入，因而利用二氧化碳驱油同时对其封存，在中国已是较为成熟的技术。2023 年 7 月，齐鲁石化建设的中国首条百万吨输送规模、百公里输送距离、百公斤输送压力的高压常温密相二氧化碳输送管道投运，每年减排二氧化碳逾 100 万吨，相当于植树近 900 万棵、近 60 万辆经济型轿车停开一年，未来 15 年预计可封存二氧化碳上千万吨，增产石油 300 万吨。

---

①　碳捕捉：将二氧化碳从工业生产、能源利用或大气中分离出来，加以存储和利用，实现永久减排。

二氧化碳是齐鲁石化第二化肥厂正常生产产生的尾气，通过劳模工作室、劳动竞赛等微创新，解决二氧化碳压缩机防喘振系统运行不经济、使用生产现状二氧化碳原料用于干气密封导致过滤器频繁堵塞等问题，形成适配企业的二氧化碳捕捉技术体系：二氧化碳经过冷却、压缩、回收、提纯，变为纯度达 99% 以上的液态，然后运输至胜利油田利用和封存，实现产能增加、含水下降、环保增效的安全绿色生产效果。

与油品管道相比，二氧化碳输送管道的设计施工、安全运输难度更大。齐鲁石化科技人员自主创新攻克多项核心技术，比如，研发中国首台低温液相二氧化碳管输离心增压泵、高效二氧化碳密相常温高压往复注入泵两种关键装备，将二氧化碳输送管道设计压力增至 12 兆帕，相当于指甲盖大小的面积承受 120 公斤重量；采用耐腐蚀不锈钢材料作为关键部件，在井筒里添加缓释剂，有效防止二氧化碳对注采管柱的腐蚀。

进一步看，作为世界上最大的煤电、钢铁和水泥生产国，中国在燃煤电厂、燃气电厂、水泥窑、化工厂、天然气处理等场景推广应用碳捕捉技术，可避免碳约束下大量基础设施提前退役而产生高额的搁浅成本。另外，中国海域二氧化碳地质封存潜力巨大，盆地级封存潜力达 2.58 万亿吨。

在发展非化石能源方面，中国可再生能源发电装机规模全球最大、发展速度全球最快，提前 6 年半实现在气候雄心峰会上所承诺的"中国到 2030 年，风电、太阳能发电总装机容量达到 12 亿千瓦以上"的目标。中国加快建设以沙漠、戈壁、荒漠地区为重点的大型风电光伏基地，集群化发展海上风电，广泛建设城乡屋顶光伏、乡村风电等分布式新能源；推进大型水电站升级改造和小水电站绿色改造，常规水电装机容量超 3.7 亿千瓦，近 4000 座小水电站完成改造升级；坚持采用最先进的技术、最严格的标准发展核电，在运核电机组长期保持安全稳定运行，代表"中国名片"的自主三代核电技术"华龙一号"首批机组陆续投运，核能清洁供暖、供热等综合利用取得突破；因地制宜开展农林生物质、沼气、城镇生活垃圾等新能源转化，建成一批以地热能为主的集中供暖项目。

在推动传统能源和新能源协同发展方面，中国构建适应新能源占比逐渐提高的新型电力系统，在资源富集地稳步实施风光水（储）一体化、风光火（储）一体化建设，在煤矿工业场地、采煤沉陷区、电厂闲置空地、油气矿区等区域建设新能源发电项目，开发海上风电为油气平台提供绿色电力，在传统加油站、加气站建设油气电氢一体化综合交通能源服务站。

乌东德、白鹤滩、溪洛渡、向家坝、三峡、葛洲坝 6 座大型水电站，沿长江干流自上而下排列，构成世界最大清洁能源走廊：跨越 1800 多千米，水位落差超 900 米，总计 110 台水轮发电机组运转，浩浩江水带来滚滚绿电，截至 2024 年末，累计发电突破 3.8 万亿千瓦时，相当于节约标准煤超 28.9 亿吨，减排二氧化碳超 30.4 亿吨。长江流域是中国水资源配置的战略水源地，多年平均水资源量达 9959 亿立方米，约占全国的 36%，形成总库容 919 亿立方米的梯级水库群和战略性淡水资源库，航运保畅、水资源保障、生态保护等效益综合释放，生态调度涵盖促进鱼类繁殖、分层取水水温调节、防治水华、库区排沙减淤、抑制沉水植物过度繁殖等领域，有力推进长江流域生态保护修复。

内蒙古锡林郭勒盟苏尼特右旗是典型的荒漠半荒漠草原牧业旗，既依赖畜牧业谋求乡村振兴，又要防治"草原过牧"带来的环境风险。京东方能源科技股份有限公司在此实施总投资约 9.3 亿元的"20 万千瓦牧光储+治沙综合示范项目"，项目投产至今光伏发电 8.1 亿度，减少二氧化碳排放约 50 万吨。项目抬高光伏支撑架，为羊群活动留出充足空间，实现"板上发电、板下放牧"牧光互补。储能系统电芯选用磷酸铁锂材料，能量密度大，充放电速度快，充放电次数多，通过"光储"联合优化调度运行，解决同类电力系统综合效率不高、"源网荷储"各环节协调不够等问题。项目光伏组件形成物理屏障，减少地表暴晒和水分蒸发，挡风固沙，改善板下植物生长环境，实现"板上发电、板下修复"治沙。一排排蓝色光伏板下，曾经荒芜的漫漫黄沙重焕生机，蜕变为一座"能源绿洲"。作为京蒙协作助力内蒙古乡村振兴十佳企业，京东方能源探索的"光伏+储能+治沙+养殖"生态修复与产业振兴协同发展模式得到当地政府和周边地区的借鉴复制。

2024 年底，宁夏银川市永宁县闽宁镇建成具备 24 小时绿电供应能力的"纯绿电小镇"，由"发、储、传、用"的新型储能系统替代煤电，成为当地乡村振兴的"催化剂"。受外部环境影响，新能源供电波动性大，项目公司开发源网荷储控制系统，在白天光伏大发时段存储多余电量，晚上风电和储能互相配合补充电量，形成"存有余补不足"的新能源经济效益。通过自建具备并/离网无缝切换与离网运行能力的区域电网，保障可靠供电及区域能源安全。采用"村集体+企业+农户"模式，为村民建设屋顶光伏，村民每年获得屋顶租赁费，促进绿色生产生活方式转变。充沛的绿电资源为闽宁产业园的智能制造、农特产品精深加工、设施农业等现代产业提供能源保障。

中国海上风电资源丰富、发电小时数高、距离电力负荷中心近、消纳空间足，150 米高度近海风能资源技术可开发量超 15 亿千瓦，深远海风能资源技术可开发量超 12 亿千瓦。中国海上风电机组设计制造体系完备，比如，东方电气自主研制的 26 兆瓦级海上风电机组是全球单机容量最大、叶轮直径最长的海上全中国制造风电机组，发电机、叶片、轴承、电控系统等关键配套技术均达世界领先水平；浙江省舟山 LHD 潮流能发电站实现兆瓦级大功率稳定并网发电，世界单台容量最大潮流能发电机组"奋进号"总并网电量超 478 万千瓦时，连续运行时间居国际前列，带动海洋牧场、海洋装备制造、特种材料、交通运输、海洋工程、电力配送、海水综合利用等上下游产业集聚发展。

2025 年 3 月，中国最大核能供热商用示范工程——国家电投"暖核一号"完成第六个供暖季任务，保障烟台海阳市、威海乳山市两市城区 40 万居民清洁温暖过冬，节约原煤 48 万吨，减排二氧化碳 88 万吨、二氧化硫 5676 吨、氮氧化物 5366 吨，相当于 500 万棵树一年的清洁效益。"暖核一号"核能供暖实现零碳热源的双城互通共享，开创"核电厂+政府平台+长输管网公司+供热公司"的供热商业新模式，其原理是抽取核电机组部分做过功的蒸汽作为热源，在物理隔绝的情况下进行多次热量交换，通过市政供热管网将热量送到居民家中，这个过程中只有热量传递，没有物质交换，供热公司还增加辐射监测、应急管理等手段，确保供暖安全可靠。

**案例 4-2　　　　北京城市副中心：绿色低碳能源转型促国家
绿色发展示范区建设**

规划建设北京城市副中心，是以习近平同志为核心的党中央作出的
重大决策部署，习近平总书记多次对北京城市副中心规划建设作出重要
指示。《国务院关于支持北京城市副中心高质量发展的意见》明确提出，
建设国家绿色发展示范区，为建设和谐、宜居、美丽的大国首都作出贡
献。《北京城市副中心建设国家绿色发展示范区实施方案》强调，探索可
复制可推广的绿色发展、低碳转型实施路径和推进模式。近年来，北京
城市副中心在全市率先开展用能和碳排放综合评价试点，建立绿电消纳
工作机制，可再生能源利用比例高于全市平均水平，可再生能源供热面
积近 400 万平方米，备案光伏装机容量超 150 兆瓦，行政办公区、城市绿
心公园实现 100% 绿电覆盖。

城市绿心公园在为市民提供休闲空间和改善城市环境的同时，也在灌
溉养护、交通运输、日常办公、园区照明、建筑空调、游乐设施方面产生
碳排放。为此，既通过建设地源热泵能源站、分布式光伏、水蓄能等实现
区域"增绿"，又通过建筑绿色化、交通电气化、智慧能源管理和碳资产管
理等促进区域"减碳"，2025 年实现区域全面"零碳"目标。

在能源低碳化供给方面，城市绿心公园对本地可再生能源充分挖掘，
能用尽用。一是城市绿心公园三大地标（北京艺术中心、北京城市图书
馆、北京大运河博物馆）及配套建筑按照公共建筑绿建三星标准，均采
用地源热泵系统作为能量来源，以热泵为主的能源站承担园区 80% 以上
供热量，每年减少二氧化碳排放 1.2 万吨；二是在城市绿心公园铺设屋顶
光伏，构建交直流微电网，采用"自发自用、余电上网"策略，实现建
筑用电优先使用光伏发电，开展绿色电力交易试点示范，以绿电外购提
升区域可再生能源供应和消费比重；三是老旧厂房按照公共建筑二星标
准，更新改造为公共服务、文化展示、体育休闲等多功能综合体，内部
摆渡车、观光车、小型货车、清洁车、巡逻车等全部配置为电动车，在
公共停车场按停车位的 20% 设置充电桩，引导车主有序错峰充电。

城市绿心公园开发以能耗数据为核心的能碳管理智慧平台，接入域

内能源站、用水、用气等能耗数据，开展多维数据智能分析，实现区域用能集中优化，通过以电折碳的方式，实时跟踪区域碳排放情况。城市绿心公园联合通州区电力公司、首都碳监测服务平台，打造碳资产管理服务平台，形成园区"电碳一张图"，建立碳积分机制，推进碳普惠应用。

案例 4-3　　　　　新疆：打造国家大型绿氢供应和出口基地

氢能是一种清洁高效、可再生循环利用的能源，具有来源多样、用途广泛、能量密度大等优势。新疆拥有优质的光伏和风电资源，累计新能源装机容量 5089 万千瓦，占全网总装机容量的 41%，加之煤炭等矿产资源丰富，有突出的绿氢制取和场景应用优势。2023 年 6 月，中国首个万吨级绿氢炼化项目——中石化库车 2 万吨绿氢示范项目顺利产氢，贯通光伏发电、绿电输送、绿电制氢、氢气储存、氢气输运、绿氢炼化等绿氢生产利用全流程，每年减排二氧化碳 48.5 万吨，开创中国化工行业深度脱碳新路径。

加速发展氢能产业，新疆政策频出。2023 年，新疆发布《自治区氢能产业发展三年行动方案（2023~2025 年）》《自治区支持氢能产业示范区建设的若干政策措施》，将乌鲁木齐市、克拉玛依市、哈密市、伊犁州列为首批氢能产业示范区。同年，新疆发起成立氢能产业发展联盟。2024 年 3 月，新疆印发《关于加快推进氢能产业发展的通知》，营造产业生态按下"快车键"，例如，允许在化工园区外建设太阳能、风能等可再生能源电解水制氢项目和制氢加氢站；太阳能、风能等可再生能源电解水制氢项目不需取得危险化学品安全生产许可。

自此，新疆氢能产业发展走上快车道。例如，开疆云能源公司在乌鲁木齐市天山区布局氢能快递专用车，尺寸与电动三轮车一致，换装的氢瓶存入专门机柜，快递小哥输入密码，取出氢瓶即可更换；源网荷储新能源科技（上海）有限公司克拉玛依氢储能调峰电站将光伏发出来的绿电，通过电解水制出绿氢，再通过绿氢燃料电池发电，年产绿电 3.6 亿千瓦时，可提供 48 万平方米的零碳供暖。

从实践看，氢能车更耐寒，比较适合新疆冬季的寒冷天气。随着氢能规模扩大、成本下降、产业链条贯通，新疆氢能的应用场景将越来越广泛，有望率先建成集绿氢制、储、运、加、用为一体的跨区域产业集群。

案例 4-4　　　　虚拟电厂：从概念走向规模化应用的
绿色能源系统新方案

虚拟电厂是资源聚合类新型经营主体，不实际生产电，而是通过信息通信技术和软件系统，聚合分布式光伏、分散式风电、新型储能、可调节负荷等电力资源，形成虚拟的集中能源系统，实时监测、分析和智能控制分散的能源资源，实现能源高效利用和供需动态平衡，成为实现碳中和目标的关键支柱。

2021 年 12 月，中国首个网地一体虚拟电厂管理平台——深圳虚拟电厂管理平台上线。2022 年 8 月，深圳挂牌成立中国首家虚拟电厂管理中心，设在南方电网深圳供电局。深圳虚拟电厂管理平台通过能源互联网技术，汇集充电桩、空调、光伏等点多、面广、单体容量小的分布式电力资源，优化调控特定时段内的电力负荷，提供多时段交易功能，成为用户与大电网互动的"云端桥梁"，截至 2025 年 3 月，累计实施电力负荷调节 101 次，调节电量超 560 万千瓦时，按照深圳家庭平均每户年度用电 3500~4500 千瓦时进行测算，相当于 1500 户家庭一年用电量，等效减少碳排放约 4681 吨。

2024 年 7 月，重庆市上线中西部地区首个省级虚拟电厂平台，构建 280 万千瓦的需求响应资源池，度夏高峰期可根据缺口大小动态调整入网企业的电力需求响应规模。重庆虚拟电厂平台采取"1+N"方式运营：建设 1 个全市统一的虚拟电厂运营服务平台，为市内充换电设施、冻库、铁塔基站、楼宇空调、分布式屋顶光伏等 N 个虚拟电厂提供资源接入、资格审核、运行监测、能力校核等服务，实现全市虚拟电厂"统一管理、统一调控、统一服务"。

二　能源绿色消费和节能提效稳步推进

中国将绿色电力证书作为用能单位消费绿色电力的唯一凭证和环境属性的唯一证明，将绿电消费作为评价、认证和标识绿色产品的重要依据和内容，引导全社会优先使用绿色能源和采购绿色产品服务，鼓励具备条件的企业形成低碳、零碳的能源消费模式。2022 年北京冬奥会、2023 年杭州亚运会均实现 100%使用绿色电力。中国将能耗强度下降作为约束性指标，并向碳排放双控转变，2013～2023 年，通过综合施策，累计节约能源消费约 14 亿吨标准煤，减少二氧化碳排放约 30 亿吨。工业领域大力推广技术节能、管理节能、结构节能，推广先进能效产品，淘汰落后产能，推动生产工艺革新、流程再造和智能化升级，2013～2023 年，规上工业单位增加值能耗累计下降超 36%。实施高耗能行业节能降碳改造，推动重点行业大中型企业能效达到世界先进水平。建立固定资产投资项目节能审查、节能监察等制度，开展万家企业节能低碳行动、重点用能单位百千万行动、能效"领跑者"引领行动。推广节能咨询、诊断、设计、融资、改造、托管等"一站式"综合服务模式，节能服务产业年产值超过 5000 亿元，比 2013 年翻了一番。

中国建筑节能协会统计数据显示，建筑业建造能耗占全国能源消费总量的 22.8%，在全国能源相关碳排放中所占份额为 48.3%。2025 年政府工作报告提出，适应人民群众高品质居住需要，完善标准规范，推动建设安全、舒适、绿色、智慧的"好房子"。"推广绿色节能建筑"是破解中国在全球规模最大的城镇化进程中，避免形成高碳锁定效应的关键举措。通过强化新建建筑节能标准要求，培育绿色建材产业，推进既有建筑节能改造，发展智慧化的超低能耗、近零能耗建筑，目前，节能建筑占城镇既有建筑面积比例超过 64%。

依托国家"东数西算"战略，青海移动推进算网强基、产业融合、产品雁阵、共链融创四大计划，建设"基础资源+计算+平台+数据+模型+应用"六位一体绿色算力体系。位于海东市的中国移动（青海）高原大数据中心通过液冷技术与绿电直供体系闭环，实现"绿电直供—智慧管控—高效转化"全链条减碳，PUE（电源使用效率）值降至 1.14 以下，成为世界海拔最高的零碳算力枢纽。位于格尔木市的中国移动柴达木绿色微电网算力中心灵活调配源网荷储资源，是全球首个规模化利用荒漠化土地和光伏能源进行"自发、自储、自用、自保"的 100%绿电稳定供给算力中心。

杭州市后亚运"十大攀登行动"提出，实施绿色低碳发展攀登行动。作为浙江首个省级新区，钱塘新区将节能降碳塑造为营商优势。钱塘新区医药港多能综合利用系统实现蒸汽驱动的溴化锂制冷机组与大型电制冷机组协同运行，耦合冰蓄冷、电化学等储能模块，在保证区内集中供冷安全可靠运行的同时，灵活开展区域电网调峰，落户企业基本不用自建工艺环境所需的空调主机系统，减少传统分散式用能，为区内战略性产业发展和城市高品质建设的用能腾出空间。例如，作为空客、波音、庞巴迪和中国商飞的合格供应商，西子航空建立中国航空零部件第一家"零碳工厂"，对多种新能源和储能技术进行有机整合，为不同生产场景提供电、冷、热、压缩空气等多种能源形式。

纵观人类历史，从薪柴、煤炭到石油天然气，每一次能源革命都伴随着生产力的巨大跃迁。当前，中国正基于能源供给创新场景突破新型储能、节能管理、能源物联网等关键性、前瞻性、战略性技术，抢占能源新质生产力制高点。作为热管理领域的绿色创新引领者，北京安兴高科新能源发展有限公司通过自主创新，在高效相变储能材料、高热流密度液冷技术、储能控温整体解决方案、用能一体化全生命周期解决方案等领域拥有专利技术 50 余项，完成 300 多个具有国际先进水平的相变控温、调峰节能项目，典型用户不乏中国移动、中国铁塔、国家电网、中国铁路、华润集团、国家税务总局等政府机构和知名企业，以相对较低的建设运营成本实现更高的节能效率和能源负荷动态稳定性。同时，开发"探卫士"智慧碳排放管控平台，对碳排放设施动态管理和达标预警。

案例 4-5　　　　　**海南博鳌东屿岛：打造零碳示范区的绿色**
发展全球"实验室"

面对气候变化的严峻挑战，博鳌亚洲论坛 2025 年年会聚焦加快落实可持续发展目标，设置"在世界转型中实现可持续发展""应对气候变化：问题与方案""携手促进亚洲能源转型""加快构建新能源体系，共创世界绿色未来"等多个议题，共谋绿色发展之策。

作为博鳌亚洲论坛的核心舞台和中国首个国家级零碳示范区，2019～2024 年，海南博鳌东屿岛全口径二氧化碳排放量从 1.2 万吨锐减至 470 吨，堪称应对气候变化的"实验室"。遵循"区域零碳、资源循环、环境自然、智慧运营"理念，博鳌东屿岛建立可再生能源利用、建筑绿色化更新、交通绿色化营运、新型电力系统建设、物资循环利用、水资源循环利用、园林景观生态化改造、运营管理智慧化相结合的"八位一体"区域降碳布局，全年生产绿电约 3200 万度，远超示范区每年约 1700 万度的用电需求，余电上网并储备负碳资源 7720 吨/年，成为全球热带地区近零碳发展的标杆案例。

漫步于博鳌东屿岛，减碳科技随处可见。比如，博鳌亚洲论坛国际会议中心等主要建筑运用屋面太阳能光伏板、外墙光伏百叶、碲化镉发电玻璃和光伏地砖等进行光能发电，采用光储直柔系统储能，使建筑所需能源达到自给自足；厨房经电气化改造，实现零化石能源使用；空调系统采用磁悬浮变频离心式冷水机组，噪声更低，能效提升 20% 以上；数字孪生平台实时监控能耗，无人会议室自动断电，AI 调控空调系统；建筑废弃物制成景观花园，雨水收集系统灌溉园林；骑行发电充电，碳积分兑换礼品……

此外，博鳌东屿岛通过园林绿化，实现调节小气候、涵养水源、削减污染物、降低碳排放等综合功能。系统修复红树林湿地，利用连接管涵养和改善水质，运用自然潮汐实现内湖、内河的生态连通，适当保留裸露泥滩，形成林、滩、沟、湖动态变化的湿地格局，搭建完整的红树林"生物链"。博鳌亚洲论坛 2025 年年会期间产生的碳排放量经过核算后，由红树林湿地修复项目全额抵消，实现"办会零负担"。

第 2 节　中国构建清洁高效的交通运输体系的创新举措、主要成效和典型案例

一　交通运输结构持续优化

中国加大投资铁路和水路基础设施力度，建设连接主要生产、消费区域的干线铁路，将集疏运体系与大型工矿企业、物流园区及港口的铁路专用线建设相结合，形成高效的"点对点"运输网络，推动大宗货物"公转铁""公转水"，提高货物运输效率，降低运输过程中的能耗和碳排放。促进交通物流与电子商务、制造业等产业深度融合，利用数字科技优化运输流程，提高物流效率。开展"一单制""一箱制"多式联运，推广"一次委托、一口报价、一单到底、一票结算"全程运输服务产品，提高铁路、水路在综合运输中的承运比重。据中国集装箱行业协会数据，2016~2023 年，铁水联运量从 274 万标箱增至 1170 万标箱，沿海港口铁水联运占比从 2.9%提升至 8%，铁路集装箱发运量从 751 万标箱增至 3323 万标箱，集装箱运量占铁路装车数比重从 8.4%提升至 25.5%。

案例 4-6　　国家铁路集团：建设"绿色长廊"，添彩美丽中国

铁路具有运量大、运输稳定、运输速度快、运输成本低、环境污染小等优点，是资源节约型和环境友好型的运输方式。国家铁路集团探索生态优先、绿色发展为导向的高质量发展路径，构建铁路安全屏障并美化沿线环境，全国铁路线路绿化率超 87.9%。

发挥绿色低碳运输的先导作用

国铁集团实施长三角、珠三角两个重要经济带的海铁联运增量方案，较传统运输，海铁联运模式下货运总成本降低 25%~50%，运输时间缩短50%。推进"散改集"运输，降低货物在运输过程中湿损、被盗及污染的风险，提升货物周转率。国铁集团建成 171 个铁路物流基地，融入各地

的物流园区、产业园区、港口及边境口岸，持续完善铁路场站多式联运、仓配中心等综合服务功能。例如，广州铁路局打造"海铁联运一体化服务云平台"，同步共享铁路与港口信息，实现"前港后站、一体运作"。

铁路建设从"工程优先"转向"生态优先"

绿色环保选线选址方面，国铁集团科学规划布局铁路线路和枢纽设施，确保铁路与自然、人文环境有机融合，例如，广汕高铁全线绕避罗浮山风景区核心区，广州站至广州南站联络线全线绕避珠江生态区。生态保护和节能降碳方面，国铁集团严格控制施工范围，优化取、弃土场和施工便道等临时设施，加强文明施工管理，制定穿越自然保护区、风景名胜区、水源保护区、居民生活区的专项施工方案，优化水污染处理工艺，广泛采用清洁能源，例如，中老铁路野象谷站加装数十千米的野象防护栏，减少铁路对野生亚洲象和原始森林的影响；青藏铁路建设野生动物通道，让藏羚羊迁徙与钢铁动脉和谐共存。绿色低碳转型方面，国铁集团采用新型节能材料、工艺、技术和装备建设铁路站房，广泛采用卫星地图、无人机、远程视频等先进科技手段养护线路。

打造万里铁道生态长廊

国铁集团通过林木管护、绿化造林、保护沿线生态、美化沿线环境等方式，构建"线-网-面"生态网络，使铁路成为区域生态系统的有机组成部分，实现"修一条铁路、绿一片山川"的复合价值。例如，兰新高铁沿线的防风固沙林带守护着铁路安全，在戈壁滩上筑起绿色长城；京雄城际铁路两侧生态廊道串联白洋淀湿地与城市绿肺，形成京津冀生态屏障；贵南高铁科学选择优良乡土树种，合理调控林分密度和乔灌草比例，提升高铁两侧廊道的绿化水平，让旅客透过车窗就可饱览"四季常绿、月月有花"的壮美景色；沪苏湖高铁沿线的光伏发电与铁路电网并网，年输送清洁能源超 2 亿千瓦时。

科技创新成为铁路绿色转型的核心引擎

2024 年，全球最快高铁 CR450 动车组样车下线，轻量化设计与能耗优化技术使单位能耗降低 10%，标志着中国高铁向更智能、更绿色迈进。氢能源智能城际动车组试运行，实现"零碳排放"突破。智能调度系统通过算法优化列车运行图，每年减少冗余能耗超 5%。全国铁路电气化率提升至 74.9%，年减碳量相当于种植 47 亿棵冷杉。铁路货运绿色效益持续释放，比如，2024 年中欧班列开行 1.9 万列，较公路运输减少碳排放约 1256 万吨；多式联运"一单制"服务推动社会物流成本降低 600 亿元，形成"效率提升—成本下降—低碳循环"闭环。

二　交通基础设施绿色化水平不断提升

中国实施绿色公路建设专项行动，大力推动废旧路面材料再生利用，高速公路、普通国省道沥青路面材料循环利用率分别达 95%、80% 以上，干线公路绿化里程超过 57 万千米，比 2012 年增加约 20 万千米。各地开展（近）零碳高速服务区建设，例如，浙江嘉兴常台高速嘉绍大桥服务区在屋顶、车棚铺设光伏板，多场景发电配合一体化储能系统，为南来北往的新能源车快速补能，基本实现自发自用；河南鸡商高速将军县服务区协同开展降碳与减污，利用光伏改造和智慧能源管理实现运营期零碳排放，并开展污水处理回用、雨水调蓄利用及垃圾压缩处理等环境治理工作。

高速公路线路长、沿线空间广阔，具备多样场景布设光伏的条件。比如，全长 161.9 千米的济青中线济潍段是中国首条零碳高速路，布设边坡光伏一体化装置，兼顾边坡固土与光伏发电功能。利用道路两侧的隔离空间安装光伏系统，有效利用闲置土地，为高速公路提供稳定的绿电供应。以 25 年运营周期测算，预计总发电量约 17 亿千瓦时，碳减排量约 152 万吨，实现总体零碳运营。

近年来，中国主要港口推进港作机械"油改电"，五类专业化泊位（集装箱、客货滚装、邮轮、3 千吨级以上客运、5 万吨级以上干散货专业化泊位）岸电设施覆盖率超 75%，推广太阳能、风能和氢能等，提升清洁能源供给比例，治理港区和靠港船舶的油污水、生活污水、干散货码头扬尘和粉尘，保护修复港口岸线，同步建设绿色港口和美丽港口。例如，张家港港打造用能体系低碳化、作业机械清洁化、环境治理精准化、现场业态景观化、运输结构合理化的"双碳五化"绿色港口建设路径，上海港、厦门港、福州港等完成港机设备"油改电""油改气"，青岛港完成桥吊机房、仓库、办公楼、变电所等设施光伏建设全覆盖，日照港实施"退港还海""退港还城"海洋生态修复工程。

案例 4-7 天津港：奋力打造世界一流智慧绿色枢纽港口"升级版"

2019 年 1 月，习近平总书记在天津港视察时强调，要志在万里，努力打造世界一流的智慧港口、绿色港口，更好服务京津冀协同发展和共建"一带一路"。牢记总书记嘱托，天津港在建设中国式现代化港口新征程上阔步前行：从全球首创集装箱码头自动化升级，到获评智慧绿色"双五星"港口；从全球首批港口风机拔地而起，到年发绿电能力近 3 亿千瓦时；从单一物流运输节点，到打造联通国内国际双循环的重要战略支点，年集装箱吞吐量、货物吞吐量稳居全球港口前十……

以安全环保、节能减排、去污降碳、添绿增美为目标，天津港推进陆海双向的绿色港口建设，推动风力、光能、氢能等绿色能源替代，实现码头岸电应建尽建、应接尽接，中国首个防波堤风电项目并网发电，数十台大型风力发电机布满港口。天津港第二集装箱码头打造"智慧零碳"码头，码头操作系统全部国产化，全自动 ED 算法提升卸船、集港的场地找位效率和场地资源分配合理性，建成风光储荷一体化绿色能源系统，实现 100% 使用电能、电能 100% 为绿电、绿电 100% 自产自足。深度调整运输结构，打造"公转铁+散改集"双示范港口，煤炭实现 100% 铁路运输，开通津晋新能源重卡双重零碳物流试点通道。构建港区充电设施"一张网"，港区内部倒运车辆实现 100% 清洁运输。

2025 年 1 月，天津港联合天津东疆综合保税区、天津市电力公司、国家电网天津双碳运营公司、交通运输部水运科学研究院联合发布《天津港东疆"零碳港区"建设方案（码头物流区）》，提出以能源消费电动化、能源供应绿色化、生产工艺智能化、能碳管控精细化、全链物流低碳化、减污降碳协同化的"六化"为驱动，努力打造中国首个涵盖码头作业区及物流加工区的综合性"零碳港区"。

中国加大绿色机场改造升级力度，在现有建筑节能改造和智慧能源管理系统开发上形成变革性突破。例如，北京大兴国际机场建成全球规模最大的浅层地源热泵利用系统，配备光伏发电站，采用集散控制模式的智能照明控制系统，联合国开发计划署认为大兴国际机场节能减排新路径为全球公共建筑提供了可借鉴经验；重庆江北国际机场光伏建设项目规划装机容量 30 兆瓦，是目前中国民用机场建设规模最大的分布式光伏发电项目，覆盖江北机场约 28 万平方米的区域，年发电量约占江北机场年用电总量的 10%；兰州中川国际机场 T3 航站楼采用"大跨度钢结构+玻璃幕墙"设计方案，辅以仿生采光天窗，通过精确计算当地光照特点，优化天窗角度，使自然光利用率提升至 35%，大幅降低照明与空调能耗，年节电量超 200 万度。

各地加速构建充电基础设施体系，提升充电服务的经济性和便捷性，更好促进新能源汽车产业发展和提振新能源汽车消费，截至 2025 年 1 月底，中国充电基础设施累计数量超 1300 万台。同时，各地增加移动充电设备，满足用户出行高峰的需求。加强信息服务，通过路况信息板、导航 App、小程序等多种渠道，为用户提供充电桩布局和使用状态等实时信息。

三 低碳交通运输工具全面普及

各地在城市公交、出租、环卫、物流配送、民航机场以及党政机关等大力推广新能源汽车，截至 2024 年末，中国新能源汽车保有量达 3140 万辆，占全球保有量超过 50%；新能源公交车超过 55 万辆，占公交车总量的 80% 以上；新能源出租汽车超过 20 万辆。

各地强化"轨道+公交+慢行"融合发展，因地制宜构建以城市轨道交通和快速公交为骨干、常规公交为主体的公共交通出行体系，截至 2024 年 11 月，中国共有 54 个城市开通运营城市轨道交通线路 313 条，运营里程超过 1 万千米。同时，共享单车满足绿色出行"最后一公里"需求，以便捷、环保的特性迅速成为民众的重要选择。

第 3 节　中国倡导践行绿色生活方式的创新 举措、主要成效和典型案例

一　生态文明教育蓬勃开展

习近平总书记强调："要加强生态文明宣传教育，把珍惜生态、保护资源、爱护环境等内容纳入国民教育和培训体系，纳入群众性精神文明创建活动，在全社会牢固树立生态文明理念，形成全社会共同参与的良好风尚。"新时代以来，中国把强化公民生态文明意识摆在更加突出的位置，持续开展全国节能宣传周、中国水周、全国城市节约用水宣传周、全国低碳日、全民植树节、六五环境日、国际生物多样性日、世界地球日、"美丽中国，我是行动者"系列活动等主题宣传活动，推进绿色生活理念进家庭、进社区、进工厂、进农村。编写生态环境保护读本，在中小学校开展生态资源基本国情教育。发布《公民生态环境行为规范（试行）》，让生态环保思想成为社会主流文化。

南京市受邀在联合国中国青少年环境大会上介绍生态文明教育经验，两次被央视《新闻联播》报道，全年共举办各类生态文明教育主题活动309 场，这是南京市 2024 年生态文明教育交出的"成绩单"。南京市将珍惜生态、保护资源、爱护环境等内容纳入教育培训体系，建成 40 余家集科普、实践、体验于一体的生态文明教育基地和生物多样性体验地，策划"美丽南京"精品体验线路；组建习近平生态文明思想宣讲团、生态文明教育公益讲师团，研发具有地方特色的生态文明课程体系，为公众提供志愿宣讲服务；上线生态环境在线教育系统，宣教人员化身"主播"和"导游"，拍摄短视频或开展直播，带领观众线上打卡；招募环境小记者，以实地采访、调查研究、新闻报道等方式，提升青少年生态环境素养。

作为四川省首个国家生态文明建设示范市，巴中市实施习近平生态文明思想传播工程，推出《生态巴中》周播专题栏目，在《巴中日报》每周刊发《生态》专版。《生态巴中》栏目设置聚焦环境热点、探访生态

巴中、环保督察进行时、百企百村变美记、生态环境时讯五个板块，通过视频、音频、海报、漫画等多种形式，在广播、电视、微信公众号、抖音等多平台同步传播，增强公众对生态文明的关注度和理解度。在全省率先编制市级中小学生态环境保护教育读本，将相关课程纳入学业水平测试，实现生态文明教育从娃娃抓起，美丽中国老区样板在巴中正一步步变为现实。

展示场馆类生态文明教育基地通过图文影像、模型展示、数字可视化系统与现场解说等方式，面向公众提供沉浸式"环保课堂"。例如，广东清远市北江生态文明展示馆立足清远粤北生态屏障的定位和北江流域贯穿城市的特点，以北江为叙事主体，围绕"清"主题词，建成"风物清嘉""清峦叠翠""清波流远""清远更清"四个展厅，采用声光电技术和互动科技，辅以实物标本和沙盘模型，结合"生态文明服务官"① 志愿讲解，开展沉浸式生态研学和环保公益活动。

杭州市乔司职业高级中学制定生态学校章程，将生态文明理念贯穿教育教学全环节，建设生态友好、资源节约的绿色校园，环保理念成为全校师生行为准则。成立生态委员会，推动和监督校园环境持续改善。通过课堂教学、实践活动、专业课程等多种形式普及生态文明知识，服装专业师生利用边角料制作环保产品，建筑专业师生将实训废料转化为学习资源，实现专业技能教学与生态文明教育深度融合。与政府部门、行业协会合作，定期举办垃圾分类、节能减排、资源循环利用等环保主题活动，提升学生的生态文明素养。

广西南宁市明月湖构建"生态修复+环境教育+社区共建"模式，实现从"环境治理项目"向"生态文明展示窗口"的跨越。打造"渗、滞、蓄、净、用、排"一体化水循环系统，应用弱电介导强化水环境生态修复技术，实现水中营养盐快速脱除与生物多样性保护，水质稳定达地表水 Ⅳ 类标准，形成集生态保护、景观体验、文体休闲、商业潮玩、艺术展示于一体的生态湿地公园，荣获 2023 年国家环境保护科学技术一

---

① "生态文明服务官"是清远市生态环境宣教与科研服务志愿者、志愿服务品牌的统称，通过组建生态文明志愿者团队，经培训担任展馆讲解员，承担生态环境宣教任务。

等奖。同时，明月湖构建场景化、全龄段的生态文明宣教体系，推出湿地景观参观路线，沿线设置湿地净化工艺流程、水生植物功能简介等解说牌，举办明月湖生态保护修复主题的摄影大赛、故事征集活动，通过视频号、抖音、小红书等网络平台发布精美视频和图片，让市民感受湿地景观美好和了解生态文明知识。打造"心小志·江小愿"志愿服务品牌，联合周边政企单位、社区和居民共同开展巡湖护绿、垃圾分类宣传、义务植树、杂草清理等志愿活动。

二　绿色生活创建广泛开展

中国广泛开展节约型机关、绿色医院、绿色家庭、绿色学校、绿色社区、绿色建筑等创建行动，全国 70%县级及以上党政机关建成节约型机关，数百所高校实现水电能耗智能监管，超百个城市参与绿色出行创建行动。广泛开展生活垃圾分类工作，居民主动分类的习惯逐步形成。颁布实施《中华人民共和国反食品浪费法》，大力推进粮食节约和反食品浪费工作，深入开展"光盘"行动，节约粮食蔚然成风。

山东省泰安市成立常务副市长任组长的节约型机关创建领导小组，出台实施方案，建立联席会议、"回头看"考核等制度，将节约型机关创建列入市县机关综合绩效考核和文明单位创建评价标准。从绿色低碳办公、制止餐饮浪费、生活垃圾分类、塑料污染治理等关键领域入手，引导机关干部养成绿色低碳、勤俭节约的行为习惯。召开节约型机关创建现场观摩会，编发典型经验汇编，发挥示范带动作用。市政中心对地源热泵、空调风机、照明设施、茶水炉等节能改造，建设"充、光、电、储"一体化新能源充电站，公共机构能耗监管平台完成市县"一张网"建设。建立"虚拟公物仓"，盘活闲置资产，集约配置房产，建立公车全生命周期数字化管理机制，淘汰老旧燃油车，新增公务车辆全部配备新能源车。

全球医院能耗量和碳排放量在公立机构中名列前茅，中国医院的建筑能耗是一般公共建筑能耗的 1.6~2 倍。在医疗服务质量与生态责任的双重命题下，南京市第一医院（河西院区）交出合格的"绿色答卷"：通过"综合节能改造+数智能源管理+能源托管运维"综合施策，年综合节能率突破 15%。硬件层面，采用磁悬浮离心式冷水机组替代原有低效冷机，风冷热泵和空气源热泵替代传统真空锅炉，优化冷热源输配系统，加装零阻力过滤器和住院楼节能膜，部署数据智能采集终端及智控设备，确保制冷、采暖、生活热水、多联机、末端用能系统的无缝对接、数据集成和节能降耗。软件层面，建立数字孪生大模型，实现"监-管-控"一体化集中管理，AI 实时分析人流密度、温湿度等参数，自动生成运行策略并下发控制指令，在保障末端需求的同时降低能耗。

清华大学早在 1998 年便提出"绿色大学"建设构想，如今勾勒出绿色教育、绿色科技、绿色校园组成的绿色清华"三联画"。其一，清华大学打造全方位、多层次、国际化的绿色教育体系，各院系每学年累计开设超 200 门绿色课程，超过一半的绿色课程面向非环境专业学生，与耶鲁大学等国际名校合作开设环境专业双学位项目，组织师生广泛参与环境科技竞赛、绿色社会实践、绿色社团等活动；其二，清华大学成立多个绿色发展相关的研究机构，开展学术研究、技术攻关、社会服务、人才培养等产学研用合作，形成一大批绿色科研成果；其三，清华大学广泛应用太阳能、地热能等可再生能源，完善能源管理体系，回收利用废弃自行车等固废，投用雨水收集池、中水处理站等环保设施。如今的清华园，绿化覆盖率超 50%，成为首都的一叶"绿肺"。

2018 年 11 月，习近平总书记走进上海市虹口区市民驿站嘉兴路街道第一分站，强调"垃圾分类工作就是新时尚"。2023 年 5 月，习近平总书记回信勉励嘉兴路街道垃圾分类志愿者，强调要"用心用情做好宣传引导工作，推动垃圾分类成为低碳生活新时尚"。嘉兴路街道发布《嘉兴路街道低碳生活新时尚实践区建设三年行动计划（2024～2026 年）》，成立来自机关、企事业单位、"两新"组织等的优秀青年组成的低碳生活志愿者服务队，打造"牢记嘱托——打造低碳生活"宣讲路线，举办"'碳'寻美好生活"主题论坛、生态艺术策展、闲置物品循环公益市集三个主线活动和系列辅线活动，以互动课堂、户外路演、快闪集市、小品演出、现场游戏、情景互动等方式，推动城市文明程度和市民生态素养"双提升"。

三　绿色消费活力涌动

中国加快推动消费模式绿色转型，实施税收减免和财政补贴，积极推广新能源汽车、高能效家用电器等绿色低碳产品，完善绿色产品认证采信推广机制，健全政府绿色采购制度，实施能效、水效标识制度，建设绿色流通主体，支持共享经济、二手交易等新模式蓬勃发展，绿色消费品类、载体和用户群体持续扩大。苏宁易购数据显示，自 2024 年 8 月新一轮家电以旧换新补贴启动以来，截至 2025 年 2 月，节能洗干一体机、智能新风空调、嵌入式蒸烤一体机销量分别增长 129%、135%、228%。

凭借高颜值、高性能、大空间等高性价比优势，"中国造"新能源车产销两旺。汽车梯次循环利用持续加快，中国具备资质的报废汽车回收企业中，3/4 以上形成新能源车拆解能力，2024 年，中国二手车累计交易量达 1961.42 万辆，报废汽车回收量达 846 万辆，分别增长 6.52%、64%，越来越多消费者选择"先出旧、再买新"的绿色消费方式。

年轻人热衷于将闲置物品挂到线上二手交易平台"赚钱回血"，同时乐于在平台上淘选"心头好"。根据闲鱼发布数据，注册用户数突破 6 亿，日均交易额突破 10 亿元，2024 年有超过 1 亿人售卖闲置物品，每天有 400 万件闲置物品在线发布。淘得到限量版手办、珍稀版本书籍、下架衣服的线下二手商店成为年轻人喜爱的消费新空间。二手物品商店走进校园，帮助大学生处理闲置物品，考研笔记、潮玩盲盒、生活用品等成为热销品。一些二手物品商店采用寄售模式，卖方将物品先寄存于店内直至出售，形成可供消费者选择的多品类货源，交易过程甚至比线上更便捷高效。

第 4 节　中国促进传统产业绿色低碳转型的创新举措、主要成效和典型案例

一　制造业的生态底色越来越鲜亮

中国加快构建绿色制造体系，全面开展清洁生产，扎实推进重点行

业节能降碳改造，加快电机、锅炉等重点用能设备更新换代，推广绿色低碳环保工艺和设备，创新绿色产品设计，建设绿色工厂、绿色产业链供应链。按照"横向耦合、纵向延伸、循环链接"原则，优化园区企业、产业和基础设施空间布局，建设绿色园区。开展数字化绿色化协同转型发展综合试点，智能制造、服务型制造等融合发展新业态新模式不断涌现。

2024 年，中国制造业绿色发展表现为"四增三降"：第一个"增"指用地集约化、原料无害化、生产清洁化、废物资源化、能源低碳化的国家级绿色工厂达 6430 家，实现产值占制造业总产值比重约 20%；第二个"增"指大宗工业固废综合利用率超 55%，较上年增加 1.2 个百分点；第三个"增"指退役动力电池综合利用量突破 30 万吨，同比增长 33%；第四个"增"指共有近 3 万种电器电子产品达到国家污染管控要求，同比增长 10%；"三降"指钢铁、水泥、玻璃等重点行业规上工业单位增加值能耗持续下降，工业领域主要污染物排放强度持续下降，每万元工业增加值用水量持续下降。

作为同时入选 2024 年国家级"绿色工厂""绿色供应链管理企业"名单的标杆，格力电器自 2013 年就提出"让天空更蓝、大地更绿"的理念，将绿色低碳理念融入企业研发生产方方面面，超过 60 个产品获得"绿色设计产品"认证。格力电器采用绿色环保水性漆生产工艺，降低挥发性有机化合物排放，建立绿色采购标准，推动上下游企业共同实施绿色制造。格力光储直柔空调系统是以空调为能源和信息中心，集光伏发电、储能调电、空调用电、智能管电于一体的源储网荷一体化生态系统，为用户带来舒适、绿色的生活环境。构建"绿色设计—绿色制造—绿色回收"循环发展模式，累计拆解废旧电子电器 6800 万套（台），减少碳排放 103 万吨。

2025 年政府工作报告提到，建立一批零碳园区、零碳工厂。伊利集团是中国食品行业第一家发布"双碳"目标及路线图的企业，已建立 5 家零碳工厂，推出 6 款零碳产品。伊利集团推行"种养一体化"生态农业模式，牧场周边种植低碳饲料，具有良好的固碳能力，牧场配置自动化设备和低碳管理系统，采用低碳饲料喂养奶牛，降低 20%～30% 奶牛瘤胃产生的甲烷排放。开展包装全生命周期碳排放评价，使用以可再生和可循环材料为主的包装，2025 年基本实现包装材料 99% 可回收。液态奶事业部自研 AI 低碳生产平台，利用碳核算模型动态调节能源供需，实现减碳可算可见。

福建省晋江经济开发区以时尚鞋服、纺织新材、健康食品等为主导产业，拥有安踏、恒安等龙头企业。创新"垂直工厂"模式，楼上设立生产车间、办公室、实验室，楼下设立库房，让一栋楼成为一座立体垂直工厂，形成"上下楼就是上下游，产业园就是产业链"的园区生态，提高工业用地容积率，促进园区土地集约高效利用。集成推广绿色环保材料，布局屋顶光伏、储能、充电桩等绿色能源，建设废气、余热回收处理设施，助力企业向"绿"生长。培育绿色制造领跑企业，引导企业开展设备换芯、生产换线、机器换人等智能化改造，将绿色低碳理念贯穿于产品设计、原料采购、生产、运输、回收处理的全过程，带动产业链供应链向新、向绿发展。

2024 年 12 月，上海闵行开发区发布《上海闵行经济技术开发区碳排放报告（2024）》，这是首个国家级经济开发区发布的年度碳排放报告。得益于产业能级提质增效、科技创新迭代升级、节能降耗持续推进、能源结构清洁低碳，闵行开发区实现从传统制造园区向绿色智能制造和研发创新园区的焕新蜕变。出台《零碳示范园区创建行动方案》《绿色低碳"领跑者"实施方案》，成立全市首个政府引导、园区搭台、企业主体的绿色共建联盟，开展碳排放核算，布局可再生能源、绿证绿电交易、碳金融，支持因企制宜的减污降碳工作，形成以装备制造、生物医药、新材料为主导的现代化产业体系，外资及合资企业占比超八成，产业"含新含绿指数"不断提升。

案例 4-8　华为：全环节全链条探索绿色低碳循环的"最优解"

华为集团把环保法规遵从、能源资源利用效率提升、自然环境保护等作为标准，融入研发、运营、采购、制造、供应链等各个环节，以创新使能产业链绿色发展。至今，华为数字能源装备和服务助力客户累计实现绿色发电 9979 亿度，节约用电 461 亿度；华为主力产品平均能效提升为 2019 年（基准年）的 2.6 倍；累计 78 万台终端设备通过以旧换新延长生命周期；ICT 业务电子废弃物填埋率为 0.5%，实现智能终端业务电子废弃物零填埋。进一步看，华为在产品设计源头即考虑安全环保以及可再生材料的选用，再生塑料和生物基塑料广泛运用于华为智能终端产品。华为自动化堆叠极简设计产品包装，持续推进说明书轻量化，逐步消除包装材料中的一次性塑料，选用可循环利用的再生纸和符合可持续发展管理原则的负责任森林所提供的纸张原料。

华为建设总部、园区、工厂等光伏电站，引入清洁能源，降低自身运营过程中的碳排放。华为核查供应商碳排放数据，倒逼供应商系统化节能减排。通过使用清洁能源交通工具、减少纸质单据、简化包装、推广循环周转箱等措施，实现绿色运输。采取取消纸质购物单、取消快递外包防水袋、减少纸箱和胶带使用、推广使用零塑包装、提升包装实装率等措施，优化绿色物流作业。推出一站式换新计划，消费者通过旧设备回收获得的代金券可以用来购买华为新产品。

华为提出，科技与自然共生，企业所做的一切，受益于地球，也有益于地球。通过持续推进节能减排，加强可再生能源使用，探索循环经济创新模式，减少对大自然的索取，为客户提供对环境更为友好的产品，正是华为的核心价值观与核心竞争力。

二 农业生产方式加快绿色转型

中国健全耕地保护制度和轮作休耕制度，全面落实永久基本农田特殊保护，耕地减少势头得到初步遏制。稳步推进黑土地保护，全国耕地质量稳步提升，平均等级达到 4.76，比 10 年前提高 0.35 个等级。多措并举推进农业节水和化肥农药减量增效，在粮食产量连年丰收情况下，农田灌溉用水有效利用系数达 0.57，比 10 年前提高 0.05，化肥年用量从 2015 年的 6022 万吨下降到 5000 多万吨。发展种养加结合、农牧渔结合、产加销一体等循环农业模式，强化农业废弃物资源化利用，畜禽粪污综合利用率达 78%，秸秆综合利用率超 88%，农膜回收率稳定在 80%以上。

统筹推进农业生产和农产品两个"三品一标"①，实施地理标志农产品保护工程，绿色、有机、名特优新、地理标志农产品总数达7.8万个，有效促进农业提档升级、农民增收致富。

2020年7月，习近平总书记来到吉林省四平市梨树县考察，走进国家百万亩绿色食品原料（玉米）标准化生产基地的玉米地，察看玉米长势。总书记强调，要认真总结和推广"梨树模式"，采取有效措施切实把黑土地这个"耕地中的大熊猫"保护好、利用好，使之永远造福人民。"梨树模式"通过秸秆覆盖还田、免耕播种等技术，以种养循环解决黑土地变"瘦"、变"薄"、变"硬"的问题，实现保土、保水、养地。吉林省成立黑土地保护工作领导小组，组建专家委员会，出台政策，实践形成玉米秸秆条带还田保护性耕作、玉米秸秆全量还田地力保育、玉米秸秆深翻还田滴灌减肥、玉米秸秆还田坐水种保苗增产、水稻稻草全量粉碎翻压还田、坡耕地保土提质、玉米秸秆堆沤培肥、玉米秸秆全量深混还田、玉米秸秆全量粉耙还田散墒增温、米豆轮作黑土地保护培肥等黑土地保护十大模式，黑土地保护性耕作面积超3800万亩，稳居全国首位。

河南省开封市兰考县实施土地流转"800+分红"②、"三化"土地托管③、村民自营"五统一"服务④等运营方式，推进高标准农田建设。开发集高标四情⑤、农事服务、数字乡村、绿色循环等功能于一体的"5G+高标准农田指挥调度平台"，实现监测预警、精准调控、自动灌溉、运营管理、决策处置等核心环节闭环贯穿。上线"农田易管家"农事服务小程序，农户可向农业专家在线咨询，专家给出指导意见并开具科

---

① 农业生产"三品一标"为品种培优、品质提升、品牌打造和标准化生产，农产品"三品一标"为绿色、有机、地理标志和达标合格农产品。
② 土地流转"800+分红"模式：成片连方土地按照800元/亩/年流转，由经营主体进行规模化种植，收益除去流转费和经营成本，剩余部分按比例分红。
③ "三化"土地托管模式：村集体通过市场化方式选择社会化托管主体，后者提供专业化"耕种管收销"全过程服务。扣除服务费后，村集体与农户按约定比例分红。
④ 村民自营"五统一"服务：对不愿流转或托管的农户，村集体提供低成本的统一农资、统一耕种、统一管理、统一收获、统一销售"五统一"服务，帮助农户降本增效。
⑤ 高标四情：高标准农田土壤墒情、作物苗情、病虫情和气候环境情况的实时监测、数据分析和精准管理。

技种田"处方单"，农户根据"处方单"向农事服务中心购买农资农服。

云南省大理州宾川县按照"先建后补"模式建设自压滴灌型高效节水灌溉工程，由当地农民专业合作社投建运维。用水总量控制指标根据项目区可供水量和灌溉定额，将初始水权量依据耕地面积和作物灌溉需求定额分配到用水户。按照确保灌区管理单位正常运转、工程良性运行、用水主体有承担水费能力的原则，运营方和用水户协商水价，实行超定额累进加价。为降低农户用水成本、提高种粮积极性，实行分类水价制度，粮食作物水价低于经济作物水价。随着农田灌溉条件改善和水资源科学分配，在干旱少雨自然条件下靠天降雨浇灌的"雷响地"变为一片绿洲，当地企业、农户开始规模化发展现代高效农业。

河北省沧州黄骅市积极探索盐碱地农业绿色发展模式，以"秸秆还田+深耕深翻+增施有机肥+增施土壤调理剂"等方式建设高标准农田，耕地面积从 1980 年的 77 万亩增加到目前的超过 140 万亩。实施全国小麦（黄骅旱碱麦）绿色高质高效项目、渤海粮仓科技示范工程项目，采取淋盐压碱、降盐蓄墒等措施降低盐分，测土配方施肥、有机肥和无机肥配合施用等措施科学施肥，选育抗旱、耐盐、耐碱、抗病、高产的小麦新品种，实施旱碱麦轮作耕种，培育新型农业经营主体，推动面粉、面花、挂面等黄骅旱碱麦加工产品规模化经营，昔日"十年九不收"的盐碱地渐成沃野良田。

湖北省孝感市云梦县是中国越冬露地蔬菜生产优势区，每年发往各地的蔬菜有 90 万余吨，年综合产值超 37 亿元。云梦县与武汉大学、华中农大等合作，引进蔬菜新品种 400 多个，焕新"种子芯片"。作为湖北省地膜科学使用回收项目试点，云梦县建立"农户捡拾交售、镇级网点组织回收、龙头企业加工利用"废弃农膜回收利用体系，农民送交废弃农膜到回收点获得购膜补助，从而引导农民主动使用成本相对更高的可回收地膜。探索"空中菜园"新模式，在大棚配置立体水培架，智能系统自动化调温、调湿、通风、补光、施肥、滴灌，水肥一体机根据蔬菜生长周期动态配比营养液，废水集中过滤供下次循环使用，节水率达 70%，肥料利用率提升 50%，突破季节与土地的束缚，水培蔬菜产量相较传统种植方式翻了数倍。

案例 4-9　　"双昌"（重庆荣昌区和四川内江隆昌市）
　　　　　　现代农业合作示范园区："三个融合"
　　　　　　　　促绿色农业互利共赢

内江荣昌现代农业高新技术产业示范区是唯一一个以农业农村为主的川渝毗邻地区功能平台。"双昌"现代农业合作示范园区由荣昌和内江在毗邻地区共建，规划总面积 19.6 万亩，涉及荣昌区和隆昌市的"七镇一街道"。两地成立由区（市）委、区（市）政府分管负责人任指挥长的合作示范园区建设指挥部，建立工作专班、联席会议制度，确保合作事项有人抓、可落地、见成效。

其一，产业融合。结合两地的资源禀赋和产业基础，按照坡上猪场-油茶和果树种养循环、水田稻渔综合种养、旱地高粱-油菜轮作的绿色农业进行布局，推行"生产+科技+加工+服务"一体化发展，形成园区名称、规划设计、主导产业、建设标准、政策标准、管理服务、科技服务"七统一"共建机制。例如，突出荣昌猪、内江猪地方优良品种保护开发，共建国家优质生猪战略保障基地和种猪供种高地；建成 40 万亩"宜机宜耕、能排能灌、高产稳产、旱涝保收"的高标准农田，共建国家级稻渔综合种养示范区，实现"一水两用、一田双收、绿色循环"；培育休闲观光、科普教育、农事体验、美食文化等农旅新业态。

其二，科技融合。依托西南大学、重庆市畜牧科学院、内江农科院等高校、科研院校和国家生猪大数据中心、国家生猪技术创新中心等国家级平台，两地围绕生猪、稻渔、柑橘等特色产业深化产学研合作，在合作园区建立博士专家工作站、科研试验基地、科技专家大院，普及开展现代化生猪养殖、水稻新品种和新技术推广、鱼菜和稻渔共生等绿色农业新质生产力项目。

其三，党建融合。例如，荣昌区龙集镇与隆昌市石碾镇共建"新风小院"，组织两镇村民共同学习绿色农业专业知识技能，促进两地村民友好往来；荣昌区安富街道普陀村党总支与隆昌市石燕桥镇三合村党委签订缔结友好村合作协议，探索党建引领人才共育、产业共兴、绿色发展的创新路径；荣昌与隆昌共同出资、共同出人、共同建设园区科技文化馆，设立绿色农业科普展示区、农特产品及非遗展示区、党校（职业技术）培训区等功能载体。

三 服务业绿色化水平不断提升

中国累计创建超过 600 家提供绿色服务、引导绿色消费、实施节能减排的绿色商场。推进数据中心节能降碳技术改造和设备更新升级，累计建成 246 家国家级绿色数据中心，在电能利用效率、可再生能源利用率、水资源利用效率等方面达到世界领先水平。实施快递包装绿色转型"七项行动"[①]，强化行业塑料污染治理，引导生产商、消费者使用可循环快递包装和可降解包装，2024 年，快递中转环节循环包装实现全覆盖。推动展览场馆使用绿色建筑、节能改造和循环使用办展设施，在广交会等重点展会开展绿色搭建、绿色运营、绿色餐饮、绿色物流等试点。全面实施铁路电子客票，推广电子发票应用，大幅减少票纸用量。倡导餐厅、宾馆、酒店不主动提供一次性用品。

南翔印象城是上海单体体量最大的商业购物中心，从建筑、设计、空间、体验、场景等多角度，探索绿色商场发展路径。以森林、湿地、高山为主题，设置三个玻璃盒组合的超 1000 平方米植物园，栽培 200 多种热带植物。打造屋顶主题花园，将凌空跑道、儿童互动乐园、萌宠乐园、篮球场等置于屋顶空间，丰富户外绿色消费体验。构建集地铁、公交场站枢纽于一体的绿色交通网络，方便消费者绿色出行。上线智慧停车管理系统，减少驾车找车位的碳排放。建设楼宇自控系统、能源再生系统，动态调整商城冷暖气。实施垃圾分类回收和追踪，引入智能机器人清洁作业，减少废弃物排放。

阿里巴巴集团《环境、社会和治理报告（2024）》显示，银泰百货

---

① 快递包装绿色转型"七项行动"：快递包装减量化专项指导行动、电商平台企业引领行动、快递包装供应链绿色升级行动、可循环快递包装推广行动、快递包装回收利用和处置行动、快递包装监管执法行动、快递包装绿色转型主题宣传行动。

获评"绿色商场"门店 40 家，清洁电力使用比例达 47.3%，碳减排 30.4 万吨。2021 年以来，银泰百货积极参与绿电交易，上线集能源管理、环境品质监测、配电控制、商户预付费充值等功能于一体的智慧能源管理系统。在绿化用水、生活用水、中央空调用水等环节部署节水设备，将收集的雨水、空调冷凝水回收利用。广泛采用可土壤降解、堆肥降解的绿色包装袋，以及环境友好的减量设计纸箱、环保填充物和环保胶带。发起"空瓶记"环保活动，消费者用化妆品空瓶兑换消费权益，空瓶被专业机构制成艺术作品展示，并由第三方机构回收循环利用。

雄安城市计算中心被誉为雄安孪生数字城市之眼、智能城市之脑、生态城市之芯。充分利用自然通风和采光，合理布置国际首例园林化生态机房大厅、中国首创模块化集装箱机房大厅。屋顶自建光伏系统，绿电直接并入建筑内部公共区域低压供电系统，成规模使用磷酸铁锂离子电池进行削峰填谷，低谷电价时电池系统充电储能，高峰、尖峰电价时释放能源。采用能源站、间接冷却塔和蓄冷罐实现不间断供冷，末端系统采用全国领先的液冷散热技术，供配电网络搭载电力监控、空调控制、机器人巡检等智能系统，动态监测与智能分析电源使用效率、温湿度、空调能耗状态等关键指标，及时优化能耗。

顺丰集团对外承诺，善用科技力量，推动绿色低碳变革，在 2030 年实现自身碳效率相较于 2021 年提升 55%，每个快件包裹的碳足迹相较于 2021 年降低 70%。顺丰集团将科技力量注入每个快件的全生命周期提效减碳：收派员配置便携型智能穿戴设备，结合内嵌物流地图，简化收派件路径，提高收派效率；开发全自动化分拣及场地管理系统，提升仓储和转运的运营效率，降低过程能耗及出错率；通过逻辑算法及智慧地图，结合快件的时效、距离等因素，整合货运线路和运力资源，利用预见性导航与节油节电算法，精准匹配车辆与货物，减少运输能耗；成立包装实验室，开发全生物降解胶袋、免胶纸的防盗拉链纸箱、可循环使用的包装箱等绿色包装，打造气候友好型快递包装循环生态圈。顺丰减碳行动路线图见图 4-1。

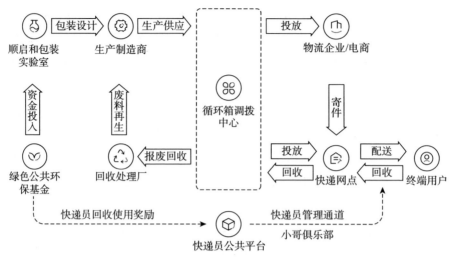

图 4-1　顺丰减碳行动路线图（图片来源：顺丰集团）

案例 4-10　京东物流：打造行业领先的物流供应链绿色发展新模式

2025 年 1 月，国家发展改革委等部门发布《绿色技术推广目录（2024 年版）》，京东物流上线的供应链碳管理平台（京碳惠），采取"分布式碳账簿"管理模式，采用自研的 MRV-T（碳足迹监测、报告、核查与跟踪）数字化减碳技术，通过传感器获取终端碳排放数据，为运单提供基于时空和地理维度的最小颗粒度双因子碳核算和减碳模型，成为物流行业唯一入选的绿色技术。

通过 AI 算法提效、绿色能源及运输设备应用、包装材料循环使用等方式，京东物流坚持在仓储、物流运输、包装材料等各环节不断减碳。绿色仓储方面，建成中国首个"碳中和"物流园区，多个分拣中心、大件仓、物流园区铺设屋顶光伏，总装机容量达 114.48 兆瓦。绿色运输方面，京东物流干线及终端运输环节投入新能源车超 8000 辆，平均每年可减少碳排放超 3.5 万吨，在京津冀地区投入首批数十辆氢能源重卡物流车，成为行业首家规模化投用氢能源卡车的物流企业。绿色包装方面，京东物流发布原厂直发包装认证标准，督促发件商开展循环包装精细化运营。

京东物流通过减碳激励机制支持环境友好产品，做大绿色消费市场，增强品牌商对绿色产品的投入决心。2017 年以来，京东物流实施"青流计划"，携手上下游伙伴共同开展供应链端到端的环保行动，开展"你的名字""箱爱计划""减碳先锋""益起捡跑""盒以为家"等环保公益活动，建立消费者碳账户，后者通过"京东快递"小程序下单寄件后，领取减碳量积分，在京东商城购买带有"减碳特权"标识的商品时，使用减碳量积分兑换商家提供的折扣、减免等权益。

第 5 节　中国大力发展绿色低碳产业的创新举措、主要成效和典型案例

一　绿色科技创新成为新质生产力的重要支撑

锚定 2035 年建成科技强国的奋斗目标，中国以高水平科技自立自强为主线，强化战略规划、政策措施、科研力量、重大任务、资源平台、区域创新等方面统筹。2023 年，党中央进一步加强对科技工作的集中统一领导，成立中央科技委员会，重组科学技术部，实现国家科技领导和管理体制的系统性重塑、整体性重构。2024 年，中国在全球创新指数排名中的位置升至第 11 位，研发经费投入总量跃居全球第二，全球百强科技创新集群数量蝉联世界第一，制造业增加值规模连续 14 年位居全球首位，研发人员、高水平论文、PCT 国际专利申请量连续位居世界第一，科技进步贡献率达到 60% 以上。

同时，中国绿色科技取得一系列重要进展：资源能源清洁高效利用方面，以燃煤发电污染物超低排放技术、先进燃煤发电技术和现代煤化工技术为代表的煤炭清洁高效转化与利用技术取得重要突破，深水油气、致密气、页岩气、致密油、煤层气的勘探开发技术取得重大进展，掌握第三代核电技术的大部分关键核心技术，风电、光伏发电等可再生能源技术与产业发展迅速；绿色资源技术领域，复杂低品位多金属资源选冶技术取得进步，大宗工业固废资源化利用、生活垃圾焚烧发电、重金属固废安全处置等一批关键技术突破；打好污染防治攻坚战方面，环境工程技术向多领域、多学科、多行业交叉融合发展，电除尘、脱硫脱

硝、污水处理、土壤污染防治、畜禽粪污收集利用等工艺技术水平达到或接近国际先进水平；生态保护修复方面，开展生态监测预警、荒漠化防治、水土流失治理、石漠化治理、退化草地修复、生物多样性保护、生态安全保障等技术研发，多级气候灾害预警、防御和服务技术系统基本建成。

二 绿色低碳产业已成经济增长新引擎

中国建成全球最大、最完整的新能源产业链，风电、光伏发电等清洁能源设备生产规模居世界第一，为全球提供 70% 的光伏组件和 60% 的风电装备。新能源汽车年销量从 2012 年的 1.3 万辆快速提升到 2024 年的突破 1000 万辆，产销量连续 10 年位居全球第一，保有量占全球一半以上。中国节能环保产业质量效益持续提升，年产值超过 8 万亿元，培育一批百亿级龙头企业，形成覆盖节能、节水、环保、可再生能源等各领域的绿色技术装备制造体系，环保装备与物联网、人工智能等新一代信息技术深度融合，综合能源服务、合同能源管理、合同节水管理、环境污染第三方治理、碳排放管理等新业态新模式发展壮大。各地积极探索生态产品价值实现路径，都市农业、生态旅游、森林康养、精品民宿、田园综合体等生态产业快速发展。

2024 年，光伏行业经历下行周期，但华晟新能源科技股份有限公司异军突起，订单增长、产能饱满、销售畅旺，跻身全球光伏一级组件制造商。创业之初，华晟新能源放弃当时同质化竞争的主流技术路线，选择做下一代异质结光伏电池，攻关出电池功率更高的光转化材料，建成全球单体产能最大的异质结光伏电池及组件一体化工厂。发起异质结技术产业化协同创新平台，线上随时讨论分享新技术，每个季度举办线下会议，把自身作为实验室，邀请社会科技力量参与验证和应用异质结产业化过程中的各种新技术、新设备、新工艺。得益于异质结的技术路线优势，华晟新能源从产品出海走向技术出海，比如，保加利亚帕扎尔吉克市 650 兆瓦太阳能园区使用的设备全部产自华晟新能源，这也是海外最大的采用异质结技术的光伏园区。

按照"技术同源、体系融通、产业共链"思路，中车集团构建轨道交通装备和清洁能源装备"双赛道双集群"格局，强化从轨道交通到清洁能源、从整机到部件的产业共链引领保障能力，将轨道交通积累的电力电子、控制算法等核心技术向新能源产业平移，打造以风电整机为龙头，发电机、叶片、塔筒、变流器、齿轮箱、变压器等关键零部件为配套，适应丰富场景的"风光储氢一体化"全产业链，风电装备年销售额超 300 亿元。作为国务院国资委首批"AI+"行动单位中唯一的装备制造企业，中车集团围绕业务全流程、管理全覆盖、客户全周期、产业全领域、行业全生态，打造端到端贯穿产业链、供应链和创新链的中车"斫轮"大模型，携手中国电信开发 DeepSeek 大模型的深度集成应用，为风电装备的研发设计、生产制造、运维服务等提供数智支撑。

2024 年 9 月，吉利集团发布《台州宣言》，宣布通过"战略聚焦、战略整合、战略协同、战略稳健、战略人才"五大举措，为用户提供"可油可电可醇"的卓越产品与灵活能源服务。2024 年，吉利汽车总销量突破 217 万辆，其中新能源车型销量突破 88 万辆，双双超越全年销售目标，总收入达历史新高（2402 亿元）。吉利汽车上线"云、数、智"一体化超级云计算平台，形成空间设计、智能能源、全域安全、AI 智能、驾控性能等新能源汽车全栈开发体系。进一步看，吉利汽车制定《2025年碳减排 50% 行动路线》，旗下整车基地全部获评国家级绿色工厂。吉利西安智能环保工厂自建 52 兆瓦光伏电站，实现 100% 使用可再生能源，年均发电量 4750 万千瓦时，每年可减排二氧化碳 2.7 万吨，相当于植树造林 3196 公顷，加之配建水资源循环设施、29.6 万平方米的工厂绿化区、全面采用低挥发性原辅材料，实现制造全周期零废水排放、零废物填埋、零有害物排放，成为中国整车企业首个零碳工厂。

盈峰环境科技集团自 2007 年研发中国第一台纯电动扫路车，到如今实现清扫、清洗、垃圾收转运、市政应急等新能源环卫车全系覆盖，市场占有率连续多年稳居行业第一。"为环卫装备插上'智慧'的双翼"是盈峰环境绿色化、智能化融合的路线图，开发智慧环卫云平台，采用物联网集成、视频指挥调度、安全驾驶检测等核心技术，为环卫车产品运营管理提供远程服务，日活用户突破 3 万，日均收运垃圾量近 3 万吨。

"智慧环卫作业舱"可搭载不同的新能源环卫装备，具备优化清扫路线、调整作业强度、数据智能分析、人机语音交互、环卫运营云管理等功能，节能、节水效率提升 15.2%，新能源环卫车出勤率提升 17.5%。

博格华纳驱动系统（苏州）有限公司为全球品牌车企生产零部件，从设计、工艺、运营到供应链等全过程落实"能源强度每年降低 5%"的节能降碳目标，在苏州碳普惠服务中心支持下，取得国际权威认证机构颁发的"零碳工厂"认证。苏州工业园区是中国首批碳达峰试点园区，区内企业绿色能源应用、碳减排意愿强烈。苏州工业园区、苏州供电公司共同成立碳普惠服务中心，联合光伏投资者、政府机构、银行、减碳需求企业、上海环境能源交易所等，以分布式光伏为切入点，构建中国首个区域性市场化自愿减排交易体系，实现数字核证、场外交易、抵押融资、在线核销、核查协助等碳中和全流程线上服务（见图 4-2），对园区内广泛、小型的减碳行为进行量化、核证和价值变现，截至 2024 年末，累计核发碳减排量超 23.5 万吨，实现碳减排量交易超 3.4 万吨。

案例 4-11　　比亚迪：技术创新驱动全球新能源汽车行业变革升级

2024 年，比亚迪新能源汽车全球销量 427.2 万辆，同比增长 41%，蝉联中国汽车市场车企销量冠军和全球新能源汽车市场销量冠军，实现营业收入 7771.02 亿元，同比增长 29.02%，首次突破 7000 亿元大关，超越特斯拉的营收表现。比亚迪新能源汽车累计纯电行驶里程突破 1500 亿公里，减少碳排放量相当于种植 5.04 亿棵树。这些数字背后，是比亚迪对"企业价值"的重新定义。

"研发之王"是比亚迪的决胜特色。2024 年，比亚迪研发投入达 542 亿元，超过纯利润（402.5 亿元）。截至 2024 年末，比亚迪累计研发投入超 1800 亿元，研发人员超 12 万人，全球专利申请量超 4.8 万项，授权专利超 3 万项，大大提升车辆性能和安全性，构筑坚实的技术壁垒。进一步看，自 2008 年推出全球首辆插电式混合动力汽车以来，比亚迪在电池、电机、电控等核心技术领域持续布局，成为中国少数能自产电池等关键零部件的车企。

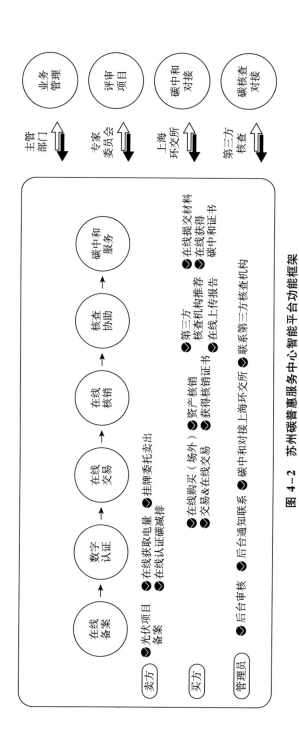

图 4-2　苏州碳普惠服务中心智能平台功能框架

早在 1998 年，比亚迪在荷兰鹿特丹成立欧洲分公司，但其电池产品只深藏在诺基亚、摩托罗拉等手机里，并未广为人知。2013 年，比亚迪纯电动大巴 K9 获得欧盟整车认证，比亚迪品牌在海外市场崭露头角。2021 年，比亚迪启动"乘用车出海"计划。2024 年，比亚迪海外出口 41.7 万辆，同比增长 71.9%，遍布六大洲 100 多个国家和地区，在日本、泰国、巴西、新加坡、哥伦比亚等多个市场夺得销冠。值得关注的是，比亚迪在进入不同国家时，愈加重视适应当地市场环境，比如，比亚迪泰国工厂从开工到投产历时仅 16 个月，年产能约 15 万辆，针对当地消费者需求推出定制车型，与当地企业合作建立销售服务网络。

从比亚迪的出海实践看出，如今中国新能源汽车出海已经迎来全新时代，最明显的特点是技术驱动、品牌全球化、本土化战略和全球价值链参与。

三　全国碳市场建设进展显著

按照党中央、国务院的决策部署，在借鉴国际碳市场建设经验、总结地方试点碳市场建设实践的基础上，全国碳排放权交易市场从发电行业入手，于 2021 年 7 月启动上线交易，现纳入重点排放单位 2257 家，年覆盖二氧化碳排放量约 51 亿吨，占全国二氧化碳排放的 40% 以上，成为全球覆盖温室气体排放量最大的市场。2024 年 1 月，全国温室气体自愿减排交易市场启动。强制碳市场对重点排放单位排放严格管控，自愿碳市场鼓励社会广泛参与，两个碳市场独立运行，通过配额清缴抵销机制衔接。基于碳排放强度控制目标的配额分配方法展现碳市场机制的灵活性和适用性优势，为全球碳市场机制创新贡献"中国方案"。

2024 年 1 月，国务院颁布《碳排放权交易管理暂行条例》，这是中国应对气候变化领域的首部专项法规。生态环境部印发《碳排放权交易管理办法（试行）》，发布登记、交易、结算三项规则，制修订碳排放核算报告和核查指南、配额分配方案等规范性文件，与《条例》共同形成涵盖"行政法规+部门规章+规范性文件+技术规范"的多层级制度体系。各级部门、重点排放单位、注册登记机构、交易机构、技术服务机构等各司其职，保障全国碳排放权交易全环节顺畅运行。截至 2023 年末，2021 年、2022 年度配额清缴完成率分别为 99.61%、99.88%，较第一个履约周期进一步提升，位于国际主要碳市场前列。建立"国家—省—市"三级碳排放数据联审机制，对关键数据实施月度存证，形成问题"及时发现—移交督办—核实整改"的闭环管理工作机制。全国碳市场管理平台、注册登记系统、交易系统等实现互联互通。中国碳排放权交易市场体系架构见图 4-3。

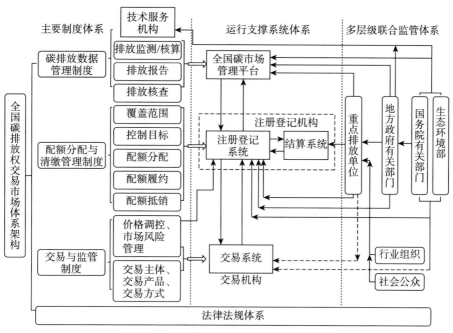

图 4-3　中国碳排放权交易市场体系架构

全国碳市场压实企业碳减排主体责任，在全社会树立"排碳有成本、减碳有收益"的低碳意识。重点排放单位基本开展元素碳含量实测。碳市场控制温室气体排放、促进能源结构调整的导向作用日益显现，2023年中国火电碳排放强度较 2018 年下降 2.38%，电力碳排放强度下降 8.78%。碳排放权交易价格为开展气候投融资、碳资产管理、配额质押等锚定了基准价格，撬动更多绿色低碳投资。符合中国实际的重点行业碳排放统计核算体系基本建立，培育一大批碳技术服务领域的专业人才和相关机构。2021~2024 年中国碳市场年度成交情况见表 4-1。

表 4-1　2021~2024 年中国碳市场年度成交情况

年份	成交总量（万吨）	成交总额（亿元）	挂牌成交量（万吨）	挂牌成交额（亿元）	大宗协议成交量（万吨）	大宗协议成交额（亿元）	成交均价（元/吨）	收盘价（元/吨）
2021	17878.93	76.61	3077.46	14.51	14801.48	62.10	42.85	54.22
2022	5088.95	28.14	621.90	3.58	4467.05	24.56	55.30	55.00
2023	21194.28	144.44	3499.66	25.69	17694.72	118.75	68.15	79.42
2024	18864.61	181.14	3702.74	36.31	15161.86	144.82	96.02	97.49
2023~2024 年变化	-11.0%	25.4%	5.8%	41.3%	-14.3%	22.0%	40.9%	22.8%

数据来源：上海环境能源交易所。

　　广州碳排放权交易中心搭建聚焦自然资源领域的市场化生态产品价值实现平台，开展生态产品开发、备案、登记、流转、注销、信息披露、宣传推广、融资对接等全流程服务，设计生态系统碳汇独立交易体系和消纳应用空间，形成"生态系统碳汇+生态标签"生态碳汇产品，以及"生态数据+碳要素"多功能交易平台。通过实施生态系统碳汇计量与监测方法开发、项目备案及碳汇产品签发、碳汇产品登记划转与应用等，解决现有项目缺乏自愿减排机制所要求的覆盖范围广、应用性高等困境。

　　重庆市"碳惠通"温室气体自愿减排平台集碳履约、碳中和、碳普惠等功能于一体，将生态、能源、工业、消费等领域的固碳、应用清洁能源、节能减排等成果转化为碳资产，形成绿色生活场景体系、碳积分消纳体系、个人碳账户权益系统，注册人数突破 250 万人。为用户设立个人碳账户，依据生态环境部门认可的计算方法和标准，精准核算用户在各个授权场景产生的碳减排量，转化认证为"渝碳信用分"并计入个人碳账户。联合"支付宝"完善公交地铁、网约车、新能源充电等绿色出行场景，用户每次低碳出行，均能将碳减排成果记录到个人碳账本，用户可兑换出行优惠券。明确积分权益通兑规则，个人碳账户的"渝碳信用分"有价流转至权益提供方积分账户，用于权益提供方自身的"碳中和"抵消，实现碳积分价值。

　　农业减排增汇形成碳票、农产品碳标签、碳汇交易、碳汇信贷、碳汇保险等价值实现模式。比如，厦门市同安区莲花镇的军营村和白交祠村是优质茶叶产地，厦门市产权交易中心对茶园进行碳汇测算，将碳汇资源纳入交易体系，促成两村与多家企业签订碳汇交易合同，增加农民收益，激励农民减少使用化肥和农药，提升茶园的碳汇能力和茶叶品质；通过福州（连江）碳汇交易服务平台，福建恒捷实业有限公司购买福建亿达食品有限公司的 1000 吨海洋渔业碳汇，以渔业碳汇收益权作为质押，在兴业银行获得"海洋碳汇贷"；福建环融环保股份公司通过海峡股权交易中心购买漳州市南靖县龙山镇农田碳汇，后者将连续淹水的灌溉方式调整为间歇灌溉，减少土壤产生的甲烷量，通过秸秆还田、减施化肥、有机肥施用等实现土壤固碳。

案例 4-12　　南京市高淳区：农业碳汇开辟绿水青山就是金山银山的转化通道

高淳区地处茅山、天目山两大山脉的结合部，太湖、水阳江两大流域的交汇点，呈现"三山两水五分田"的自然地理格局，生态涵养区面积达 70%。稻田是温室气体甲烷的重要排放源，中国每年稻田甲烷排放量约 500 万~800 万吨。2022 年 5 月，农业农村部、国家发展改革委共同印发《农业农村减排固碳实施方案》，将稻田甲烷减排行动置于十大行动之首。在全省率先启动 GEP 核算先行试点的基础上，当年 7 月，高淳区在和睦涧村淳和水稻专业合作社 500 亩有机水稻田启动固碳减排项目。

高淳区与生态环境部南京环境科学研究所、南京农业大学、南京国环有机产品认证中心合作，构建温室气体排放和土壤固碳计量模型等关键技术体系，核算以生态方式种植"零碳水稻"减排的温室气体量，经江苏省农村产权交易中心备案认证，由高淳区碳达峰碳中和工作领导小组办公室签发全省首张农业碳票。2024 年 3 月，高淳区完成中国生物质炭有机水稻产生碳汇的"第一拍"，标号为江苏省"0000001"的碳票签出，被化学新材料行业的红宝丽集团以 75 元/吨购入。

此次碳票交易对卖出方而言，固碳减排项目通过技术革新，不仅温室气体净排放量减少 51%，产生的碳汇带来"卖空气"收益，且病虫害发生率下降 15%，土壤养分、水分保持能力得到提升，水稻亩产增产 10%，农户人均增收 1700 多元；对购买方而言，碳票上核定的碳减排量可用于农村产权交易中心碳减排市场交易，也可用于自愿碳抵消、自愿碳注销、生态环境损害赔偿等，平衡生产经营和碳排放之间的矛盾。

2024 年 5 月，高淳区开出中国首单植被综合碳汇价值保险保单，保障范围覆盖漆桥街道辖区内的所有耕地、林木等。当因自然灾害、意外事故导致农业实际碳汇量低于目标值时，街道可按照每吨 35 元的碳汇量协议价申请赔付，赔款用于植被碳汇资源的救助和生态修复。由此可见，建立农业碳汇产品价值实现机制，推动当地采取多元市场手段，在减排增（碳）汇的同时促进农业绿色发展。

四　绿色金融体系建设取得明显成效

在发展绿色生产力与建设金融强国的目标之下，中国绿色金融体系在顶层设计、产品服务创新、风险管理和信息披露、基础设施建设、绿色金融改革创新试验区建设、气候投融资试点等方面取得积极成效，形成以绿色贷款和绿色债券为主、多种绿色金融工具蓬勃发展的多层次绿色金融市场体系。截至 2024 年末，中国本外币绿色贷款余额为 36.6 万亿元，同比增长 21.7%。2024 年，中国境内绿色债券市场新增发行绿色债券 477 只，发行规模约 6814.32 亿元。2021 年 11 月，中国人民银行推出"碳减排支持工具"，通过"先贷后借"的方式，对金融机构向相关企业发放的碳减排贷款，按贷款本金的 60% 提供借款支持，利率为 1.75%，期限 1 年，可展期两次。截至 2024 年 6 月末，"碳减排支持工具"余额 5478 亿元，累计支持金融机构发放碳减排贷款超 1.1 万亿元，覆盖经营主体 6000 多家，带动年度碳减排量近 2 亿吨。

深圳市出台《深圳经济特区绿色金融条例》《深圳金融支持新能源汽车产业链高质量发展的意见》《关于加快推动绿色建筑产业与绿色金融协同发展的通知》《深圳市金融机构环境信息披露指引》《深圳市绿色投资评估指引》《深圳市绿色融资主体库管理办法》等法规政策，市银行业协会开展绿色金融效能评价，辖内金融机构开展环境信息披露，发布中国首个环境污染强制责任保险风险防控服务地方标准，国家开发银行深圳分行参与发行中国首单"债券通"绿色金融债，平安信托发行中国首单"三绿"（绿色发行主体+绿色资金用途+绿色基础资产）资产支持票据产品，平安财险深圳分公司落地中国首单红树林碳汇指数保险，兴业银行深圳分行落地中国首笔红树林保护碳汇质押融资业务，工商银行深圳市分行建立绿色专营机构并完善绿色审批通道、绿色贷款专项规模、优惠定价等保障措施……深圳正成为深化绿色金融改革创新高地。

案例 4-13　　　国家绿色金融改革创新试验区：

金融改革向"绿"而行

2017 年以来，中国人民银行、国家发展改革委等部门在浙江省湖州市、衢州市，江西省赣江新区，广东省广州市，贵州省贵安新区，新疆维吾尔自治区哈密市、昌吉州、克拉玛依市，甘肃省兰州新区，重庆市等 10 个城市（新区）设立绿色金融改革创新试验区，发挥先行先试、示范带头作用，推动绿色金融在全社会逐步实现从蓝图和理念到实践和行动的跨越。

绿色金融改革创新机制不断健全

各试验区分别建立由当地党政负责人担任组长的领导机制，制定试验区建设路线图和配套实施细则，建立工作督查问效和激励约束机制，充分发挥金融支持绿色低碳发展的资源配置、风险管理、市场定价三大功能。贵安新区成立中国首个绿色金融法庭，湖州市设立绿色金融纠纷调解中心，实现金融纠纷多元化解、快速调处，金融案件应调尽调。衢州市建立基于碳账户的转型金融 5e 数智体系（碳排放 e 本账、碳征信 e 报告、碳政策 e 发布、碳金融 e 超市、碳效益 e 评估），解决金融低碳资产识别难、企业精准减碳管理难、政府低碳转型治理难。兰州新区上线绿色金融综合服务平台——"绿金通"，整合工商、司法、税务、环保、用能等多维度企业信用信息，实现绿色融资智能认定、银企融资高效对接、企业信用数字评价、金融数据实时监控、环境权益在线评估、绿色企业（项目）认证评级等功能，促进银企高效对接合作。

各金融机构通过设立绿色金融事业部或专营机构、制定绿色金融业务规划、创新绿色金融产品和服务、开展碳核算及环境信息披露、先行先试绿色金融标准、积极参与绿色金融国际合作等多种方式，参与试验区绿色金融发展，比如，工商银行制定专项支持政策，定期召开试验区专题会议；中国人民财产保险公司在湖州落地中国首单"保险+服务+信贷"绿色建筑性能保险，打造"安全生产+环境污染防治"的"安环险"衢州模式。

创新绿色金融产品和服务

赣江新区主管的江西省投资集团发行中国首单地方国企低碳转型挂钩可续期公司债，以企业科研创新投入指标为前提，与低碳转型绩效目标挂钩，选取清洁能源发电装机容量作为关键绩效指标与发行利率挂钩，创 2023 年以来中国同期限、同品种公司债券最低票面利率。

广州天人山水旅游区是中国自然教育基地，得益于当地银行提供的绿色贷款支持，打造乡村文旅振兴样本；广州市沥滘污水处理厂发行绿色债券，打造"地下建厂，地上建园"的园林式环保设施；增城循环经济产业园利用绿色贷款建成"无废园区"，年垃圾处理量 183 万吨，年垃圾发电量 8.39 亿度。

光大银行重庆分行通过组建绿色金融行业分析师队伍、采取差异化的授信审批策略、设立绿色审批通道等方式，提高绿色信贷业务质效。2023 年 9 月，中国银行作为联席主承销商，支持重庆长安汽车金融公司 5 亿元个人汽车抵押贷款绿色资产支持证券成功发行，入池基础资产均为新能源汽车贷款，获得权威认证机构绿色债券评估最高"G-1"等级。

中国农业银行聚焦三农主责主业打造绿色银行，在高管层设立绿色金融/碳达峰碳中和工作委员会，将环境和气候的风控纳入风险管理与内部控制委员会职责，推出乡村人居环境贷、绿水青山贷、生态共富贷等绿色信贷产品，截至 2024 年末，绿色信贷余额超 4.97 万亿元，同比增长22.9%。利用政策工具并结合客情定制绿色银团贷款、绿色债券等创新业务，比如，农业银行与中央结算公司联合推出首支乡村振兴领域债券指数"中债-农行乡村振兴债券指数"，发行"碳中和"和"专项乡村振兴"双标债、"绿色""专项乡村振兴"和"革命老区"三标债；与全国碳排放权注册登记机构和交易机构合作，推出"农银碳服"结算系统，为企业绿色低碳转型提供金融支持。发布绿色金融发展（环境信息披露）年度报告，强化内部运营管理的碳足迹管理和节能降碳。

兴业银行成立"双碳"服务专班，组建碳咨询专项小组，上线"双碳大脑"管理平台，为超过 1.6 万机构客户开通碳账户，实现对碳数据的精准监测和数智管理，基于企业碳减排、碳资产持有、碳表现情况等指标，为企业减碳履约提供融资便利。兴业银行与全国碳排放权注册登记机构合作开发"中碳-兴业全国碳市场碳排放配额现货抵质押价格指数"，汇总分析用户碳账户数据，跟踪反映碳排放配额价值水平及变化趋势，为参考该指数购买碳配额的企业提供贷款，助力企业把握碳价波动窗口机会，实现碳资产价值更大化。

2024 年 6 月，北京银行南京分行为江苏振江新能源装备股份公司发放 5000 万元"绿棕收入挂钩贷款"，成为该产品首单落地业务。"绿棕收入挂钩贷款"是北京银行构建"专精特新第一行"的创新探索，将借款企业的主营收入构成分为"绿色""棕色""非绿棕"三大类，通过细分主营收入标签，将贷款的优惠利率与借款人的绿色收入绩效表现相挂钩，激励借款企业绿色转型。进一步看，北京银行将原"董事会战略委员会"更名为"董事会战略及社会责任委员会"，在总行层面成立绿色金融业务专职管理部室，分行层面成立专职团队，形成总分联动的绿色金融业务管理架构。推出"碳惠融"绿色金融综合服务方案，根据绿色属性认定结果，为企业和项目量身定制包含利率优惠、快捷审批在内的绿色贷款、绿色贴现等融资服务。

案例 4-14　　　　建设银行：打好绿色金融"组合拳"

在国家政策引导及市场需求拉动双重作用下，作为"五篇大文章"之一的绿色金融日益成为推动经济社会可持续发展的重要力量。建设银行秉持"成为全球领先的可持续发展银行"战略目标，董事会定期审查绿色金融发展情况，设立由董事长任组长的碳达峰碳中和工作领导小组和由行长任主任的绿色金融委员会，出台《绿色金融发展战略规划（2022～2025年）》《服务碳达峰碳中和行动方案》等制度，围绕运管体系、人才队伍、业务发展、数智建设、风险管控五个方面打出"组合拳"。

绿色发展贯穿于生产与生活的各个领域，需结合实际情况因地、因时、因业施策推进绿色金融创新。建设银行在标准产品发行之外，及时匹配客户需求"量体裁衣"。比如，建设银行广东省分行与广州市南沙区政府合作推出"绿色气候贷"，编制中国首份穗港澳合作的气候投融资标准；建设银行湖州分行运用对公客户 ESG 评级工具，推出"ESG 可持续发展贷"，设计贷款利率与企业可持续发展绩效指标达标情况动态挂钩的调节机制；建设银行湖北省分行推出绿色电力证书收益权质押贷款，盘活新能源项目的"环境权益"价值；建设银行黑龙江省分行通过政银企联建的"数字畜牧"产业服务平台，推出生猪养殖、肉牛养殖、奶牛养殖等绿色生产场景的纯信用线上信贷产品。截至 2024 年末，建设银行绿色贷款余额达 4.7 万亿元，实现绿色发展贷款增长稳、核心存款增长稳、关键指标表现稳。

第6节　扩绿增长：中国绿色低碳转型的经验及对发展中国家的启示

一　全面绿色低碳转型化解协同推进经济高质量发展和生态环境高水平保护的全球治理难题

以习近平同志为核心的党中央从战略高度和全局视野着眼，将全方位、全领域、全地域推进绿色低碳转型融入经济社会发展全局，既考虑"生态—环境—能源"系统的整体性改善，又考虑如何通过良好的生态环境系统支撑高质量发展，进而以"双碳"目标为引领协同推进降碳、减污、扩绿、增长。中国将绿色发展理念融入工业、农业、服务业全链条各环节，加快发展以新能源汽车、清洁能源、节能环保、绿色金融为代表的绿色低碳产业，大力推进技术创新、模式创新、标准创新，培育绿色新质生产力，积极构建绿色低碳循环发展的现代化产业体系。政府部门制定全面绿色转型的目标与政策体系，市场机制发挥财税政策、金融工具、投资机制、标准体系等激励约束作用，创新绿色生产方式和扩大绿色消费，促使社会多元主体广泛参与，形成"政府引导-市场驱动-社会参与"的现代化绿色治理体系。

二　能源绿色转型提升经济社会发展"含绿量"与"含金量"

中国提出碳达峰碳中和的目标，充分发挥国家战略规划的导向作用，一张蓝图绘到底，制定能源发展中长期规划和可再生能源发展规划，明确能源绿色低碳转型发展的目标、任务、路径。注重供需协同，供给侧做好非化石能源提质扩量，大力发展可再生能源，构建完整的风电、光伏发电等新能源产业链供应链，提升新增用能需求中非化石能源的比重，推动新能源和传统能源协同互补；消费侧坚持节能降碳，加快化石能源清洁高效利用，引导全社会使用绿色能源和实施清洁能源替代。动态完善可再生能源上网电价、消纳保障、市场配置等政策措施，营造平等、开放、包容的市场环境，吸引社会力量参与新能源开发建设。统筹发展与安全，在确保能源安全稳定供应的同时，构建清洁低碳、安全充裕、经济高效、供需协同、灵活智能的新型电力系统，提升电力系统对新能源的消纳能力。推进跨省跨区输电通道规划建设和配电网升级改造，提升电网对电力资源的承载能力和配置能力。建设全国统一的电力市场体系，通过市场交易引导绿电高效合理利用，激发经营主体活力。

三　积极引导广大人民群众践行绿色生活方式

从自觉光盘行动到全民义务植树，从主动垃圾分类到拒绝"白色污染"，从拥抱新能源汽车到掀起跑步骑行热潮，从提倡共享经济到玩转二手交易……中国积极弘扬生态文明价值理念，系统推进生态文明宣传教育，引导全民提升勤俭节约、爱护环境、保护生态的消费理念和生活习惯。完善绿色生活方式激励机制，建设绿色产品认证、标识体系，引导消费者从点滴小事做起，坚持绿色饮食、绿色穿戴、绿色办公和绿色出行等。通过生活方式绿色革命，倒逼生产方式绿色转型，将绿色生活、"无废"理念普及推广到衣食住行游用等方方面面，形成全社会共同推进绿色发展的良好氛围。

第 7 节　中国式现代化视域下进一步推进绿色低碳转型的对策建议

一　联动生活方式和消费方式全龄全面绿色转型

大力倡导简约适度、绿色低碳、文明健康的生活理念和消费方式，将绿色理念和节约要求融入文明公约、市民公约、村规民约、企业规章、学生守则、团体章程等经济社会规则，形成崇尚生态文明的浓郁社会氛围。落实绿色产品、能效、水效、碳标识等差异化激励制度，普及研发、设计、制造、包装、物流、回收等产品全生命周期节能降碳。优化党政机关、事业单位、央企国企、上市公司等绿色采购政策，引导中小企业执行绿色采购指南，拓展绿色产品采购范围和规模，将碳足迹要求纳入公共部门采购，推动规上企业建立绿色供应链。推动地方政府、市场主体发放权益型绿色消费券、绿色积分，鼓励消费者购买和"以旧换新"绿色商品。继续开展新能源汽车和绿色智能家电、节水器具、节能灶具、绿色建材下乡活动，加强配套设施建设和售后服务保障。

二　积极稳妥推进能源绿色转型

以安全、绿色、经济为约束，统筹优化电力电量保障、电力流布局、新能源布局与系统调节能力，因地制宜铺设新型电力系统。深入推进能源革命，重点区域同步实施煤炭消费总量控制、散煤替代和清洁能源发展，继续实施煤电节能降碳改造、灵活性改造、供热改造"三改联动"。促进油气勘探开发与新能源融合发展，推进二氧化碳捕集利用与封存项目建设。统筹水电开发和生态保护，推进水风光一体化开发，加快西北风电光伏、西南水电、海上风电、沿海核电等清洁能源基地建设，积极发展分布式光伏、分散式风电，开发生物质能、地热能、海洋能等新能源，推动氢能"制储输用"全链条发展，积极安全有序发展核电，加强清洁能源基地、调节性资源和输电通道的衔接协同，加快微电网、虚拟电厂、源网荷储一体化项目等智能电网建设，实现可再生能源快速增长、大规模应用和安全可靠有序替代。

三　同步推进现代化产业体系建设和产业结构绿色低碳转型

推动传统产业绿色低碳转型，推广清洁生产技术装备，更新升级传统工艺流程，健全落后产能退出机制。以科技创新、绿色智造和制造服务为驱动，融合发展战略性新兴产业、高技术产业、节能环保产业、现代高效农业和现代服务业，前瞻布局人工智能、生物医药等绿色未来产业，培育绿色低碳发展的领军企业和专精特新中小企业。鼓励合同能源管理、合同节水管理、环境污染第三方治理、碳排放管理等新产业、新业态、新商业模式创新发展，促进文旅商康养深度融合发展。推进绿色低碳科技自立自强，强化关键核心技术攻关，加强知识产权创造、保护、运用。深化数智科技在电力系统、工农业、交通运输、建筑建造运行等领域的应用，加快大中小微主体"上云用数赋智"，引导互联网平台绿色低碳发展，带动上下游市场主体提高减碳能力。聚焦生态环保项目、碳市场、资源环境要素、生态环境导向的开发项目、气候投融资、绿色消费等关键领域，推动金融机构加强绿色信贷、绿色债券、绿色基金、绿色资产证券化、绿色供应链金融等绿色金融产品服务创新。

第5章
奏响协奏曲：中国加强绿色国际合作的
举措、成效、经验和建议

2013 年，在哈萨克斯坦，习近平主席首次提出共建"丝绸之路经济带"倡议，并首次在国际场合提出"两山论"。随着共建"一带一路"迈进高质量发展新阶段，"两山论"理念日益深入人心。以人类共同的前途命运为怀，习近平主席在多个国际场合就全球绿色治理发出真诚呼吁："地球是我们的共同家园。我们要秉持人类命运共同体理念，携手应对气候环境领域挑战，守护好这颗蓝色星球""唯有携手合作，我们才能有效应对气候变化、海洋污染、生物保护等全球性环境问题"……绿色发展的春风，从东方腾起，吹向更广阔的世界。联合国前副秘书长兼环境规划署执行主任埃里克·索尔海姆认为，在成为世界第二大经济体的同时，中国也扮演着全球绿色发展的领导者角色，其他国家应该多来中国看看，可以从中国的绿色发展中得到启发。斯洛伐克驻华大使彼得·利扎克认为，绿色发展是中国送给全世界的一份"礼物"，中国和斯洛伐克在气候问题上一直保持着密切合作。

第1节 共建绿色丝绸之路的创新举措、
主要成效和典型案例

一 绿色合作政策体系不断完善

中国把绿色发展理念融入共建"一带一路"各领域，既为世界经济增长开辟新空间、搭建新平台，也为全球绿色治理给出中国方案，持续造福共建国家人民，绿色成为共建"一带一路"的鲜明底色。2015 年，中国发布《推动共建丝绸之路经济带和 21 世纪海上丝绸之路的愿景与行动》，提出"在投资贸易中突出生态文明理念，加强生态环境、生物多样性和应对气候变化合作，共建绿色丝绸之路"。而后，中国陆续发布《关于推进绿色"一带一路"建设的指导意见》《"一带一路"生态环境保护合作规划》《对外投资合作建设项目生态环境保护指南》《关于推进共建"一带一路"绿色发展的意见》等政策文件，为加强境外项目环境管理、推进共建"一带一路"绿色发展、促进绿色能源国际合作等重点领域谋划部署路线图。

二　绿色合作共识不断凝聚

中国与联合国环境规划署签署《关于建设绿色"一带一路"的谅解备忘录（2017~2022）》，与 50 多个国家及国际组织签署环保合作协议，倡导建立"一带一路"能源合作伙伴关系和全球清洁能源合作伙伴关系。中国与超过 40 个共建国家的 170 多个合作伙伴建立"一带一路"绿色发展国际联盟，举办绿色发展圆桌会、绿色创新大会、绿色金融与低碳发展论坛等主题活动，发布《"一带一路"绿色发展展望》《"一带一路"项目绿色发展指南》等政策研究报告。成立中国-东盟环境保护合作中心、中柬环境合作中心、中老环境合作办公室、中国-上海合作组织环境保护合作中心、澜沧江-湄公河环境合作中心、中非环境合作中心等双多边平台，编制并实施《中国-东盟环保合作战略》《上海合作组织成员国环保合作构想》《澜沧江-湄公河环境合作战略》。中国与共建国家开展生物多样性保护合作研究，共同维护海上丝绸之路生态安全，建设"一带一路"生态环保大数据服务平台①和"一带一路"环境技术交流与转移

---

① "一带一路"生态环保大数据服务平台汇集 60 余个共建国家的基础环境信息、环境法律法规和标准，囊括 30 余个国际权威平台公开的 200 余项指标数据，研究开发"一张图"决策支持系统和对外投资项目环境评价工具，为对外投资提供生态环境管理和绿色发展解决方案。

中心（生态环境部和深圳市人民政府合作共建）。

中国发起实施绿色丝路使者计划①，为近 120 个发展中国家培训上万名生态环保领域的官员、大学生、研究学者、技术人员，被联合国环境规划署誉为"南南合作典范"。中国实施"一带一路"应对气候变化南南合作计划，与 42 个共建国家签署 53 份气候变化南南合作谅解备忘录，与老挝、柬埔寨、塞舌尔等合作建设低碳示范区，与埃塞俄比亚、巴基斯坦、萨摩亚、智利、埃及等 30 多个共建国家开展 70 余个减缓和适应气候变化项目，2016 年以来，中方为其他发展中国家提供及动员的气候资金总额超过 1770 亿元人民币。

案例 5-1　　第三届"一带一路"国际合作高峰论坛：谋划高质量　　　　　　共建绿色丝绸之路新的金色十年

在 2023 年 10 月举办的第三届"一带一路"国际合作高峰论坛开幕式上，习近平主席宣布了中国支持高质量共建"一带一路"的八项行动，"促进绿色发展"是其中一项行动。习近平主席提出，中方将持续深化绿色基建、绿色能源、绿色交通等领域合作，加大对"一带一路"绿色发展国际联盟的支持，继续举办"一带一路"绿色创新大会，建设光伏产业对话交流机制和绿色低碳专家网络。落实"一带一路"绿色投资原则，到 2030 年为伙伴国开展 10 万人次培训。

"共建绿色丝路，促进人与自然和谐共生"是第三届"一带一路"国际合作高峰论坛的三场高级别论坛之一。论坛上，中国与 20 个共建国家的政府与环境主管部门、国际组织、研究机构、金融机构及企业等 30 余个共同发起方联合发布《"一带一路"绿色发展北京倡议》，在应对气候变化、落实"昆明-蒙特利尔全球生物多样性框架"、生态环境保护、绿色基础设施互联互通、绿色能源、绿色交通、绿色金融、合作平台等八个领域倡议加强合作。参会各方强调，共同推进建设绿色丝绸之路，加

---

①　绿色丝路使者计划起源于 2011 年启动的中国-东盟绿色使者计划。2016 年，为落实国家领导人的倡议，中国-东盟绿色使者计划正式升级为绿色丝路使者计划。升级后的绿色丝路使者计划开展生态环境管理能力建设合作活动、青年先锋活动、环保技术和产业交流合作及示范等一系列友好交流与务实合作项目。

强绿色低碳发展的政策沟通与战略对接，分享绿色发展的理念与实践，鼓励发挥"一带一路"绿色发展国际联盟平台作用，深化"一带一路"绿色发展伙伴关系。

"海洋合作"是第三届"一带一路"国际合作高峰论坛的六场专题论坛之一。论坛上，各国嘉宾围绕"共促蓝色合作 共奏丝路海韵"主题，深入交流海洋保护和海洋经济发展的成功实践及发展机遇，发布《"一带一路"蓝色合作倡议》及"一带一路"蓝色合作成果清单。《"一带一路"蓝色合作倡议》呼吁各方采取一致行动，共同保护和可持续利用海洋，共商蓝色合作大计，共享蓝色发展成果，共建美丽蓝色家园；以清洁生产、绿色技术、循环经济为基础，促进海洋产业转型升级。

三　绿色双多边合作稳步推进

中国成功举办《生物多样性公约》第十五次缔约方大会、《湿地公约》第十四届缔约方大会，积极参与二十国集团、中国-东盟、东盟-中日韩、东亚峰会、中非合作论坛、金砖国家、上海合作组织、亚太经合组织等框架下绿色发展领域合作，牵头制定《二十国集团能效引领计划》，成为二十国集团领导人杭州峰会重要成果。中国与印度、巴西、南非、美国、日本、德国、法国、东盟等多个国家和地区开展节能环保、清洁能源、应对气候变化、生物多样性保护、荒漠化防治、海洋和森林资源保护等领域双多边合作，推动联合国有关机构、亚洲开发银行、亚洲基础设施投资银行、新开发银行、全球环境基金、绿色气候基金、国际能源署、国际可再生能源署等国际组织在工业、农业、能源、交通运输、城乡建设等重点领域开展绿色低碳技术援助、能力建设和试点项目，为推动全球可持续发展作出重要贡献。

中国与东盟国家联合制定与共同实施《中国-东盟环境合作战略（2009～2015）》《中国-东盟环境合作战略（2016～2020）》《中国-东盟环境合作战略与行动框架（2021～2025）》，将环境政策对话与能力建设、应对气候变化与空气质量改善、可持续城市与海洋减塑、生物多样性保护与生态系统管理作为四大战略合作方向。成功举办10届中国-东盟环境合作论坛，开展中国-东盟生态友好城市发展伙伴关系、中国-东盟环境信息共享平台、中国-东盟绿色价值链伙伴关系、中国-东盟应对气候变化与空气质量提升计划、中国-东盟红树林保护合作伙伴关系等旗舰合作项目，与联合国机构在东盟地区共同实施以协同提升社区生计与保护生态环境为目标的示范合作。开展中国-东盟生态环境与应对气候变化使者计划、中国-东盟绿色使者计划等人才培养项目，为近 4000 名东盟国家政府官员、企业代表、研究人员、青年学者搭建合作与沟通桥梁。

绿色发展是上合组织重要合作领域之一。2021 年 9 月，上合组织成员国元首理事会会议审议通过《2022～2024 年〈上合组织成员国环保合作构想〉落实措施计划》，提出 "研究建立上合组织生态环保创新基地的可行性"。2022 年 11 月，《上合组织成员国政府首脑（总理）理事会第二十一次会议联合公报》指出，"各代表团团长注意到中华人民共和国关于建立上合组织生态环保创新基地的建议。" 2024 年 7 月，习近平主席出席 "上海合作组织+" 阿斯塔纳峰会，指出要 "用好生态环保创新基地等平台促进区域合作"。同月召开的上合组织国家绿色发展论坛上，与会方联合发布 "共建绿色发展伙伴关系，共促可持续发展倡议"，提出通过建立 "中国-上海合作组织生态环保创新基地" 等形式推动区域绿色低碳发展。中方依托生态环境部对外合作与交流中心（中国-上海合作组织环境保护合作中心），在上海、青岛建立中国-上合组织生态环保创新基地，搭建上合组织国家生态环保信息交流与共享窗口、生态环保人才培养及能力建设平台、环保技术示范推广平台、绿色投融资和产业合作平台。

2016 年 3 月，中方在澜沧江-湄公河合作首次领导人会议上提出 "愿与湄公河国家共同设立澜沧江-湄公河环境合作中心，加强技术合作、人才和信息交流，促进绿色、协调、可持续发展"，标志着澜沧江-湄公河环境合作正式纳入澜湄对话合作机制。2018 年 1 月，澜沧江-湄公河合作第二次领导人会议发表的《澜沧江-湄公河合作五年行动计划（2018～2022)》《澜沧江-湄公河合作第二次领导人会议金边宣言》，提出合力制定并实施《澜湄环境合作战略》和 "绿色澜湄计划"。后者旨在促进澜沧江-湄公河与世界联通，开展环境政策主流化、环境能力建设、环境示范合作、环境合作伙伴关系等旗舰合作项目，构建区域气候与生态政策对话平台，提升流域国家环境治理能力。

鄱阳湖和维多利亚湖分别为中国和非洲的最大淡水湖，哺育周边上千万人口，是多种野生动物的栖息天堂。拥有鄱阳湖的江西省与维多利亚湖区的乌干达、肯尼亚、坦桑尼亚相关地区合作，开启中非两大湖间跨越山海的"牵手"。江西省将鄱阳湖生态环境治理和摆脱贫困的经验做法，毫无保留地同三国各界机构和人士分享；邀请三国政府官员、环保组织成员、社区成员到鄱阳湖区域，学习种植高附加值蔬菜、养殖家禽、控制病虫害、减少农药污染、沼气发电和光伏发电等专业知识；派遣技术人员支持维多利亚湖区农村开展改厕改灶、雨水储存、种树养殖、科学捕鱼，以及发展庭院经济、循环农业、清洁能源、有机食品等绿色产业，实现生态恢复和渔民增收。

咸海曾是世界上第四大湖泊、亚洲第二大内陆咸水湖，由于气候变化和人类活动影响，水域面积仅剩下 1960 年的 10%，干涸湖底每年产生 4000 万~1.5 亿吨盐尘，严重影响中亚的生态环境。2018 年，乌兹别克斯坦创新发展部邀请中国参与咸海重度盐碱地生态治理。在丝路环境专项资金的支持下，中国科学院新疆生态与地理研究所联合中亚生态与环境研究中心、乌兹别克斯坦科学家完成《咸海干涸湖盆生态环境综合治理方案》，在咸海流域布设气象和水质自动观测站点，建设生态修复实验区、节水农业示范区、盐生植物种质资源圃，示范种植耐盐植物、滴灌棉花、节水水稻等，新疆的防治荒漠化成果在中亚获得推广和应用。

案例 5-2　　　　**中非携手推进生态友好的现代化：**
构筑新时代国际绿色合作新典范

推进绿色发展，中非始终是"同路人""行动派"，不少非洲国家积极借鉴中方"绿水青山就是金山银山"创新理念和实践经验，创造性提出"绿色就是金子"。2024 年 9 月召开的中非合作论坛北京峰会发布《中非合作论坛-北京行动计划（2025~2027）》，提出中非将在未来三年共同推进"绿色发展伙伴行动"，在新能源、气候变化、生态保护三个领域为中非绿色合作擘画新蓝图。

非洲是全球能源资源的宝库，传统能源和可再生能源储量丰富。然而，非洲却是全球能源缺口最大的地区。由于能源开发及相关基础设施所需的资金投入大、技术要求高、利润回收周期长，大多数非洲国家财政难以负担。中国在非洲实施数百个光伏、地热、锂电、风电等清洁能源项目，仅光伏电站装机容量累计超过 1.5 吉瓦。比如，作为非洲首个全套中国技术独立承建的地热项目，江西国际经济技术合作有限公司承建的肯尼亚加里萨光伏发电站是东非地区规模最大的光伏发电项目，年均发电量超 7600 万千瓦时，满足 38 万人的用电需求；山东电力建设公司总承包的摩洛哥努奥光热电站为超过百万户家庭提供清洁能源，改变该国电力长期依赖进口的局面；中企承建的马里太阳能示范村、喀麦隆光伏微电网等"小而美"清洁能源项目惠及偏远社区，提升民生福祉。

2021 年 11 月，中非合作论坛第八届部长级会议通过《中非应对气候变化合作宣言》，确定建立新时代中非应对气候变化战略合作伙伴关系。截至 2024 年 9 月，中国与 17 个非洲国家签署 19 份应对气候变化南南合作谅解备忘录。2023 年 9 月，中方在首届非洲气候峰会上宣布实施"非洲光带"项目，帮助非洲 5 万户无电贫困家庭解决用电照明问题，由生态环境部对外合作与交流中心负责实施，与乍得、圣多美和普林西比、马里、布隆迪等 10 个国家开展项目磋商，与其中 5 个国家签署合作谅解备忘录或执行协议。

为遏制北非地区沙漠扩张，非洲国家借鉴中国"三北"防护林工程建设经验，开展"绿色长城"荒漠化治理计划，旨在沿撒哈拉沙漠南缘建设长 8000 公里生态防护林带，治理 1 亿公顷荒漠化土地。中国多次举办非洲国家"绿色长城"建设专题研修班。2017 年，中国科学院新疆生态与地理研究所与泛非"绿色长城"组织秘书处签署合作备忘录，在生态系统监测、土地资源可持续利用、人才培养、技术转让等领域开展合作。至今，双方阐明非洲"绿色长城"建设区域生态环境的时空格局，揭示萨赫勒地区荒漠化动态过程与发展趋势，圈定土地退化、植被受损、风沙危害的敏感区域和重点治理区域，初步建立非洲"绿色长城"荒漠化图集和生态系统管理案例库，开发沙漠城市流沙治理、沙漠公路沙害治理、丘陵地集水造林、退化草地修复等实用治沙技术。

案例 5-3　　　　建设"绿色金砖"，做可持续发展的践行者

2022 年，中国担任金砖轮值主席国时呼吁，共同应对气候变化、加快绿色低碳转型，实现更高质量、更可持续的发展。同年开始，联合国气候变化大会进入"金砖时间"，埃及、阿联酋、阿塞拜疆、巴西等金砖新老成员和"金砖+"国家先后主办气候变化大会，接续推动全球气候治理稳步发展，为以金砖国家为代表的广大"全球南方"国家争取正当权益。同时，新开发银行秉持绿色原则，为金砖国家和其他有需要的"全球南方"国家绿色、可持续发展提供投融资支持。2024 年 10 月，在俄罗斯喀山举行的金砖国家领导人第十六次会晤上，习近平主席就建设"绿色金砖"提出中国主张。

巴西地域辽阔，水电资源集中于北部，电力需求集中在东南部大城市，解决能源分布与负荷分离矛盾的中国方案是建设特高压工程，实现"北电南送"。巴西美丽山±800 千伏特高压直流输电项目是美洲地区电压等级最高、技术最先进的国家级骨干输电项目，实现中国特高压"投资、建设、运营"和"技术、装备、标准"两个一体化全产业链、全价值链协同"走出去"，带动换流变压器、换流阀、直流控保装置等中国制造高端电力装备进入巴西市场，将亚马孙流域丰沛水电以远距离、大容量、低损耗的方式，输送至 2000 多公里外的里约、圣保罗等巴西东南部中心城市，满足超 2200 万人的用电需求。

中国与俄罗斯拥有 4300 多公里共同边界，互为最大邻国，生态环境合作是中俄新时代全面战略协作伙伴关系的重要组成部分。中俄总理定期会晤委员会环保合作分委会机制建立以来，两国跨界水体水质连续多年保持稳定，突发环境事件应急联络机制畅通有效，边境地区生态环境日益改善。中俄深化东北虎、东北豹等珍稀濒危野生动植物和迁徙候鸟保护合作，联合开展森林巡护、东北虎豹监测和生态廊道建设，保障东北虎豹在中俄边界自由迁徙。能源合作一直是中俄务实合作中分量最重、成果最多、范围最广的领域，核能是战略性优先合作方向。江苏田湾核电站是目前全球在运和在建总装机容量最大的核电基地，是中俄迄今最大的技术经济合作项目，其 7 号、8 号机组参考电站为俄罗斯列宁格勒核电站二期工程，采用与俄方合作的 VVER-1200（AES-2006）堆型，单机容量 126.5 万千瓦，是全球最具代表性的三代核电机组。

2023 年 8 月，在金砖国家领导人第十五次会晤上，中国国家电网、国能集团分别与南非电力公司签署战略合作备忘录，积极参与南非可再生能源项目投资运营。南非北开普省日照条件优良、土地开阔平坦，中国电建集团承建的撒哈拉以南非洲首座塔式熔盐光热电站（南非红石 100 兆瓦塔式熔盐光热电站），近 250 米的光塔吸收地面 4 万多面反光镜反射的太阳光，储存的高温液态盐为夜间发电提供动力，实现不间断发电，满足约 20 万户家庭用电需求；南非德阿风电站是中国企业在非洲首个集投资、建设、运营于一体的风电项目，年均发电量 7.6 亿千瓦时，运营方在每根电线杆塔顶端安置栖鸟支架，加强风电场内动植物保护。

埃及政府在"2030 愿景"框架下提出打造区域清洁能源中心战略，中资企业参与建设苏伊士湾 500 兆瓦风电项目、孔翁博 500 兆瓦光伏电站和考姆翁布太阳能光伏电站等清洁能源和绿色发展项目。埃及《消息报》撰文指出，中国企业积极参与埃及绿色能源项目，为推动埃及绿色经济发展发挥重要作用。本班光伏产业园是埃及首个由中资企业承建并参与融资的光伏发电项目，规划建设 40 座太阳能发电厂，总装机容量约 2000 兆瓦，成为世界最大的光伏产业园之一。值得关注的是，中国不仅为埃及提供先进的清洁能源技术和设备，还派遣经验丰富的技术人员，与埃及团队紧密合作，实现本土化运营。

第 2 节　中国推进重点领域绿色国际合作的创新举措、主要成效和典型案例

一　绿色能源合作践行真正的多边主义

中国持续打造市场化、法治化、国际化一流营商环境，积极促进能

源贸易和投资自由化便利化，为外资企业共享中国能源转型红利提供机遇。全面实行准入前国民待遇加负面清单管理制度，除核电站以外的能源领域外商投资准入已全面放开。出台鼓励外商投资产业目录，加大对清洁能源等领域外商投资的政策支持力度。通用电气、碧辟、西门子等跨国公司在中国能源投资规模稳步增加，法国电力集团海上风电项目、上海特斯拉电动汽车制造项目、南京 LG 新能源电池项目等外资项目相继在中国落地，取得良好成效。

2021 年 9 月，习近平主席以视频方式出席第七十六届联合国大会一般性辩论时表示，中国将大力支持发展中国家能源绿色低碳发展，不再新建境外煤电项目。中国与 100 多个国家和地区开展绿色能源合作，共同构筑安全稳定、畅通高效、开放包容、互利共赢的全球能源产业链供应链体系，一大批标志性项目和惠民生的"小而美"项目落地生根，为所在国提供清洁、安全、可靠的能源供应方案。"一带一路"能源合作伙伴关系成员国达 33 个，中国-东盟、中国-阿盟、中国-非盟、中国-中东欧、中国-中亚和亚太经济合作组织可持续能源中心六大区域能源合作平台落地见效。中国发起成立上海合作组织能源部长会议机制，聚焦能源安全、能源转型、能源可及和能源可持续发展议题，为全球能源治理变革贡献中国方案。

中亚国家传统能源储量丰富、可再生能源开发潜力大，普遍有从粗放型、高耗能发展模式向绿色低碳经济转型的强烈需求。2022 年 6 月，在"中国+中亚五国"外长会晤联合声明中，生态、环保、水资源和绿色发展合作是重要内容。2023 年《中国-中亚峰会西安宣言》明确强调拓展绿色经济合作。哈萨克斯坦风力发电的潜能高达 9200 亿千瓦时/年，札纳塔斯 100 兆瓦风电项目由中国电力国际有限公司和哈萨克斯坦维索尔投资公司共同投资，中国水电建设集团国际工程公司承建，是中亚地区最大风电场。三一重能通过"项目开发+本地化制造销售"双轮驱动，在乌兹别克斯坦推进 GW 级绿地项目开发，在哈萨克斯坦打造世界级风电装备智能制造灯塔工厂。中建三局承建的戈布斯坦光伏电站是阿塞拜疆规模最大、电压等级最高的光伏发电工程，发电量达 5 亿千瓦时/年，可供 11 万户家庭使用，减少二氧化碳排放超过 20 万吨/年，阿塞拜疆总统阿利耶夫出席并网发电仪式时，称赞这个项目是"了不起的成就"。

作为全球最大的综合性能源与化工公司，中国石油集团坚定向"油气热电氢"综合能源供应商转型，在努力供给油气能源的同时，全面参与新型能源体系建设。哈萨克斯坦阿克纠宾公司开展油田地面设施"关、停、并、转、减、智"等改造，提高设施设备运行可靠性，降低生产能耗和运行成本，布局绿氢产业，探索碳捕捉和碳交易业务，打造未来利润增长点。中油国际管道公司在中亚天然气管道沿线开展增输降耗、甲烷减排、绿色文化三大工程，建设"绿色管道"，比如，中乌管道公司针对输气量变化制定科学运行方案，实现全线能耗最优，各站场充分利用压缩机组运行产生的排烟高温热量，通过余热锅炉转化为燃料气和冬季供暖热源，减少自耗天然气使用量，借鉴中国治沙经验，建成约 22 万平方米草方格组成的沙漠"绿带"。

中国能建集团拥有国际能源署中国联络办公室、"一带一路"能源合作伙伴关系秘书处等十余个国际合作平台，承办"一带一路"能源部长会、中欧能源技术创新论坛、亚洲能源安全与转型合作论坛等国际能源会议，与德国、英国、芬兰、丹麦、瑞典等国家能源部门和企业开展先进能源技术交流合作。2024 年，中国能建海外新签合同额同比增长 14.5%，沙特、菲律宾市场突破 200 亿元，10 个国别超百亿元，装机规模突破 3 吉瓦，巴基斯坦 SK 水电站、新加坡腾格水库 60 兆瓦浮体光伏项目（世界上最大的内陆漂浮太阳能光伏系统）等"一带一路"标志性工程投产，标志着中国能建从"工程出海"向"中国方案"提供者升级。中国能建强化创新驱动、绿色低碳、数字智能、共享融合为特色的核心竞争力，"揭榜挂帅"攻关压缩空气储能、AI+能源等前沿领域，专利授权超 1800 项，主导制定近 1600 项国家标准和行业标准，通过现金流提升、成本领先、债务管控等专项行动实现海外市场提质增效。

案例 5-4　中国-中东能源合作：为双方可持续发展注入绿色动能

近年来，多个中东国家将可再生能源发展视为国家战略，比如，沙特在"2030 愿景"框架下，全力推进经济多元化和能源转型；阿联酋发布《国家能源战略 2050 更新计划》《2050 年零排放战略倡议》，提出到 2030 年可再生能源装机容量增加两倍以上，2050 年实现温室气体净零排放；阿曼提出"2040 愿景"，加速可再生能源和绿氢项目的投资、推广。从核心部件的精密制造到复杂系统的集成搭建，从电力供应的稳定保障到产业生态的悉心培育，中国技术、中国经验为中东国家能源转型和可持续发展提供重要助力。

在沙特西南部城市吉达以南约 80 公里的大漠深处，81 万多根桩基、500 多万片光伏面板汇成"蓝色海洋"，在阳光照射下反射出耀眼光芒。这是由中国能源建设国际集团、广东火电工程有限公司和西北电力设计院共同承建的阿尔舒巴赫光伏电站，采用当前最先进的 N 形双面光伏组件和平单轴自动跟踪式支架，占地面积约 53 平方千米，总装机容量 2.6 吉瓦，是中东地区规模最大的光伏项目。项目执行最严格的安全与环保标准，带动中国设备、中国技术"走出去"的同时，吸纳 10 余个国家的 50 多家分包商和供应商参与，广泛应用数字化、智能化技术，实现无人化运行，被沙方人员誉为"沙中新能源合作标杆"。预测数据显示，未来 35 年，该电站总发电量约 2822 亿千瓦时，减排二氧化碳近 2.45 亿吨，相当于在沙漠中种下 5.45 亿棵树。沙特财政大臣穆罕默德·贾丹认为，中国在绿色产业和可再生能源领域处于全球领先地位，沙特正努力拓展对华合作方式，学习中国先进技术。

阿联酋连续多年是中国在中东地区第一大出口市场和第二大贸易伙伴。阿联酋驻华大使哈马迪表示，阿中传统友谊跨越千年，双边关系不断深化，在增进国际合作、谋求共赢发展的道路上始终并肩前行。中国机械设备工程股份有限公司承建的艾尔达芙拉光伏电站装机容量 2.1 吉瓦，满足约 20 万户家庭用电需求，年均减少碳排放 240 万吨，使清洁能源在阿联酋总能源结构中的比重提高到 13% 以上。中国电建集团承建的阿联酋风电示范项目年发电量可满足 2.3 万多户家庭需求，每年减少 12 万吨碳排放，验证风能在阿联酋的经济可行性。

中东气候极端，沙尘暴、50℃ 高温是常态，传统燃油车空调开到最大仍像"蒸桑拿"，而中国电动车凭借电池热管理系统和超强制冷技术征服当地消费者。与欧美品牌相比，中国新能源车定价更亲民，令中东消费者在购买决策时更倾向于选择价格更合理、技术不打折的中国新能源车型，2024 年，中国对中东汽车出口增长 46.2%。进一步看，宁德时代为阿联酋 19GWh 储能项目供"芯"，中国电建承包全球最大光储 EPC 工程（阿联酋 RTC2.6 吉瓦光伏+10 吉瓦时储能项目），华为红海储能项目成为沙特标杆，蔚来等多家中国新能源车企在中东建研发中心和定制车型工厂……这种"光储充一体化"模式将中国新能源产业链"搬"到中东，不断巩固中国品牌在该地区的影响力。

二 海洋生态环境保护国际合作全方位开展

中国批准加入《联合国海洋法公约》《防止倾倒废物及其他物质污染海洋的公约》《南极条约》等 30 余项涉海领域多边条约。2017 年，中国在联合国首届海洋可持续发展会议上发出"构建蓝色伙伴关系"倡议，推动"珍爱共有海洋、守护蓝色家园"的国际合作，随后发布《"一带一路"建设海上合作设想》。2021 年 9 月，"积极推动建立蓝色伙伴关系"被全球发展高层对话会确定为中方在全球发展倡议框架下采取的具体举措之一。在 2022 年联合国海洋大会上，中国发布《蓝色伙伴关系原则》，发起"可持续蓝色伙伴关系合作网络"和"蓝色伙伴关系基金"，与 50 多个共建"一带一路"国家和国际组织签署政府间、部门间海洋领域合作协议。

中国牵头建立并运行东亚海洋合作平台、中国-东盟海洋合作中心、国际红树林中心、中国-太平洋岛国应对气候变化合作中心等，承建 APEC 海洋可持续发展中心、"海洋十年"海洋与气候协作中心等，举办"一带一路"国际合作高峰论坛海洋合作论坛、全球滨海论坛等活动。中国与印尼、泰国、马来西亚、柬埔寨、斯里兰卡、巴基斯坦、尼日利亚、莫桑比克、牙买加等多个国家共建海洋联合研究中心、联合实验室、联合观测站等平台，联合他国开展海洋濒危物种研究、黄海环境联合调查、珊瑚礁监测与数据收集、海洋垃圾及微塑料污染防治等项目。中国加强深海生态环境保护，建立库藏量和种类数世界领先的海洋微生物资源库，助力人类深化对深海生物生命过程的认知。中国积极参与应对南北极环境和气候变化挑战国际合作，在第 40 届南极条约协商会议上，中国牵头 10 余个国家联合提出"绿色考察"倡议，获得大会以决议形式通过。

三　中国引领生物多样性保护国际合作

作为《生物多样性公约》第 15 次缔约方大会（COP15）主席国，中国通过"昆蒙框架"实施倡议、昆明生物多样性基金等引领生物多样性保护国际合作。2024 年 1 月，中国更新发布《中国生物多样性保护战略与行动计划（2023～2030 年）》，成为"昆蒙框架"通过后第一个完成更新生物多样性战略与行动计划的发展中国家。COP16 期间，昆明生物多样性基金支持的首批 9 个小额项目获得通过。联合国《生物多样性公约》秘书处官员认为，中国为发展中国家提供可供效仿和学习的模式。

中国先后与 20 个国家的 26 个机构开展大熊猫保护合作，有效提升大熊猫保护研究能力。中国在"南南合作"框架下积极为发展中国家保护生物多样性提供支持，与东盟国家合作实施"生物多样性与生态系统保护合作计划""大湄公河次区域核心环境项目与生物多样性保护走廊计划"等项目，与非洲合作开展野生动物保护行动，支持非洲实施多个相关项目，同南非、肯尼亚等国签署有关保护野生动物合作协议。中国与法国共同发布《中法生物多样性保护和气候变化北京倡议》。中国与俄罗斯、日本等国家展开候鸟保护长期合作，与俄罗斯、蒙古国、老挝、越南等国家共建跨境自然保护地和生态廊道。中国与德国、英国、南非等分别建立生物多样性领域双边合作机制，与日本、韩国建立中日韩三国生物多样性政策对话机制。

四　绿色金融国际合作稳步发展

中国于 2016 年作为 G20 主席国倡导成立"绿色金融研究小组"并发布《2016 年 G20 绿色金融综合报告》，后于 2021 年 G20 财长与央行行长会议上升级为"G20 可持续金融工作组"。2017 年，中国人民银行参与建立中央银行与监管机构绿色金融体系网络，促进金融参与环境和气候管理。2019 年，中国作为创始成员国加入欧盟发起的可持续金融国际平台。2021 年，中国人民银行与欧盟委员会相关部门共同完成《可持续金融共同分类目录报告——减缓气候变化》，就中欧双方绿色金融分类目录开展比较与分析。2018 年，中国人民银行与国际货币基金组织联合建立"中国-国际货币基金组织联合能力建设中心"，为发展中国家政府官员提供金融培训。

2018 年，中国人民银行指导，中国金融学会绿色金融专业委员会与伦敦金融城牵头，联合多家中外机构发起《"一带一路"绿色投资原则》，已有 40 多家来自共建国家的金融机构签署该原则。2023 年 5 月，中国进出口银行联合国家开发银行、工商银行、农业银行、中国银行、建设银行、中国出口信用保险有限公司、丝路基金、中金公司、渣打（中国）、汇丰（中国）等 10 余家金融机构发布《绿色金融支持"一带一路"能源转型倡议》，呼吁有关各方持续加大对共建国家能源绿色低碳转型领域支持力度。

中国金融机构积极参与绿色金融国际合作。比如，中国工商银行参与发起"一带一路"银行间常态化合作机制，发行首支该机制下的绿色债券，与欧洲复兴开发银行、法国东方汇理银行、日本瑞穗银行等共同发布"一带一路"绿色金融指数，承办的"一带一路"银行家圆桌会成为共建国家金融机构经验交流和能力建设的重要平台；中国国家开发银行、中国进出口银行、丝路基金和世界银行国际金融公司共同为巴基斯坦卡洛特水电站提供银团贷款；中国光大集团成立"一带一路"绿色股权投资基金，支持共建国家绿色产业发展。

第 3 节　青年群体参与绿色国际合作的创新举措、主要成效和典型案例

青年创新能力强、国际视野广、专业技术强、适应速度快，是绿色国际合作的主力军、生力军和攻坚队。同时，青年正处于人生发展的起

步期，面临逆全球化、社会竞争等系列挑战，参与绿色发展，发掘人生价值，成为各国青年的迫切需求。

一　青年参与绿色基建国际合作的新进展

中国青年建造者广泛开展绿色技术研发与海外市场推广应用，降低基建碳排放和能耗，积极向全球传递绿色、减碳、韧性为鲜明特色的绿色发展的青年信心和担当。

中铁二局尼泊尔 KK 公路项目被尼泊尔财政部和亚洲开发银行授予"最佳环境保护监控团队"荣誉称号。尼泊尔 KK 公路项目为既有道路改造项目，由于中国和尼泊尔的相关环保要求存在差异，为此，中方项目部青年工程师做了大量工作，与当地政府、监理机构共同编制施工环境评估报告，制定环境保护、水土污染防治及文物保护制度，成立专门的环保管理小组，聘请尼泊尔籍青年工程师参与环保管理。正是因为这些细致准备，项目自开工以来，多次接受尼泊尔各级政府和环保部门检查，均获得好评。

中国-巴新友谊学校·布图卡学园项目位于巴布亚新几内亚首都莫尔斯比港市，是中国与巴新友谊的见证、巴新现代化教育的缩影。项目由深圳市政府援建，由中建科工公司采用绿色装配式智能建筑设计和绿色施工技术总承包，解决当地 3000 多名中小学生上学难问题。为应对高温多雨气候，中国青年工程师设计被动式节能系统，室内外空气循环系统结合大屋顶、底层架空等当地传统建筑文化设计，节电 20% 以上。为实现绿色"降本增益"，项目还采用中建科工青年科技团队自主研发的"GS-Building"钢结构装配式建筑体系，以降低粉尘、有害气体等的排放，并节约建筑耗材。项目公司还为当地青年提供就业岗位和建筑、电气、水暖等方面的职业培训，为当地发展带来为之计久远的中国智慧。

埃塞俄比亚首都亚的斯亚贝巴河岸绿色发展项目是中国第一个对外援建公园类项目，由中交一公局集团承建，集景观、建筑、市政、道路、水利、园林于一体。项目青年团队建成非洲功能最多、面积最大的城市综合广场——谢格尔公园友谊广场，采用无害化、低影响石方爆破技术，避免高噪声、高扬尘、高振动等影响，将中国温室培育技术和树木移植标准引入埃塞俄比亚，大型珍贵苗木全冠移植，成活率达 100%，采用中国先进的风积沙防渗毯进行湖底封闭，有效解决人工湖渗漏水问题，同时有利于人工湖微生态环境的形成。岸边水草丰美，湖内鱼类成群，有近百种鸟类栖居于此，埃塞俄比亚总理阿比多次向国内外推介这一"美丽工程"。谢格尔公园及周边配套设施向公众开放后，很快成为当地最受欢迎的旅游目的地。

受限于地理条件，马尔代夫首都大马累地区的生活垃圾必须先通过垃圾转运站进行收集，再船运至垃圾岛进行焚烧和填埋处理，但原有的垃圾转运站场地狭小、功能单一，不具备集装箱运输等现代化转运能力。马累岛和维利马累岛垃圾转运站是马尔代夫环保部重要的民生工程，由亚洲开发银行和马尔代夫财政部出资，中建八局承建。马尔代夫雨季漫长且降雨量大，施工环境恶劣，高盐高湿，高温高辐射，资源匮乏，劳动力组织困难，中国青年工程师迎难而上，在主砌体交接部位采用硅酮胶密封，确保砌体完成后不开裂、不渗水；所有建筑屋面结构中采用防水外加剂，提升混凝土品质和综合性能；钢结构防腐防锈采用氟碳喷涂，厚度达到 C5-M 英标最高标准；采用结构架空，减少昂贵回填，增加业主使用空间；引入中国生产的双层隔音玻璃，解决转运站运行时产生的巨大噪音问题。

中国电力建设集团承建的红海公用基础设施项目位于沙特西部的塔布克省，是世界上第一个融合多能源互补整合的大型商业化公用设施项目，包括光伏、风电、储能、内燃机发电、电网、海水淡化、供水管网、废水处理、污水管网、固体废物处理等模块。沙漠地区使用光伏发电好处是日照充足，缺点是风沙大，沙尘会影响光电转换效率，中国青年科技团队开发的自动清扫机器人定期清理光伏板上的沙尘，只需打开手机应用程序操作，机器人就开始工作。在海岛间的输电网络建设中，中国青年科技团队开发的海底自动机器人下水作业，采取严格的环境保护措施，最大程度减少对海洋生物影响。中国青年工程师建设由两片芦苇丛和一片莎草地组成的人工湿地（生物"污水处理厂"），生活污水经过预处理后，先经第一片芦苇丛滤去大颗粒杂质，然后泵入第二片芦苇丛，待重金属等物质被吸附，最后在重力作用下进入莎草地，再次过滤后流入蓄水池。

二　青年参与绿色能源国际合作的新进展

中资企业青年团队积极对接发展中国家的长远发展规划和愿景，依托各国资源禀赋，充分发挥在可再生能源、节能环保、清洁生产等领域优势，运用中国技术、产品、经验等，推动绿色能源合作蓬勃发展。

乌干达是世界人均电力消费最低的国家之一，过去全国只有 15% 左右的人口使用国家电网电力。乌干达最大水电站——卡鲁玛水电站由中国进出口银行参与融资、中国水利水电建设集团承建，设计总装机容量 600 兆瓦，2024 年初全部机组并网发电，乌干达全国电力装机总量增加近 50%，每年节约原煤 131 万吨，减少二氧化碳排放 348 万吨，电价降低 17.5%。乌干达总统穆塞韦尼表示："卡鲁玛水电站极大提升乌干达发电能力，加快工业化步伐，进而吸引更多外国投资者。"水电站地处平原，若采用中高坝地上发电厂房的传统形式，水电站所占区域及大坝储水后淹没区会对当地生态环境造成不可逆的破坏，因而中国青年工程师采取"地下厂房+长尾水隧洞"的建设方案。由于水电站紧邻动植物资源丰富的穆奇森瀑布国家森林公园，中国青年工程师充分考虑环境敏感区保护，地面大坝采用低坝设计，缩短水电站储水后新增河道淹没长度，设计专门的生态鱼道以保证鱼类生长繁殖，减少对坝区动植物的影响。

锡尔河 1500 兆瓦燃气联合循环电站是乌兹别克斯坦近年以独立电站模式开发的首个大型燃气发电项目，设计装机容量约占乌兹别克斯坦电力装机总量的 8%，由中建五局参与建设。为保障高效稳定的电力输出，项目青年技术团队采用目前世界上燃烧温度最高、单体功率最大、效率最高的 9H 级燃气轮机，全力做好不同系统间的接口工作，以燃机为中心积极推动各辅助系统的深化设计和设备生产制造，实现项目水处理系统、天然气增压系统等设计参数均居世界前列。锡尔河州是乌兹别克斯坦重要农业产地，为保护项目所在地的灌溉用水和饮用水源，项目青年技术团队设计"废水零排放"方案，采用膜式反渗透装置附加强制蒸发池技术，每年直接减少约 200 万吨的废水排放，避免对周边土壤和水源造成污染。乌兹别克斯坦总统米尔济约耶夫出席投产仪式时表示，中国企业高效推进项目履约建设，极大缓解当地电力短缺困境，对提高当地人民生活条件、推动经济社会发展具有重要意义。

波黑伊沃维克风电项目是中国-中东欧国家领导人峰会成果清单首个落地的新能源项目、波黑首个以外商特许经营方式投资建设的最大能源项目。项目由中国电建集团成都勘测设计研究院青年团队负责从工程设计、设备采购、风机安装、电气安装到调试和试运行的全流程，直至项目移交。项目青年团队应用符合欧盟标准的中国先进风电技术，"中国制造"设备占比超 90%。项目所在地还是波黑野马群的栖息地，项目青年团队与当地野马保护协会合作保护栖息地，改善野马生活环境。

越南拥有丰富的光照资源，越南政府大力支持太阳能发电，中国光伏产业具有领先优势，中越光伏合作促进当地经济社会"因绿而兴"。2023 年 12 月，在赴河内对越南进行国事访问之际，习近平主席在越南《人民报》发表题为《构建具有战略意义的中越命运共同体 开启携手迈向现代化的新篇章》的署名文章，指出"中国企业在越南建成海外最大的光伏产业集群，投资建设的光伏和风能电站为越南的能源转型发展作出积极贡献"。天合光能股份有限公司自 2014 年开始布局越南，建成两家光伏零部件和模块工厂，参与投资多个越南光伏发电项目，成为越南最大的太阳能电池板制造商之一。越南中山光伏电站坐落于越南庆和省，天合光能项目青年团队克服台风登陆、高温高湿环境等不利因素，创新采用旋转支架、双面双玻组件、组串式逆变器等技术，优化发电效率，每年可生产 6.74 万兆瓦时清洁电力，减少约 5.3 万吨二氧化碳排放。

澜湄区域电网互联互通项目由中国南方电网公司投资建设运营，初步形成区域内电力余缺互济格局，"以（电）网带（电）源"降低区域内电力资源的开发强度，为绿色电网建设提供低碳转型创新方案。澜湄国家水电出力特性与中国受入省相似，中国青年工程师创新"丰枯置换"电力互济模式，将用电负荷特性与水电出力特性匹配程度高、对清洁电力需求大的粤港澳大湾区纳入调剂范围，通过更大范围的丰、枯水期"电量置换"，实现清洁能源优化配置。南方电网发起成立澜湄区域电力技术标准促进会，项目建设采用难度更大的中国绿色电网标准，最大限度保护澜湄区域生态环境。

案例 5-5　　　　**克罗地亚塞尼风电项目：两国青年共筑中欧**
绿色能源合作样板工程

在第三届"一带一路"国际合作高峰论坛民心相通专题论坛上，由中国北方国际合作股份有限公司投资、建设和运营的克罗地亚塞尼风电项目，以音乐舞台剧方式，向各国政要嘉宾、民间组织和媒体代表分享。作为克罗地亚最大规模的新能源发电项目，塞尼风电项目年平均发电超3000 小时，贡献约 5.3 亿千瓦时绿色电力，减少二氧化碳排放约 46 万吨。克罗地亚总理普连科维奇赞誉，塞尼风电项目为本国清洁能源生产、绿色转型提供重要助力，更是欧盟与中国绿色能源合作的样板工程。

作为山地风电项目，项目青年管理团队始终将生态保护作为重中之重，在施工过程中严格遵循当地及欧盟环境保护法规，像呵护自己家园一样呵护当地生态环境。"发现野生动物出没要自觉加以保护；在动物交配、产羔、孵卵的季节，尽量减少人为活动惊扰；如发现受伤、病残、饥饿、受困、迷途的野生动物，应及时报告有关部门进行救助。"这段看似出自动物保护组织工作手册的文字，却是塞尼风电项目施工指南着重强调的行为准则。

项目青年管理团队与本地企业深度合作，先后有 50 多家当地分包商、供应商和服务商参与项目建设，涵盖设备供货、大件运输、土建施工、风机吊装、动态调试和并网测试等全流程，增强克罗地亚企业在欧洲市场的竞争力。北方国际青年科技团队研发的叶片举升装置不仅圆满完成运输巨型风机任务，相较于租用欧洲设备，为项目节省成本约 280 万美元。当地合作伙伴对中国设备的优越性能赞不绝口，在巴尔干地区其他风电项目正积极推广使用。

海外项目如何克服文化差异，是中资企业"走出去"面临的普遍难题。对塞尼项目而言，中国与欧洲风电项目建设模式不同，克罗地亚本地公司对中国设备不熟悉，人员语言沟通障碍、企业管理制度差异等，都对项目的成本和工期有巨大影响。为解决文化差异，塞尼项目中国青年团队积极参加社会公益活动和社区特色活动，增进了解当地风俗习惯和人文风情，用行动争取当地民众、政府、克罗地亚籍员工对企业肯定，进而在价值观念、思维方式、行为习惯等方面达成共识。

三 青年参与绿色交通国际合作的新进展

中资企业青年团队强化交通基础设施建设领域的高质量合作，满足合作国人民"道路通，百业兴"的期待。同时，积极推动绿色低碳交通技术与经验分享，帮助合作国加强交通减排能力建设，让绿色交通成果更好惠及各国人民。

孟加拉国由于人口密集、水网密布、经济落后等原因，成为全球交通最落后的国家之一。由中国路桥工程有限公司承建的南亚地区首条水下隧道——孟加拉国卡纳普里河底隧道项目正式通车。项目部青年建造团队充分考虑外围公共安全及地理位置和地势特点，选择在原地面的基础上吹填加固，并配套建设污水处理设施，有效处理项目产生的生活污水。项目部设立由青年工程师领衔的绿色混凝土实验室，通过数据分析、仪器检测，精密调整主体结构使用的混凝土配比，提高混凝土安全使用寿命，减少混凝土浪费和二次污染。项目部青年团队引进中交集团自主研发的节能高效环境友好型设备——泥水平衡式盾构机进行施工，自动化程度高，一次成洞，不受气候影响，在加快施工进度的同时，减少施工对环境的扰动。

由中国交通建设集团承建的加纳特码新集装箱码头项目，可以提高特码港货物吞吐量，巩固特码港作为西非大港的优势地位，为加纳及周边国家经贸发展注入新动力。加纳靠近几内亚湾，是海龟的重要栖息地。项目建设期间，为保护当地海龟的繁殖，中方青年团队在施工区布置气体、粉尘微粒、噪声等环境监测仪器，设立 30 余个监测点，实现施工全过程的环境管控。在施工区域附近的沙滩上，中国青年团队仿造海龟孵化环境，配套建造新的海龟孕育中心，完成 1.7 万只海龟的集中孵化。小海龟孵化后，中方青年志愿者还在当地另选一处海滩，由专家评估后将其统一放生。

2024 年 11 月，中国国家主席习近平同秘鲁总统博鲁阿尔特在利马总统府以视频方式共同出席钱凯港开港仪式，两国元首下达指令，宣布钱凯港"开港"，从南美洲出口至亚洲市场的货物运输时间从 35 天缩短至 25 天，物流成本大幅降低。钱凯港位于秘鲁首都利马附近，属于天然深水港，由中国港湾-中交四航局联合体承建，是中国远洋海运集团在南美首个控股绿地项目，是"一带一路"倡议在拉美的标志性项目和中国企业在秘鲁实施的第一个大型交通基础设施项目。中资企业青年团队将"让海水更清、天空更蓝、动物更亲、钱凯更美"设定为钱凯港项目的建设目标。由于施工现场紧邻一处天然湿地，为保护湿地环境及生物多样性，项目青年团队围绕世界湿地日、世界地球日等开展主题活动，和当地市政厅、海事局、社区等合作对周边湿地环境进行维护，设置环保标志、标牌，邀请当地民众及青年了解、学习和保护湿地生态，取得显著成效。

由中国路桥工程有限公司承建的塞内加尔第一条城市快速公交线路——达喀尔快速公交系统项目是塞内加尔在《巴黎气候协定》承诺框架下实施的首个助力减排的交通运输项目，获得全球绿色气候基金融资支持，运营的电动公交车由中国中车集团提供，所有车站和车辆维保基地均配有光伏发电设施，为电动公交车续航提供坚实保障。项目部中国青年管理团队重视车站周边绿化建设，施工中设置防护网保护沿线绿植，实施"补偿性造林计划"，对因施工移除树木进行登记，每移除 1 棵树，后期补种 2 棵新树。为应对当地雨季洪涝，项目部青年建造团队改造达喀尔地下 17.5 公里的排污管道，新建 40 公里排水管网。

2024 年卡塔尔亚洲杯期间，一辆辆五彩斑斓、满载各参赛球队或球迷的新能源大巴车不时驶过，这支中国"绿色军团"继 2022 年卡塔尔世界杯之后再次成为国际大赛"主角"。中国客车在卡塔尔公交车市场的占有率超过 80%，而在新能源客车领域，中国企业更是成为卡塔尔唯一的供应商。针对卡塔尔温度高、风沙大的环境特点，中国新能源汽车厂商青年科技团队专门开发适配车型，空调设计采用智能温控算法，车辆动力电池采用独立、高效的液冷系统，不仅保证车辆续航能力更长，而且提高电池安全性和使用寿命。适配车型还配备泥沙防护装置，提升电机对坑洼、砂石路面的适应性，各国球迷对于中国新能源客车的普遍印象是舒适、安静和快速。中资企业将中国新能源汽车的成熟技术、供应链服务能力和商业模式带到卡塔尔，建立本地化运营体系，实施校企合作、人才交流项目，为卡塔尔培养新能源青年技术人才，实现由单一的产品出口向产品、技术、人才与管理体系共同输出的产业布局升级。

第 4 节　携手共建美丽地球家园：中国加强绿色国际合作的经验及对发展中国家的启示

一　参与和引领全球绿色转型进程

中国的发展实践充分证明，绿色与创新是人口大国在资源环境约束条件下推进现代化的新路径，超越对外掠夺和依附发展的老路，通过科技创新提升生产效率和资源利用率，通过教育和知识迭代释放人的发展潜力，以质量变革、效率变革与动力变革系统性破解资源、人口、环境的约束。进一步看，秉持人类命运共同体理念，中国坚定落实《联合国气候变化框架公约》，以积极建设性姿态参与全球气候谈判议程，为《巴黎协定》达成和落实作出历史性贡献。提高国家自主贡献力度，将完成全球最高碳排放强度降幅，用全球历史上最短时间实现碳达峰到碳中和，充分体现负责任大国的担当。中国还积极参与海洋污染治理、生物多样性保护、塑料污染治理等领域国际规则制定，推动构建公平合理、合作共赢的全球环境气候治理体系。提出和落实全球发展倡议，加强南南合作以及同周边国家合作，在力所能及范围内为发展中国家提供支持，成为绿色发展国际合作与全球生态文明建设的重要参与者、贡献者和引领者。

二　加强政策交流和务实合作

中国积极拓展双多边对话合作渠道，加强绿色发展领域的合作平台建设，大力宣传中国绿色低碳转型的成效和经验。加强绿色投资和贸易合作，鼓励绿色低碳产品进出口。加强绿色技术合作，鼓励高校、科研机构与外方开展学术交流，积极参与国际大科学工程。加强绿色标准与合格评定国际合作，推动与主要贸易伙伴在碳足迹等规则方面衔接互认。

　　尤其是在绿色丝绸之路建设上，中国坚持发展合作共商、项目实施共建、发展成果共享，坚持高标准、可持续、惠民生的目标，不断提升对共建国家绿色发展的支持力度。中国坚定提高境外项目环境可持续性，在满足共建国家环境标准的基础上，鼓励应用国际通行规则标准或中国更严格标准。通过与共建国家开展绿色民生项目，提升所在国在就业、环境提升、应对气候变化、防灾减灾等领域的发展水平。绿色丝绸之路建设与各国可持续发展议程相互衔接和促进，在应对气候变化、环境保护、能源转型等领域合作具有很强的可行性，绿色丝绸之路成为推广习近平生态文明思想的重要国际平台。

第 5 节　世界现代化视域下进一步推进绿色国际合作的对策建议

一　以高水平国际合作推动绿色低碳转型

　　推动在双边、多边合作中落实全球发展倡议，强化共建人类命运共同体的共同责任。支持发展中国家专家在国际组织担任职务，参与国际绿色治理。推动发展中国家政府部门、社会组织、公益机构、智库等参与"一带一路"绿色发展国际联盟、绿色低碳专家网络，共建绿色国际合作政策对话和沟通平台、环境知识和信息平台、绿色技术交流与转让平台。坚持公平原则、共同但有区别的责任原则和各自能力原则，全面落实应对气候变化国际合作项目，建立青年群体广泛参与的全球气候治理体系。推动公益组织、行业商协会设立绿色发展专业机构，开展人文活动、政策解读、业务咨询、人才培训、成果展览、权益维护等公共服务。办好"一带一路"绿色创新大会，在广交会、进博会、服贸会、数博会等国际展会机制下举办绿色发展主题的对话交流、创新大赛、项目路演等活动。建设光伏产业对话交流机制，推动中国光伏企业构建属地化人才体系。

二 坚定支持发展中国家提升绿色发展能力

发挥"一带一路"科技创新行动计划、"一带一路"可持续发展技术专项合作计划等机制作用，支持发展中国家科学家、企业家、创业者等依托环境技术交流与转移基地、绿色技术示范推广基地、绿色科技园区、"一带一路"联合实验室、"一带一路"技术转移中心等平台，引领低碳、节能、节水、环保等环境友好型技术研发、推广和成果转化。在"一带一路"科技交流大会等科技人文交流活动中扩展绿色发展主题研讨会、圆桌会、路演会等项目。扩大绿色丝路使者计划的教育培训、项目合作等服务质效，引导中国高校增加生态环境相关专业的留学生培养规模，帮助发展中国家高校、科研院所搭建绿色发展人才培养体系，加强环境管理人员和专业技术人才互动交流。发挥丝路智库等新型智库作用，总结、传播和推广绿色发展中国经验，讲好绿色发展中国故事。

第6章
结语"绿水青山就是金山银山"的价值意蕴：
绿色发展共建人与自然生命共同体

　　绿色是生命的象征、大自然的底色，良好生态环境是美好生活的基础、人民共同的期盼。绿色发展是顺应自然、促进人与自然和谐共生的发展，是用最少资源环境代价取得最大经济社会效益的发展，是高质量、可持续的发展，已经成为各国普遍共识。在习近平新时代中国特色社会主义思想指引下，中国坚持绿水青山就是金山银山的理念，坚定不移走生态优先、绿色发展之路，促进经济社会发展全面绿色转型，建设人与自然和谐共生的现代化，创造举世瞩目的生态奇迹和绿色发展奇迹。作为世界上最大的发展中国家，中国秉持人类命运共同体理念，坚定践行多边主义，提出全球发展倡议、全球安全倡议，深化务实合作，积极参与全球环境与气候治理，为共建清洁美丽地球家园贡献中国智慧、中国力量。

　　绿色低碳转型是一场广泛而深刻的经济社会系统性变革，是一项长期的战略性任务，需要在新时代新战略的指引下稳中求进、久久为功。中国共产党第二十次全国代表大会擘画中国未来发展蓝图，描绘绿水长流、青山常在、空气常新的美丽中国画卷。《中共中央关于进一步全面深化改革　推进中国式现代化的决定》提出，聚焦建设美丽中国，加快经济社会发展全面绿色转型，健全生态环境治理体系，推进生态优先、节约集约、绿色低碳发展，促进人与自然和谐共生。

　　为此，提出如下四大建议：

一是进一步推进高水平生态环境保护。接续打好蓝天保卫战，确保工业企业全面稳定达标排放，强化挥发性有机物和扬尘污染综合治理，督促空气质量未达标的县区编制实施大气环境质量限期达标方案，继续推进 PM2.5 和臭氧协同控制，在跨省毗邻地区建立空气治理改善先行示范区。接续打好碧水保卫战，统筹好上下游、左右岸、干支流、城市和乡村，实施"一河（湖）一策"，充分发挥河（湖）长制作用，强化溯源整治、截污控源和污水（泥）资源化利用，落实地表水与地下水协同防治，持续打好长江保护修复攻坚战、黄河生态保护治理攻坚战，健全横向流域生态保护补偿机制。健全陆海统筹、多方共治的海洋生态环境治理体系，以沿海乡镇为单元持续开展入海排污口"查、测、溯、治"，实施渔港"一港一策"污染防治，推广生态健康养殖模式，建设数据共享的涉海工程项目和海洋倾废监督系统，实施海湾、河口、岸滩等区域塑料垃圾专项清理行动。将"无废城市"建设纳入乡镇（街道）、村（社区）等基层部门污染防治攻坚战考核内容，依法依规将固体废物产生、利用、处置纳入企业信用评价体系，推广绿色建材和建筑垃圾再生利用产品，推动生活垃圾分类网点与废旧物资回收网点"两网融合"，建设危险废物环境监管"五全"体系。

二是进一步优化绿色发展空间格局。构建以自然资源合理利用为导向的国土空间保护开发新格局，开展国土空间规划实施监测评估，确保现状耕地应划尽划、应保尽保，发展多中心、组团式的城市空间形态，引导中小城市紧凑布局，推进全域土地综合整治，建设宜居宜业和美乡村。统筹推进山水林田湖草沙海一体化保护修复，科学部署、持续实施山水工程，分类有序推进绿色矿山建设，以"陆海统筹+江海联动+一湾（岛）一策"推进美丽海湾建设。健全生物多样性调查、监测、评估和保护体系。制定国家公园法，推进国家公园治沙、治水、治山全要素治理。推广沙障治沙、光伏治沙、覆膜保水、灌木截秆等沙漠治理先进技术，宣传弘扬"三北精神"、塞罕坝精神。建立县域生态资源数据库和生态产品清单，引导自然资源资产确权登记、设权赋能、布局合理和配置高效，创新自然资源权益交易、生态产品抵押贷款、生态保护补偿、自然资源资产损害赔偿、自然资源资产账户、绿色产品期货期权、绿色保险等价值实现路径。

三是进一步推进绿色低碳转型高质量发展。将绿色理念和节约要求融入文明公约、企业规章、团体章程等经济社会规则，形成崇尚生态文明的浓郁社会氛围。引导中小企业执行绿色采购指南，将碳足迹要求纳入公共部门采购，推动规上企业建立绿色供应链。推动地方政府、市场主体发放权益型绿色消费券、绿色积分，鼓励消费者购买和"以旧换新"绿色商品。重点区域同步实施煤炭消费总量控制、散煤替代和清洁能源发展，推进二氧化碳捕集利用与封存项目建设，统筹水电开发和生态保护，推进水风光一体化开发，积极发展分布式光伏、分散式风电，推动氢能"制储输用"全链条发展，加强清洁能源基地、调节性资源和输电通道的衔接协同，加快微电网、虚拟电厂、源网荷储一体化项目等智能电网建设。促进传统产业普及推广清洁生产技术装备，健全落后产能退出机制。以科技创新、绿色智造和制造服务为驱动，融合发展战略性新兴产业、高技术产业、节能环保产业、现代高效农业和现代服务业。鼓励合同能源管理、合同节水管理、环境污染第三方治理、碳排放管理等创新发展。加强绿色低碳技术知识产权创造、保护、运用。引导互联网平台绿色低碳发展，带动上下游市场主体提高减碳能力。推动绿色金融产品服务创新。

四是进一步推进高水平绿色国际合作。推动在双边、多边合作中落实全球发展倡议，支持发展中国家政府部门、社会组织、公益机构、智库等参与"一带一路"绿色发展国际联盟、绿色低碳专家网络。全面落实应对气候变化国际合作项目，建立青年群体广泛参与的全球气候治理体系。推动公益组织、行业商协会设立绿色发展专业机构，开展人文活动、政策解读、业务咨询、人才培训、成果展览、权益维护等公共服务。办好"一带一路"绿色创新大会，在广交会、进博会、服贸会、数博会等国际展会机制下举办绿色发展主题的对话交流、创新大赛、项目路演等活动。建设光伏产业对话交流机制。支持发展中国家科学家、企业家、创业者参与环境技术交流与转移基地、绿色技术示范推广基地、"一带一路"联合实验室、"一带一路"技术转移中心等项目合作。扩大绿色丝路使者计划的教育培训、项目合作等服务质效，引导中国高校增加生态环境相关专业的留学生培养规模，帮助发展中国家高校、科研院所搭建绿色发展人才培养体系。发挥丝路智库等新型智库作用，总结、传播和推广绿色发展中国经验，讲好绿色发展中国故事。

专题报告

北京市门头沟区：
绿色发展绘就首都西大门壮美新画卷

2024 年 10 月，联合国《生物多样性公约》第十六次缔约方大会发布第二届"生物多样性魅力城市"名单，北京市门头沟区入选"自然城市"名单，成为北京首个入选的行政区。门头沟区位于北京西部，是首都生态涵养区和首都发展重要门户，拥有森林、灌丛、草甸、河流、湖泊、湿地等自然或半自然生态系统类型，孕育着丰富的生物多样性，保存着太行山狭窄森林植被带的重要种质资源。在《京津冀协同发展规划纲要》明确的京津冀协同发展"一核两翼四区多节点"空间布局中，门头沟区是"四区"中"西北部生态涵养区"的重要组成部分，多年来与相邻的河北省张家口市、保定市共同守护首都西部的生态屏障。

打造灾后重建的绿色转型发展新引擎

2023 年 11 月，习近平总书记来到门头沟区考察灾后恢复重建工作并作出重要指示。按照"一年基本恢复、三年全面提升、长远高质量发展"的总体思路，门头沟区构建"1+13+X"灾后重建规划体系，其中，"1"指灾后恢复重建整体规划，"13"指平急两用设施与应急救援、综合防灾与韧性城市、防洪及河道蓝线等 13 项专项规划，"X"指镇街层面灾后重建规划。在推进灾后重建工作中，门头沟区着力提升城乡安全韧性：立足"防"，完工 71 个水利工程，实施雨水"清管行动"，建设京西哨兵预警指挥调度平台和永定河官厅山峡现代化雨水情监测预报体系；立足"抗"，开展应急管理部全国基层综合减灾示范试点建设，打造保险业服务防灾减灾救灾体系建设示范区；立足"救"，构建预警提级响应机制，细化防汛预案和应急处置。

进而，门头沟区确定"12345"总体发展思路：锚定"一个目标"——高水平建设首都西大门，打造"绿水青山门头沟""诗情画意门头沟""专精特新门头沟""安全韧性门头沟""团结奋进门头沟"，抓住灾后恢复重建和绿色高质量转型发展"两条主线"，坚持生态立区、文化兴区、科技强区"三大发展战略"，推进暖心为民行动、安全韧性行动、提升转型行动、凝心聚力行动"四大行动"，实施涵盖干部能力提升、人才队伍培育、营商环境优化、地区形象塑造和基层治理固本的"五大基础工程"，聚力谱写中国式现代化门头沟新篇章。

建成"北京大氧吧"和"京西后花园"

北京曾是华北豹的故乡，然而自 1992 年以后，北京 30 多年没有豹活动的确切信息。为让消失数十年的华北豹再度回到北京的"家"，门头沟区依托有"华北天然动植物园"之称的百花山国家级自然保护区，启动"迎豹回家"计划，编制《门头沟区生物多样性保护》白皮书，发布"迎豹回家"Logo 和吉祥物，提升市民生物多样性保护素养，目前自然保护区已具备华北豹生存的完整生境。

门头沟区以流域水系为单元，一体化推动整沟、整村、整镇小流域综合治理和清洁小流域提质增效，配合开展永定河生态补水，增强山区林地的生态韧性，地下水位最大回升点达到 23.35 米，234 处泉眼目前有 106 处实现在流。巩固提升国家森林城市建设成果，林草覆盖率达全市最高的 93.9%，森林碳汇量、林木蓄积量、生态服务价值持续增加，生态环境质量指数保持"优"等级。

门头沟区努力探索"GDP 和 GEP 同部署、双增长，生态投入和生态富民同发力、两保障"的新发展格局，GEP 测算达 307 亿元。京西古道沉浸式生态小镇项目位于王平镇西王平村，规划面积 493.55 公顷，保护利用古村肌理，科技赋能环境体验，植入乡村旅游、文化传承、教育研学、健康休闲等主题，打造集度假宿集、文旅商街、亲子乐园、山地户外于一体的京西古道文旅目的地和北京市首个特定地域单元生态产品价值实现实验区。

大力发展绿色高端产业

门头沟区聚焦公共营商环境与垂直营商环境"双核驱动"，围绕市场、法治、政务、人才、生活服务等核心维度，完善产业政策，构建系统性、精准化、全链条的区域营商环境生态，大力发展人工智能、超高清数字视听、心血管领域医疗药械等长安街西延线专精特新绿色产业集群，入驻人工智能企业超220家、专精特新中小企业超160家。

门头沟区承建大模型赋能创新中心、北京算法登记服务中心、北京国际大数据交易所数据资产服务中心，建成全市规模最大的500P国产自主可控人工智能算力集群，打响"京西智谷"IP。深化AI+4K/8K+5G技术运用，与央视网共建AGI联合研究中心，引进华为计算视听创新中心，打造内容审核大模型和"潭柘智空"文生视频大模型，全市首个气象AI人"灵西"和政务服务AI人"门小政"惊艳亮相。建设国家医学中心阜外医院西山园区，发挥百洋医药集团科研成果转化基地作用，引入医疗药械CRO企业，盘活老旧厂房，为重点药械企业打造绿色制造空间。

保护、开发、利用自然和文化资源是门头沟区可持续发展的重点。结合灾后生态修复，深入挖掘红色文化、民间民俗、古村、古道、史前文化、长城文化、农耕文化、琉璃文化等文化资源，实施东胡林遗址、"潭戒"文物区、沿河城长城、"辽白瓷"等保护行动，打造潭柘生态文化旅游区、妙峰山民俗文化旅游区、百花山自然风景区等样板景区，建成串联山水资源、景区景点、古道村落等的步道系统，形成妙峰山徒步线、京西古道穿越线、历史山水穿越线、长城徒步穿越线等精品徒步和骑行线路。2024年，全区19家A级及以上旅游景区实现营业收入1.5亿元，同比增长27%，累计接待游客210.3万人次，同比增长36.4%。

作为北京文物古迹、文化遗产最丰富的区域之一，门头沟区拥有不可移动文物556项，居全市第一。2024年，全区各级非遗项目达145项，潭柘寺镇、斋堂镇获评北京民间艺术之乡，"非遗传承赋能乡村振兴"被文旅部评为全国文化和旅游赋能乡村振兴优秀案例。建设"诗画乡村"是培育乡村绿色新质生产力的关键一招，门头沟区针对乡村治理"红雁"、引领发展"头雁"、青年后备"雏雁"等文化能人分类开展培训，支持入乡、返乡创业者打造京西古道、五新斋堂等特色题材的"诗画乡村"示范片区。

绘就首都西大门壮美新画卷

立足生态涵养区功能定位和"高水平建设首都发展重要门户"使命职责，门头沟区应进一步携手京冀毗邻地区，共同实施中国山水工程、京津风沙源治理等重点项目，开展生态环境保护修复跨区域联防联治；做好首都西部守山护林保水工作，以"迎豹回家"工程为抓手，创建世界生物圈保护区；共建京西旅游发展联盟、京西古道文旅走廊，打磨京西文旅商康养精品线路和特色产品，形成京津冀文旅新增长极；依托首都丰富的科技、人才、金融等资源优势，探索经济区与行政区适度分离改革，破解土地要素瓶颈，打造京西地区绿色高端产业链供应链。

上海市黄浦区：
建设人与自然和谐共生的社会主义现代化国际大都市核心引领区

2025 年 3 月，国家发展改革委办公厅印发第二批国家碳达峰试点名单，确定 27 个城市和园区作为试点，黄浦区作为上海市唯一区县纳入国家试点名单。黄浦区是上海市中心城区核心区，以上海的母亲河——黄浦江命名，作为上海的"心脏、窗口、名片"，是上海的经济、行政、文化中心，承载上海 700 余年的建城史和 180 余年的开埠史，见证上海国际大都市的发展变化。

中心城区绿色低碳发展示范先行

2024 年 12 月，黄浦区发布《关于全面推进美丽黄浦建设打造人与自然和谐共生的社会主义现代化国际大都市核心引领区的行动方案》，明确 2027 年、2035 年和本世纪中叶三个时间节点的绿色低碳发展目标，进而在开发保护并重、低碳转型提速、污染防治攻坚、生态城区建设、生态系统保护、安全底线守护、生态文化厚植、绿色数治创新、多元治理构建等方面提出任务举措。2025 年 3 月，黄浦区政府 13 个部门联合发布《黄浦区可再生能源发展行动方案》，这是上海首个区级可再生能源系统性发展纲领。

黄浦区碳达峰碳中和平台构建融合建筑能耗监测、虚拟电厂、碳普惠、能源审计、能效提升等的数据底座，开发数据智能分析与资料理解抽取服务，结合数字孪生技术打造业务管理平台，推出碳普惠平台、碳地图小程序等应用场景，形成以数据汇聚、数据应用、数据普惠为核心驱动力的"双碳"治理新模式，纳入近 300 幢大型公共建筑和机关办公建筑的能耗监测数据，以及 210 幢商业建筑虚拟电厂的运营数据。

值得关注的是，黄浦区碳普惠平台打造绿色出行、循环利用、减纸减塑、节能节约、虚拟电厂等低碳场景，上线低碳商城，用户凭参与低碳行为获得的减碳积分可在指定的商场、超市、书店、药店等兑换商品，并根据市民对碳普惠平台参与程度设置进阶，完成任务就能获得数字徽章，增加趣味性，形成"践行低碳行为、获得减碳积分、积分兑换权益"正向激励闭环。黄浦区碳地图小程序集成展示区内企业节能减排、公共建筑能效提升、社区绿色生活实践，使用户能够轻松一览全区绿色低碳发展成就。

2022 年 3 月，包含党的诞生地中共一大会址、上海时尚地标新天地、浦西最大的人工湖太平湖等的"一大会址·新天地"被列入上海低碳发展（近零碳排放）实践区试点。实践区升级空调、电梯、锅炉等存量建筑设备，严格落实新建项目绿色建筑星级标准，辖内楼宇安装分项计量设备并接入区级能耗监测平台，实现建筑智慧用能。建成公交枢纽站，优化慢行交通网络，绿色出行成为便捷选择。建设新能源充电桩、智慧公共停车场，赋能道路停车收费低碳治理。在寸土寸金的有限空间插花式建设城市公园，融合"海绵城市"理念，配备雨水调蓄、净化、资源化再利用设施，配种数十种绿化树种、花灌木和宿根花卉，形成丰富稳定的植物群落。新天地商圈上线"i 天地绿心社区"，鼓励消费者通过在绿色公约商户消费、光盘行动打卡等低碳行为获取积分并兑换礼品。如今，实践区基本建成弘扬红色文化与倡导低碳生活相融合、绿色低碳转型与高质量发展相适应的国际高端商业商务街区。

作为三星级绿色生态城区和上海市总体规划确定的中央活动区，董家渡是黄浦滨江的重要组成部分，营造立体、多元、生态的公共绿色空间体系，南北绿轴以董家渡教堂和商船会馆两处历史文化建筑为基点，延续历史文脉，东西绿轴兼容大型开放性空间及可供人们驻留的小型空间，打造黄浦江边绿色公共走廊。新建项目 100% 按照绿色建筑二星级及以上标准建设，辖内楼宇接入区虚拟电厂平台，应用光伏、空气源热泵等可再生能源技术，将 BIM（建筑信息模型）技术与装配式建筑、建筑机器人结合，开展智能建造试点，绿色、健康、节能的环保理念贯穿楼宇建筑的设计、施工、运营全过程。

努力绘就生态建设"最靓底色"

黄浦区利用各种"边角料"地块，或拆或改，打造口袋公园或者立体绿化，2024 年新增绿化面积 4.7 万平方米，成为公园城市建设的亮点。比如，黄浦区文化中心屋顶绿化项目采用山脉线条艺术美学，延伸扩展建筑弧线构成，联动广场与露台，依照植物花期和开花颜色特点，首层广场以草本、松科和禾本科植物构建常绿植物景观，顶部露台以草本植物为主，整体软景植物搭配既有物种间的小变化，又形成统一软景大基调，提升视觉效果；作为融观赏、游览、休憩功能于一体的口袋公园，窠石园以古画《窠石平远图》的"山水画境"织景，彰显古趣盎然、轩敞典雅的历史底蕴与人文情怀；森邻花园将原有封闭绿地打开，利用场地内多株高大乔木打造可进入、可游玩、可休憩的林下花境。

黄浦区结合产业定位，在外滩金融集聚带发展绿色金融，完成首单"碳中和"专题债券、首只"碳中和"债券指数、首单碳配额 CCER 组合质押融资、首单"碳中和"资产支持商业票据等多个中国绿色金融产品首发。ESG 全球领导者大会落户黄浦，区内企业积极建设 ESG 行动体系。推动轻生产、低噪音、环保型企业"上楼"，打造"智造空间"，培育节能环保产业，支持企业加强研发设计，转型为以服务为主的绿色制造企业，建立产品碳足迹管理体系，通过技术创新和管理优化提升绿色竞争力。

践行"人民城市"理念的向绿而行

总的来看，黄浦区以绿色为笔，生态为墨，协同推进政策制度创新和绿色低碳先进技术示范应用，建设零碳智能楼宇和绿色城区，倡导绿色低碳的生产生活方式和消费模式，绘就一幅幅绿色生态新画卷，为城市可持续发展注入更多元、可持续的发展动力，让每位市民在这片绿意盎然的土地上感受到生活美好与城市律动，也为"一高一低"中心城市（第三产业和楼宇经济发展成熟度高、单位生产总值碳排放强度低）碳达峰碳中和探索行之有效的"黄浦模式"。

创新、质优、先进：
引育绿色新质生产力的万州探索

　　绿色发展是中国式现代化的本底，绿色生产力即新质生产力，在实践中形成并展示出对高质量发展的强劲推动力和支撑力。新质生产力特点是创新，关键在质优，本质是先进生产力。"创新"意味着绿色新动能要赋能新质生产力加速形成，"质优"意味着生态活力助推新质生产力量质双升，"先进"意味着美丽中国新画卷支撑新质生产力持续发展。

　　作为三峡库区经济中心和三峡工程中重庆移民任务最重、管理单元最多的区县，重庆市万州区积极探索绿水青山向金山银山增值转化的实现路径，在打造川渝地区生态优先绿色发展样板区上取得新突破，生态环境持续改善，现代基础设施网络织密建强，现代化产业体系加快构建，巴蜀特色区域消费中心提速打造，川渝东北创新创业高地加快建设，区域中心城市、重庆重要城市副中心能级接续提升，城乡融合发展扎实推进，区域协作合作稳步落实，努力实现高水平保护和高质量发展、高品质生活、高效能治理同频共振、联动共赢。2024 年，万州区地区生产总值达 1222.36 亿元，同比增长 6.8%，总量居渝东北区县第 1、增速居全市区县第 3，森林覆盖率 50.4%，城区空气质量优良天数 354 天（创历史新高），空气质量优良率 96.72%，长江干流万州段水质稳定保持 Ⅱ 类，实施国土绿化营造林 24 万亩，国家一级保护植物荷叶铁线蕨"野外回归"首获成功。

打造川渝东北高品质生活宜居地

护好一江水，守好一方土，美好一座城。万州区坚持共抓大保护、不搞大开发，完善源头预防、前端减排、全程监管、协同增效的生态治理链条，良好生态环境成为万州金字招牌。万州区长江过境流程80.4公里，库体水面达100平方千米，以提升全域水质为中心，聚焦长江干流和支流，深入推进"三水共治"，为流域面积50平方千米以上的21条河流治理制定"一河一策"，通过生态修复、生态补水、提标改造污水处理厂、新建和修复污水收集管网等措施，构建长江生态廊道。目前，万州区城市生活污水集中处理率达98%以上，镇乡生活污水集中处理率达85%，污泥无害化处置率达100%，工业聚集区污水应收尽收、达标排放，城市集中式饮用水水源地水质达标率达100%，万元GDP用水量、万元工业增加值用水量分别较2020年下降27.02%和13.49%，农田灌溉水有效利用系数达0.5114，长江万州段生态屏障体系基本形成。

万州区探索资源环境要素市场化配置体系，促进产业绿色转型的增量收益反哺绿色发展的前期投入。比如，磨刀溪是万州境内最大的长江支流，过去沿岸居民生态保护意识不足，水环境面临挑战，万州区与石柱县、云阳县三地政府签署磨刀溪流域上下游横向生态保护补偿协议，明确补偿方式、补偿基准、补偿标准和联防共治事项，共同保护磨刀溪流域生态环境。如今，磨刀溪水质重新稳定达标，一溪清水流入长江。随后，万州区将横向生态保护补偿改革扩展到苎溪河、瀼渡河等区内次级流域。

三峡库区首个垃圾焚烧发电厂——万州区垃圾焚烧发电厂日垃圾处理能力达800吨，每天可发电36万多度，可满足3万~4万户家庭的用电需求，已累计处置生活垃圾超230万吨，供应绿色电超8.24亿度，相当于为地球新栽超1380万棵树、减排二氧化碳超115万吨。该发电厂绿树成荫，一辆辆密闭的垃圾运输车进进出出，却闻不到臭味，这源于最大限度实现生活垃圾减量化、资源化、无害化处理，生活垃圾在垃圾池堆放滤出的水分全部被收集到污水处理系统，经过先进工艺净化达标后回用或排放；焚烧产生的烟气经过脱硝、脱硫、物理吸附、除尘等组合工艺净化达标；炉渣综合利用车间通过先进的提取技术，将炉渣中的铁、铝等金属回收利用，其余部分作为建筑材料，飞灰经过螯合固化无害化处理后进入专门场所填埋。

人居环境既是高品质生态环境的样貌，也是发展绿色新质生产力的地利。塑造"美观、大气、协调、特色"的美丽山水城市典范是万州区满足居民美好生活需要的公共产品和民生福祉，聚焦城市建筑特色和空间环境品质提升，以长江为主线、次级河流为支线，统筹实施"坡、崖、壁、巷、道、岸、面"等生态修复和保护利用，建设"一季为主、四季兼顾，一色为主、多色互动"的滨江环湖景观，拓展亲水步道、休憩平台和观景平台等城市公共休闲空间，丰富林相、色相、季相、品相，使"城中有画，画中有山，山中有水，水中有城"的秀美城市画卷更加亮丽。

产业转型升级催生绿色新质生产力

万州湘渝盐化有限公司是中国最大的井矿盐和联碱生产基地，开展联碱装置绿色固碳、分布式光伏发电、空分尾气回收利用等多项技术改造项目，每年节约标准煤 2.9 万吨，减排二氧化碳、氮氧化物及烟尘近 5 万吨，产能增加 30 万吨。万州九龙万博新材料科技公司采用设备大型化、数智化赋能传统生产模式，一条生产线年产氧化铝 90 万吨，每吨氧化铝能耗由过去的 92 立方米降至 83 立方米，减少生产环节的非必要人工干预，获得国家级智能制造优秀场景等荣誉。施耐德万州基地是一家国家级绿色工厂，所有设备互联互通，从产品装配、测试到包装全程智能化和绿色化，生产效率较传统生产方式提高 139.18%，产品不良率降低 34%，运营成本降低 28.5%，单位能耗降低 14.74%……"设备换芯""生产换线""机器换人"，近 200 个绿色智造项目正"燃"动万州"高大上"的产业结构转型。

通过科技创新的转化应用，形成以生产要素创新性配置和产业深度转型升级为特征的产业创新，是形成绿色新质生产力的关键环节。万州区加快构建"5+10+X"现代化工业体系①，以"四链"融合提升产业韧性和质量，在生产方式数字化、能源消费低碳化、资源利用循环化、生产过程清洁化等产业新赛道突破，一手做节能降碳的"减法"，一手做培育绿色新质生产力的"加法"。2024 年，万州区规上工业产值和增加值同比分别增长 13.0% 和 11.5%，均高于市区 GDP 增速，万州经开区获批成渝地区双城经济圈产业合作示范园区、重庆市产业转移示范园区，九龙万博、金龙铜管 2 家企业年产值均突破百亿元，百亿级工业企业实现"零"的突破，建成国家级绿色工厂 4 家、市级绿色工厂 9 家，产业"含金量""含绿量"进一步提升。

金融支撑绿色新质生产力的加快形成

自 2022 年获批成为重庆主城区外唯一建设绿色金融改革创新试验区核心区，万州区用足、用活、用好绿色金融政策工具，在能源、化工、建材、有色金属、农业、交通运输等重点行业，制定重庆首批转型金融万州标准，建立高耗能产业、重点产业、特色产业企业转型金融项目库，引导辖内银行机构将企业转型进展与授信额度、贷款利率直接挂钩，建立重庆首个企业碳账户平台，建设碳数据云上"一组库"、碳核算"一本账"、碳披露"一张网"，推出重庆首批"碳挂钩"金融产品，2024 年发放转型金融贷款 80.9 亿元，重庆三峡银行绿色信贷余额增至 321.81 亿元。

育绿色新质生产力促高质量发展

万州区因"万川毕汇"而得名，因"万商云集"而闻名，因"万客来游"而扬名，高质量发展的底色和成色在于生态优先、绿色发展，为

---

① 万州区"5+10+X"现代化工业体系："5"即先进材料、食品加工、装备制造、医药化工、新型能源五大重点产业，"10"即围绕重点产业细分的铜及铜合金材料、铝及铝合金材料、绿色建材、粮油加工、特色食品、汽车及零部件、船舶及配套、照明电气、医药、化工 10 个特色产业链条，"X"即若干未来产业。

此，提出"建设绿色新质生产力高地"的三大建议。

一是立足要素资源优势，构建绿色新质生产力驱动的现代化产业体系。健全政府部门推动、龙头企业带动、上下游企业联动、大院大所大才驱动的产学研用合作长效机制，构建科技企业"微成长、小升高、高变强"梯次培育体系，完善"众创空间+孵化器+加速器"全链条孵化体系，提升科技创新的内生绿色动力。做强新型工业化主战场、主阵地、主平台，推动园区产城景智融合发展，实施"绿色亩均论英雄"改革，推动重点产业绿色转型，支持大中小微企业产研创新、梯度发展、做大做强。

二是坚持从实际出发，以绿色新质生产力为画笔绘就山水万州美好家园新画卷。迭代升级生态环境治理体系，坚决守住万州的蓝天、碧水、净土。强化生态系统跨区域联保，持续推进长江"十年禁渔"，推进国土绿化示范试点建设、长江岸线林相景观提升。推动林业碳汇开发，用好转型金融市场化碳账户平台，丰富转型金融产品供给。依托重点行业清洁生产和节能减排场景，跨区域按需配置绿色科技创新资源。发挥绿色新质生产力高地的创新溢出和辐射带动效应，提升区域协作合作的绿色绩效。

三是构建与绿色新质生产力相适应的新型生产关系，加快形成全民生态自觉。发挥人在绿色科技创新中的能动作用，实施"平湖人才"计划、"百千万"引才工程、产业工人队伍建设等人才项目，建设青年发展型城市，促进以人才为核心的产学研用金服融合发展，健全争先创优促绿的激励措施，提升驾驭绿色新质生产力的创新创业能力。

以"绿"为底，向"美"而行：
绿色制造的"宁波样本"

　　节约能耗成本超 115 万元/年、二氧化碳减排 872.04 吨/年，标准煤降耗 303.85 吨/年，这是宁波更大集团微改造一级能效压缩空气站后的运营效果。作为高新技术企业和国家级绿色工厂，更大集团把"碳中和"目标分解成资源利用、供应链合作、企业文化、环境治理、能源利用五个方面，将绿色、低碳、环保的理念贯穿千余种产品的研发设计、原料采购、生产、包装、回收"全生命周期"。宁波象山海螺水泥有限公司通过绿色技改创新、能源消耗降低、固废资源化利用等措施，每年处置消化 32 万吨粉煤灰、20 万吨脱硫石膏、26 万吨粉末等工业废料，全自动操控的生产流水线、错落有致的现代化厂房、整洁有序的生产环境，改变传统水泥企业粉尘飞扬、噪声不绝的脏乱差印象。

　　这是浙江省宁波市制造企业"刀刃向内"、以绿色发展促提质增效的缩影。截至 2024 年末，宁波市累计创建国家级绿色工厂 122 家，数量居中国副省级城市第 2；省级绿色工厂 82 家，数量居全省各地市第 1；国家级绿色工业园区 4 家、绿色供应链管理企业 16 家、市级绿色工厂 832 家、区（县、市）级绿色工厂 2529 家，完成绿色化改造的规上制造企业达 5033 家，覆盖率 48.3%。

聚力攻坚"大美宁波"建设体制机制改革

　　宁波市将生态文明基础体制更加完备、生态环境治理体系更加高效、绿色低碳发展机制更加鲜明、全域美丽先行优势更加突出作为总目标，以牵引性举措、突破性抓手打造"污水零直排""固废趋零填埋""生态红线之内无违规活动""环境监管覆盖无盲区"等标志性改革成果。2024年7月，《宁波市生态环境分区管控动态更新方案》发布，9365平方千米的市域面积细致划分为254个环境管控单元，实行分类管理，实际可准入三类工业项目土地面积同比增加110.19平方千米，逾3000家企业可享受"区域环评+环境标准"改革红利，重大项目保障能力、绿色发展格局得到提升。

绿色制造蔚然成风

宁波市出台新型工业化行动纲要，将绿色低碳发展作为新型工业化六大"先行示范"路径之一，提出到2027年实现规上工业企业绿色化改造全覆盖、龙头企业省级以上绿色工厂建设全覆盖、重点高碳行业企业清洁生产审核全覆盖等"三个全覆盖"目标，将加强对高碳行业减碳指导、强化绿色金融支持、培育绿色化改造服务商作为重点任务，做大做强新材料、新装备等绿色低碳产业，打造"源网荷储"新型电力系统，发展"能源+产业+污染物处置"循环经济，建设石化园区国家级减污降碳协同试点，推广绿色保险、排污权抵质押贷款、碳资信等绿色金融产品。

宁波出台《宁波市星级绿色工厂评价办法》，明确绿色化改造认定标准和动态管理办法，增加碳管理碳认证、绿色电力占比等特色指标，建立"国家级—省级—市级—县级"绿色工厂和"国家—省—市"绿色园区梯队培育模式。印发《宁波市"零碳（近零碳）工厂"评价办法（试行）》，督促年用能量1000吨标煤以上的高耗能企业开展节能降碳、清洁能源替代、绿电交易。将绿色发展指标纳入企业亩均效益综合评价、企业技术改造项目补贴评审等政策，市财政每年安排专项资金支持企业绿色低碳改造，推出"绿色工厂提升贷"，2024年为471家企业提供专项贷款381亿元。

作为以大港口、大工业、大物流著称的临港工业强区，宁波经济技术开发区持续推进重点产业全流程、清洁化、低碳化改造，提能提效产业平台，2024 年，1028 家规上工业企业实现总产值 5857.27 亿元，高新技术产业、装备制造业、战略性新兴产业增加值分别增长 10.1%、18.8%、16.1%，均高于全部规上工业增加值增速，占规上工业比重分别达 65.3%、48.6%、29.8%，入选国家环境健康管理试点城市名单。作为中国最大的烧结钕铁硼磁钢供应商，宁波科宁达工业有限公司搭建数字化车间，扩容厂区光伏发电，数智管理产品碳足迹，参与西门子等重点客户的"零碳先锋计划"，实现单位产值碳排放强度比基准年份降低25%。随着国家电网宁波经开区舟山港风光储一体化项目投运，浙江省首个绿电码头诞生，为舟山港绿色、低碳、可持续发展注入新动能。宁波绿能港拥有全球单罐容量最大的 LNG 储罐，将每年为浙江省提供 600 万吨液化天然气，推进宁波经开区油气全产业链绿色发展。

宁波市是中国纺织服装业重要出口地，拥有 2 万余家纺织企业，年产值超千亿元，通过数智化平台建设、设施设备升级和"无废工厂"打造，2024 年循环利用废纺织料超 30 万吨，减少碳排放量 108 万吨。2025年浙江省"国际无废日"主题活动上，宁波率先发布无废纺织建设指南，首次明确印、染、纺、织四类行业的全周期"无废行为准则"，即通过环境保护、原料控制、固废处理和循环利用、生活办公低碳化、厂区绿色建设、制度建设、无废评估等综合施策，推动设施设备能源消耗最小化、原料产品循环利用效益最大化、固废资源利用最优化，"无废纺织工厂"环境效能和制造效益处于全球领先水平。

作为钢铁工业清洁生产环境友好企业，宁波钢铁有限公司累计投资超 40 亿元，实施焦炉/烧结/锅炉/热风炉/加热炉烟气脱硫脱硝、电动重卡运输、废钢废渣处理等百余个项目，被生态环境部与中国钢铁工业协会评为全流程超低排放改造公示企业。宁波钢铁开发包括三维大屏展示、环保日常业务管理和环保 App 的智慧环保管控系统，自动生成环保数据报表，实现无组织排放溯源、实时预警环境异常、精准定位问题点等污染源清单化管理。宁波钢铁建设宁钢展览馆、创新成果展示厅、研学影音厅、凌霄花廊景观道等景点，将生产环节改造为百炼成钢、铁水梨花、裂变成材等主题景观，获批 AAA 级工业旅游景区，在钢铁森林的碧水栈桥间向大众展现新时代"钢铁智造"的绿色魅力。

绿色转型引领制造业高质量发展

青山不墨千秋画，绿水无弦万古琴。今天的宁波，诗画江南遍地有景，和谐美好的人居环境、蓝天碧水的生态基底渐次铺展，一座座"绿色工厂"汇聚起澎湃动能，以"美"的韵味生动彰显"八八战略"的实践伟力。作为制造业大市，宁波市加快绿色转型升级，既是现实需要，又是长久之计，是打造智造创新之都的必然选择。宁波市要进一步加强政策牵引，"一业一策""一企一策"精细谋划绿色发展路径，以科技创新促进数字化绿色化协同发展，以兼并重组、整体腾退、搬迁入园、改造提升等方式接续整治"高耗低效"企业，创建星级绿色工厂和减污降碳标杆企业，培育世界级先进制造业集群，努力探索"生态优先、节约集约、绿色低碳、美美与共"的新型工业化创新路径。

苏州逐"绿"向"新"：
厚植绿水青山新优势

 2024 年地区生产总值 2.67 万亿元，同比增长 6.0%，规上工业增加值同比增长 9.2%，规上工业企业高新技术产业产值 2.57 万亿元，这里，是东部地区重要中心城市苏州。蓝天白云成为常态，绿水青山举目可见，太湖湖滨国家湿地公园观测到 114 种鸟类，东太湖湿地公园观测到 125 种鸟类，生动诠释"环境好不好，鸟儿先知道"绿色发展优势，这里，是"上有天堂下有苏杭"的苏州。围绕"美丽苏州"中心目标，依照规划、管控、修复、发展的路径，苏州市努力打造人与自然和谐共生的现代化市域范例，空气质量在全省率先达到国家二级标准，连续六年在全省污染防治攻坚战综合考核中位列第一方阵，建成 5 个国家生态文明建设示范区，人民群众对生态环境满意率从 2015 年的 81.7% 上升到 2023 年的 92.5%，"绿水青山就是金山银山"理念引领的高质量发展图景日渐清晰。

太湖生态岛之秀美折射生态文明建设之深功

 苏州市拥有太湖三分之二水面、四分之三岸线、五分之四岛屿，太湖治理的主战场在苏州。自 2008 年《太湖流域水环境综合治理总体方案》实施以来，苏州市累计实施治太工程项目 5600 多个，总投资超 840 亿元。2023 年以来，苏州出台《苏州市推进新一轮太湖综合治理行动方案》，深入开展工业污染治理，累计完成太湖流域涉磷企业整治 6876 家，

26 家污水处理厂、603 家工业企业实现分质分类处理。太湖东部区域水质 2018 年由Ⅳ类提升至Ⅲ类且保持至今，太湖连续 17 年实现安全度夏，2023 年首次被生态环境部评价为优良湖泊。市内长江岸线开发利用率控制在 50% 以内，长江干流苏州段水质稳定达Ⅱ类，27 个省考及以上通江河道断面水质全部达到或好于Ⅲ类。

苏州市太湖生态岛地处太湖中心区域，涵盖西山岛等 27 个太湖岛屿和水域，是维护太湖生态系统的关键节点和生态屏障，也是长三角核心区重要生态服务功能的支撑点和供给地。2021 年 8 月，江苏省首例以立法形式保护太湖岛屿的《苏州市太湖生态岛条例》正式施行，提出要将太湖生态岛建成低碳、美丽、富裕、文明、和谐的生态示范岛。苏州发布《太湖生态岛发展规划（2021～2035 年)》《太湖生态岛自然资源领域生态产品价值实现机制试点实施方案》，提出"全球可持续发展生态岛的中国样本"愿景：把太湖生态岛建成"碧水青山萤舞果香的美丽岛、永续循环节能韧性的低碳岛、生态经济民生幸福的富足岛、绿色创新技术引领的知识岛、地景天成情感共鸣的艺术岛"。

苏州市建立太湖生态岛"天－空－地－人"生态环境智慧监控平台，开展生态产品开发利用价值核算，编制自然资源资产负债表，吴中区连续三年蝉联中国 GEP 百强区县榜首。融入环太湖科创圈，与百度共建中国首个"自动驾驶生态示范岛"，与比亚迪、小鹏等共建新能源汽车智能驾驶体验中心，构建"岛外产业集聚区、岛内场景实验地"的"飞地经济"绿色发展模式。打造"环太湖 1 号公路"IP，在 186 公里的公路上融合山水风光、乡村风情、人文风貌，形成集研学、赛事、民宿、文创等多业态于一体的太湖国家旅游度假区核心区。

消夏湾湿地是西山岛最大湖湾，因春秋时期吴王夫差在此避暑消夏而得名，自然禀赋良好，山上为经济林，沿太湖边为万亩良田，周边村庄密集，汇水区面积约 18 平方千米。作为全国水污染防治部际协调小组评选的农业面源污染防治典型案例，消夏湾湿地生态安全缓冲区依照"控源＋生态净化＋多功能利用"技术路线，开发三道湿地拦截处理体系：从山间流淌下来的雨水和污水，通过既有或专门修筑的沟渠，进入三处雨污水截留湿地，随着导流渠道汇入生态缓冲塘，实现面源污染先由多到少，再由少到集中；经物理过滤后，水流沿着管道注入强化型直流湿地进行生物处理；出水的水质优于地表Ⅲ类水标准，经由清水廊道汇入浅滩湿地完成净化补充后渗入消夏江，最终注入太湖。

姑苏区人民法院"太湖流域环境资源法庭太湖生态岛巡回审判点"、吴中区人民法院"太湖生态岛巡回审判点"落户金庭镇，太湖生态岛建成全省首个集修复示范、法治警示、科普交流和监测监控等功能于一体的生态环境损害赔偿修复基地。采用异地修复、劳务代偿等替代性修复模式，强化生态环境损害的治理修复主体责任，传播生态环境资源司法理念，为破解"企业污染、群众受害、政府买单"的困局提供解决方案。

现代化产业焕"绿颜"

苏州推进传统制造业节能减排、两化融合、产品结构调整，引导重点企业更新改造传统工艺和设备，加强清洁生产升级。推动龙头企业联合上下游企业、园区内企业、行业间企业协同探索产品物流循环链、能源多级利用链、废弃物利用链、温室气体消减链等循环经济。发展节能环保产业，培育超 7000 家咨询服务、环保产品、环保工程、环境治理与资源化利用等领域的环保企业，占江苏省总量的 20%，年产值约 3000 亿元。融合"一般工业固废回收处置+危险废物回收处置+再生资源回收处置"三大"收运处"网络，形成收集、分类、运输、处置等各环节全闭环且可追溯的工业固废治理体系。

苏州工业园区努力探索产业结构绿色低碳转型、能源清洁高效利用、企业节能降碳改造，先后获评循环经济试点园区、低碳工业园区试点、国家级绿色园区、国家首批碳达峰试点园区和国家能源局能源绿色低碳转型典型案例，建成全省首家生态环境监测智能实验室，部署基于 DeepSeek 大模型赋能的生态环境监测数智中枢，零编码动态生成生态环境监测可视化报告，集聚 ESG 产业规上企业超 300 家、绿色及近零碳工厂企业超 120 家。

国家电网苏州供电公司共打造 16 个微电网。苏州零碳智慧虚拟电厂完成市场化注册，预计每年发电 2.8 亿千瓦时，相当于减少标准煤消耗

8.5 万吨。苏州工业园区循环经济产业园通过污水处理、污泥处置、餐厨垃圾处理、热电等环保设施有机互联，构建以"污水处理—污泥处置/有机废弃物处理—热电联产/生物天然气利用"为核心的循环经济链。其中，污水处理厂是全市规模最大的"光伏+污水处理"综合应用项目，在4万平方米污水处理池上建设72兆瓦光伏电站，每年产出绿电580万度，减少标煤消耗约1700吨，降低二氧化碳排放量4700余吨，有效遮挡部分污水处理池水面，显著抑制池内水体藻类生长。

近年来，苏州新能源产业基础日益牢固、细分领域优势领先、创新动能竞相迸发。苏州在2024年推进新型工业化工作会议上明确提出，用3年左右时间，把新能源打造成为下一个万亿级主导产业。截至2023年末，苏州拥有新能源企业637家，其中规上企业430家，实现工业总产值3576.42亿元，同比增长20%，拥有国家级、省级企业技术中心96家，高新技术企业292家，形成"5+1"新能源（光伏、风电、智能电网、动力电池及储能、氢能和智慧能源）产业体系。

精绘绿色发展"工笔画"

作为一座拥有2500年历史的古城，苏州拥有丰富的生态资源，灵秀山水、小桥流水，勾勒出江南水乡的独特风情和自然风貌，走在苏州大街小巷，随处可见郁郁葱葱的树木、清澈见底的河流和五彩斑斓的花朵，仿佛在向人们诉说着这座城市的绿色故事。在推进中国式现代化苏州新实践中，苏州形成"生态美促进产业兴、产业兴带动百姓富、百姓富守住生态美"绿色发展路径，实现经济发展与生态保护互促共赢，为其他城市提供宝贵经验，期待苏州在生态环境保护修复、传统产业低碳转型、绿色产业迭代升级等"啃硬骨头"领域续写辉煌篇章，为世界展示一个充满生机与活力的绿色现代城市。

以"强生态"引领"强省会"，
打造全国文明典范城市的贵阳实践

2023 年 11 月，贵阳市政府召开新闻发布会，宣布贵阳成功创建国家生态文明建设示范区，成为全省第一个成功创建的地级市、全国第三个成功创建的省会城市。贵阳市实施绿色经济"一二三四"战略路径①，聚焦"一城一战一整改"②，同步推进"六个生态"③ 建设，出台中国首部生态文明建设地方性法规，组建中国首个环保法庭、环保审判庭，深入打好"蓝天、碧水、净土、固废治理、农村环境整治"五大攻坚战，构建"生态环境一本账、环境管理一张图、污染监督一张网"的现代环境治理体系，发展绿色山地高效农业和战略性新兴产业，联动避暑旅游与康养旅居发展，久久为功推动生态文明宣传教育，不断满足人民群众日益增长的优美生态环境和高质绿色经济的需要。

良好生态即是民生福祉

2024 年，贵阳市环境空气质量优良天数比例达 99.5%，PM2.5 浓度

---

① 贵阳市绿色经济"一二三四"战略路径："一"为坚持生态立市"一个战略"；"二"为"两个统筹"，即统筹发展和生态、统筹发展和安全；"三"为加快生态城市、文明城市、创新城市"三城"建设；"四"为实施绿色生产、绿色消费、绿色生活、绿色文明"四个绿色行动"。

② "一城一战一整改"："一城"指高质量建设生态文明示范城市，"一战"指深入打好污染防治攻坚战，"一整改"指全力抓好生态环保督察反馈问题整改。

③ "六个生态"：生态城市、生态治理、生态保护、生态经济、生态文化、生态制度。

同比下降 16.6%，空气质量在中国 168 个重点城市中位居前列；覆盖市区两级的建设用地土壤环境管理机制基本建成，重点建设用地安全利用率保持 100%；28 个地表水国、省控断面水质达标率、优良率，15 个县级以上集中式饮用水水源地水质达标率，6 个地下水国考点位水质达标率均为 100%；入选全国"无废城市"建设名单，绿色建筑占新建建筑比例达 100%，生活垃圾焚烧发电处理能力达 4900 吨/日，生活垃圾资源化利用率达 86.4%；森林覆盖率稳定在 55% 以上，共有大中小微各类公园 1025 个，建成区人均公园绿地面积超 14.85 平方米。

南明河是贵阳市"母亲河"，传统的集中式污水处理厂难以应对山地城市地形高差，截污管网在喀斯特地貌中无法有效收集污水。依据适度集中、就地处理、就近回用的新理念，贵阳市沿南明河流域新建及改扩建下沉式再生水厂 24 座，日污水总处理规模达百万吨级，将处理后的达标水回补河道生态基流，年补水量超 4.5 亿立方米。下沉式再生水厂拆分为地下处理层、操作层与地面景观层，解决臭气、噪声等邻避问题，实现土地集约利用。通过生物干化、稳定化技术将污泥转化为绿化用土和建材原料，实现无害化与资源化。如今，南明河水质稳定达地表水 Ⅳ 类标准，全年 80% 时间可达地表水 Ⅲ 类标准，沉水植物覆盖率上升至 85%，水生植物种类突破 23 种，底栖动物种类达 33 种，浮游动物达 16 种，优势鱼类达 29 种，生态系统健康指数接近"非常健康"状态，成为生态环境部"第二批美丽河湖"优秀案例，治理保护经验入选生态环境部"推进生态环境重大工程实施"典型案例。

红枫湖是贵阳市重要的饮用水水源地，实施沿湖村寨生活污水治理、退湖进园、退湖进城、农业产业结构调整、一级保护区围网"五大工程"，以及拆除违章建筑、拆除养殖场、依法整治农家乐、强化司法保障"四大举措"，消除污染"存量"，严控污染"增量"，管理污染"变量"，水质从 2008 年劣 Ⅴ 类提升到 Ⅱ 类，入选 2024 年贵州省美丽幸福河湖。"护水"之后兼顾"富民"：大冲村农家乐生意红火、右二村蒙德里安色系建筑"吸粉"无数、芦荻哨村阳光玫瑰葡萄直供上海市场……"上岸"后的红枫湖村民不断拓宽"两山"转化通道。

作为国家森林城市，贵阳市建立"林长+检察长""林长+庭长""林长+警长"协作机制，严厉打击破坏森林资源违法行为，加强林业灾害防治，在环城林带、阿哈湖绿核、自然保护地、矿山迹地等重点区域种植乡土树种 614.67 万株，打造"一心、两带、千园"生态景观①，组织湿地保护、森林探秘等自然教育活动，开展森林乡镇、森林乡村、森林村寨、森林人家创建，以全域森林带动全域旅游，形成"山中有城、城中有山、绿带环绕、森林围城、城在林中、林在城中"的山水林城格局。

深耕绿色经济高质量发展

贵阳市第十一次党代会将生态立市作为首位战略，将绿色经济作为主路径，围绕绿色生产、绿色消费、绿色生活、绿色文明"四个绿"作出部署。通过提升重点产业绿色化、高端化、智能化水平，2024 年绿色经济增加值占 GDP 比重近 50%，创建绿色工厂累计达 88 家（国家级 41家、省级 47 家），占全省的 30%，绿色园区 11 个（国家级 9 个、省级 2个），占全省的 26.8%。

2024 年夏季，"中国避暑之都"贵阳市上榜"马蜂窝"全国"避暑+游玩"热度涨幅榜第一名。作为中国首批青年发展型试点城市，贵阳市统筹文商旅融合发展，路边音乐会破圈引流，青云市集、曹状元街等特色街区昼夜人潮涌动，推广使用绿色产品，建立绿色消费积分制，"年轻态、新玩法"成为绿色消费新风尚。探索生活垃圾"分、投、收、转、处"贵阳模式，推动基层一线解决垃圾分、投难点，获得住建部点赞。

2024 年 10 月，贵州省首个村级联户林场在贵阳市花溪区燕楼镇旧盘村组建，按照"分股不分山、分利不分林"经营方式，将全村 295 户村民的山林交由联户林场统一经营管理，集中整合村级森林资源，培育壮大村级集体经济。进一步看，贵阳市把握新一轮集体林权制度改革机遇，以规模化种植、产业化经营为抓手，提高林下经济利用面积和林下经济产值为目标，盘活林地资源，发展食用菌、中药材等林下产业。2024 年，

---

① "一心、两带、千园"生态景观："一心"指阿哈湖国家湿地公园，"两带"指南明河生态带和环城林带，"千园"指森林公园、湿地公园、山体公园、城市公园、社区公园等各类公园。

开阳县杠寨国有林场成为全省首批林业碳票持有方，建成林下经济利用林地总面积157.92万亩，林下经济全产业链产值达112.74亿元，全省排名第1。

围绕乡村全面振兴，贵阳市因地制宜发展现代山地特色高效绿色农业，实施"4个10万+100万+5000万"产业项目①，培育种养大户、农民合作社、家庭农场、龙头企业四类新型农业经营主体，开展智慧农业、智慧农机、智慧气象等创新应用，推进农业核心技术突破和科技成果转化，生态特色食品产业年产值达204.65亿元，农机装备总量达31.12万台（套），主要农作物耕种收综合机械化率提升至61.88%。

共商全球发展绿色转型

生态文明贵阳国际论坛是中国唯一以生态文明为主题的国家级国际性论坛，自2009年创办以来已成功举办12届。论坛始终紧扣党中央、国务院关于生态文明建设的决策部署，积极回应国际社会对生态文明建设热点问题的关切，持续推动生态文明与可持续发展理念传播和实践探索，深化同国际社会在生态环境保护、应对气候变化等领域的广泛交流和务实合作，推动共建共享共融共赢，持续打造"知名品牌、著名平台"。

党中央、国务院非常关心支持生态文明贵阳国际论坛，习近平总书记2013年、2018年两次向论坛年会致贺信，2015年、2021年视察贵州期间对论坛举办作出重要指示，指出生态文明贵阳国际论坛是以生态文明为主题的国家级国际性论坛，要创新方式，继续办好。

论坛创办以来，党和国家领导人出席论坛并发表主旨演讲，多位外国政要、前政要出席论坛，数千名政府官员、诺贝尔奖获得者、著名学者、商业领军者、民间组织负责人等各界人士参与论坛，共商应对人类面临挑战的解决方案，引起国内外广泛关注，获得高度赞誉。

---

① "4个10万+100万+5000万"产业项目：建设蔬菜保供示范基地10万亩、果树提质增效10万亩、发展林下种植10万亩、新增生猪产能10万头，新增水产品100万斤，肉鸡产能5000万羽。

提升绿色发展能级

今天，爽眼、爽口、爽心、爽身、爽购、爽游"爽爽的贵阳"魅力不断凸显，生态优势成为贵阳最大的比较优势。未来，贵阳市要聚焦增绿、节能、降碳、环保"四个关键"，确保各项环境质量指标走在全国前列，筑牢长江、珠江上游生态安全屏障，需求导向推进绿色创新技术研发应用，有序做好碳达峰、碳中和工作，实施绿色工业提质、山地绿色农业增效、现代服务业创新、数字经济牵引、能源结构优化"五大工程"，壮大生态利用型、循环高效型、低碳清洁型、环境治理型产业，打响"电动贵阳""数智贵阳""低碳贵阳""无废城市""西南绿色消费中心"等绿色名片，发挥生态文明贵阳国际论坛的主场外宣、合作传播、文化交流功能，讲好贵阳绿色发展故事，加快建设环境共同改善、素质共同提升、生活共同富裕的全国文明典范城市。

哈尔滨：
探索"冰天雪地也是金山银山"
转化新路径

2023年9月，习近平总书记在黑龙江考察时指出，把发展冰雪经济作为新增长点，推动冰雪运动、冰雪文化、冰雪装备、冰雪旅游全产业链发展。2024年春节期间，哈尔滨市一夜之间"翻红"，8天假期累计接待游客1009.3万人次，旅游总收入164.2亿元，两项指标均创历史峰值，"尔滨"一跃成为旅游"顶流"名片。地处高寒地带，气候严寒，过去被认为是发展劣势，如今，哈尔滨市以冰雪经济为切入点，把曾经的"短板"变成"长板"，人们从过去"怕冷猫冬"变成现在"迎客盼冷"，寒冷清寂的冬季变成人气红火的旺季，在冰天雪地塑造高质量发展新优势。

"来到哈尔滨，我们真切感受到'冰天雪地也是金山银山'"，2025年2月7日，中国国家主席习近平在哈尔滨第九届亚洲冬季运动会开幕式欢迎宴会上致辞时说，"冰雪文化和冰雪经济正在成为哈尔滨高质量发展的新动能和对外开放的新纽带"。1996年哈尔滨市首次举办亚冬会时，GDP刚过500亿元，冰雪经济占比仅0.3%。到2024年，哈尔滨市GDP突破6000亿元，冰雪经济占比近30%，中国冰雪运动发源地如今热"雪"沸腾，工业城市绿色转型重获新机。

亚冬会引领构建"冰雪经济生态圈"

秉持"绿色、共享、开放、廉洁"的办赛理念，第九届亚冬会创造筹办时间最短、场馆利旧率最高、参赛规模最大等多项纪录，得到国际奥委会、亚奥理事会等各方高度赞誉。绿色是哈尔滨亚冬会鲜明底色，通过生态修复工程将废弃矿坑改造为滑雪训练基地，利用 AI 技术对雪场运营碳排放实时监控，将赛事场馆分布式光伏发电系统并入城市电网，测试赛及正赛均为绿电供应，竞赛场馆（场地）全部采用节能环保材料和绿色低碳技术。

哈尔滨市建立冰雪资源资产核算体系，将年均 120 天有效冰雪期等生态要素纳入 GEP 核算，让每一片冰雪都透射出经济价值，实现"冷资源"向"热动能"质变。哈尔滨银行、中国移动黑龙江公司等多家企业将持有的"龙江绿碳"无偿捐赠给第九届亚冬会组委会，助力亚冬会实现碳中和。"哈尔滨绿色厨房"计划借势亚冬会应运而生，五常大米获得碳中和认证，冰雪冷储技术延长蓝莓等寒地水果产业链，零下 30℃ 极寒环境成为生物医药的天然试验场。哈尔滨市上线东北地区首个碳普惠平台（"碳惠冰城 美丽中国"微信小程序），全方位采集和核算用户碳减排数据，建立用户绿色生活激励回馈机制。

从"靠天吃饭"到"借雪生金"，哈尔滨市建立"冰雪赛事+装备制造+文化旅游+教育培训"全产业链。哈尔滨冰雪装备产业园吸引安踏、探路者、波司登等头部品牌入驻，钛合金速滑冰刀、3D 打印滑雪板、碳纤维滑雪头盔等"哈尔滨制造"不仅服务赛事，更出口全球十余个国家，在国际中高端产品市场崭露头角，形成"研发—制造—应用"产业生态。

冰雪旅游四季火爆

"双亚冬之城"光环给火爆出圈的"尔滨"又添一把火，催生绿色旅游消费新场景：大批东南亚游客北上，跨越 50 摄氏度温差，感受"冰雪奇缘"；总投资 23.5 亿元、100 万平方米的冰雪大世界单日客流量首次突破 10 万人次；亚冬会吉祥物"滨滨"和"妮妮"文创产品售卖火爆，热门徽章、冰箱贴供不应求。2024 年，哈尔滨新开通 7 条国际航线及吉隆坡至哈尔滨旅游包机，新登记住宿类经营主体 8784 家，同比增长208.4%。亚冬会期间，哈尔滨市入境游订单同比激增 157%，游客人均消费超万元，游客人数及消费额均达历史峰值。

哈尔滨冰雪大世界运用声光电互动技术，用真冰、真雪呈现冰雕经典景观和历届亚冬会元素，游客在盛夏时节可依托室内冰雪项目尽享冰雪文化魅力，冰雪旅游告别"季节限定"，这是哈尔滨市树立"游客为本""服务至上"理念，构建"引客""留客""宠客"多层次旅游服务新格局，持续叫响"冰雪之冠上的明珠"旅游品牌的一个实践案例。进一步看，哈尔滨市聚焦亚冬会比赛项目及冬季体育赛事，串联竞赛场馆、冰雪赛事和冰雪景区，打造"跟着赛事去旅行"IP，以"约会哈尔滨·冰雪暖世界"为主题，举办国际冰雪节、太阳岛雪博会、冰灯艺术游园会、冰雪嘉年华、亚布力滑雪节等品牌活动，依托冬捕冬钓、年货大集、年猪村宴等东北民俗资源，推出美食、服饰、文创、展演等文创项目，建设"尔滨"礼物创意店、无人售货机、特许经营店等绿色特产销售网络，丰富市民游客赏冰玩雪新趣味和新体验。

在开发中保护、在利用中修复

亚布力滑雪场始建于1974年，承办过包括两届亚冬会、世界大学生冬季运动会在内的国际级赛事25次、国家级赛事350余次，是中国竞技滑雪运动的摇篮，被誉为"中国雪之门"。实施生态银行模式，将碎片化的森林、冰雪等生态资源整合评估，引入社会资本实行股份制运营，每条雪道周边保留原生林带，造雪系统采用智能节水技术，雪场径流经生态滤池净化后回补湿地，保护区域生物多样性，用旅游收入反哺生态保护资金。

哈尔滨市湿地名录面积为4.05万公顷，现有国际重要湿地1处、湿地类型省级自然保护区8处、国家级湿地公园13处、省级湿地公园2处，在《湿地公约》第十三届缔约方大会上荣获全球首批"国际湿地城市"称号。哈尔滨市秉承"以江为纲、以水定城"的可持续发展理念，成立湿地保护管理领导小组，开展湿地水系治理、"三沟一河"（何家沟、马家沟、信义沟、阿什河）和沿江两岸整治，建成以市级湿地宣教馆为主体、各湿地保护地宣教中心和湿地学校为分支的生态环境宣教网络，打造"万顷松江湿地、百里生态长廊"国际湿地名城。

冰雪经济创新"两山"转化路径

2024 年 11 月，国务院办公厅印发《关于以冰雪运动高质量发展激发冰雪经济活力的若干意见》，提出以冰雪运动为引领，带动冰雪文化、冰雪装备、冰雪旅游全产业链发展，推动冰雪经济成为新增长点，到 2027 年冰雪经济总规模达 1.2 万亿元。作为中国冰雪经济中心，哈尔滨市已在精心规划"后亚冬时代"新蓝图：利用自然资源、文化禀赋、地方符号，打造具有情感价值的冰雪体验旅游项目，与周边城市形成资源互补、协同发展的冰雪旅游产品矩阵和精品线路，发展"冰雪＋夜经济""冰雪＋沉浸式科技""冰雪＋文创"等绿色消费新场景，推出雪地温泉度假、冰雪婚礼、雪地亲子运动会、家庭滑雪挑战赛、冰雪研学等满足不同消费群体的定制服务，引育产学研主体研制满足运动员竞技、训练、测试、康复和人民群众多样化冰雪运动需求的装备器材，鼓励高校科研院所开设冰雪运动、冰雪经济相关的专业和课程，建立冰雪经济岗位标准，促进冰雪经济国际交流合作，打造国家级冰雪运动示范区和冰雪旅游度假胜地、冰雪人才培育基地、冰雪装备器材制造基地、国际冰雪赛事之都。

特大城市高品质推进美丽城市
建设的"青岛经验"

　　作为常住人口 1034 万、年地区生产总值 1.67 万亿元的特大城市，青岛气候温和湿润，冬无严寒，夏无酷暑，山、海、湾、城浑然一体，被联合国评为最适合人类居住的城市之一，获评全国文明城市、中国最具幸福感城市、中国美好生活城市等荣誉称号。连续四年在山东省污染防治攻坚战成效考核中获"优秀"等次，7 个区（市）建成国家生态文明建设示范区或"两山"基地，李村河入选全国美丽河湖，成为中国北方城市内陆河流治理的样板，灵山湾、崂山湾分获国家、省级美丽海湾称号，连续两年进入中国城市生态环保营商竞争力全国前十，成功承办上合组织国家绿色发展论坛，被生态环境部在美丽中国新闻发布会上点赞，陆海统筹、河海共治的生态优势正转化为青岛市高质量发展胜势。徜徉在青岛的红瓦绿树、碧海蓝天、绿水青山之间，466 条大小河流纵横交织，497 座湖库星罗棋布，905.2 公里的漫长海岸线上分布着 49 个海湾，深刻感受到大省大市勇挑大梁，绿色发展先行，打造美丽中国建设地方标杆的生态魅力。

共建共治生态环境保护新格局

　　乘坐飞机俯视青岛大地，大沽河如同一条舞动的银练贯通南北，至胶州湾奔流入海，成为空港入青第一景。经过多年治理和管理维护，179.9 千米、横跨多个区市的大沽河成为生机盎然、游人接踵的省级美丽幸福河湖。2017 年，青岛率先在全省实行河（湖）长制，列入对各区

（市）经济社会发展综合考核，逐段落实河湖管护责任主体，配备河湖管理员、民间（义务）河（湖）长、志愿者，做到有人管事、有钱办事、有章理事。至今，城市建成区基本消除黑臭水体，11 个国省控河道断面全面达标，18 处城镇以上集中式饮用水水源地水质达标率保持 100%，创建 31 条（段）省级美丽幸福河湖。

海湾是近岸海域具有代表性的地理单元，是生态保护重地、休闲旅游胜地和经济发展高地。作为中国首个推行湾长制的城市，青岛构建市、区、镇三级湾长体系，湾长与河长结成紧密工作搭档，接力监测和巡查入海河流水质，清理拆除养殖设施，整治入海排污口，增殖放流各类苗种，实现从陆源污染到海洋生态的全链条治理。目前，全市近岸海域优良水质比例连续 5 年达 100%，湾内调查发现共有陆地及海洋生物3511 种。

美丽海湾建设不仅造就"湾美滩净"，也带来海岸沿线产业升级。过去小岛湾北岸以传统渔业养殖为主，即墨区对小岛湾北侧海岸带和小管岛综合整治，建设滨海步行道、海上观光平台等设施，打造美丽海岸线。如今的小岛湾，聚集 50 余家"国字号"科研院所和 90 余个市级及以上创新平台，形成以海洋高技术服务、海洋生物、海洋高端装备三大主导产业和海洋文旅、涉海总部经济为特色的"3+2"绿色产业体系，成为青岛经略海洋的新名片。

超前布局碳达峰碳中和

作为国家碳达峰试点城市，青岛在绿色低碳转型上多有先行先试，比如，发布《碳达峰碳中和标准体系建设指南》，构建"基础通用标准""碳减排标准""碳清除标准""碳市场标准"四个标准子体系；率先出台税务助力"双碳"系列文件，精准推送减污降碳"红利账单"；在中国同类城市中率先出台碳金融发展三年行动方案，完成全省首单企业间用能权交易；开展绿色低碳高质量发展统计监测，完善全社会能源消费总量核算方案，探索碳排放核算办法。

青岛高新区的污水源热泵、余热回收利用等可再生能源供热面积达

426.24万平方米，占总供热面积的44%，推进"绿电倍增"工程，已建、在建光伏总装机容量达70兆瓦，年节省煤炭近15万吨，年减排二氧化碳约37万吨。鼓励有条件的企业建设"无废工厂"，引导小微企业采用"拼团"打包方式统一管理和转运危废，减少企业危废处置成本。近5年，青岛高新区二氧化硫排放总量降低93.4%，氮氧化物排放总量降低30.3%，单位工业增加值能源消费总量下降39.3%，单位工业增加值二氧化碳排放量下降45.5%，工业增加值年均增速14.7%、工业总产值年均增速13.7%，基本完成阶段性"碳达峰"目标的同时，绿色低碳发展强劲动力凸显。

绿色发展动能澎湃

锚定"双碳"目标，青岛市引导企业绿色化改造，截至2024年末，累计获评国家级绿色制造名单企业65家、绿色工厂47家、绿色供应链管理企业14家。在数智技术赋能绿色工厂构建方面，海克斯康制造智能技术有限公司是绿色工厂解决方案提供商，融合行业尖端测量仪器和专业软件系统，构建智慧运维、能源管理、楼宇监控、智能照明、智慧工厂等多维场景"一张图"的智慧工厂管理平台，实现数据实时采集、分析和控制，综合能耗可下降40%。

在工业企业与污染治理机构合作方面，污水处理厂需要购买碳源，将污水中的溶解性氮转化为氮气从水中排出，而啤酒废液是可生化性极好的高浓度有机物，也是城市污水处理厂碳源的绝佳补充。青岛啤酒集团在中国首创啤酒高浓废水与市政污水协同处理减污降碳资源化利用关键技术，每年为污水处理厂提供1.5万吨生产过程中产生的废液，减少二氧化碳排放1.23万吨。在该模式下，啤酒工厂废水处理流程简化，废水处理成本显著降低，污水处理厂减少碳源采购费用，实现"变废为宝"双赢。

在加强绿色制造能力和绿色产品供给能力方面，海尔智家构建绿色设计、绿色制造、绿色营销、绿色回收、绿色处置、绿色采购的"6-Green"战略模式，比如，海尔灯塔工厂开发设备电力负荷智能调度大模型，能源消耗降低 35%，二氧化碳排放减少 36%，提高经营韧性和减少碳排放；海尔再循环互联工厂是家电再循环产业首座互联工厂，每年有 200 万台废旧家电于此拆解，产出循环新材料 3 万吨，减少二氧化碳排放 1.7 万吨。中车青岛四方机车车辆股份有限公司研制全球首列商用碳纤维地铁列车，引入轻质新材料替代钢、铝合金等金属材料，采用新型地板布、水性漆等环保材料，排水系统采用中转式真空集便系统，电力牵引采用低压能耗分时管理，车辆整体减重 11%，运行能耗降低 7%。

书写绿水青山新答卷

锚定绿色低碳、品质环境、和谐生态、健康韧性、宜居典范、生态文化、现代制度、开放窗口"八美之城"战略任务，青岛始终不渝把美丽城市建设摆在突出位置，大力推动生态文明体制改革，纵深推进污染防治攻坚，一体治理山水林田海岛湾，以生态"含绿量"提升发展"含金量"，奋力蹚出一条山海城相融、人与自然和谐共生的美丽中国"青岛样板"高质量发展新路。

一江碧水向东流：
生态优先、绿色发展的武汉实践

"一城秀水半城山"，得天独厚的生态资源优势，是大自然对武汉最好的"馈赠"，也是武汉推动生态优先、绿色发展最丰厚的基础。近年来，武汉市全面实施绿色低碳转型，加快培育绿色新质生产力，让人民群众共享自然之美、生命之美、生活之美，2024 年，全市 22 条主要河流86.8%的断面水质达到或优于Ⅲ类，142 个湖泊达到或优于《地表水环境质量标准》Ⅳ类标准，无劣Ⅴ类湖泊，9 座大、中型水库和 41 个集中式饮用水源地水质均达到或优于Ⅲ类标准，一幅山清水秀、天蓝地绿的江城壮美新画卷蔚然铺展。

打造水环境流域综合治理样板

2018 年 4 月，习近平总书记在武汉主持召开深入推动长江经济带发展座谈会并强调，必须从中华民族长远利益考虑，把修复长江生态环境摆在压倒性位置，共抓大保护、不搞大开发，努力把长江经济带建设成为生态更优美、交通更顺畅、经济更协调、市场更统一、机制更科学的黄金经济带。

武汉市打好长江大保护十大标志性战役①，开展长江高水平保护十大

---

① 武汉市长江大保护十大标志性战役：沿江化工企业关改搬转、城市黑臭水体整治、农业面源污染整治、非法码头整治、非法采砂整治、饮用水源地保护、沿江企业污水减排、磷石膏污染整治、固体废物排查、城乡垃圾治理。

攻坚提升行动①，落实长江十年禁渔属地责任，实施河湖流域水环境"清源、清管、清流"三清行动，设置市、区、街道、社区四级河湖长，推行"河湖长+检察长"等协作机制，打造"小小河湖长""江城河小青"等民间护河（湖）志愿服务品牌，建设幸福河湖试点和示范社区，更新村规民约，"河湖治理、人人有责"深入人心。

"两江四岸"② 不仅是武汉市发展的主轴，也是彰显山水城市独特魅力的窗口。武汉市整体打造集安全廊、生态廊、文化廊、交通廊、发展廊于一体的百里长江生态廊道，以"连断点、补空点、提亮点、优服务"为建设思路，提档升级防洪设施，护净水、显绿岸、塑绿城，重筑生态空间，建设历史文化风貌展示区，加强与城市慢行道交通联系，利用江滩建休闲空间，一体打造生活岸线、生态岸线、景观岸线，还江于民、还岸于民、还景于民。

共抓长江大保护，关键在"共"字。2022 年 5 月，武汉经济技术开发区管委会和仙桃市人民政府签署《通顺河③流域跨市断面水质考核生态补偿协议》。按照"谁超标、谁赔付，谁受益、谁补偿"原则，施行通顺河上下游"双向生态补偿"，上游来水水质达到或优于目标要求，下游地区向上游地区给予生态补偿，否则上游地区向下游地区给予污染补偿，补偿资金专用于通顺河流域水污染防治。2023 年，通顺河上游来水水质优于目标要求，武汉市给予仙桃市生态补偿资金 300 万元。2024 年，武汉市又向孝感市和随州市分别兑现生态补偿资金 610 万元和 700 万元，将生态补偿由长江支流扩展至干流。

---

① 武汉市长江高水平保护十大攻坚提升行动：沿江化工企业关改搬转绿色转型攻坚提升行动、长江入河排污口溯源整治攻坚提升行动、城镇污水处理提质增效及黑臭水体治理攻坚提升行动、城乡生活垃圾无害化处理攻坚提升行动、船舶和港口污染防治攻坚提升行动、农业农村绿色发展攻坚提升行动、国土绿化和湿地保护修复攻坚提升行动、国土空间生态修复攻坚提升行动、水资源保障攻坚提升行动、长江流域非法矮围整治攻坚提升行动。

② 两江四岸："两江"为长江、汉江，"四岸"为长江南岸、长江北岸、汉江东岸、汉江西岸。

③ 通顺河是湖北省的重要河流，西起潜江市泽口闸，流经潜江市和仙桃市，进入武汉市，全长 195 公里，其中武汉段河道长 68 公里，汇水面积 824 平方千米，经黄陵矶闸入长江。

武汉市虽为"百湖之市"，但超 99%的水资源来源于长江和汉江的过境水，且长江武汉段水功能区已无较大纳污能力，面临资源型和水质型缺水的双重压力。武汉市大力推动再生水循环利用，放开再生水水价，采取"一企一价"定价机制，实施污水处理及再生水产品增值税即征即退政策，推出"节水贷"等绿色金融产品，选树节水型小区、节水型机关、节水型企业。2024 年，武汉市再生水利用量突破 5 亿米^3，工业用水重复利用率达 94.02%，再创历史新高，入选全国再生水重点利用城市及全国第二批区域再生水循环利用试点城市。

建好全球首个人口超千万的"国际湿地城市"

武汉市拥有 165 条河流、166 个湖泊、145 公里长江岸线，建有 5 个湿地自然保护区、6 个国家湿地公园、70 余座湖泊公园、40 余处小微湿地，是拥有国家湿地公园最多的省会城市，既有河流、湖泊、沼泽等自然湿地，也有库塘等人工湿地，生态系统结构完整，生物多样性丰富。市、区两级人民政府建立湿地保护联席会议制度，打造各具特色的湿地保护样板区，建成智慧湿地管理系统，形成覆盖 4 万公顷重要湿地和 8.7 万公顷湖泊的"空-天-水-岸"一张网，开展"湿地小卫士""自然笔记"等自然教育活动，东湖、后官湖、安山等湿地公园成为市民亲近自然的"生态绿心"，年均接待市民游客超 5000 万人次。

斧头湖横跨武汉、咸宁，水质下降的症结在于夏季水草生长过于茂密、养殖户将鱼塘水抽排入湖、畜禽养殖企业的尾水小范围泄漏，两市建立联防联治机制，精准施治后的水质升至Ⅲ类。汤逊湖是亚洲最大城中湖，雨污混流水、初期雨水的污染物浓度高，通过在排污口分流井安装视频监控、水质检测、雨量监测、管道水位监测等设备，符合排放标准的雨水通过管道正常排湖，一旦系统监测发现管道水污染物浓度超标，井内堰门自动打开，水流"改道"新修的引流管进入最近的市政污水管网，再输送到污水处理厂处理。实施东湖水环境提升工程，在湖中构建水下生态系统，沉水植物覆盖率超 70%，游船、帆船等水上游览体验项目吸引大量游客前来打卡。

美丽生态激活美丽经济

2024 年 11 月，随着一辆东风岚图在武汉下线，中国新能源汽车年产量首次突破 1000 万辆。武汉与东风汽车相互成就，武汉经开区 318 国道的 13 公里路段被命名为东风大道，布局 7 家整车企业、10 余个整车工厂、500 多家零部件企业、14 家省级及以上汽车研发机构，新能源车年产量超百万，成为全球汽车工业密集度最高的轴线。2021 年，东风汽车向新能源与智能驾驶领域转型，至今集聚 300 多家上下游合作商，本地配套率达 41%。东风汽车累计有效专利超 2.44 万件，智能网联与新能源专利占比 35%，连续三年蝉联中国车企发明专利授权量榜首，武汉正成为全球新能源汽车技术变革的策源地。

2023 年，武汉经开区在环太子湖畔启动建设智能汽车软件园，在自动驾驶、车规级芯片、智能座舱、车联网等领域重点布局，这是继上海之后中国第二家以智能汽车命名并形成规模的软件园。如今，以武汉东软软件园为核心，领军软件加速区、科创邻里生活区、车载芯片创新区、算力服务区集聚 200 余家汽车软件企业、3 万余名软件人才，形成"汽车工厂"到"最强大脑"跨越。

2024 年，武汉市有 32 家工厂、1 家供应链管理企业、1 家园区获评国家绿色制造体系示范，分别占全省的 45%、50%、50%，绿色成为这座工业重镇的一抹亮色。以极致能效领跑者、低碳冶金示范者、绿色能源先行者、低碳产品引领者为目标，武汉钢铁有限公司累计投资超 150 亿元用于绿色低碳环保改造，产品吨钢综合能耗、碳排放强度连续 8 年下降；建成 4 个固废处理中心和 4 个固废回用生产线，一般固废综合利用率达 100%；钢渣尾渣在炼铁工序中推广应用，减少二氧化碳排放 2.8 万吨/年；建成全球最大的取向硅钢制造基地，每年减少碳排放约 200 万吨；绿电采购逾 10 亿千瓦时，成为全省最大的绿电使用机构；建成年发电量 4500 万千瓦时的华中地区规模最大的分布式屋顶光伏站，每年减少二氧化碳排放 2.65 万吨。

2021 年 7 月，全国碳排放权交易市场上线交易，全国碳排放权注册登记结算系统选址武汉。如今，沙湖边的中碳登大厦聚集 60 多家碳交易、碳评级、碳认证、碳核算、碳资产管理等专业机构，初步形成"一栋楼就是产业链、上下楼就是上下游"的千亿级碳产业集群，便利武汉企业和市民享受"减碳红利"。2024 年末，武汉 2 笔由公众积攒的碳普惠减排量共计 2000 吨，在湖北碳排放权交易中心完成交易，获得碳收益 8.7 万元，这是中国首笔个人碳资产变现。

在中部地区绿色发展中挑大梁

武汉城市发展史是一部理水营城的历史，从东汉末年却月城、夏口城隔江对峙，到明中期汉水改道三镇分立，到 20 世纪顺江拓展，再到现在砥砺迈向"绿水青山就是金山银山"的人与自然和谐共生之路，武汉市要继续统筹好山、水、路、岸、产、城等空间关系，扎实推进长江高水平保护，加快建设安全韧性现代水网，发掘水环境改善带来的产业变革和营商环境新红利，培育绿色低碳产业链供应链，在城市更新和乡村振兴中创造绿色建筑、节能环保等新产业的新增长点，拓展绿色生活和碳普惠应用场景，加快建成中部地区绿色低碳示范城市。

鄂尔多斯：
库布齐沙漠"光伏蓝"赋能"生态绿"

在我国第七大沙漠——库布齐沙漠，一块块亮晶晶的蓝色光伏板连在一起成为"蓝色海洋"，带来源源不断的生态效益、经济效益、社会效益。昔日风沙漫天，今朝"风光"无限，茫茫大漠正上演一场"光伏长城"防沙治沙的壮美场景。库布齐沙漠是离首都北京最近的沙漠，总面积 2116 万亩，位于内蒙古自治区鄂尔多斯市北部，是黄河"几字弯"攻坚战的主战场，过去由于特殊的地理条件和十年九旱的气候特点，植被稀少，沙尘暴频发，不断侵袭和危害沙区人民，曾被称为"死亡之海"。新中国成立后，鄂尔多斯人以空前的治沙热情，构筑绿化带、淤地坝、光伏治沙带、锁边林"四道防线"，锻造出艰苦奋斗、锲而不舍、改革创新的"库布齐精神"，沙漠治理率达 40%。

2023 年，习近平总书记考察内蒙古时发出打好"三北"工程攻坚战总动员令，强调筑牢我国北方重要生态安全屏障，是内蒙古必须牢记的"国之大者"，要求在"三北"工程六期规划基础上，结合正在布局实施的新能源大基地建设，把防沙治沙与风电光伏开发一体规划设计，在保护治理中实现开发。2017 年和 2019 年，习近平总书记先后向第六届、第七届库布齐国际沙漠论坛和《联合国防治荒漠化公约》第十三次缔约方大会致贺信指出，库布齐沙漠治理为国际社会治理环境生态、落实 2030 年议程提供了中国经验。

生态屏障和绿电基地一体建设

鄂尔多斯市编制"三北"工程六期建设方案，以建设库布齐沙漠中北部和南部2个"沙戈荒"新能源大基地为牵引，引导三峡、华能、大唐、国能、蒙能、隆基等20余家头部企业通过赞助捐款、投资产业、异地治理等方式参与光伏治沙带建设，形成国家投入为主、地方配套为辅、社会广泛参与的多元投入新格局，光伏方阵周边营造乔木林防风，光伏板间种植低矮灌木林固沙，因地制宜开展板下空间开发利用，种植高产牧草、农作物等增加植被，项目区林草植被覆盖率达40%以上。至今，建成光伏项目1002万千瓦时，实现光伏治沙60万亩，在建、拟建项目全部建成后将实现光伏治沙200万亩，占库布齐沙漠总面积的10%左右，基本构筑阻止风沙侵蚀、护卫黄河安澜的绿色生态屏障。

前瞻的战略路径、丰富的资源禀赋、高效的消纳体系、强大的外送通道共同构筑鄂尔多斯市新能源变革的坚实底座。作为西部地区资源富集城市，鄂尔多斯市"脚下有煤炭，头顶有风光"，风能、太阳能开发潜力高达1.5亿千瓦以上，是中国七大陆上新能源基地之一。2023年12月，中国首个千万千瓦级大型风光基地项目——库布齐沙漠鄂尔多斯中北部新能源基地项目先导工程100万千瓦光伏项目全容量并网发电，项目全部建成后，每年将向京津冀地区输送绿电约200亿千瓦时以上，可节约标煤约656万吨、减排二氧化碳约1994万吨。截至2024年12月，鄂尔多斯累计建成新能源装机规模1419万千瓦，占全市电力总装机规模的28%，较2021年翻一番。

鄂尔多斯市加强本地电网主网架建设，建成500千伏变电站15座、220千伏变电站80座、110千伏变电站250座，形成以500千伏特高压为引领、220千伏为支撑、110千伏辐射的供电网络格局。建成1600万千瓦至天津和山东的2条特高压外送通道，在建至京津冀、上海、江苏、华东的4条外送通道，力争在"十五五"新增2条外送通道，到2030年形成"2+4+2"特高压绿电外送格局。统筹推进保障性并网、高载能产业大规模绿电替代、源网荷储一体化、风光制氢一体化、园区绿色供电、火电灵活性改造、全额自发自用等市场化消纳新能源项目，因地制宜发展分布式新能源、清洁能源保供、新能源市场化交易等增量项目，预计到 2030 年，绿电外送和本地消纳规模达 6000 万千瓦以上。美国多家媒体报道称，库布齐沙漠荒凉一隅变身大规模光伏基地，旨在产生足够能源为京津冀地区供电，这是中国建设可再生能源强国努力的一部分。

"风光氢储车" 全产业链发展

鄂尔多斯市积极推动 "装机+装备" 双向赋能，以商招商，产业链招商，构筑 "上游材料—关键装备—配套零部件—多元应用—运维服务—回收利用" 新能源全产业链条。2022 年 4 月，鄂尔多斯零碳产业园一期项目建成投产，80% 的能源直接来自风电、光伏和储能，20% 的能源通过电网回购绿电，实现 100% 零碳能源供给。至今，园区引进新能源头部企业 54 家，实施新能源产业项目 150 多个，建成光伏装备 47.5GW、储能装备 13GWh、风机装备 10GW、氢燃料电池系统超万台套、新能源车 4 万辆的产能规模，初步形成电池及储能、氢燃料电池及绿氢设备制造、新能源汽车制造等产业链，光伏关键组件产业链完整度达 100%，主辅材园区配套超 40%，电池片产能占内蒙古自治区 100%，大尺寸组件、高效电池片、氢燃料电池系统及电堆等 9 类产品填补内蒙古自治区空白。

进一步看，作为国家首批碳达峰试点城市，鄂尔多斯市依托绿电优势，开展 "光伏制氢一体化+氢能环网" 创新实践，引进绿氢、绿氨、绿醇、绿色航煤等 "化工+新能源" 耦合项目，延伸发展 "绿电+工业硅" "绿电+电解铝" "绿电+新型煤化工" 等先进材料产业，促进资源型产业绿色低碳转型。

建设荒漠化防治与绿色发展的创新高地

2022 年 7 月，国务院批复同意鄂尔多斯市以 "荒漠化防治与绿色发展" 为主题，建设国家可持续发展议程创新示范区。针对 "生态建设产业化程度低，制约荒漠化防治提质增效" "资源型产业链条短，制约经济转型升级和绿色发展"两大问题，鄂尔多斯市实施荒漠化防治提质增效、资源节约集约高效利用、现代能源经济高质量发展提速、人才和科技创新驱动发展、城乡区域协调发展促进"五大行动"，努力打造"绿、业、新、富"可持续发展的创新典范。高标准建设荒漠化防治国际技术创新中心、院士专家工作站、研究院、种质资源库等创新载体，稳步推进产学研用深度融合。与"三北"工程研究院、清华大学天津高端装备研究院等合作，设立防沙治沙装备产业园，开展关键技术攻关，智能飞播无人机、光伏清洗机器人、智能植树机器人、智能沙障铺设机械等创新成果从实验室走向生产线。建设中国种类最全、规模最大的储能试验实证基地，开展光热储能、压缩空气、重力储能、钠离子电池等应用场景实证，推进多种储能技术路线实证，积极承担储能国家重大科技战略任务。目前，鄂尔多斯市在新能源领域科技成果转化率达 60%，引领示范效应愈加显现。

共建共享，绿富同兴

鄂尔多斯市坚持利企惠民，推进光伏治沙与配套产业协同发展，出台《推进"三北"六期等重点生态工程建管创新九条措施》，落实资金统筹、以工代赈、建管一体等激励措施，培育新能源产业链供应链，探索板上发电、板下修复、板间种植、场间养殖的"草光互补""林光互补"等治沙用沙新模式，开辟"板上产绿电、板下生绿金、板外带旅游"三产融合发展新赛道。建立"基地＋企业＋合作社＋农牧民"多层次利益联结机制，光伏治沙项目前期通过流转、租赁沙化土地为农牧民带来土地增值红利，项目建设期吸纳农牧民参与施工安装、组件清洗、生态治理等获取劳务收益，项目运营期通过种苗订单、劳务派遣、产品购销等方式，稳定提供就近就业岗位，相关农牧民人均年增收 2 万元以上。

守护一方"温暖担当"

2024 年 12 月，鄂尔多斯作为中国唯一代表城市，受邀参加《联合国防治荒漠化公约》第十六次缔约方大会，库布齐沙漠"光伏+治沙"模式赢得国际社会广泛关注。作为中国重要的煤炭基地、煤电基地、西气东输基地、陆上新能源基地，鄂尔多斯温暖千座城、点亮万家灯：在北京，每5盏灯里就有1盏来自鄂尔多斯的能源点亮；在京津冀地区，有一半家庭的天然气来自鄂尔多斯……近年来，鄂尔多斯市统筹新能源开发与沙漠高效治理，形成以集约利用沙地、规模光伏发电、立体生态修复为特色的"光伏+治沙"新模式，在保障国家能源安全方面担当作为，为中国能源绿色低碳转型先行示范。

展望未来，鄂尔多斯市要锚定全球新能源产业高地目标，推动洁净煤、绿色煤电、煤基燃料、煤化工等产业高端化、多元化、低碳化发展，建设电压等级高、输送容量大、运行灵活高效的高比例清洁电力外送基地，以源网荷储一体化、园区绿色供电、风光制氢一体化等创新模式促进绿色能源与地方产业协同发展，构建集能源生产、装备制造、应用示范于一体的"风光氢储车"现代化新能源产业体系，探索传统能源绿色转型、煤炭清洁转化利用、新能源高比例内用外输、新能源全链集群发展等绿色发展新路径。

深圳市盐田区大梅沙碳中和先行示范区：建设全球低碳社区标杆

王　石

大梅沙碳中和先行示范区（以下简称"示范区"）是深圳市首批近零碳排放试点项目，位于盐田区梅沙街道，由全部的大梅沙社区、部分滨海社区和部分东海岸社区组成，面积约 3.2 平方公里，常住人口 1.98 万人，2023 年接待游客 1800 万人次。与传统园区、住宅区等不同，示范区是完全开放、功能复合、没有单一物业管理的社区，包括 22 个住宅小区、13 个总部办公楼、4 所学校、1 座大型医院和商场。

2022 年 3 月，深圳市盐田区生态环境局与深石集团签署《共建大梅沙碳中和先行示范区战略合作框架协议》。深石集团秉持"碳中和不是目的，美好生活才是"的价值观，以大梅沙万科中心碳中和实验园区为中心，构建"建筑改造+能源替代+循环经济"三位一体的碳减排体系，围绕"一个轴心、四个维度"[①]，落实碳中和社区改造，在 COP28、COP29 大会上作为典型案例展示，入选生态环境部绿色低碳典型案例及 C40"绿色繁荣社区试点"，其经验被纳入《绿色繁荣社区建设指南》国际标准。

围绕"减替抵运"[②] 打造碳中和社区

示范区内，深石集团打造了多个标杆低碳示范点。其中，采用绿色

---

① "一个轴心、四个维度"：一个轴心指"生活可以更美好"，四个维度指绿色低碳、生物多样性、运动健康、艺术与美。

② "减"即节能节费，包括建筑围护结构改造、设备提效改造、物联网管理节能等；"替"即光伏、风电等新能源替代火电；"抵"即碳抵消；"运"即能源运营。

建筑技术建造的大梅沙万科中心获得中国首个 LEED 铂金级认证（办公建筑）、三星级绿色建筑标识证书。2022 年 5 月启动改造升级，当年 10 月改造完成后更名为生物圈三号·大梅沙万科中心碳中和实验园区（以下简称"园区"），于 2024 年获得 WELL Community 和 WELL Core 双铂金级认证，成为广东省首家入选中国绿色低碳典型案例的园区，近两年荣获国家级、省市及主流媒体颁发的绿色创新类奖项 14 个。目前，园区年总用电量约 650 万度，通过叠加光伏发电、储能系统、生物质循环利用等低碳措施，绿电占比由 17.5% 提升至 85%，实现年均碳减排超 800 吨，总体碳排放较改造前下降 93%，成为具有国际示范意义的城市建筑碳中和案例。大梅沙碳中和先行示范区 2023~2028 年降碳目标和重点项目见表 1。

进一步看，园区绿色低碳技术改造的关键点在于：一是清洁能源替代，光伏总装机容量达 742.57kWp，平均年发电量约 7.2 万千瓦时，满足园区绝大部分白天负荷需求；二是储能调节能力提升，储能预制舱是深圳供电局承担的首个国家重点研发计划项目的示范系统，储能总容量 400kWh（能量）/200kW（功率），实现电能削峰填谷，为极端天气等应急场景提供电力保障；三是高效消纳与互动用能，借助智能微电网，本地光伏消纳率达 90%，部署 V2G 车网互动桩、光储充车棚、电力魔方超充示范站等，实现能源系统与交通系统深度耦合；四是全域智能监控，部署约 200 块智能电表，实现对各楼层、功能区的用电行为实时采集和分项分析；五是算法驱动调度优化，构建光伏预测、建筑能耗预测、储能控制等大模型算法，开发智能决策系统，动态预测用能与发电情况，制定收益最优的能源调度策略；六是绿化垃圾循环利用，结合雨水收集系统（年节水 5 万吨），构建"黑水虻—社区堆肥—共建花园"循环模式；七是创新材料应用，使用废弃易拉罐与工业废铝制成的"发泡支撑泡沫铝"作为部分建筑材料，将竹材用于家具与装饰；八是参与城市双碳大脑开发，建设工业、建筑两大领域碳监测体系，服务政府碳治理、企业碳减排和公众碳普惠。

盐田区行政文化中心与深石集团合作开展"近零碳机关"（深圳市第四批近零碳排放建筑试点）建设，完成屋顶光伏总装机容量 477kWp，年发电量约 50 万度，年减碳 226 吨；配置 V2G 充电桩和 1160 度电化学储

表1 大梅沙碳中和先行示范区2023~2028年降碳目标和重点项目

类目		2023年 项目	2023年 数值(吨)	2024年 项目	2024年 数值(吨)	2025年 项目	2025年 数值(吨)	2026年 项目	2026年 数值(吨)	2027年 项目	2027年 数值(吨)	2028年 项目	2028年 数值(吨)	降碳目标
设施改造	建筑节能改造							工商业建筑节能完成率30%	4408	工商业建筑节能完成率50%	7347	工商业建筑节能完成70%,小区节能完成70%	10847	21%
设施改造	新能源设施	万科中心、华大时空中心	1030	盐田区外国语学校、大梅沙小学屋顶光伏	280	工商业屋顶光伏项目(酒店,办公,商业,学校)完成30%;停车场车棚光伏项目完成30%	442	工商业屋顶光伏项目完成40%,停车场车棚光伏,小区棚光项目完成30%;波浪能投产30%	633	波浪能投产50%	1436	工商业屋顶光伏项目完成70%;工商业、小区光伏车棚项目完成70%;波浪能投产70%	2195	4%
聚合运营	碳汇	科普馆垃圾收集、大梅沙小区厨余收集	1086	科普馆垃圾收集处理持续运营	1086	盐田区环境园开始运行,15吨/天的垃圾处理规模	1906	盐田区环境园持续运营	1906	盐田区环境园持续运营	1906	盐田区环境园持续运营	1906	4%
聚合运营	虚拟电厂			万科中心、华大时空中心	2373	盐田外国语学校、梅沙小学;零碳机关;盐田区其他新增设施	4015	盐田区新增新能源设施	5103	盐田区新增新能源设施	5443	东莞科学城光伏、大鹏LNG冷能和3.2平方千米光伏微电网	5553	11%

能系统，年节约电费 27 万元，实现电动车与电网能量高效互动；构建能耗全景监控、智能调度、柔性互动、虚拟电厂四大场景，提升能源调度效率，降低尖峰负荷冲击；AI 优化空调系统运行，预计年节能率 13%，年减碳 130 吨。

虚拟电厂聚合分布式能源、储能及可控负荷资源，提升电网灵活性，有效解决深圳市面临的可再生能源大规模接入、电动汽车保有量激增、极端气候导致电力供需矛盾等挑战。作为深圳市首批负荷聚合商，深石集团采用物联网与人工智能技术，完成对示范区储能、充电桩、冰蓄冷空调机组、中央空调机组等可调控负荷控制，实现 10 秒内调频响应，精准跟踪调度指令准确率达 95%。深石集团虚拟电厂全链条参与资源聚合、市场交易、跨省结算等电网调度，累计接入精准响应负荷近 2 兆瓦，涵盖商业办公楼宇、政府公共建筑等多类型应用场景，努力打造全球领先的虚拟电厂范式和新型电力系统"深圳经验"。

黑水虻技术推动社区减碳

在大梅沙万科中心碳中和实验园区，从 2018 年开始，黑水虻厨余垃圾回收站每天处理厨余垃圾 200 公斤；在盐田区循环经济环保科普教育基地，每天完成 3 吨的厨余垃圾处理量；在深能国家级示范环境园，配置日处理 15 吨有机固渣的高标准黑水虻养殖生产线，年运行时间超过 8400 小时。作为纯生物质垃圾处理手段，黑水虻垃圾处理技术实现零碳排放，成虫具有药用价值，可制成高蛋白宠物粮，以及作为化妆品重要成分，拥有不俗的商业价值。

Verra（全球最大的自愿碳市场标准制定机构）在碳信用计划——核证碳标准（VCS）中，发布深石集团协助其战略合作伙伴万科公益基金会于 2022 年第三季度提交的黑水虻方法学，标志着黑水虻等生物多样性技术纳入国际碳抵消体系，为有机废弃物处理低碳转型提供可量化的市场激励机制，向国际业界展示中国已有公益组织利用黑水虻技术开展社区减碳，有利于类似项目通过 VCS 认证获得国际碳市场融资。

绿色健康与绿色叙事

示范区山海资源得天独厚，深石集团创办深潜海岸赛艇俱乐部，联合盐田体育馆、盐田攀岩馆、深圳登山协会、深圳自行车协会等在地资源，因地制宜发展赛艇、徒步、滑翔伞等体育健身项目，开展城市户外运动多项赛（盐田）、深圳海滨公路自行车公开赛、深圳盐田山海半程马拉松、十峰勇士人车接力赛、为爱同行35千米公益徒步、深圳100越野挑战赛等10余项赛事，极大增加人流量，带动周边消费，使得绿色健康理念深入人心。

示范区打造生物圈三号文化艺术交流平台，扶持具有先锋意识的青年艺术家，聚焦生物多样性保护、ESG实践、气候行动等时代命题，以装置艺术、数字影像、生态雕塑等多元形式诠释可持续发展理念，展陈设计、材料选择、能源供给均采用环保解决方案，形成可复制的绿色艺术运营范式。通过"大梅沙社区客厅"建立公众参与机制，与善淘慈善快闪商店等合作，联合构建"二手闲置物"交互系统，邀请艺术家利用废弃物创作艺术装置，引导市民用咖啡渣作画、电子废料创作声光装置，感受物品全生命周期的碳足迹。

绿色发展的先锋实践与未来蓝图

示范区实践证明，绿色不仅是生态底色，更是经济新引擎，通过科技赋能、资源循环与社群共创，实现"人与自然共生"的愿景，为落实中国"双碳"目标提供鲜活样本。目前，示范区的创新模式已走出大梅沙，迈向其他城市和国家，助力全球绿色繁荣。正如深石集团创始人所言，我们希望每个城市都有"生物圈三号"，这是对美好生活的追求。

参考文献

1. 新华社国家高端智库，习近平生态文明思想研究中心．让世界读懂美丽中国的"绿色密码"——习近平生态文明思想的中国实践与世界贡献，2024.

2. 国务院新闻办公室．新时代的中国绿色发展白皮书，2023.

3. 于洪君，史志钦，杨东平，刘洋．2024 年"一带一路"青年发展报告，人民出版社，2024.

4. 刘洋，方宁．成渝地区双城经济圈建设五周年研究报告，社会科学文献出版社，2024.

5. 中共生态环境部党组．聚焦建设美丽中国 深化生态文明体制改革，求是，2024（21）．

6. 许勤华．绿色"一带一路"是习近平生态文明思想在全球生态治理中的重要实践，人民日报，2025-02-18.

7. 郭威．协同推进全面绿色转型，经济日报，2025-02-13.

8. 周向军．深刻把握习近平生态文明思想的理论根基．光明日报，2023-12-01.

9. 金佳绪，刘淼．"绿水青山就是金山银山"——习近平推动生态环境保护的故事，新华网．

10. 江南，窦瀚洋．走进安吉，看"绿水青山就是金山银山"，人民日报，2023-12-08.

11. 高敬．不断书写新的绿色奇迹——新中国成立 75 周年生态环境保护成就综述，新华网．

12. 邵长军．深刻把握中国式现代化的中国特色，人民日报，2023-01-31.

13. 杨小明，王彬．全面理解我国生态文明建设仍处于压力叠加、负重前行的关键期，中国环境报，2023-09-11．

14. 金轩．践行绿水青山就是金山银山理念的浙江实践和启示，经济日报，2024-11-27．

15. 朱智翔．踩下污染"急刹车"挂上逐绿"前进档"浙江实施 5 轮"811"行动绿色发展之路越走越宽广，中国环境报，2024-08-15．

16. 洪恒飞，江耘．浙江湖州：多元化探索生态产品价值转化模式，科技日报，2024-12-13．

17. 林云龙，曹坚等．75 年，浙江的 75 个"第一"·生态文明建设，浙江日报，2024-09-29．

18. 专题调研组．总结推广浙江"千万工程"经验 推动学习贯彻习近平新时代中国特色社会主义思想走深走实，求是，2023（11）．

19. 刁凡超，吕忠梅：生态环境法典出台后，环保法将完成历史使命，澎湃新闻．

20. 陈杭，杜燕．"北京蓝"何以成为中外环境治理新范式？中国新闻网．

21. 王际娣．探索建立生态保护"湾区标准"，小康，2024（4）．

22. 阮锡桂，陈旻．福建深入践行习近平生态文明思想，久久为功扎实推进生态省建设，持续深化国家生态文明试验区建设，实现"高颜值"和"高质量"协同并进——向绿 向美 向未来，福建日报，2024-12-05．

23. 吴琼，苏小环．拼出蓝天！江苏这一企业被生态环境部点赞，上观新闻．

24. 寇江泽，姚雪青．水生态环境保护发生重大转折性变化 持续深入打好碧水保卫战，人民日报，2024-03-18．

25. 张黎．十年治水再现河湖安澜秀水长清，中国环境报，2022-09-08．

26. 刘桂环，谢婧，王夏晖，文一惠．以流域生态保护补偿助推水生态产品价值实现，中国环境报，2022-05-23．

27. 吴琼，洪叶．浅湖深治，唱响新时代"太湖美"，新华日报，2025-01-26．

28. 张腾扬．白洋淀生态修复记，人民日报，2022-05-27．

29. 张濛，王莹，陈俊廷 . 护云岭"明珠"绘绿水青山——云南推进高原湖泊保护治理高质量发展纪略，人民长江报，2024-08-24.

30. 朱蕾，杨钰洁，刘泉 . 护好洱海清波 绘就一幅山清水秀的大美画卷，大理日报，2025-01-20.

31. 光明日报调研组 . 人湖共生 再现五百里滇池——云南昆明滇池保护治理与经济社会协同发展的探索实践，光明日报，2024-12-16.

32. 朱利中 . 筑牢美丽中国的大地之基，经济日报，2024-05-25.

33. 杨秀峰 . 我国固体废物与化学品环境治理体系和治理能力大幅提升，中国经济网 .

34. 杜莹 . 南京市一项目入选中国"无废城市"减污降碳协同增效典型案例首批推荐名单，中共江苏省委新闻网 .

35. 刘毅，董丝雨，刘军国 . 为海洋"减塑"助百姓增收，人民日报，2023-11-26.

36. 国务院新闻办公室 .《中国的海洋生态环境保护》白皮书，2024.

37. 王立彬，康淼，高敬，陈炜伟 . 深学笃行"厦门实践"为美丽中国开新局——专访三部委负责人和厦门市主要负责人，新华网 .

38. 胡静漪，李筱盼，朱智翔 . 浙江构建全国首个入海河流上下游协同治理考核体系，浙江日报，2025-03-06.

39. 上海市海洋局 . 上海书写现代海洋城市建设新篇章，中国自然资源报，2024-12-10.

40. 肖和勇 . 福建发力治理海漂垃圾 守护美丽海湾，新华网 .

41. 黎越，梁冰 . 海口成为全省首个省级全域美丽海湾城市 雕琢海洋肌理 守好蔚蓝底色，海口日报，2025-02-28.

42. 生态环境部 . 中国噪声污染防治报告，2024.

43. 鞠文韬 . 长三角一体化丨下好一盘棋守护碧水蓝天，"绿色同心圆"越绘越大，澎湃新闻 .

44. 纪文慧 ."多规合一"绘就美丽中国，经济日报，2024-07-17.

45. 南京市规划和自然资源局 . 南京推动"三大工程"、深化"多规合一"改革的实践与探索，城乡规划，2023（S1）.

46. 施洁 . 蒙山县创新推动生态价值多元转化案例，南方自然资源，2024 (2).

47. 自然资源部.国家生态保护修复公报（2024），2024.

48. 刘斯文.守护高原生态 呵护江河之源——三江源国家公园的鲜活样本与生动示范，中国绿色时报，2024-10-09.

49. 安璐.保护自然秘境 乐享国宝家园——大熊猫国家公园的保护升级与发展提档，中国绿色时报，2024-10-10.

50. 吴林锡，陈沫.青山长青虎豹归——东北虎豹国家公园设立三周年纪实，吉林日报，2024-11-11.

51. 李涛.西海岸新区统筹推进海洋生态保护修复，打造绿色可持续的海洋生态环境 生态养海 人海共荣，青岛西海岸报，2024-10-22.

52. 陈汉儿.一加一减，重塑"海上森林"，福建日报，2025-03-13.

53. 黎明，江堂龙，林晓钦.广东：绿美崛起正当时 生态文明绘华章，中国绿色时报，2025-01-23.

54. 马爱平.从茫茫荒原到莽莽林海 人工修复缔造塞罕坝生态奇迹，科技日报，2023-12-07.

55. 中共国家林业和草原局党组.奋力谱写"三北"工程新篇章，人民日报，2024-06-05.

56. 熊伟.卫星视角看黄河"几字弯"攻坚战，地图，2024（3）.

57. 董峻，初杭，胡璐等.塔克拉玛干的奇迹：绿锁流沙，新华每日电讯，2024-12-30.

58. 刘侠，滕继濮.成都：打造生态宜居的公园城市实践样本，科技日报，2025-03-13.

59. 白锋哲，房宁，杨丹丹，刘云.宜居宜业绘和美，农民日报，2024-12-30.

60. 覃金香，黄金丹."456"模式合力绘就和美乡村新画卷，人民网.

61. 董陈磊，蔡秦.让绿水青山"生金淌银"——丽水深化生态产品价值实现机制改革拓宽"两山"转化通道，丽水日报，2024-10-23.

62. 李瑶.绿水青山"变现生金"，延庆报，2025-03-04.

63. 闫捍江，张磊.大兴安岭 开辟生态文明发展新路径，黑龙江日报，2025-02-17.

64. 张龙飞，罗智敏，张伟，董涵.自然资源资产组合供应的九江实践，凤凰网.

65. 余丽，郏恬甜. 温岭以土地综合整治赋能高质量发展，浙江日报，2025-03-18.

66. 江苏省自然资源厅. 江苏昆山张浦镇："三连跳"，跳出城乡融合全域焕新，中国自然资源报，2024-09-01.

67. 欧阳易佳. 绿水青山可生金"打开"生态产品价值实现的多种方式，人民网.

68. 杨林. 加快健全生态产品价值实现机制，光明日报，2025-02-13.

69. 欧阳志云. 推动国家公园高水平保护和高质量发展，人民日报，2024-12-06.

70. 国务院新闻办公室.《中国的能源转型》白皮书，2024.

71. 刘津农，周怿. 碳捕手"为促进绿色发展保驾护航，工人日报，2024-07-24.

72. 于江艳. 新疆氢能应用"加速跑"，新疆日报，2024-07-02.

73. 许晋豫. 闽宁"纯绿电小镇"背后的"链式反应"，新华每日电讯，2025-03-26.

74. 王浩. 数说世界最大清洁能源走廊（经济新方位），人民日报，2024-05-15.

75. 刘靖寰，陈婧. 高原绿算点亮数字未来——青海移动绿色算力实践周年纪实，西海都市报，2025-03-27.

76. 朱俐娜. 政策护航 多地实践 虚拟电厂从概念走向规模化应用，中国城市报，2025-03-17.

77. 齐慧. 现代交通迈向智能化绿色化，经济日报，2024-09-02.

78. 陈梦竹，高莹. "绿"镜下的中国铁路，万里生机！人民铁道，2024-08-16.

79. 韩万里. 以生态笔墨勾勒交通强国绿色图景，多彩贵州网.

80. 韩鑫. 高速公路 逐绿而行，人民日报，2024-11-15.

81. 张广艳. 天津港打造世界一流智慧绿色枢纽港口"新"向万里 扬帆远航，滨城时报，2025-01-17.

82. 柴亚娟，王俊涛，葛政涵，吴颖岚，谭唯. 气候大会里的中国"零碳社区样本"，南方 Plus.

83. 王珂，窦皓，张腾扬．绿色消费成年轻人"心头好"，人民日报，2025-02-17.

84. 李德尚玉，卢陶然．伊利集团：从"零碳工厂"到全球样本，引领行业可持续发展，21经济网．

85. 宋晓娜，秦睿．逐绿而行 向绿而兴——推进农业绿色发展综述，农村工作通讯，2024（17）.

86. 王欣，李林，程爱华，聂杰杰．农田盖上"被子"甜菜长在"空中"，湖北日报，2025-03-28.

87. 左永华．贞丰县：探索荒山绿色发展模式助力群众增收，黔西南日报，2024-12-07.

88. 陈丽丽．银泰百货2024财年减排30.4万吨，40家门店获评绿色商场，潮新闻．

89. 蒋洪强，张伟，程曦．深化绿色科技创新，推动新质生产力发展，中国环境报，2024-03-14.

90. 杨玉华，王菲，吴慧珺．追光逐新——光伏独角兽华晟新能源的成长故事，新华网．

91. 生态环境部．全国碳市场发展报告（2024），2024.

92. 中共南京市委改革办，高淳区委改革办．高淳探索农业碳汇开发交易新机制，南京日报，2024-06-26.

93. 吴秋余．绿色金融助力经济社会高质量发展，人民日报，2024-10-03.

94. 中国人民银行研究局课题组．绿色金融改革创新试验区建设进展及经验，中国金融，2023（6）.

95. 周巍．多维度把握全面绿色转型内在逻辑，经济日报，2025-03-12.

96. 张代蕾，张晓茹．不负青山不负人——共建清洁美丽世界的中国动力，新华网．

97. 新华社记者．综述：从"绿色长城"看非洲防治荒漠化进展与挑战，新华网．

98. 邹松．绿色合作，助力南非加快能源转型，建筑时报，2023-12-14.

99. 黄培昭．中企积极参与埃及绿色项目建设，人民日报，2024-10-18.

100. 李嘉宝．中国-中东能源合作向"新"逐"绿"，人民日报海外版，2025-01-25.

101. 新华社记者．中国和非洲最大淡水湖"牵手记"，新华网．

102. 陈思．打好绿色发展攻坚战 建设壮美首都西大门——访门头沟区委书记喻华锋，前线，2024（11）．

103. 王月华，汪琳玮．绿色为笔，生态为墨，鲜亮"底色"这样绘就，黄浦报，2024-12-27.

104. 冯瑄．以"绿"为底 向"美"而行——解读关键词"大美宁波"，宁波日报，2024-10-28.

105. 惠玉兰．"美丽苏州"厚植绿水青山新优势，苏州日报，2024-12-22.

106. 卢志佳．贵阳南明河综合治理"生态痛点"演绎美丽蝶变，新华网．

107. 蒋世良，黎敬程．贵阳：生态立市 奏响绿美乐章，贵州画报，2024（9）．

108. 顾钱江，王春雨，杨思琪，刘赫垚．冰天雪地也是金山银山，瞭望，2025（12）．

109. 李自成．从哈尔滨亚冬会看冰雪赋能绿色发展，中国环境网．

110. 光明日报联合调研组．冰雪经济"热"力无限——基于黑龙江省冰雪经济发展状况的调研与思考，光明日报，2025-02-06.

111. 吴帅．以生态"含绿量"提升发展"含金量"，青岛日报，2025-04-08.

112. 封满楼，肖玲玲．青岛高新区：基本完成"碳达峰"目标 超前布局"碳中和"，青岛财经网．

113. 刘成．青岛构建绿色发展体系，经济日报，2025-01-15.

114. 金文兵，黄师师．武汉探索生态优先绿色发展新路子，武汉晚报，2024-11-04.

115. 陶磊，杨光明，刘洋．武汉：以高质量保护擦亮国际湿地城市名片，中国绿色时报，2024-11-01.

116. 金文兵．点"绿"成金 武汉奋力谱写人与自然和谐共生美丽篇章，长江日报，2025-01-05.

后　记

　　坚持走生态优先、绿色发展之路，是立足新发展阶段、贯彻新发展理念、构建新发展格局的必然要求。在习近平生态文明思想指引下，各地正用实际行动不断扩大中国"绿色版图"，扩绿、兴绿、护绿，这不仅筑牢了中华民族永续发展的生态屏障，更让亿万群众真切感受到天更蓝、山更绿、水更清的幸福生活。

　　绿色发展的蓝图已经绘就。《中华人民共和国国民经济和社会发展第十四个五年规划和2035年远景目标纲要》提出，展望2035年，我国将基本实现社会主义现代化……广泛形成绿色生产生活方式，碳排放达峰后稳中有降，生态环境根本好转，美丽中国建设目标基本实现。《中共中央　国务院关于加快经济社会发展全面绿色转型的意见》进一步明确坚定不移走生态优先、节约集约、绿色低碳高质量发展道路，以碳达峰碳中和工作为引领，协同推进降碳、减污、扩绿、增长，深化生态文明体制改革，健全绿色低碳发展机制，加快经济社会发展全面绿色转型，形成节约资源和保护环境的空间格局、产业结构、生产方式、生活方式，全面推进美丽中国建设，加快推进人与自然和谐共生的现代化。

　　思想伟力无远弗届，真理之树永远常青。以"绿水青山就是金山银山"理念为重要内容的习近平生态文明思想为东方大地带来一场变革性实践，取得举世瞩目的突破性进展和标志性成就并惠及全球。中国尊重自然、顺应自然、保护自然，以绿色发展共建地球生命共同体。在中国式现代化的新时代新征程上，中国坚定不移走绿色、低碳、可持续发展之路，中国智慧、中国担当、中国方案、中国行动推动世界走向绿色发展的现代化，必将为保护地球家园做出新的更大贡献。

与此同时，丝路国际智库坚定履行新型智库的使命责任，保持昂扬的"进行时"，持续记录、研究、传播中国绿色发展的好案例、好经验、好模式，为全面推进美丽中国建设和共建清洁美丽世界提供更多时效性强、针对性强、质量高的智库成果。

需要说明的是，本书在编写过程中，参考借鉴了一些机构和学者的研究实践成果和资料数据，编委会在"参考文献"中进行了标注，并在此表示真诚感谢。请相关版权所有人与本书编委会联系（邮箱：158950711@qq.com），以便致奉谢意和薄酬。如有争议内容，也请有关人员及时与我们联系，本书再版时将予以调整。本书封面照片拍摄者为丝路国际智库曹震。

由于时间仓促和编撰者知识面有限，错误与疏忽之处在所难免，希望各位读者及时给我们反馈意见。我们也非常愿意与读者就绿色发展各项议题进行广泛深入的交流、探讨和合作。

中国绿色发展相关法规政策规划

Chief Editors
Yang Dongping, Xu Jin, Liu Yang

2025 GREEN DEVELOPMENT REPORT

（English Version）

**Chinese practice, Chinese innovation, and Chinese solutions of
"Lucid Waters and Lush Mountains Are Invaluable Assets"**

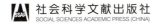

社会科学文献出版社
SOCIAL SCIENCES ACADEMIC PRESS (CHINA)

Editorial Committee

Consultants: Shang Yong, Bai Gengsheng, Yang Bangjie, Gu Boping

Chief Editors: Yang Dongping, Xu Jin, Liu Yang

Vice Chief Editors: Zhou Xiangyu, Zhang Hongxia, Zhang Chaonan, Jiang Tao, Sun Xiansheng, Wang Yanchun

Editorial Board (in alphabetical order of surname):
Ben Shenglin, Bi Xulong, Chen Honglian, Cui Fengjun, Cui Mingmo, Ding Junfa, Fang Chenguang, Gao Yuanyuan, Han Xiaoyan, He Dexu, He Xia, Jiang Hua, Kong Jingyuan, Li Houqiang, Li Ruidong, Liang Liping, Liu Chaohua, Liu Jinyu, Liu Jingjing, Liu Linqing, Liu Shuguo, Liu Yunzhong, Pang Chaoran, Tang Renwu, Wang Shi, Wang Xiaokang, Wang Zhishen, Wang Zhongmin, Wen Xiaojun, Wu Jinhua, Xia Jun, Xu Deshun, Yang Jiaqi, Yang Nianchun, Yang Tao, Yang Zaiping, Zhang Hui, Zhou Daoxu, Zhou Weimin

Writing Group Members*:
Li Chuan, Wang Yanzhen, Li Xingli, Lin Shisong, Lin Shibin, Fan Yu, Liu Lixiang, Miao Bo, Zeng Liangwei, Guo Yong, Fang Ning, Wang Tianquan, Pu Yang, Ting Yuning, Jiang Jiaqing, Dai Cheng, Kang Houping, Huang Chao, Deng Chaoming, Long Xicheng, Li Chong, Lin Sen, He Shuang

Compiling Organization: Silk Road International Think Tank, Southwest Medical University

Supporting Organizations: Silk Road Youth Forum, Silk Road Encyclopedia (Magazine), China Industrial Energy Conservation and Cleaner Production Association, China City News, China Carbon Neutrality 50 Forum, China Environment (Magazine), Urban Insight (Magazine), Shanghai Source-Grid-Load-Storage Industry Co., Ltd., Huaxin Insurance Brokers Co., Ltd., CITIC Environmental Investment Group Co., Ltd., Research Institute for Environmental Innovation (Suzhou) , Tsinghua, China-Russia Regional Cooperation Development Investment Fund Management Co., Ltd., China National Environmental Protection Group

---

* The English version is translated by: Wu Jinhua, Lin Shisong, Lin Shibin, Fan Yu, Liu Lixiang, Dahlia A. Ducreay.

Exhibition on Green Development Achievements: 20 Years After the Proposal of "Lucid Waters and Lush Mountains Are Invaluable Assets" Philosophy

Yucun Village, Anji County, Huzhou, Zhejiang:
Birthplace of the "Lucid Waters and Lush Mountains Are Invaluable Assets" Philosophy

Photo by: Cao Zhen, Huang Wenya, Silk Road International Think Tank

Yongding River After Ecological Restoration:
Reviving year-round water flow across its full length with crystal-clear waters and lush banks

Photo by: Mentougou District Culture and Tourism Bureau, Beijing

Xianghu Lake National Tourism Resort, Hangzhou, Zhejiang:
China's Prime Eco-Lake Scenic Area

Photo by: Fang Chenguang

Baiyangdian Lake: Restoring Purity Throughout, Forging a Green Development
"Xiong'an Benchmark" for Integrated Water-City Symbiosis and Interdependent Urban-Lake Coexistence

Photo by: Wang Weiqian, Xiongan Media Center

Donghu Greenway in Wuhan, Hubei:
China's First 5A-Level Tourist Attraction Greenway within Urban Area

Photo by: Tian Chunyu

Huahong Canal:
Hunan Provincial "Beautiful Rivers and Lakes" Award Recipient

Photo by: Yueyang Junshan District Integrated Media Center

Mount Fanjing, Tongren, Guizhou:
Inscribed on the World Heritage List and IUCN Green List

Photo by: Yang Xiangyang, Dai Cheng

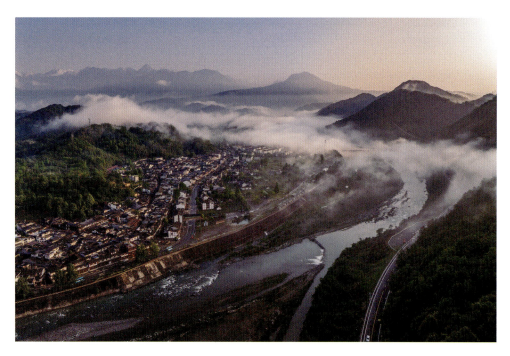

Haiwozi Ancient Town, Longmen Mountain Tourism Resort Area, Pengzhou, Chengdu, Sichuan:
The Most Beautiful Ancient Town

Photo by: Pengzhou Municipal People's Government Office

Wugong Mountain & Mingyue Mountain Tourism Area, Yichun, Jiangxi:
National Scenic and Historic Area

Photo by: Zheng Dehua

Ulan Mod Grassland on the Southern Slope of the Greater Khingan Range

Photo by: Bi Lige, Xing'an League Media Convergence Center, Inner Mongolia Autonomous Region

Saihanba Mechanized Forest Farm, Hebei:
China's Model in Global Environmental Governance

Photo by: Lin Xinmin

Dalad Banner PV Pilot Base, Inner Mongolia:
Kubuqi Desert Control Exemplar

Photo by: Ordos Forestry and Grassland Bureau, Dalad Banner Media Convergence Center

Sonid Right Banner 200MW Pasture-PV-Storage & Desert Control Project:
BOE Energy's Integrated Demonstration Initiative

Photo by: Zhang Shilin, XilinGol League Media Convergence Center, Inner Mongolia

Ulan Tologoi Sand Control Station, Uxin Banner, Ordos, Inner Mongolia:
Exemplary Case of the Campaign against Maowusu Sandy Land

Photo by: Sar Us Culture & Tourism Investment Development Co., Ltd., Uxin Banner

Golden Pebble Beach Gold Coast, Dalian:
Model Beautiful Bay of Liaoning Province

Photo by: Tian Dawei

Beautiful Bay, Yingkou, Liaoning:
Spectacular Biodiversity Conservation in "Bird-Flying Wetlands"

Photo by: Zhang Peiren

Beihai Coastal National Wetland Park (Fengjia River Basin) Water Environment Improvement Project:
Selected into China's Top 10 Nature-based Solutions for Ecological Restoration

Photo by: Wei Shankang, Department of Ecology and Environment of Guangxi Zhuang Autonomous Region

Caozhuang Village, Jingqiao Township, Lishui District, Nanjing:
Jiangsu Provincial Beautiful Countryside

Photo by:Zhu Hongsheng, Lishui District Converged Media Center

Dongtumen Village, Bailuquan Township, Luquan District, Shijiazhuang:
Model Village of Hebei Provincial Beautiful Countryside

Photo by: Zhang Xiaofeng, *Shijiazhuang Daily*

Duoyi Village, Nanmei Lahu Ethnic Township, Linxiang District, Lincang, Yunnan:
A Picturesque Haven

Photo by: Linchang High-Tech Industrial Development Zone Management Committee

Yongfeng Model Beautiful Village, Zhaoyang District, Zhaotong, Yunnan

Hongyanzi Tea Plantation, Dehong Village, Huguo Township, Naxi District (selected as a national pilot area for the "Five Good and Two Suitable" harmonious and beautiful villages initiative), Luzhou, Sichuan

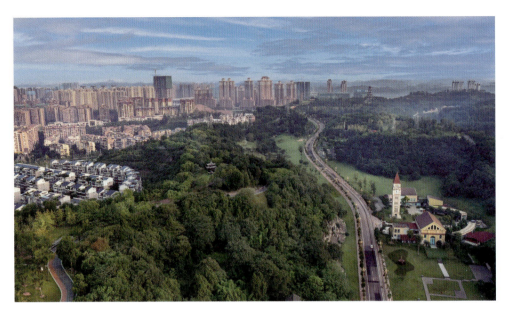

Jianyang:
A Park City Where Urban and Mountain Landscapes Intertwine, and People Live in Harmony with Waters

Photo by: Publicity Department of the CPC Jianyang Municipal Committee, Sichuan Province

National Sliding Centre "Snow Dragon" and Beijing Winter Olympic Village
Powered by Green Energy

Photo by: Culture and Tourism Bureau of Yanqing District, Beijing

Green Heart Forest Park at Beijing Sub-center,
Powered by Integrated Renewable Energy

Photo by: Capital Library (Beijing, China)

Suzhou Industrial Park:
Pioneering China's Low-Carbon Model Park

Photo by: Cheng Yugan

Changshou Economic and Technological Development Zone:
Selected as a National Model Case of "Waste-Free Parks"

Photo by: Chongqing Changshou Economic and Technological Development Zone Management Committee

"Taihu Star":
World's First Eco-Dredging Intelligent Platform Ship with China's Complete Independent Intellectual Property Rights

Photo by: Lv Feng

Egypt's New Administrative Capital CBD Project:
Applying China-Developed Green Technologies, Equipment, and Standards

Photo by: China Construction Eighth Engineering Division Corp., LTD

"Blue Sea Pathfinders" Youth Volunteer Team:
Lighting Up the Highlands with Green Initiatives in Malaysia

Photo by: China Construction Malaysia Sdn Bhd

Silk Road Youth Forum · Malaysia-China Cooperation Conference (Green Development Creates a Better Future for All)

Photo by: Silk Road International Think Tank

The Belt and Road Initiative 10th Anniversary Silk Road Youth Plant New Trees:
Co-Creation of Silk Road Youth Friendship Forest

Photo by: Silk Road International Think Tank

Lucid Waters and Lush Mountains Are Invaluable Assets[*]

(August 24, 2005)

We pursue harmony between humanity and nature, and harmony between economy and society. To put it simply, we want both lucid waters and lush mountains as well as invaluable assets.

Zhejiang's terrain consists of "70% mountains, 10% water, and 20% farmland". Many places feature "lucid waters meander away, lush mountains open in array" and enjoy excellent ecological advantages. If these ecological environment advantages can be transformed into advantages for ecological agriculture, ecological industry, ecological tourism, and other ecological economies, then lucid waters and lush mountains will indeed become invaluable assets. Lucid waters and lush mountains can bring invaluable assets, but invaluable assets cannot buy back lucid waters and lush mountains. Lucid waters and lush mountains may conflict with invaluable assets, yet they can be dialectically unified. When we cannot have both fish and bear's paw (have our cake and eat it too), we must understand opportunity costs, be adept at making choices, learn to discard and retain, do what should be done and refrain from what should not be done, and unswervingly implement the Scientific Outlook on Development to build a resource-conserving, eco-friendly society where humans and nature coexist harmoniously. In making choices, we must identify the right direction, create favorable conditions, and allow lucid waters and lush mountains to continuously bring invaluable assets.

---

* Note: On August 24, 2005, Xi Jinping, then Secretary of the Zhejiang Provincial Committee of the Communist Party of China, published a commentary titled "Lucid Waters and Lush Mountains Are Invaluable Assets" in the "Zhijiang Xinyu" column of Zhejiang Daily, which was later included in the book *Zhejiang, China: A New Vision for Development* published by Zhejiang People's Publishing House in 2007.

Selected Important Statements by General Secretary Xi Jinping on "Lucid Waters and Lush Mountains Are Invaluable Assets"

Lucid waters and lush mountains are invaluable assets. In the past, we said we want both lucid waters and lush mountains as well as invaluable assets, but in fact, lucid waters and lush mountains are invaluable assets.

> —Xi Jinping, then Secretary of Zhejiang Provincial Committee of the CPC, during research in Yucun Village, Anji County, Zhejiang Province, August 2005

China has clearly placed ecological environmental protection in a more prominent position. We want both lucid waters and lush mountains as well as invaluable assets. We would rather have lucid waters and lush mountains than invaluable assets, because lucid waters and lush mountains are actually invaluable assets. We will never sacrifice the environment for temporary economic development. We have proposed the strategic task of building an ecological civilization and a beautiful China to leave a beautiful homeland with blue skies, green lands, and clean waters for future generations.

> —President Xi Jinping's response during a speech at Nazarbayev University in Kazakhstan in September 2013

Lucid waters and lush mountains and invaluable assets are not in opposition to each other. The key lies in people and in our approach.

> —General Secretary Xi Jinping emphasized when participating in the review of the Guizhou delegation at the National People's Congress in March 2014

We must implement the development concepts of innovation, coordination, green development, openness, and sharing, and accelerate the formation of spatial patterns, industrial structures, production methods, and lifestyles that conserve resources and protect the environment, thus giving nature time and space to recuperate.

—General Secretary Xi Jinping's important speech at the National Conference on Ecological and Environmental Protection in May 2018

Lucid waters and lush mountains are invaluable assets, and improving the ecological environment is developing productive forces. Good ecology itself contains immense economic value that can continuously create comprehensive benefits and achieve sustainable economic and social development.

—President Xi Jinping's important speech at the opening ceremony of the International Horticultural Exhibition 2019 Beijing China in April 2019

Lucid waters and lush mountains are invaluable assets. Protecting the ecological environment is protecting productive forces, and improving the ecological environment is developing productive forces—this is a simple truth. We must abandon development models that damage or even destroy the ecological environment and short-sighted practices that sacrifice the environment for temporary development.

—President Xi Jinping's important speech at the Leaders Meeting on Climate in April 2021

Nature is the basic condition for human survival and development. Respecting, adapting to, and protecting nature are inherent requirements for building a comprehensive socialist modernized country. We must firmly establish and practice the concept that lucid waters and lush mountains are invaluable assets, and plan development from the strategic perspective of harmonious coexistence between humanity and nature.

—General Secretary Xi Jinping's report at the 20th National Congress of the Communist Party of China in October 2022

When we say lucid waters and lush mountains are invaluable assets，if ecology is not managed well，they won't be "invaluable assets" but will instead become money-losing ventures.

——General Secretary Xi Jinping emphasized when participating in the review of the Jiangsu delegation at the National People's Congress in March 2023

Let us take active measures，starting with planting trees，to cultivate lucid waters and lush mountains that are invaluable assets for everyone and paint a new picture of a beautiful China.

——General Secretary Xi Jinping at the Capital's Voluntary Tree Planting Activity in April 2023

The next five years are an important period for building a beautiful China. We must thoroughly implement Xi Jinping's Thought on Ecological Civilization with Chinese Characteristics for the New Era，adhere to the people-centered approach，firmly establish and practice the concept that lucid waters and lush mountains are invaluable assets，place the construction of a beautiful China in a prominent position in building a strong country and national rejuvenation，promote significant improvement in urban and rural living environments，achieve remarkable results in building a beautiful China，support high-quality development with high-quality ecological environment.

——General Secretary Xi Jinping emphasized at the National Conference on Ecological and Environmental Protection in July 2023

China adheres to the concept that lucid waters and lush mountains are invaluable assets，firmly follows a path of civilized development that ensures production development，affluent lives，and sound ecology，and has achieved remarkable accomplishments in building a beautiful China that have attracted worldwide attention.

——President Xi Jinping's congratulatory letter to the Green Development Forum of Shanghai Cooperation Organization in July 2024

Table of Contents

Main Report

Special Report

Table of Contents

Preface 1

Lucid Waters and Lush Mountains Are Invaluable Assets: Building a Community of Life on Earth and a Clean, Beautiful World

Gu Xiulian

On August 15, 2005, Xi Jinping, then Secretary of the Zhejiang Provincial Committee of the CPC, first proposed the important concept and scientific judgment that "lucid waters and lush mountains are invaluable assets" during his research in Yucun Village, Anji County, Huzhou City, Zhejiang Province. This theory elevates environmental protection from a "cost burden" to a "strategic asset" and profoundly reveals the dialectical relationship between ecological protection and economic development. It forms a green development perspective of "unswervingly following the path of ecological priority and green development, promoting comprehensive green transformation of economic and social development, and accelerate the advancemen of modernization featuring harmonious coexistence between humanity and nature", becoming the most classic proposition of Xi Jinping's ecological civilization thought.

"Lucid waters and lush mountains are invaluable assets" represents a profound transformation in a country's development concept and approach. More importantly, it reflects the Communist Party of China's profound insight into the laws governing human civilization development, natural laws, and economic and social development laws and leads China's development to new frontiers. In November 2012, the 18th National Congress of the Communist Party of China incorporated ecological civilization construction into the Five-sphere Integrated Plan of socialism with Chinese characteristics, making the CPC the first ruling party in the world to include ecological civilization construction in its action program. In October 2017, the 19th National Congress of the CPC adopted the

"Amendment to the Constitution of the Communist Party of China", which for the first time, incorporated "enhancing the awareness that lucid waters and lush mountains are invaluable assets" into the Party Constitution. Furthermore, the report delivered at the Congress explicitly stated that "building an ecological civilization is a plan of vital importance for the sustainable development of the Chinese nation for millennia to come" and "we must firmly establish and practice the concept that lucid waters and lush mountains are invaluable assets". The report of the 20th National Congress of the Communist Party of China, when elaborating on the work of the past five years and the great changes in the new era over the past decade, pointed out that upholding the concept that lucid waters and lush mountains are invaluable assets and adhering to the integrated protection and systematic governance of mountains, rivers, forests, farmlands, lakes, grasslands, and deserts, comprehensive ecological environmental protection has been strengthened in all aspects, regions, and processes. Ecological environmental protection has undergone historic, transformative, and holistic changes, making our motherland's sky bluer, mountains greener, and waters clearer. Also, this concept transcends the Western traditional development path of "pollution first, treatment later" and has gained recognition and support from the international community. In February 2013, the 27th Governing Council of the United Nations Environment Programme adopted a draft decision to promote China's ecological civilization concept and released the report "Lucid Waters and Lush Mountains Are Invaluable Assets: China's Ecological Civilization Strategy and Action" in 2016.

Since the 18th National Congress of the Communist Party of China, guided by Xi Jinping's Thought on Socialism with Chinese Characteristics for a New Era, China has adhered to the concept that lucid waters and lush mountains are invaluable assets, created world-renowned ecological and green development miracles, and made major strides in building a beautiful China. In 2024, the average PM2. 5 concentration in Chinese cities at and above the prefecture level was 29. 3 micrograms per cubic meter, down 2. 7% year-on-year, stably meeting standards for five consecutive years. The proportion of days with good or excellent air quality reached 87. 2%, up 1. 7 percentage points year-on-year. The proportion of surface water sections with good quality reached 90. 4%, exceeding 90% for the first time, up 1 percentage point year-on-year. The proportion of good quality in offshore sea areas was 83.7%, achieving the 14th Five-Year Plan target ahead of schedule. The water quality of the main stream of the Yangtze River has remained stable at Class II for five consecutive years, and the main stream of the Yellow River for three consecutive years. Clean energy consumption, including natural gas, hydropower, nuclear power, wind power, and solar power, accounted for 28.6% of total energy consumption, up 2.2 percentage points. National energy consumption per 10,000 yuan of GDP decreased by 3.8% compared to the previous year. The national carbon emission trading market had a carbon emission quota transaction volume of 189 million tons and a transaction value of 18.11 billion yuan.

Xi Jinping's Thought on Ecological Civilization is a scientific answer to the questions of the times, the world, and the people regarding ecological civilization construction against the historical background of complex and profound changes in the world, the country, and society in an unprecedented century of changes. It provides ideological inspiration and development paths for sustainable green development of humanity. Therefore, deeply studying and interpreting the era background, core essence, rich connotations, and global contributions of Xi Jinping's Thought on Ecological Civilization, and systematically organizing and summarizing the innovative practices of "lucid waters and lush mountains are invaluable assets", helps us profoundly understand the essential characteristics and basic laws of socialist ecological civilization construction. It also helps us accurately grasp the profound connotation and essential meaning of this important thought, thereby more consciously following the Chinese path to modernization featuring harmonious coexistence between humanity and nature, and more firmly drawing a new picture of a beautiful China and building a community of life on Earth and a clean, beautiful world under the guidance of Xi Jinping's Thought on Ecological Civilization.

The 2025 Green Development Report takes "China's Practice, Innovation, and Solutions for 'Lucid Waters and Lush Mountains Are Invaluable Assets'" as its theme. It is jointly compiled and published by the Editorial Committee jointly built by the Silk Road International Think Tank and relevant institutions, comprehensively interpreting the theoretical innovation, institutional innovation, mechanism innovation, and practical innovation over the twenty years since the proposal of the important concept that "lucid waters and lush mountains are invaluable assets". It provides a high-quality think tank outcome with novel perspectives, complete systems, rigorous logic, and readability and verifiability for respecting nature, adapting to nature, protecting nature, promoting the coordinated unity of economic development and ecological protection, and building a prosperous, clean, and beautiful world.

Lucid waters ripple and lush mountains adorn. We look forward to more organizations, readers, and the public promoting the concept that "lucid waters and lush mountains are invaluable assets" and becoming communicators and practitioners of green development! We hope that more Chinese and international research institutions, think tank, and scholars will make green development their research object, thus producing more effective think tank outcomes that provide decision-making references and theoretical foundations for ecological civilization construction and high-quality green development.

Preface 2
Lucid Waters and Lush Mountains Are Invaluable Assets: China's Green Development Practice and Global Value

Ling Wen

Lucid waters and lush mountains are an important component of people's happy lives. A good ecological environment is the fairest public good and the most inclusive well-being for the people. Entering the new era and new journey, China's ecological environmental protection still faces structural, root-cause, and trend-based pressures. The accumulation of pressures and moving forward under heavy burdens remain key characteristics of China's ecological civilization construction period. This makes it even more important to ensure the scientific practice of the concept that "lucid waters and lush mountains are invaluable assets" and to cultivate and develop new quality productive forces to empower high-quality green development.

General Secretary Xi Jinping has always attached great importance to ecological environmental work. Whether working at the central or local level, he has treated ecological civilization construction as a major task to personally promote ecological environmental governance and green development. More than 40 years ago, while working in Zhengding County, Hebei Province, he emphasized that we would rather not have money than have pollution and strictly prevent the relocation of pollution and rural pollution. During his work in Fujian and Zhejiang, he conducted systematic practical exploration and theoretical thinking on ecological environmental protection, proposing forward-looking judgments such as "ecological prosperity begets civilizational prosperity" and "lucid waters and lush mountains are invaluable assets". He led the comprehensive treatment of Xiamen's Yundang Lake and Fujian's creation of an ecological province, built "Green Zhejiang", and deeply promoted the Thousand Villages Demonstration and Ten Thousand Villages Renovation Project.

Since the 18th National Congress of the Communist Party of China, the CPC Central Committee with Comrade Xi Jinping at its core has treated ecological civilization construction as a fundamental plan concerning the sustainable development of the Chinese nation. It has coordinated and promoted the Five-sphere Integrated Plan and the Four-Pronged Comprehensive Strategy, vigorously promoting theoretical innovation, practical innovation, and institutional innovation in ecological civilization. The critical battle against pollution continues to advance, central ecological environmental protection inspections have been fully implemented, the protection of the Yangtze and Yellow Rivers has been deeply carried out, integrated protection and systematic governance of mountains, rivers, forests, farmlands, lakes, grasslands, and deserts have been implemented, and the natural protected area system has been accelerated. China's ecological civilization construction has undergone historic, transformative, and holistic changes. Spatial patterns, industrial structures, production methods, and lifestyles that conserve resources and protect the environment are gradually forming, laying a solid foundation for the fundamental improvement of the ecological environment by 2035 and the basic realization of the goal of building a beautiful China.

Great thoughts guide great practices. Since the new era, as the world's largest developing country, China has achieved remarkable major achievements in ecological civilization construction, fundamentally due to the strong leadership of the CPC Central Committee with Comrade Xi Jinping at its core and the scientific guidance of Xi Jinping's Thought on Ecological Civilization. Xi Jinping's Thought on Ecological Civilization inherits and develops the materialist, dialectical, and practical ecological philosophical thinking and methods contained in Marxist ecological views. It draws on ecological wisdom from excellent traditional Chinese culture, learns from the experiences and lessons of Western industrialization processes, systematically explains and scientifically plans the strategic positioning, goals and tasks, overall ideas, major principles, and institutional guarantees of ecological civilization construction, and provides fundamental guidance and action guidelines for building a beautiful China in the new era.

Furthermore, green and low-carbon development is the direction of international trends and the general trend. Xi Jinping's Thought on Ecological Civilization has brought China a transformative practice of "lucid waters and lush mountains are invaluable assets", achieved breakthrough progress and landmark achievements that benefit the world, and contained insightful thoughts and profound insights on the development of human civilization and a clean, beautiful world. China advocates that the international community should pursue harmonious coexistence between humanity and nature, prosperous green development, a love for nature, the spirit of scientific governance, and cooperation in response—this is the embodiment of the concept of building a community with a shared future for mankind in the field of ecological civilization and provides classic cases and important guidance for the sustainable development of human civilization.

Currently, the academic community at home and abroad takes green development as an important research topic, with China's green development practice being a research hotspot. However, research and interpretation centered on Xi Jinping's Thought on Ecological Civilization, especially think tank reports on China's green development, still need to be further enriched and enhanced to help more readers systematically understand China's ecological civilization construction and green development practical experience and latest achievements. The Silk Road International Think Tank, in conjunction with relevant institutions, has formed an editorial committee to compile and publish the 2025 Green Development Report. Based on the integration of think tank achievements in green Silk Road construction and green international cooperation, it summarizes China's main achievements and innovative measures in ecological environmental protection, building green development space, green and low-carbon transformation, and green international cooperation. It deeply analyzes over 200 typical cases of green development that have been recommended by relevant departments, specially researched by the Editorial Committee, and have certain influence domestically and internationally. It elaborates on innovative practices of youth participation in green international cooperation and present to readers the magnificent epic of China's new era green development under the leadership of the Communist Party of China. It uses think tank achievements to interpret the

Chinese solution for harmonious coexistence between humanity and nature, and provides decision-making references and theoretical foundations for advancing Chinese-style modernization and building a community with a shared future for mankind.

General Secretary Xi Jinping pointed out, "Only by working hand in hand can we effectively address global environmental issues such as climate change, marine pollution, and biological protection" and "Only by walking side by side can we make the concept of green development deeply rooted in people's hearts and make the global path of ecological civilization stable and far-reaching". We look forward to more domestic and international research institutions and experts and scholars taking China's green development solution as their research object, promoting China's mature experience in ecological civilization construction and green development to various parts of the world, facilitating the transformation of the global environmental governance system and the green transformation of development modes, showcasing a trustworthy, lovable, and respectable image of China, and enabling the international community to better read and understand China.

Preface 3
Lucid Waters and Lush Mountains Create Invaluable Assets, A Beautiful China Is in Sight

Du Xiangwan

The year 2025 marks the 20th anniversary of the introduction of the "lucid waters and lush mountains are invaluable assets" concept. As an original theory rooted in the land of China, aligned with China's realities, and embodying Chinese character, the "lucid waters and lush mountains are invaluable assets" concept scientifically elucidates the symbiotic relationship between green, high-quality socio-economic development and high-level protection of the ecological environment. It profoundly reveals the fundamental truth that protecting the ecological environment is to protect productivity, and improving the ecological environment is to develop productivity. This concept systematically reconstructs the imbalanced relationship, prevalent since the Industrial Revolution, between the growth of human productivity and the intensification of ecological crises, and effectively resolves the "binary paradox" of development versus protection. Particularly since the 18th National Congress of the Communist Party of China , the Party Central Committee with Comrade Xi Jinping at its core has regarded the advancement of ecological civilization as a fundamental endeavor crucial for the sustainable development of the Chinese nation. It has undertaken a series of pioneering initiatives with unprecedented determination, intensity, and effectiveness. China's achievements in green development have garnered global attention, becoming a significant hallmark of the historic accomplishments and transformations in the cause of the Party and the country in the new era.

Inheriting the Marxist View of Development and Fine Traditional Chinese Culture

The conception, practice, formation, and development of the "lucid waters and lush mountains are invaluable assets" concept has undergone a process of refining local experiences, proposing philosophical concepts, and elevating theoretical thought.

Comrade Xi Jinping has always attached great importance to green development. During his tenures in Zhengding, Xiamen, Ningde, Fujian, Zhejiang, and Shanghai, he prioritized related work as a major agenda item. In April 1997, during a research visit to Changkou Village, Sanming City, Fujian Province, Comrade Xi Jinping pointed out: "Green mountains and lucid waters are priceless treasures. Mountainous areas must paint a good 'landscape painting' and effectively manage their mountains, waters, and fields." In 2002, while serving as Governor of Fujian Province, Comrade Xi Jinping proposed that Fujian should build China's first ecological province. In July 2004, at an on-site meeting for Zhejiang Province's "Thousand Villages Demonstration and Ten Thousand Villages Renovation" initiative, Comrade Xi Jinping, then Secretary of the Zhejiang Provincial Party Committee, noted that this initiative, as an "ecological project", was an effective vehicle for advancing the construction of an ecological province, protecting "lucid waters and lush mountains" and bringing "invaluable assets". On August 15, 2005, during an inspection tour in Yucun Village, Anji County, Huzhou City, Zhejiang Province, Comrade Xi Jinping, with a forward-looking strategic vision, first proposed the "lucid waters and lush mountains are invaluable assets" concept. This concept inherits the Chinese people's understanding, love, and reverence for beautiful nature. As a spiritual treasure that carries forward the basic principles of Marxism and embodies the essence of traditional Chinese culture, this concept possesses profound intellectual power and vibrant vitality.

Since the new era, the connotations and practice of the "lucid waters and lush mountains are invaluable assets" concept have continuously deepened. The 19th National Congress of the CPC incorporated "must establish and practice the concept that lucid waters and lush mountains are invaluable assets" into its report, making it one of the basic policies for upholding and developing socialism with Chinese characteristics in the new era. The Amendment to the Constitution of the Communist Party of China, adopted at the 19th National Congress of the CPC, included "enhancing the awareness that lucid waters and lush mountains are invaluable assets" in the Party Constitution, clearly demonstrating the CPC's firm resolve to lead people of all ethnic groups in China towards green development. In November 2021, "We must adhere to the concept that lucid waters and lush mountains are invaluable assets" was written into the Resolution of the CPC Central Committee on the Major Achievements and Historical Experience of the Party over the Past Century, becoming an important guiding principle for marching towards the second centenary goal of building a great modern socialist country in all respects.

Furthermore, Xi Jinping's Thought on Ecological Civilization, with the "lucid waters and lush mountains are invaluable assets" concept at its core, guides China to stride confidently on the path of modernization characterized by green development. Lucid waters and lush mountains are not only natural and ecological wealth but also social and economic wealth. Protecting the ecological environment means safeguarding natural value, increasing natural capital, and fostering new quality productive forces. This effectively breaks the path dependency of the traditional development model of "pollute first, treat later", transforming ecological and environmental protection from a "cost expenditure" into a "development dividend", and providing theoretical guidance and practical pathways for sustainable development in China and globally.

Think Tank Achievements Elaborate China's Green Development Solutions

Under the strong leadership of the Party Central Committee with Comrade Xi Jinping at its core, all regions, departments, and sectors in China have coordinated industrial restructuring, pollution control, and ecological protection, addressed climate change, and actively and prudently advanced towards caroon peaking and achieving carbon neutrality. The green and low-carbon transition has shown new vitality, and the foundation for high-quality development has become more distinct. In the first quarter of 2025, China's green development continued its steady, positive trajectory. The "lucid waters and lush mountains are invaluable assets" concept has gained broader consensus and spurred wider action. Newly installed capacity for wind and solar power generation totaled 74. 33 MkW, accounting for 86. 7% of the total newly installed power generation capacity. The total installed capacity of wind and solar power reached 1. 48 billion kW, historically surpassing that of thermal power. The total sales revenue of green and low-carbon industries increased by 13. 6% year-on-year, 11. 5 percentage points higher than the average level in 2024. The number of newly established green and low-carbon enterprises grew by 19. 3% year-on-year, an increase of 12. 3 percentage points compared to the same period last year. The total amount spent by enterprises on environmental governance services increased by 11% year-on-year, with the manufacturing sector's spending up by 16. 5%. Sales revenue from the promotion services for green technologies such as energy conservation and environmental protection increased by 28. 9% and 17. 6% year-on-year, respectively. Investment in green governance continued its rapid growth.

On the occasion of the 20th anniversary of the "lucid waters and lush mountains are invaluable assets" concept, the Silk Road International Think Tank, in collaboration with relevant institutions, established an Editorial Committee to compile and publish the 2025 Green Development Report (Chinese and English versions). This report serves both as a retrospective, summarizing the achievements and experiences of various regions in China in practicing Xi Jinping's Thought on Ecological Civilization over the past two decades, and as a prospective guide, disseminating Xi Jinping's Thought on Ecological Civilization, constructing China's knowledge system for green development, and offering recommendations for building a Beautiful China and a beautiful world. It holds significant academic and social value. On May 20, 2025, the 2025 Green Development Report was pre-released at the China National Convention Center in Beijing and received widespread attention and recognition from government officials, industry leaders, academics, researchers, investors, media professionals, and the public at home and abroad. The Editorial Committee incorporated feedback from all parties to finalize the currently published Chinese and English reports, thereby further enriching the body of think tank achievements in researching and interpreting Xi Jinping's Thought on Ecological Civilization.

Knowledge and action must be unified, and action is paramount. Success-fully writing this grand chapter of a Beautiful China requires persistent effort and long-term dedication. It necessitates leveraging the principal role of the people, deepening the popularization and dissemination of Xi Jinping's Thought on Eco-logical Civilization, and consistently treating green development as the funda-mental solution to ecological and environmental problems, thereby simultane-ously achieving prosperity for the people and a beautiful ecology. We hope that more professional institutions will focus on green development as a research sub-ject, produce more practical think tank achievements, and serve as active communicators and exemplary practitioners of the "lucid waters and lush mountains are invaluable assets" concept.

Preface 4

The 20th Anniversary of the Important Concept of "Lucid Waters and Lush Mountains Are Invaluable Assets": Theoretical Innovation and Action Guidelines for Building a Beautiful China in the New Era

Yang Dongping and Liu Yang

Since the advent of industrial civilization, humanity has created enormous material wealth while simultaneously accelerating resource extraction, disrupting the Earth's ecological balance, and intensifying contradictions between humans and nature. In recent years, climate change, biodiversity loss, advancing desertification, and frequent extreme weather events have posed serious challenges to human survival and development. Yucun, a village in Anji County, Huzhou City, Zhejiang Province, is the birthplace of the concept that "Lucid waters and lush mountains are invaluable assets". In 2005, Xi Jinping, then Secretary of the Zhejiang Provincial Party Committee, first proposed the concept that "Lucid waters and lush mountains are invaluable assets" in Yucun, charting a course for the village's transformation from a "quarrying-based economy" to a "green economy", while providing theoretical support for the nationwide construction of ecological civilization. Over the past 20 years, Yucun has vigorously developed ecological agriculture, rural tourism, cultural and creative industries, and homestay accommodations. It has established a green development paradigm where environmental protection and specialized industry cultivation advance side by side. The village has earned numerous honors, including National Civilized Village, China's Beautiful Leisure Villagee, Key National Rural Tourism Village, and the "Best Tourism Village" award from the UN World Tourism Organization. Yucun has become a model for rural revitalization, demonstrating to the world that lucid waters and lush mountains can be seamlessly integrated with economic prosperity and enhance each other.

Building an ecological civilization concerns people's well-being and the future of the nation. Since the founding of the People's Republic of China, the country has progressively developed a law-governed understanding of eco-civilization development while implementing synchronized policy measures. Particularly since the 18th National Congress of the Communist Party of China (CPC), the CPC Central Committee with Comrade Xi Jinping at its core has positioned ecological civilization construction as a fundamental strategy concerning the sustainable development of the Chinese nation, and has planed and implemented a series of foundational, pioneering, and far-reaching initiatives. The path of ecological civilization has become increasingly steadfast and expansive, continually creating new green miracles across China. Green has become the distinctive backdrop of the new era, and green development has emerged as a prominent feature of Chinese modernization.

Perfecting Ecological Civilization Systems and Mechanisms to Form a Chinese Solution for Green Development

Systems and mechanisms are vital forces for safeguarding lucid waters and lush mountains and realizing economic prosperity. Since the 18th National Congress of the CPC, China has issued and implemented the "Opinions on Accelerating the Construction of Ecological Civilization" and the "Overall Plan for the Reform of the Ecological Civilization System", along with dozens of specific reform plans. These have gradually established fundamental systems for ecological environmental protection, natural resource asset property rights, territorial space development and protection, spatial planning, resource total quantity management and comprehensive conservation, paid use of resources and ecological compensation, ecological civilization performance evaluation and accountability, and other foundational systems. The "four beams and eight pillars" institutional framework of ecological civilization construction with Chinese characteristics has been essentially formed. The comprehensive deepening of reforms in the field of ecological civilization has transitioned from local exploration and breakthrough to systematic integration and comprehensive deepening. The modernization level of ecological environmental governance systems and governance capabilities has significantly improved.

After decades of exploration, China has essentially formed a practical, effective, and rigorous system of ecological environmental protection laws. From the first inclusion of "The state protects the environment and natural resources, and prevents and controls pollution and other public hazards" in the Constitution in 1978, to the passage of the Environmental Protection Law in 1989, ecological environmental protection work has gradually entered the track of rule of law. Since the beginning of the 21st century, China has promulgated a series of laws, regulations, departmental rules, normative documents, and local regulations and rules in the field of ecological environmental protection. Since the new era began, the Central Committee has required the use of the strictest systems and most rigorous legal measures to protect the ecological environment. The responsibility system for ecological environment—led by Party committees, guided by government, centered on enterprises, and jointly participated in by social organizations and the public—has become increasingly tight and sound, with the whole Party and country continuously enhancing their consciousness and initiative in promoting ecological civilization construction. Currently, China has over 30 effective laws on ecological environment, more than 100 administrative regulations, and over 1,000 local regulations, which cover pollution prevention and control in areas such as air, water, soil, and noise, as well as important ecosystems and elements including the Yangtze River, wetlands, and black soil.

Environmental Protection Building a Beautiful China

In August 1973, the State Council convened the first national conference on environmental protection, and ecological environmental protection was placed on the national agenda. The reform and opening up stimulated development vitality, but while China's high-speed economic development achieved tremendous success, environmental issues also accumulated. From establishing environmental protection as a basic national policy, to implementing sustainable development strategies, to building a resource-conserving and eco-friendly society, the strategic importance of ecological environmental protection has continuously increased. To address environmental challenges, China has invested substantial funds, scientific research resources, and social resources in key governance areas such as the treatment of the three major lakes—Taihu, Chaohu, and Dianchi—and in vigorously addressing acid rain and other pollution issues.

Since the 18th National Congress of the CPC, under the leadership of the Central Committee, China has prioritized resolving prominent ecological and environmental problems as a key livelihood area, launching an unprecedented and massive critical battle against pollution that has yielded precise, science-driven, and legally sound solutions and experiences for pollution control. The quality of the ecological environment has significantly improved, continuously enhancing people's sense of gain, happiness, and security. In 2023, China's total environmental pollution control investment reached 872. 34 billion yuan, accounting for 0. 7% of the GDP and 1. 7% of total social fixed asset investment. Furthermore, China is the first developing country to launch large-scale PM2. 5 control and the country with the fastest improvement in air quality globally. The fundamental improvement of rivers and lakes has brought the proportion of good-quality surface water sections close to developed country levels. Soil environmental risks have been effectively controlled, urban and rural waste classification and centralized collection and treatment capabilities continue to improve, the use of chemical fertilizers and pesticides continues to decrease, and the "zero import" target for solid waste has been achieved on schedule.

Ecological Protection, Restoration, and Territorial Space Governance Building Solid Ecological Security Barriers

At the founding of the People's Republic of China, the national forest coverage rate was only 8. 6%, and people suffered greatly from rampant wind and sand erosion. Since the 1950s, the CPC Central Committee called for "greening the motherland" and initiated ecological protection and restoration efforts. In 1978, the CPC Central Committee and the State Council made a strategic decision to build large-scale protective forests in key areas affected by wind and sand in the Northwest, North, and Northeast regions. To date, a green Great Wall stretching thousands of miles has been built in northern China, achieving a historic transformation in key governance areas from "advancing sand and retreating humans" to "advancing green and retreating sand". Also, projects such as natural forest protection and returning farmland to forests and grasslands have turned barren mountains into embroidered landscapes and deserts into oases. As General Secretary Xi Jinping has pointed out, human lifelines depend on fields,

fields depend on water, water depends on mountains, mountains depend on soil, and soil depends on forests and grasslands—this community of life is the material foundation for human survival and development.

Since the new era began, China has approached ecological protection from the perspective of ecosystem integrity, scientifically delineated red lines for ecological protection, established a natural protected area system with national parks as the mainstay, strengthened ecological protection of major rivers, important lakes, wetlands, and coastal zones, coordinated the integrated protection and systematic governance of mountains, rivers, forests, fields, lakes, grasslands, and deserts, implemented major projects for the protection and restoration of important ecosystems, regularly conducted national ecological status surveys and assessments, and scientifically carried out large-scale national land greening actions. The ecological protection and restoration of territorial space has gradually shifted from single-element to systematic governance, from engineering-dominated measures to natural recovery, from end-of-pipe treatment to whole-chain management, and from reliance on fiscal support to diversified investment. A comprehensive "blueprint" for ecological protection and restoration—from mountain tops to oceans, from plateaus to plains, from national to local levels—has taken shape.

Green and Low-Carbon Transition Steadily Advancing Carbon Peaking and Carbon Neutrality

New quality productive forces are green productive forces, and promoting the green and low-carbon transformation of economic and social development is a key link in achieving high-quality development. Under the guidance of Xi Jinping's Thought on Ecological Civilization, China is comprehensively constructing green production and lifestyle models that cover production, distribution, circulation, and consumption across all fields and territories. With innovation-driven development as the lead to shape new momentum and advantages for economic development, and with rigid resource and environmental constraints pushing deep industrial structure adjustments, China is promoting key regions such as the Yangtze River Economic Belt, Yellow River Basin, Beijing-Tianjin-Hebei region, Yangtze River Delta, Guangdong-Hong Kong-Macao Greater Bay Area, and Chengdu-Chongqing Economic Circle to take the lead in building green development highlands under the guidance of the concept of "step up conservation of the Yangtze River and stop its over-development". China has incorporated carbon peaking and carbon neutrality into the overall layout of ecological civilization construction and the overall economic and social development framework, established a national carbon emissions trading market and a national greenhouse gas voluntary emissions reduction trading market, explored paths to realize the value of ecological products, coordinated efforts to reduce carbon emissions and pollution while expanding greenery and promoting growth, and accelerated the construction of a modern economic system featuring green, low-carbon, and circular development.

From 2012 to 2024, China supported an average annual economic growth of 6.17% with an average annual energy consumption growth of about 3%, with energy intensity cumulatively decreasing by more than 29.4%, making China one of the countries with the fastest reduction in energy intensity globally. In 2024, the proportion of non-fossil energy consumption in China's total energy consumption increased by 1.8 percentage points compared to the previous year, with the proportion of hydropower, nuclear power, wind power, and solar power generation increasing to 32.6%. China has promoted large-scale equipment upgrades and the replacement of old consumer goods with new ones, providing more green, low-carbon, and energy-efficient equipment and products to facilitate people's production and livelihoods. At the national level, China has cumulatively cultivated 6,430 green factories, which has driven local levels to cultivate more than 16,000 provincial and municipal green factories, continuously improving the green manufacturing system. At the national level, China has cultivated 491 green industrial parks, with energy consumption per unit of industrial added value at two-thirds of the national average, water consumption per 10,000 yuan of industrial added value at one-quarter of the national average, and an average industrial solid waste disposal and utilization rate exceeding 95%, becoming demonstration models of green and low-carbon development.

Jointly Building a Clean and Beautiful World and a Green Silk Road

"Humanity lives in the same global village, and in the same time and space where history and reality converge. We are increasingly becoming a community of shared future where we are all interconnected". General Secretary Xi

Jinping, with a broad global vision and profound humanitarian concern, has proposed the Global Development Initiative, Global Security Initiative, and Global Civilization Initiative, emphasizing "improving global environmental governance, actively addressing climate change, and building a community of life between humans and nature", thus providing solid support for jointly creating a harmonious and livable home for humanity. As a responsible major developing country, China is working hand in hand with the world to advance global environmental and climate governance, jointly implement the United Nations 2030 Agenda for Sustainable Development, and maintain a fair, reasonable, and win-win global environmental governance system. China is extensively engaged in green international cooperation, sharing green technologies, experiences, and resources, strengthening international cooperation in green standards and conformity assessment, enhancing the environmental sustainability of overseas projects, encouraging the import and export of green and low-carbon products, and injecting powerful momentum into the global green and low-carbon transition. China is leading the comprehensive, balanced, and effective implementation of the "Kunming-Montreal Global Biodiversity Framework" and supporting biodiversity conservation in developing countries. China is conducting multi-level exchanges and cooperation in ecological environmental protection, building platforms such as the Shanghai Cooperation Organization （SCO） Environmental Protection Information Sharing Platform, expanding channels and mechanisms for multilateral and bilateral dialogue and cooperation, and transforming consensus into practical actions and positive results for global green development.

As the most welcomed international public good and the largest international cooperation platform, the Belt and Road Initiative is a path for both open development and green development. In May 2017, President Xi Jinping pointed out at the first Belt and Road Forum for International Cooperation: "We should practice the new concept of green development, advocate green, low-carbon, circular, and sustainable production and lifestyle, strengthen ecological and environmental protection cooperation, build ecological civilization, and jointly achieve the 2030 Sustainable Development Goals. " China actively promotes the construction of a Green Silk Road. It has signed a "Memorandum of Understanding on Building a Green Belt and Road" with the United Nations Environment Programme (UNEP), jointly launched the Green Development Partnership Initiative with 31 participating countries, established the Belt and Road Energy Cooperation Partnership with 32 participating countries, implemented the Green Investment Principles for the Belt and Road, deepened cooperation in green infrastructure, green energy, green transportation and other fields, increased support for the Belt and Road Initiative International Green Development Coalition, hosted the Belt and Road Green Innovation Conference, established a photovoltaic industry dialogue and exchange mechanism and a green and low-carbon expert network, and actively helped participating countries explore green development models that best suit their national interests.

Think Tank Achievements Interpreting "Lucid Waters and Lush Mountains Are Invaluable Assets"

Striding forward on the new journey of green development, the Silk Road International Think Tank, together with relevant institutions, has formed an Editorial Committee to compile and publish the 2025 Green Development Report (in Chinese and English) to explain the theoretical innovation, institutional innovation, mechanism innovation, and practical innovation of China's green development centered on the concept that "lucid waters and lush mountains are invaluable assets". Overall, the compilation and publication of this report has the following value and significance.

1. Twenty-Year Review and Achievements Summary

In the twenty years since the concept that "lucid waters and lush mountains are invaluable assets" was proposed, China has incorporated "the Beautiful China Initiative" into its goal of building a great modern socialist country, "ecological civilization" into the "five-sphere integrated plan", "harmony between humans and nature" into its modernization approach, "green" into the new development concept, and "pollution prevention and control" into the three critical battles. China has firmly followed the path of green development and provided developing countries with a Chinese solution for balancing economic development and ecological protection that is both referenceable and operational. Guided by Xi Jinping's Thought on Ecological Civilization leading the construction of a community with a shared future for mankind, this report forms think

tank achievements on green development with a 20-year research perspective,
while also considering the latest results and strategic goals through data analysis,
status summaries, challenge identification, and countermeasure suggestions.
This further enriches the system of relevant think tank achievements at home and
abroad.

2. Leadership, Demonstration, and Innovative Achievements

At the sprint stage with only ten years remaining until the basic realization
of socialist modernization by 2035, at the critical period when the 14th Five-
Year Plan is about to conclude and the 15th Five-Year Plan is waiting to be
planned, at the new starting point of the 20th anniversary of the proposal and
practice of the concept that "lucid waters and lush mountains are invaluable assets", and in combination with the strategic deployment proposed by the Third
Plenary Session of the 20th CPC Central Committee to "focus on building a
beautiful China, accelerate the comprehensive green transformation of economic
and social development, improve the ecological environment governance system, promote ecological priority, economical and intensive use, and green and
low-carbon development, and promote harmony between humans and nature",
this report summarizes the Chinese practice, Chinese innovation, and Chinese
solutions of "lucid waters and lush mountains are invaluable assets", proposes
countermeasures and future prospects, and provides a pathway guide, decision-
making reference, and theoretical basis for green high-quality development for
Chinese and international political, industrial, academic, research, investment, media sectors, and readers at large.

3. Decision-Making and Future Planning References

Facing the unprecedented changes in a century, this report fully grasps the
global trends of green development and, combining problem-oriented, strategy-
oriented, demand-oriented, and innovation-oriented approaches, focuses on
five major areas—institutional mechanism construction, ecological environmental protection, territorial space governance, green and low-carbon transformation, and green international cooperation—and several hot topics. It conducts
pioneering empirical research on the top-level design, practical innovation,
and typical cases of China's green development, polishes and launches a batch
of high-quality think tank achievements with international influence, cheers for

China's green development, tells the Chinese story of green development well, and advances a series of work on achievement compilation, publication, release, dissemination, discussion, activities, and projects, thereby building a "global think tank + industry-academia-research-application cooperation platform" for green development.

Lucid waters meander away, lush mountains open in array. Under the scientific guidance of Xi Jinping's Thought on Ecological Civilization, China has forged a bright path of green development, and the dream of a beautiful China with blue skies, green land, clean water, and harmony between humans and nature is becoming reality step by step. In the new era and new journey, China unswervingly follows the path of green, low-carbon, and sustainable development. Chinese wisdom, Chinese responsibility, Chinese solutions, and Chinese actions are propelling the world toward a new era of ecological civilization and will make new and greater contributions to protecting our Earth home.

The Silk Road International Think Tank and Silk Road Youth Forum are international exchange platforms dedicated to serving the "Belt and Road" Initiative, upholding the principles of "Unity, Friendship, and Progress". They organize annual conferences, thematic forums, and roundtable dialogues, and conduct a series of green development-themed exchange activities including the Silk Road Youth Forum－Malaysia-China Cooperation Conference (Green Development Creates a Better Future), China-US International Symposium on Ecological Civilization Construction, and the "A Decade of BRI: Youth Planting for the Future" Friendship Forest co-building activity. They carry out research on the concept that "Lucid Waters and Lush Mountains Are Invaluable Assets", and have launched the "Protect the Earth, Guard the Future: Silk Road Youth Carbon Peak and Carbon Neutrality Initiative". These platforms communicate China's stories and Chinese solutions to people from all sectors at home and abroad, especially Silk Road youth. To date, more than 100 distinguished guests have attended related activities and projects, including Vice Chairpersons of the Standing Committee of the National People's Congress of China, Vice Chairpersons of the Chinese People's Political Consultative Conference, as well as the Deputy Prime Minister of Nepal, the Nepali Ambassador to China, the Dominican Ambassador to China, the Sierra Leonean Ambassador to China, the Jamaican Ambassador to China, the Belarusian Minister-Counsellor to China, and the Comorian Ambassador to China. We look forward to strengthening green development exchanges and cooperation with more government departments, international organizations, enterprises and institutions, contributing more high-quality think tank research, scientific and technological innovation, industry-finance cooperation, and other effective results to promote Chinese-style modernization, and widely promoting China's new practices, new results, and new experiences in green development to developing countries and Belt and Road youth, helping to build a community with a shared future for mankind and the process of world modernization.

Main Report

Chapter 1
Harmonious Coexistence Between Humans and Nature: China's Green Development Solutions

General Secretary Xi Jinping profoundly pointed out that we must stand at the height of responsibility for human civilization, respect nature, adapt to nature, protect nature, explore the path of harmonious coexistence between humans and nature, promote the coordinated unity of economic development and ecological protection, and jointly build a prosperous, clean, and beautiful world. The report of the 20th National Congress of the Communist Party of China clearly stated that "Chinese modernization is modernization featuring harmonious coexistence between humans and nature" and that we must "unswervingly follow a civilized development path that ensures production development, affluent lives, and sound ecology to achieve sustainable development of the Chinese nation". From General Secretary Xi Jinping's proposal of the concept that "lucid waters and lush mountains are invaluable assets" to the establishment of the "dual carbon" goals, China has elevated ecological civilization construction to an unprecedented strategic height and achieved a leap from concept to action and a transformation from passive to proactive, making important contributions to global ecological civilization construction. In the new era, China has proven through practical actions that green development is not a burden but an opportunity, not an expedient measure but a long-term strategy.

Section 1　The Historical Background and Practical

Needs of Green Development

I. Major Challenges Faced by Countries Worldwide, Especially Developing Countries, in Coordinating Environmental Protection and Economic Development

1. Severe Challenges to the Global Ecological Environment

In recent years, the Earth, on which humans depend for survival, has faced a triple crisis of climate change, biodiversity loss, and pollution and waste. From 2024 onwards, extreme weather events such as heavy rainfall, heat waves, and droughts have occurred frequently in many parts of the world, posing serious challenges to human sustainable development. The Sixth Assessment Report of the United Nations Intergovernmental Panel on Climate Change indicates that global warming over the past 50 years has been occurring at an unprecedented rate compared to the past 2,000 years. Continuous warming has intensified the instability of the climate system, leading to more frequent and stronger extreme weather events with wider impact areas. With the economic and social development of various countries, constraints on various natural resources have become increasingly evident. Coupled with the uneven global distribution of natural resources, this has exacerbated social unrest caused by resource competition. Some countries' excessive exploitation and utilization of natural resources has led to worsening pollution of water, soil, air, and noise and brought enormous risks to human health and sustainable development, while destroying or altering biological habitats and causing declines in species populations.

2. Global Environmental Governance and Green Development Have Yet to Form Broad Consensus and Clear Pathways

Governments around the world have recognized the adverse effects of ecological and environmental problems on humanity and have made unremitting efforts to address them. However, global environmental governance is a complex systematic project requiring close cooperation among all countries. Based on their own interests and stages of development, countries often have different priorities and positions on environmental governance, making it difficult to form broad consensus and effective implementation of global environmental agreements or measures in a short period of time. Youth are the main responsible parties and participants in global environmental governance, but bilateral and multilateral cooperation involving youth is generally insufficient. Global environmental governance requires substantial financial investment, but funding channels are limited and primarily rely on government commitments or financial arrangements in transnational agreements, while market investment forces remain far from adequate.

II. China's Ecological Civilization Development Remains in a Critical Period Marked by Overlapping Pressures and Significant Challenges

Looking back at history, a good ecological environment has been an important guarantee for the Chinese nation's ability to endure and develop, and the advocacy of "unity of heaven and humanity" is a distinctive feature of Chinese civilization. Since the reform and opening up, China has established resource conservation and environmental protection as basic national policies and sustainable development as a national strategy, and has vigorously promoted the construction of socialist ecological civilization. Since the beginning of the new era, under the guidance of Xi Jinping's Thought on Socialism with Chinese Characteristics for a New Era, the whole Party and the people of all ethnic groups across the country have adhered to the concept of "lucid waters and lush mountains are invaluable assets", unswervingly followed the path of ecological priority and green development, promoted the comprehensive green transformation of economic and social development, created an ecological miracle and a green development miracle that attracted worldwide attention, and made major strides in the construction of a beautiful China. Also, China's green development remains in a critical period of moving forward under heavy burden, a window period for solving problems under compounding pressures, a period of quality and efficiency improvement for enhancing welfare, and a period of transformative breakthroughs to overcome bottlenecks. Environmental capacity is limited, ecosystems are fragile, and the structural, root, and trend-based pressures on ecological and environmental protection have not yet been fundamentally alleviated. People's expectations for a beautiful ecological environment and high-quality ecological products are higher, while their tolerance for ecological and environmental problems is lower.

First, with the overlap of green development goals and tasks, the difficulty of work has further increased. Green development has evolved from the original focus on winning the critical battle against pollution to comprehensive efforts in stronger pollution prevention and control, green and low-carbon transformation, ecological protection of territorial space, carbon peaking and carbon neutrality, safeguarding the security baseline for Beautiful China, international cooperation, and other higher standards and long-term mechanisms. The comprehensiveness, systematicity, complexity, and arduousness of tasks have undergone tremendous changes, and green development has entered the deep water zone of tackling tough challenges.

Second, the pressure to balance economic development and environmental protection continues to increase, with deeper contradictions becoming more prominent. Currently, global trade growth is slowing, and economic recovery is sluggish. The International Monetary Fund's Global Economic Outlook 2025 predicts that global economic growth will remain at 2.8% in 2025, the same as in 2024, still below the pre-COVID-19 average level of 3.2%. The increasing complexity, severity, and uncertainty of the external environment exacerbate deep-seated domestic contradictions, including insufficient effective demand, overcapacity in some industries, weak social expectations, numerous risk factors, and bottlenecks in the domestic economic cycle. Under realistic pressures, there have even been arguments that ecological and environmental protection efforts should be relaxed to make way for economic development.

Third, the pressure for environmental improvement and industrial structure adjustment has increased, making the task of green transformation more arduous. For example, under the influence of El Niño, extreme weather events have increased. In the spring of 2024, China's climate was generally characterized by warm and humid conditions, with average temperatures being the highest on record for the same period. The country experienced 14 regional torrential rain events, frequent strong convective weather in the south, and winter-spring drought in the southwest and Huanghuai-Jianghuai regions. While China produces and consumes large amounts of steel, cement, electrolytic aluminum, and some other raw materials, resource and energy utilization efficiency remains relatively low. Energy demand maintains rigid growth, with coal consumption accounting for more than half of total energy consumption. There are over 7 million road freight carriers nationwide, with road freight volume consistently maintaining about 70% of the total, creating significant pollution emission pressure.

Fourth, the international ecological and environmental governance situation is complex and severe, with the risk of global ecological crisis transmission further intensifying. In the world's new period of turbulence and transformation, the risks, challenges, and gaming pressures in global environmental governance have increased, with fierce struggles in convention negotiations on climate change and biodiversity. Some western countries have politicized ecological environment protection and incorporated it into geopolitics, even using ecological protection as an excuse to seize resources, transfer pollution, and restrict other countries' development rights. They implement "double standards" to pressure China and play the climate card in an attempt to diminish China's green development achievements.

Section 2   Review of the 20th Anniversary of the Concept "Lucid Waters and Lush Mountains Are Invaluable Assets": Zhejiang Province as a Case Study in Green Development

Since the reform and opening up, Zhejiang Province has experienced rapid economic and social development. At the beginning of the 21st century, the province's per capita GDP approached $ 3,000, but problems of water, electricity, and land shortages emerged. Ecological and environmental damage occurred from time to time, and resource and environmental constraints became increasingly tight and faced "growing pains". In 2003, Xi Jinping, then Secretary of the Zhejiang Provincial Party Committee, made a strategic decision at the Fourth Plenary Session of the 11th Zhejiang Provincial Party Committee to "leverage eight advantages" and "promote eight measures" (hereinafter referred to as the "Eight-Eight Strategy"), which became the guiding principles for Zhejiang's reform, development, and comprehensive moderately prosperous society construction. "Leveraging Zhejiang's ecological advantages, creating an ecological province, and building a 'Green Zhejiang'" was one of these strategic deployments. In 2005, when visiting Yucun Village in Anji County, Huzhou City, Xi Jinping creatively and forward-lookingly made the important assertion that "lucid waters and lush mountains are invaluable assets", emphasizing that "we should not sacrifice the environment to promote economic growth, because such growth is not development".

Over the past 20 years, successive provincial party committees and governments in Zhejiang have adhered to a consistent blueprint, continuously promoting the organic integration of beautiful ecology, beautiful economy, and beautiful life, achieving the leap from "Green Zhejiang" to "Ecological Zhejiang" and then to "Beautiful Zhejiang". With 1% of the country's land, 3% of its water usage, 4.7% of its population, and 5% of its energy consumption, Zhejiang has created 6.5% of China's GDP, maintaining its economic aggregate and quality steadily in the first tier nationwide. The "high-value" ecological environment and "high-quality" economic development have progressed in tandem, with the perfect answer unfolding across the vast land of Zhejiang.

Case 1-1　　Small Village Amazes the World: Yucun's Green Transformation from "Selling Stones" to "Selling Scenery"

Yucun is under the jurisdiction of Anji County, Huzhou City, Zhejiang Province. It is named after its location on the Yuling ridge, an extension of the Tianmu Mountains, with a total area of only 4.86 km^2. Though the village is small, its reputation is significant. As the birthplace of the concept "lucid waters and lush mountains are invaluable assets", Yucun has walked a path of rural ecological revitalization over 20 years, characterized by beautiful ecology, thriving industry, and prosperous residents. In 2024, Yucun received 1.22 million visitors, achieved a village collective economic income of 22.05 million yuan, and reached a per capita income of 74,000 yuan for villagers, far exceeding the provincial and national average levels.

In the 1980s and 1990s, Yucun relied on quarrying mountains and operating cement factories, once becoming a wealthy village with a maximum annual collective income of 3 million yuan. Although "selling stones" brought temporary economic prosperity to Yucun, it left behind a devastated environment. In 1998, Anji County was listed by national environmental protection departments as a key area for treating water pollution in Taihu Lake. As an important source village, Yucun's ecological and environmental governance gradually intensified. In 2003, Zhejiang Province launched the Thousand Villages Demonstration and Ten Thousand Villages Renovation Project. Yucun resolutely stopped developing the "mining economy" and carried out environmental governance, including garbage cleanup, factory demolition, and river regulation. However, with no succeeding industries generating benefits yet, the village collective economy experienced a deficit, and villagers' income sharply decreased. How to achieve both economic development and environmental protection became an essential question for Yucun at that time.

On August 15, 2005, Xi Jinping, then Secretary of the Zhejiang Provincial Party Committee, came to Yucun during his investigation in Anji County. According to the plan, Xi Jinping would stay in the village for 20 minutes, only listening to reports without making a speech. However, when he learned that Yucun had, through democratic decision-making, shut down mines and polluting enterprises, he immediately diagnosed the village's development path and told everyone: "Ecological resources are your most valuable resources. In developing the economy, you cannot pursue everything you see as good, and you especially cannot sacrifice the environment for development. You must do some things and refrain from others, and cannot be obsessed with past development models...We used to say that we want both lucid waters and lush mountains as well as gold and silver mountains, but in fact, lucid waters and lush mountains themselves are gold and silver mountains—they have gold content." This is the scientific judgment that "lucid waters and lush mountains are invaluable assets" proposed by comrade Xi Jinping for the first time. Nine days later, he published an article titled "Lucid Waters and Lush Mountains Are Also Invaluable Assets" in the "Zhejiang, China: A New Vision for Development" column of *Zhejiang Daily*, pointing out that lucid waters and lush mountains can bring invaluable assets, but invaluable assets cannot buy back lucid waters and lush mountains. Lucid waters and lush mountains may conflict with invaluable assets, yet they can be dialectically unified.

The concept that "lucid waters and lush mountains are invaluable assets" opened the eyes of Yucun villagers, making them truly recognize that protecting the ecological environment means protecting productivity. From then on, Yucun broke free from the wait-and-see attitude of "waiting, relying, and asking", persistently reclaimed and regreened abandoned mines, strengthened ecological protection and restoration, continuously improved the living environment, transformed abandoned mines and cement factories into tourism areas, integrated moso bamboo, white tea, and tourism into an agriculture-tourism integrated business format, and converted their own homes into farmhouse restaurants and homestays, thus embarking on a path of green development. In March 2020, General Secretary Xi Jinping revisited Yucun. Seeing the changes in the village, he said: "The achievements Yucun has made now prove that the path of green development is correct, and once the right path is chosen, we must persist in following it. "

Subsequently, Yucun continued to explore an upgraded version of green development. First, enhancing environmental quality to create a picturesque Yucun. They compiled village planning, made "micro-improvement and precise enhancement" of the water environment, constructed a mountain flood disaster prevention and flood control system of "horizontal to the edge, vertical to the bottom", created a digital twin space for future rural areas, and realized a closed-loop digital management of the entire village's living environment.

Second, accelerating business model innovation to create a common prosperity Yucun. The village joined with four surrounding villages to establish the "Five Villages Joint Prosperity" company, developing together and creating differentiated tourism products to form a premium rural tourism route for tourists. The "Yucun Cloud Villager" mini-program is Yucun's initiative for "urban-rural breakthrough plan". It creates cloud interaction experiences and consumption scenarios with urban youth through cloud adoption, cloud travel, cloud co-creation, cloud festivals, and cloud social networking.

Third, creating new carriers for rural empowerment to cultivate a branded Yucun. The village guided institutions within its domain to uniformly use the "Yucun Research and Study" brand for services, launched the "Yucun Research and Study" mini-program, and created a matrix of research and study products for ecological civilization, youth rural entry, and cultural tourism experiences. Relying on the influence of the "Yucun" brand, Yucun initiated a "Global Partner" recruitment plan, joining with 24 surrounding villages to integrate 100,000 m² of entrepreneurial space, more than 20,000 m² of factory buildings, nearly 60,000 mu (about 4,000 hectares) of bamboo forests and farmland, and establishing the "Yucun Industrial Fund" of 100 million yuan. Focusing on green industries such as research and study education, rural tourism, cultural creativity, agricultural and forestry industries, digital economy, green finance, zero-carbon technology, and health care, they broadly invite global talents to jointly build new business formats for future rural areas.

Fourth, promoting low-carbon circular development to build a zero-carbon Yucun. They compiled China's first zero-carbon rural planning— "China Yucun Zero-Carbon Rural Construction Planning (2022-2035) ", proposing the development goal of achieving carbon neutrality within the village area before 2027. The "Yucun Impression" Youth Library, which was converted from an old factory building, utilizes photovoltaic power generation for carbon offsetting. Yucun conducts "green electricity green certificate" trading and purchases photovoltaic and wind power from places like Ningxia, Heilongjiang, and Anhui to achieve full village coverage with green electricity. Yucun has set up intelligent devices to monitor walking and cycling data and convert visitors' green travel into carbon credits that can be used to offset consumption in scenic areas.

I. Ecological Transformation to "Green": Consistent Pollution Prevention and Control

Over the past 20 years, Zhejiang Province has continued to advance pollution prevention and control work, including the "811" environmental pollution remediation, "Five Water Governance"①, Blue Sky Defense War, "Waste-Free City", Beautiful Bay, and other initiatives. Public satisfaction with the ecological environment has improved for 13 consecutive years, and the effectiveness of ecological environment governance has maintained a leading position nationwide. For instance, from 2002 to 2024, the proportion of water quality at or above Class III standard at provincial controlled sections in Zhejiang Province has risen from 66.4% to 98.6%, with the complete elimination of inferior Class V sections. The average PM2.5 concentration in cities with districts has decreased from 61 micrograms per cubic meter to 26.3 micrograms per cubic meter. In 2023, the safe utilization rate of key construction land in Zhejiang Province remained at 100%, the average proportion of good water quality sea area in nearshore waters was 56.3%, and the day and night compliance rates of sound environment monitoring in functional areas of cities with districts were 96.6% and 88.5%, respectively.

To address issues strongly reflected in public concerns such as sewage and odors, Zhejiang Province has filled the shortcomings of living environment infrastructure, built more than 2,000 "zero direct discharge areas" for urban residential communities, completed the renovation and upgrade of over 1,000 domestic waste transfer stations, and taken the lead nationwide in achieving "county-wide coverage" of kitchen waste treatment facilities and "zero landfill" of raw waste. Also, Zhejiang Province vigorously promotes ecological culture, takes the lead in creating green cells such as ecological civilization education bases and green schools and forms a new trend of green practices throughout society.

In 2004, Zhejiang Province initiated the first round of "811" environmental pollution remediation action, putting the brakes on the trend of environmental pollution and ecological damage across the province. Here, "8" refers to the eight major water systems in Zhejiang, while "11" refers to both the 11 prefecture-level cities in Zhejiang and the 11 provincial-level environmental protection key supervision areas designated by the Zhejiang Provincial Government at that time. In 2008, the second round of the three-year "811" environmental

---

① Five Water Governance: Treating sewage, preventing floods, draining waterlogged areas, ensuring water supply, and promoting water conservation.

protection action was launched. At this time, "8" evolved to represent eight aspects of environmental protection work objectives and eight aspects of main tasks, while "11" referred to both the 11 aspects of policy measures proposed that year and the 11 key environmental issues identified by the Zhejiang Provincial Government. In 2011 and 2016, Zhejiang launched the third round of "811" ecological civilization construction action and the fourth round of "811" Beautiful Zhejiang construction action respectively, further clarifying the path for pioneering ecological civilization. In 2023, focusing on the goals of creating an ecological civilization highland and a provincial pioneer area for Beautiful China, Zhejiang launched the fifth round of "811" ecological civilization pioneering demonstration action and carried out eight major special actions, including the modernization of territorial space governance, green and low-carbon empowerment, improvement of beautiful environmental quality, biodiversity friendliness, comprehensive quality improvement of beautiful urban and rural areas, ecological prosperity and benefiting the people, improving ecological civilization governance efficiency, and cultivating ecological self-awareness among all people. All 11 prefecture-level cities were required to create their own pioneering brands of ecological civilization, forming more landmark achievements with Zhejiang identification, demonstration promotion, and strategic leadership. Ecological governance is "always on the road". Although each round of Zhejiang's "811" action has different themes and connotations, the content of the work is consistent and progressive.

II. Pursuing "New" and Chasing "Green": Creating Benchmarks for Pollution and Carbon Reduction, and Transition

Over the past 20 years, Zhejiang Province has formulated policies for the energy conservation and environmental protection industry, green economy, and green low-carbon circular development economic system. It has implemented four rounds of the circular economy "991" action plan, adhered to the principle of "vacating cages to change birds, phoenix rebirth", continuously eliminated "scattered, messy, and polluting" industries while cultivating "high-precision, advanced" ones. The province has explored China's first cross-provincial watershed ecological compensation mechanism, taken the lead in implementing environmental rights trading such as pollution rights, water use rights, and energy use rights, and issued China's first provincial-level standard for Gross Ecosystem Product （GEP） accounting. By promoting ecological industrialization and industrial ecologicalization, Zhejiang has enhanced development quality through the conversion of old and new growth drivers, achieving breakthrough progress in building a national circular economy pilot province and demonstration area for coordinated pollution reduction and carbon reduction. The province has built a supply system of clean energy including wind, solar, water, and nuclear power and achieved high-standard development as a National Clean Energy Demonstration Province, with new energy installed capacity exceeding that of coal power. Also, Zhejiang has driven comprehensive low-carbon transformation through demonstration pilots. Through measures such as enterprise cultivation and strengthening, innovation capability upgrading, market application enhancement, and industrial cluster building, the province has formed a new energy manufacturing base characterized by scale, high-end, and intelligence. The scale of the photovoltaic industry, the number and scale of photovoltaic auxiliary material enterprises rank among the top in the country, and the annual total revenue of the new energy vehicle industry has exceeded one trillion yuan.

III. Turning "Green" into "Gold": Improving the Value Realization Mechanism of Ecological Products

In May 2021, the Central Committee of the Communist Party of China and the State Council issued the Opinions on Supporting Zhejiang's High-Quality Development to Build a Demonstration Zone for Common Prosperity, which clearly requires Zhejiang to "broaden the conversion channel of lucid waters and lush mountains into invaluable assets, establish and improve the value realization mechanism of ecological products, and explore and improve the Gross Ecosystem Product accounting and application system with Zhejiang characteristics". The Zhejiang Province Ecological Environment Protection Regulations dedicates a special chapter to "ecological product value realization" and constructs a basic legal framework for the realization of ecological product value. Furthermore,

Zhejiang Province has formed a series of innovative paths for the realization of ecological product value in the field of natural resources, with ecological protection, restoration, and enhancement as the work foundation, and property rights construction, asset allocation, operation, and maintenance as the main means, thus promoting the transformation from "resources to assets to capital" in an organized fasion.

For example, Huzhou City has constructed an accounting mechanism of "Gross Ecosystem Product (GEP) + Value of Ecological Products (VEP) for specific territorial units". Through natural resource rights confirmation and registration and pilot accounting of ecological product total value, the city has mastered the distribution and total amount of ecological assets in its domain, conducted GEP accounting for key ecological townships, and included GEP accounting results in the performance evaluation of local governments and the natural resource asset departure (mid-term) audit of leading cadres. Financial institutions in Huzhou City have developed green financial products such as GEP project loans, VEP green loans, VEP green enterprise loans, and VEP agricultural benefit loans. By calculating the baseline ecological value before project construction and the final value after construction and operation, they use future ecological benefits as collateral to provide low-interest credit loans to relevant enterprises and farmers, with ecological value-added income specifically used for ecological protection or returned to entities that contribute to ecological protection.

Additionally, Zhejiang Province has "packaged" fragmented and idle ecological resources such as mountains, waters, forests, fields, lakes, and houses. With the help of more than 40 "Two Mountains" cooperatives at city, county, and township levels, the province has deepened the interest connection between social capital and village collectives and farmers. The province has cumulatively developed more than 200 projects with a total investment of 56 billion yuan, driven over 2,000 village collectives, increased collective income by more than 670 million yuan, and benefited 80,000 rural households. New models such as Anji's "Two Investments, Three Returns"[1] and Quzhou's rural asset savings

---

[1] Two Investments, Three Returns: Farmers invest in rural assets and resources to achieve rental income, salary income, and dividend income.

dividend① have been created to achieve ecological prosperity and benefit the people.

Table 1-1　Pioneering Green Development Experiences in
Zhejiang Province Since the 21st Century

SN	Green Development Pioneering Experiences	Overview
1	First proposal of the concept "lucid waters and lush mountains are invaluable assets"	On August 15, 2005, Xi Jinping, then Secretary of the Zhejiang Provincial Committee of the CPC, first proposed the scientific judgment that "lucid waters and lush mountains are invaluable assets" during his research in Yucun Village, Anji County, Huzhou City, Zhejiang Province.
2	Leading the nation in the number of practice innovation bases of "Lucid Waters and Lush Mountains Are Invaluable Assets"	Currently, Zhejiang has established 49 national ecological civilization construction demonstration cities and counties and 14 practice innovation bases of "Lucid Waters and Lush Mountains Are Invaluable Assets".
3	First "Ecology Day" in China	During the 2003 "Two Sessions" in Anji County, members of the Political Consultative Conference proposed establishing an "Ecology Day". In September 2003, the People's Congress Standing Committee of Anji County passed a resolution designating March 25 of each year, beginning in 2004, as "Ecology Day".
4	Release of China's first "River Chief System" appointment document	In 2003, Changxing County issued a "River Chief System" appointment document, establishing a three-tiered "River Chief System" at county, township, and village levels. In July 2017, the Standing Committee of the 12th Zhejiang Provincial People's Congress approved the Zhejiang Province River Chief System Regulations, the first local legislation in China specifically regulating the River Chief System.
5	Taking the lead in implementing the Green Rural Revival Program	In 2003, Zhejiang Province launched the Green Rural Revival Program, which has transformed villages with poor environmental conditions and lagging development into ecologically livable, prosperous, and civilized green homes and benefited tens of millions of farmers.

---

① Rural Asset Savings Dividend: Two Mountains cooperatives and village committees sign whole-village operation and development cooperation agreements, storing idle agricultural land, idle rural houses, forest land, mountain ponds, reservoirs, and other rural assets to attract village collectives and farmers to participate in whole-village operation, with farmers receiving dividends from asset savings, asset transfer, and project operation.

Continued Table

SN	Green Development Pioneering Experiences	Overview
6	First cross-provincial river basin ecological compensation mechanism pilot in China	In 2011, a cross-provincial river basin ecological compensation mechanism pilot was launched in the Xin'an River, after which the water quality of the Xin'an River significantly improved.
7	First provincial-level long-term beautiful development plan in China	In August 2020, Zhejiang Province issued the Planning Outline for Deepening Ecological Civilization Demonstration Creation and Building a Beautiful Zhejiang at a High Level in the New Era (2020–2035).
8	Ranking first in Green Development Index	In April 2018, Renmin University of China released the "Green Road—China's Economic Green Development Report 2018", measuring provincial (autonomous regions, municipalities) green development, with Zhejiang ranking first.
9	First batch of national ecological counties	In June 2006, Anji County was included in the list of ecological counties released by the National Environmental Protection Administration.
10	First in China to introduce provincial-level ecological compensation measures	In September 2005, Zhejiang Province issued "Several Opinions on Further Improving the Ecological Compensation Mechanism".
11	World's first large-scale "Zero-Waste" sporting event	The 2023 Hangzhou Asian Games formulated the "Zero-Waste Asian Games Implementation Guide", aiming to promote the reduction of solid waste and maximum utilization of event materials during the Hangzhou Asian Games.
12	China's first biodiversity-friendly township pilot project	In June 2022, the Education and Communications Center of the Ministry of Ecology and Environment awarded Longguang Township in Haishu District, Ningbo City, the designation of "Biodiversity-Friendly Township". Longguang Township is located at the eastern foothills of Siming Mountains, known as the "Green Lungs of Eastern Zhejiang", with a forest coverage rate of 86%, making it a "green treasure house" of biodiversity in East China.
13	First to achieve provincial, municipal, and county-level full coverage of the "Green Ruler"	In 2021, Zhejiang Province's "Three Lines and One List"① ecological environment zoning control plans were fully released at provincial, municipal, and county levels.

---

① Three Lines and One List: ecological protection red line, environmental quality bottom line, resource utilization upper limit line, and ecological environment access list.

**Case 1-2   Thousand Villages Demonstration and Ten Thousand
Villages Renovation Project: Drawing a Picture of
"Green, Prosperous, and Beautiful"
Rural Revitalization**

In June 2003, Xi Jinping, then Secretary of the Zhejiang Provincial Party Committee, based on extensive research and considering provincial conditions, agricultural situations, and development stage characteristics, made the strategic decision to implement the Thousand Villages Demonstration and Ten Thousand Villages Renovation Program (hereinafter referred to as the "Green Rural Revival Program"). He proposed selecting about 10,000 administrative villages from among the province's nearly 40,000 villages for comprehensive renovation, with about 1,000 of them to be built into demonstration villages of comprehensive moderate prosperity. During his work in Zhejiang, Xi Jinping personally formulated the goals, implementation principles, and investment methods for the "Green Rural Revival Program", and established a "Four Ones" working mechanism, namely: implementing a system where the "top leader" takes overall responsibility and establishes hierarchical responsibility; forming a work coordination group for the "Green Rural Revival Program" led by the deputy secretary of the provincial party committee; holding an annual on-site meeting for the "Green Rural Revival Program" attended by the main leaders of the provincial party committee and government to deploy work; and regularly commending a group of advanced collectives and individuals in the "Green Rural Revival Program".

Over the past 20 years, successive provincial party committees and governments in Zhejiang have continued to deepen the "Green Rural Revival Program" according to comrade Xi Jinping's strategic blueprint and important instructions. The renovation scope has continuously expanded from the initial approximately 10,000 administrative villages to all administrative villages in the province; the content has been continuously enriched, from the leading start of "Thousand Villages Demonstration and Ten Thousand Villages Renovation", to the deepening and upgrading of "Boutique in a Thousand Villages, Beauty in Ten Thousand Villages", and further to the iterative upgrade of "Future in a

Thousand Villages, Common Prosperity in Ten Thousand Villages", forming a vibrant scene of "Thousand Villages Toward the Future, Ten Thousand Villages Pursuing Common Prosperity, Urban-Rural Integration, and Creating Harmony and Beauty Throughout the Region".

During his work in Zhejiang, comrade Xi Jinping emphasized the need to closely integrate village renovation with the construction of green ecological homes, so as to simultaneously promote environmental renovation and ecological construction, play the "ecological card" and follow the path of ecological village establishment and ecological prosperity. Zhejiang Province has integrated these important concepts and requirements throughout the entire process and at all stages of implementing the "Green Rural Revival Program". Starting with the renovation of "dirty, disorderly, and poor" environments, the province has promoted the "three major revolutions"[1] in rural environments, carried out agricultural non-point source pollution control, built "zero-waste villages", remediated heavily polluting and high-energy-consuming industries, shut down "small, scattered, and disorderly" enterprises, cultivated new "Beautiful Countryside+" industries, and continuously opened channels for converting the value of "lucid waters and lush mountains are invaluable assets". The urban-rural resident income ratio has narrowed from 2.43 in 2003 to 1.83 in 2024, and "cities with more beautiful countryside, countryside making cities more desirable" has become a vivid portrayal of Zhejiang's urban-rural integrated development.

Xi Jinping has always been concerned about the Green Rural Revival Program. Since becoming General Secretary, he has made important instructions and comments multiple times. Various regions have learned from Zhejiang's Green Rural Revival Program experiences and achieved significant results in rural living environment improvement and rural construction. The "Green Rural Revival Program" has gained international recognition, won the "Champions of the Earth Award" of the United Nations in September 2018, and contributed Chinese solutions to creating a harmonious and livable human home. The "Opinions on Learning and Applying the Experience of the 'Thousand Villages

---

[1]   "Three Major Revolutions" in rural environment: Toilet revolution, garbage revolution, and sewage revolution.

Demonstration and Ten Thousand Villages Renovation' Project to Effectively Promote Comprehensive Rural Revitalization", issued by the CPC Central Committee and the State Council in January 2024, further emphasizes that the "Green Rural Revival Program", starting from rural environmental remediation and progressing from point to area with iterative upgrades, has built thousands of beautiful villages and benefited tens of thousands of farmers through 20 years of continuous effort, creating successful experiences and practical examples for advancing comprehensive rural revitalization.

Section 3   China's Green Development System Reform, Mechanism Development, and Legal Guarantees

I. Systematic Reshaping of the Ecological Civilization Institutional System

Since the new era, the CPC Central Committee with Comrade Xi Jinping at its core has integrated institutional construction throughout all areas of ecological civilization construction by adhering to comprehensive layout, systematic construction, and multi-level advancement. The Party has written "the Chinese Communist Party leads the people in building socialist ecological civilization" and "enhancing the awareness that lucid waters and lush mountains are invaluable assets" into the Party Constitution. The constitutional amendment passed in March 2018 incorporated ecological civilization into the Constitution, achieving a high degree of unity among the Party's propositions, the state's will, and the people's aspirations, fully demonstrating the important position of ecological civilization construction in the Party and state affairs, and indicating the Chinese Communist Party's firm will and strong determination to strengthen ecological civilization construction.

China has successively issued and implemented the "Opinions on Accelerating the Construction of Ecological Civilization", the "Overall Plan for the Reform of the Ecological Civilization System", and dozens of specific reform plans, initially establishing a basic institutional framework for ecological civilization that includes strict prevention at the source, strict management during

the process, compensation for damages, and severe punishment for consequences. Notably, ecological civilization institutional construction in the new
era increasingly emphasizes system integration and collaborative efficiency. It
covers various aspects of ecological civilization construction such as natural resource management and ecological environment supervision, as well as key regions and environmental elements. It focuses not only on the interrelationships
among various environmental elements but also on the coordination and cooperation among various institutions. For example, China has issued the "Air Pollution Prevention and Control Action Plan", the "Water Pollution Prevention
and Control Action Plan", and the "Soil Pollution Prevention and Control Action Plan" to concentrate on solving prominent ecological environment problems. Also, it has implemented fiscal, financial, investment, pricing policies, and standard systems supporting green and low-carbon development,
built a new energy system, developed green and low-carbon industries, improved green consumption incentive mechanisms, and scientifically guided
green and low-carbon transformation. This reflects the calculation of overall,
long-term, and comprehensive accounts in ecological environment protection,
not sacrificing the big picture for small gains, neglecting one aspect for another, spending tomorrow's resources today, or seeking shortsighted, immediate
gains.

Meanwhile, under the unified deployment of the CPC Central Committee
and the State Council, various regions are supported to explore and experiment
with ecological civilization system and mechanism innovations according to local
conditions. In 2016, the General Office of the CPC Central Committee and the
General Office of the State Council issued the "Opinions on Establishing Unified and Standardized National Ecological Civilization Experimental Zones".
The four provinces of Fujian, Jiangxi, Guizhou, and Hainan successively carried out experimental zone construction and gradually formed a batch of institutional achievements with replicable and promotable value, with reform experiences being promoted "from point to area".

In 2012, the report of the 18th National Congress of the Communist Party
of China identified "green development, circular development, and low-carbon development" as important pathways for ecological civilization construc-

tion. In 2017, the report of the 19th National Congress of the Communist Party of China formally proposed establishing and improving an economic system for green, low-carbon, and circular development. In February 2021, the State Council issued the "Guidelines on Accelerating the Establishment and Improvement of a Green, Low-Carbon, and Circular Development Economic System", proposing to implement green planning, green design, green investment, green construction, green production, green circulation, green living, and green consumption in all aspects and throughout the entire process, thus establishing development on the basis of efficient resource utilization, strict ecological environment protection, and effective control of greenhouse gas emissions.

The report of the 20th National Congress of the Communist Party of China dedicated a special chapter to "Promoting Green Development and Promoting Harmony between Humanity and Nature", stating that it is necessary to firmly establish and practice the concept that lucid waters and lush mountains are invaluable assets, and to promote development that prioritizes ecology, conservation, efficiency, and green and low-carbon approaches. The "Decision of the Central Committee of the Communist Party of China on Further Comprehensively Deepening Reform and Advancing Chinese Modernization" mentions "green" 14 times and includes a special chapter of "Deepening Ecological Civilization System Reform". It requires improving the ecological civilization institutional system, coordinating the promotion of carbon reduction, pollution reduction, green expansion, and growth, actively responding to climate change, and accelerating the improvement and implementation of institutional mechanisms embodying the concept that lucid waters and lush mountains are invaluable assets.

In August 2024, the CPC Central Committee and the State Council issued the "Opinions on Accelerating the Comprehensive Green Transformation of Economic and Social Development". This is the first systematic deployment at the national level for comprehensive green transformation and covers different areas including regional development, industrial structure, energy, transportation, and urban-rural construction. Through implementing key tasks across "Five Domains and Three Critical Links"①, China aims to basically establish a green, low-carbon, and circular development economic system by 2035.

Case 1-3 Fujian: Deepening the Development of the National Ecological Civilization Experimental Zone and Building a Protection and Governance Framework from Mountaintops to Oceans

Fujian Province is an important cradle and practice ground for Xi Jinping's Thought on Ecological Civilization. During his work in Fujian Province, General Secretary Xi Jinping proposed a series of innovative concepts for ecological civilization construction, personally deployed, participated in, and promoted major practices in ecological civilization construction, laying a solid foundation for Fujian Province to lead the country in ecological civilization construction. Today, Fujian Province's forest coverage rate has maintained first place in the country for 45 consecutive years. While maintaining stable excellence in water, air, and ecological environment quality and continuing to rank among the top in

---

① The "Five Domains" are: constructing a green, low-carbon, high-quality development spatial pattern, optimizing the spatial pattern of national land development and protection, and creating green development highlands; accelerating the green and low-carbon transformation of industrial structure, promoting the green and low-carbon upgrading of traditional industries, vigorously developing green and low-carbon industries, and accelerating the coordinated transformation of digitalization and greening; steadily promoting the green and low-carbon transformation of energy, strengthening the clean and efficient use of fossil energy, vigorously developing non-fossil energy, and accelerating the construction of a new power system; promoting the green transformation of transportation, optimizing transportation structure, building green transportation infrastructure, and promoting low-carbon transportation tools; promoting the green transformation of urban and rural construction and development, implementing green planning and construction methods, vigorously developing green and low-carbon buildings, and promoting green development in agriculture and rural areas. The "Three Critical Links" are: implementing a comprehensive conservation strategy, vigorously promoting energy conservation, carbon reduction, and efficiency improvement, strengthening resource conservation and efficient utilization, and vigorously developing a circular economy; promoting the green transformation of consumption patterns, promoting green lifestyles, increasing the supply of green products, and actively expanding green consumption; leveraging the supporting role of scientific and technological innovation, strengthening applied basic research, accelerating the development of key technologies, and carrying out innovative demonstration and promotion.

the country, Fujian creates about 4.3% of the national economic output with approximately 1.3% of the country's land and 3% of energy consumption.

Changting County in Longyan City, Fujian Province, was once one of the most severely affected areas by soil erosion in the red soil region of southern China, characterized by "bare mountains, turbid waters, poor fields, and impoverished people". In November 1999, Xi Jinping, then Deputy Secretary of the Fujian Provincial Party Committee and Acting Governor, visited Changting County to understand the soil erosion situation. He said: "We must persevere, plan comprehensively, and strive to complete land remediation and benefit the people with the support of the nation, province, and city over 8 to 10 years." The following year, Xi Jinping, as Governor of Fujian Province, listed "carrying out comprehensive treatment of soil erosion focusing on the severely eroded areas of Changting" as one of the 15 practical projects for the people of the entire province. Over the past 25 years, Changting County has implemented measures such as closing mountains for afforestation, improving vegetation, subsidizing coal burning, developing green industries, transferring surplus rural labor, and ecological migration relocation. The soil erosion rate decreased from 31.5% in 1985 to 6.44% in 2023, far below the level of developed countries. The forest coverage rate increased to 79.55%, achieving decisive victory in soil erosion control. The improvement of the ecological environment has driven the revitalization of ecological industries in Changting County. In 2024, the county received 10.4487 million tourists and achieved tourism revenue of 9.181 billion yuan. It has been selected multiple times as one of the "Top Ten Counties" in Fujian Province's county-level economic development.

Changting County is a microcosm of Fujian Province's green development. As early as 2000, Xi Jinping, then Governor of Fujian Province, proposed the forward-looking strategic concept of building an ecological province. In 2001, he personally served as the head of Fujian Province's ecological province construction leadership group. In 2002, Xi Jinping formally proposed the strategic goal of building an ecological province in the provincial government work report. In the same year, Fujian Province issued the "Master Plan for the Construction of Fujian Ecological Province", becoming one of the first batch of pilot ecological provinces in China. In 2016, Fujian Province was approved as the country's first national ecological civilization experimental zone, extending green development from local exploration and breakthrough to series integration and comprehensive deepening.

Over the past 25 years, Fujian Province has implemented pollution prevention and control as "one chess game", deeply implemented the "four major projects" of blue sky, clear water, blue sea, and clean soil, established a classification mechanism for marine floating garbage treatment by district, category, and layer, launched an ecological cloud platform covering provincial, municipal, and county levels, and took the lead in exploring the establishment of environmental monitoring and law enforcement agencies by river basin. The province has systematically constructed a development pattern characterized by coastal industrial conservation, efficient aggregation, key ecological protection in mountainous areas, and mountain-sea collaborative linkage. The annual total output value of forestry is about 800 billion yuan, and the annual total output value of marine industries exceeds 1.2 trillion yuan. In the fields of biomedicine, new materials, new energy, and other areas, 4 national-level and 17 provincial-level strategic emerging industry clusters have been cultivated. The province has built the country's first marine and agricultural carbon sink trading platform, taken the lead in issuing technical guidelines for the calculation of the total value of ecological products that integrate land and sea and are applicable to the whole province, and established a comprehensive green value conversion system.

In 2014, during his inspection tour in Fujian, General Secretary Xi Jinping expressed his heartfelt wish for the province to strive to build a "New Fujian" characterized by "active mechanisms, superior industries, affluent people, and beautiful ecology". In July 2024, Fujian Province issued the "Implementation Plan for Building a Strong Ecological Province at a Higher Starting Point and Writing the Fujian Chapter of Beautiful China Construction". In October 2024, during his inspection tour in Fujian, General Secretary Xi Jinping pointed out the need to deepen the construction of the national ecological civilization experimental zone, build a protection and governance framework from mountaintops to oceans, strengthen comprehensive governance of key areas, key river basins, and key sea areas, and expand ecological environmental capacity. Towards green, beauty, and the future, Fujian Province continues to advance its ecological province strategy to build a high-level national ecological civilization experimental zone with clear goals, clear paths, and firm steps.

II. Providing Strong Legal Guarantees for Building a Beautiful China

Since the new era, under the scientific guidance of Xi Jinping's Thought on Ecological Civilization and Xi Jinping's Thought on Rule of Law, China's ecological civilization rule of law construction has entered the period with the strongest legislative force, the strictest regulatory law enforcement standards, and the most significant implementation effects of legal systems. The Civil Code, passed in May 2020, establishes the green principle as a basic principle of civil activities, devotes a special chapter to provisions on environmental pollution and ecological damage liability, and establishes an ecological environmental damage compensation system. To date, China has formed a "1+N+4" legal system in the ecological environment field, which consists of one basic, comprehensive environmental protection law, several specific laws concerning air, water, solid waste, soil, noise, ocean, wetlands, grasslands, forests, deserts, etc., and four special regional laws including the Yangtze River Protection Law, the Yellow River Protection Law, the Black Soil Protection Law, and the Qinghai-Xizang Plateau Ecological Protection Law.

The Environmental Protection Law of the People's Republic of China revised in 2014 establishes the basic concepts, principles, and systems that must be followed in ecological civilization construction in legal form. The new Environmental Protection Law strengthens supervision over the performance of environmental protection duties by governments at all levels, stipulates that governments at all levels are responsible for the environmental quality in their jurisdictions, establishes an environmental quality assessment system, adds administrative seizure and detention and other enforcement measures, and provides for strict administrative penalties such as continuous daily fines. It is known as the "most stringent" environmental protection law in history. China has built the world's only environmental judicial system that covers all levels of judicial organs from the Supreme People's Court and the Supreme People's Procuratorate. It has handled a series of ecological and environmental cases that serve as exemplary models worldwide. The United Nations Environment Programme website has opened a special column for China's environmental resource trials. China implements the procuratorial public interest litigation system, with environmental protection public interest litigation accounting for more than half of the public interest litigation cases handled by procuratorial organs. The new Environmental Protection Law specifically adds a chapter on information disclosure and public participation. Environmental protection public organizations and volunteers are growing in number and playing an active role.

The "Decision of the Central Committee of the Communist Party of China on Further Comprehensively Deepening Reform and Advancing Chinese Modernization" proposes compiling an ecological environment legal code, indicating that the legislative approach for ecological environment legislation has shifted from "enacting one when one is mature" to coordinated advancement, and from primarily creating to coordinating creation with cleanup, compilation, and interpretation, with greater emphasis on enhancing the sustainable development capacity of the rule of law.

Orders must be trusted, and laws must be enforced. Since the new era, China has emphasized administration and law enforcement according to law in the field of ecological environment, advanced the legalization of institutions, functions, authorities, procedures, and responsibilities, and placed all law enforcement activities within the track of the rule of law. The country has established systems for information sharing, case reporting, and case transfer among comprehensive administrative law enforcement agencies for ecological environment protection, public security organs, procuratorial organs, and judicial organs, strengthening the connection between ecological environment administrative law enforcement and criminal justice. This forms a joint effort in the investigation and handling of illegal acts that destroy the ecological environment. A number of illegal issues in the field of ecological environment protection have been severely investigated and dealt with, thus effectively deterring similar environmental violations.

III. Continuously Improving the Environmental Governance System

At the responsibility level, China strengthens the Party's comprehensive leadership and implements systems such as ecological civilization construction goal evaluation and assessment, effectiveness assessment of critical battles against pollution, natural resource asset departure audit for leading cadres, river and lake chief systems, forest chief system, lifelong accountability for ecological environmental damage, ecological environmental damage compensation, and other systems. The country strictly implements the requirements of "party and government with the same responsibility", "one post with dual responsibilities", and "those who manage development must manage environmental protection, those who manage production must manage environmental protection, those who manage industries must manage environmental protection". The consciousness and initiative of the whole Party and the whole country in promoting ecological civilization construction continue to increase. Since the establishment of the central ecological environmental protection supervision system in 2015, two rounds of supervision covering 31 provinces (autonomous regions and municipalities) and the Xinjiang Production and Construction Corps (XPCC) have been completed. The second round of supervision also included two departments of the State Council and six central enterprises within the scope of supervision. With the strong promotion of central ecological environment protection supervision, problems such as ecological damage in the Qilian Mountains National Nature Reserve in Gansu, illegal villa construction in the northern foothills of the Qinling Mountains in Xi'an, Shaanxi, illegal mining in Muli, Qinghai, and illegal golf course and villa construction in Changbai Mountain, Jilin, have been resolved.

At the management level, China established the Ministry of Natural Resources, which exercises unified control over land use regulation and ecological conservation and restoration across all territorial spaces. Additionally, the Ministry of Ecology and Environment has been established to uniformly oversee the supervision of pollutant emissions and environmental law enforcement. In the 2018 State Council institutional reform, the environment-related administrative penalty matters from six ministries and commissions were integrated, and a specialized environmental law enforcement supervision agency was established to centrally exercise environmental law enforcement authority. The country implemented a vertical management system for ecological and environmental monitoring, supervision, and law enforcement at the provincial level and below, while advancing comprehensive administrative law enforcement reform for ecological and environmental protection. This has strengthened the independence, uniformity, and authority of environmental monitoring, supervision, and law enforcement.

IV. Exploring and Optimizing Market Regulation Mechanism for Ecological Resources

In the new era, China has continuously improved the market-based allocation system for resource and environmental factors, innovated price formation mechanisms in key areas such as water and energy conservation, sewage and waste treatment, and air pollution control, implemented more than 50 tax and fee preferential policies, and incorporated carbon emission rights, energy use rights, water use rights, and pollution discharge rights into the overall reform of market-based allocation of production factors. China has established a unified natural resource confirmation, registration, and paid-use system, and improved the price formation mechanism for natural resources. The country has enhanced the ecological protection compensation system, with the government mobilizing various forces to provide incentive-based compensation to ecological protectors through financial payments, industrial cooperation, and other means. As of November 2024, a total of 24 provinces (autonomous regions and municipalities) across the country have established 28 cross-provincial watershed ecological protection compensation mechanisms. Central-level ecological protection compensation funds have grown from several billion yuan annually to nearly 200 billion yuan, while local compensation funds have reached nearly 100 billion yuan.

In recent years, China's green finance system development has achieved remarkable results and formed a multi-level green financial product and market system including green credit, green bonds, green insurance, green funds, and green trusts, providing strong momentum for serving the green and low-carbon development of the real economy. By the end of 2024, China's green loan balance in domestic and foreign currencies reached 36.6 trillion yuan, ranking first globally, with a year-on-year growth of 21.7%, 14.5 percentage points higher than the growth of all loans. Loans directed toward projects with direct and indirect carbon reduction benefits accounted for 67.5% of green loans. With the support of green finance, China's new energy, electric vehicle, and battery industries now occupy the largest global market share, while wastewater and solid waste treatment capabilities rank among the world's highest. Additionally, China has proposed initiatives and launched multiple international cooperation mechanisms for green finance. They play a leading role in forming global consensus on sustainable finance, improve the compatibility of green finance standards, and provide capacity building for developing countries.

Section 4   Experiences and Insights from China's Green Development Since the 18th National Congress of the Communist Party of China

Practice and effectiveness prove that Xi Jinping's Thoughts on Ecological Civilization systematically address major theoretical and practical questions regarding why to build ecological civilization, what kind of ecological civilization to build, and how to build it. China's green development experience and enlightenment are concentrated in "Four Significant Shifts"[①], "Five Major Relationships"[②], and

---

① Four Significant Shifts: from focused remediation to systematic governance, from passive response to active action, from participant to leader in global environmental governance, and from practical exploration to scientific theoretical guidance.

② Five Major Relationships: the relationships between high-quality development and high-level protection, between key breakthroughs and coordinated governance, between natural restoration and artificial restoration, between external constraints and internal drivers, and between "Dual Carbon Commitments" and autonomous actions.

"Ten Adherences" ①.

I. Adhering to the People-Centered Development Philosophy

The people-centered approach is the governing philosophy of the Communist Party of China. A good ecological environment is the fairest public good and the most inclusive well-being for the people. As China's modernization advances and people's living standards continue to rise, their need for a beautiful ecological environment becomes more urgent, with ecological environment increasingly prominent in people's happiness index. China responds to people's growing needs for a beautiful ecological environment by adhering to ecology for the people, benefiting the people, and serving the people. The country vigorously promotes green production and lifestyle, focuses on solving prominent environmental problems that harm people's health, continuously improves ecological environment quality, provides more high-quality ecological products, and allows people to gain more sense of fulfillment, happiness, and security in a beautiful ecological environment.

II. Focusing on the Sustainable Development of the Chinese Nation

Ecological prosperity begets civilizational prosperity; ecological degradation leads to civilizational decline. Nature is the basic condition for human survival and development. Only by respecting, conforming to, and protecting nature can sustainable development be achieved. Based on the reality of limited environmental capacity and fragile ecosystems, China plans both for current development and for future generations and regards ecological civilization construction as a fundamental strategy related to the sustainable development of the Chi-

---

① Ten Adherences: upholding the Party's comprehensive leadership over ecological civilization construction; upholding that ecological prosperity begets civilizational prosperity; upholding harmony between humans and nature; upholding that lucid waters and lush mountains are invaluable assets; upholding that good ecological environment is the most inclusive public well-being; upholding that green development is a profound revolution in the development concept; upholding systematic governance of mountains, rivers, forests, fields, lakes, grasslands, and deserts; upholding the strictest systems and most rigorous rule of law to protect the ecological environment; upholding the transformation of building a beautiful China into conscious actions of all people; upholding the path of jointly building global ecological civilization.

nese nation. China promotes the transformation of lucid waters and lush mountains into invaluable assets, allows natural wealth and ecological wealth to continuously generate economic and social wealth, achieves simultaneous improvement in economic, ecological, and social benefits, and builds modernization featuring harmony between humanity and nature.

III. Adhering to a Systematic Approach to Coordinated Advancement

Green development represents a comprehensive and revolutionary transformation of production methods, lifestyles, thinking patterns, and values. China applies a systematic approach throughout the entire process of economic and social development and ecological environmental protection and properly handles relationships between development and protection, the overall situation and local conditions, and current and long-term interests. The country constructs a scientifically moderate and orderly spatial layout system, a green, low-carbon, and circular economic system, and an institutional system that combines constraints and incentives. China coordinates industrial structure adjustment, pollution control, ecological protection, and climate change response, collaboratively advances carbon reduction, pollution reduction, green expansion, and growth, promotes ecological priority and green development, and forms spatial patterns, industrial structures, production methods, and lifestyles that conserve resources and protect the environment.

IV. Jointly Pursuing Global Sustainable Development

Protecting the ecological environment and addressing climate change are common responsibilities of all humanity. Only through unity, cooperation, and joint efforts of all countries in the world to promote green and sustainable development can we maintain the overall balance of Earth's ecology and safeguard the only home of all humanity. Standing at the height of responsibility for human civilization, China actively participates in global environmental governance, committing to strive to peak carbon emissions before 2030 and achieve carbon neutrality before 2060. With these carbon peaking and carbon neutrality goals guiding green transformation, China engages in bilateral and multilateral international cooperation for green development with a more active stance, promotes the construction of a fair, reasonable, and win-win global environmental governance system, and contributes wisdom and strength to global sustainable development.

Case 1-4   Chengdu-Chongqing Economic Circle Jointly
Building an Ecological Barrier in the Upper Reaches
of the Yangtze River: A Model of Cross-Regional
Green Collaborative Development

On January 3, 2020, General Secretary Xi Jinping proposed at the sixth meeting of the Central Financial and Economic Committee to promote the construction of the Chengdu-Chongqing Economic Circle and form an important growth pole for high-quality development in the western region. As one of China's most economically active regions with the highest degree of openness and strongest innovation capabilities, the Chengdu-Chongqing Economic Circle, located in the southwest hinterland, connects east and west, links north and south, and holds an important position in the country's regional coordinated development strategy. According to the "Master Plan for the Construction of the Chengdu-Chongqing Economic Circle", the spatial scope of the Chengdu-Chongqing Economic Circle includes 29 districts and counties in Chongqing and 15 cities in Sichuan. It covers a total area of 185, 000 km², with a resident population of 98. 5358 million, and a regional GDP of 8. 6 trillion yuan in 2024, accounting for 1. 9%, 7. 0%, and 6. 5% of the national totals respectively.

Starting at night at the Clear Stream for Three Gorges, I'll miss you in vain upon reaching Yuzhou. The Chengdu-Chongqing Economic Circle is a fertile ecological land rich in natural resources, water energy resources, and mineral resources. Both located in the upper reaches of the Yangtze River, they share the same mountain ranges and water sources. Their atmospheric, water, and soil environments influence each other. The two regions are particularly water-rich, with rivers and lakes interconnected. There are 81 cross-boundary rivers with basin areas larger than 50 km², with a total length exceeding 10, 000 km. They form an ecological community with a shared destiny and hold an important strategic position in the ecological security of the Yangtze River Basin. Also, the

Yangtze River in this region flows through ecologically fragile mountainous areas, densely populated urban areas, and industrial clusters, with various ecological and environmental risks overlapping and intertwined, while ecological governance points are scattered, widespread, and substantial. Over the past five years, the Chengdu-Chongqing Economic Circle has adhered to the concept that "lucid waters and lush mountains are invaluable assets" and the principle of "prioritizing protection over large-scale development". The region has worked together to build an ecological barrier in the upper reaches of the Yangtze River. It explores new paths for green transformation and development and plays a demonstration role in ecological environmental protection in western China.

Make Coordinated Efforts to Protect and Restore the Ecological Environment

Over the past five years, Sichuan and Chongqing have adhered to unified environmental protection standards and a single negative list for both regions, signed more than 120 cooperation agreements, jointly issued work plans and key tasks, established special working groups, joint conference mechanisms, joint law enforcement, and other collaboration mechanisms, and formed a path for building a beautiful Chengdu-Chongqing with regional ecological co-construction, joint pollution control, policy consultation, and development promotion.

In September 2020, China's first cross-provincial joint river chief office—the Sichuan-Chongqing River Chief System Joint Promotion Office—was officially established. The director of the Joint River Chief Office is concurrently held by the deputy directors of the provincial river chief offices of Sichuan and Chongqing, with a one-year rotation system in place. Both sides send staff to work together each year to study and solve key and difficult issues across regions, watersheds, and departments. They have established provincial-level river chief joint conference, joint inspection, joint supervision, cross-provincial river environmental pollution joint prevention and control, watershed ecological environment accident consultation and disposal, and other systems. They have drawn up a water system map of cross-boundary rivers between Sichuan and Chongqing and developed "river-specific" plans. They have carried out special campaigns against sewage "three discharges" (illegal discharge, direct discharge, disorderly discharge) and "clearing four irregularities" (irregular occupation, extraction, dumping, and construction), and jointly built a cross-boundary watershed horizontal ecological protection compensation mechanism to promote the transformation of water environment governance from "sectional treatment" to "whole-domain treatment".

The Jialing River is the largest tributary of the upper Yangtze River, with a basin area of 112,000 km² in Chongqing and Sichuan Province, accounting for 70% of the total area of the Jialing River Basin. On November 25, 2021, the 29th meeting of the Standing Committee of the Fifth Chongqing Municipal People's Congress voted to pass the "Decision of the Standing Committee of the Chongqing Municipal People's Congress on Strengthening Collaborative Protection of the Water Ecological Environment in the Jialing River Basin". On the same day, the 31st meeting of the Standing Committee of the 13th Sichuan Provincial People's Congress voted to pass the "Regulations on Ecological Environment Protection in the Jialing River Basin of Sichuan Province". Both the "Decision" and the "Regulations" came into effect on January 1, 2022. Sichuan and Chongqing have achieved "five unifications" (unified planning, unified standards, unified monitoring, unified responsibility, and unified prevention and control measures) in 13 aspects, namely information sharing, ecological protection compensation, special planning, water pollution control, water ecological restoration, water resource protection, standards, monitoring, river and lake chiefs, emergency response, law enforcement, justice, and people's congress supervision. Meanwhile, the ecological and environmental departments of Sichuan and Chongqing jointly issued joint water environment treatment plans for important tributaries of the Jialing River, such as the Qiong River, Tongbo River, and Nanxi River, forming a library of regulations and policies comprising "regulations+decisions+joint treatment plans".

The ecological and environmental departments of Sichuan and Chongqing have established working mechanisms for information sharing, early warning and forecasting, environmental impact assessment consultation, and joint law enforcement for the atmospheric environment. They have collaboratively revised emergency response plans for heavily polluted weather, carried out special actions for joint prevention and control of air pollution in adjacent areas, and jointly compiled and issued air pollutant emission standards for the cement, ceramics, and glass industries. These efforts focus on coordinated prevention and control of ozone and PM2. 5 pollution and coordinated control of transportation, industrial, dust, and domestic pollution. Basic information on air stations, hourly reports of urban air automatic monitoring data in adjacent areas of Sichuan and Chongqing have been included in the first batch of cross-boundary shared government data resources between Sichuan and Chongqing. The economic and information departments and ecological and environmental departments of Sichuan and Chongqing require all cement clinker production lines in both regions to implement staggered production to shorten the operation time of cement clinker facilities and reduce excess capacity, with each cement clinker production line having an annual staggered production baseline of 140 days + X days (where X is the number of kiln shutdown days adjusted in real time based on factors such as environmental protection, energy consumption, carbon reduction, and environmentally sensitive periods).

Sichuan and Chongqing coordinated the construction of "waste-free cities", issued China's first cross-regional "waste-free city cell" evaluation standard, implemented a pilot program for intra-provincial approval of cross-provincial transfer of solid waste in Gaozhu New Area (jointly built by Guangan District of Sichuan Province and Yubei District of Chongqing), and established China's first cross-provincial joint prevention and control mechanism for solid and hazardous waste and new pollutants. The ecological and environmental departments of Sichuan and Chongqing have established a "white list" cooperation mechanism for cross-provincial transfer of hazardous waste. Every December, the ecological environment departments of both regions propose "white lists" for the coming year, including hazardous waste management units, corresponding categories and quantities of hazardous waste to be received, under conditions ensuring controllable environmental risks. After consultation and formal notification between the two parties, approval can be directly granted based on the "white list" without further consultation between the ecological and environmental departments, which significantly reduces consultation procedures and shortens approval time from about one month to five working days.

Jointly Building a Carbon Peaking and Carbon Neutrality Demonstration Zone

Sichuan and Chongqing have jointly issued a joint action plan for carbon peaking and carbon neutrality and worked together to reduce emissions, coordinate pollution control, and jointly increase greenery in industries, clean energy, transportation, construction, science and technology, agriculture and forestry, finance, and other fields.

First, they are jointly building an important clean energy base in China. Sichuan and Chongqing have strengthened cooperation in hydropower, shale gas, gas storage, natural gas pipelines, energy facilities, and other fields to continuously enhance energy mutual protection capabilities. For example, Sichuan hydropower sends about 20,000 MkWh of electricity to Chongqing annually, while Chongqing thermal power sends 500~800 MkWh of electricity to Sichuan during the dry season. Sichuan and Chongqing are rich in hydrogen energy resources and gather hundreds of upstream and downstream enterprises and research institutes in hydrogen "production, storage, transportation, refueling, and utilization". In November 2021, the "Chengdu-Chongqing Hydrogen Corridor" was officially opened, with more than 900 hydrogen fuel cell vehicles traveling daily between Chengdu, Chongqing, and surrounding cities. It drives the construction of a hydrogen energy and fuel cell industry highland in the surrounding cities that is based in Chengdu-Chongqing and radiates to the western region.

Second, carbon finance reform is steadily advancing. Liangjiang New Area launched the Chongqing Climate Investment and Financing Matchmaking Platform, and compiled a list of priority support for climate-friendly projects and carbon-neutral supply chain standards for the automotive and electronic information industries. Based on the "carbon accounts" of controlled emission enterprises in the district, it has constructed a carbon finance ecological chain of "carbon emission reduction-carbon accounting-carbon certification-carbon financing". Sichuan and Chongqing jointly created a "Carbon Neutrality Service Platform" as a public service carrier integrating voluntary emission reduction cooperation, carbon neutrality services, green mechanism research, and carbon market capacity building. Chongqing has formed China's only local carbon market that comprehensively promotes industrial emission reduction, with controlled industrial enterprises in the carbon market accounting for 87% of the city's total emissions, covering all seven greenhouse gases specified for national control.

Chapter 2
Build a Beautiful China: Measures, Achievements, Experiences, and Recommendations for China's Ecological Environmental Protection

General Secretary Xi Jinping emphasized: "There is no substitute for ecological environment, which we take for granted when it exists but find hard to recover once lost. In ecological environmental protection and construction, we must establish a big-picture, long-term, and holistic view, adhere to prioritizing protection, adhere to the basic national policies of conserving resources and protecting the environment, protect the ecological environment as we would protect our eyes, treat the ecological environment as we would treat our lives, and promote the formation of green development methods and lifestyles. " The report of the 19th National Congress of the Communist Party of China positioned pollution prevention and control as one of the three major critical battles for decisively building a moderately prosperous society in all respects, injecting green momentum to the comprehensive construction of a moderately prosperous society. In 2018 and 2021, the "Opinions of the CPC Central Committee and the State Council on Comprehensively Strengthening Ecological Environmental Protection and Resolutely Fighting the Critical Battle Against Pollution" and the "Opinions of the CPC Central Committee and the State Council on Deeply Fighting the Critical Battle Against Pollution" were successively issued. Under the leadership of the CPC Central Committee, China has prioritized resolving prominent ecological and environmental problems as a key livelihood area, launching an unprecedented and massive critical battle against pollution that has yielded precise, science-driven, and legally sound solutions and experiences for pollution control. The quality of the ecological environment has significantly improved.

Section 1   Innovative Measures, Main Achievements, and Typical Cases of China's "Blue Sky Defense Battle"

I. Innovative Measures for Environmental Air Governance

Air quality is the most direct and inclusive indicator of the critical battle against pollution. The status of a relatively heavy industrial structure, coal-dominated energy structure, and road-dominated transportation determines the long-term, complex, and arduous nature of China's atmospheric environmental problems. The blue sky defense battle is the top priority of the critical battle against pollution. With the release of the "Air Pollution Prevention and Control Action Plan" in 2013, the "Three-Year Action Plan for Winning the Blue Sky Defense Battle" in 2018, and the "Action Plan for Continuously Improving Air Quality" in 2023, China has successively issued three "Ten Rules for the Atmosphere" since the 18th National Congress of the Communist Party of China to continuously exert efforts and persist for long-term success.

Since the new era, China has comprehensively strengthened the response to heavily polluted weather and regional joint prevention and control, formulated emergency response plans, promoted full coverage of emergency emission reduction lists for enterprises involved in air pollution, implemented differentiated control of long-term large-scale heavily polluted weather in autumn and winter in phases, and carried out supervision and assistance to improve air quality in key regions. It has orderly promoted clean heating transformation in northern regions, completing treatment of about 41 million households using scattered coal, eliminated nearly 50 million high-emission vehicles, increased the proportion of new energy buses to over 70% by 2024, and continuously improved the level of clean transportation for bulk goods.

China comprehensively uses differentiated management policies in finance, pricing, taxation, environmental protection, and other areas to stimulate the internal driving force of market entities to participate in air pollution control. The country has built the world's largest clean coal power system and clean steel production system, with more and more enterprises achieving synergy between green transformation and profit growth. For example, China has introduced e-lectricity price policies for ultra-low emissions from coal-fired power plants, as well as differentiated electricity and water prices for ultra-low emissions in industries such as steel and cement. Central and local air pollution prevention and control funds support renovation projects, and enterprises that complete renovations enjoy tax reduction and exemption benefits such as environmental tax and purchase tax. Ultra-low emission and grade A environmental performance enterprises are exempt from production restrictions or shutdowns during heavy pollution weather warnings, with "no disturbance without cause" for environmental inspections to ensure that green, high-quality production capacity can operate to its full potential. To date, China has eliminated more than 1 billion tons of backward coal production capacity, 300 million tons of steel production capacity, and 400 million tons of cement production capacity; more than 95% of coal-fired power units and more than 45% of crude steel production capacity have completed ultra-low emission renovations, and coal-fired boilers have been reduced from nearly 500,000 to less than 100,000; enterprises that have completed ultra-low emission renovations have a profit margin 1.7 percentage points higher than other enterprises.

Case 2-1   "Beijing Blue": A Successful Pathway to Air
Pollution Control in a Mega City

Beijing's air pollution control is more complex and arduous than that of many developed countries' cities in history, having characteristics of both coal pollution and motor vehicle pollution. Beijing has learned from the pollution control experiences of developed countries and, based on its own compound pollution characteristics, has moved from coal-smoke pollution control to comprehensive prevention and control of industry, motor vehicles, dust, and other sources. The city has implemented 16 phases of air pollution control measures, a five-year clean air action plan, a three-year blue sky defense battle action plan, and the "One Microgram" action, with various measures advancing in a phased manner and environmental benefits gradually being released.

Beijing has established an urban air quality prediction and forecasting system to provide technical support for precise pollution control and assist residents in green travel. When air pollution is about to arrive, Beijing can carry out pollution response in advance to achieve peak shaving and speed reduction with precise control. Beijing has conducted three rounds of PM2. 5 source analysis since 2013 to quantitatively analyze the composition of PM2. 5 sources and the impact of regional transport, thus providing guidance for targeted haze control. Beijing has developed an atmospheric environment monitoring big model—the "Three Supervisions" big model. Utilizing big data, artificial intelligence, and other advanced technologies, this initiative aims to achieve a coordinated working mechanism among "regulatory departments for overall planning and dispatching, monitoring departments for intelligent sensing, and inspection and law enforcement departments for precise law enforcement".

In 2013, Beijing began implementing the national environmental quality standard— "Ambient Air Quality Standard" to conduct monitoring of PM2. 5 and ozone in the ambient air. After years of joint prevention and control with Tianjin, Hebei, and surrounding provinces and cities, various air pollutant concentrations have significantly decreased. In 2021, Beijing's air quality comprehensively met standards for the first time, with annual average PM2. 5 concentration decreasing by 63. 1% compared to 2013, an average annual decrease of 7. 9%, far exceeding the rate of decrease in developed countries' cities during the same period. In 2024, Beijing's PM2. 5 concentration was 30. 5 micrograms per cubic meter, a year-on-year decrease of 6. 2%, stably meeting the national second-level standard for four consecutive years; the number of days with good or excellent air quality reached 290, an increase of 19 days year-on-year. Against the backdrop of continuous increases in regional GDP, resident population, motor vehicle ownership, and energy consumption, Beijing has transformed from being deeply plagued by haze more than a decade ago to now having "Beijing Blue" as a beautiful background color for the capital of a major country. The United Nations Environment Programme issued an assessment report, "A Review of 20 Years' Air Pollution Control in Beijing", stating that Beijing has achieved remarkable results in improving air environmental quality. No other city or region in the world has achieved such good results in such a short time, with many experiences and practices worth learning and referencing.

Case 2-2   Guangdong: Collaborative Interconnection to Win the Blue Sky Defense Battle in the Bay Area, Exploring "Bay Area Standards" for Ecological Protection

Surrounded by mountains on three sides and converged by three rivers, he Guangdong-Hong Kong-Macao Greater Bay Area boasts a long coastline, excellent port clusters, vast sea areas, and lush mangrove forests, together weaving an ecological picture of "mountains and seas connecting cities, harmony between humanity and nature". Building a world-class beautiful bay area is an important part of building a beautiful China pioneering zone. Guangdong Province focuses on "carrying out six major actions, improving two systems, and strengthening one guarantee"[1] and takes the lead in trying out ecological environment management systems, standard systems, and cooperation models that align with international standards. The province has established a regional product carbon footprint management and low-carbon product certification system. This deepens rule alignment and mechanism docking with Hong Kong and Macao in key areas such as joint prevention and control of air pollution, marine environmental protection, climate change response, solid waste disposal, and achieves high-level mutual benefit and win-win results.

In terms of systematic pollution control, Guangdong Province adheres to PM2.5 as the main line, follows the work approach of "controlling vehicles, reducing dust, and using less oil and gas", and implements a list of key tasks for air pollution prevention and control, strengthened regional joint prevention and control program for winter and spring seasons, restriction measures for Chi-

---

[1] Note: "Six major actions" refer to industrial green and low-carbon transformation action, clean, low-carbon, and efficient energy development action, green and low-carbon transportation system construction action, quality and efficiency improvement and emission intensity reduction action, refined comprehensive governance action, and regional coordination action for air pollution. "Two systems" refer to the legal and standard system and the atmospheric environmental management system. "One guarantee" refers to increasing the guarantee for measure implementation.

na III diesel trucks, announcements on high-pollution fuel prohibition zones, and other measures. The province conducts inspections of products containing volatile organic compounds, deepens comprehensive management of storage tanks, upgrades enterprises' simple and inefficient pollution treatment facilities, and urges key enterprises in steel, cement, glass, and other industries to implement in-depth treatment for ultra-low emissions. It conducts remote sensing monitoring of diesel vehicles, road spot checks, and inspections of major vehicle users, refines inspection of motor vehicle emission testing institutions, and prevents and controls mobile source pollution. In 2024, the concentration of the six main air pollutants in Guangdong Province met standards across the board for the tenth consecutive year, with the proportion of days with good or excellent air quality at 95.8%, improving by 1 percentage point year-on-year. Days with severe or worse pollution were zero, and PM2.5 concentration was 21 micrograms per cubic meter, maintaining overall good air quality.

In November 2024, Guangdong issued the "Guangdong's Action Plan for Continuous Improvement of Air Quality", emphasizing that the path to continue fighting the blue sky defense battle is to "deeply advance the optimization and adjustment of industrial structure, energy structure, and transportation structure, strengthen multi-pollutant coordinated emission reduction and non-point source pollution prevention and control, enhance joint prevention and control of air pollution, and improve atmospheric environmental management capabilities". The air quality improvement demonstration zone in the Guangdong-Hong Kong-Macao Greater Bay Area is expected to be fully built in 3-5 years.

II. Main Achievements in Air Quality Management Governance

In 2024, the average PM2.5 concentration in key cities across China was 29.3 micrograms per cubic meter, a year-on-year decrease of 2.7%. The proportion of days with severe or worse pollution was 0.9%, a year-on-year decrease of 0.7 percentage points. The proportion of days with good or excellent air quality has reached over 86% for five consecutive years. Blue skies and white clouds have become the norm in people's daily lives, making China the country with the fastest air quality improvement in the world. PM2.5 concentrations in the Beijing-Tianjin-Hebei region, the northern slope of Tianshan Mountains urban agglomeration, the Chengdu-Chongqing region, the Fenwei Plain, the middle reaches of the Yangtze River urban agglomeration, and the Yangtze River Delta region decreased year-on-year by 3.4%, 13.4%, 10.8%, 4.8%, 4.4%, and 0.9% respectively. These six major regions collectively account for 52%, 39%, and 57% of the country's population, land area, and economic total, respectively. This improvement is hard-won under the heavy task of stabilizing growth. Coordinated control of PM2.5 and ozone has achieved initial results. Compared with 2019, before the COVID-19 pandemic, China's PM2.5 concentration has decreased by 19.4%, and ozone concentration has decreased by 2.7%, remaining stable at 144-145 micrograms per cubic meter for three consecutive years, with the continuous rise in ozone since 2015 preliminarily controlled.

Case 2-3 　　　Nanjing Iron and Steel Group: Building a Green and Beautiful Steel Plant, Being a Global Pioneer in Green Steel

At a press conference held by the Ministry of Ecology and Environment in February 2025, the head of the Department of Atmospheric Environment of the Ministry introduced the progress of work in continuously deepening the blue sky defense battle, using Nanjing Iron and Steel as an example to explain how enterprises achieve environmental protection and profit win-win in green transformation. Nanjing Iron and Steel has made low-carbon green circular development its core strategy, prioritizing the use of clean energy, adopting advanced processes and equipment with high resource utilization rates, low pollutant emissions, and comprehensive utilization of waste, achieving a clean and tidy factory appearance, beautiful environment, and urban-industrial integration. The group has been awarded honors such as green development benchmark enterprise, green factory, and environmentally friendly enterprise with clean production.

Ultra-Low Emissions, Adding "Green" and Increasing "Efficiency"

Nanjing Iron and Steel has built more than 100 energy-saving, emission-reducing, and environmental protection treatment projects of international advanced level. It has successively added 11 sets of desulfurization and denitrification facilities, completed upgrades of 112 sets of dust collectors, and through a combination of "organized ultra-low emissions", "unorganized ultra-low e-missions", and "clean logistics", achieved the environmental protection goal of "not seeing ore where minerals are used, not seeing coal where it is burned, not seeing materials during transportation, not seeing molten iron when it is tapped, and not seeing dust on green leaves".

In terms of "organized ultra-low emissions", Nanjing Iron and Steel a-dopts advanced "three-dry technology" (dry dust removal, dry desulfuriza-tion, dry coke quenching) to significantly reduce exhaust gas emissions. In terms of "unorganized ultra-low emissions" renovation, Nanjing Iron and Steel has built fully enclosed shelters for iron ore powder and coal yards, as well as coal silos and coke silos, added dust removal facilities, and achieved tight cov-ers on iron tapping troughs and dust-free iron tapping workshops. In terms of clean logistics, Nanjing Iron and Steel has built tubular belts to transport blast furnace water slag to the ultra-fine powder processing plant in an enclosed man-ner. All logistics vehicles have been replaced with "China VI" emission stand-ard vehicles, and electric heavy trucks and electric locomotives are universally used for material transportation.

Intelligent Empowerment, Smart Supervision

With significant environmental protection investments, to master real-time data from numerous environmental protection facilities and solve complex man-agement issues of "whether they exist, whether they are used, and whether they are good", Nanjing Iron and Steel has built an intelligent operation center and launched a "smart environmental protection management and control plat-form" loaded with multiple big models. This achieves real-time precise control with "one screen to see the whole domain, one click to know indicators, one network to manage environmental protection", enhancing dynamic management and compliance early warning of environmental protection facilities.

Factory Garden, "Green Pearl"

Nanjing Iron and Steel has comprehensively planned and upgraded the fac-tory environment, renovated the greening, beautification, purification, and lighting of the factory area, and formed a landscape effect with flowers in three seasons, evergreen in four seasons, rich colors, and distinct layers. The company has created more than 20 industrial tourism attractions such as the Nanjing Iron and Steel Museum, Nanjing Steel Party Building Exhibition Hall, Culture and Sports Park, and Future Steel Intelligent Manufacturing Hall, winning honors such as National Industrial Tourism Demonstration Base and Top Ten Cases of Digital Innovation Demonstration in Culture and Tourism.

Section 2   Innovative Measures, Main Achievements, and Typical Cases of China's "Clear Water Defense Battle"

Water is the foundation of survival and the source of civilization. With a deep concern for the country's rivers and mountains, General Secretary Xi Jinping has always been concerned about water. When conducting research and investigations in various places, he always makes inspecting water ecological environment protection a key part of his itinerary, and provides on-site guidance for related work. Since the 18th National Congress of the Communist Party of China (CPC), the CPC Central Committee with comrade Xi Jinping at its core has prioritized addressing prominent water ecosystem issues as a key area for people's well-being, implementing water pollution prevention and control actions with the most resolute determination and strongest measures. The battle to protect clear waters has achieved remarkable results, with water environmental quality now at its best level since monitoring records began. In 2024, the proportion of surface water sections with good quality across the country reached 90. 4%, exceeding 90% for the first time, a year-on-year increase of 1 percentage point, approaching the level of developed countries, and an improvement of 28. 8 percentage points compared to 2012. The proportion of good quality in offshore sea areas was 83. 7%, achieving the target of the 14th Five-Year Plan ahead of schedule. The main stream of the Yangtze River has maintained stable Class II water quality for 5 consecutive years, and the main stream of the Yellow River for 3 consecutive years. A magnificent picture of peaceful rivers and lakes with clear waters unfolds across the vast land of China.

I. The Institutional Mechanisms for Water Ecological Environment Governance Have Been Rapidly Improved

In 2019, the Ministry of Ecology and Environment established seven major river basin and sea area ecological environment supervision and management bureaus[①], mainly responsible for ecological environment supervision and administrative law enforcement in river basins. It addresses issues such as overlapping responsibilities and multi-headed management that have long existed in river basin and sea area ecological environment supervision. China has established a river and lake chief system with the party and government leadership responsibility system as its core for all rivers and lakes. The main leaders of party committees and governments in 31 provinces, autonomous regions, and municipalities serve as provincial general river chiefs, and more than 1.2 million river and lake chiefs at five levels—provincial, municipal, county, township, and village—have taken up their posts to fully take charge of water resource protection, water area shoreline management, water pollution prevention, water environment governance, water ecological restoration, etc. The seven major river basins—the Yangtze River, Yellow River, Huaihe River, Haihe River, Pearl River, Songhua River-Liaohe River, and Taihu Lake—have all established provincial river and lake chief joint conference mechanisms to regularly consult on issues and deploy joint actions. The river and lake chief system has been implemented in 110 large-scale water diversion projects including the South-to-North Water Diversion Project and the Yangtze-to-Huaihe Water Diversion Project. Various regions have established systems for river and lake chiefs' performance of duties, supervision and inspection, assessment and accountability, positive incentives, as well as coordination mechanisms such as "river and lake chief+po-

---

①　Note: The seven major river basins and sea areas ecological environment supervision and management bureaus under the Ministry of Ecology and Environment of the People's Republic of China include the Yangtze River Basin Ecology and Environment Administration, Yellow River Basin Ecology and Environment Administration, the Huaihe River Basin Ecology and Environment Administration, Haihe River Basin and North Sea Ecology and Environment Administration, Pearl River Basin and South China Sea Ecology and Environment Administration, Songliao River Basin Ecology and Environment Administration, and Taihu Lake Basin and East China Sea Ecology and Environment Administration.

lice chief" and "river and lake chief+chief prosecutor". The river and lake chief system has been promoted in enterprises, schools, communities, and rural areas, significantly enhancing public awareness of caring for rivers and lakes.

**Case 2-4   River and Lake Chief System Effectiveness Upgrade:
The Answer Sheet of Chaohu Lake
Governance for City-Lake Symbiosis**

Chaohu Lake is situated east of the Yangtze River, west of the Dabie Mountains, connected to the Huaihe River, and is one of China's five major freshwater lakes. In July 2011, the State Council approved Anhui Province's dissolution of the prefecture-level Chaohu City and some administrative division adjustments, making Chaohu Lake an inner lake of Hefei City. In March 2012, Anhui Province specially established the Anhui Chaohu Management Bureau, a management institution for Chaohu Lake governance. Since the new era, Anhui Province and Hefei City have jointly established a funding pool, project library, and think tank for ecological protection and governance around Chaohu Lake. Chaohu Lake governance has taken the path of joint governance across the basin and ecological restoration, opening a new chapter of symbiotic development between a city and a lake. In August 2020, during his inspection in Anhui, General Secretary Xi Jinping pointed out: "Chaohu Lake is a treasure for the people of Anhui and the most beautiful and dynamic place in Hefel. Chaohu Lake must be well governed, the ecological wetlands must be well protected, and Chaohu Lake should become the best calling card of Hefei. "

Hefei City has a total of 39 first-level tributaries flowing into Chaohu Lake from all directions. Whether these tributaries are polluted directly affects the water quality of Chaohu Lake. Hefei City has implemented three major projects of "Clear Waters, Safe Banks, and Prosperity for the People" to construct a basin-wide water pollution prevention and control system: Urban sewage quality and efficiency improvement to address point source pollution, key river treatment to tackle line source pollution, big data management to address agricultural non-point source pollution, and phosphorus control actions to curb internal source pollution. Also, Hefei City has cultivated emerging industries through scientific and technological innovation, from new display technologies to integrated circuits, from artificial intelligence to new energy vehicles, developing a modern green industrial system represented by "chips, screens, automobiles, and integrated" and "integrated devices, terminals, bio, and intelligence". In 2024, the water quality of the entire Chaohu Lake stabilized at Class IV, with the blue-green algae bloom area at its smallest in ten years. The Shiba Liangqing Wetland construction, characterized by resident relocation, fishery withdrawal, and ecological restoration, was selected as an outstanding case of United Nations ecological restoration action.

Hefei City has deepened and improved the river and lake chief system for Chaohu Lake, increasing the proportion of city committee standing committee members serving as river chiefs. It also appointed deputy city leaders as directors of the river chief office. The city has established "district total river chiefs" for different districts and initiated cross-checking patrols by river chiefs through the "Three Observations and Three Comparisons"① activities, and implemented monthly evaluations and incentive subsidies for river environment management involving participation from river chiefs. The Chaohu City Party School and the City River Chief Office jointly established Anhui Province's first river and lake chief education and training base—the River Chief Administrative School, to regularly conduct professional courses for river and lake chiefs at all levels, and issue completion certificates through a credit system assessment. River and lake chief system water culture science popularization bases have been built to foster research and study tourism routes characterized by water areas, wetlands, parks, and science popularization. A "River and Lake Chief Day" for Chaohu has been established, the "All-People Water Protection" mini-program has been launched, and "river and lake chief system integral supermarkets" have been built where goods can be exchanged for river and lake management and protection points. These efforts aim to guide all sectors of society to actively participate in river patrol and protection.

Since the new era, China has constructed a fixed pollution source supervi-

---

① Three Observations and Three Comparisons: look at appearance, compare environment; look at indicators, compare water quality; look at management, compare internal operations.

sion system centered on the pollutant discharge permit system, which has basically achieved full coverage of fixed pollution source discharge permits. Comprehensive investigation and remediation of sewage outlets entering rivers and seas in the Yangtze River, Bohai Sea, and Yellow River have been carried out, weaving an integrated monitoring network in the air, on the ground, and underwater. China has established a rigid constraint system for water resources. It adheres to the principle of determining cities, land, population, and production based on water availability, implements national water conservation actions, strictly controls water resource argumentation and water intake permits, promotes agricultural water conservation and efficiency, industrial water conservation and emission reduction, urban water conservation and loss reduction, actively develops the water conservation industry, and promotes contract water conservation management. A dual-control indicator system for total water consumption and intensity that covers provincial, municipal, and county levels has been established, and water allocation for important cross-provincial rivers has been basically completed. Since 2014, while China's GDP has nearly doubled, total water consumption has remained generally stable within 610 billion cubic meters; in 2024, water consumption per 10,000 yuan of GDP and water consumption per 10,000 yuan of industrial added value decreased by 4.4% and 5.6% year-on-year, respectively; the national average irrigation water consumption per mu (about 664 m^2) of farmland has decreased to below 350 cubic meters, achieving steady increases in irrigation area and grain production while maintaining stable agricultural water use.

Case 2-5 Cross-Provincial Basin Ecological Compensation: Constructing a Long-term Basin Protection Mechanism with Shared Responsibility, Development Results, and Quality Ecological Products

General Secretary Xi Jinping pointed out: "Comprehensively establish an ecological compensation system. We should improve the inter-regional interest compensation mechanism to form a positive situation where beneficiaries pay and protectors receive reasonable compensation. We should improve the vertical ecological compensation mechanism and increase transfer payments for forests, grasslands, wetlands, and key ecological function areas. We should promote the experience of the Xin'an River water environment compensation pilot, and encourage various forms of compensation between upstream and downstream basins, including funds, industries, and talents. We should establish and improve market-oriented, diversified ecological compensation mechanisms, and carry out ecological product value realization mechanism pilots in the Yangtze River Basin. "

Since the new era, 18 provinces and 13 basins (river sections) in China have explored cross-provincial horizontal ecological protection compensation between upstream and downstream basins, with central financial guidance funds exceeding 20 billion yuan in total. Relevant provinces have established water pollution prevention and control collaboration groups and joint prevention and control mechanisms for water pollution emergencies, formulated river basin ecological environment joint protection plans, and conducted joint monitoring and cross-border water environment joint investigations. Except for three basins (river sections) that newly signed cross-provincial compensation agreements in 2021 and are just starting, the other 10 basins (river sections) involving 23 assessment sections have maintained stable water quality that meets or exceeds agreement target requirements, with significant decreases in characteristic pollutant concentrations at some assessment sections compared to before policy implementation. Meanwhile, all 31 provinces (autonomous regions and municipalities) have carried out intra-provincial basin ecological compensation mechanism construction, with 14 provinces including Zhejiang, Chongqing, Shandong, and Tianjin achieving full coverage of intra-provincial basin ecological compensation.

The source of living water comes from Xin'an, winding thousands of times down to Qiantang. The Xin'an River originates in Huangshan City, Anhui Province, flows eastward into the Xin'an River Reservoir in Hangzhou City, then continues northeast to join the Qiantang River, with a main stream length of 373 km and a basin area of more than 11,000 km^2. The Xin'an River Reservoir is Hangzhou's second water source, with 60% of the reservoir's water coming from upstream Xin'an River replenishment. The famous tourist attraction Qiandao Lake is located here, with very important ecological and economic value. In

2007, the Xin'an River Basin was listed as a national pilot for cross-provincial basin ecological compensation mechanism construction. In 2012, Zhejiang Province and Anhui Province signed the "Agreement on Horizontal Ecological Compensation for Upstream and Downstream of the Xin'an River Basin". After three rounds of pilots, Zhejiang and Anhui established a compensation assessment system based mainly on P value (composed of four indicators—permanganate index, ammonia nitrogen, total nitrogen, total phosphorus, as well as water quality stability coefficient and indicator weight coefficient), forming the "Xin'an River Model" for common ecological environment protection across the entire basin. Anhui Province delivers nearly 7 billion cubic meters of clean water to Qiandao Lake each year. According to the assessment by the Environmental Planning Institute of the Ministry of Ecology and Environment, the total value of ecosystem services in the Xin'an River is 24.65 billion yuan, with the total value of water ecological services at 6.45 billion yuan, realizing that green mountains have "value" and clear waters contain "gold". In 2023, the fourth round of ecological compensation in the Xin'an River Basin was launched to transform the model of one-party compensation and one-party receipt in the first three rounds to both parties jointly contributing funds and jointly allocating them, strengthen industrial and talent docking cooperation between the two places through "Ten Cooperation Items between Zhejiang and Anhui", and jointly build the Xin'an River-Qiandao Lake ecological environment common protection cooperation zone.

Table 2-1 Key Points of Four Rounds of Horizontal Ecological Compensation Schemes in the Xin'an River Basin

Pilot Period	First Round (2012-2014)	Second Round (2015-2017)	Third Round (2018-2020)	Fourth Round (2023-2027)
Basic Principles	Protection priority, reasonable compensation; maintain water quality, strive for improvement; local government leadership with central supervision; monitoring-based, promote governance by compensation.			
Compensation Funds	Mainly fiscal transfer payments, with the Central Government and the two provinces of Zhejiang and Anhui jointly establishing the Xin'an River Basin Water Environment Compensation Fund.		Mainly fiscal transfer payments, with the two provinces of Zhejiang and Anhui establishing the Xin'an River Basin Water Environment Compensation Fund.	

Continued Table

Pilot Period	First Round (2012-2014)	Second Round (2015-2017)	Third Round (2018-2020)	Fourth Round (2023-2027)
Pilot Funds	The Central Government contributes 300 million yuan annually, and Zhejiang and Anhui provinces each contribute 100 million yuan annually.	The Central Government contributes in a declining manner: 400 million yuan in the first year, 300 million yuan in the second year, and 200 million yuan in the third year. Zhejiang and Anhui provinces each contribute 200 million yuan annually.	Zhejiang and Anhui provinces each contribute 200 million yuan annually.	In 2023, Zhejiang and Anhui provinces jointly contributed 1 billion yuan. From 2024 onwards, a gradual increase mechanism is established with reference to the annual economic growth rates of the two provinces. If $P \leqslant 0.95$, Zhejiang contributes 60% and Anhui contributes 40%. If $0.95 < P \leqslant 1$, Zhejiang and Anhui each contribute 50%. If $P > 1$ or a major water pollution incident occurs in the Anhui section of the Xin'an River Basin, Zhejiang contributes 40% and Anhui contributes 60%.
Assessment Basis	Based on joint water quality monitoring data at the boundary section between Zhejiang and Anhui provinces (four indicators: permanganate index, ammonia nitrogen, total phosphorus, and total nitrogen), calculate the compensation index P value.			While maintaining the P value assessment of the first three rounds, introduce the industry and talent compensation index M value.
Assessment Method	Joint monitoring by Zhejiang and Anhui provinces, verification by China Environmental Monitoring Station, and submission to relevant national departments.			
Compensation Method	If $P \leqslant 1$, Zhejiang funds are allocated to Anhui; if $P > 1$, Anhui funds are allocated to Zhejiang. Central Government funds are all allocated to Anhui.	If $P \leqslant 1$, Zhejiang transfers 100 million yuan to Anhui; if $P > 1$, Anhui transfers 100 million yuan to Zhejiang; if $P \leqslant 0.95$, Zhejiang transfers an additional 100 million yuan to Anhui. Central Government funds are all allocated to Anhui.	If the water quality meets assessment standards that year, Zhejiang transfers 200 million yuan to Anhui; if water quality fails to meet assessment standards, Anhui transfers 200 million yuan to Zhejiang.	If $M > 1.25$, the compensation fund allocation ratio between Zhejiang and Anhui is 0.25 : 0.75; if $1 < M \leqslant 1.25$, the compensation fund allocation ratio between Zhejiang and Anhui is 0.2 : 0.8; if $M \leqslant 1$, the compensation fund allocation ratio between Zhejiang and Anhui is 0.15 : 0.85.

II. Progress in the Protection and Governance of Rivers and Lakes

China adheres to the watershed-based approach, with river and lake systems as the framework, aiming for "safe rivers and tranquil lakes, clear waters with jumping fish, green banks with beautiful scenery, and environments suitable for both living and working". It coordinates upstream and downstream areas, both riverbanks, main and tributary streams, and above and below ground systems to jointly address water disaster prevention, water resource conservation, aquatic ecosystem restoration, and water environment governance. China deeply integrates economic and social development with river and lake protection and management, establishes mechanisms to realize the value of river and lake ecological products, and promotes the transformation of ecological and resource advantages into development and economic advantages. To date, China has built over 3,200 distinctive "happy rivers and lakes", completed health assessments of more than 10,000 rivers and lakes, established health records for each river and lake, and implemented rolling "one river (lake), one policy" plans. China has strengthened spatial management and control of river and lake shorelines and clearly defined management boundaries for 1,230,000 km of rivers and 1,996 lakes nationwide, while carrying out campaigns against the "four irregularities" (irregular occupation, extraction, dumping, and construction) that encroach upon rivers and lakes. China has implemented the Mother River Rejuvenation Action, strengthened the management of river and lake ecological flow, and carried out river and lake water system connectivity and ecological water replenishment. The Beijing-Hangzhou Grand Canal, which had been cut off for a hundred years, has had continuous water flow throughout its entire length for four consecutive years. The Yongding River, which had been cut off and dried up for 26 years, now has water year-round throughout its entire length. Groundwater levels in the north China groundwater over-exploitation areas have risen significantly.

The Yangtze River and Yellow River are the mother rivers of the Chinese nation, and making the Yangtze River and Yellow River into happy rivers that benefit the people is the starting point and goal of the national river strategy. China has enacted the Yangtze River Protection Law to strengthen the governance of the Yangtze River shoreline, illegal docks, illegal sand mining, and pollution and implement small hydropower clean-up, river and lake wetland protection and restoration, a ten-year fishing ban on the Yangtze River. The Yellow River Protection Law has been enacted to improve the basin water and sediment regulation and flood disaster reduction system, strengthen water resource conservation and intensive use, implement water ecological protection and restoration, and strengthen soil erosion control. The governance and protection of the Yangtze River and Yellow River have achieved historic accomplishments and undergone historic changes, with effective prevention of water-related disasters.

China has implemented special actions for the environmental protection of centralized drinking water sources. It follows the requirement of "one water source, one set of plans, one implementation to the end", implements problem list management systems for domestic non-point source pollution, industrial enterprise pollution discharge, agricultural non-point source pollution, tourism and catering pollution, transportation crossing, etc., and legally cleans up illegal construction projects in drinking water source protection zones. In 2023, the proportion of compliant sections (points) for drinking water sources in cities at or above the prefecture level nationwide was 96.5%, and for county-level towns it was 94.8%, maintaining a high level. The ecological environment quality of water sources of the South-to-North Water Diversion Project and those along its route has significantly improved, ensuring reliable protection of people's drinking water safety.

Case 2-6   Lake Shore Co-governance, Basin Joint Governance:
Singing the "Beautiful Taihu Lake"
of the New Era

Lake governance is a recognized global challenge, and Taihu Lake governance is particularly difficult. The Taihu Lake Basin is located in the core area of the Yangtze River Delta, one of the most economically vibrant, densely populated, and highly urbanized regions in China. In the past, under the extensive economic development model, various types of wastewater were discharged into

Taihu Lake, resulting in the serious consequences of the blue-green algae out-break in Taihu Lake in 2007. Taihu Lake governance is a "major national mat-ter" that General Secretary Xi Jinping has repeatedly emphasized and attached great importance to. During the 2023 National Two Sessions, when participat-ing in the deliberation of the Jiangsu delegation, General Secretary Xi Jinping asked about the Taihu Lake governance situation and earnestly said, "When we say lucid waters and lush mountains are invaluable assets, if ecology is not managed well, they won't be invaluable assets but will instead become money-losing ventures. "

Multiple Measures Have Been Taken to Restore the Rippling Blue Waters

Pollution is in the water, but the root cause is on the shore. On the basis of fully implementing the national "Overall Plan for Comprehensive Water Envi-ronment Treatment in the Taihu Lake Basin", Jiangsu Province issued the "Action Plan for Promoting a New Round of Comprehensive Treatment of Taihu Lake" in 2023, prepared "river-specific" water quality compliance improve-ment plans for 40 rivers within its jurisdiction, and conduced "dual source" tracing of pollution sources and blue-green algae sources. With source control and sewage interception and phosphorus and nitrogen control as the main direc-tions of attack, comprehensive remediation of phosphorus-related enterprises, rural domestic sewage, and main rivers entering the lake has been carried out. High-intensity treatment projects, such as sewage treatment plants and pipeline networks construction, sediment dredging, and blue-green algae collection, have also been implemented. For internal source reduction, a blue-green algae emergency prevention and control system has been established that combines "blocking, diverting, collecting, and controlling". "Diverting water from the Yangtze River to Taihu Lake" increases the water resource supply in the basin, promotes ecological restoration in the basin, and constructs an ecological wet-land circle around Taihu Lake.

Along the 142-kilometer shoreline near Taihu Lake in Wuxi, there are 83 blue-green algae collection platforms and 13 algae-water separation stations. These facilities utilize integrated technologies of "enclosed algae blocking and diversion + deep well pressurized algae control" to construct a model of blue-green algae collection, disposal, and utilization featuring scientific monitoring, professional teams, mechanized collection, pipeline transportation, factory-based processing, harmless disposal, and information-based management. In March 2024, the "Star of Taihu Lake", an ecological dredging integrated intelligent platform ship independently designed and developed in China, was put into use, pioneering a new path for large-scale river and lake dredging and on-site sediment solidification on water. From 2007 to 2024, Wuxi cumulatively removed 22.56 million tons of blue-green algae, accounting for over 90% of the total amount removed from the entire Taihu Lake. This is equivalent to directly removing pollutants such as 6,023 tons of total nitrogen and 1,511 tons of total phosphorus from the lake body.

Making Room for New Growth, Cultivating New Quality Productive Forces

The Taihu Lake region of Jiangsu Province accounts for 20% of the province's land area, supporting more than 30% of the population and more than 40% of the economic total. In recent years, industrial pollution prevention and control has been deepened, with all 230 chemical enterprises in the Taihu Lake primary protection zone completely eliminated, crude steel production reduced by 4.619 million tons, tens of thousands of "scattered, disorderly, and polluting" enterprises shut down, more than 20,000 phosphorus-related enterprises remediated, and a cumulative reduction of more than 4,000 tons in the use of raw phosphorus. The catalogue of prohibited and restricted industries and products in the Taihu Lake Basin and the implementation opinions on high-quality development of traditional and future industries have been issued. Two national-level strategic emerging industry clusters have been built in Suzhou and Changzhou, with a cumulative construction of 24 national-level green industrial parks, 200 green factories, and 56 green supply chain management enterprises. To promote the reduction and efficiency of chemical fertilizers and pesticides, all field plots with suitable conditions in the primary and secondary protection zones of Taihu Lake have completely eliminated direct seeding rice, all straw in the main rivers entering the lake is removed from the fields, and ecological healthy aquaculture is implemented in fisheries to foster a green transition in agriculture and fisheries. New business models combining "river and lake+culture, sports, and tourism" are being advanced. The thriving of water sports such as sailing and rowing visibly embodies the positive effects of "Happy Rivers and Lakes", enjoyed by locals and tourists alike.

An emerald lake mirrors the wide horizon's gleam, vast waters and clouds stretch far across rivers and stream. In 2024, Taihu Lake's overall water quality reached Class III, the best level recorded in 30 years. It also met the national 'good lake' standard throughout the entire year for the first time. The intensity of blue-green algae blooms has steadily decreased; notably, no blooms were detected during the first half of the year, another first occurrence. Taihu Lake has also marked its 17th consecutive year of ensuring a safe summer. Furthermore, the watershed ecosystem has become healthier, with the lake's aquatic biodiversity index reaching the 'Excellent' grade for the first time.

Case 2-7   Baiyangdian's Ecological Transformation: City and Wetland in Symbiotic Harmony, Creating a Tapestry of Shared Beauty

Baiyangdian is the largest freshwater lake on the North China Plain, with a basin area of more than 30,000 km^2, involving more than 30 counties (cities, districts), 143 scattered lakes and more than 3,700 crisscrossing ditches and trenches. Thus, it has significant importance for maintaining ecological security in north China. After the 1970s, due to drought, reduced upstream water inflow, increased industrial and agricultural water use, and other reasons, despite being at the "end of nine rivers", Baiyangdian also faced challenges of declining water levels and pollution. In February 2017, General Secretary Xi Jinping made a special trip to Baiyangdian during his on-site inspection of the construction planning of Xiong'an New Area and emphasized that in building Xiong'an New Area, Baiyangdian must be well restored and protected. In April 2017, the Central Committee of the Communist Party of China and the State Council decided to establish Hebei Xiong'an New Area. This is a plan for the millennium and a major national event. Baiyangdian thus welcomed the largest systematic ecological governance in its history. The "Master Plan for the Xiong'an New Area in Hebei" published in April 2018 clearly stated that the ecological environment of Baiyangdian should be strengthened in terms of governance and protection, gradually restoring Baiyangdian's function as the "kidney of north China".

By 2021, Baiyangdian was fully cleared, with water quality improved to Class III surface water standard and maintained at that level for three consecutive years, creating a "Xiong'an model" of green development with water-city integration and city-lake interdependence, namely: Adhering to systematic governance of 'source control-sewage interception-river treatment' in the basin, implementing water quality target management for rivers entering the lake, comprehensively treating industrial pollution sources, strengthening urban and rural sewage collection and treatment, effectively treating agricultural non-point source pollution, creating good river and lake ecological environments, and ensuring that rivers entering the lake meet water quality standards.

Exploring Multi-source Ecological Water Replenishment Mechanisms

Since the late 1990s, relevant departments have diverted water to Baiyangdian more than a dozen times to maintain it from drying up, but under the long-term state of resource-based water shortage, the water crisis in Baiyangdian has not been fundamentally resolved. Since the establishment of Xiong'an New Area, comprehensive remediation of rivers entering the lake has been carried out, with Zhulong River, Xiaoyi River, Tang River, Fu River, Cao River, Ping River, Pu River, and Baigou Diversion River basically connected. Key projects such as "Yellow River to Baiyangdian" and "Yangtze River to Baiyangdian" have been implemented, enabling Yellow River water, water from rivers along the central route of the South-to-North Water Diversion Project, upstream reservoir water, reclaimed water, and other sources to provide ecological replenishment for Baiyangdian. The water level of Baiyangdian is maintained at around 7 meters, reaching the target water level required by the "Baiyangdian Ecological Environment Governance and Protection Plan (2018-2035)". The lake area has been restored to about 300 km^2, with more than 100 million cubic meters of water released to the downstream river (Zhaowang New River), which has effectively improved the hydrodynamics and water circulation of Baiyangdian.

Exploring New Paths for Internal and External Source Treatment

Since 2017, pollution enterprises throughout the Baiyangdian Basin have been investigated and banned, the construction of centralized sewage treatment facilities in 37 provincial-level and above industrial parks in the basin has been completed, and all aquaculture and large-scale livestock and poultry farms in Xiong'an New Area have withdrawn. In June 2020, the Baiyangdian Basin Ecological Environment Monitoring Center was inaugurated. This involved establishing 61 assessment monitoring sections throughout the basin, building 42 automatic water quality monitoring stations, and having upstream cities install online wastewater monitoring systems for all basin discharge points entering the lake and for 852 key water-related enterprises, thereby creating a dense watershed monitoring network.

Sewage treatment capacity has been continuously upgraded and expanded, with Baoding City's daily sewage treatment capacity exceeding 1.75 million tons, an increase of nearly 50% compared to 2015. The Baoding Lugang Phase II Sewage Treatment Plant, with a daily treatment capacity of 100,000 tons, is the largest fully underground sewage treatment facility in the Baiyangdian Basin that adopts a "ground green leisure space + underground pollution treatment" model. In addition to traditional sewage treatment units, the rain and sewage storage and regulation system combines urban drainage, flow regulation, and emergency sewage treatment functions. An environmental education base exhibition hall is set up inside the underground box, serving as a window for the public to understand sewage treatment processes and environmental protection knowledge.

Past practices in Baiyangdian, such as building dikes and embankments in some lake zones for aquaculture and lotus farming, along with converting other zones into cropland, severely fragmented the water body. This caused sediment to accumulate, reduced the open water surface, hindered natural water flow, and consequently degraded the water quality. Since 2019, Xiong'an New Area has implemented ecological projects such as connecting the hundred lakes, dredging, and returning farmland to the lake. Natural restoration has been implemented in dredged areas, with submerged plants planted and benthic aquatic animals released. The newly constructed Fu River and Xiaoyi River wetlands adopt a near-natural ecological pollution treatment model, namely: After upstream river water enters the wetland, it first passes through a pre-sedimentation ecological pond to reduce the concentration of suspended solids in the incoming water, then enters a subsurface wetland, where strong purification of pollutants is achieved through the combined action of "substrate-microorganisms-plants" in the three-level bed, and finally passes through an aquatic plant pond for further improvement of water quality.

Case 2-8   Yunnan: "One Lake, One Policy" for Precise
Pollution Control in Plateau Lakes

Yunnan Province is located in the southwestern frontier of China and is an important ecological security barrier and water conservation area in the upper reaches of the Yangtze River. Anchoring the goal of being a "pioneer in ecological civilization construction", it strengthens coordination in legislation, policy, technology, funding, and supervision, promotes the treatment of polluted water, agricultural non-point source pollution, garbage, and improvement of water ecology through "three treatments and one improvement". The water quality of nine major plateau lakes[1] is generally improving, with a compliance rate of 100% for water quality at main outflow and cross-border river sections, and water quality at the outflow and cross-border sections of the six water systems [2] all at Class II or above, achieving "clear water flowing out of Yunnan".

Protecting the Clear Waves of Erhai Lake

As Yunnan's second-largest plateau freshwater lake, Erhai Lake has always been a place of concern for General Secretary Xi Jinping. During his inspections of Yunnan in January 2015 and January 2020, he twice made important instructions on the protection and governance of Erhai Lake, emphasizing that "Erhai Lake must be well protected". Over the past decade, Dali Prefec-

---

[1]   Yunnan's Nine Major Plateau Lakes: Dianchi Lake, Erhai Lake, Fuxian Lake, Chenghai Lake, Lugu Lake, Qilu Lake, Yilong Lake, Xingyun Lake, and Yangzong Lake.

[2]   Yunnan's Six Major Water Systems: Yangtze River (Jinsha River), Pearl River (Nanpan River), Red River (Yuan River), Lancang River (Mekong River), Nujiang River (Salween River), and Irrawaddy River (Dayingjiang River).

ture has revised the Regulations of Dali Bai Autonomous Prefecture in Yunnan Province on the Conservation and Management of Erhai Lake five times, implementing scientific legislation, strict law enforcement, fair justice, and universal law-abiding throughout the entire process of Erhai Lake protection and governance. Through measures such as sewage interception and treatment, improving water quality entering the lake, the "three prohibitions and four promotions" [1] to prevent agricultural non-point source pollution, and ecological restoration, Dali has comprehensively advanced the integrated protection of mountains, water, forests, fields, lakes, grasslands, and sand in the Erhai Lake basin. The prefecture established the Erhai Lake Conservation and Watershed Ecological Civilization Promotion Association, designated the first Saturday of each month as "Erhai Protection Day", and regularly organizes public science education and volunteer services…Erhai Lake's water quality has maintained excellent levels for consecutive years, with lake transparency increasing to2. 29 meters. The water quality excellence rate of 27 main rivers entering the lake has reached 100%, and Ottelia acuminata, known as a "water quality indicator organism" that had disappeared for more than 20 years, is now blooming around the lake.

Relying on platforms such as the National Field Scientific Observation and Research Station for Erhai Lake Ecosystem, Erhai "Science and Technology Cottage", and expert workstations, Dali Prefecture has established mechanisms for scientific research coordination and expert consultation, continuously conducting scientific research to address key challenges in Erhai Lake governance. The "Digital Erhai" platform encompasses six major functional modules: intelligent sensing, data center, decision support, collaborative management, information services, and business applications. It collects real-time monitoring data on water quality, rainfall, meteorology, and pollution control facility operations, quantitatively analyzes Erhai Lake's water quality trends for the up-

---

[1] Three Prohibitions and four Promotions: Prohibiting the sale and use of nitrogen and phosphorus fertilizers and highly toxic pesticides with high residual levels; prohibiting the cultivation of water and fertilizer-intensive crops; promoting organic fertilizer as a substitute for chemical fertilizers, green pest and disease control, green ecological planting, and standardized livestock and poultry farming.

coming seven days, provides timely warnings and responses, and achieves interconnection, intercommunication, and deep integration of monitoring data, expert opinions, administrative decisions, and work measures.

Clear Waters Return to Dianchi Lake

Dianchi Lake is Yunnan's largest freshwater lake, known as the "Pearl of the Plateau". In the mid-20th century, influenced by various factors, Dianchi Lake's water quality began to deteriorate, with some areas declining to worse than Class V by the 1990s. In January 2020, General Secretary Xi Jinping visited the Xinhai Peninsula Ecological Wetland at Dianchi Lake in Kunming to learn about the lake's protection, governance, and water quality improvement. He pointed out that Dianchi Lake is a gem embedded in Kunming, and emphasized the need to maintain unwavering determination, treating mountains, waters, forests, fields, lakes, and grasslands as a living community, and strengthening comprehensive, systematic, and source-based governance to further improve Dianchi Lake treatment. In recent years, Kunming City has adhered to the concept that "Dianchi Lake is for protection, not development", adopting measures such as "retreat, reduction, adjustment, treatment, and management", and maintaining Class IV water quality throughout the lake for seven consecutive years.

Water replenishment and sewage interception are key measures to address Dianchi Lake's scarce water resources, high environmental pressure, and weak self-purification capacity. Kunming has built multiple cross-regional water diversion projects, 29 water purification plants, and 7,864 km of municipal drainage pipeline networks, processing over 2.5 million cubic meters of sewage daily. The Niulan River-Dianchi Lake Water Replenishment Project alone has supplemented Dianchi Lake with 4.553 billion cubic meters of water and provided 605 million cubic meters of emergency water supply for the city. Following the principle of "minimizing human intervention and maximizing natural restoration", 62,900 mu (about 4,193.33 hectares) of wetland-based ecological belts have been built around Dianchi Lake, with an average width of about 200 meters, further buffering sewage inflow and purifying water quality.

Technology empowerment is an important tool for overcoming ecological restoration challenges in Dianchi Lake. The Longmen Algae-Water Separation Station is China's first station specifically designed for treating blue-green algae blooms in lakes and reservoirs. Through processes including "algae-water collection-physical filtration-pressurized sedimentation-efficient air flotation-tail water utilization-algal sludge dewatering-environmental disposal", algae-rich water is treated to Class III surface water standards, and algal sludge is processed to "turn waste into treasure" as organic fertilizer. The Dianchi Plateau Lake Research Institute of Kunming has developed a complete set of ecological restoration technologies such as "habitat improvement-aquatic plant restoration-turbid-clear transformation", which have been demonstrated in the Dabokou area of Dianchi Lake. The overall water quality in the Dabokou area has basically reached Class III, with the distribution area of submerged plants increasing from less than 10% in 2015 to over 50%, and Ottelia acuminata and water birds becoming increasingly abundant.

III. Significant Achievements in Water Environment Management in Other Areas

China has continuously implemented special environmental protection actions for urban and rural black and odorous water body remediation and conducted dynamic investigations of black and odorous water bodies. Those with larger areas and stronger public reactions are included in the regulatory list. Resource recovery and ecological treatment methods are prioritized. Additionally, a systematic approach of 'itemized listing and progressive resolution' is employed, where each identified water body is tracked individually until it is successfully remediated. Monitoring and spot checks are strengthened, a mechanism to prevent the recurrence of blackness and odor has been established, and follow-up supervision is conducted using integrated methods such as satellite remote sensing and water quality monitoring. Currently, black and odorous water bodies in urban built-up areas at and above the prefecture level have been basically eliminated. Over 3,000 larger rural black and odorous water bodies have been treated, with the treatment rate of nationally monitored rural black and odorous water bodies reaching 82.3%. The water quality sampling compliance rate of completed treatment bodies exceeds 97%. What were once "ditches of black water" have transformed into pools of green water and bays of clear water, effectively promoting urban-rural integrated development.

The Ministry of Water Resources, together with relevant departments and provinces, has advanced comprehensive treatment of groundwater over-extraction in the recipient areas of the eastern and middle routes of the South-to-North Water Diversion Project Phase I, the north China region, and other key areas, forming a systematic treatment model of "one reduction and one increase". By implementing integrated strategies such as scientifically mapping groundwater overdraft areas, boosting water savings in crucial fields, tightly controlling development scale and intensity, increasing recharge from diverse sources, replenishing groundwater from rivers and lakes, and strictly managing groundwater use, China has steadily reduced groundwater overdraft levels. Compared with 2015, in 2024, the area of groundwater over-extraction has decreased by 19,500 km^2 (6.8%), the area of severe over-extraction has decreased by 88,300 km^2 (51%), and the over-extraction volume has decreased by 5 billion cubic meters (31.9%).

Section 3   China's Innovative Measures, Main Achievements, and Typical Cases in Marine Ecological Environment Protection

China is a firm promoter and active participant in marine ecological environment protection. Since the new era, General Secretary Xi Jinping has made a series of important statements on marine ecological environment protection, emphasizing that "we should care for the ocean as we care for life". China has incorporated marine ecological environment protection into the national ecological environment protection system and established a land-sea coordinated marine ecological environment governance system. The overall marine ecological environment quality has improved, ecosystem service functions in some sea areas have significantly enhanced, marine resources are being orderly developed and utilized, and the path of transforming blue seas and silver beaches into invaluable assets is becoming increasingly broader.

Case 2-9   Xiamen "Mountain-Water-Sea-City" Integration:
Creating a Window for Building a Beautiful
China in the New Era

The comprehensive treatment of Yundang Lake is an important origin of Xi Jinping's Thought on Ecological Civilization, and Xiamen City is an important nurturing ground and pioneering practice area for this thought. During his work in Xiamen, General Secretary Xi Jinping personally planned, deployed, and promoted the comprehensive governance of Yundang Lake. With forward-looking strategic vision, he creatively proposed the 20-character guideline of "governing the lake according to law, intercepting and treating sewage, dredging and building embankments, activating water bodies, and beautifying the environment", pointing out a high-quality development path of harmonious coexistence between humans and the ocean.

With the comprehensive treatment of Yundang Lake as a starting point, Xiamen City has anchored the goal of building a beautiful Xiamen, strengthening goal coordination, departmental coordination, policy coordination, regional coordination, and governance coordination. Adhering to integrated land-sea planning, river-sea linkage, and systematic management, the city deeply engages in the critical battle against nearshore marine pollution. It carries out ecological restoration of urban and rural land spaces in an all-around, region-wide, and all-element manner, effectively tackling challenges common to bay-type cities, such as tight resource constraints, high pollution emissions, and numerous conflicts between human activities and the marine environment.

Furthermore, Xiamen City has listed the comprehensive management of marine floating garbage as a project to benefit the people, incorporating it into the assessment of party and government leaders' ecological and environmental protection objectives. The city has established a "four-modernization" governance mechanism for marine floating garbage, featuring institutionalized responsibility implementation, normalized maritime sanitation, systematic comprehensive governance, and informationized forecasting, achieving garbage collection at sea and disposal on land. This has been included in the National Ecological Civilization Pilot Zone reform measures and experience practice list by the National Development and Reform Commission. The municipal and district finances invest nearly 100 million yuan annually for vessel and vehicle maintenance, personnel expenses, and outsourced services for cleaning vessels to ensure effective operation of marine area and beach cleaning and garbage transfer. A marine debris monitoring, early warning, and forecasting system has been launched. Drones are used for aerial surveillance of key shoreline sections to accurately predict the drift trajectories and distribution areas of debris entering the sea. Discovered problems are promptly reported for rectification. Through comprehensive measures, the proportion of excellent and good water quality in Xiamen's near-shore marine areas has increased from 50% in 2019 to over 95% in 2024, and the rate of excellent water quality at swimming beaches is 100% in 2024, both reaching the best levels in history.

As one of China's first 14 marine economy development demonstration zones, Xiamen City leverages its marine resource advantages to connect marine economy policies related to government services, industrial layout, ecological environment, regional coordination, and factor support. The city has built a marine high-tech industrial park, cultivated marine scientific research and innovation carriers and talent highlands, and developed marine emerging industries characterized by "leading enterprises as leaders + specialized and innovative enterprises building brands+cultivation and strengthening of science and technology-based small and medium-sized enterprises". Since 2020, the added value of Xiamen's marine strategic emerging industries has grown at an average annual rate of 11.3%, exceeding the average annual GDP growth rate. As of September 2024, Xiamen has more than 10,000 marine-related enterprises, including 28 national high-tech enterprises, 30 industrial chain leading enterprises, and 13 listed companies.

I. The Multi-departmental Collaborative, Central-Local Joint Marine Ecological Environment Protection Working Mechanism Has Been Basically Established

In 2018, the State Council's institutional reform integrated marine environmental protection responsibilities into ecological and environmental departments, and marine protection, restoration, and development and utilization responsibilities into natural resources departments. Departments such as transportation, maritime affairs, fisheries, forestry and grassland, coast guard, and the military participate in marine ecological environment protection according to their respective functions, enhancing the coordination of land and sea pollution prevention and control and the integrity of ecological environment protection. Ecological environment regulatory agencies have been established in the Haihe River Basin-North Sea area, the Pearl River Basin-South China Sea area, and the Taihu Lake Basin-East China Sea area. The specific responsibility for protecting the ecological environment of nearshore marine areas lies with the respective coastal provinces, autonomous regions, and municipalities. Meanwhile, China has gradually established a "three-in-one" marine environmental protection judicial system integrating criminal, civil, and administrative litigation, as well as a marine environmental public interest litigation system with Chinese characteristics, building a solid judicial defense line for marine ecological environment protection.

II. Major Progress Has Been Made in Comprehensive Governance of Key Sea Areas

The Bohai Sea is China's semi-enclosed inland sea with insufficient water exchange capacity and self-purification capacity. Since 2018, China has continuously carried out two rounds of key comprehensive governance in the Bohai Sea. By focusing on the "1+12" cities around the Bohai Sea[①], China has established cross-regional, cross-departmental collaborative governance, consultation and notification, joint prevention and control mechanisms for near-shore sea areas, strengthened total nitrogen treatment in rivers entering the sea, effectively investigated, monitored, traced, and treated sewage outlets entering the sea, carried out protection and restoration of coastal wetlands and ecological coastlines, and achieved integrated land-sea coordinated pollution control of "watershed-estuary-near-shore sea area". In 2023, the proportion of excellent and good water quality in the near-shore areas of the Bohai Sea reached 83.5%, an increase of 18.1 percentage points compared to 2018. The 49 rivers entering

---

① The "1+12" cities around the Bohai Sea: "1" refers to Tianjin Municipality, and "12" refers to Dalian, Yingkou, Panjin, Jinzhou, Huludao, Qinhuangdao, Tangshan, Cangzhou, Binzhou, Dongying, Weifang, and Yantai.

the sea around the Bohai Sea have completely eliminated Class V inferior water quality at national-controlled cross-sections, and the ecological environment quality of the Bohai Sea continues to improve.

Zhejiang Province has issued the "Action Plan for Ecological Restoration and Enhancement of the Hangzhou Bay Marine Area". It established China's first assessment system for coordinated upstream-downstream governance of rivers flowing into the sea. Provincial, municipal, and county levels coordinate to effectively manage key control sections of main river streams and tributaries. Furthermore, systems such as financial rewards and penalties based on the water quality of rivers entering the sea and horizontal ecological compensation mechanisms within basins have been established. Comprehensive, basin-wide joint governance has been initiated for rivers flowing into the sea, including the Qiantang River, Cao'e River, and Yong River. Notably, the whole-basin control range is "stricter than strict". Even at the Nanjiang River in Dongyang City, a fourth-level tributary of the Qiantang River about 180 km from the estuary, key control cross-sections have been set up, demonstrating Zhejiang's precision and determination to manage every drop of water well.

Guangdong Province has a sea area of 420,000 km^2, three times its land area, with a winding coastline stretching 4,084 km. Guangdong Province has completed the "investigation, monitoring, and tracing" of sewage outlets entering the sea in the Pearl River Estuary, developed a key monitoring system for sewage outlets entering the sea, and implemented total volume reduction and control of pollutants such as chemical oxygen demand, ammonia nitrogen, and total phosphorus based on scientific calculations of total environmental capacity. Also, following the principle of "one bay, one policy", differentiated protection and restoration measures are adopted for different types of bays, creating beautiful bays each with distinctive characteristics.

Case 2-10   Creating a Beautiful Marine Ecological Space: Shanghai Writes a New Chapter for a Modern Marine City

Shanghai was born and thrived because of the sea. "Strengthening marine ecological protection, reinforcing near-shore marine pollution control and marine ecological restoration, constructing an integrated protection and restoration pattern coordinated between land and sea, river and sea, and enhancing marine safety resilience" are key to building a modern strong marine city and a demonstration base for building a strong marine nation. In October 2022, Shanghai issued an implementation plan for building a modern marine city, proposing to implement marine ecological protection and restoration actions. In January 2023, Shanghai issued the "Implementation Opinions of the Shanghai Municipal People's Government General Office on Strengthening the Management of Overlapping Areas between the Yangtze River Estuary and Sea in Shanghai City", requiring "implementation of ecological protection and restoration of the Yangtze River Estuary and coastline". In March 2024, the Shanghai Municipal Government held a meeting of the Leading Group for the Construction of a Modern Marine City, requiring systematic promotion of ecological protection and restoration of the Yangtze River Estuary-Hangzhou Bay. In May 2024, Shanghai issued the "Implementation Opinions on Comprehensively Promoting the Construction of Beautiful Shanghai and Building a Modernized International Metropolis Where Humanity and Nature Coexist in Harmony", requiring "phased promotion of ecological protection and restoration of the coastlines of Lingang, Fengxian, Jinshan along the northern shore of Hangzhou Bay and the Yangtze River Estuary". In July 2024, Shanghai issued the "Decision on Thoroughly Implementing the Spirit of the Third Plenary Session of the 20th CPC Central Committee, Further Deepening Comprehensive Reform, and Fully Playing the Leading and Demonstrative Role in Promoting Chinese-style Modernization", proposing key reform tasks for marine ecological environment protection in the next stage...With the issuance of one policy after another, Shanghai is firmly moving towards "maritime power".

Shanghai cleverly applies the "addition and subtraction method" in land-sea coordinated ecological environment protection. For example, the city has carried out sewage interception and pipeline integration, river dredging, and ecological restoration for the Suzhou Creek and Huangpu River, which were once plagued by pollution, significantly improving water quality. The Shanghai Wusongkou Ancient Battery Fort, located at the confluence of the Yangtze Riv-

er and Huangpu River, has undergone ecological restoration and cultural reconstruction, transforming from a disorderly "steel slag dump" into a wetland park
with water purification functions. Benchmarking "the highest standards and the
highest levels", Shanghai took the lead in building an intelligent control system
for the Yangtze River fishing ban, achieving a closed-loop management cycle of
intelligent discovery, intelligent warning, comprehensive judgment, command
and dispatch, territorial supervision, timely investigation and handling, and
information sharing.

Chongming Island, known as the "Gateway to the Yangtze River and an
Island in the East China Sea", is located at the mouth of the Yangtze River and
has been positioned by the Shanghai Municipal Government as a "world-class
ecological island". In recent years, Chongming Island has carried out ecological restoration of tidal flat natural wetlands, effectively controlled the expansion
of invasive alien species (Spartina alterniflora), gradually restored native species such as reeds and Scirpus mariqueter, promoted the conversion of old and
new growth drivers, supervised non-compliant enterprises to return tidal flats
and water to the people, completely eliminated black and odorous water bodies
and inferior Class V water bodies, and achieved a 100% compliance rate for
surface water environmental function zones, an air quality excellence rate of
91.9%, and forest coverage twice the city's average. The connection between
river and sea, the merging of water and sky, and the gathering of thousands of
birds have become the "new normal". Chongming District, taking the construction of a carbon neutrality demonstration zone as a starting point, coordinates emission reduction, source control, carbon fixation, and carbon sink enhancement. The district conducts research, registration, confirmation of
rights, accounting, and refined management of characteristic ecological products in six ecosystems including tidal flats, oceans, forests, rivers and lakes,
farmland, and towns. It develops new energy sources such as fishery-photovol-
taic complementary systems and onshore wind power, with renewable energy
generation accounting for 32% of the district's total electricity consumption. The
district focuses on developing two leading industries—urban modern green agriculture and marine equipment—complemented by three advantageous industries: high-quality tourism, characteristic sports, and health services, accel-

erating the construction of a green and low-carbon ecological industrial system. The "world-class ecological island" has been rejuvenated through the "dual carbon" goals.

III. Joint Governance of Land-based Pollution

1. Strengthening Pollution Prevention and Control of Rivers Entering the Sea

China continues to enhance the quality and effectiveness of urban sewage treatment, build separate rainwater and sewage pipeline networks, strengthen supervision of the sewage treatment industry, and reduce the impact of urban production and domestic sewage on the water quality of rivers entering the sea. By the end of 2023, the length of urban drainage pipelines nationwide reached 952,500 km, an increase of 4.27% year-on-year. The sewage treatment capacity was 227 million cubic meters per day, an increase of 4.84% year-on-year. The sewage treatment rate was 98.69%, an increase of 0.58 percentage points from the previous year. The domestic sewage centralized collection rate was 73.63%, an increase of 3.57 percentage points from the previous year. Sewage treatment plants in coastal cities at and above the prefecture level have basically completed upgrades to the Class A discharge standard. Meanwhile, rural environmental improvement efforts have been carried out. From 2021 to 2024, coastal provinces completed comprehensive environmental improvement in more than 17,000 administrative villages, compiled 170 livestock and poultry breeding pollution prevention and control plans for major livestock counties, and achieved a rural domestic sewage treatment rate exceeding 45%.

River chiefs and bay chiefs coordinate and collaborate, while departments such as oceanic, coast guard, and maritime affairs conduct regular law enforcement, using drones for comprehensive bay inspections, strengthening supervision of marine engineering projects, including total nitrogen reduction as an important indicator in cross-regional compensation agreements for rivers entering the sea, and implementing "river-specific" governance for rivers entering the sea. In 2023, the average concentration of total nitrogen at national-controlled cross-sections of rivers entering the sea decreased by 12.2% year-on-year, and the proportion of excellent and good water quality in near-shore sea areas reached 85%, an increase of 3.1 percentage points year-on-year, achieving the "sixth consecutive increase" since 2018, with inferior Class V cross-sections basically eliminated.

2. Guarding the Key Gates for Coastal Pollution Entering the Sea

China coordinates the investigation, monitoring, tracing, and remediation of sewage outlets entering the sea, establishing a whole-chain governance system for near-shore water bodies, sewage outlets, sewage pipelines, and pollution sources, achieving whole-process supervision and management of "near-shore water bodies-sewage outlets into the sea-sewage channels-polluting units". Following the requirement of "investigating all outlets, investigating as much as possible", China has clarified the number, distribution, discharge characteristics, responsible entities, and other information of various types of sewage outlets entering the sea, investigated more than 53,000 sewage outlets entering the sea, and completed the remediation of more than 16,000 sewage outlets entering the sea. China has built a unified information platform for sewage outlets entering the sea, standardized the setup and management of sewage outlets entering the sea, and strictly prohibited the establishment of new sewage outlets in areas such as natural protected areas, important fishery waters, sea bathing beaches, and ecological protection red lines.

Case 2-11   Jiangsu: Taking Sewage Outlets Remediation
as the Entry Point to Develop the "Jiangsu Model"
for Marine Ecological Governance

The coastal area of Jiangsu Province (Nantong City, Lianyungang City, and Yancheng City) is located in the Yellow Sea area, with a 954-kilometer coastline, a sea area of 37,500 km^2, and a coastal land area of 35,900 km^2. In 2019, Jiangsu Province launched a "net-like investigation" of sewage outlets entering the sea. Through a combination of "drone aerial photography+satellite remote sensing + manual survey", each suspected outlet underwent a three-level verification model at county, city, and province levels, making Jiangsu the earliest province outside the Bohai Sea region to complete a comprehensive investigation of sewage outlets entering the sea. Adhering to the principles of simultaneous monitoring and tracing, and tracing all outlets, detailed records of key information about sewage outlets entering the sea were kept, effectively clarifying "who is discharging, what is being discharged" and "where the wastewater comes from and where it goes".

Jiangsu Province has established a closed-loop supervision mechanism for the entire process of setting up, registering, remediating, and de-registering sewage outlets entering the sea, as well as monitoring and supervision inspections. First, following the requirements of "legally banning a batch, cleaning and merging a batch, standardizing and remediating a batch", the province has remediated sewage outlets entering the sea with "one outlet, one policy". For example, in areas with concentrated substandard outlets, observation wells have been built at the end of rainwater pipes, water quality monitoring before discharge has been increased, and immediate sewage control and interception facilities have been installed to enhance the ability to prevent and handle pollution risks. Combined with the ecological transformation of seawater aquaculture ponds, classified remediation of seawater aquaculture sewage outlets have been carried out, scattered outlets have been cleaned and merged, aquaculture tail water has been collected and treated uniformly, and direct discharge into rivers and the sea have been strictly prevented. The remediation of land and sea sewage outlets have been combined with the remediation of rivers entering the sea, and incorporated into urban and rural infrastructure construction and comprehensive environmental governance for both symptomatic and root-cause treatment. Second, the province has established a provincial-level information management platform for outlets discharging into the sea, created electronic files for each such outlet, and achieved full process management of monitoring, source tracking, and remediation information for these outlets.

3. Systematic Clean Up and Remediation of Marine Debris

China has established a system for monitoring, intercepting, collecting, salvaging, transporting, and treating marine garbage to continuously conduct monitoring and surveys of marine garbage and microplastics, comprehensively plan and construct land-based reception, transfer, and treatment facilities for marine garbage, and implement special clean-up actions in 11 key bays and marine garbage clean-up actions in coastal cities. Each coastal city has implemented systems such as "maritime sanitation" to prevent marine garbage from entering the sea through multiple links and measures. The average density of marine garbage and near-sea microplastics in China's near-shore sea areas is generally at a medium to low level.

Case 2-12   Fujian: Comprehensive Treatment of Marine
Floating Debris Drives the Development
of Beautiful Bays

Fujian is a major maritime province with a coastline of 3,752 km, ranking second in the country. Over the years, Fujian has continued to deepen the construction of an ecological province, making marine floating garbage treatment a livelihood project for five consecutive years. It has continuously exerted efforts in seven aspects: plans, mechanisms, projects, models, teams, standards, and platforms for marine floating garbage treatment. The province has strengthened source control of marine floating garbage, established a smart supervision system for marine floating garbage, controlled the source generation on shore, intercepted garbage entering the sea in watersheds, and reduced the stock of garbage on the sea surface, creating a whole-chain governance path of "managing on shore, intercepting in water areas, and cleaning on the sea surface". All coastal counties and districts have established professional maritime sanitation teams, achieving full coverage of marine floating garbage cleanup in continental coastlines and inhabited islands. By the end of 2023, Fujian Province had cleaned up approximately 470,000 tons of marine floating garbage, with the distribution density of marine floating garbage in key shoreline sections decreasing by more than 60% compared to before remediation (2020), showing the effectiveness of beautiful bay construction with clean beaches and blue seas.

Ningde City has a coastline of 1,046 km and a sea area of 44,500 km^2, accounting for about one-third of Fujian Province. It has a long history of marine aquaculture, which is the "mainstay industry" for coastal residents to get rid of poverty and become prosperous. Ningde City has promoted comprehensive remediation of marine aquaculture, transforming traditional "wooden + white foam float ball" fish rafts into recyclable and reusable environmentally friendly high-density plastic fish rafts, and setting up centralized garbage collection facilities and garbage transfer yards at designated points. The city has implemented land-sea coordination of garbage cleaning in coastal villages and marine floating garbage, assigning responsibility to a second-level subsidiary established by the Ningde City Construction Group. A "Smart Ocean" big data system covering responsible entities such as fish rafts, fishing boats, fishing ports, and law enforcement departments has been built, realizing an efficient management model of "marine floating garbage discovered in the first time-personnel dispatched with early warning in the first time-environmental sanitation forces cleaning in the first time".

IV. Precise Prevention and Control of Marine Pollution

1. Strict Control of Marine Engineering Waste Disposal

Starting from the source, China continues to optimize the environmental impact assessment management of marine projects, legally incorporate marine engineering into the pollutant discharge permit management, and strictly control projects such as sea reclamation and sea sand mining. China has strengthened pollution prevention and control in offshore oil and gas exploration and development, with the state uniformly exercising the authority over environmental impact assessment approval and pollutant discharge supervision. Following the principles of scientific, reasonable, economic, and safe selection, China has designated dumping areas, scientifically and carefully evaluated the operation status of dumping areas, and ensured the safety of ecological environment and navigation depth in dumping areas. China strictly implements a dumping permit system and comprehensively uses means such as ship automatic identification systems and online monitoring of marine dumping for off-site supervision to minimize the impact of waste dumping on the marine ecological environment.

2. Systematic Management of Marine Aquaculture Pollution

As the world's largest aquaculture country, China continuously strengthens environmental supervision of seawater aquaculture through formulating emission standards, strengthening environmental impact assessment management, promoting classified remediation of sewage outlets, and monitoring tail water. The local authorities are required to clean up and rectify illegal and improperly set fish farm wastewater discharge outlets according to the principle of "abolishing a batch, merging a batch, and standardizing a batch". They should also promote environmental protection upgrades for pond farming, intensive factory farming, cage culture, and other methods to improve the aquaculture environment. All coastal provinces, cities, and counties have issued plans for aquaculture waters and tidal flats, scientifically delineating prohibited areas, restricted areas, and aquaculture areas for seawater aquaculture. China has carried out special remediation activities to prevent ship water pollution, implemented joint supervision of the transfer and disposal of ship water pollutants, and coastal provinces (autonomous regions, municipalities) have basically completed the construction of port ship pollutant reception, transfer, and disposal facilities. China continues to conduct supervision and inspection of ship fuel quality and strengthen the supervision of shore power facility equipment and use for berthed ships.

V. Striving to Build Beautiful Bays

The "Outline of the 14th Five-Year Plan (2021–2025) for National Economic and Social Development and Vision 2035 of the People's Republic of China" clearly calls for advancing the protection and development of beautiful bays. The "Opinions on Comprehensively Advancing the Building of a Beautiful China" incorporates beautiful bays into the overall framework of building a Beautiful China. "The 14th Five-Year Plan for Marine Ecological Environment Protection" has systematically divided China's coastal waters into 283 bays and deployed 1,682 specific tasks. Accordingly, China has taken bays as the basic units for development, with the goal of creating beautiful bays characterized by "clear waters, clean beaches, abundant fish and birds, and harmony between humans and the ocean". China has established basic standards for beautiful bay construction, created management platforms for beautiful bay development, encouraged business entities and social capital to participate, and implemented "bay-specific approaches" to advance pollution prevention and control in coastal waters, ecological protection and restoration, and shoreline environmental improvement. In 2023, among the nation's 283 bays, 126 showed improved water quality compared to the average of the previous three years, and none of the 24 typical marine ecosystems monitored were classified as being in an "unhealthy" state for three consecutive years.

Case 2-13   Shenzhen: Building a Global Marine Center City
Through Comprehensive Bay Governance

Shenzhen is located in southern Guangdong Province on the eastern shore of the Pearl River Estuary, adjacent to Hong Kong. It has a sea area of 2,297 km^2 and a coastline of 311.4 km (including the Shenzhen-Shanwei Special Co-operation Zone). The marine area is divided by Hong Kong's Kowloon Peninsula into eastern and western parts. The eastern part includes Daya Bay, Dapeng Bay, and Red Bay (within the Shenshan Special Cooperation Zone), while the western part comprises the Pearl River Estuary and Shenzhen Bay. Each bay possesses distinct natural endowments and abundant marine biological resources. The region features diverse and important coastal wetlands, including mangroves, salt marshes, and coral reefs. It is home to China's only national nature reserve located within an urban core-the Futian Mangrove Nature Reserve-which serves as a vital habitat for international migratory birds in the Eastern Hemisphere and a crucial "stopover site" along their north-south migration routes. In recent years, Shenzhen has implemented "bay-specific approaches" to strictly control land-based pollution entering the sea, continuously reduce the total amount of pollutants entering the western sea area and set total emission limits for pollutants in the eastern sea area. The city has achieved effective results in classified management of sea discharge outlets, land-sea coordinated monitoring, and joint law enforcement.

First, Shenzhen has integrated "Beautiful Bay" indicators with pollution control and cleaning projects and pollution prevention tasks, incorporating them into ecological civilization assessments at both municipal and district levels. The city has established a 24-hour remote dispatch patrol system for drones with "fixed-route cruising+targeted aerial inspection" and China's first district-level comprehensive ecological environment dynamic monitoring platform. It has built a three-dimensional observation network of "sea-land-air" with marine monitoring buoys, ground wave radar, and satellite remote sensing. Shenzhen has also established a comprehensive governance mechanism for coastline and marine garbage with multi-party participation from government departments, subdistricts, communities, social organizations, and volunteers to effectively guarantee human, material, and financial resources. This has formed a land-sea coordinated environmental supervision pattern guided by water quality monitoring data, with basic coverage of coastal waters, complete supervision of coastlines, efficient routine inspections, and tracking and handling of emergencies.

Second, Shenzhen has created a high-standard coastal leisure belt that integrates recreation, fitness, sightseeing, and nature experience, with interconnected parks and corridors of different themes, achieving full connectivity of shorelines for public access to the sea. The city has established China's first privately initiated Mangrove Foundation and conducted "mountain-sea-forest-river" nature education activities to mobilize citizens to actively participate in biodiversity protection.

Case 2-14   Hainan's Beautiful Bays: Creating a "Blue Calling Card" of Environmental Excellence, Ecological Beauty, and Governance Effectiveness

Hainan Island has over 1,900 km of diverse and picturesque coastline, with abundant ecological, tourism, cultural, and other green resources. In early 2023, Hainan Province issued the "Opinions on Strengthening the Protection and Construction of Beautiful Bays", specifying measures to "advance the construction of beautiful bays across the province in batches and by types in a progressive manner". Based on the five national indicators for beautiful bay construction (proportion of excellent water quality in bays, cleanliness of bays, marine biological protection, coastal wetland and shoreline protection, and environmental conditions of beaches and coastal tourist resorts), Hainan added six provincial characteristic indicators: public satisfaction, elimination of inferior Class V water in rivers flowing into the sea, standardized management of sewage outlets into the sea, local environmental and relevant departmental work performance, enhancement of domestic and international influence, and implementation of major strategies. The province has adopted "bay-specific approaches" to promote the creation of beautiful bays throughout the province.

Haikou City has followed the construction concept of "each bay with its own beauty, advancing progressively". By focusing on key environmental issues such as agricultural and rural pollution, marine aquaculture, and marine floating garbage, the city has strengthened land-sea coordination and collaborative governance of watersheds and sea areas, implemented zoned management and ecological restoration, simultaneously enhanced the ecological landscape function and disaster prevention function of the coast, created fishing-tourism integrated wetlands, and implemented garbage collection actions by fishing vessels. This has formed a "ecological conservation type" beautiful bay calling card. Haikou Bay has been selected as a national excellent case of beautiful bays, while Puqian Bay (Haikou section) and Chengmai Bay (Haikou section) have been included in the provincial list of beautiful bays, making Haikou the first city in Hainan Province with beautiful bays across its entire area.

Sanya Bay is located in the southern part of Sanya's main urban area, with a sea area of 75 km^2 and a coastline of 35.7 km. Sanya has established a multi-departmental coordination mechanism involving comprehensive law enforcement, public security, marine affairs, environmental sanitation, and ecological environment departments, achieving a beautiful bay construction mechanism with "full regional coverage, full process coverage, and uninterrupted personnel presence". With "daily cleaning" as the basic model for beach and marine garbage management, Sanya has linked the construction of beautiful bays with the "waste-free city" initiative to strictly control garbage from entering rivers and seas, strengthen marine biodiversity protection, carry out large-scale coral reef ecological restoration and stock enhancement activities in the bay area, and build a 15-kilometer coastal park along the bay. This extends the "ecology + tourism+economy" value chain, returning scenery and greenery to the people, and transforming Sanya Bay into an ideal venue for marine sports such as sailing, yachting, diving, and coastal tourism and vacation.

Section 4   China's Innovative Measures, Main Achievements, and Typical Cases in Environmental Management of Solid Waste and Chemicals

I. In-depth Advancement of "Waste-Free City" Construction

Since the General Office of the State Council issued the "Pilot Work Plan for 'Waste-Free City' Construction" in December 2018, localities have issued more than 400 "waste-free city" policies. For example, Shanghai promulgated regulations on "waste-free city" construction, six provinces including Shandong have written "waste-free city" construction into local regulations, and Jiangsu and others have issued provincial-level reward measures for "waste-free city" construction. Nineteen provinces including Zhejiang, Jilin, and Chongqing are promoting whole-area "waste-free city" construction, while the Guangdong-Hong Kong-Macao Greater Bay Area, the Yangtze River Delta region, and the Chengdu-Chongqing Economic Circle are promoting regional "waste-free city" joint construction. Various localities have built over 25,000 "waste-free cells" targeting government agencies, enterprises, and schools, forming a societal "waste-free" culture transmission chain. To date, 113 prefecture-level and above cities and 8 special regions across the country have cumulatively released more than 3,700 "waste-free city" construction projects, with investments exceeding 1 trillion yuan. In terms of source reduction, in 2023, the industrial solid waste generation intensity of 109 prefecture-level cities participating in "waste-free city" construction averaged 2.03 tons per 10,000 yuan, a decrease of 6.8% compared to 2020. In terms of resource utilization, Guizhou has developed mature consumption channels for phosphogypsum building materials and ecological restoration, with a comprehensive utilization rate reaching 91.8%; Chongqing has reused construction waste soil for backfilling, completing ecological restoration of historical mining sites and closed mines covering an area of 241 hectares...

Case 2-15   Hebei：Creating New Green "Waste-Free City" Scenarios

During the "14th Five-Year Plan" period, Hebei Province launched construction in all cities based on the inclusion of Shijiazhuang, Tangshan, Baoding, Hengshui, and Xiong'an New Area in the national "113+8" "waste-free city" construction list. Hebei took the lead in China in conducting heavy metal emission rights confirmation, publishing benchmark prices for heavy metal trading, carrying out multiple batches of heavy metal emission rights transactions, and supporting comprehensive utilization projects for solid waste such as steel blast furnace dust, consuming and utilizing 7.8 million tons of solid waste annually. The province has issued construction guidelines for eight types of "waste-free cells", including "waste-free communities", "waste-free villages", "waste-free hospitals", "waste-free shopping malls", "waste-free construction sites", "waste-free government agencies", "waste-free schools", and "waste-free scenic areas", with nearly a thousand various "waste-free cells" built cumulatively.

Various localities in Hebei have built distinctive "waste-free cities" based on their economic and social development foundations. For example, Xiong'an New Area has put into operation China's first hidden semi-underground neighborhood-friendly waste treatment facility and created a "waste-free lake" demonstration in Baiyangdian; Shijiazhuang City has created a solid waste management pilot in logistics parks guided by "recyclable packaging" and "smart systems"; Zhangjiakou City has extended the wind power industry circular chain to carry out resource utilization of new energy solid waste; Chengde City has built a green sand and gravel aggregate recycling base around Beijing using the national industrial solid waste comprehensive utilization base as a platform; Handan City, led by the construction of a national demonstration base for comprehensive utilization of bulk solid waste, continuously improves the utilization efficiency of fly ash, metallurgical slag, and other materials.

The treatment of industrial solid waste such as boiler slag, industrial sludge, desulfurization ash, fly ash, dust, steel slag, and water slag has been a traditional challenge for steel enterprises. Shougang Jingtang Limited Iron & Steel Co., Ltd., combining the characteristics and uses of industrial solid waste, has constructed a solid waste hierarchical full-quantity disposal, utilization, and consumption system with the goal of "legal compliance, full disposal, maximum benefit", consuming more than 1 million tons of solid waste annually. It has been selected as a typical case of "waste-free enterprises" by the Ministry of Industry and Information Technology and the Ministry of Ecology and Environment (the only steel enterprise selected in the province). As an important steel production base, Tangshan promotes the "solid waste not leaving the factory" model for steel enterprises within the city, with an industrial solid waste utilization and disposal capacity of 11.577 million tons per year.

Anping County in Hengshui City is a national-level livestock farming county, producing 1.02 million tons of farming waste and about 400,000 tons of various crop straws annually. Solid waste pollution problems such as on-site burning of crop straw and open-air storage of livestock manure once troubled the entire county. Hebei Yufeng Jingan Breeding Co., Ltd. ("Yufeng Jingan") in Anping County has pioneered a new path: Pre-burying pipelines under pig houses so that manure does not leave the pens but is directly transported to the biogas power plant. Pig manure undergoes anaerobic fermentation to produce biogas, which is used for power generation or purified into biomethane. The biogas slurry is fermented again to become liquid organic fertilizer, and the biogas residue is transformed into solid organic fertilizer, achieving a "gas, electricity, heat, fertilizer" joint production circular agriculture model with zero discharge of wastewater and waste. Yufeng Jingan has further undertaken centralized treatment and resource utilization of livestock manure throughout the county. It consumes 100,000 tons of manure and 70,000 tons of straw annually, produces 18 million cubic meters of biogas, achieves grid-connected power generation of 15.12 MkWh, purifies 6,360,000 m^3 of biomethane, and produces 250,000 tons of organic fertilizer. Green development has become a new growth point for the company's revenue.

Case 2-16   Nanjing Qixia District Kitchen Waste Collection and Treatment Integration Project: Integrated Pollution Reduction and Carbon Reduction with Synergistic Effects

In recent years, Qixia District has comprehensively explored new paths for waste reduction, resource utilization, and harmless treatment. It promotes the integration of renewable resource recovery networks and garbage classification recovery networks, establishes "professional+occupational" recovery channels, implements "district transfer + central collection" transportation forms, and forms an "chain-style operation, closed-loop management" operating system with renewable resource trading markets as the leader, sorting and processing centers as carriers, and urban and rural recovery points as terminals.

Previously, most of Qixia District's kitchen waste relied on external terminal facilities for disposal, with 58.6% sent to waste incineration plants, 34.2% sent to garbage transfer stations, and 7.2% sent to fertilizer plants for utilization and disposal. However, kitchen waste has characteristics of high organic content, high water content, and easy decomposition, which can easily produce odors, wastewater, debris, and residue during processing. The Qixia District kitchen waste collection and treatment integration project was jointly built through government-enterprise cooperation, establishing a collection network covering more than 800 kitchen waste generation points across 9 subdistricts in the district and a centralized kitchen waste disposal plant. It adopts "mechanical pretreatment+wet anaerobic digestion technology" for processing: after collection, kitchen waste is first sent to the pretreatment workshop, where oil and residue are separated. After passing through homogenization tanks and digestion tanks, it enters anaerobic fermentation tanks. The separated oil is purified to produce biodiesel, aviation kerosene, and other products. The liquid and solid phases are mixed to produce biogas for power generation. Wastewater enters the back-end sewage treatment system for compliant discharge, and the biogas residue is transported externally for incineration.

By establishing an efficient, centralized collection and transportation system, implementing meticulous pre-treatment and sorting, adopting advanced resource utilization and disposal technologies, and creating a closed-loop management mechanism, this project transitions food waste treatment in Qixia District from a decentralized to a centralized model. It not only solves the problems of large quantities and difficult treatment of kitchen waste but also creates high-value industrial raw materials, organic fertilizers, and clean energy, achieving a win-win situation for ecological environmental protection and economic and social development. It was evaluated as a typical case of pollution reduction and carbon reduction synergistic effect in China's "waste-free cities" in 2023 by the Basel Convention Regional Centre for Asia and the Pacific (BCRC China), being the only case listed in Nanjing and the only selected case in Jiangsu Province in the field of domestic waste.

II. Continuous Improvement of Hazardous Waste Supervision and Disposal Capacity Shortcomings

In recent years, China has revised and issued policies such as the "Identification Standards for Solid Wastes General Rules", "Measures for the Transfer of Hazardous Wastes", "National Catalogue of Hazardous Wastes", and "Exclusion List for Hazardous Waste Management" to enhance the informatization level of hazardous waste supervision. The country has carried out the "1+6 +20" key projects for hazardous waste (1 national hazardous waste technology center, 6 regional technology centers, and 20 regional special hazardous waste centralized disposal centers), clarified the procedures and time limits for cross-provincial transfer approval of hazardous waste, simplified approval conditions, and optimized cross-provincial transfer management pilot work for waste lead-acid batteries and other items. The national hazardous waste centralized utilization and disposal capacity exceeds 200 million tons per year, an increase of 50% compared to 2020, generally matching the waste generation situation. More than 780,000 enterprises have been included in the national solid waste information system management, an increase of nearly 15 times compared to 2018 when the information system was launched.

China has implemented a hazardous waste cross-provincial utilization permit exemption management system, achieving sharing of hazardous waste utilization and disposal capabilities and complementary advantages. The country has launched "waste-free group" construction, supporting pilot enterprises to implement hazardous waste "point-to-point" targeted utilization exemption management, sharing of hazardous waste utilization and disposal facilities within the group, and other policies to enhance the level of hazardous waste resource utilization within the group. For example, Xuzhou City has built a hazardous waste smart supervision platform, creating a complete information chain and traceable, visualized smart supervision mechanism for hazardous waste that is "traceable in source, traceable in destination, and fully recorded throughout the process". The Xuzhou Hazardous Waste Disposal Center, through the hazardous waste smart supervision platform, integrates data such as waste generator information and disposal plans, attaching an "ID card" to each package of hazardous waste awaiting disposal, and using high-temperature rotary kiln hazardous waste slag incineration technology to decompose and transform hazardous waste.

III. Breakthroughs in Large-Scale Utilization of Bulk Solid Waste

Since the new era, China has coordinated the comprehensive utilization and disposal of bulk solid waste, established China Resources Recycling Group Co. , Ltd. , broken through relevant technical bottlenecks, driven the formation of a number of circular economy deep processing industrial clusters, expanded channels for large-scale utilization of bulk solid waste, and enhanced the level of comprehensive utilization of complex and difficult-to-use bulk solid waste. In 2023, China's typical bulk industrial solid waste comprehensive utilization volume reached 2.258 billion tons, with a comprehensive utilization rate of 53.32%, an increase of 10.52 percentage points compared to 2012.

Ordos issued China's first prefecture-level city "Green Mine Construction Regulations", published policy documents such as the "Ordos Green Mine Construction Evaluation Indicators", and built green mine demonstration zones, exemplary mines for whole-mountain and whole-gully treatment, and concentrated contiguous treatment areas with a "mine-specific" approach. Each year, more than 60 million tons of coal gangue are comprehensively utilized for ecological restoration and land reclamation of coal mine goafs, subsidence areas, etc. , promoting the recovery and deep utilization of associated resources such as kaolin and pyrite, and developing high-tech utilization products from coal gangue such as chemicals, cement, soil improvement, fertilizers, and fiber materials, forming a coal gangue comprehensive utilization industrial chain of large-scale ecological governance and high-value comprehensive utilization.

As a major province in the phosphorus chemical industry, Yunnan produces about 23 million tons of phosphogypsum annually. The province implements a "waste determines production" model, carrying out three major projects: phosphogypsum waste pit ecological restoration and utilization, phosphorus building gypsum building materials promotion, and phosphogypsum roadbed material application. The comprehensive utilization rate of phosphogypsum has increased to over 50%, exceeding the national average. Kunming has established a special leadership group headed by municipal government leaders, signed the "Phosphogypsum Three-Year Action Goal Responsibility Letter" between the municipal government and district/county governments where phosphogypsum is produced, established project cooperation and ecological compensation mechanisms among phosphorus chemical enterprises, and set up a phosphogypsum environmental statistics information platform. Each year, 14 million tons of phosphogypsum achieve comprehensive disposal and utilization with multi-stakeholder participation.

Case 2-17   Zhejiang "Blue Cycle": Exploring a New Model for Comprehensive Management of Marine Plastic Waste

According to a report released by the United Nations Environment Programme, plastic products are the largest, most harmful, and most persistent part of marine debris, accounting for at least 85% of the total marine debris. The United Nations has listed the prevention and significant reduction of marine debris as an indicator of sustainable development. Zhejiang Province has a sea area of 260,000 km^2 and 4,350 islands, with heavy tasks and great pressure in managing marine plastic pollution.

In 2019, Jiajiang District in Taizhou City, Zhejiang Province, introduced the "Marine Cloud Warehouse" smart pollution control model and installed intelligent facilities in central fishing ports and Dachen fishing ports to recycle ship-generated pollutants such as oily tank washing water, engine room bilge water, and oily ballast water. In 2021, Jiajiang District expanded the types of ship pollutants treated using the digital platform "Yushengxin", an eco-friendly fishery management platform. In 2022, Jiajiang District, as the only pilot in the province, took the lead in implementing the upgraded "Blue Cycle" model, namely: through "government guidance + market operation", combined with the characteristics of marine garbage generation and distribution, establish a digital management platform and physical collection network, absorb public participation in marine plastic waste collection, have professional companies process the collected marine plastic into high-value raw materials for sale, and establish a "Blue Alliance Common Prosperity Fund" for secondary distribution of value to achieve ecological protection and increase income for the people. The "Blue Cycle" model solves the problem of "no one collecting" with "high returns", solves the problem of "low value" with "high credit", and solves the problem of "sustainability" with "high feedback". It has been replicated and promoted in all coastal counties (cities and districts) in Zhejiang and coastal provinces, winning the 2023 United Nations "Champions of the Earth Award".

Many manufacturing enterprises actively fulfill their social responsibility to protect the marine ecological environment and are willing to purchase higher-priced recycled marine plastic pellets to replace virgin plastic pellets, but the difficulty lies in how to solve problems such as marine plastic traceability and material recycling certification. Zhejiang Province has constructed a new governance mechanism of "market-oriented garbage collection-internationally certified value addition-high-value resource utilization" and employed blockchain and Internet of Things technologies to ensure visualized traceability of marine plastic waste collection, regeneration, re-manufacturing, resale, and other links, conduct carbon labeling and carbon footprint identification, and obtain certification from international authoritative certification bodies. This achieves high premiums and high returns for plastic waste recycling and utilization, increasing public enthusiasm for participating in marine garbage collection. To prevent non-marine plastic waste from entering the "Blue Cycle", Zhejiang equips front-line collectors with video recorders to record the source of plastic waste.

Zhejiang Province has established "Little Blue Home" marine plastic waste collection and storage stations in coastal cities for pre-treatment of marine plastic waste, which significantly reduces subsequent transportation and disposal costs. Taizhou City has constructed a credit evaluation system around front-line collection personnel's historical trustworthiness records, daily management, garbage collection operation management, environmental protection training records, etc. Personnel who continuously engage in marine plastic waste collection and have "excellent" credit evaluations can receive financial subsidies, accident insurance, major illness medical insurance, green loans, and other rewards.

IV. Continuous Strengthening of Heavy Metal and Tailings Pond Management

In recent years, China has continuously strengthened the classified management of heavy metal pollutants such as lead, mercury, cadmium, chromium, arsenic, thallium, and antimony, implemented enterprise heavy metal pollutant emission total control systems, explored heavy metal pollutant emission total replacement management exemptions, and strictly managed the access of key industry enterprises such as heavy non-ferrous metal mining and selection, heavy non-ferrous metal smelting, lead-acid battery manufacturing, electroplating, chemical raw material and chemical product manufacturing, and leather tanning processing. The country has legally promoted the exit of backward production capacity and strengthened enterprise cleaner production transformation. From 2021 to 2024, China has cumulatively implemented more than 730 projects to eliminate backward production capacity in heavy metal-related industries, completed more than 240 heavy metal deep treatment projects, and included 11,345 enterprises in the regulatory list of key heavy metal-related industries.

China has a large number of tailings ponds, with those in the Yangtze River Economic Belt and Yellow River Basin accounting for 43% of the total, and the overall situation is complex. In recent years, China has clarified the main responsibility of tailings pond operation and management units and the regulatory responsibility of ecological and environmental departments, and refined the whole-process pollution prevention and control of tailings ponds. According to the level of environmental risk, tailings ponds are divided into three grades,

establishing a graded list of tailings pond environmental risks and a differentiated regulatory mechanism. 7,820 tailings ponds have been included in the environmental regulatory system. Annual flood season tailings pond environmental
risk hazard investigation and rectification are carried out to promote "pond-spe-
cific" pollution control in key areas, and the environmental safety level of tailings ponds has significantly improved.

V. Important Steps in New Pollutant Management

After the General Office of the State Council issued the "Action Plan for
the Control of New Pollutants" in 2022, China established an inter-ministerial
coordination group for new pollutant control led by the Ministry of Ecology and
Environment and composed of 15 departments, formed an expert committee on
new pollutant control, and all provinces issued new pollutant control work
plans. Requirements for new pollutant control have been incorporated into the
revision of industrial structure adjustment guidance catalogs, the implementation of cleaner production, and the issuance of green product evaluation standards, initially forming a working mechanism of national coordination, provincial responsibility, and municipal and county implementation. Currently, China has completed a baseline survey of 122 industries, more than 70,000 enterprises, and more than 4,000 chemical substances with high hazards and high
environmental detection, preliminarily grasping the distribution of potential new
pollutants. For 14 types of new pollutants with prominent environmental and
health risks, whole-life-cycle environmental risk control measures such as prohibition, restriction, and emission limitation have been implemented. More
than 20,000 new chemical substances have been approved for registration, and
more than 3,200 environmental risk control measures have been proposed.

Section 5　China's Innovative Measures, Main Achievements, and Typical Cases in Other Fields of Ecological Environment Protection

I. Continuously Deepening the Battle for Clean Soil

Soil is the "foundation of life and mother of all things". Compared to air and water pollution, soil pollution has characteristics of concealment, lag effect, and complexity. Since the 18th National Congress of the Communist Party of China, China has solidly advanced the battle for clean soil, conducting the Second National Pollution Source Census, detailed investigations of soil pollution conditions, and surveys of soil pollution conditions in key industrial enterprise sites. These efforts have identified the area and distribution of polluted agricultural land and their impact on agricultural product quality, screened and investigated more than 100,000 potentially contaminated sites, and basically grasped the soil and groundwater pollution status and environmental risks of key industrial enterprise sites. Various regions have strengthened soil pollution prevention and control, completely banned the import of foreign garbage and cumulatively reduced solid waste imports by about 100 million tons. The safe utilization rate of contaminated farmland and the safe utilization rate of contaminated plots both exceed 90%, effectively curbing the trend of worsening soil pollution. China has included more than 16,000 enterprises in the list of key soil pollution monitoring units, implemented 124 soil pollution source control projects, and driven thousands of key monitoring units to implement green transformation. The country has established a priority monitoring plot system, incorporating nearly 10,000 potentially high-risk plots into the soil pollution risk control or remediation list.

II. Overall Improvement in Sound Environment Quality

With the rapid development of Chinese cities, increasing population density, growing number of motor vehicles, and more frequent industrial, commercial, and construction activities, noise sources continue to multiply. In 2023, noise disturbance issues accounted for 61.3% of the complaints and reports received by the national ecological environment complaint and report management platform, ranking first among all environmental pollution factors. China has built and networked more than 3,800 automatic monitoring stations, legally designated sound environment functional zones and areas with concentrated noise-sensitive buildings, and established a full-process noise control mechanism of "planning-environmental assessment-design-construction-acceptance-operation and maintenance". The country has comprehensively regulated noise in industrial, construction, transportation, social life, and other fields, strengthened quality supervision and certification regulation of noise-related products, jointly built "quiet communities that eliminate noise and allow peaceful sleep", and strictly handled noise pollution violation cases, achieving positive progress in noise pollution control. Currently, about 119,000 enterprises nationwide have incorporated industrial noise into pollution discharge permits, 2,132 quiet communities have been built, and the daytime compliance rate of sound environment functional zones has risen from 94.6% in 2020 to 95.8% in 2024, while the nighttime compliance rate has increased from 80.1% in 2020 to 88.2% in 2024.

Section 6   Pollution Reduction and Emission Control: China's Experience in Ecological Environmental Protection and Lessons for Developing Countries

I. Adhering to Environmental Protection for the People, Striving Tirelessly to Meet People's Needs for a Beautiful Ecological Environment

From the implementation of China's first pollution control project after the water pollution incident at Beijing's Guanting Reservoir in 1972, to the comprehensive pollution prevention and control of "Three Rivers" and "Three Lakes" in the 1990s, to the vigorous promotion of total reduction of major pollutants at the beginning of the 21st century, China has continuously intensified its pollution prevention and control efforts, striving to create a good production and living environment for the people. Especially since the 18th National Congress of the Communist Party of China, the entire Party and all ethnic groups across the country have adhered to the concept that "lucid waters and lush mountains are invaluable assets", resolutely declared war on pollution, advanced the battles for blue skies, clear waters, and clean soil, and solved a large number of prominent environmental issues related to people's livelihoods. The people's sense of gain, happiness, and security regarding the ecological environment has continuously strengthened, and the green foundation and quality of Chinese-style modernization have been enriched. China has continuously improved its ecological environmental protection policy and institutional system, established an enterprise emission permit system covering all fixed pollution sources, and strengthened environmental legislation, environmental justice, and environmental law enforcement to control pollution according to law, thus protecting the ecological environment with the strictest systems and the most rigorous legal framework. China has established a systematic, complete environmental management structure with clear responsibilities and effective supervision to strictly implement the principle that "both Party and government share responsibility, with one position bearing dual responsibilities". It has implemented the main responsibility for ecological environmental protection and restoration, deepened cross-regional cooperation in pollution control, and constructed a new pattern of joint governance, joint prevention, and joint control.

II. Adhering to Systematic Governance, Zoned Implementation, and Precise Pollution Control

China adheres to the integrated ecological protection and restoration of mountains, rivers, forests, farmlands, lakes, and grasslands, strengthens whole-chain governance from source to end, enhances environmental infrastructure and professional team building, and implements differentiated precise control by zones and categories. Pollution control no longer focuses on isolated indicators such as emission reduction volume and emission standards, but on comprehensive assessment indicators centered on environmental quality, improvement effectiveness, and long-term mechanisms, demonstrating a determination to respond to people's concerns about the ecological environment with visible results.

In winning the battle for blue skies, China focuses on improving air quality, reducing heavily polluted weather, and addressing prominent atmospheric environmental issues around people, with reducing fine particulate matter (PM2.5) concentration as the main line. It promotes the reduction of nitrogen oxides and volatile organic compounds, strengthens area-source air pollution control, and carries out regional joint prevention and control. In winning the battle for clean waters, China comprehensively coordinates both banks, upstream and downstream, land and water, surface and underground, rivers and oceans, water ecology and water resources, pollution prevention and ecological protection. It implements comprehensive governance with watersheds as units, transforming from sewage treatment to comprehensive water environment remediation, with "treating poor-quality water" bidding farewell to black and odorous conditions, and "protecting good-quality water" enhancing quality. In marine ecological environmental protection, China has improved marine ecological monitoring, early warning, and regulatory systems, comprehensively investigated and rectified sewage outlets into the sea, strictly controlled and reduced land-based pollutants, strengthened classified remediation of marine pollution, promoted marine plastic waste management, protected marine ecosystems and biodiversity, and promoted continuous improvement of marine ecological environmental quality and demonstration of beautiful bays. In solid waste management, China has deeply promoted the construction of "waste-free cities" and comprehensive utilization of bulk solid waste, strictly adhered to the bottom line of ecological environmental risk prevention and control of "one waste, one repository, one heavy metal"[①], improved the effectiveness of domestic waste classification and disposal, strengthened source reduction and efficient utilization of solid waste, enhanced the disposal capacity of hazardous waste, medical waste, construction waste, etc., promoted coordinated control of new pollutants, and solved problems such as large amounts of solid waste generation, inefficient utilization, illegal transfer and dumping, and difficulties in site selection for disposal facilities.

Case 2-18   Yangtze River Delta Region: Make Coordinated
Efforts to Protect and Restore the Ecological
Environment, Drawing a "Concentric Circle"
of Green Development

In August 2020, at a symposium on solidly promoting the integrated devel-

---

① Note: "One waste" refers to hazardous waste, "one repository" refers to tailings ponds, and "one heavy metal" refers to heavy metals.

opment of the Yangtze River Delta held in Hefei, Anhui, General Secretary Xi Jinping pointed out that the Yangtze River Delta region is the head of the Yangtze River Economic Belt, which should not only take the lead in economic development but also set a good example in ecological protection and construction. In November 2023, General Secretary Xi Jinping emphasized at a symposium on deepening the integrated development of the Yangtze River Delta: "The Yangtze River Delta region should further make coordinated efforts to protect and restore the ecological environment". Subsequently, by establishing a regional ecological environmental protection cooperation group, planning with one map, and using one standard for environmental protection, the ecological environmental protection of Shanghai, Jiangsu, Zhejiang, and Anhui has changed from "solo" to "symphony", moving toward the fast track of green development. Since May 1, 2024, the "Regulations on Promoting High-Quality Development of the Demonstration Zone of Green and Integrated Ecological Development of the Yangtze River Delta", which were separately approved by the Standing Committees of the People's Congresses of Shanghai, Jiangsu, and Zhejiang, have been implemented simultaneously in the three places, forming a long-term mechanism that "does not break administrative affiliation but breaks administrative boundaries" to make coordinated efforts to protect and restore the ecological environment.

Cross-boundary Water Bodies Joint Protection and Governance

Qingpu District of Shanghai, Wujiang District of Suzhou City in Jiangsu Province, and Jiashan County of Jiaxing City in Zhejiang Province are adjacent to each other, with crisscrossing waterways and scattered lakes, known as "the most Jiangnan of Jiangnan". In November 2019, the three places jointly established the Yangtze River Delta Ecological Green Integrated Development Demonstration Zone. By making coordinated efforts to protect and restore the ecological environment, the proportion of Class III or better surface water sections in the Yangtze River Delta Ecological Green Integrated Development Demonstration Zone rose from 75% in 2019 to 96.2%, and the water environmental quality of key cross-boundary water bodies such as "one river and three lakes" (Taipu River, Dianshan Lake, Yuandang Lake, and Fenhu Lake) reached or exceeded the 2025 target ahead of schedule.

73% of the Yuandang Lake shoreline belongs to Wujiang District and 27% to Qingpu District. In the past, due to different administrative affiliations, there were unclear responsibility divisions in the governance of Yuandang Lake between the two places. Now, the two places jointly implement the Yuandang Lake ecological shoreline connection project, adopting measures such as water system connection, river obstacle clearance, and bank slope remediation for Yuandang Lake and its surrounding tributaries. They have opened up the provincial "dead-end road" (Yuandang Bridge), which reduces the travel time between the two places from 40 minutes to 5 minutes and brings residents of both places a comfortable experience of slow walking on the bridge and "cross-domain seamlessness".

As the largest artificial waterway in the Taihu Lake basin, the Taipu River is a flood discharge channel for upstream Wujiang District and a drinking water source for Qingpu District and Jiashan County. In the past, due to different functional positioning and water control standards, segmented governance brought environmental risks. In 2019, the three places established a joint river chief system, jointly formulated "one set of standards" for joint water quality monitoring, joint law enforcement for water pollution control, and joint inspection by river chiefs, forming a mechanism of joint decision-making, joint protection, and integrated control.

Joining Hands to Win the Blue Sky Defense Battle

In 2018, the Yangtze River Delta regional environmental meteorology integration business platform went online, covering three major functions: precise control of air pollution, forecasting and early warning of heavily polluted weather, and medium and long-term regulation of the atmospheric environment. The environmental meteorology departments of the three provinces and one municipality not only share relevant data but also understand air pollution sources within and outside the region through analysis of pollutant transport channels. In 2022, the Yangtze River Delta regional air quality prediction and forecast result map went online, with "one map" releasing air quality prediction data for the three provinces and one municipality for the next 7 days. This is the first time in China that cross-provincial administrative region air quality forecast results have been jointly publicly released at the local level. Now, on the Wechat public accounts and other new media platforms of the ecological and environmental departments of the three provinces and one municipality, this digital visualization report is continuously updated, providing precise basis for joint response to heavily polluted weather and collaborative pollution control. In 2024, the average PM2.5 concentration in 31 cities in the Yangtze River Delta region was 33 micrograms per cubic meter, down 0.9% year-on-year, reaching the national secondary standard for five consecutive years; the average ozone concentration was 161 micrograms per cubic meter, down 1.2% year-on-year; the average proportion of good air quality days was 82.1%, with no heavily polluted days or worse.

Section 7   Countermeasures and Suggestions for Further Promoting High-Level Ecological Environmental Protection from the Perspective of Chinese-Style Modernization

I. Continue to Implement the Blue Sky Defense Battle

1. Strengthen Multi-Pollutant Emission Reduction and Area-Source Pollution Control

Continue to promote ultra-low emission retrofits in key industries such as steel, cement, coking, glass, lime, mineral wool, non-ferrous metals, and coal-fired boilers, ensuring that industrial enterprises fully and stably meet emission standards. Continuously carry out special remediation and third-party operation and maintenance of restaurant oil fumes and odors. Popularize the enclosed management of manure transportation, storage, and treatment in large-scale livestock and poultry farms, and steadily promote the prevention and control of atmospheric ammonia pollution. Strengthen comprehensive control of volatile organic compounds throughout the entire process and all links. Deepen comprehensive dust pollution control, promote prefabricated green buildings, and adopt dust prevention measures for urban public bare land, bulk cargo terminal material yards, etc., after surveying and filing. Promote comprehensive remediation of the mine ecological environment and universally build green mines. Improve the straw collection, storage, transportation service, and resource utilization system, and strengthen grid-based supervision of straw burning.

2. Accelerate Clean and Low-Carbon Development in Energy and Transportation Sectors

On the premise of ensuring energy security and supply, key regions will continue to implement total coal consumption control and reduction substitution, and include coal-fired boiler and tea water stove, commercial stove, grain drying equipment, agricultural product processing, and other coal-fired facility replacement projects in the equipment and facility update plan. Promote the replacement of coal with electricity and gas in industrial furnaces with "supply-determined transformation" as the orientation. Comprehensively use subsidies, taxes and fees, freight rates, transportation capacity allocation, land and sea use guarantees, and other levers to guide long-distance transportation of bulk goods to prioritize rail and water transportation, and short-distance transportation to prioritize enclosed belt corridors or new energy vehicles and vessels. Strengthen the construction of railway special lines and intermodal transfer facilities, and promote "external collection and internal distribution" logistics methods such as rail-road-water intermodal transportation. Popularize the replacement of new energy in public transportation, taxis, urban logistics distribution, environmental sanitation, and other vehicles, and cultivate clean transportation enterprises and zero-emission freight vehicle fleets. Severely crack down on the illegal sale of non-standard oil products and ensure the quality of finished oil products at private gas stations.

3. Improve the Air Environment Supervision and Law Enforcement System

Urge counties and districts that have not met air quality standards to prepare time-limited plans for achieving air environment quality standards and disclose them to the public. Continue to promote the coordinated control of PM2. 5 and ozone. Improve the joint prevention and control mechanism for air pollution in key regions such as the Beijing-Tianjin-Hebei region, the Yangtze River Delta region, the Guangdong-Hong Kong-Macao Greater Bay Area, the Chengdu-Chongqing economic circle, the urban agglomeration in the middle reaches of the Yangtze River, northeast China, the Fenwei Plain, the urban agglomeration on the northern slope of Tianshan Mountains, and within provincial administrative regions. Establish air governance improvement demonstration zones in cross-provincial adjacent areas and carry out joint cross-checking law enforcement on a regular basis. Improve the emergency management system for heavily polluted weather at the provincial, municipal, and county levels, and carry out clean transformation and emergency emission reduction of air-related enterprises in a list-based manner. Integrally improve the air quality monitoring network in cities, key towns, and key areas such as airports, ports, railway freight yards, logistics parks, industrial parks, and highways, and strengthen data networking, sharing, and release. Scientifically evaluate the amount of sand and dust in various places and the effectiveness of sand fixation and retention, and strengthen the construction of meteorological and air quality monitoring networks and the linkage of intervention measures in sand source areas and sand and dust path areas. Regularly update and announce the list of key air environment polluters to force enterprises to assume the main responsibility for pollution control. Stably operate automatic monitoring equipment for pollution sources and strengthen supervision and law enforcement based on data support.

II. Continue to Fight the Battle for Clear Waters

1. Strengthen Water Pollution Control Capacity Building

Coordinate upstream and downstream, both banks, main and tributary streams, cities and villages, strengthen source tracing and remediation and sewage interception and source control, give full play to the role of the river (lake) chief system, strengthen the remediation of sewage outlets into rivers (lakes), strictly control direct discharge of wastewater from towns, industries, agriculture, etc. , systematically promote the shortcomings of urban and rural and park sewage collection and treatment facilities and upgrade and transformation, optimize sewage and sludge resource utilization, promote rain and sewage separation in places with conditions, upgrade the implementation of comprehensive treatment of heavily polluted rivers, and establish a long-term mechanism to prevent the return of black and odorous conditions. Strengthen coordinated prevention and control of surface water and groundwater. Carry out water body endogenous pollution control and ecological restoration according to local conditions to enhance the self-purification function of rivers and lakes. With scenario application as the orientation, innovatively break through bottleneck technologies that restrict the continuous improvement of the water ecological environment.

2. Promote Comprehensive Governance of Rivers and Lakes

Implement "river-specific approaches", strictly implement hard measures such as water resource use control, water resource argumentation, water intake permit supervision, carrying capacity evaluation, and overload treatment, construct good connectivity of rivers and lakes, strengthen shoreline protection and utilization, strengthen cross-regional joint prevention and control of watershed pollution, and achieve sustainable use of river functions. Accelerate the treatment of sloping farmland and the construction of ecological clean small watersheds to promote water and soil quality and efficiency improvement in watersheds. Popularize the trading of pollution rights, carbon emission rights, and water rights, and improve the horizontal watershed ecological protection compensation and ecological product value realization mechanism. Fight the critical battle for the protection and restoration of the Yangtze River, strengthen the prevention and control of total phosphorus pollution with the Three Gorges Reservoir area and upstream, Tuojiang River, Wujiang River, etc. as the focus, strengthen the prevention and control of agricultural non-point source pollution with tributaries such as the Hanjiang River, Wujiang River, Jialingjiang River, Ganjiang River, and lakes such as Poyang Lake and Dongting Lake as the focus, promote the ecological restoration of the Yangtze River shoreline, implement the ten-year fishing ban in key waters of the Yangtze River basin, and effectively restore the biodiversity of aquatic life in the Yangtze River. Fight the critical battle for ecological protection and governance of the Yellow River, carry out the "waste clearing action" in the Yellow River basin, promote comprehensive water environment governance of water quality poor river sections of the main stream and main tributaries, second and third-level tributaries, and other "capillaries", strengthen soil and water loss control in the middle and lower reaches, implement wetland protection and restoration in the Yellow River Delta, carry out deep water-saving and water control actions, and maintain the water source conservation function of the upper reaches through determining livestock by grass and determining grazing. Rectify and clean up behaviors that skirt the rules for lakeside development in the name of real estate, tourism, health care, etc. Carry out lake water resource utilization, water pollution prevention and control, water ecological restoration, aquatic life protection, etc. according to local conditions, establish a total water intake control system covering important lake watersheds, and resolutely curb the "great leap forward in lake creation".

III. Improve the Marine Ecological Environment Governance System with Land-Sea Coordination and Multi-Party Joint Governance

1. Deepen Classified Remediation of Pollution in Key Marine-Related Fields

Continuously carry out "investigation, measurement, tracing, and treatment" of sewage outlets into the sea with coastal townships as units, realize "one map" of geographical distribution, discharge characteristics, responsible subjects, and pollution permits, and construct a whole-chain governance system of "nearshore water bodies-sewage outlets into the sea-sewage pipelines-pollution sources". Fight the critical battle for comprehensive governance of key sea areas, establish a coordinated and integrated governance system for coastal areas, watersheds, and sea areas, strengthen the shortcomings of sewage collection and treatment facilities in coastal urban and rural areas, implement artificial wetland purification and ecological expansion projects in coastal areas, and achieve simultaneous improvement of the ecological environment of rivers entering the sea and key sea areas. Enhance the operational efficiency of pollution collection and transfer facilities for ships, fishing ports, etc. , connect with relevant public facilities in cities, and timely collect, clean, transfer, and dispose of garbage generated by fishing ports and visiting fishing vessels. Strictly implement environmental impact assessment access and review for seawater aquaculture, fill the gaps in environmental protection facilities for seawater aquaculture, promote the layout of seawater aquaculture from nearshore to deep and distant seas, and promote ecological and healthy aquaculture models. Build a data-sharing supervision system for marine engineering projects and marine waste dumping. Implement special plastic waste cleanup actions in areas such as bays, estuaries, and shorelines.

2. Solidly Promote the Construction of Beautiful Bays

Implement "bay-specific approaches" to progressively advance comprehensive ecological environment governance, focusing on bays and beaches adjacent to coastal medium and large cities, routinely investigate and rectify pollution sources entering the sea around seawater bathing beaches and coastal tourism resort areas, and resolutely ban illegal and unreasonably set sewage outlets. Implement long-term supervision of shoreline and marine floating garbage, and promote simultaneous improvement of bay water body and shoreline environmental quality. Strengthen environmental quality monitoring, forecasting, and information release of seawater bathing beaches, increase marine environmental protection publicity efforts, and enhance the public's sense of gain and happiness in approaching, loving, and protecting the sea. Incorporate beautiful bays into the overall planning layout of coastal beautiful cities, and explore paths for building beautiful bays with distinctive characteristics.

IV. Deepen the Construction of "Waste-Free Cities"

1. Improve the Fine Management System for Solid Waste

Incorporate the construction of "waste-free cities" into the assessment content of the critical battle against pollution for townships (subdistricts) and villages (communities). Incorporate the generation, utilization, and disposal of solid waste into the enterprise credit evaluation system in accordance with laws and regulations. Incorporate hazardous waste from small and micro enterprises and social sources into the statistical system, forming "one account" for the management of major categories of solid waste. Promote source reduction and resource utilization of industrial solid waste, popularize the construction of green factories, green parks, green mines, and cultivate "waste-free enterprises". Comprehensively investigate and inventory historical legacy solid waste storage sites and implement graded and classified rectification. Promote green building materials and construction waste recycling products, and universally apply new construction methods that are prefabricated and intelligent. Establish incentive mechanisms for broad farmer participation in agricultural and rural waste management, and strengthen the recycling of waste agricultural materials. Promote the "integration of two networks" of domestic waste classification points and waste material recycling points. Deepen the construction of the "five-all"[①] system for environmental supervision of hazardous waste.

2. Improving the Resource Utilization and Reuse Level of Waste

On the premise of meeting environmental quality standards and requirements, expand the application of bulk solid waste comprehensive utilization products in the construction field. Develop deep processing industrial chains for renewable resources such as scrap steel, non-ferrous metals, waste paper, and waste plastics. Support the development of remanufacturing industries for high-frequency consumables such as auto parts, engineering machinery, machine tools, and cultural and office equipment, and explore high-end equipment re-manufacturing for shield machines, aircraft engines, industrial robots, power generation equipment, and others. Address the shortcomings in county-level domestic waste incineration treatment capacity, and rationally plan and construct treatment facilities for kitchen waste, agricultural and forestry biomass, and other materials. Promote new circular economy models such as energy cascade utilization, water resource recycling, and comprehensive utilization of solid waste within enterprises, within industrial parks, and between industries. Use fiscal rewards and subsidies, green finance, and other levers to strengthen the recycling and utilization of low-value recyclable materials. Explore pathways for the recycling and utilization of new types of waste such as retired wind power equipment, photovoltaic equipment, data centers, and communication base stations.

---

① "Five-all": all-domain investigation, all-round cleanup, all-quantity disposal, all-process supervision, and all-around improvement.

Chapter 3
Fortifying Ecological Security Barriers: China's Measures, Achievements, Experiences and Recommendations for Building a Green Development Spatial Pattern

Humans and nature form a community of life. President Xi Jinping has pointed out that we must organically integrate natural restoration and artificial restoration, implementing measures according to local conditions, time requirements, and regional categories to find the best solutions for ecological protection and restoration. Since the new era began, China has adhered to a systems approach, proceeding from the integrity of ecosystems to promote the integrated protection and restoration of mountains, rivers, forests, farmlands, lakes, grasslands and deserts. A "blueprint" for ecological protection and restoration from mountaintops to oceans, from plateaus to plains, and from national to local levels has basically taken shape. Meanwhile, China has actively improved its territorial space system, strengthened the coordinated planning and management of production, living, and ecological spaces, intensified ecological system protection and restoration efforts, effectively expanded ecological environmental capacity, and promoted the rapid accumulation of natural and ecological wealth, providing strong support for sustainable and healthy economic and social development.

Section 1   China's Innovative Measures, Main Achievements and Typical Cases in Optimizing the Pattern of Territorial Space Protection and Development

I. Achieving "Integration of Multiple Plans" in Territorial Space Planning

Land is the spatial carrier for green development. Territorial space planning serves as the guide for national spatial development and the blueprint for sustainable development and provides the basic foundation for various development, protection, and construction activities. In 2018, the CPC Central Committee and the State Council implemented reform measures to integrate spatial planning responsibilities previously divided among different departments—including major function zone planning, land use planning, urban-rural planning, and marine functional zoning—into the Ministry of Natural Resources, making it responsible for establishing and supervising the implementation of the territorial space planning system, thus achieving "integration of multiple plans". Subsequently, the "Outline of the National Territorial Space Planning (2021-2035)" was issued, and the "five-level three-category" territorial space planning system[①] was implemented. The planning compilation and approval system, implementation supervision system, regulatory policy system, and technical standard system for "integration of multiple plans" were gradually established, initially forming a "one map" approach for national territorial space development and protection, which plays an active role in supporting urbanization development and rural revitalization, and promoting the rational use and effective protection of territorial space.

Since 2022, China's first national-level territorial spatial plan incorporating the "integration of multiple plans" —the "Outline of the National Territorial Space Planning (2021-2035)" —has been issued, and local general plans, detailed plans, and special plans at all levels have been coordinated and ad-

---

①   "Five-level three-category" territorial space planning: "Five-level" refers to national, provincial, municipal, county, and township levels of territorial space planning; "three categories" refers to master plans, detailed plans, and related special plans.

vanced. To date, all provincial territorial space plans have received approval from the State Council, and over 80% of municipal and county territorial space master plans have been approved for implementation. Territorial space planning for key regions and river basins such as the Yangtze River Economic Belt (Yangtze River Basin), Beijing-Tianjin-Hebei region, Chengdu-Chongqing Twin City Economic Circle, and the Yellow River Basin coastal zone and nearshore waters is being accelerated to improve construction and development rules within and outside urban development boundaries, and promote the formulation of village planning for villages with conditions and needs. Planning leads and sets the framework. Local governments have strengthened the integration of planning and land policies, achieving "unified review and unified certification" for planned land use, improving approval efficiency and regulatory service levels. Following the principle of "unified data, unified standards, unified technical processes", they overlay information on population, land use, property rights, and industries to optimize spatial layout according to local conditions.

Case 3-1   Nanjing: Advancing Territorial Space Governance
             System and Governance Capacity Modernization
             Through "Integration of Multiple Plans"

In January 2023, Nanjing began implementing the "Nanjing Territorial Space Planning Regulations", which brings the entire chain of territorial space planning compilation, implementation, and supervision into the legal framework and addresses at the source the problems of overlap and contradiction between plans caused by differences in compilation concepts, methods, and control measures. Based on administrative authority, Nanjing designated "master plan-detailed plan-special plan" units across the entire city and established a territorial space planning system with administrative management logic as the main body, functional organization logic as support, integration of administration and function, and a combination of top-down and bottom-up approaches. With the goal of "facilitating project approval, serving project enterprises, and optimizing the business environment", Nanjing constructed a business integration processing model of "unified systems, unified processes, and unified per-

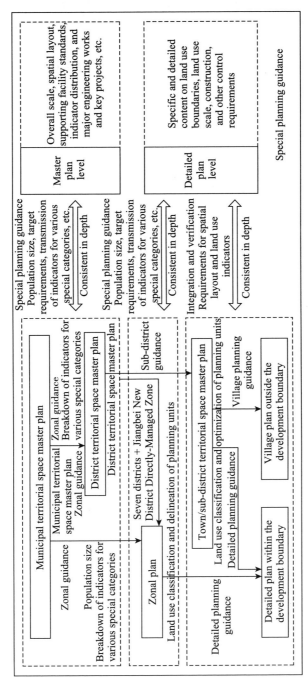

Figure 3 – 1   Schematic Diagram of the Linkage and Transmission Relationship Between Nanjing's Territorial SpaceMaster Plan, Special Plan, and Detailed Plan (Source: Nanjing Bureau of Planning and Natural Resources)

sonnel" to promote deep integration of land supply and planning permits.

Adhering to a development model of "ancient capital prominence, central (urban) area upgrading, sub-city concentration, and new city support", Nanjing plans cluster-style and connotative development for the central urban area and surrounding urban townships. Agricultural production is concentrated in grain production functional zones and important agricultural product protection zones, promoting concentrated and contiguous farmland. The city designs ecological functional areas and green corridor systems with water as the vein, connecting ecological space with urban space and integrating with agricultural space.

Nanjing integrates territorial space planning with historical and cultural city protection, adhering to the principles of "protection first, protecting all that should be protected, activation and utilization, promoting protection through use, combining long-term and short-term goals, and integrated development". Following the approach of "strict management, height control, leaving white spaces, and renewal", the city has improved the protection framework for ancient capital patterns and features, historical districts, ancient towns and villages, cultural relics and historic sites, and intangible cultural heritage. Also, Nanjing integrates territorial space planning with urban renewal, planning a batch of urban renewal demonstration projects using a "small-scale, gradual, micro-renewal" model to jointly plan, build, and share people-oriented, distinctive, and open public service spaces.

II. Coordinated Optimization of Territorial Space Layout

China has established high-standard "three zones and three lines"① designations to scientifically arrange urban, agricultural, and ecological functional spaces, and optimize the spatial pattern of major agricultural product producing areas, key ecological function areas, and urbanized areas. Coordinated delimi-

---

① Three zones and three lines: three types of spatial zones corresponding to urban space, agricultural space, and ecological space, and the three control lines designated for them: urban development boundaries, farmland and permanent basic farmland, and ecological protection red lines.

tation of urban development boundaries, farmland and permanent basic farmland, ecological protection red lines and other spatial control boundaries, as well as various marine protection lines, has strengthened the spatial foundation for national security and development. China strives to achieve intensive and efficient production space, livable and moderate living space, and picturesque ecological space, specifically: Nationwide, China has designated no less than 1.865 billion mu (about 124.33 million hectares) of farmland and 1.546 billion mu (about 103.07 million hectares) of permanent basic farmland, completed the designation of approximately 3.04 million km^2 of terrestrial ecological protection red lines, initially designated about 150,000 km^2 of marine ecological protection red lines, and controlled urban development boundary expansion within 1.3 times the 2020 urban construction land scale.

III. Strengthening Management of Key Ecological Function Areas

China has designated county-level administrative areas that undertake important ecosystem service functions—such as water conservation, soil and water conservation, wind prevention and sand fixation, biodiversity protection, carbon sequestration and oxygen release, and coastal protection—as key ecological function areas. With a focus on protecting the ecological environment and providing ecological products, these areas limit large-scale, high-intensity industrialization and urbanization development and promote overall stability and improvement of natural ecosystems, gradual enhancement of ecological service functions, and continuous improvement in ecological product supply levels. From 2013 to 2023, transfer payments for national key ecological function areas increased from 42.3 billion yuan to 109.1 billion yuan, with cumulative investments of 790 billion yuan, covering more than 800 counties across 31 provinces, autonomous regions, and municipalities.

Case 3-2   Junshan District, Yueyang City, Hunan Province:
Green Development to "Safeguard the
Clear Waters of the Yangtze River"

In October 2024, the Ministry of Ecology and Environment, together with the Ministry of Finance, reported the results of ecological environment quality monitoring and evaluation in national key ecological function areas at the county level for 2023. Junshan District in Yueyang City, Hunan Province, became one of six counties with evaluation results showing "significant improvement". In April 2018, during his inspection in Yueyang, President Xi Jinping left earnest instructions to "safeguard the clear waters of the Yangtze River". Junshan District strictly implements the river (lake) chief and forest chief systems, vigorously carries out special pollution control actions such as "Summer Offensive" and "Dongting Clear Waters", innovatively conducts wetland ecological restoration, and contributes to "Yangtze River governance" through "Junshan's actions".

Wetlands in Junshan District account for 34.79% of the district's total land area. Utilizing its geographical advantage of proximity to Dongting Lake and the Yangtze River, the district has cumulatively restored nearly 60,000 mu (4,000 hectares) of wetlands through measures such as eliminating illegal docks, clearing European and American black poplars, restoring greenery along the Yangtze River shoreline, and planting trees to protect embankments. In July 2022, under the authorization of the Junshan District People's Government, Hunan Junshan State Farm Group completed the research, registration, verification, certification, issuance, and trading processes for Junshan freshwater wetland carbon sinks, becoming the world's first freshwater wetland restoration project to reach the international Verified Carbon Standard and be publicly listed. The project is expected to generate a total income of 46 million yuan over 40 years, benefiting 25 villages, approximately 12,000 households, and 40,000 residents in the project area and surrounding areas. In August 2024, the Junshan Wetland Ecological Carbon Sink Research Center, jointly established by the Junshan District Government and the School of Earth and Space Sciences, University of Science and Technology of China, was unveiled. This is China's first freshwater wetland ecological carbon sink research center, promoting the replication of the "Junshan experience" to the Dongting Lake area and the middle and lower reaches of the Yangtze River.

The Junshan District government has transferred the operation of 14 lakes covering 46,000 mu (about 3066.67 hectares) within its jurisdiction to the district's ecological fishery group, changing the inefficient situation of scattered farming and extensive management in the past. Implementing "lake-specific approaches" for stocking and aquaculture, the district has built modern land-based and water-based fishery infrastructure, launched a digital fishery big data platform integrating real-time video, remote diagnosis, information exchange, disease prevention and control, and project management, and created a national-level aquatics breed center and the largest fishery breeding base in Central China. This achieves the goal of "using fishery to nourish water and using water to protect fishery", with annual fishery output value reaching several hundred million yuan and the brand of "Jianghu Junshan produces good fish" gaining increasing influence. Focusing on "leisure fishery +", Junshan District integrates the development of international wetland scenic areas, urban wild fishing bases, wetland culture research and learning bases, and migratory bird habitat protection and service bases, driving high-value rural tourism with distinctive lake-fresh cuisine and high-quality ecological environment.

Case 3-3 Mengshan County, Wuzhou City, Guangxi Autonomous Region: Leading Diversified Ecological Product Value Realization Pathways with the "Sweet Economy"

As a national ecological demonstration area and national key ecological function area, Mengshan County focuses on green agriculture, new industry, wellness tourism, boutique towns, and people's well-being. The county conducts urban sewage treatment and comprehensive village environment improvement, maintaining an excellent air quality rate above 99%, with all surface water assessment sections meeting or exceeding Class I standards. In the 2022 ecological environment quality assessment of national key ecological function areas at the county level, Mengshan ranked first in Guangxi, and the Mei River basin ecological belt is being rapidly established.

Mengshan County, guided by territorial space planning, has constructed a "3+2" green economic system with three leading industries (silk and sericulture, forest products and forest chemical industry, and longevity foods) and two characteristic industries （characteristic agriculture and health & wellness tourism）. With a forest coverage rate of 82. 87%, over 90 plant nectar sources, and favorable climate conditions, Mengshan County has become a natural base for beekeeping, ranking first in Guangxi in terms of beekeeping scale. The local government provides precise support to beekeepers through methods such as rewards instead of subsidies, post-construction subsidies, enterprise credit sales, cooperative entrusting and raising-based dividends, and follow-up learning. It implements a mechanism whereby "resources become assets, funds become shares, and farmers become shareholders", guiding farmers to invest nectar plant ecological protection forests in village collective economic organizations. Professional companies use collective assets and collective venues to establish honey processing production lines, convert ecological resources into shares and issue share certificates to farmers, achieving "one industry per township" and "one product per village" industrialized operations. Farmers gain income through an "order purchasing+dividend" model.

Furthermore, through "government support + enterprise operation + farmer participation + supply and marketing system+digital empowerment", Mengshan County has built a bee industry chain that integrates breeding, processing, production, research and development, sales, and ecological tourism, with an annual output value of the bee industry exceeding 100 million yuan. Mengshan County promotes the integrated development of "bee+N", builds bee deep-processing industrial parks, collaborates with the Chinese Academy of Agricultural Sciences to develop "smart bee farms", issues traceability codes for bee products, develops green foods and healthcare products such as royal jelly, bee face masks, and bee capsules, and constructs rural tourism carriers like honey-themed villages, bee science and technology museums, and bee-themed towns, thus promoting the upgrading of the bee industry.

IV. Steady and Orderly Comprehensive Land Remediation

China has implemented pilot projects for comprehensive land remediation to protect agricultural patterns, restore ecological foundations, improve the living environment, and support rural revitalization. These include 356 township-based pilot projects in 25 provinces, as well as pilot projects of different scales in Ningbo (Zhejiang), Conghua (Guangzhou), Quanzhou (Fujian), along the Chongzuo-Aidian Port Expressway in Guangxi, and cross-township areas in Zhejiang. In addition, localities have independently launched 892 township-based pilot projects. By the end of 2023, pilot areas had completed comprehensive remediation of 3.78 million mu, resulting in 470,000 mu (about 31,333 hectares) of new farmland and a reduction of 120,000 mu (8,000 hectares) of construction land.

Hengfeng Subdistrict in Wenling City, Taizhou, Zhejiang Province, has a developed private economy but faces tight land resources. Adhering to the concept of "comprehensive remediation, comprehensive prosperity, and comprehensive renewal", it has constructed an urban-rural integrated land comprehensive remediation model. Breaking through village boundary restrictions, the street has revitalized unused construction land such as old rural homesteads, addressed shortcomings in rural infrastructure, unified planning for residential resettlement areas, industrial upgrading areas, and ecological restoration areas, and liberated 23% of rural land for industrial space. Hengfeng Street has introduced an "apartment-style housing + industrial factory buildings" resettlement model, where resettled villagers take on dual roles as "landlords + shareholders", with housing and factory buildings allocated in a 3 : 2 ratio. Factory buildings generate dividends when invested as shares, while residential properties generate rental income. Through improving educational and commercial facilities, optimizing water systems and road networks, creating ecological green corridors, the street has enhanced residents' quality of life.

Conghua District in Guangzhou City, following the principle of "easy things first, classified implementation, and gradual progress", has implemented integrated comprehensive land remediation actions including "field consolidation, river restoration, village enhancement, and industrial revitalization". The district has revitalized and optimized unused homesteads and "hollow villages", implemented comprehensive governance of the Liuxi River Basin, restored mines, and improved forest quality. It has linked natural endowments such as the Aimi Daoxiang Agricultural Park, Fengyun Hill Forest Park, and the South China National Botanical Garden ex-situ conservation demonstration area, and explored a "reserved land investment" model where village collectives invest land and properties for shares. The land is transferred to enterprises for development through rental arrangements, creating ecological design towns, Liuxi Hot Spring Square, and other special parks, and developing waterfront leisure, water sports, river and lake yachting, and other "beautiful water" business formats. This brings village collectives a 10% annual profit dividend, increasing by 10% every five years, forming a "forest-under-the-mountains-and-waters city" ecological economic model of "land appreciation-collective income increase-villager benefit".

Zhangpu Town in Kunshan City, Jiangsu Province, is both an industrial powerhouse and an agricultural stronghold, as well as the town with the largest number of traditional villages in Kunshan City. It has constructed a stock land comprehensive remediation model of "urban-rural integration, comprehensive renewal". In 2024, its regional GDP exceeded 32 billion yuan, attracting more than 800 foreign-funded enterprises and 2,000 private enterprises, with comprehensive strength ranking among the top thousand towns nationwide. Kunshan City has established a leading group for the Zhangpu Town comprehensive land remediation pilot project involving 12 municipal departments. At the town level, detailed working groups have been formed, generating a planning layout map, a project plan package, and a time arrangement table. The town implements integrated projects including river ecological environment remediation, rural idle resource and asset revitalization, infrastructure improvement, and historical culture protection and landscape enhancement. Relying on a cooperation model of "leading enterprises+strong village companies+agricultural bases+specialized farmers", the town uses the land indicators freed up for industrial park construction, promoting the integration of primary; secondary, and tertiary industries and broadening channels for increasing farmers' income.

Section 2 China's Innovative Measures, Main Achievements and Typical Cases in Ecological System Protection and Restoration

I. Regular National Ecological Status Surveys and Assessments

Since the beginning of the 21st century, China has completed four national ecological status surveys and assessments. The results of the fourth survey and assessment show that the national ecological status is generally stable and improving, with the ecological system pattern being stable overall, ecological system quality continuously improving, ecological system service functions constantly strengthening, and biodiversity protection levels gradually increasing. In 2024, China launched its fifth survey and assessment work, scheduled to last two years. From previous ecological status surveys, these assessments examine China's ecological status and its changing trends and spatial-temporal distribution characteristics in different periods, including changes in national ecological system patterns, quality, and functions, as well as the ecological status and changes in national major strategic areas such as the Yangtze River Economic Belt, Yellow River Basin, Beijing-Tianjin-Hebei region, Guangdong-Hong Kong-Macao Greater Bay Area, and Yangtze River Delta region. These surveys provide important support for ecological protection red line delineation and promote the formation of major function zone strategies and the layout of major ecological protection and restoration projects.

II. Scientific Delineation of Ecological Protection Red Lines

China has incorporated areas with extremely important ecological functions, extremely fragile ecology, and potential important ecological value into ecological protection red lines, including optimized and integrated nature reserves, achieving control of important ecological spaces with a single red line. To date, China's terrestrial ecological protection red lines account for more than 30% of the terrestrial national territory. Through delineating ecological protection red lines and formulating ecological protection and restoration plans, China has consolidated the "three regions and four belts" ecological security pattern based on the Qinghai-Xizang Plateau ecological barrier area, Yellow River key ecological area (including the Loess Plateau ecological barrier), Yangtze River key ecological area (including the Sichuan-Yunnan ecological barrier), Northeast forest belt, Northern sand prevention belt, Southern hilly mountain belt, and coastal belt. Furthermore, the ecological protection red line system implemented by China is the first of its kind globally and has been evaluated by the international community as a substantive step in addressing global climate change.

III. Preliminary Establishment of a New Natural Protected Area System with National Parks as the Main Body

China has accelerated the construction of a natural protected area system with national parks[1] as the main body, nature reserves as the foundation, and various natural parks as supplements. Nearly 10,000 natural protected areas of various types and levels have been established, covering more than 17% of the country's terrestrial area. As a result, 90% of terrestrial ecosystem types and 74% of key state-protected wild flora and fauna species are effectively conserved. Additionally, two national botanical gardens have been established in Beijing and Guangzhou, with 14 more candidate national botanical gardens selected and incorporated into the national botanical garden system layout, forming a plant ex-situ conservation system with national botanical gardens as the main body.

In October 2021, President Xi announced at the 15th Conference of the Parties (COP15) to the Convention on Biological Diversity that China had officially established its first batch of national parks, including Three-River-Source, Giant Panda, Northeast China Tiger and Leopard, Hainan Tropical

---

[1] Note: Based on existing protected areas, integrate and establish national parks in regions where the natural ecosystem is most critical, natural landscapes are uniquely distinctive, natural heritage is the most exquisite, and biodiversity is richest—areas that hold global value, serve as national symbols, and enjoy high public recognition. These national parks should encompass large protection zones with complete ecological processes.

Rainforest, and Wuyishan. Building on the first five national parks, China has established 44 national park candidate areas, involving more than 700 existing nature reserves, with a total area of approximately 1. 1 million km^2. China has issued the "Overall Plan for Establishing the National Park System", the "National Park Spatial Layout Plan", and other documents, formulated systems, methods, and standards for national park creation, establishment, monitoring, evaluation, funding, and projects. The country has initially established two national park management systems—direct central management and central entrusting of provincial governments—as well as coordinated linkage mechanisms between central and local governments, departments, and parks, with clear subjects, distinct responsibilities, and close cooperation.

Today, the number of flagship species in national parks continues to grow. For example, chiru have increased to more than 70,000, snow leopards have recovered to more than 1,200, and Northeast tigers and leopards have increased from 27 and 42 at the beginning of the pilot project to about 70 and 80, respectively. The wild population of Hainan gibbons has grown from fewer than 10 individuals in 2 groups 40 years ago to 42 individuals in 7 groups. Ecosystem diversity, stability, and sustainability have steadily improved. For instance, the headwaters of the Yangtze river, Yellow river, and Lancang rivers have achieved comprehensive protection, more than 70% of wild giant panda habitats are protected, and ecological corridors connecting 13 local giant panda populations have been established. Livelihoods have continuously improved, with national parks implementing wildlife damage insurance, ecological resettlement, entrance community and demonstration village construction, concentrated cattle farming, and other livelihood projects. Nearly 50,000 community residents have been employed as ecological rangers, earning an average annual wage income of 10,000 to 20,000 yuan per person.

Wuyishan National Park, spanning Fujian and Jiangxi provinces, is the only national park that is both a World Biosphere Reserve and a World Cultural and Natural "Double Heritage" site, possessing the most complete, most typical, and largest mid-subtropical primary forest ecosystem in the same latitude zone on Earth. Wuyishan National Park has established a two-level management system of "management bureau and management stations", and implemented refined grid management systems such as "forest chief+police chief", procuratorial supervision collaboration, and "negative list". The two provinces have separately issued Wuyishan National Park regulations, and the Wuyishan City Court has established China's first people's court named after a "national park", strengthening specialized and professional judicial protection for Wuyishan National Park. As the birthplace of oolong tea and black tea, Wuyishan National Park explores models such as "tea-forest" and "tea-grass", providing free seedlings to tea farmers, encouraging interplanting of precious tree species such as nanmu, red yew, and ginkgo, and interplanting green manure crops such as Chinese milk vetch, soybeans, and rapeseed according to different seasons. Supplemented by green control technology, these practices maintain tea garden ecological balance and improve tea quality. Wuyishan has created a 251-kilometer National Park No. 1 Scenic Road that links multiple scenic areas and becomes an index map for tourists to explore "Wuyi Culture". In 2023, tourism reception numbers and revenue reached 15. 5 million visitors and 21. 6 billion yuan, respectively.

The National Park of Hainan Tropical Rainforest is China's most concentrated, most diverse, best-preserved, and largest contiguous continental island tropical rainforest. It has established a National Park Research Institute and built systems such as a provincial-level smart management center, smart rainforest big data center, gibbon monitoring platform, and smart visitor service center. The park has set up a "four-in-one" tropical rainforest monitoring system comprising forest dynamic monitoring plots, satellite sample plots, random sample plots, and kilometer grid sample plots. From 2021 to 2024, Hainan Province has conducted Gross Ecosystem Product (GEP) accounting for the Tropical Rainforest National Park for four consecutive years, becoming China's first national park to complete GEP accounting, forming an ecological protection mechanism of "natural resource confirmation-GEP accounting-carbon sink trading-smart management". In July 2024, the Forestry Department of Hainan Province held a tropical rainforest carbon sink trading and project cooperation signing ceremony, marking China's first national park carbon sink trading activity.

Case 3-4   Three-River-Source National Park: Delivering a
Green Response to Protect the
"Water Tower of China"

The three-river-source, located in the hinterland of the Qinghai-Tibet Plateau, nurtures major rivers including the Yangtze, Yellow, and Lancang rivers, earning it the reputation as the "Water Tower of China" and "Source of Rivers". The Three-River-Source National Park is the first national park system pilot project and is currently China's largest and highest-altitude national park with highly concentrated biodiversity, completely incorporating the source regions of the Yellow and Yangtze rivers. In June 2024, during his inspection in Qinghai, President Xi Jinping emphasized: "The top priority is to protect the three-river-source, this 'Water Tower of China', to protect biodiversity and enhance water conservation capacity. We should strengthen the construction of a natural protected area system with national parks as the mainstay, and create exemplary protected areas that are nationally representative and globally influential. "

Institutional Innovation Resolves Protection and Development Bottlenecks

In March 2016, the "Three-River-Source National Park System Pilot Program" was released. In April of the same year, Qinghai Province established a pilot leading group co-chaired by the provincial party secretary and governor, and issued the "Deployment Opinions on Implementing the Three-River-Source National Park System Pilot Program", launching a profound transformation concerning the natural beings of the three-river-source area and the billions of people downstream. To address the drawbacks of segmented management in six categories and 15 protected areas within the pilot scope, Qinghai Province transferred ecological protection management responsibilities dispersed among forestry, land, environmental protection, housing and construction, water resources, and agriculture and animal husbandry departments to the Three-River-Source National Park Administration, completing the historic transformation of "one organization managing everything" in the national park. The province compiled the "Three-River-Source National Park Master Plan" and a "1+5" planning system including ecological protection planning, ecological experience and environmental education planning, industrial development and concession planning, community development and infrastructure construction planning, and management planning. Supporting management measures were issued, building an institutional system of "one standard measuring all", forming the "nine ones"① Three-River-Source ecological protection model.

Integrated Management and Protection of Mountains, Waters, Forests, Fields, Lakes, Grasslands, Deserts, and Ice

With the goal of "overall restoration, comprehensive improvement, ecological health, and functional stability", Three-River-Source National Park has invested more than 30 billion yuan cumulatively, enhancing grassland ecosystems, restoring desert ecosystems, and protecting lake, river, snow mountain, glacier, and wetland ecosystems. Surface water resources have increased by 33.7% compared to the multi-year average, with a net increase of 309 km^2 in water and wetland ecosystem area, and an average increase of more than 6% in water conservation. The park stably delivers nearly 100 billion cubic meters of Class I or better quality water to the middle and lower reaches annually. Grassland coverage and grass production have increased by more than 11% and 30% respectively compared to 10 years ago, wildlife populations have significantly increased, and the ecological environment in key ecological construction project areas continues to improve.

Technology Designing Ecological Blueprints

The Three-River-Source National Park Administration has cooperated with China Aerospace Science and Technology Group and others to build a "space-air-ground" integrated monitoring network covering key ecological areas, achieving "long-distance, large-range, non-contact, all-directional" near-earth real-time monitoring. The park has completed baseline surveys of wild flora and fauna resources, forming for the first time a catalog of terrestrial vertebrate species and drawing detailed distribution maps of dominant mammal and bird spe-

---

① Nine ones: one flag leading, one department managing, one type integrating, one system governing, one household one position protecting, one system monitoring, one team enforcing, one group of forces promoting, one spirit supporting.

cies. The 5G base station at Zhuonai Lake in Hoh Xil has been put into operation, connecting the central area of China's largest and highest-altitude World
Natural Heritage site to the global network via 5G. The Sonam Dargye Natural
Protection Station has achieved stable transmission of "visible light+thermal imaging" 24-hour all-directional video remote monitoring data covering nearly 600
km^2, which provides technical support for dynamically understanding the current status, changes, and habitats of wildlife populations. More than 15,000
ecological rangers have been equipped with the "Ecological Ranger APP", enabling real-time transmission of patrol information.

Coordinated Ecological Protection and Livelihood Improvement

The Three-River-Source National Park Administration has established ecological ranger positions for local herders, provided professional skills training,
and offered financial subsidies of 20,000 yuan per person per year. 23,000 herders have put down their herding whips and taken up certified positions, promptly
photographing or filming unknown animals and transmitting the images back to the
data center. The park has established township protection stations, village protection teams, and protection squads, promoting organized protection and grid
patrolling of mountains, waters, forests, grasslands, lakes, and ice. The park
guides herders to participate in family hotels, herder homes, ethnic cultural performances, and other specialized business projects through various methods such
as investment, cooperative operation, and providing services. Wildlife and livestock conflict management regulations have been introduced, alleviating conflicts
among humans, livestock, and wildlife. Today, local people have taken the ecological path and benefited from ecological development, gradually forming a
beautiful picture of harmonious coexistence between the peoples of the three-river-
source and mountains, waters, wildlife, grasses, and trees.

Case 3-5   Giant Panda National Park: Nationwide Participation
in Enhanced Protection of the
National Treasure's Home

Since the 1960s, China has successively established 67 nature reserves
with giant pandas and their habitats as the main protection objects. The wild gi-

ant panda population has increased from about 1,100 in the 1980s to nearly 1,900 at the time of the fourth national giant panda survey, with the threat level reduced from "endangered" to "vulnerable". In October 2021, China established the Giant Panda National Park in the main habitats of giant pandas across Sichuan, Shaanxi, and Gansu provinces, with a total zoned area of 22,000 km^2, creating an upgraded version of giant panda protection（a biodiversity protection demonstration zone, an ecological value realization pilot zone, and a world ecological education model）.

Collaborative Ecological Protection and Restoration

The National Forestry and Grassland Administration and the governments of Sichuan, Shaanxi, and Gansu provinces have established a bureau-province joint conference mechanism to coordinate and promote work, with the Chengdu Special Commissioner's Office performing the duties of the coordination mechanism office. The three provinces have jointly compiled the "Giant Panda National Park Master Plan（2023-2030）", and the standing committees of the three provincial people's congresses have simultaneously issued "Decisions on Strengthening the Collaborative Protection and Management of the Giant Panda National Park". The high courts of the three provinces have jointly issued "Opinions on Strengthening Judicial Collaborative Protection of the Giant Panda National Park", and public security agencies and Giant Panda National Park management agencies in adjacent areas routinely conduct cross-regional police-park collaboration. Sichuan adopts differentiated classification and dynamic control measures in core protection zones, general control zones, adjacent specific areas, and surrounding related areas. It has also pioneered in China the use of local area networks combined with ultra-short wave transmission and giant panda "face" recognition technology to achieve wireless transmission of wild monitoring real-time images and videos of wild giant pandas. Gansu has formulated "mine-specific" and "station-specific" disposal plans, completing the shutdown, demolition, restoration verification, and compensation cancellation of relevant mining areas and hydropower stations.

Developing Green Industries with Deep Local Resident Participation

Foping County in Hanzhong City, Shaanxi Province has created a "Giant Panda IP", developing tourism routes such as "National Treasure Discovery

Journey", launching creative products like "Xiong Xiaoxin" brand creative ice cream and smart building blocks, and launching the "Foping Panda Journey" online game platform to immersively showcase giant panda culture and Qinling ecological culture. The Tangjiahe National Nature Reserve in Sichuan has jointly established the Tangjiahe-Luoyigou Co-construction and Co-management Committee with the local Qingxi Township government, Luoyigou Village committees, and social organizations. This initiative has eliminated scattered farming, developed eco-friendly industry bases such as ecological planting and understory breeding that pose low threats to wildlife, registered and marketed original ecological products, provided rewards and subsidies to farmers participating in industrial structure adjustment, and moderately developed ecological tourism and wellness tourism. Such co-management, co-construction, and collaborative development of green industries are being widely explored in the Giant Panda National Park.

Flourishing Nature Education Activities

Liziba Village in Longnan City, Gansu Province falls within the jurisdiction of the Baishuijiang Branch of the Giant Panda National Park. In 2023, with the support of the Baishuijiang Nature Reserve Management Bureau and the Wenxian County government, the village formed China's first farmers' voluntary forest patrol team to drive away illegal logging and poaching personnel. Liziba Village signed the "Forest Resource Protection Commitment" with farmers, built a clean energy demonstration village, established a tea cooperative, and distributed ecological protection bonuses. Subsequently, Liziba Village formed a natural education team and established a natural education center, using its own practices as teaching materials to popularize environmental protection knowledge among villagers and tourists. The Liziba Village ecological protection case was selected as one of the "Biodiversity 100+ Global Typical Cases" announced at the NGO Parallel Forum of the 15th Conference of the Parties (COP15) to the Convention on Biological Diversity.

Other regions are also working to develop natural education courses with regional characteristics, becoming highlights of research and study tourism. For example, the Longxi-Hongkou Reserve, located in Dujiangyan City, Chengdu, is the closest national nature reserve to a mega-city. It has launched the

"Panda Classroom" brand, formed panda volunteer and panda lecturer teams, promoted textbook development, curriculum design, creative product development, and base construction, and carried out nature science popularization in school districts, scenic areas, communities, street districts, and mountain areas, becoming a natural education IP. Wenchuan County has developed natural education routes, compiled "Wenchuan Biodiversity Atlas" and "Wenchuan Natural Education Manual of the Giant Panda National Park", launched the Giant Panda National Park natural education Wenchuan area visitor reservation platform, and built high-quality academic exchange platforms, high-level publicity platforms, and high-quality visitor destinations.

Case 3-6 Northeast China Tiger and Leopard National Park: Greener Mountains Welcome the Return of Tigers and Leopards

The Northeast China Tiger and Leopard National Park is located in the southern area of Laoyeling at the junction of Jilin and Heilongjiang provinces. It borders Russia's Leopard Land National Park to the east and faces North Korea across the Tumen River to the south, making it China's only national park undertaking cross-border protection cooperation tasks. This area once had "tigers in every mountain", but a century ago, wild Northeast tigers departed, and their numbers rapidly dwindled. Achieving long-term stable reproduction of Northeast tiger and leopard populations requires not only large connected habitats and complete forest landscapes, but also healthy vegetation structures, rich biodiversity resources, complete food chains, and undisturbed breeding environments. In December 2021, the Northeast China Tiger and Leopard National Park was officially established.

The Northeast China Tiger and Leopard National Park has established a four-level grid protection system of "Management Bureau-Management Branch Bureau-Protection Center-Protection Station", and established judicial cooperation mechanisms with courts, procuratorates, and forest public security bureaus in Jilin and Heilongjiang provinces to routinely carry out special actions such as mountain and trap clearing, anti-poaching, "Green Guard", and "Green

Shield". The park implements the "one household, one position" policy for ecological rangers, recruiting village ecological rangers from park residents, with each household receiving an annual special subsidy of 10,000 yuan. The park includes in its compensation scope personal and property losses occurring within the national park, personal injuries caused by wild tigers and leopards throughout Jilin and Heilongjiang provinces, accidental injuries of ecological rangers during work, and losses caused by non-key protected wildlife. These efforts expand the types of compensable crop damage. Focusing on three major monitoring contents—flagship species, ecosystems, and human activities—the park has developed professional monitoring platforms, achieving real-time monitoring and analysis of data on tiger and leopard activity rhythms, spatiotemporal distribution trends, population activity trends, and distribution heat maps.

Through comprehensive measures, the Northeast China Tiger and Leopard National Park has created a green development miracle of "doubled numbers" of wild Northeast tigers and leopards and "ecological common prosperity" for park residents. It has become one of the regions with the most complete biological chain in China and the best-preserved original state and richest biodiversity gene pool in the same latitude zone of the Eurasian continent.

IV. Orderly Development of Marine Ecosystem Restoration

China treats marine ecosystems as a whole, adopting targeted protection, natural recovery, assisted regeneration, and ecological reconstruction approaches. Since 2016, the central government has supported coastal cities in implementing major marine ecological protection and restoration projects, including the "Blue Bay" remediation initiative, critical battle for Bohai Sea comprehensive governance and ecological restoration, coastal zone protection and restoration projects, and mangrove conservation and restoration. By the end of 2023, a cumulative 25.258 billion yuan in central government funds had been invested, driving the restoration of nearly 1,680 km of coastline and over 750,000 mu (50,000 hectares) of coastal wetlands nationwide.

The Yellow River Estuary Bay Area Coastal Wetland in Dongying City, Shandong Province, is the most complete and youngest warm temperate wetland ecosystem in the world. The local government adheres to a combined approach of systematic treatment methods, such as "mowing plus controlled flooding" and "mowing plus tilling", integrated with long-term management and protection. This involves scientifically ensuring the wetland's water supply, providing long-term care for species habitats by introducing fresh water, restoring wetlands, and creating homes for wildlife, as well as establishing a mechanism for the prevention, monitoring, early warning, and control of alien invasive species. Today, the proportion of good water quality areas in the bay has increased by more than 30% compared to the 13th Five-Year Plan period. The water quality at the Yellow River estuary cross-section has stabilized at Class II, and millions of migratory birds stop and breed here annually.

In the past, due to rising sea levels, storm surges, and reduced sediment flow into the sea, the Beidaihe shoreline experienced erosion and retreat. Qinhuangdao issued the "Qinhuangdao Coastline Protection Regulations" and "Qinhuangdao Seawater Bathing Beach Management Regulations", incorporating marine ecological restoration into the legal framework. The city established a "vegetated dunes-beach shoulder sand replenishment-artificial sand bar-offshore submerged breakwater" beach static equilibrium restoration model to solve problems of difficult maintenance and weak self-restoration capacity in traditional artificial beach nourishment models. High energy-dissipating, strong permeability pebble layering technology was adopted to protect rocky coastal erosion landforms and improve regional disaster prevention and mitigation capabilities. On the foundation of beach restoration, and a strategy that prioritizes "enclosed protection and conservation" supplemented by "biological resource restoration", native plants resistant to salinity and alkalinity and tolerant of sea breezes were selected and planted to construct ecological corridors, thereby improving the population structure of wetland species and enhancing the biodiversity and ecological landscape value of the coastal zone.

Qingdao West Coast New Area is a national-level new area themed on the marine economy. Its 309-kilometer coastline stretches and delineates the landscape, 23 harbors and bays crisscross the area, and 42 islands are scattered like stars, while its 2,129 km^2 of land and 5,000 km^2 of sea area mutually enhance and beautify each other. Focusing on six major tasks—removing illegal buildings, clearing shorelines, adjusting projects, building slow lanes, planting greenery, and preserving culture—Qingdao West Coast New Area implemented the Blue Bay remediation initiative. For instance, the Lingshan Island Marine Ecological Protection and Restoration Project was implemented. This involved carrying out the "5 + 1" engineering initiative, including vegetation community restoration, island stability protection, shoreline protection and restoration, oyster reef restoration, treatment of pollutants entering the sea, and construction of an ecological protection and restoration management platform. As a result, the carbon emission accounting for the Lingshan Island Provincial Nature Reserve was certified by the China Quality Certification Centre (CQC), making it China's first independently carbon-negative region to receive certification from an authoritative body.

Laoshi Village is a small village at the mouth of the Zhubijiang River in Haitou Town, Danzhou City, Hainan Province. The village cleared waste from farming areas, dredged rivers and ditches, restored water system connectivity and water exchange conditions, used ecological filter dams to reinforce ditch banks and riverbanks, planted native plants along rivers to strengthen soil and water conservation functions, transformed traditional shrimp pond farming models into ecological pond and salt field comprehensive utilization methods, converted cleared farming areas into coastal wetlands featuring mangrove wetlands and sand vegetation, and built ecological small islands for citizens and tourists to enjoy water access. The project was included in the list of typical marine ecological protection and restoration cases released by the Ministry of Natural Resources.

Case 3-7   Huanjiang District, Putian City, Fujian Province:
"Blue Carbon Sink Enhancement and Ecological
Restoration" to Cultivate Thriving "Sea Forests"

Known for promoting silt deposition and beach protection, providing windbreaks and dissipating wave energy, degrading pollutants, and regulating climate, mangroves are acclaimed as the "marine green lungs" and "coastal guardians", and are one of the most biodiverse ecosystems. By the end of

2023, China had cultivated about 7,000 hectares of new mangroves and restored about 5,600 hectares of existing mangroves, increasing the total mangrove area to 36,200 hectares, an increase of about 14,000 hectares since the beginning of this century, making China one of the few countries in the world with net growth in mangrove area.

Starting in 2023, bodies such as the Huanjiang District People's Court, Procuratorate and Public Security Sub-bureau established the "Mulan Stream Estuary Wetland Mangrove Protection Zone" at the Mulan Stream estuary to optimize the ecological judicial protection of the Mulan Stream basin. For ecological and environmental resource damage cases where on-site ecological restoration is not possible, the Huanjiang District People's Court guides parties to fulfill their ecological environmental restoration obligations through "afforestation and carbon sequestration" blue carbon alternative restoration methods by planting mangroves through third-party enterprises in the protection zone. To ensure that mangrove seedlings can "gain a firm foothold" in the mud, the Hanjiang District People's Court, during the execution proceedings of the aforementioned cases, introduced an "Ecological Technical Investigator" mechanism. This involves inviting agricultural and forestry experts to participate in the enforcement stage, providing professional opinions on ecological environmental assessment, evaluation, and restoration. This initiative aims to fill the "knowledge gaps" of enforcement judges in the field of ecological technology and to urge third-party companies to improve the survival rate of mangroves planted for restoration. Additionally, for ecological and environmental resource damage cases executed in winter, when it is not an appropriate season for supplementary planting and alternative restoration, the Huanjiang District People's Court used the ecological restoration funds of the case for the elimination and treatment of alien invasive species in the protection zone, thus constructing a "reduction-type" ecological judicial restoration model, which has been promoted by the Supreme People's Court.

Notably, the governance of the Mulan Stream is a pioneering exploration of water treatment work personally outlined and promoted by General Secretary Xi Jinping during his work in Fujian. Guided by General Secretary Xi Jinping's important philosophy on the governance of the Mulan Stream, Party committees and governments at all levels in Putian City introduced a series of policies and measures. They took the lead in conducting special inspections for a single river basin, pioneered the "dual river chief", "corporate river chief", "committee member river chief", and "online river chief" systems for the watershed, implemented the dual compensation mechanism of the "Mulan Stream Basin + Drinking Water Sources"; treated urban pollution sources, dredged and widened river channels, carried out people-centric greening projects, restored natural vegetation, constructed river embankments and railings, laid tree-lined paths along the river, and developed waterfront landscapes and venues, among other efforts. Consequently, the Mulan Stream was transformed into one of China's "Top Ten Most Beautiful Hometown Rivers" and successfully established as a model for green development.

The practice of the Huanjiang District People's Court shows that environmental resource adjudication by people's courts must not only legally punish environmental resource crimes but also uphold the concept of ecological restorative justice, explore diverse restoration methods, and actively guide defendants to restore damaged ecological environments, turning destroyers into guardians.

V. Steady Progress in Major Ecological Protection and Restoration Projects

1. Remarkable results achieved in the integrated protection and restoration of mountains, rivers, forests, farmland, lakes, grasslands, and deserts

China focuses on national key ecological function zones, ecological protection red lines, natural protected areas, etc., and has successively implemented ecological environment restoration and governance projects with significant ecological impacts such as the Three-North Shelter Forest Program, Yangtze River Shelter Forest Program, natural forest protection and restoration, returning farmland to forests and grasslands, mine ecological restoration, "Blue Bay" remediation actions, coastal zone protection and restoration, critical battle for Bohai Sea comprehensive governance, mangrove protection and restoration, thus promoting continuous increases in forest, grassland, wetland, river, and lake areas. Forest coverage rate and forest stock volume have maintained "double growth" for more than 30 years. China is the country with the largest increase in forest resources and the largest area of artificial afforestation in the world. Since 2000, China has consistently been the main force of global "greening", with about 25% of the world's new greening area coming from China. China is the first country in the world to achieve "zero growth" in land degradation and "double reduction" in desertified land and sandy land areas.

Focusing on key areas of ecological security barriers identified in national spatial planning, ecological protection and restoration planning, or ecologically critical areas of global significance, China continues to promote 52 integrated protection and restoration projects for mountains, rivers, forests, farmland, lakes, grasslands, and deserts (Shan-Shui Initiative in China). By the end of 2023, the completed restoration and remediation area exceeded 67,000 km^2. More than 10 provinces (autonomous regions, municipalities) including Jiangsu, Zhejiang, and Hebei have launched provincial-level Mountains-Waters Projects to comprehensively improve the quality of ecosystems in related areas.

Ulansuhai Lake in Bayannur City, Inner Mongolia, is a key core area of China's northern sand prevention belt, an important area for biodiversity conservation in the Yellow River Basin, and an important node on the migratory route of the world bird migration corridor in China. The Ulansuhai Lake Mountains-Waters Project focuses on the path of "repairing mountains-protecting water-expanding forests-protecting grasslands-adjusting fields-treating lakes-stabilizing sand" to restore the structure of the watershed ecosystem and address issues such as damaged governance functions and degradation trends. The reeds in Ulansuhai Lake are annual plants that, if not processed in time, would rot in the lake, then produce carbon dioxide and exacerbate water eutrophication. The aquatic plant resource comprehensive processing project involves professional companies purchasing harvested lake reeds at market prices to produce formaldehyde-free environmentally friendly panels with an annual output value of tens of millions of yuan, replacing timber from forest harvesting and driving the development of local transportation, packaging, materials, service, and other industries.

Fanjing Mountain in Tongren City is the highest peak in the Wuling Mountains, with 97% of its area covered by forests. It is Guizhou Province's premier tourist destination that preserves 7, 925 ancient relict, rare and endangered, and endemic species. Known as the "only oasis" at the same latitude on Earth, it is listed as a World Natural Heritage site and on the IUCN Green List of Protected and Conserved Areas (GLPCA). The Fanjing Mountain Biodiversity Conservation and Restoration Project addresses issues such as wildlife habitat compression, invasive species, and degradation of farmland ecosystems through six projects: ecosystem conservation, ecological function enhancement, river water environment comprehensive remediation, farmland ecological function enhancement, mine ecological restoration, and buffer zone construction in human activity areas. Tongren issued the "Tongren Fanjing Protection Regulations", established collaborative mechanisms for Fanjing ecological law enforcement and resource management, set up a Fanjing Mountain police district and ecological court, preserved local ethnic minority village customs and traditions, deepened integration of culture, sports, agriculture, and tourism, and built a world-class wellness tourism destination with "ecological leadership".

Jinhu National Wetland Park in Zhijiang City, Hubei Province, is the largest natural shallow lake in the middle reaches of the Yangtze River. It has implemented measures such as source pollution reduction, returning fishing to lakes, and water system connectivity, aiming to systematically treat external pollution from discharge points and internal pollution from lake aquaculture. Focusing on restoring the structure and function of the lakeside ecosystem and enhancing its ability to supply ecological products, the shoreline around the lake has been reorganized and restored, and terrestrial protection red lines have been defined around Jinhu. The Municipal River Chief Office reports water quality monitoring results monthly, and the municipal government provides reward and punishment funds to township governments and the Jinhu Wetland Management Office based on the annual water quality compliance rate.

2. Steady progress in ecological restoration of historical abandoned mines

China has introduced incentive measures for mine ecological restoration, driving local government and social investment to accelerate mine restoration in key river basins and regions such as the Yangtze River Economic Belt, Yellow

River Basin, Beijing-Tianjin-Hebei region, Fenwei Plain, and Qinghai-Xizang Plateau. Since 2022, forty-nine demonstration projects for historical abandoned mine restoration have been implemented, completing historical abandoned mine remediation on an area exceeding 4.8 million mu (320,000 hectares), effectively improving the ecological conditions of mining areas and surrounding living environments, promoting economical, intensive, and circular use of natural resources, enhancing the utilization value of abandoned mining land, and playing a leading role in industrial introduction and promoting the transformation and development of resource-based cities.

The ChinaCoal Pingshuo Mining Area is a national billion-ton coal production base, and its Antaibao Open-pit Mine is China's first Sino-foreign cooperation project after the reform and opening up. Pingshuo Group implements the "stripping-transportation-dumping-creation-reclamation" process, applying the concept of "less land occupation, good land creation, quick reclamation, and good utilization" to mine land reclamation. The location and quantity of topsoil dumping for open-pit coal mines are incorporated into the mining production plan, making land reclamation the final step in open-pit coal mining, creating the "Pingshuo Model" of mine ecological restoration for large open-pit coal mines on the Loess Plateau with "mining and restoration occurring simultaneously". Also, Pingshuo Group has built a nursery of nearly a thousand mu, marketing tree seedlings beyond its own use; planted alfalfa on leveled land to provide quality forage for local animal husbandry; and established an ecological garden with 300 solar greenhouses and 16,000 m^2 of intelligent greenhouses, annually producing 3 million kilograms of vegetables, cultivating more than 300,000 flowers, and raising over 4,000 meat lambs.

Ansteel Mining's Dagushan Iron Mine was the first iron mine to resume production in New China. After years of mining, it formed a deep pit with a vertical depth of over 400 meters and a volume of 292 million cubic meters, known as the deepest open-pit iron mine in Asia. Ansteel Mining uses tailings sand mixed with adhesives to backfill the open-pit mine, establishing tailings separation, slurry preparation, slurry transportation, and open-pit drainage systems. The agricultural and forestry land formed through ecological restoration is developed into an ecological park with four functional areas: science education display, fruit picking, vegetable planting, and seedling cultivation. This a-chieves fruit production in two seasons, flower viewing in three seasons, and year-round greenery, forming an ecological restoration model characterized by timely reclamation of mining areas, green mine construction, minimized eco-logical damage risk, and shared use of wastewater.

The Huainan mining area in Anhui Province involves repeated mining of multiple coal seams with a cumulative mining thickness of 30 meters and a maxi-mum subsidence depth of 22 meters, forming a subsidence area of 411, 500 mu (about 27, 400 hectares). The subsidence area is characterized by "large sub-sidence depth, wide subsidence range, long stabilization time, shallow groundwater level, and high water accumulation proportion". The Huainan mining area follows the general approach of "three-color map guidance"①, "three-planning integration"②, and "three-type governance"③, adhering to government-university-enterprise cooperation and industry-university-research integration, promoting innovation in governance models, processes, and tech-nologies. It achieves synchronization of resource extraction and subsidence pre-vention, combining comprehensive governance with rational utilization. Six eco-logical parks have been built, more than 6, 000 hectares of land have been re-claimed, and a 600, 000 kW water surface photovoltaic power generation project

---

① "Three-color map guidance": For unstable subsidence areas with less than 10 years of stability, Huainan Mining uses dynamic maintenance as the main means of remediation and restoration to restore land to a usable state, develop photovoltaics in deep water areas, trial floating rice beds in shallow water areas, plant floating bed rice in shallow waterlogged area and implement dy-namic restoration in non-water-covered areas, thus forming a three-dimensional systematic resto-ration and utilization model.

② "Three-planning integration": For subsidence areas stable for more than 10 years, based on the mining replacement planning, subsidence control planning, and overall spatial planning, coordinated restoration and utilization with rural environmental quality improvement is carried out, implementing road hardening, shore-based regreening, land reclamation, and landscape construction to improve the production and living environment.

③ "Three-type governance": For all stable permanent safe areas within urban planning scope, cultural tourism is developed to provide leisure space for urban residents. For all stable perma-nent safe areas in urban-rural integration areas, facility restoration and landscape enhancement are strengthened to extend the urban radiation range. For all stable permanent safe areas far from towns, infrastructure maintenance and land improvement are carried out to restore land farming functions.

has been constructed. This pioneers a new path for mine ecological restoration through fundamental treatment of permanently safe areas, systematic treatment of areas stable for more than 10 years, and dynamic treatment of unstable areas with less than 10 years of stability.

The East Hope Chongqing Copper Mine Cement Limestone Quarry is located in the heart of the Three Gorges Reservoir area. It innovates with the "stone-electricity symbiosis" and "mining-restoration integration" models, and employs open-pit terraced layered mining technology to build systems such as "cover first, then mine" land cycling and "interception-storage-irrigation" water cycling. This innovative approach involves utilizing stripped topsoil, cave-filling soil, and slope interlayer soil for factory greening and slope regreening. As a result, the region has achieved 100% ecological restoration and reduced carbon emissions by 3.07 million tons annually. To address the low survival rate of vegetation in mine restoration, East Hope Cement Company adopts the "three-year rotation method": planting sorghum in the first year, herbs and shrubs in the second year, and trees in the third year. This method has improved the soil environment and significantly increased vegetation survival rates. The restored effect is basically consistent with the surrounding unmined areas.

Section 3　China's Innovative Approaches, Main Achievements, and Typical Cases in Scientific Large-scale Land Greening Actions

I. Comprehensive Implementation of Voluntary Tree Planting by All Citizens

General Secretary Xi Jinping emphasized that all Chinese people persist in tree planting and afforestation, barren mountains have been adorned with beauty, deserts have been transformed into oases, and these achievements are world-renowned. Greening the motherland requires expanding, developing, and protecting greenery simultaneously, promoting better linkage among forest "water reservoirs, money reservoirs, food reservoirs, and carbon reservoirs". Increasing greenery means increasing advantages, and planting trees means planting for the future. Everyone must take responsibility, smooth channels for public participation, innovate forms of responsibility fulfillment, make good use of the forest chief system, mobilize forces from all aspects, and promote voluntary tree planting to continuously deepen and solidify. In April 2013, comrade Xi Jinping participated in his first capital voluntary tree planting activity after being elected General Secretary of the CPC Central Committee. Since then, every spring, General Secretary Xi Jinping has taken practical action by picking up a shovel and participating in voluntary tree planting activities with the public. This demonstrates leadership by example and expresses determination to adhere to green development. The leaders of the National People's Congress, the Chinese People's Political Consultative Conference, and the Central Military Commission have participated in voluntary tree planting activities collectively. Central and state organs have promoted the construction of economical, green, and beautiful units. In 2024, 137 ministerial-level leaders fulfilled their planting responsibilities, and 93,000 cadres and staff completed 385,000 voluntary tree plantings. All 31 provinces (autonomous regions, municipalities) and the Xinjiang Production and Construction Corps organized provincial-level leadership collective voluntary tree planting activities, and more than 400 prefecture-level cities organized city-level leadership collective voluntary tree planting activities. More than 2,600 "Internet+Voluntary Tree Planting" bases have been established to provide services for age-appropriate citizens to fulfill their responsibilities nearby, at appropriate times, and in diverse ways.

Since the inception of voluntary tree planting by all citizens, Beijing has had more than 110 million person-times fulfilling their obligations through various forms, with a cumulative planting of 220 million trees, increasing the forest coverage rate from 12.83% in 1980 to 44.95% in 2024. Combined with garden city construction, Beijing promotes diversified, normalized, and year-round voluntary tree planting, shifting from seasonal planting to year-round responsibility fulfillment, forming organizational forms such as "spring planting, summer claiming, autumn nurturing, winter protection". Citizens can make online appointments and work offline year-round, or participate through tree adoption, donations of funds and materials, fulfilling their tree planting obligations anytime, anywhere, and as they wish. Citizens are guided to create "one-meter gardens" and "half-meter balconies" and other home gardening scenes in their own courtyards, roofs, walls, gardens, balconies, etc. , which can be converted into voluntary tree planting numbers, realizing "fulfilling obligations without leaving home, adding new greenery in a small space".

Guangdong Province has implemented the "Green and Beautiful Guangdong" ecological construction action, advocating "plant a tree for happy occasions" and calling for "I plant a tree for my hometown", building themed forests such as youth forests, pioneer forests, and women's forests. In 2024, more than 24, 500 voluntary tree planting activities were organized, ranking first in the country in number of planting activities. Using highways, national and provincial roads, railways, etc. , as carriers, ancient villages, historical sites, natural parks, green demonstration points, etc. , are strung together to create an interconnected green ecological network. Guangdong has continuously raised the compensation standard for public welfare forests at or above the provincial level for 17 consecutive years, optimized differentiated compensation for public welfare forests, provided additional incentive compensation of 4 yuan per mu (about 666. 67 m^2) per year for areas with high forest quality and good forest appearance, implemented reward and punishment mechanisms for public welfare forest management and protection, established ecological product value realization incentive mechanisms, and achieved a policy forest insurance participation rate of 66%, with cumulative carbon inclusive certified emission reduction filings of 2. 47 million tons.

Due to terrain limitations, Hunan Province has difficulty finding large flat areas in various cities and prefectures to serve as stable bases for voluntary tree planting activities, making it difficult to meet citizens' needs to fulfill their voluntary tree planting responsibilities entirely through on-site planting. To address this, Hunan Province has strengthened other forms of responsibility fulfillment. For example, citizens can fulfill a certain number of tree planting tasks by participating in tree nurturing and management labor, wildlife habitat protection, desertification prevention and control, returning farmland to forests (grasslands), returning farmland to wetlands, mountain or abandoned land ecological restoration, adopting and protecting ancient and famous trees, building green corridors, donating funds for land greening, and participating in land greening public welfare activities. Some wetland parks, scenic areas, and forest farms offer ticket discounts and priority services for ecological education, nature experience, and forest wellness to holders of voluntary tree planting responsibility certificates.

II. Solid Steps in the Three-North Program Critical Battle

In 1978, the CPC Central Committee made the strategic decision to build large-scale protective forests in the northwestern, northern, and northeastern regions affected by wind and sand hazards and serious soil erosion. The Three-North Program area covers important ecological security regions such as the northern sand prevention belt and northeastern forest belt. It stretches 4,480 km and contains 84% of China's sandy lands, including eight major deserts, four major sandy areas, and vast gobi deserts. It is the area with the harshest natural conditions and most fragile ecology in China. Correspondingly, the Three-North Program area accounts for nearly half of China's terrestrial territory and contains major agricultural product regions such as the Northeast Plain, Hetao Irrigation Area, Hexi Corridor, and Xinjiang Oasis. It is also an important base for "obtaining food from forests and grasslands" and developing and utilizing solar and wind energy resources.

Under the unified command of the Three-North Program coordination mechanism of the State Council, various regions, departments, and central and private enterprises have locked yellow sand and created green forests in desert sandy lands where "yellow sand obscures the sun and birds have no trees to perch on", turning northern borderlands from yellow to green and from green to gold. In the new era, General Secretary Xi Jinping has made a series of important instructions and deployments on strengthening the Three-North Program construction, personally planning, deploying, and promoting three landmark campaigns: the Yellow River "Jiziwan" Critical Battle ("Jiziwan" refers to a Yellow River bend in the shape of the Chinese character "几"), the annihilation battle for the Horqin and Hunshandake sandy lands, and the interception battle along the Hexi Corridor-Taklamakan Desert edge. The Three-North Program has been established as a "number one" project for party committees and governments. Various Three-North regions have successively issued forest chief orders for fighting the Three-North critical battle, coordinating measures such as enclosed protection, afforestation and grass planting, desert vegetation restoration, ecological water diversion, wind power and photovoltaics, and developing green industries such as under-forest economy, Chinese medicinal materials, economic forests and fruits, and desert tourism. To date, the cumulative area treated exceeds 76 million mu (about 5.07 million hectares). Forest coverage in the project area has increased from 5.05% to 13.84%, 61% of the soil erosion area has been effectively controlled, and more than 45% of treatable sandy land has been initially treated. The Program effectively shelters 450 million mu (30 million hectares) of farmland, and 15 million people have achieved stable poverty alleviation through specialized forest and fruit industries, fundamentally realized the historic transformation from "advancing sand and retreating humans" to "advancing green and retreating sand" and built a "Green Great Wall" to resist wind and sand on China's northern border. The Three-North Program has established a Chinese benchmark for sand prevention and control, making China an important promoter and leader in global desertification prevention. The Secretariat of the United Nations Convention to Combat Desertification (UNCCD) praised that the world looks to China for desertification prevention and control.

Case 3-8　　　Yellow River "Jiziwan" Critical Battle: Thickening the "Green Foundation" for High-Quality Development in the Yellow River Basin

The Yellow River "Jiziwan" region spans northern and northwestern China, forming an "S-shaped" ecological region as the Yellow River flows through five provinces (autonomous regions): Gansu, Ningxia, Inner Mongolia, Shaanxi, and ShanxI. It contains deserts and sandy lands such as Kubuqi, Ulan Buh, Tengger, and Mu Us, and is the main source of sediment for the middle and lower reaches of the Yellow River as well as an important sand source area and path affecting sandstorms in Beijing, Tianjin, and eastern regions. Since 1978, the Yellow River "Jiziwan" region has implemented forestry ecological projects such as the Three-North, returning farmland to forests and grasslands, and Beijing-Tianjin sandstorm source control, controlling soil erosion in the Loess Plateau's hilly and gully areas. The average annual soil erosion modulus in the Yellow River Basin has decreased from 8,000 to 12,000 tons per square kilometer to 2,000 to 5,000 tons, and the average annual sediment entering the Yellow River has decreased from 1. 6 billion tons to 242 million tons, achieving "double increases" in regional forest coverage and grassland vegetation coverage and "double decreases" in desertification and sandy land areas.

Subsequently, China implemented the Yellow River "Jiziwan" Critical Battle. For sand problems, the focus is on sand fixation, dust retention, and sand blocking from entering the Yellow River, with differentiated approaches for different deserts and sandy lands. For water problems, the control of flowing sand entering the Yellow River along the riverbanks and the promotion of small watershed systematic management are prioritized. For salinization problems, salt-tolerant forest and grass germplasm resources are cultivated and promoted, and comprehensive governance of saline-alkali land is strengthened. For grassland overgrazing problems, the focus is on restoring "three-type" (degraded, desertified, saline-alkali) grasslands and increasing grazing prohibition efforts. For river and lake wetland protection problems, it is required to ensure that important wetlands along the Yellow River do not shrink in area and strictly control the number and scale of new wetlands.

In May 2020, during his inspection tour in Shanxi Province, General Secretary Xi Jinping pointed out that we must firmly establish the concept that lucid waters and lush mountains are invaluable assets and carry forward the "spirit of Youyu people". Youyu County in Shuozhou City, Shanxi Province, is located on the edge of the Mu Us Desert in the high, cold, and arid area of northwestern ShanxI. "One year of wind blowing from spring to winter, oil lamps lit during the day, doors blocked with soil at night, wind raises yellow sand, nine years of crop failure out of ten" -these few lines of folk rhyme describe the fragile ecology and development difficulties of Youyu County in the past. Following an approach of treating mountains fundamentally, adding greenery to surroundings, achieving prosperity through ecology, and comprehensive protection, Youyu County has made afforestation and ecological improvement a foundational and far-sighted project, treating it as a life and development project for all county residents. One administration has continued the work of the previous one, never interrupting afforestation for more than 70 years. The county developed methods such as the "remove one layer, dig one layer" frozen soil afforestation method and the "dig holes and replace with clay soil" seedling planting method, thus solving the problem of "frozen soil layer restricting afforestation project progress". The greening rate has climbed from less than 3% to 57%, successfully transforming "an area unsuitable for human habitation" into a national ecological demonstration zone.

Looking further, the Mu Us Desert spans four provincial regions—Inner Mongolia, Shaanxi, Ningxia, and Gansu—with a total area of 47,200 km^2. To date, 80% has been greened, showcasing China's iterative upgrading of desertification prevention and control concepts and technical approaches, and the latest achievements leading global desertification prevention and control. At the 13th Conference of the Parties （COP13） to the United Nations Convention to Combat Desertification, the treatment mode of the Mu Us Desert was described as "a miracle in the history of sand control in China and even the world". The Director General of the United Nations Organization to Combat Desertification commented on this: "The world salutes China for its practical experience in controlling the Mu Us Desert. " Uxin Banner in Ordos City, Inner Mongolia, is located in the heart of the Mu Us Desert, with its total territory accounting for about 25% of the total area of the Mu Us Desert. For more than 70 years, Uxin Banner has made controlling the Mu Us Desert its central task. Through practice, it has developed nine models for desert control, prevention, and utilization: zoned rotational grazing, sand enclosure for forest cultivation and grazing prohibition, aerial seeding, small watershed management, family grassland pastures, afforestation households, ecological migration, leading enterprise governance, and agricultural comprehensive development grassland construction. In recent years, Uxin Banner has been fully advancing the battle against desertification in the Mu Us Desert, scientifically delineating "five governance zones" （blocking and locking edges to the east and west, protection and restoration to the east, industrial revitalization to the south, precision management to the west, and desert eradication to the north）. It is developing five "million-mu （about 6,666. 67 hectares） ecological construction bases", which include areas for controlling exposed desert land, restoring degraded forests, improving desertified grasslands, promoting forestry and sand industry as well as shrub processing and utilization, and consolidating and enhancing ecological redline zones. The Banner also promotes the "work-relief" approach to drive low-income rural populations to increase income through sand control. Forest coverage and vegetation coverage have reached 32.92% and 80% respectively, with sandy land significantly reduced.

The Hetao Irrigation District in Bayannur City, Inner Mongolia, has a total of 103,600 irrigation and drainage ditches at seven levels (main canal, trunk canal, branch canal, lateral canal, sublateral canal, farm canal, field canal) with a length of 64,000 km. It is one of China's three extra-large irrigation districts and an important commercial grain and oil base. To better leverage the benefits of farmland shelterbelts, Bayannur City has explored the "canal-forest-road" afforestation model. This model involves planting trees between canals and roads, with forest belts spaced 500 meters apart. Main and auxiliary forest belts are perpendicular, forming a closed network. The belts are 2−3 meters wide, with trees planted at a spacing of 2−3 meters. Native tree species such as Xinjiang Poplar (Populus alba var. pyramidalis) and Xiaomei Drought-resistant Poplar are primarily selected, effectively resolving the conflict between farmers' reluctance to give up land and the encroachment of trees on farmland. Currently, Bayannur City has 360,000 mu (24,000 hectares) of farmland shelterbelts controlling over 10 million mu (about 666,667 hectares) of farmland, basically forming a comprehensive benefit pattern where "fields are square, forests form networks, roads are connected, canals are linked, drought can be irrigated, and waterlogging can be drained".

Shapotou District in Zhongwei City, Ningxia, is one of the direct sand heads of the Tengger Desert entering the Yellow River. In the past, the environment was harsh, the climate dry, and when winds were strong, sand flow directly entered the Yellow River. Shapotou District adopted the straw checkerboard sand control method, arranging rope-like straw checkerboard sand barriers in the desert, using plant root systems to fix sand, reducing sand flow movement, and establishing a "five-belt integrated" railway sand control system (gravel firebreak belt, irrigation afforestation belt, straw barrier plant belt, front sand barrier belt, and enclosed sand cultivation grass belt）. The district developed photovoltaic green energy in the sand control area and applied "forest-photovoltaic complementation" and "agriculture-photovoltaic complementation" technologies to restore and increase vegetation, exploring a new green sand control model of "primarily fixation, combined fixation and interception".

Case 3-9   Saihanba Mechanical Forest Farm in Hebei Province:
A Great Man-Made Restoration Project
Creating Miracles of Green Development

Located in the northernmost part of Hebei Province, Saihanba was once a natural paradise with abundant water, lush grasslands, and dense forests. It was an important part of the Mulan Hunting Grounds, the royal hunting preserve of the Qing Dynasty. Due to land reclamation at the end of the Qing Dynasty, years of warfare, and forest fires, Saihanba's original natural ecosystem was severely damaged. By the founding of New China, the primeval forests had vanished completely, transforming the area into a barren wasteland with raging sandstorms and withered vegetation.

In 1962, the Ministry of Forestry approved the establishment of the Hebei Saihanba Mechanical Forest Farm. Through the efforts of three generations, the world's largest artificial forest was built. All rocky wastelands within the forest farm have been greened, with forest area increasing from 240,000 mu (about 16,000 hectares) to 1.151 million mu (about 76,700 hectares), and forest stock volume growing from 336,000 m^3 to 10,368,000 m^3. Forest coverage increased from 11.4% to 82%, with the unit area forest stock reaching 2.76 times the national average for artificial forests. Nearly 500 million trees have been planted—if arranged at one-meter intervals, these trees would circle the earth's equator 12 times. Biodiversity has been restored, providing 284 million cubic meters of water conservation and freshwater purification annually for the downstream areas of the Luan and Liao Rivers, reducing soil erosion by 5.1355 million tons per year, sequestering 860,300 tons of carbon dioxide annually, and releasing 598,400 tons of oxygen per year. It has become a wind-sand barrier and water source guardian for north China, winning the United Nations' highest environmental honor, the "Champions of the Earth Award", and the highest honor in combating desertification, the "Land for Life Award", becoming a "Chinese model" for global environmental governance.

The people of Saihanba developed full-light seedling cultivation techniques for high-altitude cold regions to nurture high-quality seedlings. They refined comprehensive afforestation technical standards including soil backfilling, film mulching for water conservation, seedling moisture retention, and winter frost protection. They constructed forest structures with multiple tree species and multiple layers, creating mixed coniferous and broad-leaved forests with rich color gradations and varied age structures, gradually bringing the forest stands to a near-natural state. Additionally, the Saihanba Mechanical Forest Farm established an integrated "sky-space-ground" early warning and monitoring system, achieving organic integration of satellites, helicopters, drones, fire detection radar, video surveillance, mountain lookouts, and ground patrols. They also conduct scientific research and application in areas such as larch efficient cultivation technology, remote sensing monitoring, forest wetland resource value assessment, and technical prevention and control of forest pests.

In September 2021, with the approval of the CPC Central Committee, the Saihanba Spirit—centered on "remembering the mission, working hard, and green development" —became one of the first great spirits to be included in the spiritual pedigree of the Chinese Communists. The value of the Saihanba Spirit lies in: First, the sacred mission to green the nation's mountains and rivers. The spiritual strength embodied in the slogan "Revolutionary ideals are higher than heaven" inspired the people of Saihanba to persevere with unwavering tenacity, reclothing the barren land in green. Second, a profound commitment to the people's well-being through windbreak, sand fixation, and water source conservation. Actions like conserving soil and water, blocking wind and fixing sand, and improving the environment vividly embody the Communist Party of China's principle of "everything for the people". The Saihanba Mechanical Forest Farm was established in response to the call of the Party and the people, sounding the clarion call to "reclaim forests from barren mountains and restore our woodlands". Third, an entrepreneurial spirit of meeting challenges head-on and courageously taking responsibility. Afforestation in Saihanba adhered to scientific pragmatism and active exploration. With revolutionary optimism, they tackled key technical problems, formulated standards, and established procedures. They integrated "afforestation and protection" with "ecological utilization", generating an annual total value of 14.58 billion yuan from material products and ecological services (as assessed by the Chinese Academy of Sciences). This has driven income growth and poverty alleviation for local residents, earning Saihanba the honorary title of "National Role Model in Poverty Alleviation".

Case 3-10   The Hexi Corridor-Taklamakan Desert Edge
                 Containment Battle: Creating a Model for
                 Desertification Control in Arid Regions Along
                 the "Belt and Road"

The Hexi Corridor-Taklamakan Desert Edge containment battle area covers four provincial regions: Inner Mongolia, Gansu, Qinghai, and Xinjiang, with widely distributed deserts and gobi, where shifting sand dunes account for approximately 70%. It contains the Taklamakan, Badain Jaran, Tengger, and Gurbantunggut deserts, as well as two-thirds of China's wind-sand passes. It is the region with the most frequent sandstorm activity and the most severe disaster impacts in northern China, and also serves as the throat passage of the ancient Silk Road and the New Eurasian Land Bridge, thus holding a special geographical position and ecological status.

The Hexi Corridor-Taklamakan Desert Edge containment battle focuses on the key objectives of "wind prevention, sand containment, and dust control". By identifying regional wind passes, strong wind intensity and channels, sand intrusion patterns, and gaps in oasis wind-sand protection, it prioritizes treatment of protection forest gaps between the edges of the Taklamakan Desert, Tengger Desert, and Badain Jaran Desert oases. By delineating dust release source areas and tracking transmission paths, the project focuses on controlling wind erosion in major dust source areas by: deploying key projects in key areas, layer by layer and step by step, establishing a framework that combines points, lines, and areas, with multiple corridors and screens interwoven, and comprehensive prevention, treatment, and utilization.

The Taklamakan is the world's second-largest shifting desert. Since 1978, hundreds of thousands of people have been battling day and night on its edges in what can be described as a modern-day "Foolish Old Man Moving Away the Mountains". In November 2024, the 3,046 km Taklamakan Green Sand Control Protection Belt project achieved complete "connection" around the perimeter, becoming the world's longest green ecological barrier around a desert. It effectively prevents further outward movement of the desert, protects surrounding farmland, pastures, and human settlements, reduces the frequency and intensity of sandstorms in the Beijing-Tianjin-Hebei region, and creates favorable conditions for the survival, reproduction, and migration of wildlife in desert areas.

The key to the remarkable success of the Taklamakan Desert control lies in category-specific measures and scientific sand control. In terms of engineering sand control, locals use wheat straw, rice straw, reeds, branches, stones, cotton stalks, nylon nets, and other materials to create straw checkerboard barriers, forming grid-like sand barriers on shifting dunes to increase ground roughness, reducing wind force and blocking sand particles. For biological sand control, grass is grown on the desert edges surrounding oases, tree and shrub combinations are planted in protective forest belts at the forefront of oases, and farmland shelterbelts are established in the interior areas of oases. In terms of photovoltaic sand control, a three-dimensional "forest and grass+photovoltaic" model has been developed, solving the electricity problem for pumping groundwater to irrigate psammophytes, using photovoltaic panels to reduce wind speed, weaken airflow, block wind and sand, improve soil moisture conditions in sandy areas, and inhibit sandstorm occurrence. For intelligent sand control, domestically produced intelligent robots follow preset routes to navigate through deserts, dig holes, sow seeds, and cover soil, with each robot capable of completing dozens of mu (about 666.67 m^2 per mu) of sand greening tasks daily, dozens of times more efficient than traditional manual planting.

The win-win benefits of sand control and prosperity are also gradually expanding. From the bountiful apple orchards of Aksu, to the blossoming rose plantations in Yutian County, to the ecological forests of Xinjiang poplars, tamarisks, and plums standing side by side in Makit County, specialized sand industries are becoming increasingly vibrant. Desert, gobi, and wasteland areas have become strongholds for clean energy development, continuously attracting leading enterprises to develop concentrated, rationally laid-out photovoltaic sand control projects.

III. Continuous Improvement in Urban and Rural Greening and Beautification

1. Steady Progress in Building Beautiful Cities with Harmony Between Humans and Nature

China places the protection of urban ecological environments in a prominent position to promote people-centered new urbanization. Urban construction is guided by existing natural landscapes, water systems, and other unique scenic features to build livable, resilient, and smart cities. The nation is creating National Garden Cities and National Forest Cities, developing urban park systems and greenway networks, and vigorously implementing urban greening. These efforts aim to integrate cities into nature, allowing residents to see the mountains, find the water, and recall their nostalgic connections to their hometowns. From 2012 to 2024, China's urban built-up area greening coverage increased from 39.22% to 43.32%, and per capita park green space rose from 11.8m^2 to 15.65m^2.

Case 3-11   Chengdu: Building a Park City Demonstration Area That Practices the New Development Concept

On the path of Chinese modernization, urban modernization is the "main battlefield". In February 2018, during an inspection of Tianfu New District, General Secretary Xi Jinping pointed out the need to emphasize the characteristics of park cities and incorporate ecological values. In 2022, the National Development and Reform Commission and other departments jointly issued the "Overall Plan for Chengdu to Build a Park City Demonstration Area That Practices the New Development Concept", giving Chengdu the "two new" missions (exploring new practices of harmony between mountains, waters, people and cities, and new paths for the transformation and development of mega-cities),

"three high" requirements (achieving combinations of high-quality development, high-quality life, and high-efficiency governance), and "three demonstration" development positioning (demonstrating cities practicing the concept
that lucid waters and lush mountains are invaluable assets, cities where people
can live and work well, and cities with modern governance).

The concept of "park city" was first proposed in Chengdu, with the core
idea of building a city into a large park, emphasizing the harmonious unity of e-
cology with production and life. Over the past seven years, Chengdu has established a "master plan+special plans+technical guidelines" park city planning
system, solidifying the goals and measures of park city construction through legislation, forming an ecological landscape of "building cities in parks, having
parks in cities, integrating parks and cities, and harmonizing people and cities". It has become China's first sub-provincial city with a permanent resident
population exceeding 21 million and the third with an economic output exceeding 2 trillion yuan, ranking first as the "city with the strongest sense of happiness" for 16 consecutive years.

Thousands of Parks Integrate with the City, Making It Livable and Pleasant.

Chengdu uses the forest chief system as a starting point to implement the
"Five Greens Enriching the City" ecological demonstration project, focusing on
creating the "ecological green lungs" of the Giant Panda National Park Chengdu section, the "urban green heart" of Longquan Mountain Urban Forest
Park, the "vibrant green veins" of Tianfu Greenways, the "super green ring"
of the City Ring Ecological Park, and the "premium green axis" of Jinjiang
Park, consolidating the city's green ecological foundation.

Longquanshan Urban Forest Park has cumulatively increased its green and
scenic areas by 350,000 mu (approximately 23,333 hectares). The regional
forest coverage has risen from 54% to over 60%. Annually, it sequesters over
1. 2 million tons of carbon dioxide and releases over 900,000 tons of oxygen,
becoming a "natural oxygen bar" at the citizens' doorstep and winning the
World Green City Awards 2024.

Chengdu has planned and constructed a Tianfu Greenway system totaling
16,930 km (the world's longest greenway), linking urban green spaces, water

systems, forests, lakes, rivers, and countryside. Over 1,500 parks of various types and more than 9,000 kilometers of Tianfu Greenways have been built, with 3,500+ cultural tourism, sports, and science facilities integrated. This creates a unique landscape with each park having its own theme, characteristics, and story, providing citizens with rich and diverse spaces for rest and entertainment. Meanwhile, Chengdu has launched the "Tan Hui Tian Fu" green public welfare platform. This platform incorporates green travel, garbage sorting, Clean Plate campaign check-ins, low-carbon reading, and other green scenarios into the platform's incentive points system, guiding citizens to practice green lifestyles.

Ecological Orientation, Making the City Suitable for Business and Commerce

Entering the core area of Tianfu New District, the most eye-catching feature is Xinglong Lake with birds flying and fish swimming in shallow waters. An 8.84 km lakeside greenway connects parks, communities, commercial districts, and industrial parks. Under the guidance of the park city concept, Tianfu New District has compressed the scale of production land, increased the proportion of ecological space, preserved more than 80% of the original landscape, arranged industrial spaces along rivers and green areas, and attracted 26 national scientific research institutions and more than 1,000 high-tech enterprises. Looking further, the park city demonstration area is accelerating Chengdu's construction as a strong manufacturing city. Through implementing the actions of "optimizing quality, establishing distinctive parks, empowering and increasing efficiency, and filling parks with enterprises", it eliminates low-end industries and cultivates green leading industries such as biomedicine, aerospace, rail transit, artificial intelligence, robotics, low-altitude economy, hydrogen energy, cultural creation, tourism, and health care, reshaping this central western city's advantages for sustainable development.

2. Emergence of Green Ecological Livable and Harmonious Villages

China uses green development as a new engine to promote rural revitalization, strengthening ecological protection and restoration, continuously improving the rural living environment, comprehensively advancing rural greening, enhancing the protection and utilization of traditional villages, inheriting outstanding traditional culture, actively developing ecological agriculture, rural e-commerce, leisure agriculture, rural tourism, health care, and other new business forms, improving rural infrastructure completeness, public service convenience, living environment comfort, and civilization reputation, presenting a beautiful picture of clear waters, blue skies, green land, and harmonious villages throughout rural areas.

Quanzhou City in Fujian Province has established a coordination mechanism for pastoral landscape construction, with the Municipal Party Committee's Rural Affairs Office taking the lead and coordinating departments including agriculture and rural affairs, water resources, natural resources and planning, housing and urban-rural development, development and reform, culture and tourism, forestry, transportation, and others to jointly advance the work. They strengthen regional coordination, work coordination, and fund coordination through "three coordinations", emphasize contiguous construction, integrated development, and three-dimensional advancement through "three emphases", and establish a "headquarters leadership + state-owned enterprise construction + policy financing + fiscal subsidies" ecological protection facility construction and operation mechanism. They conduct "four beauty" construction—beautiful rivers, beautiful countryside, beautiful villages, and beautiful economy—and establish evaluation mechanisms for metrics such as completion rate of comprehensive river management, coverage rate of high-standard farmland, completion rate of bare house renovation, and growth rate of village collective operating income, transforming the ecological foundation of "mountains, waters, roads, and human settlements" into distinctive agricultural tourism scenic routes.

Xiabiaoyuan Village in Qinghe Community, Qushi Town, Tengchong City, Yunnan Province, is located within a world biosphere reserve (Gaoligong Mountains) and a national volcanic natural reserve. The village Party branch organized Party members and villagers to consult and determine the green village development approach of "self-design, using local materials, turning waste into treasure, and maintaining rural character". Farmer artists created distinctive rural-themed paintings on existing walls, Gleditsia sinensis trees (soapberry trees), and chimneys. Using stones, wood, and plants sourced from local fields and roadsides, they constructed an ecological sightseeing corridor along the cliff edge and an agri-tourism leisure corridor within the village. Villagers are guided to repurpose discarded items such as pig troughs, winnowing baskets, windmills, stone mills, and earthenware jars into decorative landscape features. Furthermore, villagers have voluntarily donated over 3,000 pots of bonsaI. These efforts have fostered a strong atmosphere of supporting and loving the Party and cultivated a beautiful and refreshing village environment, leading to its successful establishment as a national AAA-rated tourist attraction and a Green and Beautiful Village.

Fogang County in Qingyuan City, Guangdong Province, has launched greening activities in "four sides" (house sides, village sides, road sides, and water sides). It is also enhancing the quality of greening and beautification along the "five edges" (mountain edges, water edges, road edges, town and village edges, and scenic area edges). By fully utilizing measures such as the "Three Clearances, Three Demolitions, and Three Rectifications"① initiative, the county is constructing beautiful courtyards and increasing the overall green coverage in its villages. "Harmony" is based on "tourism suitability". Fogang County's Shijiao Town has created the "Mountain and Water Painting Dragon" rural revitalization demonstration belt, linking modern agricultural bases, "Field Green World" scenic spots, landscape greenery, and supporting service facilities such as homestays to create a comprehensive countryside complex integrating sports and leisure, cultural experiences, agricultural experiences, and agricultural sightseeing.

Dongtumen Village in Bailuquan Township, Luquan District, Shijiazhuang City, has launched "big cleaning" and "moving-style" environmental sanitation comprehensive cleaning special actions to clear accumulated garbage from

---

① Three Clearances, Three Demolitions, and Three Renovations: "Three Clearances" refers to clearing village lanes and production tools, building materials haphazardly piled up, clearing weeds and miscellaneous objects and accumulated garbage in front of and behind houses and in village lanes, and clearing silt, floating objects, and obstacles in ditches, ponds, streams, and rivers; "Three Demolitions" refers to demolishing dangerous and dilapidated houses, abandoned pig and cattle pens, and outdoor toilets, demolishing unauthorized structures and illegal buildings, and demolishing illegal commercial advertisements and signs; "Three Renovations" refers to renovating random garbage disposal, renovating random sewage discharge, and renovating water pollution.

streets and alleys, with the number of beautiful courtyard households reaching over 85%, earning recognition as a premium beautiful village in Hebei Province. The village implements Party member grid management, front-door three guarantees for environmental sanitation, and a building deposit system to maintain the results of harmonious village construction. The village guides villagers to contribute land as shares, introduces social capital to create the Tumen Pass Postal Road Small Town, and builds areas where villagers can start their own businesses, developing "tourism+" new business forms, providing stable employment for more than 350 villagers, steadily increasing village collective economic income, and earning recognition as a tourism characteristic village in Hebei Province.

Shuoliang Town in Tiandong County, Baise City, Guangxi adheres to Party building leadership, Party member demonstration, and full participation, forming the "four driving forces, five melodies playing together, six governance approaches"[①] comprehensive "456 model" of planning, consultation, construction, sharing, and co-management. All administrative villages have formulated "Village Regulations and Agreements", established repair and maintenance of garbage transfer pools, hired cleaners to conduct grid-based clean village actions, and gathered resources from all parties to participate in living environment maintenance through "six points"[②], redesigning and utilizing vacant lots, abandoned sites, and dilapidated houses within the village, turning waste into treasure, planting greenery in empty spaces, and sketching a new picture of harmonious villages with pleasant village scenery, affluent lives for the people, thriving industries, and a pleasant ecological environment.

---

① "Four forces" refers to branch leadership force, Party member pioneering force, Party-mass linkage force, and hometown elite assistance force; "five melodies" refers to regulations, cleaning, collection, beautification, and protection; "six governance approaches" refers to moral governance, legal governance, self-governance, smart governance, clean governance, and co-governance.

② "Six points": Seeking some fiscal investment, injecting some social capital, raising some collective economic funds, contributing some labor from the masses, supporting some from supporting units, and competing for some through competitions.

Section 4　China's Innovative Measures, Main Achievements, and Typical Cases in Promoting the Realization of Ecological Product Value

I. Innovative Advancement of Ecological Product Value Realization Mechanism Pilots

Beginning in 2021, the Ministry of Natural Resources selected 10 cities and counties in 6 provinces—Jiangsu, Fujian, Shandong, Henan, Guangdong, and Chongqing—to carry out pilot mechanisms for realizing the value of ecological products in the natural resources field. In May 2024, the National Development and Reform Commission established the first batch of national pilot mechanisms for realizing the value of ecological products[1], encouraging pilot areas to explore government-led, enterprise and society-participated, market-operated, and sustainable paths for realizing ecological product value over three years. To date, pilot areas have formed three typical paths for realizing ecological product value: externality sharing type, empowerment value-added type, and quota trading type[2].

In December 2024, Beijing's Yanqing District completed the city's first GEP compensation and reward fund disbursement of 20 million yuan. In 2016, Yan-

---

[1]　Note: The first batch of national pilot mechanisms for realizing the value of ecological products includes Yanqing District in Beijing, Chengde City in Hebei Province, Daxing'anling Region in Heilongjiang Province, Huzhou City and Lishui City in Zhejiang Province, Huangshan City in Anhui Province, Nanping City in Fujian Province, Fuzhou City in Jiangxi Province, Yantai City in Shandong Province, Huaihua City in Hunan Province, Guilin City in Guangxi Zhuang Autonomous Region, and Shangluo City in Shaanxi Province, totaling 12 cities and districts.

[2]　Note: Externality sharing type is aimed at ecological products that are difficult to divide and confirm rights, where the government purchases or compensates through transfer payments, financial subsidies, and other methods. Empowerment value-added type is aimed at ecological products for which natural resource property rights or powers can be clearly defined (or expanded), with ecological value reflected in the empowerment and value addition to resource products through market transactions. Quota trading type is aimed at ecological products that need total amount control for utilization or protection, converting non-standardized ecosystem services into standardized quotas (or indicators) through legal or administrative means, realizing their value through market trading of quotas.

qing District established a special group for ecological civilization system reform and collaborated with a Chinese Academy of Engineering team to carry out GEP data accounting. Later, referring to Beijing's pioneering ecosystem regulatory service value (GEP-R) accounting method (the first in the country), the district's total GEP for 2023 was finally calculated at 49. 86 billion yuan, representing the highest growth rate among Beijing's ecological conservation areas. Sihai Town, located in the deep mountains of Yanqing, had nearly 40% of its villages with weak collective economies in early 2022. The town introduced an ecological rights transaction model of "lucid waters and lush mountains usage fees", with each homestay paying 10, 000 yuan per year to the village collective, putting a price on the mountains, streams, and economic crops that villagers carefully protect. Following a model of village grouping, town-village joint operation, villager shareholding, and enterprise investment, the town has created flower sea night markets and the "Small Stream Dudu" agricultural-cultural-tourism complex. All villages with weak collective economies have shed this label, with 50% of villages achieving annual collective incomes exceeding 500, 000 yuan.

Heilongjiang Province's Daxing'anling Region has a forest coverage rate of 86. 26%, serving as an important ecological barrier and green gene bank in northern China. Chinese Academy of Forestry expert team calculations show the ecological product value of Daxing'anling's forests, wetlands, and grasslands reaches 802. 144 billion yuan per year. Since 2021, the Daxing'anling Region has accelerated exploration of ecological product value realization paths in cold temperate zone areas, conducting natural resource rights confirmation surveys, ecological product directory compilation, forest carbon storage and carbon change measurement, formulation of local standards for GEP accounting, trial calculation of total ecological product value, and layout of forest understory economy, characteristic cultural tourism, new energy, and other ecology-led industries. The region is creating a regional public brand for Daxing'anling ecological products, establishing an ecological product traceability system, and premium-selling ecological products that are included in the ecological product directory and meet ecological product certification standards, with a hundred-billion-level forest understory industry cluster taking shape.

Shangluo City in Shaanxi Province, located in the heart of the Qinling

Mountains, is "China's Climate Health and Wellness Capital". It simultaneously evaluates ecological asset stock and ecological product flow, considers ecological product supply and utilization simultaneously, and promotes the synchronous association of "ecological assets-ecological product supply-ecological product utilization-ecological product value". Using increased income for the masses, increased benefits for enterprises, and revenues for the government as standards, it has constructed a "five-by-four" ecological product value realization system[①], built a climate ecological monitoring center and big data display platform, developed business systems for ecological value assessment, high-impact weather warnings for mountainous scenic areas, dynamic ecological environment monitoring, ecological health and wellness, and other services, achieving a "one-map" display of Qinling climate ecological big data, and developing green industries such as "meteorology+tourism", "meteorology+health and wellness", and "meteorology+research and learning".

Case 3-12   Lishui City, Zhejiang Province: Ecological Product Value Realization Mechanism Reform Making Lucid Waters and Lush Mountains "Produce Gold and Silver"

China's first township and village-level GEP accounting, first land transfer including GEP appreciation, first large-scale public institution activity carbon neutrality transaction, first batch of green financial innovation products such as "ecological credit loans" and "ecological collateral loans" ...These are the achievements of Lishui City's ecological product value realization mechanism reform.

---

① "Five-by-four" ecological product value realization system: "Four key points" are ecological products, value, realization, and mechanism; "four major attributes" are material supply, cultural services, regulatory services, and finance; "four forms of expression" are market realization for material supply products such as agricultural specialty products, market and government purchase realization for tourism health and public service products, government compensation and policy-based trading market realization for fully public products and quasi-public products respectively, and financial market realization for financial attributes based on security property rights; "four difficulties" are accounting difficulty, trading difficulty, monetization difficulty, and mortgage difficulty; "four types of long-term mechanisms" are top-level design, mechanism construction, typical cases, and work effectiveness.

Institutional innovation, quantifying value

In August 2019, Lishui City issued technical methods for ecological product value accounting, forming technical processes, indicator systems, and accounting methods for ecological product function quantity and value accounting. Subsequently, Lishui City established a leading group for ecological product value realization mechanism reform, established a four-level (city, county, township, village) dual accounting, dual assessment, and dual evaluation mechanism for GDP and GEP, compiled natural resource asset balance sheets, implemented a fiscal reward and compensation mechanism linked to ecological product quality and value, and expanded "GEP into planning, into decision-making, into trading, into assessment, into monitoring, into projects, into finance, into justice, into ecological damage compensation" and other "nine into" application scenarios.

Based on GEP accounting, Lishui City established government procurement and market-oriented trading mechanisms for ecological products. Relying on city and county state-owned enterprises," Two Mountains Cooperatives" were established, and "Ecological Prosperity Village Companies" were formed in townships (subdistricts), becoming operating entities for dispersed ecological resource collection and storage. Following the principles of "four unifications" for ecological product collection and storage, trading, investment attraction, and services, the city established the province's first regional ecological product trading center, constructed platforms for ecological resource asset development operation services and ecological product market-oriented trading, and completed various ecological resource, ecological product, and green property rights transactions totaling over 5.8 billion yuan. Thus, by establishing ecological product value accounting and trading mechanisms and clarifying ecological product prices, Lishui City formed "one account" for green development.

Ecological credit, value realization

Lishui City pioneered China's ecological credit system, compiling positive and negative lists of ecological credit behaviors from five dimensions: ecological protection, ecological management, green living, ecological culture, and social responsibility. It set up application scenarios such as exchanging ecological credit points for daily items and incentives for trustworthiness, and provided "ecological credit loan" services linked to ecological credit, with financial institutions within the city offering preferential policies in loan amounts, interest rates, and processing procedures to borrowers with good ecological credit. The city launched "ecological collateral loan" products using future income rights of GEP, national park forest land easement income, public welfare forest compensation income rights, forest rights, water withdrawal rights, and other collateral. These initiatives aim to use ecological credit as collateral, transform ecological resources into assets, and further convert these assets into capital. As of the end of June 2024, the balance of "ecological collateral loans" reached 32. 555 billion yuan.

**Case 3-13   Nanping City, Fujian Province:" Forest Eco-Bank"
Realizing Ecological Product Value**

Nanping City in Fujian Province has established a "Forest Ecological Bank · Four Ones" forestry shareholding cooperative management model, forming pathways to realize ecological product value through cultivating new forms of "Water Beauty Economy", enhancing the brand value of "Wuyi Mountain and Water", trading forestry carbon sink products, and comprehensive land development. Forest coverage has increased to 78. 89%, the proportion of Class II and above high-quality water in main streams and small watersheds has increased to 100%, air quality remains among the best in the country, and the total emissions of major pollutants and carbon emission intensity continue to decline, with green momentum growing stronger.

Nanping City has built village-level forest resource operation platforms, figuratively described as "Forest Eco-Banks", which gather non-forested land and forested land scattered among individual households into the "Forest Eco-Bank", integrate and package them into concentrated and contiguous resource packages, and rely on the technical and management advantages of state-owned forest farms (forestry enterprises) for scale management and professional operation. The "Forest Eco-Bank" calculates the total amount of guaranteed income for shareholding cooperative management of non-forested and forested land, issues equity certificates to each forest farmer on a household basis, with the equity in the hands of forest farmers equivalent to fixed "deposits" stored in the "Forest Eco-Bank", allowing them to receive "savings interest" according to the cooperative agreement. The "Forest Eco-Bank" adopts a revenue distribution model of "guaranteed income + annual dividend + main harvest dividend", and solves the problems of long forestry production cycles and forest farmers' low short-term income, with benefits 30% higher than individual forest farmer management.

Each county (city, district) builds a county-level forest land and forest stock resource database, achieving "one-key search" for key data such as forest resource site quality, stand conditions, resource ownership, understory space, and management income, providing support for market-oriented investment and management of forestry. Taking Shaowu City as an example, forest understory spaces that meet the conditions for developing understory economy and have circulation willingness are registered for storage, entered into the "Forest Eco-Bank", and a forest understory space resource database is established. Following the model of forest rights certification, a "forest understory space management right certificate" sub-directory is added to the real estate system, issuing "forest understory space management right certificates", and launching "Fulin · Forest Understory Management Right Loan", solving the problem that "understory economy operators who are not forest rights certificate holders find it difficult to obtain credit support".

II. Broadening the Transformation Pathways of Nationally owned Resources Assets

China uses pilot mechanisms for the commissioned agency of ownership rights of eight types of natural resource assets owned by all people (including natural ecological spaces) —land, minerals, oceans, forests, grasslands, wetlands, water, and national parks—as entry points, guiding localities to explore paths and methods for multi-element allocation of natural resource assets, promoting the combined allocation of usufructuary rights for "land+" and "water domain+" and other resource assets, and promoting the efficient use and value appreciation of natural resource assets.

Ningxia Autonomous Region has constructed a natural resource asset reporting framework system with "resource+asset", "physical quantity+value quantity", and "special report+report system" as core contents, built a dedicated
management information system, and compiled inventory, accounting, and
balance sheets of natural resources assets owned by all people covering the entire region, providing data support on physical attributes, value attributes, and
value quantities for the transformation of natural resource assets. The "Rice-
Fish Space" primary-secondary-tertiary industry integration project in Helan
County has completed the iterative upgrade from traditional cultivation to three-
dimensional cultivation and breeding of rice, fish, crabs, and ducks, and
further to the integration of primary, secondary, and tertiary industries through
land consolidation, using fish to treat alkaline soil, circular farming, and unified prevention and control measures. Ningxia government departments commissioned professional assessment institutions to reassess the land price of state-
owned agricultural land used by Ningxia Agricultural Reclamation Group according to current land prices, optimizing the group's capital structure through capital contribution assessment and capital increase, significantly reducing its as-
set-liability ratio and continuously increasing total assets.

Jiujiang City in Jiangxi Province has explored a path for combined supply
of natural resource assets: "rights confirmation and registration-assignment of
responsibilities-full-element reserve and empowerment-overall assessment-market
mechanism-green finance-innovative distribution-protection and restoration".
The city has compiled a list of natural resources for which the Jiujiang municipal
government acts as an agent in fulfilling the ownership responsibilities of natural
resource assets owned by all people, clarifying "who manages what" for natural resource assets, and incorporating them into the "one map" management of
spatial planning to clarify "what exists" and "how much exists" of natural resource assets. A natural resource asset rights confirmation information database
has been established to clarify "where" natural resource assets are located.
Package marketable natural resource assets with market demand into high-quality "asset packages" to solve the challenge of "how to allocate" natural resource assets. Establish natural resource asset protection and value conversion
centers, centralizing the rights of natural resource "asset packages" to a single

entity through collection, redemption, leasing, and other methods to solve the problem of "multi-headed reserves" of natural resource assets. Build a publicly owned natural resource asset trading system to achieve multi-category, one-stop, full-process online trading of natural resource assets.

Section 5   Long-term Stability: China's Experience in Shaping Green Development Spatial Patterns and Its Implications for Developing Countries

I. Optimizing National Land Space Development and Protection Pattern

China's first national-level territorial spatial plan incorporating the "integration of multiple plans" —the "Outline of the National Territorial Space Planning (2021-2035)" —has been issued and implemented. The preparation of local general plans, detailed plans, and special plans at all levels is being promoted in a coordinated manner. The "five-level, three-category" land spatial planning system has made decisive progress, and a unified, clear in responsibility, scientifically efficient national land spatial planning "one map" has generally taken shape. In particular, the "three zones and three lines" as the core content and important component of land spatial planning, represents the spatial bottom line for ensuring and maintaining national food security, ecological security, and healthy urbanization development, contributing "China's solution" to other countries in handling the relationship between humans and nature, development and protection. China has innovated policy measures such as comprehensive land remediation, redevelopment of inefficient urban land, linking the increase and decrease of urban and rural construction land, and market entry of collective operational construction land. By strictly controlling total volume, revitalizing existing resources, optimizing structure, and improving efficiency, China promotes the economical and intensive use of land, mineral, marine, and other resources. By learning from and applying the experience of the "Green Rural Revival Program", China enhances the quality of human settlements, protects and inherits traditional culture, and forms a closed-loop process of "resource-asset-capital-fund-protection and restoration", thus constructing a comprehensive pattern of protection, restoration, and governance of land space from mountaintops to oceans.

II. Integrated Protection and Restoration of Mountains, Rivers, Forests, Farmlands, Lakes, Grasslands, and Deserts

China follows the concept of mountains, rivers, forests, farmlands, lakes, grasslands, and deserts as a life community, constructing a cross-departmental, cross-regional, and cross-watershed ecological protection and restoration system. This achieves a transition from single-element to systematic governance, from engineering measures to natural restoration, from end-of-pipe treatment to whole-chain management, and from reliance on fiscal funds to diversified investment. China has established a natural protected area system with national parks as the main body, effectively planning, constructing, managing, supervising, protecting, and restoring cross-administrative region, large-scale natural spaces. National parks implement zoned control, with strict management in core protection areas and development of suitable green industries in general control areas, allowing contemporary people to enjoy beautiful homes with blue skies, green land, clean water, and birds singing among flowers, while leaving valuable natural heritage for future generations. China promotes greening, flourishing, and protecting greenery simultaneously, strengthening nationwide mobilization, participation of all people, and involvement of the whole society in tree planting. National land greening has shifted from "quantity growth" to "quality improvement".

From the experience of the "Three-North" Program, we can learn the following lessons: first, balancing water with greenery, and adjusting water with greenery to construct a dynamic balance between water resources and large-scale, high-density artificial afforestation, and to reconstruct a healthy circulation network of "precipitation-surface water-groundwater-ecological water use" in arid areas; second, spatial optimization, exploring composite land resource utilization, reserving sufficient space for ecological construction, and achieving spatial efficiency through methods such as forest-field inlays; third, coordination between heaven and humanity, grasping the balance point between artificial intervention and natural restoration, and establishing a positive mechanism of "short-term artificial intervention for foundation building, long-term natural restoration for efficiency enhancement".

III. Ecological Product Value Realization Broadens the Transformation Path of "Lucid Waters and Lush Mountains are Invaluable Assets"

The flourishing of plants and trees constitutes the wealth of a nation. China has constructed ecological product value accounting systems, ecological product price systems, and ecological product trading systems according to local conditions, enhancing the supply capacity of ecological products and transforming the ecological products and services contained in lucid waters and lush mountains into realistic environmental productivity. Establish regional natural resource survey and monitoring systems, clarify resource bases, and carry out natural resource rights registration and empowerment. According to characteristics such as public welfare and commercial nature, comprehensively plan matters such as natural resource asset reserves, allocation, value realization, and revenue management. Form subject-clear, boundary-clear combined targets and overall allocation mechanisms, promote combined supply and value realization of natural resource assets, and advance more efficient ecological industrialization and industrial ecologicalization.

Section 6　Policy Recommendations for Further Optimizing Green Development Spatial Patterns from the Perspective of Chinese-style Modernization

I. Constructing a New Pattern of National Land Space and Protection and Development Oriented by the Rational Utilization of Natural Resources

1. Optimize National Land Space Planning, Protection, and Development

Continuously conduct "three-in-one" natural resource surveys, monitoring, and early warning of quantity, quality, and ecology, improving the ability to identify and respond to ecological conditions in key areas. Improve the ecological restoration planning system at county and township levels, systematically plan the 15th Five-Year Plan for special action plans such as mountain and water governance, mine restoration, marine restoration, and mangrove protection and restoration. Conduct monitoring and evaluation of the implementation of national land spatial planning, implement the natural ecological space use control system, and maintain the seriousness of the "three zones and three lines" delimitation results. Based on resource and environmental carrying capacity and the suitability of national land space development, implement the main functional area strategy. Deeply implement the strategy of "storing grain in the land and technology", ensure that all existing farmland is delineated and protected, resolutely curb the "non-agricultural use" of farmland, and strictly control "non-grain use". Guide key areas such as metropolitan areas and urban agglomerations to form multi-center, group-style urban spatial forms, promote compact layout of small and medium-sized cities, and prevent disorderly urban sprawl. List areas that currently have no human activity and have potential important ecological value as strategic blank spaces, and develop them prudently to cope with future uncertainties.

2. Steadily Promote Comprehensive Land Remediation in All Areas

Based on national land spatial planning, with the county (city, district) as the coordinating unit and the township as the basic implementation unit, scientifically and reasonably determine the areas and promotion routes for comprehensive land remediation in all areas. Simultaneously improve the ecological, production, and living environments of rural areas, promote the integration of primary, secondary, and tertiary industries in rural areas, and build beautiful villages suitable for living and working. Focus on micro-adjustments to plots with scattered layout, incomplete supporting facilities, and inconvenient farming, to achieve no reduction in the quantity of cultivated land, improvement in quality, and ecological improvement. For cultivated land already included in the ecological protection red line, permanent basic farmland surrounded by the ecological protection red line, and original scattered construction land, implement supplementary balance and optimization according to procedures. Actively revitalize "hollow villages", idle rural homesteads, abandoned industrial and mining land, and other scattered, inefficient, and idle construction land, consolidating small pieces of stock land into large plots. Strengthen the protection and restoration of ancient towns, ancient streets, and other heritage sites to preserve hometown nostalgia and charm, and strengthen the introduction of green industries such as agriculture, culture, and tourism.

II. Coordinated Promotion of Integrated Protection and Restoration of Mountains, Rivers, Forests, Farmlands, Lakes, Grasslands, Deserts, and Seas

1. Highlight the "China's Landscape" Project Brand

Adhere to natural restoration as the main approach and artificial restoration as supplementary, scientifically deploy and continuously implement mountains and waters projects, adapt measures to local conditions and time, implement source governance, systematic governance, scientific governance, and standardized governance, and construct a scientifically reasonable urban and rural ecological pattern. Comprehensively evaluate completed "China Mountains and Waters" projects, and summarize and promote mature experiences. Categorically and orderly build green mines, improve list-based dynamic management and supervision mechanisms, strengthen the upgrading of green and low-carbon technology processes and equipment, strictly manage third-party assessments, and promote production alongside governance. Promote the construction of beautiful bays and beautiful islands with "land-sea coordination + river-sea linkage + one bay (island) one policy", strengthen the protection and restoration of comprehensive ecological systems such as estuaries, bays, islands, and typical ecological systems such as salt marshes, and maintain the diversity, stability, and sustainability of marine ecosystems. Improve biodiversity survey, monitoring, assessment, and protection systems, and strengthen the prevention and control of invasive alien species.

2. Construct a "China Solution" for National Park Ecological Protection and Restoration

Formulate a National Park Law, determine the national park authority and its responsibilities, stipulate the institutional mechanisms for the creation, establishment, planning, construction, and management of national parks, and strengthen coordination and cooperation among multiple departments and regions. Accelerate the pace of national park creation and establishment. Establish a "sky-ground-earth" integrated ecological monitoring and early warning system "one account", to achieve data sharing and unified management of various types of natural protected areas. Construct a governance pattern of "park-locality linkage, co-construction and sharing, and ecological compensation", and enhance the effectiveness of community and resident participation. Establish ecological compensation mechanisms such as commercial forest redemption, easement management compensation, ecological management positions, wildlife damage compensation and insurance claims by zone and category, and innovate ways to transform ecological product values.

3. Steadily Promote the Deep and Solid Implementation of the "Three-North" Program

Focus on key areas such as the three major symbolic battle areas, carry out joint prevention, control, and treatment of key areas, and achieve comprehensive governance of sand, water, and mountains. Promote effective sand control models, establish a cross-departmental joint review mechanism for key projects, and implement closed-loop management throughout the process of project reserve, construction, and monitoring and evaluation. Construct a diversified construction and operation mechanism with investments from governments at all levels as the main body, and broad participation from state-owned enterprises, state-owned forest farms, and social institutions. Implement the "list champions" mechanism to guide domestic and international scientific and technological forces to participate in the Three-North Program and jointly break the scientific and technological code of "desert becoming oasis". Adhere to the integrated planning of sand control effects and water resource conservation, and promote advanced technologies such as barrier sand control, photovoltaic sand control, film water conservation, and shrub cutting. Vigorously publicize and promote the "Three-North Spirit" and Saihanba Spirit, and use exemplary power to mobilize more forces to participate, telling the Chinese story of sand prevention and control.

III. Holistically Building a Long-term Mechanism for Ecological Product Value Realization

Establish county-level ecological resource databases and ecological product lists, determine the timing, methods, scale, and purposes of natural resource asset allocation with unified rights and responsibilities orientation, explore methods such as collection and storage, leasing, exchange, and equity participation, and guide the rights registration, empowerment, rational layout, and efficient allocation of natural resource assets. Improve the national standard system for ecological product value accounting, and quantify the economic value and spatiotemporal distribution characteristics of various ecological products. Layout professional trading markets and online trading platforms, innovate value realization paths such as natural resource rights trading, ecological product mortgage loans, ecological protection compensation, natural resource asset damage compensation, natural resource asset accounts, green product futures and options, and green insurance, allowing reasonable returns for protecting lucid waters and lush mountains. Construct mechanisms for the industrialized operation and development of ecological products, and scientifically develop and utilize renewable marine energy, geological heritage, geothermal energy, mineral water, and other natural resources. Establish risk prevention mechanisms to control natural risks, market risks, policy risks, and other risks in ecological product trading.

Chapter 4

High-Quality Development: China's Measures, Achievements, Experiences, and Recommendations for Green and Low-Carbon Transition

In September 2020, President Xi Jinping made a major declaration at the general debate of the 75th United Nations General Assembly that China would strive to peak carbon dioxide emissions before 2030 and achieve carbon neutrality before 2060. The CPC Central Committee has incorporated carbon peaking and carbon neutrality into the overall layout of ecological civilization construction and the overall economic and social development. In January 2024, General Secretary Xi Jinping emphasized in his speech at the 11th collective study session of the Political Bureau of the 20th CPC Central Committee: "Green development is the foundation of high-quality development, and new quality productive forces are themselves green productive forces." Promoting the green and low-carbon development of the economy and society is a key link in achieving high-quality development. In grasping the dialectical unity of high-quality development and high-level protection, China adheres to the new development concept of innovation, coordination, green, openness, and sharing, promoting deep adjustment of industrial structure through rigid constraints of resources and environment, continuously optimizing industrial spatial layout through strengthened regional collaboration, changing the traditional production and consumption mode of "mass production, mass consumption, and mass emissions", and promoting development to achieve effective quality improvement and reasonable quantity growth in green transformation.

Section 1 Innovative Measures, Main Achievements, and Typical Cases of China's Green and Low-Carbon Energy Transition

I. Accelerated Construction of a New Energy Supply System

Under the guidance of the new energy security strategy of "Four Revolutions and One Cooperation"[①], China adheres to establishing first and breaking later, planning as a whole, and on the basis of continuously enhancing energy supply guarantee capacity, accelerates the construction of a new energy system, walking out an energy transition path that conforms to national conditions and adapts to the requirements of the times. In 2024, China's clean energy consumption ratio reached 28.6%, an increase of 13.3 percentage points compared to 2013, with coal consumption ratio cumulatively decreasing by 14.5 percentage points; total installed power generation capacity reached 3.35 billion kW, and the proportion of non-fossil energy power generation installed capacity to total installed capacity was 58.2%. Over the past decade, newly added clean energy power generation has accounted for more than half of the total increase in social electricity consumption, continuously enhancing the "green content" of China's energy.

In terms of clean and efficient utilization of fossil energy, China aims to promote clean and low-carbon development of coal power, building safe, intelligent, green, and modernized coal mines, carrying out energy-saving retrofits for coal power, implementing stricter energy-saving standards for new coal power units, achieving world-leading levels in power generation efficiency and pollutant emission control. The average coal consumption for power supply in coal power has decreased to 303 g of standard coal per kWh, and the emission levels of sulfur dioxide and nitrogen oxides from advanced units are comparable to the

---

① Four Revolutions and One Cooperation: "Four Revolutions" refers to energy consumption revolution, energy supply revolution, energy technology revolution, and energy system revolution; "One Cooperation" refers to energy cooperation.

limits for natural gas power units. China promotes the replacement of coal with natural gas, electricity, and renewable energy in end-use energy consumption, actively advances clean heating in northern regions during winter, orderly promotes the efficient use of natural gas in urban gas, industrial fuel, gas power generation, transportation, and other fields, develops combined cooling, heating, and power generation with natural gas, builds green oil and gas fields, promotes the transformation and upgrading of the petroleum refining industry, implements special actions for upgrading the quality of refined oil products, achieving a "triple upgrade" from National III to National VI standards, walking the path of refined oil quality upgrading in less than 10 years that developed countries took more than 30 years to accomplish.

Case 4-1　　　Technological Innovation in Carbon Capture[①]
at Qilu Petrochemical: Achieving Win-Win
in Petroleum Production Increase and
Carbon Emission Reduction

Most oil is stored in the pores and fissures of rocks, previously mainly driven out by water, but low-permeability oil has very tight rocks that water cannot enter. Therefore, using carbon dioxide for oil displacement while simultaneously sequestering it has become a relatively mature technology in China. In July 2023, the high-pressure normal-temperature dense-phase carbon dioxide transportation pipeline with one million tons of transportation scale, 100 km of transportation distance, and one hundred kilograms of transportation pressure built by Qilu Petrochemical, the first of its kind in China, was put into operation. It reduces carbon dioxide emissions by more than one million tons annually, equivalent to planting nearly 9 million trees or about 600,000 economy cars not operating for a year. Over the next 15 years, it is expected to sequester tens of millions of tons of carbon dioxide and increase oil production by 3 million tons.

Carbon dioxide is tail gas generated during normal production at Qilu Petrochemical's Second Fertilizer Plant. Through micro-innovations such as

---

① Carbon Capture: Separating carbon dioxide from industrial production, energy use, or the atmosphere for storage and utilization, achieving permanent emission reduction.

model workshops and labor competitions, they solved problems such as the un-economical operation of the carbon dioxide compressor anti-surge system and frequent clogging of filters due to the use of carbon dioxide raw materials for dry gas sealing, forming a carbon dioxide capture technology system adapted to the enterprise, namely: Carbon dioxide is cooled, compressed, recovered, and purified to become liquid with a purity of over 99%, and then transported to Shengli Oilfield for utilization and storage, achieving safe green production effects of increased capacity, decreased water content, and increased production.

Compared to oil pipelines, the design, construction, and safe transportation of carbon dioxide pipelines present higher difficulties. Qilu Petrochemical's scientific and technological personnel have independently innovated to overcome multiple core technologies. For example, they have developed China's first low-temperature liquid-phase carbon dioxide pipeline transmission centrifugal booster pump and high-efficiency carbon dioxide dense-phase normal-temperature high-pressure reciprocating injection pump, two key equipment pieces, increasing the design pressure of the carbon dioxide transportation pipeline to 12 MPa, e-quivalent to a thumbnail-sized area bearing a weight of 120 kilograms; using corrosion-resistant stainless steel materials as key components and adding slow-release agents in well bores to effectively prevent carbon dioxide corrosion of injection and production strings.

Looking further, as the world's largest producer of coal power, steel, and cement, China's promotion and application of carbon capture technology in scenarios such as coal-fired power plants, gas-fired power plants, cement kilns, chemical plants, and natural gas processing can avoid high stranded costs caused by the premature retirement of large amounts of infrastructure under carbon constraints. Additionally, China's offshore carbon dioxide geological storage potential is enormous, with basin-level storage potential reaching 2.58 trillion tons.

In developing non-fossil energy, China has the world's largest installed capacity of renewable energy power generation and the fastest development speed, achieving the goal promised at the Climate Ambition Summit that "by 2030, China's wind power and solar power installed capacity will reach more than 1.2

billion kW" six and a half years ahead of schedule. China is accelerating the construction of large-scale wind and photovoltaic bases focusing on desert, Gobi, and wasteland areas, developing offshore wind power in clusters, and extensively building distributed new energy sources such as urban and rural rooftop photovoltaics and rural wind power. Also, it is promoting the upgrading and transformation of large hydropower stations and green transformation of small hydropower, with conventional hydropower installed capacity exceeding 370 MkW and nearly 4,000 small hydropower stations completing upgrading. China is adhering to the use of the most advanced technology and the strictest standards to develop nuclear power and maintain safe and stable operation of nuclear power units in operation over the long term. The first batch of units of "Hualong One", China's indigenous third-generation nuclear power technology representing the "China Card", has successively been put into operation, achieving breakthroughs in comprehensive utilization of nuclear energy such as clean heating and heat supply. Moreover, China is developing new energy conversion of agricultural and forestry biomass, biogas, urban domestic waste, and other sources according to local conditions, and building a number of centralized heating projects with geothermal energy as the main source.

In promoting the coordinated development of traditional energy and new energy, China is constructing a new type of power system adapted to the gradually increasing proportion of new energy, steadily implementing wind-photovoltaic-hydro (storage) integration and wind-photovoltaic-thermal (storage) integration in resource-rich areas, building new energy power generation projects in coal mine industrial sites, coal mining subsidence areas, idle power plant spaces, oil and gas mining areas, and other areas, developing offshore wind power to provide green electricity for oil and gas platforms, and building oil-gas-electricity-hydrogen integrated comprehensive transportation energy service stations at traditional gas stations and filling stations.

The six large hydropower stations of Wudongde, Baihetan, Xiluodu, Xiangjiaba, Three Gorges, and Gezhouba are arranged from upstream to downstream along the main stream of the Yangtze River, thus forming the world's largest clean energy corridor that spans more than 1,800 km, with a water level drop of over 900 meters, and a total of 110 hydro-turbine generators in operation, the vast river water brings rolling green electricity. As of the end of 2024, the cumulative power generation has exceeded 3.8 trillion kWh, equivalent to saving more than 2.89 billion tons of standard coal and reducing carbon dioxide emissions by more than 3.04 billion tons. The Yangtze River Basin is China's strategic water source for water resource allocation, with an average annual water resource volume of 995.9 billion cubic meters, accounting for about 36% of the national total, forming a cascade reservoir group with a total storage capacity of 91.9 billion cubic meters and a strategic freshwater resource reservoir. The comprehensive benefits of shipping smoothness, water resource security, ecological protection, and others are released, with ecological regulation covering areas such as promoting fish reproduction, layered water temperature adjustment, preventing water blooms, reservoir sand discharge and siltation reduction, and inhibiting excessive proliferation of submerged plants, powerfully promoting ecological protection and restoration in the Yangtze River Basin.

Sonid Right Banner in Xilingol League, Inner Mongolia, is a typical desert and semi-desert grassland pastoral banner, which both relies on animal husbandry to seek rural revitalization and needs to prevent environmental risks brought by "grassland overgrazing". BOE Energy Technology Co., Ltd. implemented the "200,000 kW pastoral-photovoltaic-storage + sand control comprehensive demonstration project" with a total investment of about 930 million yuan. Since the project's commissioning, photovoltaic power generation has reached 810 MkWh, reducing carbon dioxide emissions by about 500,000 tons. The project raises the photovoltaic support frame, leaving sufficient space for sheep activities, achieving the complementarity of "power generation above the panels, grazing below the panels". The energy storage system uses lithium iron phosphate material for battery cells, which has high energy density, fast charging and discharging speed, and numerous charging and discharging cycles. Through joint optimization and dispatch operation of "photovoltaic and storage", it solves problems such as low comprehensive efficiency of similar power systems and insufficient coordination among "source-grid-load-storage" links. The photovoltaic modules form a physical barrier, reducing surface exposure and water evaporation, blocking wind and fixing sand, improving the plant growth environment under the panels, and achieving "power generation above the panels, restoration below the panels" for sand control. Under rows of blue photovoltaic panels, the once desolate vast yellow sand has been rejuvenated and transformed into an "energy oasis". As one of the top ten enterprises helping Inner Mongolia's rural revitalization through Beijing-Inner Mongolia collaboration, BOE Energy's exploration of the collaborative development model of "photovoltaic+energy storage+sand control+breeding" for ecological restoration and industrial revitalization has been emulated and replicated by local governments and surrounding areas.

By the end of 2024, Minning Town in Yongning County, Yinchuan City, Ningxia, built a "pure green electricity town" with 24-hour green electricity supply capability to replace coal power with a new type of energy storage system of "generation, storage, transmission, use", becoming a "catalyst" for local rural revitalization. Affected by the external environment, new energy power supply has large fluctuations. The project company developed a source-grid-load-storage control system, storing excess electricity during daytime when photovoltaic generation is high, and supplementing electricity at night with wind power and energy storage complementing each other, forming the economic benefit of "storing surplus to supplement deficiency" for new energy. Through self-built regional power grids with seamless on/off-grid switching and off-grid operation capabilities, reliable power supply and regional energy security are ensured. Using the "village collective+enterprise+farmer" model, rooftop photovoltaics are built for villagers, who receive annual roof rental fees, promoting the transformation to green production and lifestyle. Abundant green electricity resources provide energy security for modern industries such as intelligent manufacturing, deep processing of agricultural specialty products, and facility agriculture in Minning Industrial Park.

China's offshore wind power resources are abundant, with high power generation hours, proximity to power load centers, and sufficient consumption space. The technically developable volume of near-sea wind energy resources at 150 meters height exceeds 1.5 billion kW, and that of deep and distant sea wind energy resources exceeds 1.2 billion kW. China's offshore wind turbine design and manufacturing system is complete. For example, the 26-megawatt offshore wind turbine independently developed by Dongfang Electric is the world's largest single-capacity, longest rotor diameter fully domestically produced offshore wind turbine, with key component technologies such as generators, blades, bearings, and electronic control systems reaching world-leading levels. The LHD tidal current energy power station in Zhoushan, Zhejiang Province, has achieved megawatt-level high-power stable grid connection. The world's largest single-capacity tidal current energy generator "Fenjin" has a total grid-connected electricity exceeding 4.78 MkWh, with continuous operation time ranking among the international forefront, driving the clustering and development of upstream and downstream industries such as marine ranching, marine equipment manufacturing, special materials, transportation, marine engineering, power distribution, and comprehensive seawater utilization.

In March 2025, China's largest nuclear energy heating commercial demonstration project, State Power Investment Corporation's "Nuanhe No. 1", completed the task of the sixth heating season, ensuring clean and warm winters for 400,000 residents in urban areas of Haiyang City, Shandong Province, and Rushan City, Weihai, saving 480,000 tons of raw coal consumption, reducing emissions of 880,000 tons of carbon dioxide, 5,676 tons of sulfur dioxide, and 5,366 tons of nitrogen oxides, equivalent to the clean effect of 5 million trees in one year. "Nuanhe No. 1" nuclear energy heating achieves zero-carbon heat source intercommunication and sharing between two cities, creating a new commercial heating model of "nuclear power plant+government platform+long-distance pipeline company + heating company". Its principle is to extract some steam that has done work from nuclear power units as a heat source, exchange heat multiple times under physical isolation, and deliver heat to residents' homes through municipal heating pipelines. In this process, there is only heat transfer, no material exchange. The heating company also adds radiation monitoring, emergency management, and other measures to ensure safe and reliable heating.

Case 4-2   Beijing Municipal Administrative Center: Green and
Low-Carbon Energy Transition Promotes the
Construction of a National Green Development
Demonstration Zone

Planning and building Beijing Municipal Administrative Center is a major decision made by the CPC Central Committee with Comrade Xi Jinping at its core. General Secretary Xi Jinping has made important instructions on the planning and construction of Beijing City Sub-Center many times. The "State Council's Opinions on Supporting the High-Quality Development of Beijing Municipal Administrative Center" clearly proposes to build a national green development demonstration zone, contributing to the construction of a harmonious, livable, and beautiful capital of a great nation. The "Implementation Plan for Building a National Green Development Demonstration Zone in Beijing Municipal Administrative Center" emphasizes exploring replicable and promotable implementation paths and promotion models for green development and low-carbon transformation. In recent years, Beijing Municipal Administrative Center has taken the lead in the city in carrying out comprehensive evaluation pilots for energy use and carbon emissions, establishing a mechanism for green electricity consumption, with renewable energy utilization ratio higher than the city average, renewable energy heating area of nearly 4 million m^2, registered photovoltaic installed capacity exceeding 150 megawatts, and 100% green electricity coverage in the administrative office area and urban green heart park.

While providing leisure space for citizens and improving the urban environment, the urban green heart park also generates carbon emissions in irrigation and maintenance, transportation, daily office, park lighting, building air conditioning, and recreational facilities. To this end, the park achieves regional "greening" through the construction of ground source heat pump energy stations, distributed photovoltaic, water energy storage, and other facilities, and promotes regional "carbon reduction" through building greening, transportation electrification, smart energy management, and carbon asset management, aiming to achieve comprehensive "zero carbon" in the region by 2025.

In terms of low-carbon energy supply, the urban green heart park fully excavates and utilizes local renewable energy: First, the three landmarks of the urban green heart park (Beijing Performing Arts Center, Beijing Library, and the Grand Canal Museum of Beijing) and supporting buildings, built to three-star green building standards for public buildings, all use ground source heat pump systems as energy sources, with heat pump-based energy stations carrying more than 80% of the park's heating, reducing carbon dioxide emissions by 12,000 tons annually; second, rooftop photovoltaics are installed in the urban green heart park, constructing AC/DC microgrids, and adopting the strategy of "self-generation and self-use, surplus electricity to the grid", achieving priority use of photovoltaic power generation for building electricity use. Carrying out green electricity trading pilot demonstrations to increase the supply and consumption proportion of renewable energy in the region through external purchase of green electricity; third, old factory buildings are renovated according to two-star standards for public buildings, updated into multifunctional complexes for public services, cultural exhibitions, sports and leisure, etc. All shuttle cars, sightseeing cars, small freight vehicles, cleaning vehicles, patrol vehicles, etc. in the park are configured as electric vehicles, and charging piles are set up at 20% of the parking spaces in public parking lots, guiding car owners to charge in an orderly manner during off-peak hours.

The urban green heart park develops an energy and carbon management intelligent platform with energy consumption data as the core, accessing energy consumption data from energy stations, water use, gas use, etc. within the domain, conducting multi-dimensional data intelligent analysis, achieving centralized optimization of regional energy use, and real-time tracking of regional carbon emissions through the method of converting electricity to carbon. The urban green heart park, in conjunction with the Tongzhou District Power Company and the Capital Carbon Monitoring Service Platform, has created a carbon asset management service platform, forming an "electricity-carbon map" of the park, establishing a carbon credit mechanism, and promoting carbon inclusive applications.

Case 4-3   Xinjiang: Building a National Large-Scale Green
Hydrogen Supply and Export Base

Hydrogen energy is a clean, efficient, renewable, and cyclically usable energy source with advantages such as diverse sources, wide applications, and high energy density. Xinjiang possesses high-quality photovoltaic and wind power resources, with a cumulative new energy installed capacity of 50. 89 MkW, accounting for 41% of the total grid installed capacity. Combined with abundant coal and other mineral resources, it has outstanding advantages in green hydrogen production and scenario application. In June 2023, China's first ten-thousand-ton level green hydrogen refining project, Sinopec Kuqa 20, 000-ton green hydrogen demonstration project, successfully produced hydrogen. This project connects the entire process of green hydrogen production and utilization including photovoltaic power generation, green electricity transmission, green electricity hydrogen production, hydrogen storage, hydrogen transportation, and green hydrogen refining. It reduces carbon dioxide emissions by 485, 000 tons annually, creating a new path for deep decarbonization in China's chemical industry.

To accelerate the development of the hydrogen energy industry, Xinjiang has issued frequent policies. In 2023, Xinjiang released the "Three-Year Action Plan for Hydrogen Energy Industry Development in the Autonomous Region (2023-2025)" and "Several Policy Measures to Support the Construction of Hydrogen Energy Industry Demonstration Zones in the Autonomous Region", designating Urumqi City, Karamay City, Hami City, and Ili Prefecture as the first batch of hydrogen energy industry demonstration zones. In the same year, Xinjiang initiated the establishment of a hydrogen energy industry development alliance. In March 2024, Xinjiang issued the "Notice on Accelerating the Development of the Hydrogen Energy Industry", pressing the "fast forward button" for creating an industrial ecology. For example, it allows the construction of renewable energy electrolysis water hydrogen production projects and hydrogen production and refueling stations outside chemical industrial parks; renewable energy electrolysis water hydrogen production projects do not require dangerous chemical production safety licenses.

Since then, Xinjiang's hydrogen energy industry development has been on a fast track. For example, Kaijiangyun Energy Co., Ltd. has deployed hydrogen energy express delivery special vehicles in Tianshan District, Urumqi City, which are the same size as electric tricycles, and the replaced hydrogen cylinders are stored in special cabinets where delivery personnel can input passwords to take out and replace hydrogen cylinders. The Karamay hydrogen energy storage peak-shaving power station developed by Source Grid Load Storage New Energy Technology (Shanghai) Co., Ltd. converts green electricity generated by photovoltaic into green hydrogen through water electrolysis, and then generates electricity through green hydrogen fuel cells, producing 360 MkWh of green electricity annually, providing zero-carbon heating for 480,000 m^2.

From practice, hydrogen energy vehicles are more cold-resistant, making them more suitable for Xinjiang's cold winter weather. As hydrogen energy scale expands, costs decrease, and industry chains connect, the application scenarios for hydrogen energy in Xinjiang will become increasingly widespread, and it is expected to be one of the first to build a cross-regional industrial cluster integrating green hydrogen production, storage, transportation, refueling, and use.

Case 4-4 Virtual Power Plants: A New Green Energy System Solution Moving from Concept to Scale Application

Virtual power plants are a new type of resource aggregation business entity that does not actually produce electricity, but rather uses information and communication technology and software systems to aggregate distributed photovoltaic power, dispersed wind power, new energy storage, and adjustable loads and other power resources to form a virtual centralized energy system. They monitor, analyze, and intelligently control dispersed energy resources in real time to achieve efficient energy utilization and dynamic balance of supply and demand, becoming a key pillar for achieving carbon neutrality goals.

In December 2021, China's first integrated grid-and-local virtual power plant management platform—the Shenzhen Virtual Power Plant Management

Platform—was launched. In August 2022, Shenzhen established China's first virtual power plant management center, located at the Southern Power Grid Shenzhen Power Supply Bureau. The Shenzhen Virtual Power Plant Management Platform uses energy internet technology to gather distributed power resources such as charging piles, air conditioners, and photovoltaic systems, which are numerous, widespread, and individually small in capacity. It optimizes the control of power loads during specific time periods and provides multi-period trading functions, serving as a "cloud bridge" between users and the main power grid. As of March 2025, it has implemented power load adjustments 101 times, adjusting more than 5.6 MkWh of electricity. Based on Shenzhen's average household annual electricity consumption of 3,500 to 4,500 kWh, this is equivalent to the annual electricity consumption of 1,500 households, effectively reducing carbon emissions by approximately 4,681 tons.

In July 2024, Chongqing launched the first provincial-level virtual power plant platform in central and western China, building a demand response resource pool of 2.8 MkW. It can dynamically adjust the scale of power demand response for connected enterprises according to shortfalls during summer peak periods. The Chongqing virtual power plant platform adopts a "1+N" operation method, namely: Building one unified virtual power plant operation service platform for the entire city to provide resource access, qualification review, operation monitoring, capability verification and other services for N virtual power plants such as charging and battery swap facilities, cold storage, telecommunications towers, building air conditioning, and distributed rooftop photovoltaic systems, achieving "unified management, unified control, and unified service" of virtual power plants across the city.

II. Steady Progress in Green Energy Consumption and Energy Efficiency Improvement

China has established green power certificates as the sole credential for energy-consuming units to consume green power and the only proof of environmental attributes. Green electricity consumption is used as an important basis and content for evaluating, certifying, and labeling green products, guiding the whole society to prioritize the use of green energy and the procurement of green products and services, and encouraging qualified enterprises to form low-carbon and zero-carbon energy consumption models. The 2022 Beijing Winter Olympics and the 2023 Hangzhou Asian Games both achieved 100% use of green electricity. China has made energy intensity reduction a binding target and is transitioning to dual control of carbon emissions. From 2013 to 2023, through comprehensive measures, China cumulatively saved about 1.4 billion tons of standard coal in energy consumption, reducing carbon dioxide emissions by about 3 billion tons. The industrial sector strongly promotes technical energy conservation, management energy conservation, and structural energy conservation, promotes advanced energy-efficient products, eliminates backward production capacity, and promotes production process innovation, process reengineering, and intelligent upgrading. From 2013 to 2023, the energy consumption per unit of added value in industries above designated size cumulatively decreased by more than 36%. China implements energy conservation and carbon reduction retrofits in high-energy-consuming industries and promotes large and medium-sized enterprises in key industries to reach world-advanced energy efficiency levels. China has established systems for energy conservation review and energy conservation supervision of fixed asset investment projects, and launched energy conservation and low-carbon actions for ten thousand enterprises, key energy-using units, and energy efficiency "leader" initiatives. China promotes "one-stop" comprehensive service models including energy conservation consulting, diagnosis, design, financing, renovation, and trusteeship. The annual output value of the energy conservation service industry exceeds 500 billion yuan, doubling compared to 2013.

According to statistics from the China Association of Building Energy Efficiency, the construction energy consumption in the building industry accounts for 22.8% of the total national energy consumption, and accounts for 48.3% of the national energy-related carbon emissions. The 2025 Government Work Report proposes to adapt to the people's need for high-quality housing by improving standards and regulations and promoting the construction of safe, comfortable, green, and smart "good houses". "Promoting green and energy-efficient buildings" is a key measure to break through China's avoidance of high-carbon lock-in effects in the world's largest urbanization process. By strengthening energy efficiency standards for new buildings, cultivating the green building materials industry, promoting energy-saving renovations of existing buildings, and developing intelligent ultra-low energy consumption and near-zero energy consumption buildings, the proportion of energy-efficient buildings in existing urban building areas now exceeds 64%.

Relying on the national "East Data, West Computing" strategy, China Mobile Qinghai Company is advancing four major plans: algorithm-network strengthening, industrial integration, product formation, and collaborative innovation chain, aiming to build a six-in-one green computing power system of "basic resources+computing+platform+data+models+applications". Located in Haidong City, China Mobile (Qinghai) Plateau Big Data Center achieves a closed loop of "green electricity direct supply-smart management-efficient conversion" through liquid cooling technology and a green electricity direct supply system, reducing its power usage effectiveness (PUE) value to below 1.14, becoming the world's highest-altitude zero-carbon computing power hub. Located in Golmud City, China Mobile Qaidam Green Microgrid Computing Center flexibly allocates source-grid-load-storage resources and is the world's first computing center that uses desertified land and photovoltaic energy on a large scale to achieve "self-generation, self-storage, self-use, and self-protection" with 100% stable green electricity supply.

Hangzhou's post-Asian Games "Ten Climbing Actions" proposes to implement green and low-carbon development climbing actions. As Zhejiang's first provincial-level new district, Qiantang New District has shaped energy conservation and carbon reduction into a business advantage. The multi-energy comprehensive utilization system at Hangzhou Medical Port Town in Qiantang New District achieves collaborative operation of steam-driven lithium bromide refrigeration units and large-scale electric refrigeration units. This system is coupled with energy storage modules such as ice thermal storage and electrochemical storage. While ensuring the safe and reliable operation of centralized cooling within the zone, it flexibly participates in regional power grid peak shaving. Consequently, tenant enterprises largely do not need to build their own air conditioning host systems required for their process environments. This reduces traditional decentralized energy consumption, thereby freeing up energy capacity for the development of strategic industries and high-quality urban construction within the area. For example, as a qualified supplier for Airbus, Boeing, Bombardier, and COMAC, XIZI Aviation has established China's first "zero-carbon factory" for aviation components, organically integrating various new energy and energy storage technologies to provide different forms of energy such as electricity, cooling, heating, and compressed air for different production scenarios.

Throughout human history, from firewood and coal to oil and natural gas, each energy revolution has been accompanied by a huge leap in productivity. Currently, China is making breakthroughs in key, forward-looking, and strategic technologies such as new energy storage, energy management, and energy Internet of Things based on innovative energy supply scenarios, seizing the commanding heights of new quality productive forces in energy. As a green innovation leader in the field of thermal management, Beijing Anxing High-tech New Energy Development Co., Ltd. has, through independent innovation, acquired more than 50 patents in high-efficiency phase change energy storage materials, high heat flux density liquid cooling technology, energy storage temperature control integrated solutions, energy integration whole life cycle solutions and other fields. It has completed more than 300 phase change temperature control and peak shaving energy-saving projects with international advanced levels. Typical users include China Mobile, China Tower, State Grid, China Railway, China Resources Group, State Taxation Administration and other government agencies and well-known enterprises, achieving higher energy efficiency and dynamic stability of energy loads at relatively low construction and operation costs. Also, the company has developed the "Explorer" intelligent carbon emission management and control platform for dynamic management and compliance early warning of carbon emission facilities.

Case 4-5　　　Dongyu Island in Boao, Hainan: Building a
Zero-Carbon Demonstration Zone as a
Global "Laboratory" for Green Development

Facing the severe challenges of climate change, the Boao Forum for Asia Annual Conference 2025 focused on accelerating the implementation of sustainable development goals, setting up multiple topics such as "Achieving Sustainable Development in a Transforming World", "Addressing Climate Change: Problems and Solutions", "Working Together to Promote Asia's Energy Transition", "Accelerating the Construction of a New Energy System, Creating a Green Future for the World Together", and other issues to jointly plan strategies for green development.

As the core stage of the Boao Forum for Asia and China's first national-level zero-carbon demonstration zone, from 2019 to 2024, the total carbon dioxide emissions of Dongyu Island in Boao, Hainan sharply decreased from 12,000 tons to 470 tons, making it a "laboratory" for addressing climate change. Following the concept of "regional zero carbon, resource circulation, natural environment, and intelligent operation", Boao Dongyu Island has established an "eight-in-one" regional carbon reduction layout combining renewable energy utilization, green building updates, green transportation operations, new power system construction, material recycling, water resource recycling, ecological transformation of garden landscapes, and intelligent management operations. The island produces about 32 MkWh of green electricity annually, far exceeding the demonstration zone's annual electricity demand of about 17 MkWh. The surplus electricity is fed into the grid and reserves negative carbon resources of 7,720 tons per year, becoming a benchmark case of near-zero carbon development in global tropical regions.

Walking on Boao Dongyu Island, carbon reduction technology can be seen everywhere. For example, the Boao Forum for Asia International Conference Center and other main buildings use rooftop solar photovoltaic panels, photovoltaic louvers on exterior walls, cadmium telluride power generation glass, and photovoltaic floor tiles for power generation, and adopt optical storage direct flexible systems for energy storage, making the building's energy needs self-sufficient; kitchens have been electrified to achieve zero fossil energy use; the air conditioning system uses magnetic levitation variable frequency centrifugal water chillers, which are quieter and improve efficiency by more than 20%; the digital twin platform monitors energy consumption in real time, automatically cuts power to empty meeting rooms, and AI controls the air conditioning system; construction waste is made into landscape gardens, and rainwater collection systems irrigate gardens; bike riding generates electricity for charging, and carbon credits can be exchanged for gifts...

In addition, Boao Dongyu Island uses garden landscaping to achieve comprehensive functions such as regulating the microclimate, conserving water sources, reducing pollutants, and reducing carbon emissions. The island systematically restores mangrove wetlands, using connecting culverts to conserve and improve water quality, utilizing natural tides to achieve ecological connectivity of inner lakes and rivers, appropriately retaining exposed mudflats, and forming a wetland pattern with dynamic changes of forests, beaches, ditches, and lakes, building a complete mangrove "biological chain". The carbon emissions generated during the Boao Forum for Asia Annual Conference 2025 have been fully offset after accounting by the mangrove wetland restoration project, achieving "zero burden conferences".

Section 2 China's Innovative Measures, Main Achievements, and Typical Cases in Building a Clean and Efficient Transportation System

I. Continuous Optimization of Transportation Structure

China has increased investment in railway and waterway infrastructure, built trunk railways connecting major production and consumption regions, combined collection and distribution systems with dedicated railway lines for large industrial and mining enterprises, logistics parks, and ports, formed an efficient "point-to-point" transportation network, promoted the shift of bulk cargo from "road to rail" and "road to water", improved cargo transportation efficiency, and reduced energy consumption and carbon emissions in the transportation process. China promotes the deep integration of transportation logistics with e-commerce, manufacturing, and other industries, uses digital technology to optimize transportation processes, and improves logistics efficiency. China conducts "one-document" and "one-container" multimodal transport, promotes "one-time entrustment, one-price quote, one-document through, one-ticket settlement" whole-process transportation service products, and increases the proportion of railway and waterway transportation in comprehensive transportation. According to data from the China Container Industry Association, from 2016 to 2023, rail-water intermodal transportation volume increased from 2.74 million TEUs to 11.7 million TEUs, the proportion of rail-water intermodal transportation in coastal ports rose from 2.9% to 8%, railway container shipments increased from 7.51 million TEUs to 33.23 million TEUs, and the proportion of container volume in railway loading increased from 8.4% to 25.5%.

Case 4-6   China State Railway Group: Building "Green Corridors", Adding Beauty to Beautiful China

Railways have advantages such as large capacity, stable transportation, fast speed, low cost, and minimal environmental pollution, making them a resource-conserving and environmentally friendly mode of transportation. China State Railway Group explores a high-quality development path oriented towards ecological priority and green development, builds railway safety barriers, and beautifies the surrounding environment, with a national railway line greening rate exceeding 87.9%.

Playing a Leading Role in Green Low-Carbon Transportation

China State Railway Group has implemented sea-rail combined transport increase plans for the Yangtze River Delta and Pearl River Delta, two important economic belts. Compared with traditional transportation, the sea-rail combined transport mode reduces total freight costs by 25%-50% and shortens transportation time by 50%. It promotes the transformation from "bulk to container" transportation, reducing the risk of moisture damage, theft, and pollution of goods during transportation, and improving cargo turnover rate. China State

Railway Group has built 171 railway logistics bases, integrating them into local logistics parks, industrial parks, ports, and border crossings, and continuously improving comprehensive service functions such as multimodal transport at railway stations and distribution centers. For example, China Railway Guangzhou Group has created a "sea-rail integrated service cloud platform", sharing information between railways and ports simultaneously, achieving "front port, back station, integrated operation".

Railway Construction Shifts from "Engineering Priority" to "Ecological Priority"

In terms of green and environmentally friendly route selection and site selection, China State Railway Group scientifically plans and layouts railway lines and hub facilities to ensure organic integration of railways with natural and cultural environments. For example, the Guangzhou-Shanwei High-Speed Railway bypasses the core area of the Luofu Mountain Scenic Area, and the connecting line from Guangzhou Station to Guangzhou South Station bypasses the Pearl River Ecological Zone. In terms of ecological protection and energy conservation and carbon reduction, China State Railway Group strictly controls the construction scope, optimizes temporary facilities such as borrow and spoil grounds and construction access roads, strengthens civilized construction management, formulates special construction plans for crossing nature reserves, scenic spots, water source protection areas, and residential areas, optimizes water pollution treatment processes, and widely adopts clean energy. For example, the China-Laos Railway's Wild Elephant Valley Station has installed dozens of kilometers of wild elephant protection fences to reduce the impact of railways on wild Asian elephants and primary forests; the Qinghai-Xizang Railway has built wildlife passages to allow the harmonious coexistence of chiru migration and the steel transportation artery. In terms of green and low-carbon transformation, China State Railway Group adopts new energy-saving materials, processes, technologies, and equipment to build railway stations, and widely uses advanced scientific and technological means such as satellite maps, drones, and remote video to maintain lines.

Creating a Ten-Thousand-Mile Railway Ecological Corridor

China State Railway Group constructs a "line-network-area" ecological network through forest management, afforestation, protection of surrounding e-cology, and beautification of surrounding environment, making railways an or-ganic part of the regional ecosystem and achieving the compound value of "building one railway, greening a landscape". For example, the windbreak and sand-fixing forest belts along the Lanzhou-Xinjiang High-Speed Railway pro-tect railway safety and build a green wall on the Gobi Desert; ecological corri-dors on both sides of the Beijing-Xiong'an Intercity Railway link the Baiyangdian Wetland with urban green lungs, forming an ecological barrier for the Beijing-Tianjin-Hebei region; the Guiyang-Nanning High-Speed Railway scientifically selects excellent native tree species, rationally controls forest density and the ratio of trees, shrubs, and grasses, enhancing the greening level of corridors on both sides of the high-speed railway, allowing passengers to enjoy the mag-nificent scenery of "evergreen throughout the seasons, flowers every month" through the window; photovoltaic power generation along the Shanghai-Suzhou-Huzhou High-Speed Railway is connected to the railway power grid, transmit-ting more than 200 MkWh of clean energy annually.

Scientific and Technological Innovation Has Become the Core En-gine of Railway Green Transformation

In 2024, the world's fastest high-speed train, the CR450 EMU prototype, was unveiled. Lightweight design and energy consumption optimization technolo-gy reduced unit energy consumption by 10%, marking China's high-speed rail's advancement toward greater intelligence and greenness. Hydrogen-powered in-telligent intercity EMUs are undergoing trial operations, achieving a break-through in "zero carbon emissions". The intelligent dispatching system optimi-zes train operation diagrams through algorithms, reducing redundant energy consumption by more than 5% annually. The national railway electrification rate has increased to 74.9%, with annual carbon reduction equivalent to planting 4.7 billion fir trees. Railway freight transport continues to release green bene-fits. For example, in 2024, China-Europe freight trains made 19,000 trips, reducing carbon emissions by about 12.56 million tons compared to road trans-port; the multimodal transport "one-document system" service reduced social logistics costs by 60 billion yuan, forming a closed loop of "efficiency improve-ment-cost reduction-low-carbon cycle".

II. Continuous Improvement in the Level of Green Development in Transportation Infrastructure

China has implemented special actions for green highway construction and vigorously promoted the recycling of old road surface materials. The recycling rate of asphalt pavement materials for expressways and ordinary national and provincial roads has reached over 95% and 80% respectively. The length of trunk highway greening exceeds 570,000 km, an increase of about 200,000 km compared to 2012. Various regions are building (near) zero-carbon expressway service areas. For example, the Jiashaodaqiao Service Area of Changtai Expressway in Jiaxing, Zhejiang, has installed photovoltaic panels on roofs and car sheds, with multi-scenario power generation combined with integrated energy storage systems, which provide fast energy replenishment for new energy vehicles traveling north and south, and basically achieve self-generation and self-use; the General County Service Area of Jishang Expressway in Henan coordinates carbon reduction and pollution reduction, achieves zero-carbon emissions during the operation period through photovoltaic renovation and smart energy management, and carries out environmental management such as wastewater treatment and reuse, rainwater storage and utilization, and garbage compression processing.

Expressways have long routes and spacious surrounding areas, providing conditions for deploying photovoltaic systems in various scenarios. For example, the 161.9-kilometer-long Jiwei section of the Central Line between Jinan and Qingdao is China's first zero-carbon expressway, equipped with integrated slope photovoltaic devices that combine slope soil stabilization and photovoltaic power generation functions. Photovoltaic systems are installed in isolation spaces on both sides of the road, effectively utilizing idle land and providing stable green electricity supply for expressways. Based on a 25-year operation cycle, the total power generation is expected to be about 1,700 MkWh, with a carbon emission reduction of about 1.52 million tons, achieving overall zero-carbon operations.

In recent years, China's major ports have promoted the conversion of port machinery from "oil to electricity", with shore power facilities covering more than 75% of five types of specialized berths (container, ro-ro, cruise, passenger berths above 3,000 tons, and specialized dry bulk cargo berths above 50,000 tons). They promote solar, wind, and hydrogen energy to increase the proportion of clean energy supply, treat oily water, domestic sewage, dust, and powder from port areas and docked ships, protect and restore port shorelines, and simultaneously build green ports and beautiful ports. For example, Zhangjiagang Port has created a "dual carbon five transformations" green port construction path featuring low-carbon energy systems, clean machinery operations, precise environmental governance, scenic business formats, and rational transportation structure. Shanghai Port, Xiamen Port, Fuzhou Port, and others have completed the conversion of port machinery equipment from "oil to electricity" and "oil to gas". Qingdao Port has completed full coverage of photovoltaic construction for bridge crane rooms, warehouses, office buildings, substations, and other facilities. Rizhao Port has implemented marine ecological restoration projects such as "returning port to sea" and "returning port to city".

Case 4-7   Tianjin Port: Striving to Build an "Upgraded Version" of a World-Class Smart Green Hub Port

In January 2019, during his inspection of Tianjin Port, General Secretary Xi Jinping emphasized the need to aim high and strive to build a world-class smart port and green port that better serves the coordinated development of Beijing-Tianjin-Hebei and the joint construction of the "Belt and Road". Bearing in mind the General Secretary's instructions, Tianjin Port is striding forward on the new journey of building a Chinese-style modernized port: From the world's first container terminal automation upgrade to being rated as a "double five-star" smart and green port; from the erection of the world's first batch of port wind turbines to an annual green electricity generation capacity of nearly 300 MkWh; from a single logistics transportation node to an important strategic fulcrum connecting domestic and international dual circulation, with annual container throughput and cargo throughput consistently ranking among the top ten ports in the world...

With the goals of safety and environmental protection, energy conservation and emission reduction, pollution and carbon reduction, and adding greenery and beauty, Tianjin Port is promoting the construction of a green port with both land and sea directions, promoting the replacement of wind power, solar energy, hydrogen energy, and other green energies, achieving shore power construction and connection wherever possible, with China's first breakwater wind power project connected to the grid and dozens of large wind power generators filling the port. Tianjin Port's Second Container Terminal has built a "smart zero-carbon" terminal, with all terminal operating systems domestically produced. The fully automated ED algorithm improves the efficiency of ship unloading and port entry site positioning and the rationality of site resource allocation. It has built a wind-solar-storage-load integrated green energy system, achieving 100% use of electricity, 100% green electricity, and 100% self-production and self-sufficiency of green electricity. The port has deeply adjusted its transportation structure, creating a "road to rail+bulk to container" dual demonstration port, with coal achieving 100% railway transportation, and opening a pilot zero-carbon logistics channel for Tianjin-Shanxi new energy heavy trucks. The port has built a "single network" of charging facilities in the port area, with 100% clean transportation for internal port transfer vehicles.

In January 2025, Tianjin Port, together with Tianjin Dongjiang Comprehensive Bonded Zone, Tianjin Electric Power Company, State Grid Tianjin Carbon Peaking and Carbon Neutrality Operation and Service Center, and the China Waterbone Transport Research Institute of the Ministry of Transport jointly released the "Dongjiang Zero-Carbon Port Area Construction Plan of Tianjing Port (Terminal Logistics Area)". Driven by "six transformations" —electrification of energy consumption, greening of energy supply, intelligent production processes, refined energy and carbon management, low-carbon throughout logistics, and coordinated pollution and carbon reduction—they are striving to build China's first comprehensive "zero-carbon port area" covering terminal operation areas and logistics processing areas.

China has intensified the green renovation and upgrading of airports, achieving transformative breakthroughs in existing building energy conservation renovation and intelligent energy management system development. For example, Beijing Daxing International Airport has built the world's largest shallow geothermal heat pump utilization system, equipped with photovoltaic power stations, and adopted an intelligent lighting control system with a distributed control mode. The United Nations Development Programme believes that Daxing International Airport's energy-saving and emission-reduction path provides replicable experience for global public buildings; Chongqing Jiangbei International Airport's photovoltaic construction project has a planned installed capacity of 30 megawatts, making it the largest distributed photovoltaic power generation project currently under construction at a Chinese civil airport, covering an area of approximately 280,000 m^2 at Jiangbei Airport, with annual power generation accounting for about 10% of Jiangbei Airport's total annual electricity consumption; Lanzhou Zhongchuan International Airport's T3 terminal adopts a "large-span steel structure+glass curtain wall" design scheme, supplemented by bionic skylight windows. Through precise calculation of local lighting characteristics and optimization of skylight angles, the utilization rate of natural light is increased to 35%, which significantly reduces lighting and air conditioning energy consumption, with annual electricity savings exceeding 2 MkWh.

Various regions are accelerating the construction of charging infrastructure systems, enhancing the economy and convenience of charging services, better promoting the development of new energy vehicle industries and stimulating new energy vehicle consumption. As of the end of January 2025, the cumulative number of charging infrastructure facilities in China exceeded 13 million. Also, various regions are increasing mobile charging equipment to meet user demand during travel peaks. They are strengthening information services, providing users with real-time information on charging pile layout and usage status through multiple channels such as road condition information boards, navigation apps, and mini-programs.

III. Comprehensive Adoption of Low-Carbon Transportation Tools

Various regions are vigorously promoting new energy vehicles in urban public transport, taxis, environmental sanitation, logistics and distribution, civil aviation, airports, and party and government agencies. As of the end of 2024,

China's new energy vehicle ownership reached 31. 4 million, accounting for more than 50% of global ownership; new energy buses exceeded 550,000, accounting for more than 80% of total buses; and new energy taxis exceeded 200,000.

Various regions are strengthening the integrated development of "rail+bus+ slow traffic", constructing public transportation systems based on local conditions with urban rail transit and bus rapid transit as the backbone and conventional buses as the main body. As of November 2024, fifty-four cities in China have opened and operated 313 urban rail transit lines, with an operating mileage exceeding 10,000 km. Shared bicycles meet the "last mile" demand for green travel and quickly become an important choice for the public with their convenient and environmentally friendly characteristics.

Section 3　China's Innovative Measures, Main Achievements, and Typical Cases in Advocating and Practicing Green Lifestyles

I. Vigorous Development of Ecological Civilization Education

General Secretary Xi Jinping emphasized: "We must strengthen ecological civilization publicity and education, incorporate content such as cherishing ecology, protecting resources, and taking care of the environment into the national education and training system and into mass spiritual civilization creation activities, firmly establish the concept of ecological civilization throughout society, and form a good trend of participation by the whole society. " Since the new era, China has placed strengthening citizens' ecological civilization consciousness in a more prominent position. It continuously carries out themed publicity activities such as National Energy Conservation Publicity Week, China Water Week, National Urban Water Conservation Publicity Week, National Low-Carbon Day, National Tree Planting Day, World Environment Day (June 5), International Biodiversity Day, World Earth Day, "Beautiful China, I am an Actor" series activities, and promotes the concepts of green living in families, communities, factories, and rural areas. China has compiled ecological environmental protection readers and conducted education on basic national conditions of ecological resources in primary and secondary schools. It has released the "Citizen Ecological Environment Behavior Norms (Trial)", making ecological and environmental protection ideas the mainstream culture of society.

China was invited to share ecological civilization education experiences at the United Nations Chinese Youth Environmental Conference, reported twice by CCTV's "News Network", and holding a total of 309 ecological civilization education-themed activities throughout the year—this is Nanjing's "report card" for ecological civilization education in 2024. Nanjing City has incorporated content such as cherishing ecology, protecting resources, and caring for the environment into its education and training system, building more than 40 ecological civilization education bases and biodiversity experience sites that integrate science popularization, practice, and experience, and planning "Beautiful Nanjing" premium experience routes. It has established a Xi Jinping's Thought on Ecological Civilization lecture group and an ecological civilization education public welfare lecturer team, developed a distinctive local ecological civilization course system, and provided volunteer lecture services to the public. It has launched an online ecological environment education system, where education personnel become "hosts" and "guides" to film short videos or conduc live broadcasts to lead viewers to online check-in locations. It recruits environmental young reporters to enhance youth ecological environment literacy through on-site interviews, research investigations, and news reporting.

As Sichuan Province's first national ecological civilization construction demonstration city, Bazhong City has implemented the Xi Jinping's Thought on Ecological Civilization communication project, launched the weekly special program "Ecological Bazhong", and published a weekly "Ecology" special edition in the Bazhong Daily. The "Ecological Bazhong" column is divided into five sections: focusing on environmental hotspots, visiting ecological Bazhong, environmental supervision in progress, the beautification record of hundreds of enterprises and villages, and ecological environment news. It is disseminated simultaneously across multiple platforms such as radio, television, Wechat public accounts, and Douyin accounts through various forms including videos, audio, posters, and cartoons, enhancing public attention to and understanding of ecological civilization. Taking the lead in compiling city-level ecological environment protection education readers for primary and secondary school students in the province, and including relevant courses in academic level tests, Bazhong is implementing ecological civilization education starting from childhood, and the beautiful China old area model is gradually becoming a reality in Bazhong.

Exhibition hall-type ecological civilization education bases carry out immersive "environmental protection classrooms" for the public through graphic images, model displays, digital visualization systems, and on-site explanations. For example, the North River Ecological Civilization Exhibition Hall in Qingyuan City, based on Qingyuan's positioning as the northern ecological barrier of Guangdong and the characteristic of the North River flowing through the city, takes the North River as the narrative subject and centers around the theme word "Qing" (clear/clean). It has built four exhibition halls: "Clear and Beautiful Scenery", "Clear Mountain Ranges", "Clear Flowing Waves", and "Clearer Qingyuan". It employs sound, light, and electrical technology and interactive technology, supplemented by physical specimens and sand table models, combined with "Ecological Civilization Service Officer"① volunteer explanations, to conduct immersive ecological research and environmental protection public welfare activities.

Hangzhou Qiaosi Vocational High School has formulated an ecological school charter, integrated ecological civilization concepts throughout the education and teaching process, built an ecologically friendly and resource-saving green campus, and made environmental protection concepts the code of conduct for all teachers and students. It has established an ecological committee to promote and supervise continuous improvement of the campus environment. It popularizes ecological civilization knowledge through various forms such as classroom teaching, practical activities, and specialized courses. Fashion major

---

① Note: "Ecological Civilization Service Officer" is the collective name for Qingyuan City's ecological environment publicity, education, and scientific research service volunteers and volunteer service brand. By forming ecological civilization volunteer teams and training them as exhibition hall guides, they undertake ecological environment publicity and education tasks.

teachers and students use scraps to make environmentally friendly products, and construction major teachers and students transform training waste materials into learning resources, achieving deep integration of professional skills teaching and ecological civilization education. In cooperation with government departments and industry associations, the school regularly holds environmental protection-themed activities such as garbage sorting, energy conservation and emission reduction, and resource recycling, enhancing students' ecological civilization literacy.

Mingyue Lake in Nanning, Guangxi, has constructed a model of "ecological restoration+environmental education+community co-building", achieving a leap from an "environmental governance project" to an "ecological civilization showcase window". It has created an integrated water cycle system of "infiltration, retention, storage, purification, use, and discharge", applied weak electric field-mediated enhanced water environment ecological restoration technology, and achieved rapid removal of nutrients in water and protection of biodiversity, with water quality stably meeting Class IV surface water standards. It has formed an ecological wetland park integrating ecological protection, landscape experience, cultural and sports leisure, commercial trend play, and artistic display, winning the 2023 National Environmental Protection Science and Technology First Prize. Also, Mingyue Lake has built a scenario-based, all-age ecological civilization education system, launched wetland landscape tour routes with interpretive signs along the route explaining wetland purification process and aquatic plant function introductions, held photography competitions and story collection activities themed on Mingyue Lake ecological protection and restoration, and released beautiful videos and pictures through Wechat Channel, Douyin, rednote and other network platforms, allowing citizens to experience the beauty of wetland landscapes and learn about ecological civilization knowledge. It has created the "Small Hearts, Big Dreams" volunteer service brand, joining with surrounding government and enterprise units, communities, and residents to carry out volunteer activities such as lake patrol and greenery protection, garbage classification promotion, voluntary tree planting, and weed clearing.

II. Widespread Promotion of Green Lifestyle

China widely carries out creations such as economical government agencies, green hospitals, green families, green schools, green communities, and green buildings. 70% of county-level and above party and government organs have built economical agencies, hundreds of universities have achieved intelligent monitoring of water and electricity consumption, and more than a hundred cities have participated in green travel creation actions. China extensively carries out domestic waste classification work, with residents' habits of actively sorting gradually forming. China has promulgated and implemented the "Anti-Food Waste Law of the People's Republic of China" to vigorously promote food conservation and anti-food waste work and deeply carry out the "Clean Plate" campaign, with food conservation becoming a prevailing trend.

Taian City, Shandong Province, has established a leading group for the creation of economical agencies headed by the executive deputy mayor, issued implementation plans, established joint conference and "look-back" assessment systems, and included the creation of economical agencies in the comprehensive performance assessment of municipal and county organs and the evaluation standards for the creation of civilized units. Starting from green and low-carbon office practices, stopping food waste, household waste sorting, and plastic pollution control, government agencies are guiding civil servants to develop green, low-carbon, and frugal behavior habits. They have held on-site observation meetings for creating economical government agencies, compiled typical demonstration experiences, and played a demonstrative role. The municipal government center has upgraded ground-source heat pumps, air conditioning fans, lighting facilities, and water heaters for energy efficiency, built integrated "charging, solar, electric, and storage" new energy charging stations, and completed the "single network" construction of the public institution energy consumption monitoring platform at both city and county levels. A "virtual public property warehouse" has been established to revitalize idle assets and optimize property allocation. A digital lifecycle management mechanism for official vehicles has been implemented to eliminate old fuel vehicles and ensure all new government vehicles are equipped with new energy technology.

Globally, hospitals rank among the top energy consumers and carbon emitters among public institutions, with Chinese hospitals consuming 1.6 to 2 times more energy than general public buildings. Facing the dual challenges of healthcare quality and ecological responsibility, Nanjing First Hospital (Hexi Campus) has presented a satisfactory "green report card": Through "comprehensive energy-saving renovation + digital intelligent energy management + energy trusteeship operation and maintenance", the annual comprehensive energy-saving rate exceeds 15%. At the hardware level, the hospital has replaced original low-efficiency cooling machines with magnetic levitation centrifugal water chillers, substituted traditional vacuum boilers with air-cooled heat pumps and air-source heat pumps, optimized cooling and heating source distribution systems, installed zero-resistance filters and energy-saving films in inpatient buildings, and deployed intelligent data collection terminals and smart control equipment to ensure seamless integration, data integration, and energy conservation across cooling, heating, domestic hot water, multi-connected, and terminal energy systems. At the software level, a digital twin model has been established to achieve integrated "monitoring-management-control" centralized management. AI analyzes pedestrian flow density, temperature, humidity, and other parameters in real-time, automatically generates operation strategies and issues control instructions to reduce energy consumption while ensuring terminal needs are met.

Tsinghua University proposed the concept of building a "Green University" as early as 1998, and has since outlined a "triptych" of green education, green technology, and green campus that makes up "Green Tsinghua". First, Tsinghua University has created a comprehensive, multi-level, and internationalized green education system, with various departments offering over 200 green courses each academic year, more than half of which are available to non-environmental majors. The university has established environmental dual-degree programs in cooperation with international institutions such as Yale University, and organizes students and faculty to participate extensively in environmental technology competitions, green social practices, and green community activities. Second, Tsinghua University has established multiple research institutes related to green development, conducting academic research, technological break-throughs, social services, talent cultivation, and industry-university-research-application cooperation, resulting in numerous green scientific research a-chievements. Third, Tsinghua University extensively applies solar energy, geo-thermal energy and other renewable energy sources, improves its energy man-agement system, recycles waste such as abandoned bicycles, and uses environ-mental protection facilities like rainwater collection pools and reclaimed water treatment stations. Today, the Tsinghua campus has a green coverage rate ex-ceeding 50%, becoming a "green lung" of the capital.

In November 2018, General Secretary Xi Jinping visited the first branch of the Jiaxing Road Neighborhood Community Center in Hongkou District, Shang-hai, emphasizing that "waste sorting is a new fashion". In May 2023, Gener-al Secretary Xi Jinping replied to a letter from waste sorting volunteers in Jiaxing Road Subdistrict, emphasizing the need to "earnestly conduct publicity and guidance work, and promote waste sorting as a new low-carbon lifestyle fash-ion". Jiaxing Road Subdistrict has released the "Three-Year Action Plan for Building a Low-Carbon Lifestyle Practice Area in Jiaxing Road Subdistrict (2024-2026)", established a low-carbon lifestyle volunteer service team com-posed of outstanding young people from government agencies, enterprises, public institutions, and new types of organizations, created a "Remember the Instructions—Creating a Low-Carbon Life" lecture route, and organized a "Seeking a Better Life through Carbon Reduction" themed forum, ecological art exhibitions, idle item recycling public welfare markets, and a series of sup-porting activities. Through interactive classrooms, outdoor performances, flash markets, short plays, on-site games, scenario interactions and other forms, they are promoting the "dual improvement" of urban civilization and citizens' ecological literacy.

III. Surging Vitality in Green Consumption

China is accelerating the green transformation of consumption patterns by implementing tax exemptions and financial subsidies, actively promoting green and low-carbon products such as new energy vehicles and high-efficiency household appliances, improving the certification and promotion mechanism for green products, enhancing government green procurement systems, implementing energy and water efficiency labeling systems, building green circulation entities, and supporting the vigorous development of new models such as the sharing economy and second-hand transactions. The categories, carriers, and user groups of green consumption continue to expand. Data from Suning. com shows that since the launch of the new round of home appliance trade-in subsidies in August 2024, sales of energy-efficient washer-dryer combos, intelligent fresh air conditioners, and built-in steam-bake combination ovens have increased by 129%, 135%, and 228% respectively as of February 2025.

With advantages such as appealing design, high performance, large space, and high cost-performance, "Made in China" new energy vehicles have strong production and sales figures. The recycling and circular use of automotive products continues to accelerate. Among qualified end-of-life vehicle recycling enterprises in China, more than 3/4 have developed new energy vehicle dismantling capabilities. In 2024, China's cumulative transaction volume of used cars reached 19. 6142 million units, and the recovery of scrapped vehicles reached 8. 46 million units, increasing by 6. 52% and 64% respectively. More and more consumers are choosing the green consumption method of "first disposing of the old, then buying new".

Young people are enthusiastic about listing idle items on online second-hand trading platforms to "make money back", while also enjoying finding their favorite items on these platforms. According to data released by Xianyu, the number of registered users has exceeded 600 million, with daily transaction volume exceeding 1 billion yuan. In 2024, more than 100 million people sold idle items, with 4 million idle items being listed online every day. Second-hand stores selling limited-edition figurines, rare books, and discontinued clothing have become new consumer spaces favored by young people. Second-hand item stores have entered university campuses, helping college students dispose of idle items, with graduate entrance exam notes, trendy blind boxes, and daily necessities becoming bestsellers. Some second-hand stores adopt a consignment model, where sellers deposit items in the store until they are sold, creating a multi-category source of goods for consumers to choose from, making the transaction process more convenient and efficient than online platforms.

Section 4   China's Innovative Measures, Main Achievements, and Typical Cases in Promoting Green and Low-Carbon Transition of Traditional Industries

I. The Ecological Foundation of Manufacturing Is Becoming Increasingly Prominent

China is accelerating the construction of a green manufacturing system, comprehensively implementing cleaner production, steadily promoting energy conservation and carbon reduction in key industries, accelerating the updating and replacement of key energy-using equipment such as motors and boilers, promoting green, low-carbon, and environmentally friendly processes and equipment, innovating green product design, and building green factories and green industrial chain supply chains. Following the principles of "horizontal coupling, vertical extension, and circular connection", industrial parks are optimizing the spatial layout of enterprises, industries, and infrastructure to build green parks. Comprehensive pilot programs for coordinated digital and green transformation development have been launched, with intelligent manufacturing, service-oriented manufacturing, and other integrated development models continuously emerging.

In 2024, China's green development in manufacturing demonstrated "four increases and three decreases", namely: The first "increase" refers to 6,430 national-level green factories characterized by land-intensive use, harmless raw materials, clean production, waste resource utilization, and low-carbon energy, accounting for about 20% of the total manufacturing output value; the second "increase" indicates that the comprehensive utilization rate of bulk industrial solid waste exceeded 55%, an increase of 1.2 percentage points over the previous year; the third "increase" shows that the comprehensive utilization of retired power batteries exceeded 300,000 tons, a year-on-year increase of 33%; the fourth "increase" means that nearly 30,000 types of electrical and electronic products met national pollution control requirements, a year-on-year increase of 10%. The "three decreases" refer to the continuous decline in energy consumption per unit of added value in key industries such as steel, cement, and glass, the continuous decrease in the emission intensity of major industrial pollutants, and the ongoing reduction in water consumption per 10, 000 yuan of industrial added value.

As a benchmark simultaneously selected for the 2024 national-level "Green Factory" and "Green Supply Chain Management Enterprise" lists, Gree Electric Appliances proposed the concept of "making the sky bluer and the earth greener" as early as 2013, integrating green and low-carbon concepts into every aspect of the company's research and development and production, with more than 60 products obtaining "Green Design Product" certification. Gree Electric Appliances adopts environmentally friendly water-based paint production processes to reduce the emission of volatile organic compounds, establishes green procurement standards, and promotes the joint implementation of green manufacturing among upstream and downstream enterprises. Gree's photovoltaic storage direct flexible air conditioning system is an integrated ecological system centered on air conditioning, integrating photovoltaic power generation, energy storage, air conditioning power consumption, and intelligent power management, bringing users a comfortable and green living environment. The company has constructed a "green design-green manufacturing-green recycling" circular development model, dismantling 68 million sets of waste electrical and electronic equipment, reducing carbon emissions by 1. 03 million tons.

The 2025 Government Work Report mentioned establishing a number of zero-carbon parks and zero-carbon factories. Yili Group is the first company in China's food industry to publish dual carbon goals and a roadmap, having established 5 zero-carbon factories and launched 6 zero-carbon products to date. Yili Group implements an "integrated farming and breeding" ecological agriculture model, planting low-carbon feed around dairy farms with good carbon sequestration capabilities. The farms are equipped with automated equipment and low-carbon management systems, using low-carbon feed to reduce methane emissions from cows' rumens by 20%-30%. The company conducts carbon emission assessments throughout the packaging lifecycle, using packaging primarily made of renewable and recyclable materials, and aims to achieve 99% recyclable packaging materials by 2025. The liquid milk business division has independently developed an AI low-carbon production platform, using carbon accounting models to dynamically adjust energy supply and demand, making carbon reduction calculable and visible.

Fujian Province's Jinjiang Economic Development Zone has fashion footwear and apparel, textile new materials, and healthy food as its leading industries, with leading enterprises such as Anta and Hengan. The zone has innovated a "vertical factory" model, establishing production workshops, offices, and laboratories upstairs, with warehouses downstairs, turning one building into a vertically integrated factory, forming an industrial park ecosystem where "going up and down floors means moving upstream and downstream, and the industrial park is the industrial chain", improving the volume rate of industrial land and promoting intensive and efficient use of land in the park. It integrates and promotes green and environmentally friendly materials, deploys rooftop photovoltaics, energy storage, charging piles and other green energy sources, and builds waste gas and waste heat recovery and treatment facilities, helping enterprises grow "greener". The zone cultivates leading enterprises in green manufacturing, guiding companies to undertake intelligent transformations such as equipment core replacement, production line renewal, and machine replacement, integrating green and low-carbon concepts throughout product design, raw material procurement, production, transportation, recycling, and processing, driving the industrial chain and supply chain to develop in new and green directions.

In December 2024, Minhang Development Zone released the "Shanghai Minhang Economic and Technological Development Zone Carbon Emission Report (2024)", the first annual carbon emission report issued by a national-level economic development zone. Thanks to the quality improvement and efficiency enhancement of industries, iterative upgrades in scientific and technological innovation, continuous progress in energy conservation and consumption reduction, and a clean and low-carbon energy structure, Minhang Development Zone has achieved a fresh transformation from a traditional manufacturing park to a green intelligent manufacturing and R&D innovation park. The zone has issued the "Action Plan for Creating a Zero-Carbon Demonstration Park" and the "Implementation Plan for Green and Low-Carbon Leaders", established the city's first government-guided, park-facilitated, enterprise-oriented green co-construction alliance, conducted carbon emission accounting, deployed renewable energy, green certificate and green electricity trading, and carbon finance, and supported company-specific pollution and carbon reduction work. This has formed a modernized industrial system dominated by equipment manufacturing, biomedicine, and new materials, with foreign-funded and joint ventures accounting for more than 80%, continuously enhancing the industrial "new and green index".

Case 4-8　　　　Huawei: Exploring the "Optimal Solution" for
Green, Low-Carbon, and Circular Development
Throughout All Processes and Chains

Huawei Group integrates environmental compliance, energy and resource efficiency improvement, and natural environment protection as standards into research and development, operations, procurement, manufacturing, supply chain, and other aspects, enabling the green development of the industrial chain through innovation. To date, Huawei Digital Energy has helped customers achieve 997.9 billion kWh of green power generation and save 46.1 billion kWh of electricity; the average energy efficiency of Huawei's main products has improved to 2.6 times that of 2019 (the base year); a cumulative 780,000 terminal devices have extended their lifecycles through trade-ins; the landfill rate of electronic waste from ICT business is 0.5%, and zero landfill for electronic waste from the smart terminal business. Looking further, Huawei considers safety, environmental protection, and the use of renewable materials at the source of product design, with recycled plastics and bio-based plastics widely used in Huawei's smart terminal products. Huawei employs automated stacking and minimalist design for product packaging, continuously promotes lightweight instruction manuals, gradually eliminates single-use plastics from packaging materials, and selects recyclable recycled paper and paper raw materials provided by responsibly managed forests that comply with sustainable development management principles.

Huawei has built photovoltaic power stations at its headquarters, campuses, factories, and other locations, introducing clean energy to reduce carbon emissions in its own operations. Huawei verifies suppliers' carbon emission data, pressuring suppliers to systematically reduce energy consumption and emissions. Through using clean energy transportation tools, reducing paper documents, simplifying packaging, promoting circular turnover boxes, and other measures, Huawei achieves green transportation. By eliminating paper shopping lists, eliminating express delivery outer waterproof bags, reducing the use of cardboard boxes and tape, promoting zero-plastic packaging, and improving packaging loading rates, Huawei optimizes green logistics operations. The company has launched a one-stop renewal plan, allowing consumers to purchase new Huawei products using vouchers obtained through recycling old devices.

Huawei proposes that technology and nature coexist, and that everything the company does benefits from the earth and also benefits the earth. Continuously promoting energy conservation and emission reduction, increasing the use of renewable energy, exploring innovative circular economy models, reducing demands on nature, and providing more environmentally friendly products to customers are at the core of Huawei's values and core competitiveness.

II. Agricultural Production Methods Are Accelerating Green Transition

China has improved its arable land protection system and crop rotation and fallow system, fully implemented special protection for permanent basic farmland, and initially curbed the trend of arable land reduction. Steady progress has been made in black soil protection, with national arable land quality steadily improving, reaching an average grade of 4.76, an increase of 0.35 grades compared to 10 years ago. Multiple measures have been taken to promote agricultural water conservation and the reduction and efficiency improvement of chemical fertilizers and pesticides. Under conditions of continuous bumper grain harvests, the effective utilization coefficient of farmland irrigation water has reached 0.57, an increase of 0.05 compared to 10 years ago, and the annual use of chemical fertilizers has decreased from 60.22 million tons in 2015 to over 50 million tons. China has developed circular agricultural models that integrate planting, breeding, and processing, agriculture, animal husbandry, and fisheries, and production, processing, and sales, strengthening the resource utilization of agricultural waste. The comprehensive utilization rate of livestock and poultry manure has reached 78%, the comprehensive utilization rate of crop straw exceeds 88%, and the agricultural film recovery rate remains stable at over 80%. China has coordinated the advancement of agricultural production and agricultural product "three products and one mark"[1]. Coupled with the implementation of the protection program for agricultural products with geographical indications, the total number of green food, organic products, products that are famous, distinctive, high-quality, or new, and agricultural products with geographical indications has reached 78,000. This has effectively promoted industrial upgrading and modernization, while also increasing farmers' incomes and helping them achieve prosperity.

In July 2020, General Secretary Xi Jinping visited the national million-mu green food raw material (corn) standardized production base in Lishu County, Siping City, Jilin Province, to inspect the growth of corn. The General Secretary emphasized the need to carefully summarize and promote the "Lishu Model", and take effective measures to protect and utilize the black soil, the "giant panda of arable land", so that it can benefit the people forever. The "Lishu Model" addresses the problems of black soil becoming "thin", "shallow", and "hard" through techniques such as straw mulching and no-till planting, achieving soil conservation, water conservation, and land nourishment through planting and breeding cycles. Jilin Province has established a black soil protection work leading group, formed an expert committee, issued policies, and developed ten major black soil protection models including corn straw strip return conservation tillage, corn straw full return land conservation, corn straw deep turning return drip irrigation fertilizer reduction, corn straw return planting with water conservation for seedling growth and yield increase, rice straw full crushing and pressing return, sloping land soil conservation and

---

[1]　Note: "Three products and one mark" for agricultural production refers to variety improvement, quality enhancement, brand building, and standardized production; "three products and one mark" for agricultural products refers to green, organic, geographical indication, and standard-compliant agricultural products.

quality improvement, corn straw pile fermentation and fertilization, corn straw full deep mixing return, corn straw full powdered return soil loosening and temperature increasing, and rice-bean rotation black soil protection and fertilization. The area of black soil conservation tillage exceeds 38 million mu (about2. 53 million hectares), ranking first in the country.

Lankao County, Kaifeng City, Henan Province has implemented land transfer operations such as the "800+ dividend" model①, "Three Modernizations" land trusteeship②, and villager self-operation "Five Unifications" service ③ to promote the construction of high-standard farmland. The county has developed a "5G+ High-Standard Farmland Command and Dispatch Platform" integrating high-standard four conditions④, agricultural services, digital villages, green recycling, and other functions, achieving closed-loop management of monitoring and early warning, precise regulation, automatic irrigation, operational management, decision-making, and disposal. The county has launched the "Farmland Easy Manager" agricultural service mini-program, where farmers can consult agricultural experts online. Experts provide guidance and issue "prescriptions" for scientific farming, and farmers purchase agricultural materials and services from agricultural service centers based on these "prescriptions".

Binchuan County in Dali Prefecture, Yunnan Province has built self-pressurized drip irrigation high-efficiency water-saving irrigation projects according

---

① The "800+ dividend" land transfer model: Contiguous plots of land are transferred at 800 yuan/mu/year, with large-scale planting by operating entities. After deducting transfer fees and operating costs from the revenue, the remaining portion is distributed as dividends according to predetermined proportions.

② The "Three Modernizations" land trusteeship model: Village collectives select social trusteeship entities through market-oriented methods, which provide professional "plowing, planting, managing, harvesting, and selling" whole-process services. After deducting service fees, the village collective and farmers share dividends according to agreed proportions.

③ Villager self-operation "Five Unifications" service: For farmers unwilling to transfer or entrust their land, village collectives provide low-cost unified agricultural materials, unified farming, unified management, unified harvesting, and unified sales services, helping farmers reduce costs and increase efficiency.

④ High-standard four conditions: Real-time monitoring, data analysis, and precise management of soil moisture, crop growth, pest and disease conditions, and climate and environmental conditions in high-standard farmland.

to the "build first, subsidize later" model, with local farmers' professional co-operatives investing in construction, operation, and maintenance. Total water usage control indicators are based on available water and irrigation quotas in the project area, with initial water rights allocated to water users according to culti-vated land area and crop irrigation requirement quotas. Following the principle of ensuring normal operation of irrigation area management units, good project operation, and water users' ability to afford water fees, operators and water us-ers negotiate water prices with a progressive increase for usage exceeding quo-tas. To reduce farmers' water costs and increase enthusiasm for grain produc-tion, a classified water price system has been implemented, with grain crop water prices lower than economic crop water prices. As farmland irrigation con-ditions improve and water resources are scientifically allocated," thunder echo fields" that relied on rainfall for irrigation in dry conditions have been trans-formed into oases, with local enterprises and farmers beginning to develop mod-ern efficient agriculture on a large scale.

Huanghua City in Cangzhou, Hebei Province actively explores green agri-cultural development models for saline-alkali land, building high-standard farm-land through methods such as "straw return + deep plowing + increased organic fertilizer+increased soil conditioner", with cultivated land area increasing from 770,000 mu（about 51,333.33 hectares）in 1980 to over 1.4 million mu（a-bout 93,333.33 hectares）currently. By implementing projects such as the Na-tional Wheat（Huanghua Drought-Alkali Wheat）Green, High-Quality, and High-Efficiency Project and the Bohai Granary Science and Technology Demon-stration Engineering Project, salinity has been reduced through measures like salt leaching and alkali suppression, and salt reduction combined with moisture conservation. Scientific fertilization methods have been adopted, including soil testing for formula fertilization and the combined application of organic and inor-ganic fertilizers. New wheat varieties that are drought-resistant, salt-tolerant, alkali-tolerant, disease-resistant, and high-yielding have been selected and bred. Drought-alkali wheat rotation cropping has been implemented, and new types of agricultural business entities have been cultivated. These efforts pro-mote the scale operation of Huanghua drought-alkali wheat processed products like flour, decorative flour products（mianhua）, and dried noodles. Consequently, the saline-alkali land, once characterized by "crop failure in nine out of ten years," is gradually transforming into fertile fields.

Yunmeng County in Xiaogan City is an advantageous area for winter open-field vegetable production in China, with over 900,000 tons of vegetables sent to various regions each year and annual comprehensive output value exceeding 3.7 billion yuan. Yunmeng County has cooperated with Wuhan University, Huazhong Agricultural University, and others to introduce more than 400 new vegetable varieties, renewing the "seed chip". As a pilot project for scientific use and recycling of agricultural film in Hubei Province, Yunmeng County has established a waste agricultural film recycling and utilization system of "farmers collecting and selling, township-level outlets organizing recycling, and leading enterprises processing and utilizing". Farmers receive subsidies for purchasing films when they deliver waste agricultural films to recycling points, guiding farmers to actively use relatively more expensive recyclable films. Exploring a new "sky garden" model, vertical hydroponic racks are configured in greenhouses. Intelligent systems automatically regulate temperature, humidity, ventilation, supplementary lighting, fertilization, and drip irrigation. An integrated water and fertilizer machine dynamically proportions nutrient solutions according to the vegetable growth cycle. Wastewater is centrally filtered for reuse in the next cycle, achieving a water-saving rate of 70% and increasing fertilizer utilization by 50%. This breaks through the constraints of seasons and land, with hydroponic vegetable yields multiplying several times compared to traditional planting methods.

Case 4-9   "Double Chang" (Rongchang District, Chongqing City and Longchang City, Neijiang, Sichuan Province) Modern Agricultural Cooperation Demonstration Park: "Three Integrations" Promote Win-Win Cooperation in Green Agriculture

The Neijiang-Rongchang Modern Agricultural High-tech Industry Demonstration Zone is the only functional platform in the adjacent areas of Sichuan and Chongqing that focuses on agriculture and rural areas. The "Double Chang" Modern Agricultural Cooperation Demonstration Park is jointly built by

Rongchang and Neijiang in their adjacent areas, with a total planned area of 196,000 mu (about 13,100 hectares), involving "seven towns and one sub-district" in Rongchang District and Longchang City. Both regions established a construction command headquarters for the cooperation demonstration park, led by district (city) committee and government deputy leaders, and established special working groups and joint meeting systems to ensure cooperation matters are effectively implemented and yield results.

First, industrial integration. Combining the resource endowments and industrial foundations of both areas, they developed green agriculture based on hillside pig farms with oil tea and fruit trees in a circular farming system, comprehensive rice-fish farming in paddy fields, and dryland sorghum-rapeseed rotation. They promoted integrated development of "production+technology+processing+services", forming a "seven unified" joint construction mechanism covering park naming, planning and design, leading industries, construction standards, policy standards, management services, and technological services. For example, they highlight the protection and development of excellent local pig breeds like Rongchang and Neijiang pigs, jointly building a national strategic support base for high-quality pigs and a highland for breeding pig supply. 400,000 mu (about 26,666.67 hectares) of high-standard farmland, characterized as "suitable for mechanization and cultivation, capable of drainage and irrigation, high-yielding and stable-yielding, and ensuring harvests despite drought or flood," have been developed. A national-level integrated rice-fish farming demonstration zone has been co-established, achieving "dual use of water, dual harvest from one field, and green circulation". New agri-tourism formats are also being cultivated, including leisure sightseeing, science popularization and education, farming experiences, and food culture.

Second, technological integration. Relying on research institutions and universities such as Southwest University, Chongqing Academy of Animal Sciences, Neijiang Academy of Agricultural Sciences, and national-level platforms such as the National Pig Big Data Center and the National Pig Technology Innovation Center, the two regions deepened industry-university-research cooperation around characteristic industries such as pigs, rice-fish farming, and citrus. They established doctoral expert workstations, scientific research and experimental bases, and scientific expert centers in the cooperation park to popularize modern pig farming, new rice varieties and technology promotion, fish-vegetable and rice-fish symbiosis, and other green agricultural projects representing new quality productive forces.

Third, Party building integration. For example, Rongchang District's Longji Town and Longchang City's Shinian Town jointly built "New Wind Courtyards" and organized villagers from both towns to learn green agricultural knowledge and skills together, thus promoting friendly exchanges between villagers; the Party General Branch of Putuo Village in Anfu Subdistrict, Rongchang District signed a friendship village cooperation agreement with the Party Committee of Sanhe Village in Longchang City's Shiyanqiao Town to explore innovative paths for Party-led talent cultivation, industrial co-prosperity, and green development; Rongchang and Longchang jointly funded, staffed, and built a park science and culture center, and established functional carriers such as green agriculture science popularization exhibition areas, specialty agricultural products and intangible cultural heritage exhibition areas, and Party school (vocational technical) training areas.

III. Continuous Improvement in Green Service Industry Levels

China has cumulatively created over 600 green shopping malls that provide green services, guide green consumption, and implement energy conservation and emission reduction. It has been promoting energy conservation and carbon reduction technology upgrades and equipment updates in data centers, with a cumulative total of 246 national-level green data centers built, achieving world-leading levels in electricity utilization efficiency, renewable energy utilization rate, and water resource utilization efficiency. China has been implementing "seven actions" for green transformation of express delivery packaging[1],

---

[1]   Seven actions for green transformation of express delivery packaging: Special guidance action for express delivery packaging reduction, e-commerce platform enterprise leadership action, green upgrade action for express delivery packaging supply chain, promotion action for recyclable express delivery packaging, recovery and disposal action for express delivery packaging, supervision and enforcement action for express delivery packaging, and thematic publicity action for green transformation of express delivery packaging.

strengthening plastic pollution control in the industry, guiding producers and consumers to use recyclable express delivery packaging and degradable packaging, with recyclable packaging achieving full coverage in express delivery transfer links in 2024. The country has been promoting the use of green buildings, energy-saving renovations, and recycling of exhibition facilities in exhibition venues, and conducting pilots in green construction, green operations, green catering, and green logistics at key exhibitions such as the Canton Fair. China has been fully implementing electronic railway tickets and promoting the application of electronic invoices, which has significantly reduced paper ticket usage. It advocates that restaurants, guesthouses, and hotels do not proactively provide disposable items.

Nanxiang Impression City is Shanghai's largest single-volume commercial shopping center, constructing a green mall development path from multiple angles including architecture, design, space, experience, and scenarios. With forests, wetlands, and mountains as themes, it has set up a plant garden of over 1000 m² with three glass box combinations, cultivating more than 200 species of tropical plants. Rooftop theme gardens are created, and amenities such as sky running tracks, children's interactive playgrounds, pet parks, and basketball courts are placed in the rooftop space to enrich the outdoor green consumption experience. A green transportation network integrating subway and bus station hubs is constructed to facilitate green travel for consumers. An intelligent parking management system has been launched to reduce carbon emissions from driving around searching for parking spaces. Building automation systems and energy regeneration systems are constructed to dynamically adjust the mall's heating and cooling. Waste sorting, recycling, and tracking are implemented, and intelligent robots are introduced for cleaning operations to reduce waste emissions.

Alibaba Group's "Environmental, Social, and Governance Report（2024）" shows that Intime Department Store has been awarded 40 "Green Mall" stores, with clean electricity usage reaching 47.3%, and carbon reduction of 304,000 tons. Since 2021, Intime Department Store has actively participated in green electricity transactions, launching a smart energy management system that integrates energy management, environmental quality monitoring, power distribution control, merchant prepaid recharging, and other functions. Water-saving devices are deployed in areas such as landscaping irrigation, domestic water use, and central air conditioning water systems, and collected rainwater and air conditioning condensate are recycled and reused. Green packaging bags that are soil-degradable and compost-degradable are widely adopted, along with environmentally friendly reduced-design cartons, eco-friendly fillers, and eco-friendly adhesive tape. The "Empty Bottle Record" environmental protection activity has been launched. Consumers can exchange empty cosmetic bottles for consumption benefits/rewards. The empty bottles are then either made into art pieces for display by professional institutions or recycled and reused by third-party organizations.

The Xiong'an Urban Computing Center is known as the "eye" of Xiong'an's digital twin city, the "brain" of the intelligent city, and the "core" of the ecological city. It makes full use of natural ventilation and lighting, and reasonably arranges the world's first garden-style ecological computer room hall and China's first modular container computer room hall. Self-built rooftop photovoltaic systems directly feed green electricity into the building's internal low-voltage power supply system for public areas. Lithium iron phosphate batteries are used on a large scale for peak shaving and valley filling; the battery system charges and stores energy during off-peak electricity price periods and releases energy during peak and super-peak price periods. Uninterrupted cooling supply is achieved using energy stations, indirect cooling towers, and cold storage tanks. The terminal system employs nationally leading liquid cooling heat dissipation technology. The power supply and distribution network is equipped with intelligent systems such as power monitoring, air conditioning control, and robotic inspections, which dynamically monitor and intelligently analyze key indicators like power usage efficiency, temperature and humidity, and air conditioning energy consumption status, thereby optimizing energy consumption in a timely manner.

SF Group has externally committed to leveraging technological power to promote green and low-carbon transformation, achieving a 55% improvement in its own carbon efficiency by 2030 compared to 2021, and reducing the carbon footprint of each express package by 70% compared to 2021. SF Group injects technological power into the entire life cycle of each package to improve efficiency and reduce carbon emissions: Couriers are equipped with portable smart

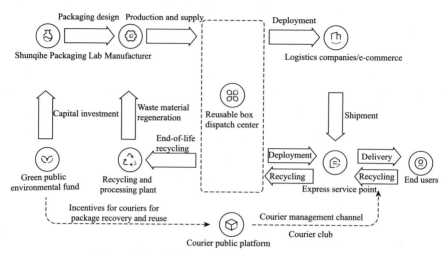

Figure 4-1   SF Express Carbon Reduction Action Roadmap（Source：SF Group）

wearable devices integrated with embedded logistics maps to simplify collection and delivery routes and improve efficiency. A fully automated sorting and site management system has been developed to enhance warehousing and transit operational efficiency, reducing process energy consumption and error rates. By utilizing logical algorithms and smart maps, combined with factors such as package timeliness and distance, freight routes and transport capacity are consolidated; predictive navigation and fuel-saving algorithms precisely match vehicles with cargo, minimizing transport energy consumption. Furthermore, a packaging laboratory has been established to develop green packaging options like fully biodegradable plastic bags, anti-theft zipper cartons that eliminate the need for adhesive tape, and reusable packaging boxes, thereby creating a climate-friendly circular ecosystem for express packaging.

Case 4-10   JD Logistics: Creating a Industry-Leading Green Development Model for Logistics and Supply Chain

In January 2025, the National Development and Reform Commission and other departments released the " Green Technology Promotion Catalog （2024）". JD Logistics launched the Supply Chain Environmental Management

Platform (SCEMP) that adopts a " distributed carbon ledger" management model and uses self-developed MRV-T (carbon footprint monitoring, reporting, verification, and tracking) digital carbon reduction technology. Through sensors to obtain terminal carbon emission data, it provides minimum granularity dual-factor carbon accounting and carbon reduction models based on time-space and geographic dimensions for waybills, becoming the only green technology selected in the logistics industry.

Through AI algorithm efficiency improvement, green energy and transportation equipment applications, packaging material recycling, and other methods, JD Logistics persists in continuously reducing carbon in warehousing, logistics transportation, packaging materials, and other links. In terms of green warehousing, JD Logistics built China's first "carbon-neutral" logistics park, with rooftop photovoltaics installed on multiple sorting centers, large item warehouses, and logistics parks, with a total installed capacity of 114. 48 megawatts. In terms of green transportation, JD Logistics has introduced over 8,000 new energy vehicles in trunk line and terminal transportation links, reducing carbon emissions by more than 35,000 tons per year on average, and introduced the first batch of dozens of hydrogen energy heavy-duty logistics vehicles in the Beijing-Tianjin-Hebei region, becoming the first logistics enterprise in the industry to deploy hydrogen energy trucks on a large scale. In terms of green packaging, JD Logistics released original factory direct delivery packaging certification standards, urging shippers to conduct refined operations for recycled packaging.

JD Logistics supports environmentally friendly products through a carbon reduction incentive mechanism, aiming to expand the green consumption market and strengthen brand owners' determination to invest in green products. Since 2017, JD Logistics has implemented the "Green Stream Plan", joining hands with upstream and downstream partners to carry out end-to-end environmental protection actions in the supply chain, launching environmental public welfare activities such as "Your Name", "Box Love Plan", "Carbon Reduction Pioneer", "Together to Pick Up and Run", and "Home with Boxes", establishing consumer carbon accounts where consumers can receive carbon reduction points after placing orders for express delivery through the "JD Express" mini program, and using these points to exchange for discounts, reductions, and other benefits provided by merchants when purchasing products with "carbon reduction privileges" on JD Mall.

Section 5   China's Innovative Measures, Main Achievements, and Typical Cases in Vigorously Developing Green and Low-Carbon Industries

I. Green Technology Innovation Has Become an Important Support for New Quality Productive Forces

Anchored in the goal of building a strong science and technology nation by 2035, China focuses on high-level scientific and technological self-reliance and self-strengthening as the main line, strengthening coordination in strategic planning, policy measures, scientific research forces, major tasks, resource platforms, regional innovation, and other aspects. In 2023, the Central Committee of the Communist Party of China further strengthened centralized and unified leadership over scientific and technological work, established the Central Science and Technology Commission, and reorganized the Ministry of Science and Technology, achieving a systematic reshaping and overall reconstruction of the national science and technology leadership and management system. In 2024, China's position in the Global Innovation Index ranking rose to 11th, with its total R&D investment ranking second globally, the number of global top 100 science and technology innovation clusters continuing to rank first in the world, and manufacturing value-added scale ranking first globally for 14 consecutive years. Research personnel, high-level papers, and PCT international patent applications consistently ranked first in the world, with the contribution rate of scientific and technological progress exceeding 60%.

China's green technology has made a series of important advances: in terms of clean and efficient utilization of resources and energy, important breakthroughs have been made in coal clean and efficient conversion and utilization technologies represented by ultra-low emission technologies for coal-fired power generation, advanced coal-fired power generation technologies, and modern coal chemical technologies; deep-water oil and gas, tight gas, shale gas, tight oil, and coalbed methane exploration and development technologies have made significant progress; most core key technologies for third-generation nuclear power have been mastered, and wind power, photovoltaic power generation, and other renewable energy technologies and industries have developed rapidly; in the field of green resource technologies, progress has been made in complex low-grade multi-metal resource selection and smelting technologies, and a batch of key technologies have been broken through in resource utilization of bulk industrial solid waste, municipal solid waste incineration for power generation, and safe disposal of heavy metal solid waste; in the fight against pollution, environmental engineering technologies are developing towards cross-integration of multiple fields, disciplines, and industries, with process technology levels for electrostatic precipitation, desulfurization and denitrification, sewage treatment, soil pollution prevention and control, and collection and utilization of livestock and poultry manure reaching or approaching international advanced levels; in terms of ecological protection and restoration, technological research and development has been carried out in ecological monitoring and early warning, desertification prevention and control, water and soil loss control, rocky desertification control, degraded grassland restoration, biodiversity protection, ecological security assurance, and other areas, and a multi-level climate disaster early warning, defense, and service technology system has been basically established.

II. Green and Low-Carbon Industries Have Become New Engines of Economic Growth

China has built the world's largest and most complete new energy industry chain, with production scale of clean energy equipment such as wind power and photovoltaic power generation ranking first in the world, providing 70% of photovoltaic modules and 60% of wind power equipment globally. Annual sales of new energy vehicles rapidly increased from 13,000 units in 2012 to over 10 million units in 2024, with production and sales ranking first globally for 10 consecutive years, and ownership accounting for more than half of the global total. China's energy conservation and environmental protection industry has continuously improved in quality and efficiency, with an annual output value exceeding 8 trillion yuan. A number of leading enterprises at the ten-billion-yuan level have been cultivated. A green technology and equipment manufacturing system covering various fields such as energy saving, water conservation, environmental protection, and renewable energy has been formed. Environmental protection equipment is deeply integrated with new-generation information technologies like the Internet of Things and artificial intelligence. New business formats and models, including comprehensive energy services, energy performance contracting, water conservation management contracting, third-party environmental pollution control, and carbon emission management, are developing and growing stronger. Various regions are actively exploring paths to realize the value of ecological products, with rapid development of urban agriculture, eco-tourism, forest wellness, boutique homestays, garden complexes, and other ecological industries.

In 2024, while the photovoltaic industry experienced a downturn, Anhui Huasun Energy Co., Ltd. emerged strongly, with increasing orders, full production capacity, and booming sales, ranking among the global first-class photovoltaic module manufacturers. From its inception, Huasun Energy abandoned the mainstream technological path of homogenous competition and chose to develop next-generation heterojunction (HJT) photovoltaic cells. It successfully tackled the development of light conversion materials with higher cell power and built the world's largest integrated factory for HJT photovoltaic cells and modules by single-plant capacity. It launched a heterojunction technology industrialization collaborative innovation platform, discussing and sharing new technologies online at any time, and holding offline meetings every quarter, using itself as a laboratory to invite social scientific and technological forces to participate in the verification and application of various new technologies, new equipment, and new processes in the industrialization of heterojunction. Benefiting from the technical route advantages of HJT, Huasun Energy has moved from exporting products to exporting technology. For example, the 650-megawatt solar park in Pazardzhik, Bulgaria, uses equipment entirely produced by Huasun Energy, which is also the largest overseas photovoltaic park adopting HJT technology.

Following the approach of "technological homology, system integration, and industrial co-chaining", CRRC Group has constructed a "dual-track, dual-cluster" pattern for rail transit equipment and clean energy equipment. This strengthens its capability to lead and guarantee industrial co-chaining from rail transit to clean energy, and from complete machines to components. Core technologies accumulated in rail transit, such as power electronics and control algorithms, are being transferred to the new energy industry. This has led to the creation of a full "wind-solar-storage-hydrogen integration" industrial chain adaptable to diverse scenarios, spearheaded by complete wind turbine units and supported by key components like generators, blades, towers, converters, gearboxes, and transformers. The annual sales of wind power equipment exceed 30 billion yuan. As the only equipment manufacturing enterprise among the first batch of "AI+" action units of the State-owned Assets Supervision and Administration Commission of the State Council, CRRC Group focuses on the full business process, comprehensive management coverage, full customer lifecycle, full industry coverage, and full industry ecology, creating the CRRC "Aizor" large model that runs end-to-end through the industrial chain, supply chain, and innovation chain, joining hands with China Telecom to develop deep integration applications of the DeepSeek large model, providing digital intelligent support for the research and development design, production and manufacturing, operation and maintenance services of wind power equipment.

In September 2024, Geely Group released the "Taizhou Declaration", announcing that through the five major measures of "strategic focus, strategic integration, strategic coordination, strategic stability, and strategic talent", it would provide users with excellent products and flexible energy services that "can use oil, electricity, or methanol". In 2024, Geely Automobile's total sales exceeded 2.17 million units, of which new energy vehicle sales exceeded 880,000 units, both surpassing the annual sales targets, with total revenue reaching a historical high (240.2 billion yuan). Geely Automobile launched a "cloud, data, intelligence" integrated super cloud computing platform, forming a full-stack development system for new energy vehicles covering spatial design, intelligent energy, full-domain safety, AI intelligence, driving and control performance, etc. Furthermore, Geely Automobile formulated the "2025 Carbon Emission Reduction 50% Action Roadmap", with all of its vehicle manufacturing bases being recognized as national-level green factories. Geely's Xi'an Intelligent Environmental Protection Factory built a 52 MW photovoltaic power station, achieving 100% use of renewable energy, with an average annual power generation of 47.5 MkWh, reducing carbon dioxide emissions by 27,000 tons annually, equivalent to planting and afforesting 3,196 hectares. With additional water resource recycling facilities, a 296,000 m² factory greening area, and comprehensive use of low-volatility raw and auxiliary materials, it has achieved zero wastewater discharge, zero waste landfill, and zero harmful substance emissions throughout the manufacturing cycle, becoming China's first zero-carbon factory for vehicle manufacturers.

Infore Environment Technology Group, since developing China's first pure electric sweeper in 2007, has now achieved full coverage of new energy environmental sanitation vehicles for sweeping, washing, garbage collection and transfer, and municipal emergency services, with market share consistently ranking first in the industry for many years. "Adding smart wings to environmental sanitation equipment" is Yingfeng Environment's roadmap for the integration of green and intelligent technologies. It has developed a smart environmental sanitation cloud platform, adopting core technologies such as Internet of Things integration, video command and dispatch, and safe driving detection, providing remote services for the operation and management of environmental sanitation vehicle products, with daily active users exceeding 30,000 and daily average garbage collection volume approaching 30,000 tons. The "Smart Environmental Sanitation Operation Cabin" can be equipped with different new energy environmental sanitation equipment, with functions such as optimizing sweeping routes, adjusting operation intensity, intelligent data analysis, human-machine voice interaction, and environmental sanitation operation cloud management, improving energy and water efficiency by 15.2% and increasing environmental sanitation vehicle attendance rate by 17.5%.

BorgWarner PowerDrive Systems（Suzhou）Co., Ltd. produces components for global brand automobile manufacturers and implements the energy conservation and carbon reduction goal of "reducing energy intensity by 5% annually" throughout the entire process from design, process, operation to supply chain. With the support of the Suzhou Carbon Inclusive Service Center, it has obtained the "Zero Carbon Factory" certification issued by an internationally authoritative certification body. Suzhou Industrial Park is one of China's first batch of carbon peak pilot parks, with strong willingness for green energy application and carbon emission reduction among enterprises in the park. Suzhou Industrial Park and State Grid Suzhou Power Supply Company jointly established a Carbon Inclusive Service Center. Collaborating with photovoltaic investors, government agencies, banks, enterprises with carbon reduction needs, and the Shanghai Environment and Energy Exchange, among others, they have used distributed photovoltaics as an entry point to build China's first market-oriented voluntary emission reduction trading system. This system enables comprehensive online services for the entire carbon neutrality process, including digital verification, over-the-counter (OTC) trading, collateralized financing, online offsetting, and verification assistance (see Figure 4-2). It quantifies, verifies, and monetizes widespread, small-scale carbon reduction behaviors within the park. As of the end of 2024, it had cumulatively issued over 235,000 tons of carbon emission reductions and facilitated transactions of over 34,000 tons of carbon emission reductions.

Case 4-11   BYD: Technological Innovation Driving Global
New Energy Vehicle Industry Transformation
and Upgrade

In 2024, BYD's global sales of new energy vehicles reached 4.272 million units, a year-on-year increase of 41%, retaining the title of sales champion in the Chinese automobile market and global new energy vehicle market, achieving operating revenue of 777.102 billion yuan, a year-on-year increase of 29.02%, exceeding the 700 billion yuan mark for the first time and surpassing Tesla's revenue performance. BYD's new energy vehicles have accumulated pure electric mileage exceeding 150 billion km, reducing carbon emissions equivalent to planting 504 million trees. Behind these numbers is BYD's redefinition of "enterprise value".

"King of R&D" is BYD's decisive characteristic. In 2024, BYD's R&D investment reached 54.2 billion yuan, exceeding its net profit (40.25 billion

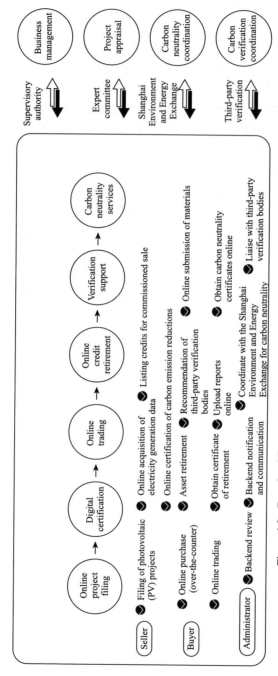

Figure 4-2　Functional Framework of Suzhou Carbon Inclusive Service Center Intelligent Platform

yuan). By the end of 2024, BYD's cumulative R&D investment exceeded 180 billion yuan, with over 120,000 R&D personnel, over 48,000 global patent applications, and over 30,000 granted patents, greatly improving vehicle performance and safety, and building solid technology barriers. Furthermore, since launching the world's first plug-in hybrid vehicle in 2008, BYD has continuously deployed in core technology areas such as batteries, motors, and electronic controls, becoming one of the few automakers in China capable of self-producing key components such as batteries.

As early as 1998, BYD established a European branch company in Rotterdam, the Netherlands, but its battery products were only deeply embedded in phones from Nokia, Motorola, and others, and were not widely known. In 2013, BYD's pure electric bus K9 obtained EU whole vehicle certification, marking the emergence of the BYD brand in overseas markets. In 2021, BYD launched its "passenger car overseas expansion" plan. In 2024, BYD's overseas exports reached 417,000 units, a year-on-year increase of 71.9%, covering more than 100 countries and regions across six continents, capturing the sales crown in multiple markets including Japan, Thailand, Brazil, Singapore, Colombia, and others. Notably, BYD has increasingly emphasized adapting to local market environments when entering different countries. For example, BYD's Thailand factory took only 16 months from groundbreaking to production, with an annual production capacity of about 150,000 units, launching customized models for local consumer needs, and cooperating with local enterprises to establish sales and service networks.

From BYD's overseas expansion practices, it can be seen that China's new energy vehicles are now entering a new era in international markets, with the most obvious characteristics being technology-driven, global branding, localization strategies, and participation in global value chains.

III. Significant Progress in Building the National Carbon Market

Following the decisions and deployments of the CPC Central Committee and the State Council, and based on international carbon market experience and local pilot practices, China's national carbon emissions trading market began with the power generation sector, launching trading in July 2021. Currently, it includes 2,257 key emission units, covering approximately 5.1 billion tons of carbon dioxide emissions annually, accounting for over 40% of China's carbon dioxide emissions, making it the world's largest market in terms of greenhouse gas emissions coverage. In January 2024, the national greenhouse gas voluntary emission reduction trading market was launched. The mandatory carbon market strictly controls emissions from key emission units, while the voluntary carbon market encourages broad social participation. The two carbon markets operate independently but are connected through an allowance surrender and offset mechanism. The allowance allocation method based on carbon emission intensity control targets demonstrates the flexibility and applicability advantages of the carbon market mechanism, contributing a "Chinese solution" to global carbon market mechanism innovation.

In January 2024, the State Council promulgated the "Interim Regulations on Carbon Emissions Trading Management", the first specialized regulation in China's climate change response field. The Ministry of Ecology and Environment issued the "Measures for the Administration of Carbon Emissions Trading (Trial)", released three rules on registration, trading, and settlement, and formulated or revised normative documents such as carbon emission accounting, reporting and verification guidelines, and allowance allocation plans, forming with the "Regulations" a multi-level institutional system covering "administrative regulations + departmental rules + normative documents + technical specifications". Various departments at all levels, key emission units, registration institutions, trading institutions, and technical service institutions fulfill their respective duties, ensuring the smooth operation of all aspects of national carbon emissions trading. By the end of 2023, the completion rates for allowance surrender in 2021 and 2022 were 99.61% and 99.88% respectively, further improving from the first compliance cycle and ranking among the top international carbon markets. A three-level "national-provincial-municipal" carbon emission data joint review mechanism has been established, with monthly verification of key data, forming a closed-loop management mechanism of "timely discovery-transfer for supervision-verification and rectification" for issues. The national carbon market management platform, registration system, and trading system

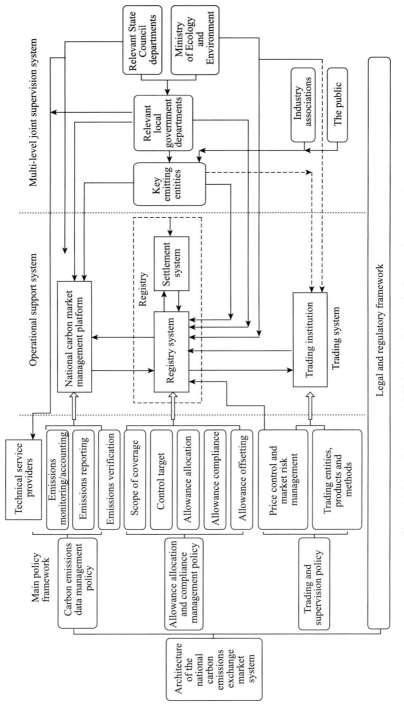

Figure 4-3　Architecture of China's carbon emissions exchange market system

have achieved interconnection （see Figure 4 – 3 Architectural Framework of China's Carbon Emissions Trading Market）.

The national carbon market reinforces enterprises' main responsibility for carbon reduction and establishes the low-carbon awareness that "carbon emissions have costs, carbon reduction has benefits" throughout society. Key emission units have basically implemented actual measurement of carbon content. The carbon market's role in controlling greenhouse gas emissions and promoting energy structure adjustment is increasingly evident. In 2023, China's thermal power carbon emission intensity decreased by 2.38% compared to 2018, and power sector carbon emission intensity decreased by 8.78%. Carbon emissions trading prices serve as benchmark prices for climate investment and financing, carbon asset management, allowance pledges, and other activities, leveraging more green and low-carbon investments. A statistical accounting system for carbon emissions in key industries that suits China's actual conditions has been basically established, aiming to cultivate a large number of professional talents and related institutions in the field of carbon technology services （see Table 4–1 Annual Transaction Overview of China's Carbon Market 2021–2024）.

The Guangzhou Emissions Exchange has established a market-oriented platform that focuses on realizing the value of ecological products in natural resources. It provides comprehensive services including ecological product development, filing, registration, circulation, cancellation, information disclosure, promotion, and financing connections. The center has designed an independent trading system for ecosystem carbon sinks with consumption applications, forming "ecosystem carbon sink + ecological label" ecological carbon sink products, as well as a multi-functional trading platform combining "ecological data+carbon elements". Through the implementation of ecosystem carbon sink measurement and monitoring method development, project filing and carbon sink product issuance, carbon sink product registration transfer and application, it resolves the challenges of existing projects lacking the broad coverage and high applicability required by voluntary emission reduction mechanisms.

Table 4-1   Annual Transaction Overview of China's Carbon Market 2021-2024
(Data Source: Shanghai Environment and Energy Exchange)

Year	Total Trading Volume (10,000 tons)	Total Trading Value (100 million yuan)	Listed Trading Volume (10,000 tons)	Listed Trading Value (100 million yuan)	Block Agreement Trading Volume (10,000 tons)	Block Agreement Trading Value (100 million yuan)	Average Trading Price (yuan/ton)	Closing Price (yuan/ton)
2021	17878.93	76.61	3077.46	14.51	14801.48	62.10	42.85	54.22
2022	5088.95	28.14	621.90	3.58	4467.05	24.56	55.30	55.00
2023	21194.28	144.44	3499.66	25.69	17694.72	118.75	68.15	79.42
2024	18864.61	181.14	3702.74	36.31	15161.86	144.82	96.02	97.49
Changes from 2023 to 2024	-11.0%	25.4%	5.8%	41.3%	-14.3%	22.0%	40.9%	22.8%

Chongqing's "Carbon Benefit Pass" greenhouse gas voluntary emission reduction platform integrates carbon compliance, carbon neutrality, and carbon inclusion functions. It converts achievements in carbon sequestration, clean energy application, and energy conservation from ecological, energy, industrial, and consumption sectors into carbon assets. The platform has formed a green lifestyle scenario system, carbon credit consumption system, and personal carbon account rights system, with registered users exceeding 2.5 million. Personal carbon accounts are established for users, and carbon emission reductions generated in various authorized scenarios are accurately calculated according to methods and standards recognized by ecological and environmental departments, then certified and converted into "Chongqing Carbon Credit Points" and credited to personal carbon accounts. In partnership with "Alipay", the platform has improved green travel scenarios such as public transit, subway, ride-hailing, and new energy charging. Users can record carbon emission reduction achievements in their personal carbon accounts for each low-carbon trip and can exchange these for travel discount coupons. Clear credit exchange rules have been established, allowing "Chongqing Carbon Credit Points" from personal carbon accounts to be transferred with value to the credit accounts of rights providers for their own "carbon neutrality" offsets, realizing the value of carbon credits.

Agricultural emission reduction and carbon sequestration have formed models such as carbon coupons, agricultural product carbon labels, carbon sink trading, carbon sink credit, and carbon sink insurance. For example, Junying Village and Baijiaoci Village in Lianhua Town, Tong'an District, Xiamen City are high-quality tea production areas. The Xiamen Property Rights Trading Center calculated the carbon sequestration of tea gardens, incorporated carbon sink resources into the trading system, and facilitated carbon sink trading contracts between the two villages and multiple enterprises, increasing farmers' income and encouraging them to reduce the use of chemical fertilizers and pesticides, enhancing both carbon sequestration capacity and tea quality. Through the Fuzhou (Lianjiang) Carbon Sink Trading Service Platform, Fujian Hengjie Industrial Co., Ltd. purchased 1,000 tons of marine fishery carbon sinks from Fujian Yida Food Co., Ltd. and used fishery carbon sink income rights as collateral to obtain a "Marine Carbon Sink Loan" from Industrial Bank. Fujian Huanrong Environmental Protection Co., Ltd. purchased agricultural carbon sinks from Longshan Town, Nanjing County, Zhangzhou City through the Haixia Equity Exchange. The latter adjusted continuous irrigation to intermittent irrigation, reduced soil methane production and achieved soil carbon sequestration through straw returning, reduced chemical fertilizer application, and organic fertilizer application.

Case 4-12   Gaochun District, Nanjing City: Agricultural
Carbon Sinks Opening a Channel for Transforming
Lucid Waters and Lush Mountains into Invaluable Assets

Gaochun District is located at the junction of Maoshan and Tianmu Mountains and the confluence of Taihu Lake and Shui Yang River watersheds, presenting a natural geographical pattern of "three mountains, two waters, and five parts farmland", with ecological conservation areas accounting for 70% of the total area. Rice paddies are a significant source of methane emissions, with China's annual rice field methane emissions reaching approximately 5 to 8 million tons. In May 2022, the Ministry of Agriculture and Rural Affairs and the

National Development and Reform Commission jointly issued the "Implementation Plan for Agricultural and Rural Emission Reduction and Carbon Sequestration", placing paddy field methane emission reduction action at the top of ten major actions. Building on its pioneering role as the province's first GEP accounting pilot, Gaochun District launched a carbon sequestration and emission reduction project in July of the same year on 500 mu (about 33. 33 hectares) of organic rice fields at the Chunhe Rice Professional Cooperative in Hexiejian Village.

Gaochun District collaborated with Nanjing Institute of Environmental Sciences of the Ministry of Ecology and Environment, Nanjing Agricultural University, and the Organic Food Development Center of the Ministry of Ecology and Environment (OFDC) to develop key technical systems such as greenhouse gas emission and soil carbon sequestration measurement models. They calculated the greenhouse gas reduction from ecological "zero-carbon rice" cultivation, which was filed and certified by Jiangsu Rural Property Rights Trading Center, with the Gaochun District Carbon Peak and Carbon Neutrality Working Group Office issuing the province's first agricultural carbon coupon. In March 2024, Gaochun District completed China's "first auction" of carbon sequestration from biochar organic rice. The carbon coupon numbered "0000001" in Jiangsu Province was purchased by Hongbaoli Group, a chemical new materials company, at 75 yuan per ton.

For sellers in this carbon coupon transaction, the carbon sequestration and emission reduction project achieved a 51% reduction in net greenhouse gas emissions through technological innovation, generating income from "selling air". Additionally, pest and disease incidence decreased by 15%, soil nutrient and water retention capacity improved, rice yield increased by 10% per mu (about 666. 67 m^2), and farmers' per capita income increased by more than 1, 700 yuan. For buyers, the certified carbon emission reductions on the carbon coupons can be used for carbon emission reduction market transactions at rural property rights trading centers, as well as for voluntary carbon offsetting, voluntary carbon cancellation, ecological environment damage compensation, etc. , balancing the contradiction between production operations and carbon emissions.

In May 2024, Gaochun District issued China's first vegetation comprehensive carbon sink value insurance policy. The policy covers all cultivated land and forests in Qiqiao Subdistrict, allowing the Subdistrict to apply for compensation at the agreed carbon sink value of 35 yuan per ton when actual carbon sequestration is lower than the target value due to natural disasters or accidents. The compensation is used for carbon sink resource rescue and ecological restoration. This demonstrates that establishing realization mechanisms for agricultural carbon sink product value promotes the adoption of diverse market means locally, facilitating both emission reduction and carbon sequestration while promoting green agricultural development.

IV. Significant Progress in Green Financial System Development

Under the dual goals of developing green productivity and building a financial powerhouse, China's green financial system has achieved positive results in top-level design, product service innovation, risk management and information disclosure, infrastructure construction, green finance reform and innovation pilot zones, and climate investment and financing pilots. This has formed a multi-level green financial market system dominated by green loans and green bonds with various green financial instruments flourishing. As of the end of 2024, China's green loan balance in domestic and foreign currencies reached 36.6 trillion yuan, a year-on-year increase of 21.7%. In 2024, 477 new green bonds were issued in China's domestic green bond market, with an issuance scale of approximately 681.432 billion yuan. In November 2021, the People's Bank of China launched the "Carbon-reduction Supporting Tool" to provide loans to financial institutions for carbon emission reduction loans issued to relevant enterprises through a "lend first, borrow later" approach. The tool provides support at 60% of the loan principal, with an interest rate of 1.75%, a term of 1 year, and the option for two extensions. As of the end of June 2024, the balance of the "Carbon-reduction Supporting Tool" was 547.8 billion yuan. It cumulatively supports financial institutions in issuing more than 1.1 trillion yuan in carbon emission reduction loans, covers more than 6,000 operating entities, and drives annual carbon emission reductions of nearly 200 million tons.

Shenzhen City has issued regulations and policies including the "Regulations of Shenzhen Special Economic Zone on Green Finance", "Opinions on Financial Support for High-Quality Development of New Energy Vehicle Industry Chain in Shenzhen", "Notice on Accelerating the Coordinated Development of Green Building Industry and Green Finance", "Guidelines for Environmental Information Disclosure by Financial Institutions in Shenzhen", "Guidelines for Green Investment Evaluation in Shenzhen", and "Administrative Measures for Shenzhen Green Financing Entity Database". The city's Banking Association conducts green finance efficiency evaluations, and financial institutions within its jurisdiction disclose environmental information. Shenzhen has released China's first local standard for environmental pollution mandatory liability insurance risk prevention and control services. The Shenzhen Branch of China Development Bank participated in issuing China's first "Bond Connect" green financial bond. Ping An Trust issued China's first "triple green" (green issuer + green fund use + green underlying assets) asset-backed note product. Ping An Property Insurance Shenzhen Branch launched China's first mangrove carbon sink index insurance. The Shenzhen Branch of Industrial Bank completed China's first mangrove protection carbon sink pledge financing business. The Shenzhen Branch of the Industrial and Commercial Bank of China established green specialized institutions and improved guarantee measures such as green approval channels, special green loan allocations, preferential pricing, etc. Shenzhen is becoming a highland for deepening green finance reform and innovation.

Case 4-13　　　　National Green Finance Reform and Innovation Pilot Zones: Financial Reform Moving Toward "Green"

Since 2017, the People's Bank of China, National Development and Reform Commission, and other departments have established green finance reform and innovation pilot zones in ten cities, including Huzhou and Quzhou in Zhejiang Province, Ganjiang New Area in Jiangxi Province, Guangzhou in Guangdong Province, Guian New Area in Guizhou Province, Hami City, Changji Prefecture, and Karamay City in Xinjiang Autonomous Region, Lanzhou New

Area in Gansu Province, and Chongqing. These pilot zones play a pioneering and demonstrative role, promoting the gradual realization of green finance from blueprint and concept to practice and action across society.

Green Finance Reform and Innovation Mechanisms Continuously Improving

Each pilot zone has established a leadership mechanism headed by local party and government leaders, formulated roadmaps and supporting implementation rules for pilot zone construction, established work supervision and incentive and restraint mechanisms, and fully leveraged the three major functions of financial support for green and low-carbon development: resource allocation, risk management, and market pricing. Guian New Area established China's first green finance court, and Huzhou City set up a green finance dispute mediation center, achieving diversified resolution and rapid handling of financial disputes, mediating all financial cases that can be mediated. Quzhou City established a 5e digital intelligent system for transition finance based on carbon accounts （carbon emission e-ledger, carbon credit e-report, carbon policy e-release, carbon finance e-supermarket, and carbon benefit e-evaluation）, resolving difficulties in identifying financial low-carbon assets, precise corporate carbon reduction management, and government low-carbon transition governance. Lanzhou New Area launched the green finance comprehensive service platform—" Green Gold Pass", integrating multidimensional enterprise credit information including business, judicial, tax, environmental protection, and energy consumption data. The platform enables intelligent recognition of green financing, efficient bank-enterprise financing connection, digital evaluation of enterprise credit, real-time monitoring of financial data, online evaluation of environmental rights and interests, and certification and rating of green enterprises （projects）, aiming to promote efficient bank-enterprise connection and cooperation.

Various financial institutions participate in green finance development in pilot zones through establishing green finance business departments or specialized institutions, formulating green finance transition plans, innovating green financial products and services, conducting carbon accounting and environmental information disclosure, pioneering green finance standards, and actively participating in international green finance cooperation. For example, Industrial and Commercial Bank of China has formulated special support policies and regularly holds special meetings on pilot zones; China People's Property Insurance Company launched China's first "insurance+service+credit" green building performance insurance in Huzhou and created the "safety production+environmental pollution prevention" "safety and environmental insurance" Quzhou model.

Innovative Green Financial Products and Services

Jiangxi Provincial Investment Group, overseen by Ganjiang New District, issued China's first perpetual bond linked to low-carbon transition for local state-owned enterprises. The bond sets enterprise scientific research and innovation investment indicators as prerequisites for its issuance, ties these to low-carbon transition performance goals, and selects clean energy power generation capacity as a key performance indicator that is also linked to the issuance interest rate. This innovative approach has resulted in achieving the lowest coupon rate among corporate bonds of the same term and variety issued in China since 2023.

Guangzhou's Tianren Mountain and Water Tourism Area is a Chinese natural education base that has created a rural cultural tourism revitalization model for Conghua District with support from local bank green loans. Guangzhou Lijiao Sewage Treatment Plant issued green bonds to create a garden-style environmental protection facility with "underground factory, above-ground park". Zengcheng Circular Economy Industrial Park used green loans to build a "waste-free park" with an annual waste treatment capacity of 1. 83 million tons and annual waste power generation of 839 MkWh.

China Everbright Bank Chongqing Branch improves the quality and effectiveness of green credit business by forming a team of green finance industry analysts, adopting differentiated credit approval strategies, and establishing green approval channels. In September 2023, Bank of China, as a joint lead underwriter, supported Chongqing Chang'an Auto Finance Company's successful issuance of 500 million yuan in green asset-backed securities for personal auto mortgage loans. All underlying assets in the pool were new energy vehicle loans, receiving the highest "G-1" rating from an authoritative certification institution for green bonds.

Agricultural Bank of China focuses on its main responsibilities in agriculture, rural areas, and farmers to build a green bank. It has established a Green Finance/Carbon Peak and Carbon Neutrality Working Committee at the executive management level and incorporated environmental and climate risk control into the responsibilities of the Risk Management and Internal Control Committee. The bank has launched green credit products such as Rural Human Settlement Environment Loans, Lucid Waters and Lush Mountains Loans, and Ecological Co-prosperity Loans. As of the end of 2024, the green credit balance exceeded 4. 97 trillion yuan, a year-on-year increase of 22. 9%. Utilizing policy tools and customizing innovative businesses such as green syndicated loans and green bonds based on client relationships, Agricultural Bank of China has worked with the Central Clearing Company to launch the first bond index in the rural revitalization field, the "ChinaBond-ABC Rural Revitalization Bond Index". It has issued dual-labeled "carbon neutrality" and "special rural revitalization" bonds, as well as triple-labeled "green", "special rural revitalization", and "revolutionary old areas" bonds. In cooperation with national carbon emission registration and trading institutions, it has launched the "ABC Carbon Service" settlement system to provide financial support for enterprise green and low-carbon transformation. The bank publishes annual reports on green finance development (environmental information disclosure) and strengthens carbon footprint management and energy conservation and carbon reduction in internal operations.

Industrial Bank has established a "dual carbon" service team and formed a carbon consulting special group. It has launched the "Dual Carbon Brain" management platform, opened carbon accounts for more than 16, 000 institutional clients, achieved precise monitoring and intelligent management of carbon data, and provided financing conveniences for enterprise carbon reduction compliance based on indicators such as enterprise carbon emission reduction, carbon asset holdings, and carbon performance. Industrial Bank has cooperated with the national carbon emission registration institution to develop the "Zhongtan-Industrial Bank National Carbon Market Carbon Emission Allowance Spot Pledge Price Index", which summarizes and analyzes user carbon account data and tracks and reflects carbon emission allowance value levels and change trends. The bank provides loans to enterprises that purchase carbon allowances with reference to this index, helping enterprises grasp carbon price fluctuation window opportunities and maximize carbon asset value.

In June 2024, Beijing Bank Nanjing Branch issued a 50 million yuan "Green-Brown Revenue Linked Loan" to Jiangsu Zhenjiang New Energy Equipment Co., Ltd., becoming the first implementation of this product. The "Green-Brown Revenue Linked Loan" is Beijing Bank's innovative exploration in building the "First Bank for Specialized, Refined, and Innovative Enterprises". It categorizes the borrowing enterprise's main business revenue into three categories:" green", "brown", and "non-green-brown", and links preferential loan interest rates to the borrower's green revenue performance by subdividing main business revenue labels, incentivizing borrowing enterprises to transition to green operations. Further, Beijing Bank has renamed its original "Board Strategy Committee" to "Board Strategy and Social Responsibility Committee", established a specialized green finance business management department at the head office level and specialized teams at the branch level, forming a head-branch coordinated green finance business management structure. The bank has launched the "Carbon Benefit Financing" green finance comprehensive service solution to provide financing services including green loans and green discounting with interest rate preferences and expedited approval, customized according to the green attribute certification results for enterprises and projects.

Case 4-14　　　　China Construction Bank: Playing a "Combination Punch" in Green Finance

Under the dual influence of national policy guidance and market demand, green finance, as one of the "five major articles", has increasingly become an important force in promoting sustainable economic and social development. China Construction Bank adheres to the strategic goal of "becoming a globally leading sustainable development bank". Its board of directors regularly reviews green finance development, and it has established a Carbon Peak and Carbon Neutrality Working Group led by the chairman and a Green Finance Committee chaired by the president. The bank has issued systems including the "Green Finance Development Strategic Plan (2022-2025)" and "Action Plan for Serving Carbon Peak and Carbon Neutrality", deploying a "combination punch" across five aspects: operational management systems, talent teams, business development, digital intelligence construction, and risk control.

Green development permeates all areas of production and life, requiring green finance innovation to be advanced according to local conditions, timing, and industry characteristics. China Construction Bank provides tailored solutions to match customer needs beyond standard products. For example, China Construction Bank Guangdong Branch cooperated with Nansha District Government in Guangzhou to launch the "Green Climate Loan" and compiled China's first Guangzhou-Hong Kong-Macao cooperative climate investment and financing standard. China Construction Bank Huzhou Branch used ESG rating tools for corporate clients to launch the "ESG Sustainable Development Loan", designing an adjustment mechanism linking loan interest rates to the achievement of enterprise sustainable development performance indicators. China Construction Bank Hubei Branch launched green power certificate income right pledge loans, activating the "environmental rights and interests" value of new energy projects. China Construction Bank Heilongjiang Branch launched pure credit online credit products for pig farming, beef cattle farming, dairy cattle farming, and other scenarios through the "Digital Animal Husbandry" industry service platform jointly built by government, banks, and enterprises. As of the end of 2024, China Construction Bank's green loan balance reached 4.7 trillion yuan, achieving stable growth in green development loans, core deposits, and key indicator performance.

Section 6   Expanding Green Growth: China's Experience in Green and Low-Carbon Transition and Its Implications for Developing Countries

I. Comprehensive Green and Low-Carbon Transition to Address Global Governance Challenges in Promoting High-Quality Economic Development and High-Level Environmental Protection

The CPC Central Committee with Comrade Xi Jinping at its core, taking a strategic and holistic view, has integrated green and low-carbon transition across all sectors, domains, and regions into the overall economic and social development framework. This approach considers both the holistic improvement of the "ecology-environment-energy" system and how a sound ecological environment system can support high-quality development, thereby using the "dual carbon" goals to coordinate carbon reduction, pollution reduction, green expansion, and economic growth. China has integrated the concept of green development into all links of the industrial, agricultural, and service sectors' value chains, accelerating the development of green and low-carbon industries represented by new energy vehicles, clean energy, energy conservation, environmental protection, and green finance. China vigorously promotes technological innovation, model innovation, and standards innovation, cultivating new green new quality productive forces and actively building a modern industrial system characterized by green, low-carbon, and circular development. Government departments formulate comprehensive green transition goals and policy systems, while market mechanisms play incentive and constraint roles through fiscal policies, financial instruments, investment mechanisms, and standards systems. By innovating green production methods and expanding green consumption, China encourages broad participation from diverse social entities, forming a modern green governance system characterized by "government guidance, market-driven approaches, and social participation".

II. Green Energy Transition Enhances the "Green Content" and "Gold Content" of Economic and Social Development

China has proposed carbon peaking and carbon neutrality goals, fully leveraging the guiding role of national strategic planning with consistent implementation. It has formulated medium and long-term energy development plans and renewable energy development plans, clarifying the goals, tasks, and pathways for green and low-carbon energy transition. China emphasizes supply-demand coordination: on the supply side, improving and expanding non-fossil energy, vigorously developing renewable energy, building complete supply chains for wind power, photovoltaic power, and other new energy industries, increasing the proportion of non-fossil energy in new energy demand, and promoting synergy and complementarity between new and traditional energy sources; on the consumption side, adhering to energy conservation and carbon reduction, accelerating the clean and efficient use of fossil fuels, and guiding society to use green energy and implement clean energy substitution. China dynamically improves policy measures for renewable energy grid-connected pricing, consumption guarantees, and market allocation, creating an equal, open, and inclusive market environment to attract social forces to participate in new energy development and construction. China coordinates development and security, ensuring stable energy supply while building a new power system that is clean, low-carbon, secure, abundant, economically efficient, supply-demand coordinated, flexible, and intelligent, enhancing the power system's capacity to absorb new energy. China promotes planning and construction of cross-provincial and cross-regional transmission channels and upgrades distribution networks to enhance the grid's capacity to carry and allocate power resources. China is building a unified national electricity market system, guiding the efficient and rational use of green electricity through market transactions and stimulating the vitality of business entities.

III. Actively Guiding the General Public to Practice Green Lifestyles

From consciously practicing the "Clean Plate" campaign to nationwide voluntary tree planting, from actively sorting garbage to rejecting "white pollution", from embracing new energy vehicles to sparking running and cycling trends, from advocating the sharing economy to engaging in second-hand transactions... China actively promotes ecological civilization values, systematically advances ecological civilization publicity and education, and guides the public to enhance consumption concepts and living habits characterized by frugality, environmental care, and ecological protection. China improves incentive mechanisms for green lifestyles, builds green product certification and labeling systems, and guides consumers to start with small actions by adhering to green diets, green clothing, green office practices, and green transportation. Through a green revolution in lifestyles, China drives the green transformation of production methods, popularizing green living and "zero-waste" concepts in all aspects of daily life including food, clothing, housing, transportation, tourism, and consumption, creating a favorable atmosphere for the whole society to jointly promote green development.

Section 7   Policy Recommendations for Further Advancing Green and Low-Carbon Transition from the Perspective of Chinese Modernization

I. Linking Lifestyle and Consumption Patterns for Comprehensive Green Transformation Across All Ages

Vigorously advocate simple, moderate, green, low-carbon, civilized, and healthy life concepts and consumption patterns, integrating green concepts and conservation requirements into economic and social rules such as civilization conventions, citizen conventions, village regulations, corporate rules, student codes, and organizational charters to form a strong social atmosphere that values ecological civilization. Implement differentiated incentive systems for green products, energy efficiency, water efficiency, and carbon labeling, and promote energy conservation and carbon reduction throughout the entire product lifecycle, including research and development, design, manufacturing, packaging, logistics, and recycling. Optimize green procurement policies for Party and government organs, public institutions, central and state-owned enterprises, and listed companies; guide small and medium-sized enterprises to implement green procurement guidelines; expand the scope and scale of green product procurement; incorporate carbon footprint requirements into public sector procurement; and promote the establishment of green supply chains by enterprises above designated size. Encourage local governments and market entities to issue green consumption vouchers and green credits, encouraging consumers to purchase green products and participate in "trade-in" programs. Continue to carry out activities promoting new energy vehicles, green and intelligent household appliances, water-saving devices, energy-saving stoves, and green building materials in rural areas, strengthening supporting facilities and after-sales service guarantees.

II. Actively and Steadily Promoting the Green Transformation of the Energy Sector

With safety, greenness, and economy as constraints, comprehensively optimize power and energy security, power flow layout, new energy layout, and system regulation capacity, establishing new power systems tailored to local conditions. Deepen the energy revolution, implementing coal consumption control, scattered coal replacement, and clean energy development simultaneously in key regions, continuing to implement the "three reforms in coordination" approach: coal power energy conservation and carbon reduction transformation, flexibility transformation, and heating transformation. Promote the integrated development of oil and gas exploration and development with new energy, and advance the construction of carbon dioxide capture, utilization, and storage projects. Coordinate hydropower development and ecological protection, promote integrated development of hydro, wind, and solar power, and accelerate the construction of clean energy bases in northwest China (wind and photovoltaic power), southwest China (hydropower), offshore wind power, and coastal nuclear power. Actively develop distributed photovoltaic and dispersed wind power, develop new energy sources such as biomass energy, geothermal energy, and ocean energy, promote the "production-storage-transportation-use" whole chain development of hydrogen energy, and actively, safely, and orderly develop nuclear power. Strengthen the coordination of clean energy bases, regulatory resources, and transmission channels, accelerate the construction of smart grid projects such as microgrids, virtual power plants, and integrated source-grid-load-storage projects to achieve rapid growth, large-scale application, and safe, reliable, and orderly replacement of renewable energy.

III. Simultaneously Promoting the Construction of a Modern Industrial System and the Green and Low-Carbon Transformation of Industrial Structure

Promote the green and low-carbon transformation of traditional industries, popularize clean production technologies and equipment, update and upgrade traditional process flows, and improve mechanisms for phasing out outdated production capacity. Driven by scientific and technological innovation, green intelligent manufacturing, and manufacturing services, develop strategic emerging industries, high-tech industries, energy conservation and environmental protection industries, modern efficient agriculture, and modern service industries in an integrated manner. Look ahead to layout green future industries such as artificial intelligence and biopharmaceuticals, and cultivate leading enterprises and specialized, refined, distinctive, and innovative small and medium-sized enterprises for green and low-carbon development. Encourage the innovative development of new industries, new business formats, and new business models such as energy performance contracting, water conservation management contracting, third-party environmental pollution treatment, and carbon emission management. Promote the deep integration of culture, tourism, commerce, health, and wellness. Advance green and low-carbon science and technology self-reliance, strengthen key core technology research, and enhance the creation, protection, and application of green and low-carbon technology intellectual property. Deepen the application of digital and intelligent technologies in power systems, industry, agriculture, transportation, building construction and operation, and other fields. Accelerate the "cloud adoption, data utilization, and intelligent empowerment" of entities of all sizes, and guide internet platforms toward green and low-carbon development, leading upstream and downstream market entities to improve their carbon reduction capabilities. Focus on key areas such as ecological and environmental protection projects, carbon markets, resource and environmental elements, eco-environment-oriented development projects, climate investment and financing, and green consumption to promote financial institutions' innovation in green financial products and services including green credit, green bonds, green funds, green asset securitization, and green supply chain finance.

Chapter 5
A Symphony of Partnership: China's Measures, Achievements, Experiences, and Recommendations for Strengthening Green International Cooperation

In 2013, it was in Kazakhstan that President Xi Jinping first proposed the initiative to jointly build the "Silk Road Economic Belt" and first introduced the "Two Mountains Theory" in an international forum. As the joint construction of the "Belt and Road" enters a new stage of high-quality development, the concept of the "Two Mountains Theory" has increasingly taken root. With a concern for the common future and destiny of humanity, President Xi Jinping has made sincere appeals regarding global green governance on multiple international occasions: "Earth is our common home. We must uphold the concept of a community with a shared future for mankind, work together to address challenges in climate and environmental fields, and safeguard this blue planet." "Only through cooperation can we effectively address global environmental issues such as climate change, ocean pollution, and biodiversity protection." The spring breeze of green development rises from the East and blows toward a broader world. Erik Solheim, former UN Under-Secretary-General and Executive Director of the UN Environment Programme, believes that while becoming the world's second-largest economy, China also plays the role of a global leader in green development. Other countries should visit China more often to gain inspiration from China's green development. Peter Lizak, Slovak Ambassador to China, believes that green development is a "gift" from China to the world, and China and Slovakia have maintained close cooperation on climate issues.

Section 1   Innovative Measures, Main Achievements, and Typical Cases in Building a Green Silk Road

I. Continuous Improvement of the Green Cooperation Policy System

China has integrated the concept of green development into all areas of the "Belt and Road" Initiative, creating new space and platforms for world economic growth while providing Chinese solutions for global green governance, continuously benefiting the people of participating countries, with green becoming a distinctive feature of the "Belt and Road" Initiative. In 2015, China issued the "Vision and Actions on Jointly Building Silk Road Economic Belt and 21st Century Maritime Silk Road", proposing to "highlight the concept of ecological civilization in investment and trade, strengthen cooperation in ecological environment, biodiversity, and climate change response, and jointly build a Green Silk Road". Subsequently, China issued policy documents such as "Guidance on Promoting Green Belt and Road Construction", "Belt and Road Ecological Environmental Protection Cooperation Plan", "Guidelines for Ecological Environmental Protection in Foreign Investment Cooperation and Construction Projects", and "Opinions on Promoting Green Development in Jointly Building the Belt and Road", providing roadmaps for strengthening environmental management of overseas projects, promoting green development in jointly building the "Belt and Road", and facilitating international cooperation in green energy and other key areas.

II. Growing Consensus on Green Cooperation

China has signed the "Memorandum of Understanding on Building a Green Belt and Road (2017-2022)" with the United Nations Environment Programme, established environmental cooperation agreements with over 50 countries and international organizations, and advocated for the establishment of the Belt and Road Energy Cooperation Partnership and Global Clean Energy Cooperation Partnership. China has established the Belt and Road Initiative International Green Development Coalition with more than 170 partners from over 40 participating countries, organized thematic events including Green Development Roundtables, Green Innovation Conferences, and Green Finance and Low-carbon Development Forums, and published policy research reports such as the "Green Development Outlook for the Belt and Road Initiative" and "Green Development Guidelines for Belt and Road Projects". China has established bilateral and multilateral platforms including the China-ASEAN Environmental Protection Cooperation Center, China-Cambodia Environmental Cooperation Center, China-Laos Environmental Cooperation Office, China-Shanghai Cooperation Organization Environmental Protection Cooperation Center, Lancang-Mekong Environmental Cooperation Center, and China-Africa Environmental Cooperation Center. It has also formulated and implemented the "China-ASEAN Environmental Cooperation Strategy", "Shanghai Cooperation Organization Member States Environmental Cooperation Vision", and "Lancang-Mekong Environmental Cooperation Strategy". China has conducted biodiversity conservation cooperation research with participating countries, jointly safeguarded the ecological security of the Maritime Silk Road, and established the "Belt and Road Ecological and Environmental Big Data Service Platform"[1] and the "Belt and Road Environmental Technology Exchange and Transfer Center" (jointly built by the Ministry of Ecology and Environment and Shenzhen Municipal People's Government).

China has launched the Green Silk Road Envoys Program[2], training tens

---

① Note: The Belt and Road Ecological and Environmental Big Data Service Platform collects basic environmental information, environmental laws, regulations, and standards from over 60 participating countries, encompasses more than 200 indicator data points published by over 30 authoritative international platforms, develops "One Map" decision support systems and foreign investment project environmental assessment tools, and provides ecological environmental management and green development solutions for foreign investment.

② Note: The Green Silk Road Envoys Program originated from the China-ASEAN Green Envoy Program launched in 2011. In 2016, to implement the national leadership's initiative, the China-ASEAN Green Envoys Program was officially upgraded to the Green Silk Road Envoy Program. The upgraded Green Silk Road Envoys Program conducts a series of friendly exchanges and practical cooperation projects, including ecological environmental management capacity building cooperation activities, youth pioneer activities, and environmental technology and industry exchange cooperation and demonstration.

of thousands of officials, university students, researchers, and technical personnel in the ecological and environmental fields from nearly 120 developing countries, which has been praised by the United Nations Environment Programme as a "model of South-South cooperation". China has implemented the Belt and Road South-South Cooperation Plan on Climate Change, signed 53 memorandums of understanding on South-South climate change cooperation with 42 participating countries, collaborated with Laos, Cambodia, Seychelles and others to build low-carbon demonstration zones, and carried out over 70 climate change mitigation and adaptation projects with more than 30 participating countries including Ethiopia, Pakistan, Samoa, Chile, and Egypt. Since 2016, China has provided and mobilized climate financing totaling over 177 billion yuan for other developing countries.

Case 5-1   The Third Belt and Road Forum for International Cooperation: Planning for a New Golden Decade of High-Quality Green Silk Road Development

At the opening ceremony of the Third Belt and Road Forum for International Cooperation held in October 2023, President Xi Jinping announced eight actions to support high-quality Belt and Road cooperation, with "promoting green development" being one of them. President Xi Jinping proposed that China will continue to deepen cooperation in green infrastructure, green energy, green transportation and other fields, increase support for the Belt and Road Initiative International Green Development Coalition, continue to hold the Belt and Road Green Innovation Conference, and establish a photovoltaic industry dialogue and exchange mechanism and a green low-carbon expert network. China will implement the Green Investment Principles for the Belt and Road and provide training for 100,000 people from partner countries by 2030.

"Building a Green Silk Road and Promoting Harmony Between Humans and Nature" was one of the three high-level forums at the Third Belt and Road Forum for International Cooperation. At the forum, China and more than 30 co-initiators, including governments and environmental authorities, international organizations, research institutions, financial institutions, and enterprises from

20 participating countries, jointly issued the "Beijing Initiative on Green Development of the Belt and Road", proposing strengthened cooperation in eight areas: addressing climate change, implementing the "Kunming-Montreal Global Biodiversity Framework", ecological environmental protection, green infrastructure connectivity, green energy, green transportation, green finance, and cooperation platforms. Participants emphasized the importance of jointly advancing the construction of a Green Silk Road, strengthening policy communication and strategic alignment for green and low-carbon development, sharing green development concepts and practices, encouraging the role of the Belt and Road Initiative International Green Development Coalition platform, and deepening Belt and Road green development partnerships.

"Marine Cooperation" was one of the six thematic forums at the Third Belt and Road Forum for International Cooperation. At the forum, guests from various countries engaged in in-depth exchanges on successful practices and development opportunities in marine protection and marine economic development around the theme "Promoting Blue Cooperation, Composing Maritime Silk Road Melodies", and released the "Belt and Road Blue Cooperation Initiative" and a list of Belt and Road blue cooperation achievements. The "Belt and Road Blue Cooperation Initiative" calls on all parties to take concerted action to jointly protect and sustainably use the oceans, jointly plan blue cooperation initiatives, share blue development results, and build a beautiful blue home together; it also promotes the transformation and upgrading of marine industries based on clean production, green technology, and circular economy.

III. Steady Progress in Green Bilateral and Multilateral Cooperation

China has successfully hosted the 15th Conference of the Parties (COP15) to the Convention on Biological Diversity and the 14th Conference of the Parties to the Ramsar Convention on Wetlands, and actively participated in green development cooperation under frameworks such as the G20, China-ASEAN, ASEAN Plus Three, East Asia Summit, Forum on China-Africa Cooperation, BRICS, Shanghai Cooperation Organization, and Asia-Pacific Economic Cooperation. China led the formulation of the "G20 Energy Efficiency Leading Program", which became an important outcome of the G20 Hangzhou Summit. China has engaged in bilateral and multilateral cooperation with India, Brazil, South Africa, the United States, Japan, Germany, France, ASEAN and other countries and regions in areas such as energy conservation, environmental protection, clean energy, climate change response, biodiversity conservation, desertification control, and marine and forest resource protection. China has promoted green and low-carbon technical assistance, capacity building, and pilot projects in key areas such as industry, agriculture, energy, transportation, and urban-rural construction through United Nations agencies, the Asian Development Bank, the Asian Infrastructure Investment Bank, the New Development Bank, the Global Environment Facility, the Green Climate Fund, the International Energy Agency, the International Renewable Energy Agency and other international organizations, making important contributions to promoting global sustainable development.

China and ASEAN countries have jointly formulated and implemented the "China-ASEAN Environmental Cooperation Strategy 2009-2015", "China-ASEAN Environmental Cooperation Strategy 2016-2020", and "China-ASEAN Environmental Cooperation Strategy and Action Framework 2021-2025", establishing four strategic cooperation directions: environmental policy dialogue and capacity building, climate change response and air quality improvement, sustainable cities and marine plastic reduction, and biodiversity conservation and ecosystem management. China has successfully held 10 China-ASEAN Environmental Cooperation Forums and carried out flagship cooperation projects including the China-ASEAN Environmentally Friendly Cities Development Partnership, China-ASEAN Environmental Information Sharing Platform, China-ASEAN Green Value Chain Partnership, China-ASEAN Climate Change Response and Air Quality Improvement Plan, and China-ASEAN Mangrove Conservation Partnership. China has also implemented demonstration cooperation with UN agencies in the ASEAN region aimed at simultaneously improving community livelihoods and protecting the ecological environment. China has conducted talent development programs such as the China-ASEAN Ecological Environment and Climate Change Response Envoy Program and the China-ASEAN Green Envoy Program, building cooperation and communication bridges for nearly 4,000 government officials, business representatives, researchers, and young scholars from ASEAN countries.

Green development is one of the important cooperation areas of the Shanghai Cooperation Organization (SCO). In September 2021, the SCO Heads of State Council Meeting reviewed and approved the "Implementation Measures Plan for the SCO Member States Environmental Protection Cooperation Vision 2022–2024", proposing to "study the feasibility of establishing an SCO ecological and environmental innovation base". In November 2022, the "Joint Communique of the 21st Meeting of the Council of Heads of Government (Prime Ministers) of SCO Member States" stated, "The heads of delegations noted the proposal of the People's Republic of China on establishing an SCO ecological and environmental innovation base". In July 2024, President Xi Jinping attended the "SCO+" Astana Summit and pointed out the need to "make good use of platforms such as the ecological and environmental innovation base to promote regional cooperation". At the SCO Green Development Forum held in the same month, participants jointly issued the "Initiative on Building a Green Development Partnership and Promoting Sustainable Development", proposing to promote regional green and low-carbon development through forms such as establishing the "China-Shanghai Cooperation Organization Ecological and Environmental Innovation Base". China, relying on the Foreign Environmental Cooperation Center, Ministry of Ecology and Environment (China-Shanghai Cooperation Organisation (SCO) Environmental Protection Cooperation Center), has established the China-SCO Ecological and Environmental Innovation Base in Shanghai and Qingdao. It has created a window for information exchange and sharing among SCO countries on ecological and environmental protection, a platform for ecological and environmental talent cultivation and capacity building, a platform for environmental technology demonstration and promotion, and a platform for green investment, financing, and industrial cooperation.

In March 2016, China proposed at the first Lancang-Mekong Cooperation Leaders' Meeting that it "is willing to establish the Lancang-Mekong Environmental Cooperation Center with Mekong countries to strengthen technical cooperation, talent and information exchange, and promote green, coordinated, and sustainable development", marking the official inclusion of Lancang-Mekong environmental cooperation in the Lancang-Mekong dialogue and cooperation mechanism. In January 2018, the "Lancang-Mekong Cooperation Five-Year Action Plan (2018-2022)" and the "Phnom Penh Declaration of the Second Lancang-Mekong Cooperation Leaders' Meeting" issued at the second Lancang-Mekong Cooperation Leaders' Meeting proposed to jointly formulate and implement the "Lancang-Mekong Environmental Cooperation Strategy" and the "Green Lancang-Mekong Plan". The latter aims to connect the Lancang-Mekong region with the world, carry out flagship cooperation projects such as environmental policy mainstreaming, environmental capacity building, environmental demonstration cooperation, and environmental cooperation partnerships, build a regional climate and ecological policy dialogue platform, and enhance the environmental governance capacity of countries in the basin.

Lake Poyang and Lake Victoria are the largest freshwater lakes in China and Africa respectively, nurturing tens of millions of people in surrounding areas and serving as havens for various wildlife. Jiangxi Province, home to Lake Poyang, has initiated cross-continental "hand-in-hand" cooperation with relevant regions of Uganda, Kenya, and Tanzania in the Lake Victoria area. Jiangxi Province has unreservedly shared its experience in Lake Poyang's ecological environmental governance and poverty alleviation with institutions and individuals from the three countries; invited government officials, environmental organization members, and community members from the three countries to the Lake Poyang region to learn professional knowledge about growing high-value-added vegetables, poultry farming, pest control, reducing pesticide pollution, biogas power generation, and photovoltaic power generation; and dispatched technical personnel to support rural areas around Lake Victoria in improving toilets and stoves, rainwater storage, tree planting and breeding, scientific fishing, as well as developing courtyard economies, circular agriculture, clean energy, organic food and other green industries, achieving ecological restoration and increased income for fishermen.

The Aral Sea was once the world's fourth-largest lake and Asia's second-largest inland salt lake. Due to climate change and human activities, its water area has shrunk to only 10% of its 1960 size, with the dried lake bed producing 40 to 150 million tons of salt dust annually, severely affecting the ecological environment in Central Asia. In 2018, the Ministry of Innovative Development of Uzbekistan invited China to participate in the ecological management of the Aral Sea's severely saline-alkaline land. With support from the Silk Road Environmental Special Fund, the Xinjiang Institute of Ecology and Geography, Chinese Academy of Sciences, together with the CAS Research Center for Ecology and Environment of Central Asia and Uzbek scientists, completed the "Comprehensive Ecological Environmental Management Plan for the Aral Sea Dried Lake Basin", established automatic meteorological and water quality observation stations in the Aral Sea basin, built ecological restoration experimental zones, water-saving agriculture demonstration zones, and salt-tolerant plant germplasm resource nurseries, and demonstrated the planting of salt-tolerant plants, drip-irrigated cotton, and water-saving rice. Xinjiang's desertification prevention and control achievements have been promoted and applied in Central Asia.

Case 5-2   China and Africa Jointly Advancing Ecologically Friendly Modernization: Creating a New Model of International Green Cooperation for the New Era

In promoting green development, China and Africa have always been "companions on the same path" and "action-oriented partners". Many African countries have actively drawn on China's innovative concept and practical experience that "lucid waters and lush mountains are invaluable assets", creatively pointing out that "green is gold". The "Forum on China-Africa Cooperation-Beijing Action Plan (2025-2027)" released at the Beijing Summit of the Forum on China-Africa Cooperation in September 2024 proposed that China and Africa will jointly promote the "Green Development Partnership Action" over the next three years, charting a new blueprint for China-Africa green cooperation in three areas: new energy, climate change, and ecological protection.

Africa is a treasure house of global energy resources, with abundant reserves of both traditional and renewable energy. However, Africa is the region with the largest energy gap in the world. Due to the large capital investment required for energy development and related infrastructure, high technical requirements, and long profit recovery periods, most African countries' finances cannot afford them. China has implemented hundreds of clean energy projects in Africa, including photovoltaic, geothermal, lithium battery, and wind power projects, with photovoltaic power station installed capacity alone exceeding 1.5 gigawatts. For example, the Garissa Photovoltaic Power Station in Kenya, built by Jiangxi International Economic & Technical Cooperation Co., Ltd., is Africa's first geothermal project independently constructed with a complete set of Chinese technology and is the largest photovoltaic power project in East Africa, with an average annual power generation exceeding 76 MkWh, meeting the electricity needs of 380,000 people; the Morocco Noor Solar Power Station, for which SEPCO Electric Power Construction Corporation is the general contractor, provides clean energy for more than one million households, changing the country's long-term dependence on imported electricity; "small but beautiful" clean energy projects built by Chinese enterprises, such as Mali's Solar Demonstration Village and Cameroon's Photovoltaic Microgrid, benefit remote communities and improve people's well-being.

In November 2021, the 8th Ministerial Conference of the Forum on China-Africa Cooperation adopted the "Declaration on China-Africa Cooperation on Combating Climate Change", establishing a new era China-Africa strategic partnership for addressing climate change. As of September 2024, China has signed 19 memorandums of understanding on South-South cooperation in addressing climate change with 17 African countries. In September 2023, China announced the implementation of the "African Light Belt" project at the first African Climate Summit to help 50,000 households without electricity in impoverished areas of Africa solve their lighting problems. The project is implemented by the Foreign Environmental Cooperation Center, Ministry of Ecology and Environment, which has conducted project consultations with 10 countries including Chad, Sao Tome and Principe, Mali, and Burundi, and signed cooperation memorandums of understanding or implementation agreements with five of these countries.

To curb desert expansion in North Africa, African countries have drawn on China's Three-North Shelterbelt Forest Program to carry out the "Great Green Wall" desertification control plan, which aims to build an 8,000-kilometer-long ecological protection forest belt along the southern edge of the Sahara Desert and manage 100 million hectares of desertified land. China has repeatedly held specialized training courses on the "Great Green Wall" construction for African countries. In 2017, the Xinjiang Institute of Ecology and Geography, Chinese Academy of Sciences signed a cooperation memorandum with the Pan-African "Great Green Wall" Organization Secretariat to cooperate in ecosystem monitoring, sustainable land resource utilization, talent cultivation, and technology transfer. To date, the two sides have clarified the spatial pattern of the ecological environment in the "Great Green Wall" construction area, revealed the dynamic process and development trend of desertification in the Sahel region, delineated sensitive areas and key governance areas for land degradation, vegetation damage, and wind-sand hazards, preliminarily established the African "Great Green Wall" desertification atlas and the African "Great Green Wall" ecosystem management case library, and developed practical sand control technologies such as desert city flowing sand control, desert road sand hazard control, hill water collection afforestation, and degraded grassland restoration.

Case 5-3   Building a "Green BRICS" as Practitioners of
Sustainable Development

In 2022, when China held the BRICS rotating presidency, it called for jointly addressing climate change, accelerating green and low-carbon transformation, and achieving higher-quality and more sustainable development. Starting that year, the United Nations Climate Change Conference entered "BRICS time", with Egypt, the United Arab Emirates, Azerbaijan, Brazil, and other new and old BRICS members and "BRICS+" countries successively hosting climate change conferences, continuously promoting the steady development of global climate governance, and striving for legitimate rights and interests for the broader "Global South" countries represented by BRICS nations. Also, the New Development Bank BRICS adheres to green principles and provides investment and financing support for the green and sustainable development of BRICS countries and other "Global South" countries in need. In October 2024, at the 16th BRICS Leaders' Meeting held in Kazan, Russia, President Xi Jinping put forward China's proposition on building a "Green BRICS".

Brazil has vast territory with hydropower resources concentrated in the north and electricity demand concentrated in large cities in the southeast. China's solution to the contradiction between energy distribution and load separation is to build ultra-high voltage projects to achieve "north-to-south power transmission". The Belo Monte (Brazil) ±800 kV Ultra-High Voltage Direct Current Transmission Project is the highest voltage and most technologically advanced national backbone transmission project in the Americas. It achieves the coordinated "going global" of China's ultra-high voltage "investment, construction, operation" and "technology, equipment, standards" in two integrated full industrial chains and value chains, driving high-end domestic power equipment such as converter transformers, converter valves, and DC control and protection devices into the Brazilian market. It transmits abundant hydroelectric power from the Amazon Basin to cities in southeastern Brazil such as Rio de Janeiro and São Paulo, more than 2,000 km away, in a long-distance, large-capacity, low-loss manner, thus meeting the electricity needs of over 22 million people.

China and Russia share more than 4,300 km of common border and are each other's largest neighbors. Ecological and environmental cooperation is an important component of the China-Russia comprehensive strategic partnership of coordination for a new era. Since the establishment of the Environmental Protection Subcommittee mechanism under the China-Russia Prime Ministers' Regular Meeting Committee, the water quality of transboundary water bodies between the two countries has remained stable for many consecutive years, the emergency contact mechanism for sudden environmental incidents has been smooth and effective, and the ecological environment in border areas has been increasingly improved. China and Russia have deepened cooperation in protecting rare and endangered wildlife such as Amur tigers and Amur leopards and migratory birds, jointly conducted forest patrols, Amur tiger and leopard monitoring, and ecological corridor construction, ensuring the free migration of Amur tigers and leopards across the China-Russia border. Energy cooperation has always been the most substantial, fruitful, and extensive field in China-Russia practical cooperation, with nuclear energy being a strategic priority direction. Jiangsu

Tianwan Nuclear Power Plant is currently the nuclear power base with the largest total installed capacity in operation and under construction in the world and is the largest technical and economic cooperation project between China and Russia to date. Units 7 and 8 reference the Leningrad Nuclear Power Plant Phase II in Russia and adopt the VVER-1200 （AES-2006） reactor type in cooperation with Russia, with a unit capacity of 1.265 MkW, making it one of the most representative third-generation nuclear power units globally.

In August 2023, at the 15th BRICS Leaders' Meeting, China's State Grid Corporation and China Energy Group respectively signed strategic cooperation memorandums with ESKOM to actively participate in the investment and operation of South Africa's renewable energy projects. South Africa's Northern Cape Province has excellent solar conditions and flat, open land. The Red Stone 100 MW Tower Molten Salt Concentrated Solar Power Station built by Power Construction Corporation of China is the first tower molten salt concentrated solar power station in sub-Saharan Africa. Its nearly 250-meter-high light tower absorbs sunlight reflected by more than 40,000 mirrors on the ground, and the stored high-temperature liquid salt provides power for nighttime electricity generation, achieving uninterrupted power generation and meeting the electricity needs of about 200,000 households; the De Aar Wind Farm in South Africa is the first wind power project in Africa that integrates Chinese investment, construction, and operation, with an average annual power generation of 760 MkWh. The operator has installed bird perches on top of each power line pole to strengthen the protection of flora and fauna within the wind farm.

The Egyptian government has proposed a strategy to build a regional clean energy center under the framework of "Vision 2030", and Chinese enterprises have participated in the construction of clean energy and green development projects such as the Gulf of Suez 500 MW Wind Power Project, the Kom Ombo 500 MW Photovoltaic Power Station, and the Kom Ombo Solar Photovoltaic Power Station. Egypt's "Al Akhbar" （newspaper） has pointed out that Chinese enterprises actively participate in Egypt's green energy projects and play an important role in promoting Egypt's green economic development. The Benban Solar Park is Egypt's first photovoltaic power generation project built and financed by Chinese enterprises, with plans to build 40 solar power plants with a total installed capacity of about 2,000 megawatts, making it one of the world's largest photovoltaic industrial parks. Notably, China not only provides Egypt with advanced clean energy technologies and equipment but also dispatches experienced technical personnel to work closely with Egyptian teams, achieving localized operations.

Section 2　China's Innovative Measures, Main Achievements, and Typical Cases in Promoting Green International Cooperation in Key Areas

I. Green Energy Cooperation Practicing True Multilateralism

China continues to create a first-class business environment that is market-oriented, law-based, and internationalized, actively promoting the liberalization and facilitation of energy trade and investment, and providing opportunities for foreign enterprises to share in the dividends of China's energy transition. China has fully implemented the pre-establishment national treatment plus negative list management system, with foreign investment access in the energy sector, except for nuclear power plants, now fully opened. China has issued a catalog of industries encouraging foreign investment and increased policy support for foreign investment in clean energy and other fields. Multinational companies such as General Electric, BP, and Siemens have steadily increased their energy investment in China, and foreign investment projects such as the Electricite De France's offshore wind power project, the Shanghai Tesla electric vehicle manufacturing project, and the Nanjing LG New Energy Battery project have successively landed in China.

In September 2021, President Xi Jinping stated in his video address to the general debate of the 76th Session of the United Nations General Assembly that China will strongly support developing countries in green and low-carbon energy development and will no longer build new coal-fired power projects abroad. China has carried out green energy cooperation with more than 100 countries and regions, jointly building a global energy industrial and supply chain system that is secure and stable, smooth and efficient, open and inclusive, and mutually beneficial and win-win. A large number of landmark energy projects and "small but beautiful" livelihood projects have taken root, providing clean, safe, and reliable energy supply solutions for host countries. The Belt and Road Energy Partnership has reached 33 member countries, with six major regional energy cooperation platforms successfully established and operating effectively: China-ASEAN, China-Arab League, China-African Union, China-Central and Eastern Europe, China-Central Asia, and the APEC Sustainable Energy Center. China initiated the establishment of the Shanghai Cooperation Organization Energy Ministers Meeting mechanism, focusing on energy security, energy transition, energy accessibility, and sustainable energy development issues, contributing Chinese solutions to global energy governance reform.

Central Asian countries possess abundant traditional energy reserves and great potential for renewable energy development, with a strong demand to transition from extensive, high-energy-consuming development models to green, low-carbon economies. In June 2022, the joint statement from the "China + Five Central Asian Countries" Foreign Ministers' Meeting highlighted ecological protection, environmental conservation, water resources, and green development cooperation as key components. The "Xi'an Declaration of the China-Central Asia Summit" in 2023 clearly emphasized expanding green economy cooperation. Kazakhstan's wind power potential reaches up to 920,000 MkWh/year. The 100 MW Zhanatas Wind Power Project, jointly invested by China Power International Company and Kazakhstan's Visor Investment Company and constructed by China Hydropower Construction Group International Engineering Company, is the largest wind farm in Central Asia. SANY Renewable Energy, through its dual-drive approach of "project development + localized manufacturing and sales", is advancing GW-level greenfield project development in Uzbekistan and building a world-class intelligent manufacturing lighthouse factory for wind power equipment in Kazakhstan. The Gobustan Photovoltaic Power Station, constructed by China Construction Third Engineering Bureau, is Azerbaijan's largest photovoltaic power project with the highest voltage level. With an annual power generation capacity of 500 MkWh, it can supply electricity to 110,000 households and reduce carbon dioxide emissions by over 200,000 tons per year. At the grid connection ceremony, Azerbaijan's President Aliyev praised the project as "a remarkable achievement".

As the world's largest integrated energy and chemical company, China National Petroleum Corporation is firmly transitioning into a comprehensive energy supplier of "oil, gas, thermal power, and hydrogen", while fully participating in the construction of new energy systems while striving to supply oil and gas energy. Kazakhstan's Aktobe Company is implementing transformations of oilfield surface facilities through "shutting down, suspending, merging, converting, reducing, and smart upgrading" to improve operational reliability, reduce production energy consumption and operating costs, develop the green hydrogen industry, explore carbon capture and carbon trading businesses, and create future profit growth points. China Oil International Pipeline Company is implementing three major projects along the Central Asian natural gas pipeline: increasing transmission while reducing consumption, methane emission reduction, and green culture, to build a "green pipeline". For example, the China-Uzbekistan Pipeline Company has developed scientific operational plans based on gas transmission volume changes to achieve optimal energy consumption across the entire line. Each station fully utilizes the high-temperature exhaust heat generated by compressor units, converting it through waste heat boilers into fuel gas and winter heating sources, reducing self-consumption of natural gas. Drawing on China's sand control experience, they have built a desert "green belt" composed of approximately 220, 000 m^2 of grass squares.

Energy China Group hosts more than ten international cooperation platforms, including the International Energy Agency China Liaison Office and the Belt and Road Energy Partnership Secretariat. It organizes international energy conferences such as the Belt and Road Energy Ministers Meeting, China-EU Energy Technology Innovation Forum, and Asian Energy Security and Transition Cooperation Forum, while conducting advanced energy technology exchange and cooperation with energy departments and enterprises from Germany, the UK, Finland, Denmark, Sweden, and other countries. In 2024, Energy China's newly signed overseas contracts increased by 14. 5% year-on-year, with the Saudi Arabian and Philippine markets exceeding 20 billion yuan, and ten countries surpassing 10 billion yuan. The installed capacity exceeded 3GW, with landmark Belt and Road projects such as Pakistan's SK Hydropower Station and Singapore's Tengeh Reservoir 60 MW floating photovoltaic project （the world's largest inland floating solar photovoltaic system） being put into operation, marking Energy China's upgrade from "engineering going global" to a provider of "Chinese solutions". Energy China has strengthened its core competitiveness characterized by innovation-driven, green and low-carbon, digital intelligence, and shared integration. It has taken the lead in tackling frontier areas such as compressed air energy storage and AI + energy, obtained over 1,800 patent authorizations, and led the formulation of nearly 1,600 national and industry standards. Through special actions such as cash flow improvement, cost leadership, and debt control, it has achieved quality and efficiency enhancement in overseas markets.

Case 5-4   China-Middle East Energy Cooperation: Injecting
Green Momentum for Sustainable
Development of Both Sides

In recent years, multiple Middle Eastern countries have regarded renewable energy development as a national strategy. For instance, Saudi Arabia is fully promoting economic diversification and energy transition under its "Vision 2030" framework; the UAE has released the "National Energy Strategy 2050 Update Plan" and "2050 Zero Emission Strategy Initiative", proposing to more than double renewable energy installed capacity by 2030 and achieve net-zero greenhouse gas emissions by 2050; Oman has proposed "Vision 2040", accelerating investment and promotion of renewable energy and green hydrogen projects. From precision manufacturing of core components to integrated construction of complex systems, from stable power supply guarantees to careful cultivation of industrial ecosystems, Chinese technology and experience provide important support for Middle Eastern countries' energy transition and sustainable development.

In the depths of the desert about 80 km south of Jeddah in southwestern Saudi Arabia, more than 810,000 pile foundations and over 5 million photovoltaic panels form a "blue ocean", reflecting dazzling light under the sunshine. This is the Al-Shuaibah Photovoltaic Power Station, jointly constructed by China Energy International Group, Guangdong Power Engineering Co., Ltd., and Northwest Electric Power Design Institute. It adopts the most advanced N-type bifacial photovoltaic modules and flat single-axis automatic tracking brackets, covering an area of approximately 53 km^2 with a total installed capacity of 2.6 GW, making it the largest photovoltaic project in the Middle East. The project implements the strictest safety and environmental protection standards. While promoting Chinese equipment and technology "going global", it has attracted more than 50 subcontractors and suppliers from over 10 countries and extensively applied digital and intelligent technologies to achieve unmanned operation. Saudi personnel have praised it as a "benchmark for Saudi-China new energy cooperation". Forecast data shows that over the next 35 years, the power station's total electricity generation will be approximately 282,200 MkWh, reducing carbon dioxide emissions by nearly 245 million tons, equivalent to planting 545 million trees in the desert. Saudi Finance Minister Mohammed Al-Jadaan believes that China holds a global leading position in green industries and renewable energy. Saudi Arabia is working to expand cooperation methods with China and learn from China's advanced technologies.

The UAE has been China's largest export market and second-largest trading partner in the Middle East for many consecutive years. UAE Ambassador to China Hamadi stated that the traditional friendship between the UAE and China spans thousands of years, with bilateral relations continuously deepening. The two countries have always moved forward side by side on the path of enhancing international cooperation and seeking win-win development. The Al Dhafra Solar PV Power Plant, constructed by China Machinery Engineering Corporation (CMEC), has an installed capacity of 2.1 GW, meeting the electricity needs of approximately 200,000 households, reducing carbon emissions by 2.4 million tons annually, and increasing the proportion of clean energy in the UAE's total energy structure to over 13%. The UAE Wind Power Demonstration Project contracted by Power Construction Corporation of China (POWERCHINA) has an annual power generation capacity that can meet the needs of more than 23,000 households, reducing carbon emissions by 120,000 tons annually, and verifying the economic feasibility of wind energy in the UAE.

The Middle East has extreme climate conditions, with sandstorms and 50℃ high temperatures being the norm. Traditional fuel vehicles with air conditioning at maximum still feel like a "steam sauna", while Chinese electric vehicles have conquered local consumers with their battery thermal management systems and superior cooling technology. Compared to European and American brands, Chinese new energy vehicles are more affordably priced, making Middle Eastern consumers more inclined to choose reasonably priced new energy vehicle models without compromising on technology. In 2024, China's automobile exports to the Middle East grew by 46.2%. Looking further, CATL is supplying "cores" for the UAE's 19 GWh energy storage project; Power China is contracting the world's largest integrated photovoltaic-storage EPC project (UAE RTC2.6 GW photovoltaic+10 GWh storage project); Huawei's Red Sea Energy Storage Project has become a benchmark in Saudi Arabia; and multiple Chinese new energy vehicle companies such as NIO are building R&D centers and customized vehicle factories in the Middle East. This "integrated photovoltaic-storage-charging" model is "relocating" China's new energy industry chain to the Middle East, continuously consolidating the influence of Chinese brands in the region.

II. Comprehensive Development of International Cooperation on Marine Ecological Environment Protection

China has ratified more than 30 multilateral treaties in the marine field, including the United Nations Convention on the Law of the Sea, the Convention on the Prevention of Marine Pollution by Dumping of Wastes and Other Matters (London Dumping Convention), and the Antarctic Treaty. In 2017, China proposed the "Building a Blue Partnership" initiative at the first United Nations Ocean Conference, promoting international cooperation to "cherish our shared oceans and safeguard our blue home", and subsequently released the "Vision for Maritime Cooperation under the Belt and Road Initiative". In September 2021," actively promoting the establishment of blue partnerships" was identified as one of China's specific measures under the Global Development Initiative framework at the High-level Dialogue on Global Development. At the 2022 United Nations Ocean Conference, China released the "Blue Partnership Principles", initiated the "Sustainable Blue Partnership Cooperation Network" and the "Blue Partnership Fund", and signed intergovernmental and interdepartmental marine cooperation agreements with more than 50 Belt and Road partner countries and international organizations.

China has led the establishment and operation of the East Asia Maritime Cooperation Platform, China-ASEAN Maritime Cooperation Center, International Mangrove Center, China-Pacific Island Countries Cooperation Center in Coping with Climate Change, and others. It has also constructed the APEC Marine Sustainable Development Center, the "Ocean Decade" Marine and Climate Collaboration Center, and hosted events such as the Subforum on Maritime Cooperation of the Belt and Road Forum for International Cooperation and the Global Coastal Forum. China has jointly established marine joint research centers, joint laboratories, joint observation stations, and other platforms with multiple countries including Indonesia, Thailand, Malaysia, Cambodia, Sri Lanka, Pakistan, Nigeria, Mozambique, and Jamaica. It has collaborated with other countries on projects such as marine endangered species research, Yellow Sea environmental joint surveys, coral reef monitoring and data collection, and prevention and control of marine debris and microplastic pollution. China has strengthened deep-sea ecological environment protection, established a world-leading marine microbial resource bank in terms of collection volume and species diversity, helping humanity deepen its understanding of deep-sea biological life processes. China actively participates in international cooperation to address environmental and climate change challenges in the Arctic and Antarctic. At the 40th Antarctic Treaty Consultative Meeting, China led more than 10 countries in jointly proposing the "Green Expedition" initiative, which was adopted by the conference in the form of a resolution.

III. China Leads International Cooperation in Biodiversity Conservation

As the presidency country of the 15th Conference of the Parties (COP15) to the Convention on Biological Diversity, China is leading international cooperation in biodiversity conservation through initiatives such as the implementation of the "Kunming-Montreal Global Biodiversity Framework" and the Kunming Biodiversity Fund. In January 2024, China updated and released the "China's Biodiversity Conservation Strategy and Action Plan (2023-2030)", becoming the first developing country to complete an updated biodiversity strategy and action plan after the adoption of the "Kunming-Montreal Global Biodiversity Framework". During COP16, the first batch of nine small-scale projects supported by the Kunming Biodiversity Fund was approved. Officials from the United Nations Convention on Biological Diversity Secretariat believe that China provides a model for developing countries to emulate and learn from.

China has conducted giant panda conservation cooperation with 26 institutions in 20 countries, effectively enhancing giant panda conservation research capabilities. Under the "South-South Cooperation" framework, China actively provides support for biodiversity conservation in developing countries. It cooperates with ASEAN countries to implement projects such as the "Biodiversity and Ecosystem Conservation Cooperation Plan" and the "Greater Mekong Subregion Core Environment Project and Biodiversity Conservation Corridor Plan". China also collaborates with Africa on wildlife protection actions, supports the implementation of multiple related projects in Africa, and has signed wildlife protection cooperation agreements with countries such as South Africa and Kenya. China and France jointly released the "China-France Beijing Initiative on Biodiversity Conservation and Climate Change". China has engaged in long-term cooperation on migratory bird protection with countries such as Russia and Japan, and has jointly established transboundary nature reserves and ecological corridors with Russia, Mongolia, Laos, Vietnam, and other countries. China has established bilateral cooperation mechanisms in the field of biodiversity with Germany, the United Kingdom, South Africa, and others, and has established a China-Japan-Korea trilateral biodiversity policy dialogue mechanism with Japan and Korea.

IV. Steady Development of International Cooperation in Green Finance

In 2016, as the G20 presidency country, China advocated for the establishment of the "Green Finance Study Group" and released the "G20 Green

Finance Synthesis Report 2016", which was later upgraded to the "G20 Sustainable Finance Working Group" at the G20 Finance Ministers and Central Bank Governors Meeting in 2021. In 2017, the People's Bank of China participated in establishing the Central Banks and Supervisors Network for Greening the Financial System (NGFS) to promote financial environment and climate management. In 2019, China joined the International Platform on Sustainable Finance initiated by the European Union as a founding member. In 2021, the People's Bank of China and relevant departments of the European Commission jointly completed the "Common Ground Taxonomy: Climate Change Mitigation", conducting comparison and analysis of green finance taxonomies between China and the EU. In 2018, the People's Bank of China and the International Monetary Fund jointly established the "China-IMF Joint Capacity Building Center", providing financial training for government officials from developing countries.

In 2018, under the guidance of the People's Bank of China, the Green Finance Committee of the Banking Accounting Society of China, together with the City of London, led multiple Chinese and foreign institutions in initiating the "Green Investment Principles for the Belt and Road (GIP)", which has been signed by more than 40 financial institutions from Belt and Road partner countries. In May 2023, the Export-Import Bank of China, together with more than 10 financial institutions including China Development Bank, Industrial and Commercial Bank of China, Agricultural Bank of China, Bank of China, China Construction Bank, China Export & Credit Insurance Corporation (Sinosure), Silk Road Fund, China International Capital Corporation (CICC), Standard Chartered (China), HSBC (China), and others, released the "Initiative for Supporting Belt and Road Energy Transition with Green Finance", calling on relevant parties to continuously increase support for the green and low-carbon energy transition in partner countries.

Chinese financial institutions actively participate in international cooperation in green finance. For example, the Industrial and Commercial Bank of China participated in initiating the Belt and Road Inter-bank Regular Cooperation Mechanism, issued the first green bond under this mechanism, and jointly released the Belt and Road Green Finance Index with the European Bank for

Reconstruction and Development （EBRD）, Crédit Agricole CIB, Mizuho Bank （Japan）, etc. The Belt and Road Bankers Roundtable hosted by ICBC has become an important platform for financial institutions in partner countries to exchange experiences and build capacity. China Development Bank, Export-Import Bank of China, Silk Road Fund, and the International Finance Corporation of the World Bank jointly provided syndicated loans for the Karot Hydropower Station in Pakistan. China Everbright Group established the "Belt and Road Green Equity Investment Fund" to support the development of green industries in partner countries.

Section 3　Innovative Measures, Main Achievements, and Typical Cases of Youth Participation in Green International Cooperation

Young people have strong innovation capabilities, broad international perspectives, strong professional skills, and quick adaptation speeds, making them the main force, new force, and assault team in green international cooperation. At the same time, youth are in the starting period of their life development and face a series of challenges such as anti-globalization and social competition. Participating in green development and discovering life value has become an urgent need for young people in various countries.

I. New Progress in Youth Participation in Green Infrastructure International Cooperation

Chinese young builders extensively conduct green technology research and development and overseas market promotion and application, reducing infrastructure carbon emissions and energy consumption, actively conveying to the world the youth confidence and responsibility for green development characterized by greenness, carbon reduction, and resilience.

China Railway Hi-tech Industry Corporation Limited's Nepal KK Highway Project was awarded the "Best Environmental Protection Monitoring Team" honor by Nepal's Ministry of Finance and the Asian Development Bank. The Nepal KK Highway Project is an existing road reconstruction project. Due to differences in relevant environmental protection requirements between China and Nepal, young Chinese engineers did a lot of work, jointly preparing construction environmental assessment reports with local governments and supervision agencies, formulating environmental protection, soil and water pollution prevention, and cultural relic protection systems, establishing a special environmental protection management group, and hiring Nepalese young engineers to participate in environmental protection management. It is precisely because of these meticulous preparations that the project has received positive reviews during multiple inspections by various levels of Nepalese government and environmental protection departments since its commencement.

The China-Papua New Guinea Friendship School (Butuka Academy) project is located in Port Moresby, the capital of Papua New Guinea, and is a testament to the friendship between China and Papua New Guinea and a microcosm of Papua New Guinea's modern education. The project, aided by the Shenzhen Municipal Government and contracted by China Construction Science and Industry Corporation Ltd, uses green prefabricated intelligent building design and green construction technology. It has solved the schooling difficulties for more than 3,000 local primary and secondary school students. To address the high-temperature and rainy climate, Chinese young engineers designed a passive energy-saving system. The indoor and outdoor air circulation system, combined with the design of large roofs and elevated ground floors that incorporate local traditional building culture, saves more than 20% of electricity. To achieve green "cost reduction and benefit increase", the project also adopts the "GS-Building" steel structure prefabricated building system independently developed by the China Construction Science & Industry youth technology team to reduce the emission of dust, harmful gases, and other pollutants, and save building materials. The project company also provides employment opportunities and vocational training in construction, electrical, water and heating, and other aspects for local youth, bringing Chinese wisdom for the long-term development of the local area.

The Addis Ababa Riverside Green Development Project in the capital of Ethiopia is China's first foreign aid park project. It was undertaken by China First Highway Engineering Co. , Ltd. This comprehensive project integrates landscape, architecture, municipal, road, water conservancy, and gardening. The youth team of the project built Africa's most functional and largest urban comprehensive square—Sheger Park Friendship Square. They adopted harmless low-impact rock blasting technology to avoid high noise, high dust, and high vibration impacts. They introduced Chinese greenhouse cultivation technology and tree transplantation standards to Ethiopia, achieving a 100% survival rate for large-scale precious seedling full-crown transplantation. They used China's advanced wind-deposited sand anti-seepage blanket for lake bottom sealing, effectively solving the problem of artificial lake water leakage while being conducive to the formation of the artificial lake's micro-ecological environment. With lush aquatic plants on the shore, schools of fish in the lake, and nearly a hundred species of birds residing here, Ethiopian Prime Minister Abiy has repeatedly promoted this "beautiful project" both domestically and internationally. After Sheger Park and its surrounding supporting facilities were opened to the public, it quickly became the most popular tourist destination in the area.

Limited by geographical conditions, household waste in the Greater Male region of the Maldives must first be collected through waste transfer stations and then shipped to waste islands for incineration and landfill disposal. However, the original waste transfer stations had small sites and single functions, lacking modern transfer capabilities such as container transportation. The Male Island and Vilimale Island waste transfer stations are important livelihood projects of the Maldives Ministry of Environment, funded by the Asian Development Bank and the Maldives Ministry of Finance, and constructed by China Construction Eighth Engineering Division Corp. , Ltd. The Maldives experiences a long rainy season with heavy rainfall, creating a harsh construction environment characterized by high salinity, high humidity, high temperatures, and high radiation, alongside scarce resources and difficulties in labor organization. Despite these conditions, young Chinese engineers rose to the challenge. They applied silicone sealant at the main masonry joints to ensure the completed masonry would not crack or leak. Waterproof admixtures were incorporated into all building roof structures to enhance the concrete's quality and overall performance. For anticorrosion and rust prevention on steel structures, fluorocarbon spray coating was applied, achieving a thickness that meets the highest C5-M British Standard. Furthermore, elevated structural designs were adopted to reduce costly backfill and increase usable space for the owner, and Chinese-manufactured double-glazed soundproof glass was introduced to address the significant noise generated during the operation of the transfer station.

The Red Sea Utilities Infrastructure Project undertaken by Power Construction Corporation of China is located in Tabuk Province in western Saudi Arabia. It is the world's first large-scale commercialized public utility project that integrates multiple energy complementary integration, including photovoltaic, wind power, energy storage, internal combustion engine power generation, power grid, seawater desalination, water supply network, wastewater treatment, sewage network, solid waste treatment, and other modules. The advantage of using photovoltaic power generation in desert areas is abundant sunlight, but the disadvantage is heavy sand, which affects photoelectric conversion efficiency. The automatic cleaning robots developed by the Chinese youth technology team regularly clean the dust on photovoltaic panels—just open the mobile phone application, and the robots start working. In the construction of power transmission networks between islands, the underwater automatic robots developed by the Chinese youth technology team operate underwater, adopting strict environmental protection measures to minimize the impact on marine organisms. Chinese young engineers built an artificial wetland (biological "sewage treatment plant") consisting of two reed thickets and a sedge field. After pretreatment, domestic sewage first passes through the first reed thicket to filter out large particles of impurities, then is pumped into the second reed thicket where heavy metals and other substances are adsorbed, and finally flows into the sedge field under gravity, where it is filtered again before flowing into the storage pool.

II. New Progress in Youth Participation in Green Energy International Cooperation

Chinese enterprise youth teams continue to connect with developing countries' long-term development plans and visions, relying on each country's resource endowments, fully leveraging advantages in renewable energy, energy conservation and environmental protection, clean production, and other fields, and applying Chinese technology, products, experience, etc. , to promote the vigorous development of green energy cooperation.

Uganda is one of the countries with the lowest per capita electricity consumption in the world, with only about 15% of the population having access to the national power grid. Uganda's largest hydropower station, the Karuma Hydropower Station, which was financed by the Export-Import Bank of China and constructed by Power China, has a total designed capacity of 600 megawatts. All generating units were connected to the grid in early 2024, increasing Uganda's total power generation capacity by nearly 50%, saving 1. 31 million tons of coal annually, reducing carbon dioxide emissions by 3. 48 million tons, and lowering electricity prices by 17. 5%. Ugandan President Museveni stated:" The Karuma Hydropower Station has greatly enhanced Uganda's power generation capacity, accelerated industrialization, and consequently attracted more foreign investors". The power station is located on plains where traditional high-dam surface powerhouse designs would cause irreversible damage to the local ecosystem through flooding. Chinese young engineers therefore adopted a construction solution consisting of "underground powerhouse+long tailrace tunnel". As the hydropower station is adjacent to the Murchison Falls National Park, which is rich in flora and fauna, Chinese young engineers fully considered the protection of environmentally sensitive areas. The ground dam features a low dam design to reduce the length of river inundation, and includes a specially designed ecological fish passage to ensure fish breeding and reduce impacts on plant and animal life in the dam area.

The Syr Darya 1500 MW Combined Cycle Gas Power Plant is Uzbekistan's first large-scale gas power project developed as an independent power plant model in recent years. With a designed capacity accounting for about 8% of Uzbekistan's total power generation capacity, it was constructed with the participation of China Construction Fifth Engineering Bureau. To ensure efficient and stable power output, the project's young technical team employed the world's highest combustion temperature, largest single-unit capacity, and highest efficiency 9H-class gas turbines. They focused on interface work between different systems, actively promoting detailed design and equipment manufacturing of auxiliary systems centered on the gas turbines, achieving world-leading design parameters for the project's water treatment and natural gas pressurization systems. Syr Darya is an important agricultural region in Uzbekistan. To protect local irrigation and drinking water sources, the project's young technical team designed a "zero wastewater discharge" solution using membrane reverse osmosis combined with forced evaporation pool technology, directly reducing wastewater discharge by about 2 million tons annually and preventing pollution of surrounding soil and water sources. Uzbekistan's President Mirziyoyev, attending the project's commissioning ceremony, stated that Chinese enterprises had efficiently advanced project implementation, greatly alleviating local power shortages, and making significant contributions to improving local people's living conditions and promoting economic and social development.

The Bosnia and Herzegovina Ivovik Wind Power Project is the first new energy project from the China-CEE Leaders' Summit outcome list to be implemented, and Bosnia and Herzegovina's largest energy project invested through foreign concession. The project was managed by a young team from PowerChina Chengdu Engineering Corporation, responsible for the entire process from engineering design, equipment procurement, wind turbine installation, and electrical installation to debugging, trial operation, and final handover. The young project team applied advanced Chinese wind power technology meeting EU requirements, with "Made in China" equipment accounting for over 90% of the project. The project site is also home to wild horse herds in Bosnia and Herzegovina. The young project team collaborated with local wild horse protection associations to protect habitats and improve the living environment for wild horses.

Vietnam has abundant solar resources, and the Vietnamese government strongly supports solar power generation. China's photovoltaic industry enjoys leading advantages, and bilateral cooperation promotes local economic and social development that "prospers through green development". In December 2023, while making a state visit to Hanoi, Chinese President Xi Jinping published an article titled "Building a China-Vietnam Community with a Shared Future of Strategic Significance and Opening a New Chapter in Our Joint Journey

Toward Modernization" in the *People's Daily of Vietnam*, mentioning that "Chinese enterprises have built the largest overseas photovoltaic industrial cluster in Vietnam, and their investments in photovoltaic and wind power stations have made positive contributions to Vietnam's energy transition and development". Trina Solar Co., Ltd. began developing its presence in Vietnam in 2014, establishing two photovoltaic component and module factories, and participating in multiple Vietnamese photovoltaic power generation projects, becoming one of Vietnam's largest solar panel manufacturers. The Vietnam Trung Son Photovoltaic Power Station, located in Khanh Hoa Province, Vietnam, was constructed by Trina Solar's young project team who overcame challenges such as typhoon landings and high temperature and humidity environments. They innovatively adopted rotating brackets, dual-sided double-glass modules, string inverters, and other technologies to optimize power generation efficiency. The project produces 67.4 MkWh of clean electricity annually, reducing carbon dioxide emissions by approximately 53,000 tons.

The Lancang-Mekong Regional Power Grid Interconnection Project, invested, constructed, and operated by China Southern Power Grid, has initially formed a pattern of power surplus and deficit mutual support in the region. The project uses "grid-led power source development" to reduce the intensity of power resource development in the region, providing an innovative low-carbon transition solution for green power grid construction. The Lancang-Mekong countries' hydropower output characteristics are similar to those of the receiving provinces in China. Chinese young engineers innovated a "wet and dry season exchange" power mutual assistance model, incorporating the Guangdong-Hong Kong-Macao Greater Bay Area, which has high demand for clean energy and compatible load characteristics with hydropower output, into the adjustment range. Through larger-scale "power exchange" during flood and dry seasons, optimal allocation of clean energy resources is achieved. China Southern Power Grid initiated the establishment of the Lancang-Mekong Regional Power Technology Standards Promotion Association. The project adopts China's more challenging green power grid standards to maximize protection of the Lancang-Mekong region's ecological environment.

Case 5-5   Croatia Senj Wind Power Project: Youth
from Both Countries Jointly Build a Model
Project for Green Energy Cooperation
between China and Europe

At the People-to-People Connectivity Thematic Forum of the Third Belt and
Road Forum for International Cooperation, the Croatia Senj Wind Power Project
invested, constructed, and operated by NORINCO International Cooperation
Ltd. was presented as a musical stage performance to government officials, civil
society organizations, and media representatives from various countries. As
Croatia's largest new energy power generation project, the Senj Wind Power
Project generates electricity for more than 3,000 hours annually on average,
contributing about 530 MkWh of green electricity and reducing carbon dioxide
emissions by approximately 460,000 tons. Croatian Prime Minister Plenkovi
épraised the Senj Wind Power Project as providing important support for the
country's clean energy production and green transition, and as a model project
for green energy cooperation between the European Union and China.

As a mountain wind power project, the young management team consistently prioritized ecological protection, strictly following local and EU environmental protection regulations during construction, and caring for the local ecological environment as if it were their own home. "If wildlife is found, it should
be protected conscientiously; during animal mating, lambing, and incubation
seasons, human activities should be reduced to avoid disturbance; if injured,
sick, hungry, trapped, or lost wildlife is found, relevant departments should
be promptly notified for rescue. " These guidelines, which seem to come from a
wildlife protection organization's manual, are actually emphasized behavioral
standards in the Senj Wind Power Project construction guidelines.

The project's young management team deeply collaborated with local enterprises, with more than 50 local subcontractors, suppliers, and service providers participating in project construction, covering equipment supply, heavy
transportation, civil engineering, wind turbine hoisting, dynamic commissioning, and grid-connection testing throughout the entire process, enhancing
Croatian enterprises' competitiveness in the European market. The blade lifting

device developed by NORINCO International's young technology team not only successfully completed the transportation of giant wind turbines but also saved the project approximately2. 8 million US dollars compared to renting European equipment. Local partners praised the superior performance of Chinese equipment and are actively promoting its use in other wind power projects in the Balkan region.

How to overcome cultural differences in overseas projects is a common challenge for Chinese enterprises "going global". For the Senj project, differences between Chinese and European wind power project construction modes, unfamiliarity of Croatian local companies with Chinese equipment, language communication barriers, and differences in corporate management systems all had significant impacts on project costs and schedule. To resolve cultural differences, the Chinese young team of the Senj project actively participated in social public welfare activities and community special events, enhancing understanding of local customs and humanistic traditions. Through action, they earned recognition from local people, government, and Croatian employees, thereby reaching consensus on values, thinking patterns, and behavioral habits.

III. New Progress in Youth Participation in Green Transportation International Cooperation

Chinese enterprise youth teams are strengthening high-quality cooperation in transportation infrastructure construction to meet the expectations of partner countries that "when roads are open, all industries prosper". At the same time, they actively promote the sharing of green low-carbon transportation technologies and experiences, helping partner countries strengthen their transportation emission reduction capabilities, allowing green transportation achievements to better benefit people of all countries.

Bangladesh, due to its dense population, abundant waterways, and economic underdevelopment, is one of the world's most backward countries in terms of transportation. The Karnaphuli River Tunnel Project, the first underwater tunnel in South Asia constructed by China Road & Bridge Corporation, has officially opened to traffic. The young construction team of the project department fully considered external public safety, geographical location, and terrain characteristics, choosing to blow-fill and reinforce the original ground, and equipped the project with sewage treatment facilities to effectively treat domestic sewage generated by the project. The project department established a green concrete laboratory led by young engineers. Through data analysis and instrument testing, they precisely adjusted the concrete proportions used in the main structure, improving concrete safety service life and reducing concrete waste and secondary pollution. The young project team introduced an environmentally friendly, energy-efficient, and highly automated earth pressure balance shield tunneling machine developed by CCCC Group for construction. This machine achieves one-pass tunneling, is unaffected by climate, and reduces environmental disturbance while accelerating construction progress.

The Ghana Tema New Container Terminal Project, constructed by China Communications Construction Group, can increase cargo throughput at Tema Port, consolidating its advantage as a major port in West Africa and injecting new momentum into the economic and trade development of Ghana and surrounding countries. Ghana, near the Gulf of Guinea, is an important habitat for sea turtles. During project construction, to protect local sea turtle breeding, the Chinese young team deployed environmental monitoring instruments for gas, dust particles, noise, and other factors in the construction area, setting up more than 30 monitoring points to achieve environmental control throughout the construction process. On beaches near the construction area, the Chinese young team replicated sea turtle hatching environments, building a new sea turtle breeding center where 17,000 sea turtles were incubated. After the baby sea turtles hatched, Chinese young volunteers selected another beach, which was assessed by experts, for their release.

In November 2024, Chinese President Xi Jinping and Peruvian President Boluarte jointly attended the opening ceremony of Chancay Port via video link from the Presidential Palace in Lima. The two heads of state issued instructions announcing the "opening" of Chancay Port, shortening the transportation time for cargo exports from South America to Asian markets from 35 days to 25 days and significantly reducing logistics costs. Chancay Port, located near Peru's capital Lima, is a natural deep-water port constructed by a consortium of China

Harbour Engineering Company and CCCC Fourth Harbor Engineering Co. , Ltd. It is the first controlling greenfield project of COSCO Shipping Group in South America, a landmark project of the "Belt and Road" Initiative in Latin America, and the first large-scale transportation infrastructure project implemented by Chinese enterprises in Peru. The Chinese enterprise youth team set "making the sea clearer, the sky bluer, animals friendlier, and Chancay more beautiful" as the construction goal for Chancay Port. As the construction site is adjacent to a natural wetland, the project's young team organized themed activities around World Wetlands Day, Earth Day, and other environmental dates to protect the wetland environment and biodiversity. They collaborated with local city halls, maritime authorities, and communities to maintain surrounding wetland environments, set up environmental protection signs and markers, and invited local people and youth to understand, learn about, and protect the wetland ecology, achieving remarkable results.

The Dakar Bus Rapid Transit System Project, constructed by China Road & Bridge Corporation, is Senegal's first urban rapid transit line and the country's first emission reduction transportation project implemented under the Paris Agreement framework. It has received financing support from the Global Green Climate Fund. The electric buses used in operations are provided by China's CRRC Group, and all stations and vehicle maintenance bases are equipped with photovoltaic power generation facilities, providing solid support for electric bus continuity. The Chinese young management team of the project department emphasized green construction around stations, setting up protective nets during construction to protect vegetation along the line, and implementing a "compensatory afforestation plan" to register trees removed due to construction, with two new trees planted for every one removed. To address local rainy season flooding, the young construction team renovated 17. 5 km of underground drainage pipes in Dakar and built 40 km of new drainage networks.

During the 2024 AFC Asian Cup in Qatar, colorful new energy buses carrying various competing teams or fans frequently passed by. This Chinese "green fleet" has once again become a "protagonist" in international competitions following the 2022 Qatar World Cup. Chinese buses have a market share of over 80% in Qatar's public transportation market, and Chinese enterprises have become the sole supplier in the new energy bus sector. To address Qatar's high temperatures and sandy environment, Chinese new energy vehicle manufacturers' young technology teams developed specially adapted vehicle models. The air conditioning design uses intelligent temperature control algorithms, and the vehicle power batteries employ independent, efficient liquid cooling systems, ensuring not only longer vehicle range but also improved battery safety and service life. The adapted models are also equipped with mud and sand protection structures, enhancing the motor's adaptability to potholed and sandy roads. Fans from various countries generally found Chinese new energy buses comfortable, quiet, and fast. Chinese enterprises have brought mature technologies, supply chain services, and business models from China's new energy vehicle industry to Qatar, establishing localized operation systems, implementing school-enterprise cooperation and talent exchange programs, and cultivating new energy young technical talent for Qatar, achieving an industrial layout upgrade from single product export to the joint export of products, technology, talent, and management systems.

Section 4　Working Together to Build a Beautiful Earth Home: China's Experiences in Strengthening Green International Cooperation and Implications for Developing Countries

I. Participating in and Leading the Global Green Transition Process

China's development practice fully demonstrates that green development and innovation provide a new path for populous countries to advance modernization under resource and environmental constraints, transcending the old path of foreign plunder and dependent development. Through scientific and technological innovation, production efficiency and resource utilization rates are improved; through education and knowledge iteration, human development potential is released; and through quality transformation, efficiency transformation, and dynamic transformation, the constraints of resources, population, and environment are systematically addressed. Furthermore, upholding the concept of a community with a shared future for mankind, China firmly implements the U-nited Nations Framework Convention on Climate Change and actively partici-pates in global climate negotiations with a constructive attitude, making historic contributions to the conclusion and implementation of the Paris Agreement. By increasing nationally determined contributions, China will achieve the world's highest reduction in carbon emission intensity and realize carbon peaking to car-bon neutrality in the shortest time in global history, fully demonstrating the re-sponsibility of a major country. China also actively participates in the formula-tion of international rules in areas such as marine pollution governance, biodi-versity conservation, and plastic pollution management, promoting the con-struction of a fair, reasonable, and win-win global environmental and climate governance system. By proposing and implementing the Global Development Ini-tiative, strengthening South-South cooperation and cooperation with neighboring countries, and providing support to developing countries within its capacity, China has become an important participant, contributor, and leader in green development international cooperation and global ecological civilization construc-tion.

II. Strengthening Policy Exchange and Practical Cooperation

China actively expands bilateral and multilateral dialogue and cooperation channels, strengthens cooperation platform construction in the field of green de-velopment, and vigorously promotes the effectiveness and experience of China's green and low-carbon transformation. China strengthens green investment and trade cooperation, improves the environmental sustainability of overseas pro-jects, and encourages the import and export of green and low-carbon products. It enhances green technology cooperation, encouraging universities and research institutions to conduct academic exchanges with foreign partners and actively participate in international big science projects. It reinforces international coop-eration in green standards and conformity assessment, promoting alignment and mutual recognition with major trading partners on rules such as carbon footprint.

Especially in building the Green Silk Road, China adheres to jointly consulting on development cooperation, jointly building project implementation, and sharing development outcomes. It adheres to the goals of high standards, sustainability, and people's livelihoods, continuously enhancing support for green development in partner countries. China firmly improves the environmental sustainability of overseas projects. While meeting the environmental standards of partner countries, it encourages the application of international common rules and standards or more stringent Chinese standards. Through implementing green livelihood projects with partner countries, China enhances the development level of host countries in areas such as employment, environmental improvement, climate change response, and disaster prevention and mitigation. The Green Silk Road construction and the sustainable development agendas of various countries promote each other, with strong feasibility for cooperation in addressing climate change, environmental protection, and energy transition. The Green Silk Road has become an important international platform for promoting Xi Jinping's Thought on Ecological Civilization.

Section 5　Policy Recommendations for Further Promoting Green International Cooperation from the Perspective of World Modernization

I. Promoting Green and Low-carbon Transition through High-level International Cooperation

Promote the implementation of the Global Development Initiative in bilateral and multilateral cooperation, strengthening the shared responsibility of building a community with a shared future for mankind. Support experts from developing countries in taking positions in international organizations and participating in international green governance. Promote the participation of government departments, social organizations, public welfare institutions, and think tanks from developing countries in the "Belt and Road" Green Development International Coalition and green low-carbon expert networks, jointly building platforms for green international cooperation policy dialogue and communication, environmental knowledge and information, and green technology exchange and transfer. Adhere to the principles of equity, common but differentiated responsibilities, and respective capabilities, comprehensively implement international cooperation projects addressing climate change, and establish a global climate governance system with broad youth participation. Promote the establishment of specialized green development institutions by public welfare organizations and industry associations to provide public services such as cultural activities, policy interpretation, business consulting, talent training, achievement exhibitions, and rights protection. Successfully host the "Belt and Road" Green Innovation Conference, and organize dialogue exchanges, innovation competitions, project roadshows, and other activities under international exhibition mechanisms such as the Canton Fair, China International Import Expo, China International Fair for Trade in Services, and China International Big Data Industry Expo. Build a dialogue and exchange mechanism for the photovoltaic industry, promoting the construction of localized talent systems by Chinese photovoltaic enterprises.

II. Firmly Supporting Developing Countries in Enhancing Their Green Development Capabilities

Leverage mechanisms such as the "Belt and Road" Science and Technology Innovation Action Plan and the "Belt and Road" Sustainable Development Technology Special Cooperation Plan to support scientists, entrepreneurs, and innovators from developing countries. Utilizing platforms such as environmental technology exchange and transfer bases, green technology demonstration and promotion bases, green science and technology parks, " Belt and Road" joint laboratories, and "Belt and Road" technology transfer centers, lead the research, development, promotion, and transformation of environmentally friendly technologies such as low-carbon, energy-saving, water-saving, and environmental protection. Expand green development-themed seminars, roundtables, roadshows, and other projects in technology and humanities exchange activities such as the "Belt and Road" Science and Technology Exchange Conference. Expand the educational training, project cooperation, and other service qualities of the Green Silk Road Envoys Program, guide Chinese universities to increase the scale of international student training in ecological environment-related majors, help universities and research institutes in developing countries build green development talent training systems, and strengthen interaction and exchange among environmental management personnel and professional technical talents. Leverage the role of new-type think tanks such as Silk Road International Think Tank to summarize, disseminate, and promote China's green development experience and tell China's green development story well.

Chapter 6
Conclusion Value Implications of "Lucid Waters and Lush Mountains Are Invaluable Assets": Green Development Building a Community of Life Between Humans and Nature

Green is the symbol of life and the background color of nature. A good ecological environment is the foundation of a good life and the common aspiration of the people. Green development is development that conforms to nature and promotes harmony between humans and nature. It achieves maximum economic and social benefits at the minimum cost to resources and the environment. It is high-quality, sustainable development and has become a consensus among countries. Under the guidance of Xi Jinping's Thought on Socialism with Chinese Characteristics for a New Era, China adheres to the concept that lucid waters and lush mountains are invaluable assets, firmly follows the path of ecological priority and green development, promotes the comprehensive green transformation of economic and social development, builds modernization featuring harmony between humans and nature, and creates world-renowned ecological and green development miracles. As the world's largest developing country, China upholds the concept of a community with a shared future for mankind, firmly practices multilateralism, proposes the Global Development Initiative and Global Security Initiative, deepens practical cooperation, actively participates in global environmental and climate governance, and contributes Chinese wisdom and strength to building a clean and beautiful earth home.

Green and low-carbon transformation is a broad and profound systemic change in the economy and society and a long-term strategic task that requires steady progress and persistent efforts under the guidance of new era strategies. The 20th National Congress of the Communist Party of China has outlined the blueprint for China's future development, depicting a beautiful China with flowing clear waters, permanent green mountains, and fresh air. The "Decision of the Central Committee of the Communist Party of China on Further Comprehensively Deepening Reform and Advancing Chinese Modernization" proposes focusing on building a beautiful China, accelerating the comprehensive green transformation of economic and social development, improving the ecological environment governance system, promoting ecological priority, economical and intensive use, and green and low-carbon development, and promoting the harmonious coexistence of humans and nature.

To this end, the following four major recommendations are proposed.

First, further promote high-level ecological environmental protection. Continue to implement the blue sky defense battle, ensure that industrial enterprises fully and stably meet emission standards, strengthen comprehensive management of volatile organic compounds and dust pollution, supervise counties and districts where air quality has not reached standards to formulate time-limited air quality improvement plans, continue to promote coordinated control of PM2.5 and ozone, and establish air treatment improvement demonstration zones in cross-provincial adjacent areas. Continue the battle for clear waters, coordinate upstream and downstream, left and right banks, main and tributary streams, cities and rural areas, implement "one river (lake) one policy", fully leverage the river (lake) chief system, strengthen source tracing and rectification, sewage interception and source control, and resource utilization of sewage (sludge), implement coordinated prevention and control of surface water and groundwater, continue to fight the battle for Yangtze River protection and restoration and the battle for Yellow River ecological protection and governance, and improve cross-regional watershed ecological protection compensation mechanisms. Improve the marine ecological environment governance system integrating land and sea with multi-party governance, continuously carry out "investigation, measurement, tracing, and treatment" of sewage outlets entering the sea with coastal townships as units, implement "one port one policy" pollution prevention and control for fishing ports, promote ecological and healthy aquaculture models, build a data-sharing supervision system for marine engineering projects and marine waste disposal, and implement special plastic garbage cleanup actions in areas such as bays, estuaries, and shores. Incorporate "waste-free city" construction into the assessment content of pollution prevention and control campaigns for townships (subdistricts), villages (communities), and other grassroots departments, legally include solid waste generation, utilization, and disposal in the corporate credit evaluation system, promote green building materials and construction waste recycling products, promote the "integration of two networks" between household waste classification points and waste material recycling points, and build a "five-complete" environmental supervision system for hazardous waste.

Second, further optimize the spatial layout of green development. Construct a new pattern of national land space development and protection oriented toward the rational use of natural resources, carry out monitoring and evaluation of national land space planning implementation, ensure that current arable land is classified and protected as much as possible, develop multi-center, group-style urban spatial forms, guide compact layouts for small and medium-sized cities, promote comprehensive land remediation across the territory, and build beautiful villages suitable for living and working. Coordinate the integrated protection and restoration of mountains, rivers, forests, fields, lakes, grasslands, deserts, and seas, scientifically deploy and continuously implement landscape engineering, promote the construction of green mines in a classified and orderly manner, advance the construction of beautiful bays with "land-sea coordination+river-sea linkage + one bay (island) one policy", improve the biodiversity survey, monitoring, assessment, and protection system, enact the National Park Law, facilitate comprehensive governance of deserts, water bodies, and mountains, promote advanced technologies such as barrier desertification control, photovoltaic desertification control, film covering for water conservation, and shrub cutting, publicize and carry forward the "Three-North" Spirit and Saihanba Spirit. Establish county-level ecological resource databases and ecological product inventories, guide the confirmation of rights, empowerment, rational layout, and efficient allocation of natural resource assets, innovate value realization pathways such as natural resource rights trading, ecological product mortgage loans, ecological protection compensation, natural resource asset damage compensation, natural resource asset accounts, green product futures options, and green insurance.

Third, further promote high-quality development of green and low-carbon transformation. Integrate green concepts and conservation requirements into economic and social rules such as civilization conventions, enterprise regulations, and group charters to form a strong social atmosphere that values ecological civilization. Guide small and medium-sized enterprises to implement green procurement guidelines, incorporate carbon footprint requirements into public sector procurement, and promote the establishment of green supply chains by enterprises above designated size. Encourage local governments and market entities to issue green consumption vouchers and green credits, encouraging consumers to purchase green products and participate in "trade-in" programs. Synchronously implement coal consumption control, scattered coal replacement, and clean energy development in key regions, promote the construction of carbon dioxide capture, utilization, and storage projects, coordinate hydropower development and ecological protection, promote integrated development of water, wind, and solar power, actively develop distributed photovoltaic and dispersed wind power, promote the development of the entire "production, storage, transportation, and use" chain for hydrogen energy, strengthen the connection and coordination of clean energy bases, regulatory resources, and transmission channels, and accelerate the construction of smart grid projects such as microgrids, virtual power plants, and source-grid-load-storage integration. Promote the universal adoption of clean production technologies and equipment in traditional industries and improve the exit mechanism for backward production capacity. Driven by technological innovation, green intelligent manufacturing, and manufacturing services, integrate the development of strategic emerging industries, high-tech industries, energy conservation and environmental protection industries, modern efficient agriculture, and modern service industries. Encourage the innovative development of energy management contracting, water conservation management contracting, third-party environmental pollution treatment, carbon emission management, and other innovative services. Strengthen the creation, protection, and application of intellectual property rights for green and low-carbon technologies. Guide the green and low-carbon development of internet platforms, leading upstream and downstream market entities to improve their carbon reduction capabilities. Promote innovation in green finance products and services.

Fourth, further promote high-level green international cooperation. Promote the implementation of the Global Development Initiative in bilateral and multilateral cooperation, support the participation of government departments, social organizations, public welfare institutions, and think tanks from developing countries in the "Belt and Road" Green Development International Coalition and green low-carbon expert networks. Comprehensively implement international cooperation projects addressing climate change and establish a global climate governance system with broad youth participation. Promote the establishment of specialized green development institutions by public welfare organizations and industry associations to provide public services such as cultural activities, policy interpretation, business consulting, talent training, achievement exhibitions, and rights protection. Successfully host the "Belt and Road" Green Innovation Conference, and organize dialogue exchanges, innovation competitions, project roadshows, and other activities under international exhibition mechanisms such as the Canton Fair, China International Import Expo, China International Fair for Trade in Services, and China International Big Data Industry Expo. Build a dialogue and exchange mechanism for the photovoltaic industry. Support scientists, entrepreneurs, and innovators from developing countries in participating in project cooperation such as environmental technology exchange and transfer bases, green technology demonstration and promotion bases," Belt and Road" joint laboratories, and "Belt and Road" technology transfer centers. Expand the educational training, project cooperation, and other service qualities of the Green Silk Road Envoys Program, guide Chinese universities to increase the scale of international student training in ecological environment-related majors, help universities and research institutes in developing countries build green development talent training systems. Leverage the role of new-type think tanks such as Silk Road International Think Tank to summarize, disseminate, and promote China's green development experience and tell China's green development story well.

Special Report

Mentougou District, Beijing: Green Development Creating a Magnificent New Picture for the Western Gateway to the Capital

In October 2024, the 16th Conference of the Parties (COP16) to the Convention on Biological Diversity of the United Nations released the list for the second "Cities with Rich Biodiversity", with Beijing's Mentougou District selected for the "Nature City" list, becoming the first administrative district in Beijing to be selected. Mentougou District is located in western Beijing, serving as an ecological conservation area and an important gateway for the capital's development. It has natural or semi-natural ecological system types including forests, shrubs, meadows, rivers, lakes, and wetlands, nurturing rich biodiversity and preserving important germplasm resources of the narrow forest vegetation belt of the Taihang Mountains. In the "one core, two wings, four districts, and multiple nodes" spatial layout of Beijing-Tianjin-Hebei coordinated development clarified in the "Beijing-Tianjin-Hebei Coordinated Development Planning Outline", Mentougou District is an important component of the "northwestern ecological conservation area" among the "four districts". For many years, it has worked together with neighboring Zhangjiakou and Baoding in Hebei Province to jointly protect the ecological barrier in the western part of the capital.

Igniting New Engines for Green Transformation and Development in Post-Disaster Reconstruction

In November 2023, General Secretary Xi Jinping visited Mentougou District to inspect post-disaster recovery and reconstruction work and made important instructions. Following the overall approach of "basic recovery in one

year, comprehensive improvement in three years, and high-quality development in the long term", Mentougou District has constructed a "1+13+X" post-
disaster reconstruction planning system. Here, "1" refers to the overall post-
disaster recovery and reconstruction plan, "13" refers to 13 special plans including dual-purpose emergency facilities and emergency rescue, comprehensive disaster prevention and resilient city, flood control and river blue line,
and "X" refers to town and street-level post-disaster reconstruction plans. In
promoting post-disaster reconstruction work, Mentougou District has focused on
enhancing urban and rural safety resilience: Based on "prevention", 71 water
conservancy projects have been completed, a "pipeline cleaning action" for
rainwater has been implemented, and the Beijing West Sentinel early warning
command and dispatch platform and the Guanting Gorge modern rainwater monitoring and forecasting system for the Yongding River have been built; based on
"resistance", a national grassroots comprehensive disaster reduction demonstration pilot project of the Emergency Management Department has been launched,
creating a demonstration zone for the insurance industry to serve disaster prevention, mitigation, and relief system construction; based on "rescue", an early
warning upgrade response mechanism has been established, with refined flood
prevention plans and emergency response procedures.

Furthermore, Mentougou District has determined a "12345" overall development approach: Anchoring "one goal" —building a high-level western
gateway to the capital, build Mentougou into a district of "Lucid Waters and
Lush Mountains", "Poetic and Picturesque Mentougou", "Specialized, Refined, Distinctive, and Innovative Mentougou", "Safe and Resilient Mentougou", and "United and Progressive Mentougou", seizing the "two main
lines" of post-disaster recovery and reconstruction and green high-quality transformation and development. It will adhere to the "three development strategies"
of establishing the district based on ecology (ecological foundation strategy),
revitalizing the district through culture (cultural vitalization strategy), and
strengthening the district with science and technology (sci-tech empowerment
strategy). Furthermore, it will advance "four key actions": heartwarming initiatives for the people, safety and resilience initiatives, upgrading and transformation initiatives, and initiatives to build cohesion and strength. Finally, it

will implement "five foundational projects" encompassing cadre capacity building, talent team cultivation, business environment optimization, regional image enhancement, and strengthening the foundations of grassroots governance, all to concentrate efforts on promoting green and high-quality development.

Building the "Beijing's Great Oxygen Bar" and the "Backyard Garden of Western Beijing"

Beijing was once home to the north China leopard, but since 1992, there has been no confirmed information about leopard activity in Beijing for over 30 years. To bring back the north China leopard that disappeared decades ago to its "home" in Beijing, Mentougou District, relying on the Baihuashan National Nature Reserve known as the "North China Natural Botanical and Zoological Garden", has launched the "Welcome Leopards Home" plan, compiled the White Paper on "Biodiversity Conservation in Mentougou District", released the "Welcome Leopards Home" logo and mascot, and improved citizens' biodiversity conservation literacy. Currently, the nature reserve has established a complete habitat suitable for north China leopards.

Mentougou District, using water systems as units, has implemented integrated small watershed comprehensive management and clean small watershed quality improvement across entire valleys, villages, and towns, supporting ecological water replenishment of the Yongding River, and enhancing the ecological resilience of mountain forests. The maximum rise in groundwater level has reached 23. 35 meters, and 106 out of 234 springs are currently flowing. Consolidating and enhancing the achievements of the National Forest City construction, the forest and grass coverage rate has reached 93. 9%, the highest in the city, with forest carbon sequestration, forest stock volume, and ecological service value continuing to increase, and the ecological environment quality index maintaining an "excellent" rating.

Mentougou District is striving to explore a new development pattern of "deploying GDP and GEP together for dual growth, and simultaneously empowering ecological investment and ecological prosperity for dual guarantees", with GEP calculated at 30. 7 billion yuan. The Western Beijing Ancient Road Immersive

Ecological Town project is located in Xiwangping Village, Wangping Town, with a planned area of 493. 55 hectares. It preserves and utilizes the ancient village texture, enhances environmental experiences through technology, and incorporates rural tourism, cultural heritage, educational research, health, and leisure themes, creating a Western Beijing ancient road tourism destination and Beijing's first ecological product value realization experimental zone for specific geographical units that integrates vacation accommodation, cultural tourism commercial streets, family parks, and mountain outdoor activities.

Vigorously Developing Green High-end Industries

Mentougou District focuses on the "dual-core drive" of public business environment and vertical business environment, improving industrial policies around core dimensions such as market, rule of law, government affairs, talent, and life services. It has constructed a systematic, precise, and full-chain regional business environment ecosystem, vigorously developing specialized, refined, distinctive, and innovative green industry clusters along the West Chang'an Street extension line in fields including artificial intelligence, ultra-high-definition digital audio-visual, and cardiovascular medical devices. More than 220 artificial intelligence enterprises and over 160 specialized, refined, distinctive, and innovative small and medium-sized enterprises have settled in the district.

Mentougou District has established the Large Model Empowerment Innovation Center, Beijing Algorithm Registration Service Center, and Data Asset Service Center of Beijing International Data Exchange. It has built the largest 500P domestically autonomous artificial intelligence computing power cluster in the city, creating the IP of "Western Beijing AI Valley". Deepening the application of AI+4K/8K+5G technology, the district has jointly established an AGI Research Center with CCTV. com and introduced Huawei Computing Audiovisual Innovation Center. It has created content review large models and the "Tanzhe Intelligent Space" text-to-video large model. The city's first meteorological AI person "Lingxi" and government service AI person "Men Xiaozheng" have made stunning debuts. The district is constructing the National Medical Center Fuwai Hospital West Mountain Campus, leveraging Baiyang

Pharmaceutical Group's scientific research transformation base, introducing medical device CRO enterprises, and revitalizing old factory buildings to create green manufacturing spaces for key pharmaceutical and device enterprises.

The protection, development, and utilization of natural and cultural resources are the focus of Mentougou District's sustainable development. Combined with post-disaster ecological restoration, the district has deeply explored cultural resources including red culture, folk customs, ancient villages, ancient roads, prehistoric culture, Great Wall culture, agricultural culture, and cloisonné culture. It has implemented protection actions for sites such as the Donghulin Site, the "Tanjie" Cultural Relics Area, Yanhecheng Great Wall, and "Liao White Porcelain". The district has created model scenic areas such as the Tanzhe Ecological Cultural Tourism Area, Miaofeng Mountain Folk Cultural Tourism Area, and Baihuashan Natural Scenic Area. It has built a trail system connecting water resources, scenic spots, ancient roads and villages, forming premium hiking and cycling routes such as the Miaofeng Mountain hiking line, Western Beijing Ancient Road traversing line, historical landscape traversing line, and Great Wall hiking traversing line. In 2024, the district's 19 A-level and above tourist attractions achieved operating revenue of 150 million yuan, a year-on-year increase of 27%, and received a total of 2.103 million visitors, a year-on-year increase of 36.4%.

As one of Beijing's regions richest in cultural relics and cultural heritage, Mentougou District has 556 immovable cultural relics, ranking first in the city. In 2024, the district had 145 intangible cultural heritage projects at various levels. Tanzhe Temple Town and Zhaitang Town were evaluated as Beijing Folk Art Villages, and "Intangible Cultural Heritage Inheritance Empowering Rural Revitalization" was selected by the Ministry of Culture and Tourism as an outstanding national case of culture and tourism empowering rural revitalization. Building "Poetic and Picturesque Villages" is a key move in cultivating rural green new quality productive forces. Mentougou District conducts classified training for cultural talents including "Red Swans" for rural governance, "Lead Swans" for development leadership, and "Young Swans" as youth reserves. It supports immigrants and returnees to create "Poetic and Picturesque Villages" demonstration areas with characteristic themes such as the Western Beijing

Ancient Road and Wuxin Zhaitang.

Drawing a Magnificent New Picture of the Capital's Western Gateway

Based on its functional positioning as an ecological conservation area and its mission to "build a high-level important gateway for the capital's development", Mentougou District should further join hands with neighboring areas in Beijing and Hebei to jointly implement key projects such as the Shan-Shui Initiative in China and the Beijing-Tianjin sandstorm source control, and carry out cross-regional joint prevention and control of ecological environment protection and restoration; perform the capital's western mountain guarding, forest protection, and water conservation work, using the "Welcome Leopards Home" project as a starting point to create a World Biosphere Reserve; jointly build the Western Beijing Tourism Development Alliance and the Western Beijing Ancient Road Cultural Tourism Corridor, refine Western Beijing cultural tourism, commercial and health care boutique routes to form a new growth pole for Beijing-Tianjin-Hebei cultural tourism; rely on the capital's rich scientific and technological, talent, and financial resource advantages to explore reforms that appropriately separate economic zones from administrative zones, break through land element bottlenecks, and create green high-end industrial and supply chains in the western Beijing region.

Huangpu District, Shanghai: Building a Core Leading Area of a Socialist Modern International Metropolis in Harmony between Humans and Nature

In March 2025, the General Office of the National Development and Reform Commission issued the second batch of national carbon peak pilot list, determining 27 cities and parks as pilots, with Huangpu District being the only district and county in Shanghai included in the national pilot list. Huangpu District is the core area of Shanghai's central urban area, named after Shanghai's mother river—the Huangpu River. As the "heart, window, and business card" of Shanghai, it is Shanghai's economic, administrative, and cultural center, carrying over 700 years of Shanghai's city-building history and over 180 years of port-opening history, witnessing the development and changes of Shanghai as an international metropolis.

Demonstration and Pioneering Green Low-carbon Development in Central Urban Areas

In December 2024, Huangpu District issued the "Action Plan for Comprehensively Promoting Beautiful Huangpu Construction and Creating a Core Leading Area of a Socialist Modern International Metropolis in Harmony between Humans and Nature", clarifying green low-carbon development goals for three time nodes: 2027, 2035, and the middle of this century. It further proposed task measures in aspects including balanced development and protection, accelerated low-carbon transformation, pollution prevention and control, ecological city construction, ecosystem protection, safety bottom line protection, ecological culture cultivation, green digital governance innovation, and pluralistic governance construction. In March 2025, 13 departments of the Huangpu District Government jointly issued the "Huangpu District Renewable Energy Development Action Plan", which is Shanghai's first district-level systematic development program for renewable energy.

The Huangpu District carbon peak and carbon neutrality platform integrates building energy consumption monitoring, virtual power plants, carbon inclusion, energy audits, energy efficiency improvement, and other data foundations. It develops intelligent data analysis and material understanding extraction services, creates business management platforms combined with digital twin technology, and introduces applications such as a carbon inclusion platform and carbon map mini-programs. This forms a new "dual carbon" governance model driven by data aggregation, application, and inclusion, incorporating energy consumption monitoring data from nearly 300 large public and government office buildings, as well as operational data from 210 commercial building virtual power plants.

Notably, the Huangpu District carbon inclusion platform has created low-carbon scenarios including green travel, recycling, paper and plastic reduction, energy conservation, and virtual power plants. It has launched a low-carbon mall where users can exchange goods in designated shopping malls, supermarkets, bookstores, pharmacies, etc., using carbon reduction points earned from participating in low-carbon behaviors. Based on citizens' participation levels in the carbon inclusion platform, progressive levels have been set up, and completing tasks earns badges, adding an element of fun and forming a positive incentive closed loop of "practicing low-carbon behavior, obtaining carbon reduction points, and exchanging points for benefits". The Huangpu District low-carbon map mini-program integrates and displays district enterprises' energy conservation and emission reduction, public building energy efficiency improvement, and community green lifestyle practices, allowing users to easily view the district's green low-carbon development achievements.

In March 2022, the "First Party Congress Site · Xintiandi" area, which includes the birthplace of the Party—the site of the First CPC National Congress, Shanghai's fashion landmark Xintiandi, and Taiping Lake (the largest artificial lake in Puxi), was listed as a pilot for Shanghai's low-carbon development (near-zero carbon emissions) practice zone. The practice zone has upgraded air conditioning, elevators, boilers, and other existing building equipment, strictly implemented green building star rating standards for new projects, installed sub-metering equipment in buildings within its jurisdiction connected to the district-level energy consumption monitoring platform, and achieved smart energy use in buildings. It has built a public transportation hub station, optimized the slow traffic network, and made green travel a convenient choice. It has constructed new energy charging piles and smart public parking lots, enabling low-carbon governance of road parking charges. In the precious limited space of the district, urban parks have been built in a scattered pattern, integrating the concept of "sponge city" with facilities for rainwater storage, purification, and resource recycling. Dozens of species of trees, flowering shrubs, and perennial flowers have been planted, forming a rich and stable plant community. The Xintiandi commercial district has launched the "i Tiandi Green Heart Community", encouraging consumers to earn points and redeem gifts through low-carbon behaviors such as consuming at green covenant merchants and participating in the Clean Plate campaign. Today, the practice zone has basically built an international high-end commercial and business district that integrates the promotion of red culture with the advocacy of low-carbon life, and aligns green low-carbon transformation with high-quality development.

As a three-star green ecological urban area and a central activity area defined in Shanghai's overall planning, Dongjiadu is an important component of Huangpu's riverside area. It creates a three-dimensional, diverse, and ecological public green space system. The north-south green axis uses the Dongjiadu Church and the Merchant Ship Association, two historical and cultural buildings, as base points, continuing the historical context. The east-west green axis accommodates both large open spaces and small spaces for people to stay and creates a green public corridor along the Huangpu River. New projects are built 100% according to green building two-star or above standards. Buildings in the jurisdiction are connected to the district virtual power plant platform and apply renewable energy technologies such as photovoltaics and air source heat pumps. BIM technology is combined with prefabricated buildings and building robots to conduct intelligent construction pilots. Green, healthy, and energy-saving environmental concepts permeate the entire process of building design, construction, and operation.

Striving to Draw the "Most Beautiful Foundation" of Ecological Construction

Huangpu District uses various "remnant" plots of land, either demolishing or renovating them to create pocket parks or vertical greenery. In 2024, it added 47,000 m^2 of green space, becoming a highlight of park city construction. For example, the Huangpu District Cultural Center rooftop greening project adopts mountain contour line artistic aesthetics, extending and expanding the arc lines of the building, linking the plaza and terrace. According to the flowering period and color characteristics of plants, the first-floor plaza uses herbs, pines, and grasses to build an evergreen plant landscape, while the top terrace mainly uses herbaceous plants. The overall soft landscape plant matching has small variations between species while forming a unified major tone, enhancing the visual effect; as a pocket park integrating viewing, touring, and leisure functions, Keshi Garden weaves scenery based on the "landscape painting realm" of the ancient painting "Picture of Distant View with Rocky Perches", showcasing the historical heritage and humanistic feelings of ancient interest and elegant spaciousness; Forest Neighbor Garden opens up the originally enclosed green space, using many tall trees on site to create an accessible, playable, and restful forest flower border.

Huangpu District develops green finance in the Bund financial cluster in line with its industrial positioning, completing the first issuance of multiple green financial products including the first "carbon neutrality" special bond, the first "carbon neutrality" bond index, the first carbon quota CCER portfolio pledge financing, and the first "carbon neutrality" asset-backed commercial paper. The ESG Global Leaders Conference has settled in Huangpu, and enterprises in the district are actively building ESG action systems. The district promotes light production, low-noise, and environmentally friendly enterprises to "move upstairs", creating "smart manufacturing spaces", cultivating energy conservation and environmental protection industries, supporting enterprises to strengthen research and development design, transforming into new manufacturing enterprises mainly based on services, establishing product carbon footprint management systems, and enhancing green competitiveness through technological innovation and management optimization.

Green Progress in Practicing the "People's City" Concept

Overall, Huangpu District uses green as its brush and ecology as its ink, collaboratively promoting policy and institutional innovation and demonstrating advanced green low-carbon technologies. It builds zero-carbon intelligent buildings and green urban areas, advocates green low-carbon production and lifestyle models and consumption patterns, and draws a series of new green ecological pictures. This injects more diverse and sustainable development momentum into the city's sustainable development, allowing every citizen to feel the beauty of life and urban rhythm on this lush land, while also exploring an effective "Huangpu Model" for carbon peaking and carbon neutrality in "high and low" cities (high maturity of tertiary industry and building economy development, low carbon emission intensity per unit of GDP).

Innovative, Quality, Advanced: Wanzhou's Exploration of Cultivating Green New Quality Productive Forces

Green development is the foundation of Chinese-style modernization, and green productivity is new quality productive forces, forming and demonstrating strong driving force and support for high-quality development in practice. The characteristic of new quality productive forces is innovation, the key is quality excellence, and the essence is advanced productivity. "Innovation" means that green new momentum should empower the accelerated formation of new quality productive forces, "quality excellence" means that ecological vitality helps boost both quantity and quality of new quality productive forces, and "advanced" means that the new picture of Beautiful China supports the sustainable development of new quality productive forces.

As the economic center of the Three Gorges Reservoir Area and the district and county with the heaviest Three Gorges Project migration tasks and the most management units in Chongqing, Wanzhou District of Chongqing City actively explores the realization path of transforming lucid waters and lush mountains into invaluable assets. It has made new breakthroughs in creating an ecological priority green development model area in the Sichuan-Chongqing region. The ecological environment continues to improve, modern infrastructure networks are being woven tightly and strongly built, a modern industrial system is being accelerated, a Bashu-characteristic regional consumption center is being built at an accelerated pace, a science and technology innovation center and Chongqing-Sichuan northeast innovation and entrepreneurship highland are being rapidly constructed, the level of the regional central city and important urban sub-center of Chongqing is continuously being elevated, urban-rural integrated development is being solidly promoted, and regional collaboration and cooperation are being steadily implemented. These efforts aim to achieve high-level protection and high-quality development, high-quality life, and high-efficiency governance in resonance and joint success. In 2024, Wanzhou District's regional GDP reached 122. 236 billion yuan, a year-on-year increase of 6. 8%, ranking first in total volume among northeastern Chongqing districts and counties and 3rd in growth rate among all districts and counties in the city. The forest coverage rate is 50. 4%, the number of days with good air quality in urban areas is 354 (a record high), and the good air quality rate is 96. 72%. The water quality of the Wanzhou section of the Yangtze River mainstream has stably maintained Class II status. The district has implemented 240, 000 mu (about 16, 000 hectares) of national land greening and afforestation, and the "wild return" of the national first-class protected plant Adiantum nelumboides has achieved its first success.

Creating a High-quality Living Place in Northeast Sichuan-Chongqing

Protecting the river, guarding the land, and beautifying the city. Wanzhou District adheres to joint efforts for major protection rather than major development, improving the ecological governance chain of source prevention, front-end emission reduction, whole-process supervision, and collaborative effectiveness. The good ecological environment has become Wanzhou's golden brand. The Yangtze River flows through Wanzhou District for 80. 4 km, with a reservoir water surface reaching 100 km^2. Focusing on improving water quality across the entire region and concentrating on the mainstream and tributaries of the Yangtze River, the district deeply promotes "three water co-governance". It has developed "river-specific approaches" for the governance of 21 rivers with basin areas of over 50 km^2. Through ecological restoration, ecological water replenishment, upgrading and transforming sewage treatment plants, and building and repairing sewage collection networks and other measures, it has constructed an ecological corridor along the Yangtze River. Currently, Wanzhou District's urban domestic sewage centralized treatment rate exceeds 98%, the township domestic sewage centralized treatment rate reaches 85%, the sludge harmless disposal rate reaches 100%, industrial cluster area sewage is collected as much as possible and discharged according to standards, the water quality compliance rate of urban centralized drinking water sources reaches 100%, water consumption per 10,000 yuan of GDP and water consumption per 10,000 yuan of industrial added value have decreased by 27.02% and 13.49% respectively compared to 2020, the effective utilization coefficient of farmland irrigation water reaches 0.5114, and the ecological barrier system of the Wanzhou section of the Yangtze River has basically taken shape.

Wanzhou District explores the market-oriented allocation system of resource and environmental elements, promoting the incremental benefits of industrial green transformation to feed back to the early-stage investment in green development. For example, Modao Creek is the largest tributary of the Yangtze River in Wanzhou. In the past, residents along the river had insufficient ecological protection awareness, and the water environment faced challenges. The governments of Wanzhou District, Shizhu County, and Yunyang County signed a horizontal ecological protection compensation agreement for the upstream and downstream of the Modao Creek basin, clarifying compensation methods, compensation benchmarks, compensation standards, and joint prevention and control matters to jointly protect the ecological environment of the Modao Creek basin. Today, the water quality of Modao Creek has stabilized again and meets standards, with clear water flowing into the Yangtze River. Subsequently, Wanzhou District expanded the horizontal ecological protection compensation reform to secondary basins such as the Zhuxi River and Rangdu River within the district.

The first garbage incineration power plant in the Three Gorges Reservoir area—Wanzhou District Garbage Incineration Power Plant—has a daily garbage processing capacity of 800 tons and can generate more than 360,000 kWh of electricity per day, meeting the electricity needs of 30,000 to 40,000 households. It has cumulatively disposed of more than 2.3 million tons of domestic waste and supplied more than 824 MkWh of green electricity, equivalent to planting more than 13.8 million new trees for the Earth and reducing carbon dioxide emissions by more than 1.15 million tons. The power plant is surrounded by lush trees, and although sealed garbage transport vehicles come and go, there is no odor. This is due to the maximization of domestic waste reduction, resource utilization, and harmless treatment. The water filtered from domestic waste accumulated in the garbage pit is entirely collected by the sewage treatment system and purified to meet standards through advanced processes before being reused or discharged; the flue gas generated by incineration is purified to meet standards through combined processes such as denitrification, desulfurization, physical adsorption, and dust removal; the slag comprehensive utilization workshop uses advanced extraction technology to recover metals such as iron and aluminum from the slag, with the remainder used as building materials, and fly ash is harmlessly treated through chelation and solidification before being landfilled in a dedicated site.

The living environment is both the appearance of high-quality ecological environment and the geographical advantage for developing green new quality productive forces. Creating a beautiful mountain and water city model with "beauty, grandeur, harmony, and characteristics" is Wanzhou District's public product and people's livelihood for meeting residents' needs for a better life. Focusing on improving urban architectural features and spatial environmental quality, with the Yangtze River as the main line and secondary rivers as branch lines, the district implements ecological restoration and protection utilization of "slopes, cliffs, walls, alleys, roads, banks, and surfaces". It builds riverside and lakeside landscapes that are "primarily focused on one season but considering all four seasons, primarily focused on one color but with multiple colors interacting", expands urban public leisure spaces such as waterfront walkways, rest platforms, and viewing platforms, and enriches forest, color, seasonal, and quality characteristics, making the beautiful city picture of "paintings in the city, mountains in the paintings, water in the mountains, and city in the water" more bright and beautiful.

Industrial Transformation and Upgrading Generate Green New Quality Productive Forces

Chongqing Xiangyu Salt Chemical Co., Ltd. is China's largest well-mined salt and combined soda production base. It has carried out multiple technical transformation projects such as green carbon fixation for combined soda facilities, distributed photovoltaic power generation, and tail gas recovery and utilization from air separation. This saves 29,000 tons of standard coal annually, reduces emissions of carbon dioxide, nitrogen oxides, and smoke and dust by nearly 50,000 tons, and increases production capacity by 300,000 tons. Chongqing Jiulong Wanbo New Materials Technology Co., Ltd. has adopted large-scale equipment and digital intelligence to empower traditional production models. One production line produces 900,000 tons of alumina annually, with energy consumption per ton of alumina reduced from 92 m^3 to 83 m^3. This reduction minimizes unnecessary manual intervention in the production process. The company has received honors such as the National Excellent Intelligent Manufacturing Scene. Schneider Wanzhou Base is a national-level green factory where all equipment is interconnected, and the entire product assembly, testing, and packaging process is intelligent and green. Production efficiency has increased by 139.18% compared to traditional production methods, the product defect rate has decreased by 34%, operating costs have decreased by 28.5%, and unit energy consumption has decreased by 14.74%... "Equipment core replacement", "production line replacement", and "machine replacement of people" are fueling the transformation of Wanzhou's "high-end" industrial structure with nearly 200 green intelligent manufacturing projects.

The key link in forming green new quality productive forces is the transformation and application of scientific and technological innovation, forming industrial innovation characterized by innovative allocation of production factors and deep industrial transformation and upgrading. Wanzhou District is accelerating the construction of a "5 + 10 + X" modern industrial system[①], enhancing industrial resilience and quality through the integration of "four chains", and making breakthroughs in new industrial tracks such as digital production meth-

---

① Wanzhou District's "5 + 10 + X" modern industrial system: "5" refers to five key industries: advanced materials, food processing, equipment manufacturing, pharmaceutical chemicals, and new energy; "10" refers to 10 specialized industrial chains subdivided around key industries: copper and copper alloy materials, aluminum and aluminum alloy materials, green building materials, grain and oil processing, specialty foods, automobiles and parts, ships and supporting facilities, lighting and electrical equipment, pharmaceuticals, and chemicals; "X" refers to several future industries.

ods, low-carbon energy consumption, circular resource utilization, and clean production processes. It is doing both "subtraction" for energy conservation and carbon reduction and "addition" for cultivating green new quality productive forces. In 2024, the above-scale industrial output value and added value of Wanzhou District increased by 13.0% and 11.5% year-on-year, respectively, both higher than the district's GDP growth rate, ranking 4th and 3rd, respectively. Wanzhou Economic and Technological Development Zone was approved as a Chengdu-Chongqing Economic Circle Industrial Cooperation Demonstration Park and a Chongqing Industrial Transfer Demonstration Park. Two enterprises, Jiulong Wanbo and GD Copper, both achieved annual output values exceeding 10 billion yuan, realizing a breakthrough from "zero" for ten-billion-yuan level industrial enterprises. The district has built 4 national-level green factories and 9 municipal-level green factories, further enhancing the industrial "gold content" and "green content".

Financial Support Accelerates the Formation of Green New Quality Productive Forces

Since being approved in 2022 as the only core area of the green finance reform and innovation pilot zone outside Chongqing's main urban area, Wanzhou has fully utilized and effectively leveraged green finance policy tools. In key industries such as energy, chemicals, building materials, non-ferrous metals, agriculture, and transportation, it has formulated Chongqing's first batch of transition finance standards for Wanzhou, established a transition finance project database for high-energy-consuming industries, key industries, and characteristic industries, guided local banking institutions to directly link enterprise transition progress with credit lines and loan interest rates, established Chongqing's first enterprise carbon account platform, built a "one group library" for carbon data in the cloud, "one account" for carbon accounting, and "one network" for carbon disclosure. It has launched Chongqing's first batch of "carbon-linked" financial products. In 2024, it issued 8.09 billion yuan in transition finance loans, and Chongqing Three Gorges Bank's green credit balance increased to 32.181 billion yuan.

Cultivating Green New Quality Productive Forces to Promote High-quality Development

Wanzhou District is named for "the convergence of ten thousand rivers", is known for "the gathering of ten thousand merchants", and is famous for "the tourism of ten thousand guests". The foundation and quality of high-quality development lie in ecological priority and green development. To this end, three major proposals for "building a highland of green new quality productive forces" have been put forward:

First, based on factor resource advantages, construct a modern industrial system driven by green new quality productive forces. Improve the long-term mechanism of government department promotion, leading enterprise driving, upstream and downstream enterprise linkage, and major institutions and talents driving industry-university-research cooperation. Construct a tiered cultivation system for science and technology enterprises to "grow from micro to small, rise from small to high, and change from high to strong". Improve the full-chain incubation system of "maker space + incubator + accelerator" to enhance the endogenous green power of scientific and technological innovation. Strengthen the main battlefield, main position, and main platform of new industrialization, promote the integrated development of industrial parks with cities, landscapes, and intelligence, implement the reform of "green output per mu (about 666.67 m^2) as the hero", promote the green transformation of key industries, and support enterprises of all sizes in product research and innovation, gradient development, and growing stronger.

Second, adhere to proceeding from reality, and use green new quality productive forces as a brush to draw a new picture of beautiful Wanzhou. Iterate and upgrade the ecological environment governance system, resolutely safeguard Wanzhou's blue sky, clear waters, and clean soil. Strengthen cross-regional joint protection of ecological systems, continue to promote the "ten-year fishing ban" in the Yangtze River, advance the construction of national land greening demonstration pilot projects, and enhance the forest landscape along the Yangtze River shoreline. Promote the development of forestry carbon sinks, make good use of the market-oriented carbon account platform for transition finance, and enrich the supply of transition finance products. Allocate green science and technology innovation resources across regions according to needs, based on key industry clean production and energy conservation and emission reduction scenarios. Give play to the innovation spillover and radiation driving effects of the highland of green new quality productive forces to enhance the green performance of regional collaboration and cooperation.

Third, construct new types of production relations adapted to green new quality productive forces, and accelerate the formation of ecological consciousness among all people. Give play to the dynamic factor of people in green science and technology innovation, implement talent projects such as the "Pinghu Talent" plan, the "Hundred-Thousand-Ten-Thousand" talent attraction project, and industrial worker team building. Build a youth development-oriented city, promote the integrated development of industry-university-research-finance-service with talent as the core, improve incentive measures for excellence and innovation, and enhance innovation and entrepreneurship capabilities to master green new quality productive forces.

With "Green" as the Foundation, Moving Toward "Beauty": The "Ningbo Model" of Green Manufacturing

Saving energy consumption costs of over 1.15 million yuan/year, reducing carbon dioxide emissions by 872.04 tons/year, and decreasing standard coal consumption by 303.85 tons/year—these are the operational effects after Ningbo Great Group's micro-renovation of its first-level energy efficiency compressed air station. As a high-tech enterprise and national-level green factory, Ningbo Great Group has broken down the "carbon neutrality" goal into five aspects: resource utilization, supply chain cooperation, corporate culture, environmental governance, and energy utilization. It has incorporated green, low-carbon, and environmentally friendly concepts throughout the "full lifecycle" of the research and development, design, raw material procurement, production, packaging, and recycling of its more than one thousand product varieties. Ningbo Xiangshan Conch Cement Co., Ltd., through green technological innovation, energy consumption reduction, and solid waste resource utilization, processes and consumes 320,000 tons of fly ash, 200,000 tons of desulfurized gypsum, 260,000 tons of powder, and other industrial waste materials annually. With its fully automated production line, well-arranged modern factory buildings, and clean and orderly production environment, it has changed the dirty, messy, and poor impression of traditional cement enterprises characterized by flying dust and continuous noise.

This is a microcosm of manufacturing enterprises in Ningbo, Zhejiang Province, cutting to the core and promoting quality and efficiency through green development. As of the end of 2024, Ningbo City has cumulatively established 122 national-level green factories, ranking second among China's sub-provincial cities. It has also established 82 provincial-level green factories, ranking first among cities in Zhejiang Province. The City has set up 4 national-level green industrial parks and 16 green supply chain management enterprises, as well as 832 city-level green factories and 2,529 district (county and city) level green factories. A total of 5,033 above-scale manufacturing enterprises have completed green transformation, reaching a coverage rate of 48.3%.

Focusing on Reform Mechanisms to Build a "Beautiful Ningbo"

Ningbo City has set comprehensive ecological civilization systems, efficient ecological environmental governance systems, distinctive green and low-carbon development mechanisms, and prominent advantages in comprehensive beauty as its overall goals. The city is using pivotal initiatives and breakthrough approaches to create landmark reform achievements such as "zero direct discharge of wastewater", "near-zero landfill of solid waste", "no illegal activities within ecological red lines", and "no blind spots in environmental supervision coverage". In July 2024, the "Ningbo Environmental Zoning Control Dynamic Update Plan" was released, dividing the city's 9,365 km^2 into 254 environmental control units under classified management. The area of land actually available for Category III industrial projects increased by 110.19 km^2 year-on-year. More than 3,000 enterprises can benefit from the "regional environmental assessment +environmental standards" reform, enhancing capacity for major project support and green development.

Green Manufacturing Gaining Momentum

Ningbo City has issued a new industrial action outline, positioning green and low-carbon development as one of six "pioneer demonstration" paths for new industrialization. The city has proposed "three full coverage" goals by 2027: complete green transformation of all above-scale industrial enterprises, complete coverage of provincial-level or higher green factory construction for leading enterprises, and complete coverage of cleaner production audits for high-carbon industries. Key tasks include strengthening carbon reduction guidance for high-carbon industries, enhancing green financial support, and cultivating green transformation service providers. The city is expanding and strengthening green and low-carbon industries such as new materials and equipment, building "source-grid-load-storage" new power systems, developing "energy+industry+pollutant disposal" circular economy, establishing a national-level pollution and carbon reduction collaborative pilot in chemical industrial parks, and promoting green financial products including green insurance, emission rights-backed loans, and carbon creditworthiness.

Ningbo has issued the "Ningbo Star-Rated Green Factory Evaluation Methods", clarifying green transformation certification standards and dynamic management approaches, adding characteristic indicators such as carbon management certification and green electricity proportion, and establishing a tiered cultivation model for "national/provincial-city-county" level green factories and "national-provincial-city" level green parks. The city has released the "Ningbo 'Zero-Carbon (Near Zero-Carbon) Factory' Evaluation Methods (Trial)", guiding high energy-consuming enterprises with annual energy consumption of over 1,000 tons of standard coal to implement energy conservation, carbon reduction, clean energy substitution, and green electricity trading. Green development indicators have been incorporated into policies such as enterprise average efficiency comprehensive evaluation and technical transformation project subsidy reviews. The municipal finance department allocates special funds annually to support enterprise green and low-carbon transformation and has launched "Green Factory Upgrade Loans", providing 38. 1 billion yuan in special loans to 471 enterprises in 2024.

As a strong industrial port district known for its large port, major industries, and extensive logistics, Ningbo Economic and Technological Development Zone continues to promote full-process, clean, and low-carbon transformation of key industries and enhance the efficiency of industrial platforms. In 2024, 1,028 above-scale industrial enterprises achieved a total output value of 585. 727 billion yuan. The added value of high-tech industries, equipment manufacturing, and strategic emerging industries increased by 10. 1%, 18. 8%, and 16. 1% respectively, all higher than the growth rate of total above-scale industrial added value, accounting for 65. 3%, 48. 6%, and 29. 8% of above-scale industry. The zone was selected for the national environmental health management pilot list. As China's largest supplier of sintered neo-dymium-iron-boron magnets, Ningbo Konit & Nihon Magnetic Materials Co., Ltd. has built digital workshops, expanded solar power generation in factory areas, digitally managed product carbon footprints, and participated in the "Zero Carbon Pioneer Program" with key customers like Siemens, achieving a 25% reduction in carbon emission intensity per unit of output compared to the base year. With the commissioning of the State Grid Ningbo Economic Development Zone Zhoushan Port wind-solar-storage integrated project, Zhejiang Province's first green electricity port has been created, injecting new momentum into the green, low-carbon, and sustainable development of Zhoushan Port. Ningbo Green Energy Port has the world's largest single-tank LNG storage capacity and will provide 6 million tons of liquefied natural gas annually to Zhejiang Province, advancing the green development of the oil and gas industry chain in Ningbo Economic Development Zone.

Ningbo City is an important export hub for China's textile and apparel industry, with over 20,000 textile enterprises and annual output exceeding 100 billion yuan. Through digital platform construction, equipment upgrades, and zero-waste factory development, more than 300,000 tons of waste textile materials were recycled in 2024, reducing carbon emissions by 1.08 million tons. At the 2025 Zhejiang Province "International Zero-Waste Day" themed activities, Ningbo took the lead in releasing zero-waste textile construction guidelines, defining for the first time the full-cycle "zero-waste code of conduct" for printing, dyeing, spinning, and weaving industries: Through comprehensive measures including environmental protection, raw material control, solid waste treatment and recycling, low-carbon office operations, green facility construction, system building, and zero-waste assessment, Ningbo promotes the minimization of facility and equipment energy consumption, maximization of raw material product recycling benefits, and optimization of solid waste resource utilization. The environmental performance and manufacturing efficiency of "zero-waste textile factories" are at globally leading levels.

As an environmentally friendly enterprise in clean steel production, Ningbo Iron & Steel Co., Ltd. has invested over 4 billion yuan in implementing more than 100 projects including desulfurization and denitrification of coke oven/sintering/boiler/hot blast stove/heating furnace flue gas, electric heavy truck transportation, and scrap steel and slag treatment. It has been recognized by the Ministry of Ecology and Environment and the China Iron and Steel Association as a publicly announced enterprise for ultra-low emission transformation across the entire process. Ningbo Steel has developed a smart environmental protection control system including 3D large-screen display, routine environmental business management, and environmental protection apps, automatically generating environmental data reports and achieving pollution source inventory management through unorganized emission tracing, real-time environmental anomaly warnings, and precise problem point location. Ningbo Steel has built attractions including the Ninggang Exhibition Hall, Innovation Achievement Exhibition Hall, Research Audio-Visual Hall, and Lingxiao Flower Gallery landscape road. The company has transformed production processes into themed landscapes such as "Steel Forged Through Hundreds of Refinements", "Molten Iron Pear Blossoms", and "Split into Materials", obtaining AAA-level industrial tourism scenic area certification and showcasing the unique charm of "steel intelligent manufacturing" in the new era among the steel forest's blue waterfront boardwalks.

Green Transformation Leading High-Quality Development of Manufacturing

Green mountains paint a timeless picture without ink; clear waters play music without strings. Today's Ningbo features scenic spots throughout its poetic Jiangnan landscape, with harmonious and beautiful living environments and blue sky and clear water ecological foundations gradually expanding. Green factories are converging to generate powerful momentum, vividly demonstrating the practical strength of the "Eight-Eight Strategy" through the charm of "beauty". As a major manufacturing city, accelerating green transformation and upgrading is both a practical need and a long-term plan, and an inevitable choice for building an innovative smart manufacturing city. Ningbo City must further strengthen policy guidance, precisely plan green development paths with "one industry, one policy" and "one enterprise, one policy" approaches, promote coordinated development of digitalization and green transformation through technological innovation, continuously remediate "high consumption, low efficiency" enterprises through mergers and reorganizations, overall relocation, park entry, and transformation and upgrading. The city should create star-rated green factories and benchmarks for pollution and carbon reduction, cultivate world-class advanced manufacturing clusters, and strive to explore innovative paths for new industrialization characterized by "ecological priority, conservation and intensive use, green and low-carbon, and shared beauty".

Suzhou Pursuing "Green" to "New": Cultivating New Advantages of Lucid Waters and Lush Mountains

With a regional GDP of 2.67 trillion yuan in 2024, a year-on-year increase of 6.0%, above-scale industrial added value increasing by 9.2% year-on-year, and above-scale industrial enterprises' high-tech industry output value reaching2.57 trillion yuan-this is Suzhou, an important central city in eastern China. Blue skies and white clouds have become the norm, lucid waters and lush mountains are visible everywhere, 114 bird species have been observed at Taihu Lake National Wetland Park, and 125 bird species at East Taihu Wetland Park, vividly illustrating the green development advantage that "birds know first if the environment is good", this is Suzhou, known as "heaven above, Suzhou and Hangzhou below". Focusing on the central goal of "Beautiful Suzhou" and following the path of planning, control, restoration, and development, Suzhou City strives to create a modern metropolitan model of harmony between humans and nature. Air quality was the first in the province to reach national second-level standards, and the city has ranked in the first echelon of provincial pollution prevention and control comprehensive assessments for six consecutive years. It has established five national ecological civilization demonstration zones, and public satisfaction with the ecological environment rose from 81.7% in 2015 to 92.5% in 2023. The high-quality development landscape guided by the concept of "lucid waters and lush mountains" is becoming increasingly clear.

The Beauty of Taihu Eco-Islands Reflects the Depth of Ecological Civilization Construction Achievements

Suzhou City owns two-thirds of Taihu Lake's water surface, three-quarters of its shoreline, and four-fifths of its islands, making it the main battlefield for Taihu Lake governance. Since the implementation of the "Overall Plan for Comprehensive Water Environment Treatment in the Taihu Lake Basin" in 2008, Suzhou City has implemented more than 5,600 Taihu treatment projects with a total investment exceeding 84 billion yuan. Since 2023, Suzhou has issued the "Suzhou Action Plan for Promoting a New Round of Comprehensive Treatment of Taihu Lake", deeply carried out industrial pollution control and cumulatively completed the remediation of 6,876 phosphorus-related enterprises in the Taihu Basin. Twenty-six sewage treatment plants and 603 industrial enterprises have achieved classified treatment. The water quality in the eastern area of Taihu Lake improved from Class IV in 2018 to Class III and has maintained this level to date. Taihu Lake has achieved safe summer passage for 17 consecutive years, and in 2023 was evaluated as an excellent lake by the Ministry of Ecology and Environment for the first time. The development and utilization rate of the city's Yangtze River shoreline is controlled within 50%, and the water quality of the Suzhou section of the Yangtze River mainstream stably reaches Class II. All 27 provincial-level or higher river section monitoring points connecting to the Yangtze River have water quality at or better than Class III.

Suzhou's Taihu Eco-Island is located in the central area of Taihu Lake, encompassing Xishan Island and 26 other Taihu islands and waters. It is a key node and ecological barrier for maintaining the Taihu Lake ecosystem, as well as a supporting point and supply area for important ecological service functions in the core area of the Yangtze River Delta. In August 2021, the "Suzhou Taihu Eco-Island Regulations", the first legislation in Jiangsu Province to protect Taihu Lake islands, officially came into effect, proposing to build Taihu Eco-Island into an ecological demonstration island characterized by low carbon, beauty, prosperity, civilization, and harmony. Suzhou released the "Taihu Eco-Island Development Plan (2021-2035)" and the "Implementation Plan for Taihu Eco-Island Natural Resource Field Ecological Product Value Realization Mechanism Pilot", proposing the vision of "a Chinese model of global sustainable development ecological island": To build Taihu Eco-Island into "a beautiful island with clear waters, green mountains, dancing fireflies, and fragrant fruits; a low-carbon island featuring sustainable cycles, energy efficiency, and resilience; a prosperous island with ecological economy and well-be-ing; a knowledge island led by green innovation technology; and an artistic is-land with natural landscapes and emotional resonance".

Suzhou City has established a "sky-air-land-human" ecological environ-ment intelligent monitoring platform for Taihu Eco-Island, carried out ecological product development and utilization value accounting, compiled natural re-source asset balance sheets, and Wuzhong District has topped China's GEP (Gross Ecosystem Product) 100 Strong Counties ranking for three consecutive years. Integrating into the Taihu Lake Science and Innovation Circle, the city has jointly built China's first "autonomous driving ecological demonstration is-land" with Baidu, and established new energy vehicle intelligent driving expe-rience centers with BYD, XPeng, and other brands, creating a new "enclave economy" model of "industrial clusters outside the island, scenario experiment grounds on the island". The city has created the "Around Taihu Lake No. 1 Road" IP, integrating mountain and water scenery, rural customs, and cultur-al features along the 186-kilometer road, forming the core area of Taihu Nation-al Tourism Resort with multiple business formats including research tours, e-vents, homestays, and cultural creativity.

Xiaoxia Bay Wetland is the largest lake bay on Xishan Island, named after King Fu Chai of Wu who avoided summer heat there during the Spring and Au-tumn Period. It has good natural endowments, with economic forests on the mountain, ten thousand mu (about 666. 67 hectares) of good fields along Taihu Lake, and dense surrounding villages, with a water catchment area of about 18 km^2. As a typical case of agricultural non-point source pollution prevention and control selected by the National Water Pollution Prevention and Control Inter-ministerial Coordination Group, the Xiaoxia Bay Wetland Ecological Safety Buffer Zone has developed a three-level wetland interception and treatment sys-tem following the technical route of "source control + ecological purification + multi-functional utilization": Rainwater and sewage flowing down from the mountains enter three rain and sewage interception wetlands through existing or specially built ditches, converging into ecological buffer ponds along diversion channels, achieving a transition from multiple sources to fewer, then from few to concentrated sources. After physical filtration, the water flows through pipes into enhanced direct-flow wetlands for biological treatment. The effluent water quality exceeds surface water Class III standards and enters shallow wetlands through clear water corridors for final purification before permeating into Xiaoxia River and eventually flowing into Taihu Lake.

The "Taihu Basin Environmental Resource Court Taihu Eco-Island Circuit Court Point" of Gusu District People's Court and the "Taihu Eco-Island Circuit Court Point" of Wuzhong District People's Court have been established in Jinting Town. Taihu Eco-Island has built the province's first ecological environment damage compensation and restoration base integrating restoration demonstration, legal warning, science education exchange, and monitoring control functions. Alternative restoration models such as off-site restoration and labor compensation have been adopted to strengthen the main responsibility for ecological environmental damage remediation and repair, spread ecological environment resource judicial concepts, and provide solutions to the dilemma of "enterprise pollution, public suffering, and government footing the bill".

Modern Industries Displaying "Green Features"

Suzhou promotes energy conservation and emission reduction, integration of informatization and industrialization, and product structure adjustment in traditional manufacturing industries, guiding key enterprises to update and transform traditional processes and equipment and strengthen cleaner production upgrades. The city encourages leading enterprises to work with upstream and downstream companies, park enterprises, and cross-industry enterprises to jointly explore circular economy approaches including product logistics circulation chains, multi-level energy utilization chains, waste utilization chains, and greenhouse gas reduction chains. Suzhou develops energy conservation and environmental protection industries, cultivating more than 7,000 environmental enterprises in fields such as consulting services, environmental protection products, environmental engineering, environmental governance, and resource utilization, accounting for 20% of Jiangsu Province's total, with an annual output value of about 300 billion yuan. The city integrates "general industrial solid waste recovery and disposal + hazardous waste recovery and disposal + renewable resource recovery and disposal" into three major "collection-transportation-disposal" networks, forming a fully closed-loop and traceable industrial solid waste management system covering collection, classification, transportation, and disposal.

Suzhou Industrial Park strives to explore green low-carbon transformation of industrial structure, clean and efficient energy utilization, and enterprise energy conservation and carbon reduction transformation. It has been successively recognized as a circular economy pilot park, a low-carbon industrial park pilot, a national-level green park, the first national carbon peak pilot park, and a typical case of energy green low-carbon transformation by the National Energy Administration. The park has built the province's first intelligent laboratory for ecological environment monitoring, deployed a DeepSeek large model-empowered ecological environment monitoring digital intelligence center, dynamically generates ecological environment monitoring visualization reports with zero coding, and aggregates more than 300 above-scale ESG industry enterprises and more than 120 green and near-zero carbon factory enterprises.

State Grid Suzhou Power Supply Company has built 16 microgrids, and Suzhou zero-carbon smart virtual power plant has completed market registration, expected to generate 280 MkWh of electricity annually, equivalent to reducing standard coal consumption by 85,000 tons. Suzhou Industrial Park Circular Economy Industrial Park has built a circular economy chain centered on "sewage treatment-sludge disposal/organic waste treatment-combined heat and power/biogas utilization" through organic interconnection of environmental protection facilities such as sewage treatment, sludge disposal, food waste treatment, and thermal power. The sewage treatment plant is the city's largest "photovoltaic + sewage treatment" comprehensive application project, building a 72 MW photovoltaic power station on 40,000 m^2 of sewage treatment pools, producing 5.8 MkWh of green electricity annually, reducing standard coal consumption by about 1,700 tons, and decreasing carbon dioxide emissions by over 4,700 tons. It effectively shields part of the sewage treatment pool water surface, significantly inhibiting algae growth in the pool water.

In recent years, Suzhou's new energy industry foundation has become increasingly solid, with advantages in subdivided fields leading and innovation momentum bursting forth. At the 2024 New Industrialization Work Conference, Suzhou clearly proposed building new energy into the next trillion-yuan leading industry within about three years. As of the end of 2023, Suzhou had 637 new energy enterprises, including 430 above-scale enterprises, achieving an industrial output value of 357.642 billion yuan, a year-on-year increase of 20%. It has 96 national-level and provincial-level enterprise technology centers and 292 high-tech enterprises, forming a "5+1" new energy industry system (photovoltaic, wind power, smart grid, power batteries and energy storage, hydrogen energy, and smart energy).

Drawing a Meticulous "Brush Painting" of Green Development

As an ancient city with a 2,500-year history, Suzhou is endowed with abundant ecological resources. Its graceful mountains, charming waters, and the quintessential small bridges over flowing streams together paint a vivid picture of the unique allure and natural beauty of a Jiangnan water town. Wandering through Suzhou's streets and alleys, one encounters lush trees, crystal-clear rivers, and a profusion of colorful flowers at every turn, as if they are collectively narrating the city's green story to all who pass by. In advancing the Suzhou new practice of Chinese-style modernization, Suzhou has formed a green development path where "ecological beauty promotes industrial prosperity, industrial prosperity drives public wealth, and public wealth preserves ecological beauty", achieving mutual promotion and win-win results between economic development and ecological protection. This provides valuable experience for other cities. We look forward to Suzhou continuing to write brilliant chapters in challenging areas such as ecological environment protection and restoration, low-carbon transformation of traditional industries, and iterative upgrading of green industries, showcasing to the world a green city full of vitality and vigor.

Leading "Strong Provincial Capital" with "Strong Ecology": Guiyang's Practice in Building a National Civilized Model City

In November 2023, the Guiyang Municipal Government held a press conference announcing Guiyang's successful creation of a national ecological civilization demonstration zone, becoming the first prefecture-level city in the province and the third provincial capital city in the country to successfully create such a zone. Guiyang City implements the green economy "one-two-three-four" strategic path[1], focuses on "one city, one battle, one rectification"[2], simultaneously promotes the construction of "six ecologies"[3], issues China's first local ecological civilization construction regulations, establishes China's first environmental protection court and environmental protection trial court, and deeply fights the "five major battles" of blue sky, clear water, clean soil, solid waste treatment, and rural environmental improvement. The city has constructed a modern environmental governance system of "one ecological environment account, one environmental management map, and one pollution supervision

---

[1] Guiyang City's green economy "one-two-three-four" strategic path: "One" refers to adhering to the "one strategy" of establishing the city based on ecology; "Two" refers to "two coordinations", namely coordinating development with ecology and coordinating development with security; "Three" refers to accelerating the construction of "three cities" -ecological city, civilized city, and innovative city; "Four" refers to implementing "four green actions" -green production, green consumption, green living, and green civilization.

[2] One city, one battle, one rectification: "One city" refers to high-quality construction of an ecological civilization demonstration city, "one battle" refers to deeply fighting the pollution prevention and control battle, and "one rectification" refers to fully addressing ecological and environmental protection supervision feedback issues.

[3] Six ecologies: Ecological city, ecological governance, ecological protection, ecological economy, ecological culture, and ecological system.

network", developed green mountain efficient agriculture and strategic emerging industries, linked cool summer tourism with health and wellness tourism development, persistently promoted ecological civilization publicity and education, and continuously meets people's growing needs for a beautiful ecological environment and high-quality green economy.

Good Ecology Equals People's Well-being

In 2024, Guiyang City's ambient air quality excellent rate reached 99.5%, with PM2.5 concentration decreasing by 16.6% year-on-year, ranking among the top cities in China's 168 key cities. The construction land soil environment management mechanism covering municipal and district levels is basically complete, with a 100% safe utilization rate of key construction land. The compliance rate and excellence rate of 28 national and provincial surface water control sections, the compliance rate of 15 county-level or above centralized drinking water sources, and the compliance rate of 6 national groundwater monitoring points are all 100%. Guiyang has been selected for the national "waste-free city" construction list, with green buildings accounting for 100% of new buildings, domestic waste incineration power generation capacity reaching 4,900 tons/day, and domestic waste resource utilization rate reaching 86.4%. Forest coverage has stabilized at over 55%, with 1,025 parks of various sizes, and per capita park green space in built-up areas exceeding 14.85 m^2.

Nanming River is Guiyang City's "mother river". Traditional centralized sewage treatment plants struggle to address mountain city terrain differences, and intercepting sewer networks cannot effectively collect sewage in karst landforms. Following the new concept of moderate concentration, local treatment, and nearby reuse, Guiyang City has built and expanded 24 submerged reclaimed water plants along the Nanming River basin with a total sewage treatment capacity of millions of tons. Treated standard water is returned to replenish the river's ecological base flow, with annual water replenishment exceeding 450 million cubic meters. The submerged reclaimed water plants are divided into underground treatment layer, operation layer, and ground landscape layer, effectively addressing NIMBY (Not in My Backyard) problems such as odor and noise and achieving intensive land use. Through biological drying and stabiliza-tion technologies, sludge is transformed into soil for greening and building ma-terial raw materials, achieving harmless treatment and resource utilization. To-day, Nanming River's water quality stably meets Class IV surface water stand-ards and can reach Class III surface water standards 80% of the time throughout the year. Submerged plant coverage has risen to 85%, aquatic plant species ex-ceed 23, benthic animal species reach 33, planktonic animal species reach 16, dominant fish species reach 29, and the ecosystem health index approa-ches "very healthy" status. It has become an outstanding case of the Ministry of Ecology and Environment's "Second Batch of Beautiful Rivers and Lakes" and its governance and protection experience has been selected as a typical case of the "Promoting Implementation of Major Ecological Environment Projects" of the Ministry of Ecology and Environment.

Red Maple Lake is an important drinking water source in Guiyang City. The implementation of "five major projects" -lakeside village domestic sewage treatment, retreat from lake to park, retreat from lake to city, agricultural in-dustry structure adjustment, and first-level protection zone enclosure nets-as well as "four major measures" -demolishing illegal buildings, dismantling breeding farms, legally regulating farmhouse restaurants, and strengthening ju-dicial guarantees-have eliminated pollution "stock", strictly controlled pollu-tion "increments", and managed pollution "variables". Water quality has im-proved from Class V inferior in 2008 to Class II, and the lake was selected as a beautiful and happy lake in Guizhou Province in 2024. "Water protection" fol-lowed by "prosperity": Dachong Village's farmhouse restaurants are thriving, Right Two Village's Mondrian color scheme buildings attract countless visitors, and Ludishao Village's Shine Muscat grapes are supplied directly to Shanghai markets...Villagers around Red Maple Lake who have "moved ashore" continue to expand channels for converting "two mountains" (lucid waters and lush mountains) into wealth.

As a national forest city, Guiyang City has established "Forest Chief + Chief Prosecutor", "Forest Chief+Court Chief", and "Forest Chief+Police Chief" collaboration mechanisms, strictly cracking down on illegal activities that damage forest resources and strengthening forestry disaster prevention. The city has planted 6. 1467 million native trees in key areas such as the around-city forest belt, Aha Lake green core, natural protected areas, and mining remnant sites, creating the ecological landscape of "one heart, two belts, and thousand parks"[1]. It organizes natural education activities such as wetland protection and forest exploration, conducts forest township, forest village, forest settlement, and forest home creation, and drives all-region tourism with all-region forests, forming a mountain-water-forest-city pattern of "mountains within the city, city within mountains, green belts surrounding, forests encircling the city, city in forest, forest in city".

Deep Cultivation of High-Quality Green Economic Development

Guiyang City's 11th Party Congress positioned ecological development as its primary strategy and green economy as its main path, making arrangements around the "four greens" of green production, green consumption, green living, and green civilization. By enhancing the green, high-end, and intelligent levels of key industries, the added value of the green economy in 2024 accounted for nearly 50% of GDP. The city has cumulatively established 88 green factories (41 national-level and 47 provincial-level), accounting for 30% of the province's total, and 11 green parks (9 national-level and 2 provincial-level), accounting for 26. 8% of the province's total.

In summer 2024, "China's Summer Resort Capital" Guiyang topped the national "cooling+travel" heat increase ranking on "Mafengwo" platform. As one of China's first batch of youth development pilot cities, Guiyang City coordinates the integrated development of culture, commerce, and tourism. Roadside concerts have gone viral, and special districts like Qingyun Market and Cao Zhuangyuan Street are bustling day and night. The city promotes the use of green products, establishes a green consumption points system, and "youthful style, new ways to play" has become a new trend in green consumption. Explo-

---

① The ecological landscape of "one heart, two belts, and thousand parks": "One heart" refers to Aha Lake National Wetland Park, "two belts" refer to the Nanming River ecological belt and the around-city forest belt, and "thousand parks" refer to various parks including forest parks, wetland parks, mountain parks, city parks, and community parks.

ring the "sorting, disposal, collection, transfer, processing" Guiyang model for domestic waste, the city promotes solving waste sorting and disposal difficulties at the grassroots level, earning praise from the Ministry of Housing and Urban-Rural Development.

In October 2024, Guizhou Province's first village-level joint household forest farm was established in Jiupan Village, Yanlou Town, Huaxi District, Guiyang City. Following the management approach of "sharing dividends without dividing mountains, sharing benefits without dividing forests", the forest resources of all 295 village households were unified under the management of the joint household forest farm, centrally integrating village-level forest resources and cultivating and strengthening the village-level collective economy. Looking further, Guiyang City is seizing the opportunity of the new round of collective forest rights system reform, using scale planting and industrial management as a starting point and aiming to increase under-forest economic utilization area and value. The city activates forest land resources, develops under-forest industries such as edible fungi and medicinal herbs. The Gangzhai State-owned Forest Farm in Kaiyang County has become the province's first batch of forestry carbon coupon holders. The total area of forest land used for under-forest economy reaches 1, 579, 200 mu (about 105, 280 hectares), with the full industrial chain value of the under-forest economy reaching 11. 274 billion yuan, ranking first in the province.

Focusing on comprehensive rural revitalization, Guiyang City develops modern mountainous characteristic efficient green agriculture according to local conditions, implements "4 × 100, 000 + 1, 000, 000 + 50, 000, 000" industrial projects[1], cultivates "four types of new agricultural management entities" - large-scale farming households, farmer cooperatives, family farms, and leading enterprises. The city conducts innovative applications such as smart agriculture, smart agricultural machinery, and smart meteorology, promotes agricul-

---

[1] "4×100, 000+1, 000, 000+50, 000, 000" industrial projects: Building vegetable supply demonstration bases of 100, 000 mu (about 6, 667 hectares), fruit tree quality and efficiency improvement of 100, 000 mu (about 6, 667 hectares), developing under-forest planting of 100, 000 mu (about 6, 667 hectares), adding pig production capacity of 100, 000 heads, adding aquatic products of 500, 000 kg, and broiler production capacity of 50, 000, 000 birds.

tural core technology breakthroughs and scientific and technological achievement transformation. The annual output value of ecological characteristic food industry reaches 20. 465 billion yuan, the total agricultural machinery equipment reaches 311, 200 units (sets), and the comprehensive mechanization rate of main crop cultivation, planting, and harvesting has increased to 61. 88%.

Joint Global Development of Green Transition

Eco Forum Global Guiyang is China's only national-level international forum themed on ecological civilization. Since its founding in 2009, it has been successfully held for 12 sessions. The forum has consistently thoroughly implemented Xi Jinping's Thought on Ecological Civilization, closely followed the central government and State Council's decisions and arrangements on ecological civilization construction, actively responded to the international community's concerns about hot issues in ecological civilization construction, continuously promoted the dissemination and practical exploration of ecological civilization and sustainable development concepts, deepened extensive exchanges and practical cooperation with the international community in ecological environment protection, climate change response, and other fields, promoted sharing, integration, joint construction, and win-win results, and continuously built a "well-known brand, famous platform".

The CPC Central Committee and the State Council are very concerned about and supportive of the Eco Forum Global Guiyang. General Secretary Xi Jinping sent congratulatory letters to the forum's annual meetings in 2013 and 2018, and during his inspections of Guizhou in 2015 and 2021, he gave important instructions on holding the forum, pointing out that Eco Forum Global Guiyang is a national-level international forum themed on ecological civilization, and should be continuously well-organized through innovative methods.

Since the forum's inception, Party and state leaders have personally attended and delivered keynote speeches, many foreign leaders and former leaders have attended, and thousands of government officials, Nobel Prize winners, renowned scholars, business leaders, NGO heads, and people from various sectors have participated in the forum, discussing solutions to challenges facing humanity, attracting widespread domestic and international attention and high acclaim.

Enhancing Green Development Capacity

Today, the charm of "Refreshing Guiyang" —refreshing to the eyes, taste, heart, body, shopping, and travel—continues to stand out, with ecological advantages becoming Guiyang's greatest comparative advantage. In the future, Guiyang City will focus on "four keys" (increasing greenery, conserving energy, reducing carbon, and environmental protection), ensuring that all environmental quality indicators lead the nation and solidifying the ecological security barrier for the upper reaches of the Yangtze and Pearl Rivers. The city will promote demand-oriented green innovation technology research and application, orderly carry out carbon peaking and carbon neutrality work, implement "five major projects" -green industrial quality improvement, mountain green agriculture efficiency enhancement, modern service innovation, digital economy traction, and energy structure optimization. Guiyang will strengthen ecological utilization, circular efficiency, low-carbon clean, and environmental governance industries, build green brands such as "Electric Guiyang", "Digital Intelligent Guiyang", "Low-carbon Guiyang", "Waste-free City", and "Southwest Green Consumption Center". The city will utilize the functions of Eco Forum Global Guiyang in home-field publicity, cooperation and dissemination, and cultural exchange, tell Guiyang's green development story well, and accelerate the construction of a national civilized model city with jointly improved environment, jointly enhanced quality, and jointly prosperous life.

Harbin: Exploring New Pathways to Transform "Ice and Snow Resources into Invaluable Assets"

In September 2023, during his inspection tour in Heilongjiang, General Secretary Xi Jinping pointed out that developing the ice and snow economy should be treated as a new growth point, promoting the development of the entire industrial chain of ice and snow sports, ice and snow culture, ice and snow equipment, and ice and snow tourism. During the 2024 Spring Festival period, Harbin City became an overnight sensation, receiving 10.093 million tourist visits over the 8-day holiday, with tourism revenue reaching 16.42 billion yuan. Both figures hit historic peaks, making "Er Bin" a top trending tourism destination. Located in a cold climate zone with harsh winters, what was once considered a developmental disadvantage has now become Harbin's strength. The city has turned its former "shortcoming" into an "advantage" by focusing on the ice and snow economy. People have shifted from "fearing the cold and hibernating in winter" to "welcoming tourists and hoping for cold weather". The once quiet and desolate winter season has transformed into a bustling peak season, creating new advantages for high-quality development in the ice and snow environment.

"Coming to Harbin, we truly experience how 'ice and snow resources can become invaluable assets'", said President Xi Jinping in his speech at the welcome banquet for the 9th Asian Winter Games opening ceremony in Harbin on February 7, 2025. "Ice and snow culture and the ice and snow economy are becoming new drivers for Harbin's high-quality development and new bonds for opening up." When Harbin first hosted the Asian Winter Games in 1996, its GDP had just exceeded 50 billion yuan, with the ice and snow economy accounting for only 0. 3% of that figure. By 2024, Harbin's GDP surpassed 600 billion yuan, with the ice and snow economy contributing nearly 30%. The birthplace of China's winter sports is now experiencing a snow "fever", and the industrial city has found new opportunities through green transformation.

The Asian Winter Games Leading the Construction of an "Ice and Snow Economic Ecosystem"

Adhering to the hosting concept of "Green, Shared, Open, and Clean", the 9th Asian Winter Games set multiple records, including the shortest preparation time, highest venue reuse rate, and largest participation scale, earning high praise from the International Olympic Committee, the Olympic Council of Asia, and others. Green development was a distinctive feature of the Harbin Asian Winter Games. Abandoned mining pits were transformed into ski training bases through ecological restoration projects. AI technology was used for real-time monitoring of carbon emissions at ski resorts. Distributed photovoltaic power generation systems at competition venues were connected to the urban power grid. Both test events and official competitions were powered by green electricity, with all competition venues using energy-efficient, environmentally friendly materials and green low-carbon technologies.

Harbin established an accounting system for ice and snow resource assets, incorporating ecological elements such as the annual average of 120 days of effective ice and snow period into its GEP（Gross Ecosystem Product）accounting. This allowed every piece of ice and snow to reflect economic value, transforming "cold resources" into "hot momentum". Multiple enterprises, including Harbin Bank and China Mobile Heilongjiang Company, donated their "Longjiang Green Carbon" credits to the Organizing Committee of the 9th Asian Winter Games free of charge, helping the Games achieve carbon neutrality. The "Harbin Green Kitchen" plan emerged in response to the Asian Winter Games. Wuchang rice received carbon neutrality certification, while ice and snow cold storage technology extended the industrial chain for local fruits like blueberries. The extreme cold environment of minus 30°C became a natural testing ground for biomedical products. Harbin launched the first carbon inclusive platform in northeast China (the "Carbon Benefits Ice City, Beautiful China" WeChat mini program), comprehensively collecting and accounting for users' carbon reduction data and establishing an incentive mechanism for users' green lifestyles.

Transitioning from "relying on nature" to "profiting from snow", Harbin has established a complete industrial chain of "ice and snow events+equipment manufacturing+cultural tourism+education and training". The Harbin Ice and Snow Equipment Industrial Park has attracted leading brands such as Anta, Toread, and Bosideng. "Made in Harbin" products, including titanium alloy speed skating blades, 3D printed skis, and carbon fiber ski helmets, not only serve competitions but are also exported to more than ten countries worldwide. These products are gaining prominence in international mid-to-high-end markets, forming a "research-manufacturing-application" industrial ecosystem.

Booming Ice and Snow Tourism Year-Round

The halo of being a "dual Asian Winter Games city" has added fuel to the already trending "Er Bin", creating new scenarios for green tourism consumption: Large numbers of Southeast Asian tourists travel north to experience a temperature difference of 50 degrees Celsius to feel the "ice and snow fantasy". The Ice and Snow World, with a total investment of 2.35 billion yuan and an area of 1,000,000 m², saw its daily visitor flow exceed 100,000 for the first time. Cultural products featuring the Asian Winter Games mascots "Bin Bin" and "Ni Ni" have seen explosive sales, with popular badges and refrigerator magnets in short supply. In 2024, Harbin opened 7 new international air routes and chartered flights from Kuala Lumpur to Harbin, while registering 8,784 new accommodation businesses, an increase of 208.4% year-on-year. During the Asian Winter Games, Harbin's inbound tourism orders increased by 157% year-on-year, with tourists spending over 10,000 yuan per person on average. Both tourist numbers and consumption reached historic peaks.

The Harbin Ice and Snow World uses interactive sound and light technology to present classic ice sculpture landscapes and elements from previous Asian Winter Games with real ice and snow. Tourists can enjoy ice and snow culture through indoor ice and snow activities even in the height of summer, freeing ice and snow tourism from being "seasonally limited". This is an example of Harbin's practice of establishing a "tourist-centered" and "service-first" concept, building a multi-level tourism service pattern of "attracting guests", "retaining guests", and "pampering guests", and continuously promoting its tourism brand as the "Pearl on the Crown of Ice and Snow". Looking further, Harbin focuses on Asian Winter Games competition events and winter sports events, connecting competition venues, ice and snow events, and ice and snow scenic areas to create an "Follow the Event for Travel" IP. With the theme of "Date Harbin-Ice and Snow Warm the World", the city hosts brand activities such as the International Ice and Snow Festival, Sun Island Snow Expo, Ice Lantern Art Garden Party, Ice and Snow Carnival, and Yabuli Ski Festival. Relying on Northeast folk resources such as winter fishing, New Year's goods markets, and village feasts, Harbin has launched creative projects including food, clothing, cultural creations, and performances. The city has built a green specialty product sales network including "Er Bin" gift creative stores, vending machines, and licensed stores, enriching citizens' and tourists' experiences of ice and snow appreciation.

Protecting While Developing, Restoring While Utilizing

The Yabuli Ski Resort, established in 1974, has hosted 25 international events including two Asian Winter Games and the Winter Universiade, as well as more than 350 national events. It is the cradle of competitive skiing in China and known as "China's Snow Gate". Implementing an ecological bank model, the fragmented ecological resources such as forests and snow are integrated and evaluated, with social capital introduced for shareholding operations. Original forest belts are preserved around each ski trail, intelligent water-saving technology is adopted for the snow-making system, and runoff from the ski resort is purified through ecological filter ponds before replenishing wetlands, protecting regional biodiversity. Tourism revenue feeds back into ecological protection funds.

Harbin has 40,500 hectares of wetlands listed in its registry, including one internationally important wetland, eight provincial-level nature reserves for wetland types, thirteen national wetland parks, and two provincial wetland parks. The city was awarded the title of "International Wetland City" at the 13th Conference of the Parties to the Ramsar Convention. Adhering to the sustainable development concept of "taking the river as the principle and letting water determine the city", Harbin established a wetland protection and management leadership group. The city has carried out wetland water system governance and remediation of "three ditches and one river" (Hejia Ditch, Majia Ditch, Xinyi Ditch, and Ashi River) as well as both banks along the river. It has built an ecological environment education network with the municipal wetland education hall as the main body and education centers and wetland schools in various wetland protected areas as branches, creating an international wetland city featuring "ten thousand mu of Songjiang wetlands and a hundred-mile ecological corridor".

Ice and Snow Economy Innovating the Transformation Path of "Two Mountains"

In November 2024, the General Office of the State Council issued the "Several Opinions on Stimulating the Vitality of the Ice and Snow Economy through High-Quality Development of Winter Sports", proposing to use winter sports as a leader to drive the development of the entire industrial chain of ice and snow culture, ice and snow equipment, and ice and snow tourism. The goal is to promote the ice and snow economy as a new growth point, reaching a total scale of 1. 2 trillion yuan by 2027. As the center of China's ice and snow economy, Harbin is meticulously planning its "post-Asian Winter Games era" blueprint: Utilizing natural resources, cultural endowments, and local symbols, Harbin aims to create ice and snow experience tourism projects with emotional value. The city will form a matrix of ice and snow tourism products and premium routes with complementary resources and collaborative development with surrounding cities. It will develop new green consumption scenarios such as "ice and snow+night economy", "ice and snow+immersive technology", and "ice and snow+cultural innovation". The city will launch customized services to meet the needs of different consumer groups, including snow hot spring resorts, ice and snow weddings, snow parent-child sports meetings, family ski challenges, and ice and snow research tours. It will foster production, education, and research entities to develop equipment that meets the needs of athletes for competition, training, testing, and rehabilitation, as well as the diverse ice and snow sports needs of the general public. The city will encourage colleges and research institutes to offer majors and courses related to ice and snow sports and the ice and snow economy, establish job standards for the ice and snow economy, and promote international exchanges and cooperation in the ice and snow economy. Harbin aims to build a national-level ice and snow sports demonstration zone and an ice and snow tourism resort, an ice and snow talent cultivation base, an ice and snow equipment manufacturing base, and an international ice and snow event capital.

The "Qingdao Experience" of High-Quality, Beautiful City Construction in a Super-Large City

As a super-large city with a permanent population of 10.34 million and a regional GDP of 1.67 trillion yuan, Qingdao enjoys a mild and humid climate with no severe cold in winter or extreme heat in summer. Mountains, sea, bay, and city blend harmoniously. The United Nations has rated it as one of the most livable cities for humans, and it has won honors such as National Civilized City, China's Most Happy City, and China's Beautiful Life City. For four consecutive years, Qingdao has achieved "excellent" ratings in the provincial assessment of pollution prevention and control. Seven districts (cities) have been built into national ecological civilization demonstration zones or "Two Mountains" bases. The Licun River has been selected as a national beautiful river and lake, becoming a model for inland river management in northern Chinese cities. Lingshan Bay and Laoshan Bay have been recognized as national and provincial beautiful bays, respectively. The city has ranked among the top ten in China's urban eco-environmental protection business competitiveness for two consecutive years and successfully hosted the Shanghai Cooperation Organization Green Development Forum. It has been praised by the Ministry of Ecology and Environment at the Beautiful China press conference. The ecological advantages of coordinated land and sea governance and joint river and sea management are being transformed into competitive advantages for Qingdao's high-quality development. Wandering among Qingdao's red-tiled roofs, green trees, blue seas, blue skies, lucid waters, and lush mountains, 466 rivers of various sizes crisscross, 497 lakes and reservoirs are scattered about, and 49 bays are distributed along the 905.2 km-long coastline. One can deeply feel the ecological charm of a major province and city shouldering major responsibilities, taking the lead in green development, and creating a local benchmark for building a Beautiful China.

Building a New Pattern of Co-Construction and Co-Governance for Ecological Environmental Protection

Looking down at Qingdao from an airplane, the Dagu River flows like a dancing silver ribbon from north to south, rushing into the sea at Jiaozhou Bay, becoming the first sight for those entering Qingdao by air. After years of management and maintenance, the 179.9-kilometer Dagu River, which spans multiple districts and cities, has become a provincial-level beautiful and happy river and lake, full of vitality and attracting crowds of visitors. In 2017, Qingdao took the lead in implementing the river (lake) chief system in the province, including it in the comprehensive assessment of economic and social development of various districts (cities). The city implemented river and lake management responsibilities section by section, equipped with river and lake managers, civilian (voluntary) river chiefs, and volunteers, ensuring that people manage affairs, money handles matters, and regulations govern affairs. To date, black and odorous water bodies have been basically eliminated in urban built-up areas, all 11 national and provincially controlled river monitoring sections have met standards, the water quality compliance rate of 18 centralized drinking water sources at or above the township level has remained at 100%, and 31 provincial-level beautiful and happy rivers and lakes have been created.

Bays are representative geographical units in coastal waters and are important areas for ecological protection, leisure tourism destinations, and economic development highlands. As the first city in China to implement the bay chief system, Qingdao has constructed a three-level bay chief system at the city, district, and township levels. Bay chiefs and river chiefs form close working partnerships, taking turns to monitor and patrol the water quality of rivers entering the sea, clearing and dismantling aquaculture facilities, rectifying sewage outlets into the sea, and releasing various seedlings to increase reproduction, achieving full-chain governance from land-based pollution to marine ecology.

Currently, the proportion of good water quality in the city's coastal waters has reached 100% for five consecutive years, and 3,511 terrestrial and marine species have been found in the bay survey.

The construction of beautiful bays has not only created "beautiful bays and clean beaches", but has also led to industrial upgrades along the coastal line. In the past, the north shore of Xiaodao Bay was dominated by traditional fishery aquaculture. Jimo District comprehensively renovated the north coastal zone of Xiaodao Bay and Xiaoguandao, building facilities such as coastal walkways and marine observation platforms to create a beautiful coastline. Today, Xiaodao Bay is home to more than 50 "national" research institutes and over 90 innovation platforms at or above the municipal level. It has formed a green industrial system featuring "3+2" with three leading industries (marine high-tech services, marine biology, and marine high-end equipment) and two characteristic industries (marine cultural tourism and marine headquarters economy), becoming a new calling card for Qingdao's maritime strategy.

Advanced Planning for Carbon Peaking and Carbon Neutrality

As a national carbon peaking pilot city, Qingdao has taken many pioneering steps in green and low-carbon transformation. For example, it has issued the "Guide for the Construction of Carbon Peaking and Carbon Neutrality Standard System", constructing four standard subsystems: "basic general standards", "carbon reduction standards", "carbon removal standards", and "carbon market standards". The city took the lead in issuing a series of tax documents to support "dual carbon" goals, precisely pushing "pollution reduction and carbon reduction benefit bills". It was the first among similar cities in China to issue a three-year action plan for carbon finance development and completed the province's first energy use rights transaction between enterprises. Qingdao has carried out statistical monitoring of green and low-carbon high-quality development, improved the accounting scheme for total energy consumption in the whole society, and explored methods for carbon emission accounting.

In Qingdao High-tech Zone, the area supplied by renewable energy sources such as sewage source heat pumps and waste heat recovery utilization reaches 4, 262, 400 m^2, accounting for 44% of the total heating area. The zone has promoted the "Green Electricity Multiplication" project, with a total installed photovoltaic capacity of 70 megawatts built or under construction, saving nearly 150,000 tons of coal annually and reducing carbon dioxide emissions by about 370,000 tons per year. The zone encourages qualified enterprises to build "waste-free factories" and guides small and micro enterprises to adopt a "group buying" packaged approach for unified management and transportation of hazardous waste, reducing enterprises' hazardous waste disposal costs. Over the past five years, Qingdao High-tech Zone has reduced sulfur dioxide emissions by 93. 4%, nitrogen oxide emissions by 30. 3%, energy consumption per unit of industrial added value by 39. 3%, and carbon dioxide emissions per unit of industrial added value by 45. 5%. With an average annual growth rate of 14. 7% in industrial added value and 13. 7% in total industrial output value, the zone has basically completed its "carbon peaking" target while demonstrating strong momentum in green and low-carbon development.

Strong Momentum in Green Development

Anchoring to the "dual carbon" goals, Qingdao has guided enterprises in green transformation. By the end of 2024, a cumulative total of 65 enterprises had been evaluated for the national green manufacturing list, including 47 green factories and 14 green supply chain management enterprises. In terms of empowering green factories with digital intelligent technology, Hexagon Manufacturing Intelligence Technology Co. , Ltd. is a provider of green factory solutions. It integrates cutting-edge industry measurement instruments and professional software systems to build a smart factory management platform with "one map" for multiple scenarios such as smart operation and maintenance, energy management, building monitoring, intelligent lighting, and smart factories. This achieves real-time data collection, analysis, and control, with comprehensive energy consumption reduced by 40%.

Regarding cooperation between industrial enterprises and pollution treatment institutions, sewage treatment plants need to purchase carbon sources to convert dissolved nitrogen in sewage into nitrogen gas for discharge from water.

Beer waste liquid is a highly biodegradable organic matter with high concentration and an excellent supplement to carbon sources for urban sewage treatment plants. The Tsingtao Brewery Group pioneered in China the key technology of collaborative treatment and resource utilization of high-concentration beer wastewater and municipal sewage for pollution reduction and carbon reduction. Each year, it provides 15,000 tons of waste liquid generated during the production process to sewage treatment plants, reducing carbon dioxide emissions by 12,300 tons. Under this model, the beer factory's wastewater treatment process is simplified, wastewater treatment costs are significantly reduced, and sewage treatment plants reduce carbon source procurement costs, achieving a win-win situation by "turning waste into treasure".

In terms of strengthening green manufacturing capabilities and green product supply capabilities, Haier Smart Home has constructed a "6-Green" strategic model encompassing green design, green manufacturing, green marketing, green recycling, green disposal, and green procurement. For example, the Haier Lighthouse Factory has developed a large model for intelligent scheduling of equipment power loads, reducing energy consumption by 35% and carbon dioxide emissions by 36%, improving operational resilience and reducing carbon emissions. The Haier Recycling Interconnected Factory is the first interconnected factory in the home appliance recycling industry, where 2 million waste home appliances are dismantled each year, producing 30,000 tons of recycled new materials and reducing carbon dioxide emissions by 17,000 tons. CRRC Qingdao Sifang Co., Ltd. has developed the world's first commercial carbon fiber metro train, introducing lightweight new materials to replace steel, aluminum alloys, and other metal materials. It adopts environmentally friendly materials such as new floor cloth and water-based paint, uses a transfer-type vacuum collection system for the drainage system, and employs low-voltage energy consumption time management for electric traction. The overall weight of the vehicle is reduced by 11%, and operational energy consumption is decreased by 7%.

Writing a New Chapter for Lucid Waters and Lush Mountains

Anchoring to the strategic tasks of building "eight beautiful cities" -green and low-carbon, quality environment, harmonious ecology, healthy resilience, livable model, ecological culture, modern system, and open window-Qingdao has consistently placed beautiful city construction in a prominent position. The city vigorously promotes the reform of the ecological civilization system, deepens pollution prevention and control, and holistically manages mountains, waters, forests, fields, lakes, islands, and bays. By increasing the "green content" of ecology to enhance the "gold content" of development, Qingdao is striving to explore a new path of high-quality development for Beautiful China's "Qingdao Model", where mountains, seas, and cities integrate, and humans coexist harmoniously with nature.

One River Flowing East:
The Practice of Ecological Priority and
Green Development in Wuhan

"A city of beautiful waters and half a city of mountains", the unique ecological resource advantages are nature's best "gift" to Wuhan, as well as the richest foundation for Wuhan to promote ecological priority and green development. In recent years, Wuhan has fully implemented green and low-carbon transformation, accelerated the cultivation of green new quality productive forces, and enabled people to share the beauty of nature, life, and living. In 2024, 86.8% of the sections of the city's 22 main rivers achieved water quality at or better than Class III, 142 lakes met or exceeded the Class IV standard of the "Surface Water Environmental Quality Standard" with no Class V+ lakes, and the water quality of 9 large and medium-sized reservoirs and 41 centralized drinking water sources all reached or exceeded Class III standards. A magnificent new picture of clear waters, blue skies, and green lands is unfolding in this river city.

Creating a Model of Comprehensive River Basin Water Environment Management

In April 2018, at a symposium on promoting the development of the Yangtze River Economic Belt held in Wuhan, General Secretary Xi Jinping emphasized that, considering the long-term interests of the Chinese nation, the restoration of the Yangtze River ecological environment must be placed in an overwhelming position. The focus should be on joint protection rather than large-scale development, striving to build the Yangtze River Economic Belt into a golden economic belt with better ecology, smoother transportation, more coordinated economy, more unified markets, and more scientific mechanisms.

Wuhan has fought ten landmark battles for the protection of the Yangtze River①, carried out ten major actions to enhance high-level protection of the Yangtze River②, implemented the responsibility for the ten-year fishing ban in the Yangtze River, and carried out "Clear Source, Clear Management, Clear Flow" actions for river and lake basin water environments. The city has established four levels of river and lake chiefs at the city, district, subdistrict, and community levels, implemented cooperative mechanisms such as "River and Lake Chiefs + Procurators", and created volunteer service brands such as "Little River and Lake Chiefs" and "Wuhan River Youth Volunteers" for civilian river (lake) protection. It has built pilot and demonstration communities for happy rivers and lakes, updated village regulations and conventions, making "everyone responsible for river and lake governance" deeply rooted in people's hearts.

"Two Rivers and Four Banks"③ is not only the main axis of Wuhan's development but also a window showcasing the unique charm of this mountain and

---

① Wuhan's Ten Landmark Battles for Yangtze River Protection: Closure, rectification, relocation, and transformation of chemical enterprises along the river, remediation of urban black and odorous water bodies, control of agricultural non-point source pollution, rectification of illegal docks/wharves, crackdown on illegal sand mining, protection of drinking water sources, wastewater discharge reduction for enterprises along the river, control/management of phosphogypsum pollution, investigation and screening of solid waste, and urban and rural waste management.

② Wuhan's Ten Major Actions to Enhance High-Level Protection of the Yangtze River: Green transformation and upgrading action for chemical enterprises along the river; source tracing and rectification action for pollutant discharge outlets into the Yangtze River; quality improvement and efficiency enhancement action for urban sewage treatment and black and odorous water body management; harmless treatment action for urban and rural domestic waste; pollution prevention and control action for ships and ports; green development action for agriculture and rural areas; national greening and wetland protection and restoration action; ecological restoration action for national land space; water resource guarantee action; and remediation action for illegal low dykes in the Yangtze River Basin.

③ Two Rivers and Four Banks: "Two Rivers" refer to the Yangtze River and Han River; "Four Banks" refer to the south bank of the Yangtze River, the north bank of the Yangtze River, the east bank of the Han River, and the west bank of the Han River.

water city. Wuhan has created a hundred-mile Yangtze River ecological corridor that integrates safety, ecology, culture, transportation, and development. With the construction concept of "connecting broken points, filling empty points, highlighting bright points, and optimizing services", the city has upgraded flood control facilities, protected clean water, displayed green shores, reshaped ecological spaces, built historical and cultural landscape exhibition areas, strengthened connections with urban slow traffic routes, used river beaches to create leisure spaces, and integrally created living shorelines, ecological shorelines, and scenic shorelines, returning the river, shores, and scenery to the people.

Joint protection of the Yangtze River hinges on the word "joint". In May 2022, the Management Committee of Wuhan Economic and Technological Development Zone and the People's Government of Xiantao City signed the "Ecological Compensation Agreement for Cross-City Section Water Quality Assessment in the Tongshun River[①] Basin". Following the principle of "who exceeds the standard pays, who benefits compensates", a "two-way ecological compensation" is implemented for the upstream and downstream of the Tongshun River. If the water quality from upstream meets or exceeds the target requirements, the downstream area provides ecological compensation to the upstream area; otherwise, the upstream area provides pollution compensation to the downstream area. The compensation funds are specifically used for water pollution prevention and control in the Tongshun River basin. In 2023, as the upstream water quality of the Tongshun River exceeded the target requirements, Wuhan provided 3 million yuan in ecological compensation funds to Xiantao City. In 2024, Wuhan also disbursed ecological compensation funds of 6.1 million yuan and 7 million yuan to Xiaogan City and Suizhou City respectively, expanding ecological compensation from tributaries to the main stream of the Yangtze River.

Although Wuhan is known as the "City of Hundred Lakes", more than

---

① Note: The Tongshun River is an important river in Hubei Province. It originates at the Zekou Sluice in Qianjiang City, flows through Qianjiang City and Xiantao City, and then enters Wuhan. The total length of the river is 195 kilometers, with the section flowing through Wuhan measuring 68 kilometers long and draining a catchment area of 824 km^2. The river eventually flows into the Yangtze River via the Huanglingji Sluice.

99% of its water resources come from transit water from the Yangtze and Han Rivers. Moreover, the water function zones of the Yangtze River in Wuhan no longer have significant capacity to accept pollution, facing dual pressures of resource-based and quality-based water shortages. Wuhan vigorously promotes the recycling and utilization of reclaimed water, liberalizing reclaimed water prices, adopting a "one enterprise, one price" pricing mechanism, implementing an immediate refund policy for value-added tax on sewage treatment and reclaimed water products, launching green financial products such as "Water-Saving Loans", and selecting water-saving communities, water-saving government agencies, and water-saving enterprises. In 2024, Wuhan's reclaimed water utilization exceeded 500 million cubic meters, with an industrial water reuse rate reaching 94. 02%, setting a new historical record. The city was selected as a national key reclaimed water utilization city and as part of the second batch of national regional reclaimed water recycling pilot cities.

Building the World's First "International Wetland City" with a Population Over Ten Million

Wuhan has 165 rivers, 166 lakes, a 145-kilometer Yangtze River shoreline, 5 wetland nature reserves, 6 national wetland parks, more than 70 lake parks, and more than 40 small wetlands. It is the provincial capital with the most national wetland parks in China. The city has both natural wetlands such as rivers, lakes, and marshes, as well as artificial wetlands such as reservoirs and ponds, with a complete ecosystem structure and rich biodiversity. City and district governments have established a wetland protection joint conference system, created wetland protection model areas with distinctive characteristics, built a smart wetland management system, and formed a "space-sky-water-shore" network covering 40,000 hectares of important wetlands and 87,000 hectares of lakes. The city conducts natural education activities such as "Wetland Little Guards" and "Nature Journal". Wetland parks such as East Lake, Houguan Lake, and Anshan have become "ecological green hearts" for citizens to get close to nature, receiving more than 50 million citizens and tourists annually.

Futou Lake spans Wuhan and Xianning, and the root cause of its water quality decline was that summer aquatic plants grew too luxuriantly, fish pond owners pumped water into the lake, and wastewater from livestock and poultry farming enterprises leaked on a small scale. The two cities established a joint prevention and control mechanism, and after precise treatment, the water quality rose to Class III. Tangxun Lake is the largest urban lake in Asia, where mixed rain and sewage water and initial rainwater have high pollutant concentrations. By installing video monitoring, water quality testing, rainfall monitoring, pipeline water level monitoring, and other equipment in the diversion wells at sewage outlets, rainwater that meets discharge standards normally flows into the lake through pipelines. Once the system detects that the pollutant concentration in the pipeline water exceeds the standard, the gate in the well automatically opens, and the water flow is "diverted" to a newly built diversion pipeline, which then enters the nearest municipal sewage network and is transported to the sewage treatment plant for processing. The East Lake water environment improvement project has constructed an underwater ecological system in the lake, with submerged plant coverage exceeding 70%, attracting a large number of tourists to visit with water tour activities such as cruises and sailboats.

Beautiful Ecology Activating Beautiful Economy

In November 2024, with a Dongfeng Lantu rolling off the production line in Wuhan, China's annual production of new energy vehicles exceeded 10 million for the first time. Wuhan and Dongfeng Motor have achieved mutual success. A 13-kilometer section of National Highway 318 in Wuhan Economic & Technological Development Zone has been named Dongfeng Avenue, hosting 7 automobile enterprises, more than 10 vehicle factories, over 500 parts companies, and 14 provincial-level or above automotive research and development institutions. The annual production of new energy vehicles exceeds one million, making it the axis with the highest density of global automotive industry. In 2021, Dongfeng Motor shifted towards new energy and intelligent driving fields, and to date has gathered more than 300 upstream and downstream partners, with a local supporting rate of 41%. Dongfeng Motor has accumulated more than 24,400 valid patents, with intelligent connectivity and new energy patents accounting for 35%. It has topped the list of patent grants among Chinese auto companies for three consecutive years, making Wuhan an emerging source of global automotive technology revolution.

In 2023, the Wuhan Economic & Technological Development Zone began building an Intelligent Automobile Software Park on the shores of Taizi Lake, focusing on key areas such as autonomous driving, automotive-grade chips, intelligent cockpits, and vehicle networking. This is China's second software park named after intelligent automobiles and formed at scale after Shanghai. Today, with Wuhan Neusoft Software Park as the core, the Leading Software Acceleration Zone, Science Innovation Neighborhood Living Zone, Automotive Chip Innovation Zone, and Computing Power Service Zone have gathered more than 200 automotive software enterprises and over 30,000 software talents, forming a leap from "automobile factory" to "most powerful brain".

In 2024, Wuhan had 32 factories, 1 supply chain management enterprise, and 1 park evaluated as national green manufacturing system demonstrations, accounting for 45%, 50%, and 50% of the provincial total respectively. Green has become a bright color in this industrial city. With the goals of being an extreme energy efficiency leader, a low-carbon metallurgy demonstrator, a green energy pioneer, and a low-carbon product leader, Wuhan Iron and Steel Co., Ltd. has invested more than 15 billion yuan in green, low-carbon, and environmental protection transformations, with its comprehensive energy consumption per ton of steel and carbon emission intensity decreasing for 8 consecutive years: It has built 4 solid waste treatment centers and 4 solid waste recycling production lines, achieving a 100% comprehensive utilization rate of general solid waste. Steel slag tailings are promoted and applied in the ironmaking process, reducing carbon dioxide emissions by 28,000 tons per year. The company has built the world's largest grain-oriented silicon steel manufacturing base, reducing carbon emissions by about 2 million tons annually. It has purchased more than 1,000 MkWh of green electricity, becoming the largest green electricity user in the province. It has built Central China's largest distributed rooftop photovoltaic station with an annual power generation of 45 MkWh, reducing carbon dioxide emissions by 26,500 tons annually.

In July 2021, the national carbon emission rights trading market went online, and the national carbon emission rights registration and settlement system was located in Wuhan. Today, the China Carbon Registration Building by Sha Lake has gathered more than 60 professional institutions for carbon trading, carbon rating, carbon certification, carbon accounting, carbon asset management, and other services, initially forming a trillion-yuan carbon industry cluster where "one building is an industrial chain, and going up and down floors means upstream and downstream", facilitating Wuhan enterprises and citizens to enjoy "carbon reduction dividends". In late 2024, two batches of carbon offset credits amounting to 2,000 tons, accumulated by the public in Wuhan, were successfully traded at the Hubei Carbon Emissions Trading Center, generating carbon revenue of 87,000 yuan, marking China's first personal carbon asset monetization.

Playing a Major Role in Green Development in the Central Region

The history of Wuhan's urban development is a history of water management and city planning, from the opposing cities of Queyue and Xiakou across the river in the late Eastern Han Dynasty, to the separation of three towns after the Hanshui River changed course in the mid-Ming Dynasty, to the riverside expansion in the 20th century, and now to the determined path toward harmonious coexistence between humans and nature embodied in the concept that "lucid waters and lush mountains are invaluable assets". Wuhan City must continue to effectively coordinate the spatial relationships between mountains, water, roads, shorelines, industries, and urban areas. It must solidly advance high-level protection of the Yangtze River and accelerate the construction of a safe, resilient, and modern water network. The city should explore new dividends for industrial transformation and business environment improvement brought by enhancements in the water environment, and cultivate green, low-carbon industrial and supply chains. New growth points, such as green buildings and energy conservation/environmental protection, should be created in urban renewal and rural revitalization. Green lifestyle and carbon inclusive application scenarios should be expanded to accelerate the city's development into a green, low-carbon demonstration city in the central region.

Ordos: Harnessing the Photovoltaic Power of the Kubuqi Desert to Empower Ecological Sustainability

In China's seventh largest desert—the Kubuqi Desert, shimmering blue photovoltaic panels connect to form a "blue ocean", bringing continuous ecological, economic, and social benefits. Where sandstorms once raged, today "wind and light" resources abound, as the vast desert stages a magnificent scene of "photovoltaic Great Wall" preventing sand encroachment. The Kubuqi Desert is the closest desert to the capital Beijing and covers a total area of 21.16 million mu (about 1.41 million hectares). Located in the northern part of Ordos City, Inner Mongolia Autonomous Region. It is the main battlefield of the Yellow River "Jiziwan" Critical Battle. In the past, due to special geographical conditions and a climate characterized by drought in nine out of ten years, vegetation was sparse, sandstorms frequent, constantly invading and endangering the people of the sandy areas, earning it the name "Sea of Death". After the founding of New China, the people of Ordos, with unprecedented enthusiasm for sand control, built "four lines of defense" —greenbelts, silt dams, photovoltaic sand control belts, and edge-locking forests. They forged the "Kubuqi Spirit" of hard work, perseverance, and innovation, with the desert governance rate reaching 40%.

In 2023, during his inspection of Inner Mongolia, General Secretary Xi Jinping issued a general mobilization order to fight the Three-North Program campaign, emphasizing that building an important ecological security barrier in northern China is an essential "national matter" that Inner Mongolia must remember. He called for efforts, building on the plan for Phase VI of the Three-North Program and in conjunction with the ongoing planning and implementation

of large-scale new energy bases, to integrate the planning and design of desertification prevention and control with wind and photovoltaic power development,
thereby achieving development through protection and governance. In 2017 and
2019, General Secretary Xi Jinping successively sent congratulatory letters to
the 6th and 7th Kubuqi International Desert Forums and the 13th Conference of
the Parties to the United Nations Convention to Combat Desertification (UNC-
CD), pointing out that Kubuqi Desert governance has provided Chinese experience for the international community in managing the environmental ecology and
implementing the 2030 Agenda.

Integrated Construction of Ecological Barriers and Green Power Bases

Ordos City has formulated the Phase VI construction plan for the Three-
North Program. Spearheaded by the development of two large-scale new energy
bases in the "sandy, Gobi, and barren lands" of the central-northern and
southern Kubuqi Desert, the city has guided more than 20 leading enterprises
such as China Three Gorges Corporation, China Huaneng Group, China Da-
tang Corporation, China Energy Group, Inner Mongolia Energy Group, and
Longi Green Energy Technology Co., Ltd. to participate in the construction of
photovoltaic sand control belts through sponsorship donations, industrial investment, and off-site treatment. This approach has formed a new pattern of diversified investment, with national input as the mainstay, supplemented by local
supporting funds, and involving broad social participation. Wind-breaking tree
forests are established around photovoltaic arrays, low shrub forests for sand fixation are planted between photovoltaic panels, and the space beneath the panels
is developed and utilized according to local conditions, planting high-yield forage grasses, crops, and other vegetation to increase coverage. The forest and
grass vegetation coverage rate in the project area has reached over 40%. To
date, 10.02 MkWh of photovoltaic projects have been completed, achieving
photovoltaic sand control over 600,000 mu (about 40,000 hectares). After all
under-construction and planned projects are completed, photovoltaic sand control will reach 2 million mu (about 133,333 hectares), accounting for about
10% of the total area of the Kubuqi Desert, basically constructing a green eco-

logical barrier to prevent sand from invading the north and protect the tranquility of the Yellow River.

Forward-looking strategic pathways, abundant resource endowments, efficient consumption systems, and strong outbound transmission channels collectively build a solid foundation for Ordos City's new energy transformation. As a resource-rich city in China's western region, Ordos City has "coal beneath its feet and wind and light above its head", with wind and solar energy development potential of over 150 MkW, making it one of China's seven major onshore new energy bases. In December 2023, China's first large-scale wind and solar power base project with a capacity of 10 MkW—the Ordos Central North Kubuqi Desert New Energy Base Project—achieved full-capacity grid connection for its pilot 1 MkW photovoltaic project. Once the project is fully completed, it will transmit more than 20,000 MkWh of green electricity to the Beijing-Tianjin-Hebei region annually, saving about 6.56 million tons of standard coal and reducing carbon dioxide emissions by about 19.94 million tons. As of December 2024, Ordos had built a cumulative new energy installed capacity of 14.19 MkW, accounting for 28% of the city's total power installed capacity, doubling compared to 2021.

Ordos City has strengthened the construction of the local power grid's main framework, completing fifteen 500kV substations, eighty 220kV substations, and two hundred and fifty 110kV substations, forming a power supply network pattern led by 500kV ultra-high voltage, supported by 220kV, and radiating 110kV. Two ultra-high voltage outbound transmission channels with a capacity of 16 MkW to Tianjin and Shandong have been completed, with four outbound channels under construction to Beijing-Tianjin-Hebei, Shanghai, Jiangsu, and East China. There are efforts to add two more outbound channels during the 15th Five-Year Plan, forming a "2+4+2" ultra-high voltage green electricity outbound transmission pattern by 2030. The city has coordinated the advancement of guaranteed grid connection, large-scale green electricity substitution in high-load industries, integration of source-grid-load-storage, wind-solar-hydrogen integration, green power supply in industrial parks, flexible transformation of thermal power, and full self-generation and self-consumption market-based new energy consumption projects. It has developed distributed new energy, clean energy supply guarantee, new energy market-based transactions, and other in-cremental projects according to local conditions. By 2030, the scale of green e-lectricity outbound transmission and local consumption is expected to reach more than 60 MkW. Multiple U. S. media outlets have reported that the transforma-tion of a desolate corner of the Kubuqi Desert into a large-scale photovoltaic base, aimed at generating enough energy to power the Beijing-Tianjin-Hebei re-gion, is part of China's efforts to build a renewable energy powerhouse.

Development of the Complete "Wind-Solar-Hydrogen-Storage-Vehicle" Industrial Chain

Ordos City actively promotes the dual empowerment of "installed capacity+equipment", attracting businesses through existing ones, and recruiting along the industrial chain to build a complete new energy industrial chain of "upstream materials-key equipment-supporting components-diversified applications-operation and maintenance services-recycling and utilization". In April 2022, the first phase of the Ordos Zero-Carbon Industrial Park was completed and put into oper-ation, with 80% of energy coming directly from wind power, photovoltaics, and energy storage, and 20% of energy through grid repurchase of green electricity, achieving 100% zero-carbon energy supply. To date, the park has attracted 54 leading new energy enterprises, implemented more than 150 new energy industry projects, and built production capacities of 47.5GW of photovoltaic equipment, 13GWh of energy storage equipment, 10GW of wind turbine equipment, over 10,000 sets of hydrogen fuel cell systems, and 40,000 new energy vehicles. It has preliminarily formed industrial chains such as batteries and energy storage, hydrogen fuel cells and green hydrogen equipment manufacturing, and new ener-gy vehicle manufacturing. The completeness of the photovoltaic key component industrial chain has reached 100%, with over 40% of main and auxiliary materi-als supported by the park. Battery cell production capacity accounts for 100% of the Inner Mongolia Autonomous Region, while large-size components, high-effi-ciency battery cells, hydrogen fuel cell systems and stacks, and nine other prod-uct categories have filled gaps in the Inner Mongolia Autonomous Region.

Looking further, as one of the first national carbon peak pilot cities, Ordos City relies on its green electricity advantages to carry out innovative practices in photovoltaic hydrogen production integration + hydrogen energy ring network. It has introduced "chemical + new energy" coupling projects such as green hydrogen, green ammonia, green alcohol, and green aviation fuel, extending to develop business models like green electricity + industrial silicon, green electricity + electrolytic aluminum, green electricity + new coal chemical advanced materials, promoting the green and low-carbon transformation of resource-based industries.

Building an Innovation Highland for Desertification Control and Green Development

In July 2022, the State Council approved Ordos City to build a national sustainable development agenda innovation demonstration zone with the theme of "desertification control and green development". In response to two major issues— "low industrialization of ecological construction, constraining the quality and efficiency improvement of desertification control" and "short resource-based industrial chains, constraining economic transformation and upgrading and green development" —Ordos City has implemented five major actions: improving the quality and efficiency of desertification control, conserving and efficiently using resources, accelerating the high-quality development of modern energy economy, driving development through talent and technological innovation, and promoting coordinated urban-rural regional development. It strives to create an innovative model of "green, industry, new, and prosperous" sustainable development. The city has built innovation carriers such as an international technological innovation center for desertification control, academician expert workstations, research institutes, and germplasm resource banks to high standards, steadily promoting the deep integration of industry, academia, research, and application. In collaboration with the Three-North Program Research Institute, Tianjin Research Institute for Advanced Equipment, Tsinghua University and other organizations, a sand prevention and control equipment industrial park has been established to tackle key technologies. Innovative achievements such as intelligent aerial seeding drones, photovoltaic cleaning robots, intelligent tree-planting robots, and intelligent sand barrier laying machinery have moved from laboratories to production lines. The city has built China's most comprehensive and largest energy storage test and demonstration base, conducting application scenario demonstrations for solar thermal storage, compressed air, gravity storage, sodium-ion batteries, and other technologies, promoting the demonstration of multiple energy storage technology routes, and actively undertaking major national scientific and technological strategic tasks in energy storage. Currently, Ordos City's technology achievement transformation rate in the new energy field has reached 60%, with increasingly prominent leading demonstration effects.

Co-building and Sharing, Green Prosperity

Ordos City adheres to benefiting enterprises and people, promoting the coordinated development of photovoltaic sand control and supporting industries. It has issued "Nine Measures for Innovation in the Construction and Management of Phase VI of the Three-North Program and Other Key Ecological Projects", implementing incentive measures such as fund coordination, work-for-relief programs, and integrated construction and management. It has cultivated new energy industry chain supply chains, explored new models of sand control and sand utilization such as "grass-photovoltaic complementation" and "forest-photovoltaic complementation" with power generation above panels, restoration beneath panels, planting between panels, and farming between arrays, opening up a new track for the integrated development of three industries: "green electricity production above panels, green gold generation beneath panels, and tourism development outside panels". The city has established a multi-level interest linkage mechanism of "base + enterprise + cooperative + farmers and herdsmen". In the early stage of photovoltaic sand control projects, farmers and herdsmen gain land value-added dividends through land transfer and leasing. During the project construction period, farmers and herdsmen participate in construction installation, component cleaning, ecological management, and other activities to obtain labor income. During the project operation period, stable nearby employment positions are provided through seedling orders, labor dispatch, product purchase and sales, and other means, increasing the per capita income of farmers and herdsmen by more than 20,000 yuan.

Safeguarding a Community-Centered Responsibility

In December 2024, Ordos, as China's only representative city, was invited to participate in the 16th Conference of the Parties to the United Nations Convention to Combat Desertification (UNCCD), with the Kubuqi Desert's "photovoltaic+sand control" model winning widespread attention from the international community. As an important national coal base, coal power base, west-to-east gas transmission base, and onshore new energy base, Ordos warms thousands of cities and lights up tens of thousands of homes: in Beijing, one out of every five lights is powered by energy from Ordos; in the Beijing-Tianjin-Hebei region, half of households get their natural gas from Ordos. In recent years, Ordos City has coordinated new energy development with efficient desert governance, forming a new "photovoltaic+sand control" model characterized by intensive use of sandy land, large-scale photovoltaic power generation, and three-dimensional ecological restoration. It takes responsibility for ensuring national energy security and leads by example in China's green and low-carbon energy transition.

Looking to the future, Ordos City aims to anchor the goal of becoming a global new energy industry highland, promoting the high-end, diversified, and low-carbon development of clean coal, green coal power, coal-based fuels, coal chemical industry, and other industries. It will build a high-proportion clean power transmission base with high voltage levels, large transmission capacity, and flexible and efficient operation. Through innovative models such as source-grid-load-storage integration, green power supply in industrial parks, and wind-solar-hydrogen integration, it will promote the coordinated development of green energy and local industries to build a modern new energy industrial system integrating "wind-solar-hydrogen-storage-vehicle" energy production, equipment manufacturing, and application demonstration. It will explore and practice new paths for traditional energy green transformation, clean conversion and utilization of coal, high-proportion internal use and external transmission of new energy, and full-chain cluster development of new energy.

Dameisha Carbon Neutrality Pilot Demonstration Zone, Yantian District, Shenzhen: Building a Global Low-Carbon Community Benchmark

Wang Shi

The Dameisha Carbon Neutrality Pilot Demonstration Zone (hereinafter referred to as the "Demonstration Zone") is one of Shenzhen's first near-zero carbon emission pilot projects. Located in Meisha Subdistrict, Yantian District, it comprises the entire Dameisha community, parts of the Binhai community, and parts of the East Coast community. The zone covers an area of approximately 3. 2 km², with a permanent population of 19,800 and 18 million visitors in 2023. Unlike traditional industrial parks or residential areas, the Demonstration Zone is a fully open, mixed-use community without a single property management entity. It includes 22 residential communities, 13 headquarters office buildings, 4 schools, 1 large hospital, and a shopping mall.

In March 2022, the Yantian District Ecology and Environment Bureau of Shenzhen signed a "Strategic Cooperation Framework Agreement on Jointly Building the Dameisha Carbon Neutrality Pilot Demonstration Zone" with Deeprock Group. Upholding the value that "carbon neutrality is not the goal, a better life is", Deeprock Group has built a three-in-one carbon reduction system of "building renovation + energy substitution + circular economy" centered on the Dameisha Vanke Center Carbon Neutral Experimental Park. Focusing on "one core, four dimensions"[1], the group has implemented carbon-neutral community transformation, which was showcased as a typical case at COP28 and COP29 conferences, selected as a typical case of green and low-carbon development by

---

[1] One core, four dimensions: The "one core" refers to "life can be better", and the "four dimensions" refer to green and low-carbon, biodiversity, sports and health, art and beauty.

the Ministry of Ecology and Environment, and included in the C40 "Green Prosperity Community Pilot". Its experience has been incorporated into the international standard "Green Prosperity Community Construction Guide".

Creating a Carbon-Neutral Community Based on "Reduction, Substitution, Offsetting, and Operation" ①

Within the Demonstration Zone, Deeprock Group has created multiple low-carbon demonstration sites. Among them, the Dameisha Vanke Center, built using green building technology, received China's first LEED Platinum certification (for office buildings) and a three-star green building certification. Renovation and upgrade began in May 2022, and after completion in October of the same year, it was renamed Biosphere 3-Dameisha Vanke Center Carbon Neutral Experimental Zone (hereinafter referred to as the "Park"). In 2024, it received both WELL Community and WELL Core Platinum certifications, becoming the first park in Guangdong Province to be selected as a typical case of China's green and low-carbon development. In the past two years, it has won 14 green innovation awards from national, provincial, and municipal authorities and mainstream media. Currently, the Park's annual total electricity consumption is approximately 6. 5 MkWh. Through the implementation of low-carbon measures such as photovoltaic power generation, energy storage systems, and biomass recycling, the proportion of green electricity has increased from 17. 5% to 85%, achieving annual carbon emission reductions of over 800 tons. Overall carbon emissions have decreased by 93% compared to pre-renovation levels, making it an urban building carbon neutrality case with international demonstration significance (see Table 1: 2023-2028 Carbon Reduction Targets and Key Projects of Dameisha Carbon Neutrality Pilot Demonstration Zone).

---

① Note: "Reduction" refers to energy and cost savings, including building envelope structure renovation, equipment efficiency improvement, and IoT management for energy conservation; "Substitution" refers to replacing fossil fuels with new energy sources such as photovoltaic and wind power; "Offsetting" refers to carbon offsetting; "Operation" refers to energy operation.

Table 1　2023–2028 Carbon Reduction Targets and Key Projects of Dameisha Carbon Neutrality Pilot Demonstration Zone

Category		2023		2024		2025		2026		2027		2028		Carbon Reduction Target (%)
		Item	Numerical Value (tons)	Item	Numerical Value (tons)	Item	Numerical Value (tons)	Item	Numerical Value (tons)	Item	Numerical Value (tons)	Item	Numerical Value (tons)	
	Building Energy Efficiency Retrofiting							30% completion rate for energy efficiency retrofits in commercial and industrial buildings	4408	50% completion rate for commercial and industrial buildings	7347	70% completion for commercial and industrial building energy efficiency; 70% completion for residential area energy efficiency	10847	21%
Facilities Transformation & Upgrading	New Energy Facilities	Vanke Center, BGI Time-Space Center	1030	Rooftop Solar PV at Yantian Foreign Language School & Meisha Primary School	280	Completion of 30% commercial and industrial rooftop solar PV projects (hotels, offices, commercial, schools); Completion of carport PV at parking lots (parking garageseds	442	Commercial and industrial rooftop solar PV projects: 40% completed; parking loted PV projects (including residential areas): 30% completed; wave energy projects: 30% operational	633	70% operational	1436	Commercial and industrial rooftop solar PV projects: 70% completed; parking loted PV projects (including residential areas): 70% completed; wave energy projects: 70% operational	2195	4%

Continued Table

Category	2023 Item	2023 Numerical Value (tons)	2024 Item	2024 Numerical Value (tons)	2025 Item	2025 Numerical Value (tons)	2026 Item	2026 Numerical Value (tons)	2027 Item	2027 Numerical Value (tons)	2028 Item	2028 Numerical Value (tons)	Carbon Reduction Target (%)
Carbon Sink	science education pavilion garbage collection and kitchen waste collection in Dameisha residential area	1086	continued operation of garbage collection and treatment at the science education pavilion	1086	Yantian District Environmental Park starts operation, 15 tons/day waste treatment capacity	1906	Yantian District Environmental Park continues operation	1906	Yantian District Environmental Park continues operation	1906	Yantian District Environmental Park continues operation	1906	4%
Aggregated Operations — Virtual Power Plant			Vanke Center, BGI Time-Space Center	2373	Yantian Foreign Language School, Meisha Primary School; Zero-Carbon Government Buildings; Other new facilities in Yantian District	4015	New energy facilities added in Yantian District	5103	New energy facilities added in Yantian District	5443	Dongguan Science City Solar PV; Dapeng LNG Cryogenic Energy Utilization; and 3.2 km^2 Photovoltaic Microgrid System	5553	11%

Looking further, the key points of the Park's green and low-carbon technological transformation are: First, clean energy substitution, with a total photovoltaic installation capacity of 742. 57kWp and an average annual power generation of about 72,000 kWh, meeting most of the Park's daytime load demands; second, improved energy storage regulation capability, with the energy storage prefabricated cabin being the first demonstration system of a national key R&D program undertaken by Shenzhen Power Supply Bureau (China Southern Power Grid), having a total storage capacity of 400kWh (energy) /200kW (power), achieving peak shaving and valley filling of electricity, and providing power guarantee for emergency scenarios such as extreme weather; third, efficient consumption and interactive energy use, utilizing an intelligent microgrid to achieve a 90% local photovoltaic consumption rate, deploying V2G vehicle-to-grid interactive charging piles, photovoltaic-storage-charging carports, and power cube superfast charging demonstration stations to realize deep coupling of energy and transportation systems; fourth, comprehensive intelligent monitoring, deploying approximately 200 smart meters to achieve real-time collection and categorical analysis of electricity consumption behaviors in various floors and functional areas; fifth, algorithm-driven dispatch optimization, building big model algorithms for photovoltaic prediction, building energy consumption prediction, and energy storage control, developing intelligent decision-making systems to dynamically predict energy use and power generation, and formulate optimal revenue energy dispatch strategies; sixth, recycling of green waste, combining with rainwater collection systems (saving 50,000 tons of water annually) to build a "black soldier fly-community composting-co-built garden" circular model; seventh, innovative material applications, using "foam-supported aluminum foam" made from discarded cans and industrial waste aluminum as building materials, and bamboo for furniture and decoration; eighth, participation in the development of urban dual carbon brain, establishing carbon monitoring systems for industrial and building sectors, serving government carbon governance, enterprise carbon reduction, and public carbon incentives.

The Yantian District Administrative and Cultural Center has collaborated with Deeprock Group to develop a "Near-Zero Carbon Government Office" (fourth batch of near-zero carbon emission building pilots in Shenzhen). They completed rooftop photovoltaic installations with a total capacity of 477kWp, generating about 500,000 kWh annually and reducing carbon by 226 tons per year. Also, they configured V2G charging piles and a 1,160 kWh electrochemical energy storage system, saving 270,000 yuan in electricity bills annually and achieving efficient energy interaction between electric vehicles and the grid. They built four major scenarios of energy consumption panoramic monitoring, intelligent dispatching, flexible interaction, and virtual power plant to improve energy dispatch efficiency and reduce peak load impact. Moreover, they optimized air conditioning system operation with AI, expecting an annual energy-saving rate of 13% and annual carbon reduction of 130 tons.

The virtual power plant aggregates distributed energy resources, energy storage, and controllable load resources. This enhances grid flexibility and effectively addresses challenges faced by Shenzhen, including large-scale integration of renewable energy, rapid growth in electric vehicle ownership, and power supply-demand conflicts caused by extreme climate conditions. As one of Shenzhen's first load aggregators, Deeprock Group uses Internet of Things (IoT) and artificial intelligence technologies to control adjustable loads such as energy storage, charging piles, ice storage air conditioning units, and central air conditioning units in the Demonstration Zone, achieving frequency response within 10 seconds and reaching a dispatch instruction accuracy rate of 95%. Deeprock Group's virtual power plant participates in the entire chain of grid dispatch, including resource aggregation, market trading, and cross-provincial settlement. It has connected nearly 2 megawatts of precisely responsive loads, covering multiple application scenarios such as commercial office buildings and government public buildings. The project aims to create a globally leading virtual power plant model and contribute the "Shenzhen experience" to the development of new power systems.

Black Soldier Fly Technology Promotes Community Carbon Reduction

In the Dameisha Vanke Center Carbon Neutral Experimental Park, since 2018, the black soldier fly food waste recycling station has processed 200 kilograms of food waste daily; at the Yantian District Circular Economy Environmental Protection Science Education Base, it completes 3 tons of food waste processing daily; at the Shenzhen Energy National Demonstration Environmental Park, a high-standard black soldier fly breeding production line is configured to process 15 tons of organic solid waste daily, with an annual operation time exceeding 8,400 hours. As a pure biomass waste treatment method, black soldier fly waste treatment achieves zero carbon emissions. The adult flies have medicinal value and can be made into high-protein pet food and important cosmetic ingredients, thus possessing considerable commercial value.

Verra, the world's largest voluntary carbon market standard-setting organization, published the black soldier fly methodology submitted by Deeprock Group's strategic partner, the Vanke Foundation, in the third quarter of 2022 under its carbon credit program—the Verified Carbon Standard (VCS). This marks the inclusion of biodiversity technologies such as black soldier fly into the international carbon offset system, providing a quantifiable market incentive mechanism for the low-carbon transformation of organic waste treatment. It demonstrates to the international community that Chinese public welfare foundations are already using black soldier fly technology to reduce carbon in communities, facilitating similar projects to obtain international carbon market financing through VCS certification.

Green Health and Green Narrative

The Demonstration Zone has exceptional mountain and sea resources. Deeprock Group has established the Deep Diving Coast Rowing Club and collaborated with local resources such as Yantian Sports Center, Yantian Climbing Gym, Shenzhen Mountaineering & Outdoor Sport Association, and Shenzhen Cycling Association to develop sports and fitness activities including rowing, hiking, paragliding, and others according to local conditions. They have organized more than 10 events, including Urban Outdoor Sports Multiple Events (Yantian), Shenzhen Coastal Road Cycling Race, Shenzhen Yantian Shanhai Half Marathon, Ten Peaks Braveheart Human-Vehicle Relay Race, Walk for Love 35km Charity Hike, and Shenzhen 100 Mountain Running Race. These have greatly increased the flow of people, boosted surrounding consumption, and deeply instilled green and healthy concepts.

The Demonstration Zone has created the Biosphere 3 Cultural and Art Exchange Platform to support pioneering young artists, focusing on contemporary issues such as biodiversity protection, ESG practices, and climate action. It interprets sustainable development concepts through various forms including installation art, digital imaging, and ecological sculpture. The exhibition design, material selection, and energy supply all adopt environmentally friendly solutions, forming a replicable green art operation paradigm. Through the "Dameisha Community Living Room", a public participation mechanism has been established. Collaborating with initiatives like the Buy42 Charity Flash Store, they jointly host "second-hand idle item" interactive systems, invite artists to create art installations using waste materials, and guide citizens to paint with coffee grounds and create sound and light installations with electronic waste, allowing them to experience the carbon footprint of items throughout their entire life cycle.

Green Development: Pioneer Practices and Future Blueprint

The Demonstration Zone practice proves that green is not only an ecological foundation but also a new economic engine. Through technological empowerment, resource recycling, and community co-creation, it realizes the vision of "humans coexisting with nature" and provides a vivid example for implementing China's "dual carbon" goals. Currently, the innovative model of the Demonstration Zone has moved beyond Dameisha to other cities and countries, helping to promote global green prosperity. As the founder of Deeprock Group said, we hope every city will have a "Biosphere 3" —this is the pursuit of a better life.

References

1. National Center for Research (NCR), Xi Jinping's Thought on Ecological Civilization Research Center. Helping the World Understand the "Green Code" of Beautiful China—Chinese Practice and Global Contribution of Xi Jinping's Thought on Ecological Civilization, 2024

2. The State Council Information Office. White Paper "China's Green Development in the New Era", 2023

3. Yu Hongjun, Shi Zhiqin, Yang Dongping, Liu Yang. 2024 Belt and Road Youth Development Report, People's Publishing House, 2024

4. Liu Yang, Fang Ning. Report on the Fifth Anniversary of The Construction of the Chengdu-Chongqing Economic Circle, Social Sciences Academic Press, 2024

5. CPC Ministry of Ecology and Environment Party Leadership Group. Focus on Building a Beautiful China and Deepening Ecological Civilization System Reform, Qiushi, 2024 (21)

6. Xu Qianhua. Green "Belt and Road" is an Important Practice of Xi Jinping's Thought on Ecological Civilization in Global Ecological Governance, People's Daily, February 18, 2025

7. Guo Wei. Coordinated Promotion of Comprehensive Green Transformation, Economic Daily, February 13, 2025

8. Zhou Xiangjun. Deeply Grasping the Theoretical Foundation of Xi Jinping's Thought on Ecological Civilization. Guangming Daily, December 1, 2023

9. Jin Jiaxu, Liu Miao. "Lucid Waters and Lush Mountains Are Invaluable Assets" —Stories of Xi Jinping Promoting Ecological Environmental Protection, Xinhua Net

10. Jiang Nan, Dou Hanyang. Visiting Anji to See "Lucid Waters and Lush

Mountains Are Invaluable Assets", People's Daily, December 8, 2023

11. Gao Jing. Continuously Writing New Green Miracles—A Comprehensive Review of Ecological and Environmental Protection Achievements on the 75th Anniversary of the Founding of the People's Republic of China, Xinhua Net

12. Shao Changjun. Deeply Understanding the Chinese Characteristics of Chinese-Style Modernization, People's Daily, January 31, 2023

13. Yang Xiaoming, Wang Bin. Comprehensively Understanding That China's Ecological Civilization Construction Is Still in a Critical Period of Pressure Accumulation and Moving Forward Under Heavy Burden, China Environment News, September 11, 2023

14. Jin Xuan. Zhejiang's Practice and Enlightenment of Implementing the Concept That Lucid Waters and Lush Mountains Are Invaluable Assets, Economic Daily, November 27, 2024

15. Zhu Zhixiang. Stepping on the Pollution "Emergency Brake" and Shifting into the "Forward Gear" of Green Pursuit: Zhejiang Implements Five Rounds of "811" Actions, Making the Road of Green Development Broader, China Environment News, August 15, 2024

16. Hong Hengfei, Jiang Yun. Huzhou City, Zhejiang Province: Exploring Diversified Models for Converting Ecological Products into Value, Science and Technology Daily, December 13, 2024

17. Lin Yunlong, Cao Jian et al. 75 Years, Zhejiang's 75 "Firsts" in Ecological Civilization Construction, Zhejiang Daily, September 29, 2024

18. Special Research Group. Summarizing and Promoting Zhejiang's "Green Rural Revival Program" Experience to Promote In-depth Implementation of Xi Jinping's Thought on Socialism with Chinese Characteristics for a New Era, Qiushi, 2023 (11)

19. Diao Fanchao. Lv Zhongmei: After the Enactment of the Ecological Environment Code, the Environmental Protection Law Will Complete Its Historical Mission, The Paper

20. Chen Hang, Du Yan. How Did "Beijing Blue" Become a New Paradigm for Environmental Governance at Home and Abroad?, China News Service

21. Wang Jidi. Exploring the Establishment of "Bay Area Standards" for Ecological Protection, Insight China, 2024 (4)

22. Ruan Xigui, Chen Min. Fujian Deeply Practices Xi Jinping's Thought on Ecological Civilization, Persistently Promotes Ecological Province Construction, Continuously Deepens the Construction of National Ecological Civilization Experimental Zone, and Achieves Coordinated Progress of "High Aesthetic Value" and "High Quality" —Towards Green, Beauty and the Future, Fujian Daily, December 5, 2024

23. Wu Qiong, Su Xiaohuan. Striving for Blue Skies! This Jiangsu Enterprise Was Praised by the Ministry of Ecology and Environment, Shanghai Observer

24. Kou Jiangze, Yao Xueqing. Major Transformative Changes in Water Ecological Environment Protection, Continuously Deepening the Battle for Clear Waters, People's Daily, March 18, 2024

25. Zhang Li. A Decade of Water Management Restores River and Lake Tranquility and Clear Waters, China Environment News, September 8, 2022

26. Liu Guihuan, Xie Jing, Wang Xiahui, Wen YihuI. Promoting the Realization of Water Ecological Product Value Through Basin Ecological Protection Compensation, China Environment News, May 23, 2022

27. Wu Qiong, Hong Ye. Shallow Lake Deep Governance, Singing the New Era "Beautiful Taihu", Xinhua Daily, January 26, 2025

28. Zhang Tengyang. The Story of Baiyangdian Ecological Restoration, People's Daily, May 27, 2022

29. Zhang Meng, Wang Ying, Chen Junting. Protecting the "Pearl" of Yunling Mountain and Drawing Lucid Waters and Lush Mountains—Records of Yunnan's High-Quality Development in Highland Lake Protection and Governance, People's Yangtze River News, August 24, 2024

30. Zhu Lei, Yang Yujie, Liu Quan. Protecting Erhai's Clear Waves and Drawing a Beautiful Picture of Clear Waters and Lush Mountains, Dali Daily, January 20, 2025

31. Guangming Daily Research Group. Human-Lake Coexistence, Reappearance of Five Hundred Li Dianchi Lake—Exploration and Practice of Dianchi Lake Protection, Governance, and Coordinated Economic and Social Development in Kunming, Yunnan, Guangming Daily, December 16, 2024

32. Zhu Lizhong. Building a Solid Foundation for Beautiful China, Economic Daily, May 25, 2024

33. Yang Xiufeng. China's Environmental Governance System and Capability for Solid Waste and Chemicals Have Been Significantly Enhanced, China Economic Net

34. Du Ying. A Project in Nanjing City Selected for the First Batch of Recommended Cases of China's "Waste-Free City" Pollution Reduction and Carbon Reduction Synergy, News of Jiangsu Provincial Committee of the Communist Party of China

35. Liu Yi, Dong Siyu, Liu Junguo. Reducing Plastics in the Ocean and Increasing Income for the People, People's Daily, November 26, 2023

36. The State Council Information Office. White Paper "Marine Eco-Environment Protection in China", 2024

37. Wang Libin, Kang Miao, Gao Jing, Chen Weiwei. Deeply Learning and Practicing the "Xiamen Practice" to Open a New Chapter for Beautiful China—Interviews with Officials from Three Ministries and Commissions and Main Officials of Xiamen City, Xinhua Net

38. Hu Jingyi, Li Xiaopan, Zhu Zhixiang. Zhejiang Establishes the Nation's First Assessment System for Collaborative Governance of Rivers Entering the Sea in Upstream and Downstream Areas, Zhejiang Daily, March 6, 2025

39. Shanghai Ocean Administration. Shanghai Writes a New Chapter in the Construction of a Modern Ocean City, China Natural Resources News, December 10, 2024

40. Xiao Heyong. Fujian Makes Efforts to Govern Marine Floating Garbage to Protect Beautiful Bays, Xinhua Net

41. Li Yue, Liang Bing. Haikou Becomes the Province's First Provincial-Level Beautiful Bay City in All Areas, Carving Marine Texture and Protecting the Blue Background, Haikou Daily, February 28, 2025

42. Ministry of Ecology and Environment. Annual Report on Prevention and Control of Noise Pollution in China, 2024

43. Ju Wentao. Yangtze River Delta Integration | Playing a Chess Game to Protect Blue Waters and Clear Skies, the "Green Concentric Circle" Is Growing Larger, The Paper

44. Ji Wenhui. "Integration of Multiple Plans" Draws a Beautiful China, Economic Daily, July 17, 2024

45. Nanjing Bureau of Planning and Natural Resources. Nanjing's Practice and Exploration in Promoting "Three Major Projects" and Deepening "Integration of Multiple Plans" Reform, Urban and Rural Planning, 2023 (S1)

46. Shi Jie. Case of Innovative Promotion of Diversified Transformation of Ecological Value in Mengshan County, Southern Natural Resources, 2024 (2)

47. Ministry of Natural Resources. National Ecological Protection and Restoration Bulletin (2024), 2024

48. Liu Siwen. Protecting Plateau Ecology and Safeguarding the Source of Rivers—The Vivid Example and Demonstration of Three-River-Source National Park, China Green Times, October 9, 2024

49. An Lu. Protecting Natural Sanctuaries and Enjoying the Homeland of National Treasures—Protection Upgrade and Development Enhancement of Giant Panda National Park, China Green Times, October 10, 2024

50. Wu Linxi, Chen Mo. Green Mountains Stay Green and Tigers and Leopards Return—A Record of the Third Anniversary of the Establishment of Northeast China Tiger and Leopard National Park, Jilin Daily, November 11, 2024

51. Li Tao. West Coast New District Coordinates the Promotion of Marine Ecological Protection and Restoration, Creating a Green and Sustainable Marine Ecological Environment, Ecological Sea Cultivation, and Human-Sea Harmony, Qingdao West Coast News, October 22, 2024

52. Chen Han'er. Adding and Subtracting, Reshaping the "Sea Forest", Fujian Daily, March 13, 2025

53. Li Ming, Jiang Tanglong, Lin Xiaoqin. Guangdong: The Time for Green and Beautiful Rise Is Now, Drawing a Chapter of Ecological Civilization, China Green Times, January 23, 2025

54. Ma Aiping. From Vast Wilderness to Dense Forests, Artificial Restoration Creates Saihanba's Ecological Miracle, Science and Technology Daily, December 7, 2023

55. CPC State Forestry and Grassland Administration Party Leadership Group. Striving to Write a New Chapter of the Three-North Shelterbelt Forest Program, People's Daily, June 5, 2024

56. Xiong Wei. Satellite Perspective on the Yellow River "Jiziwan" Critical Battle, Map, 2024 (3)

57. Dong Jun, Chu Hang, Hu Lu, et al. The Miracle of Taklamakan: Green Locks on Flowing Sand, Xinhua Daily Telegraph, December 30, 2024

58. Liu Xia, Teng Jipu. Chengdu: Creating a Practical Example of an Ecologically Livable Park City, Science and Technology Daily, March 13, 2025

59. Bai Fengzhe, Fang Ning, Yang Dandan, Liu Yun. Creating Livable and Business-Friendly Harmonious Environments, Farmers' Daily, December 30, 2024

60. Qin Jinxiang, Huang Jindan. "456" Model Jointly Draws a New Picture of Beautiful Rural Villages, People's Daily Online

61. Dong Chenlei, Cai Qin. Making Lucid Waters and Lush Mountains "Produce Gold and Silver" —Lishui Deepens the Reform of Ecological Product Value Realization Mechanism to Broaden the "Two Mountains" Transformation Channel, Lishui Daily, October 23, 2024

62. Li Yao. Turning Lucid Waters and Lush Mountains into "Monetary Gold", Yanqing Daily, March 4, 2025

63. Yan Hanjiang, Zhang Lel. Greater Khingan Range, Opening a New Path for Ecological Civilization Development, Heilongjiang Daily, February 17, 2025

64. Zhang Longfei, Luo Zhimin, Zhang Wei, Dong Han. Jiujiang's Practice of Combined Supply of Natural Resource Assets, Phoenix New Media

65. Yu Li, Ji Tiantian. Wenling Empowers High-Quality Development Through Comprehensive Land Remediation, Zhejiang Daily, March 18, 2025

66. Jiangsu Provincial Natural Resources Department. Zhangpu Town, Kunshan City, Jiangsu Province:" Three Jumps" to Achieve Urban-Rural Integration and All-Around Renewal, China Natural Resources News, September 1, 2024

67. Ouyang Yijia. Lucid Waters and Lush Mountains Can Produce Gold," Opening Up" Various Ways to Realize the Value of Ecological Products, People's Daily Online

68. Yang Lin. Accelerating the Improvement of Ecological Product Value Realization Mechanism, Guangming Daily, February 13, 2025

69. Ouyang Zhiyun. Promoting High-Level Protection and High-Quality Development of National Parks, People's Daily, December 6, 2024

70. The State Council Information Office. White Paper "China's Energy Transition", 2024

71. Liu Jin'nong, Zhou Yi. "Carbon Catchers" Escort the Promotion of Green Development, Workers' Daily, July 24, 2024

72. Yu Jiangyan. Xinjiang Hydrogen Energy Application "Accelerating", Xinjiang Daily, July 2, 2024

73. Xu Jinyou. The "Chain Reaction" Behind the "Pure Green Electricity Town" in Minning, Xinhua Daily Telegraph, March 26, 2025

74. Wang Hao. Data Tells the Story of the World's Largest Clean Energy Corridor (New Direction of Economy), People's Daily, May 15, 2024

75. Liu Jinghuan, Chen Jing. Plateau Green Computing Illuminates the Digital Future—One-Year Record of Green Computing Practice by China Mobile in Qinghai, March 27, 2025

76. Zhu Lina. Policy Support and Multi-regional Practice: Virtual Power Plants Move from Concept to Scale Application, China City News, March 17, 2025

77. Qi Hui. Modern Transportation Moves Towards Intelligence and Green Development, Economic Daily, September 2, 2024

78. Chen Mengzhu, Gao Ying. China's Railways Under a "Green" Lens, Vitality Over Thousands of Miles!, People's Railway, August 16, 2024

79. Han Wanli. Using Ecological Brushwork to Outline the Green Vision of a Strong Transportation Nation, Colorful Guizhou Net (www. gog. cn)

80. Han Xin. Expressways, Pursuing Green Development, People's Daily, November 15, 2024

81. Zhang Guangyan. Tianjin Port Creates a World-Class Smart Green Hub Port, Setting Sail for "New" Horizons, Bincheng Times, January 17, 2025

82. Chai Yajuan, Wang Juntao, Ge Zhenghan, Wu Yinglan, Tan Wei. China's "Zero-Carbon Community Sample" at the Climate Conference, South Plus

83. Wang Ke, Dou Hao, Zhang Tengyang. Green Consumption Becomes Young People's "Favorite", People's Daily, February 17, 2025

84. Li Deshangyu, Lu Taoran. Yili Group: From "Zero-Carbon Factory" to

Global Example, Leading the Industry's Sustainable Development, 21jingjI. com

85. Song Xiaona, Qin RuI. Pursuing Green and Thriving in Green—A Summary of Promoting Green Agricultural Development, Rural Work Newsletter, 2024 (17)

86. Wang Xin, Li Lin, Cheng Aihua, Nie Jiejie. Farmland Covered with "Blankets", Sugar Beets Growing in the "Air", Hubei Daily, March 28, 2025

87. Zuo Yonghua. Zhenfeng County: Exploring Green Development Models for Barren Mountains to Help Increase Residents' Income, Qianxinan Daily, December 7, 2024

88. Chen Lili. Intime Department Store Reduces Emissions by 304,000 Tons in Fiscal Year 2024, 40 Stores Rated as Green Shopping Malls, TideNews

89. Jiang Hongqiang, Zhang Wei, Cheng XI. Deepening Green Technology Innovation, Promoting the Development of New Quality Productive Forces, China Environment News, March 14, 2024

90. Yang Yuhua, Wang Fei, Wu Huijun. Chasing Light and Pursuing Innovation—The Growth Story of Photovoltaic Unicorn Huasun Energy, Xinhua Net

91. Ministry of Ecology and Environment. National Carbon Market Development Report (2024), 2024

92. CPC Nanjing Municipal Committee Reform Office, Gaochun District Committee Reform Office. Gaochun Explores New Mechanisms for Agricultural Carbon Sink Development and Trading, Nanjing Daily, June 26, 2024

93. Wu Qiuyu. Green Finance Helps High-Quality Economic and Social Development, People's Daily, October 3, 2024

94. Research Bureau of the People's Bank of China Task Force. Progress and Experience of Green Finance Reform and Innovation Pilot Zones, China Finance, 2023 (6)

95. Zhou Wei. Grasping the Internal Logic of Comprehensive Green Transformation from Multiple Dimensions, Economic Daily, March 12, 2025

96. Zhang Dailei, Zhang Xiaoru. Not Letting Down Green Mountains or People—China's Momentum in Building a Clean and Beautiful World,

Xinhua Net

97. Xinhua News Agency Reporters. Overview: Examining Africa's Progress and Challenges in Combating Desertification from the Perspective of the "Green Great Wall", Xinhua Net

98. Zou Song. Green Cooperation Helps South Africa Accelerate Energy Transition, Construction Times, December 14, 2023

99. Huang Peizhao. Chinese Enterprises Actively Participate in Egypt's Green Project Construction, People's Daily, October 18, 2024

100. Li Jiabao. China-Middle East Energy Cooperation Pursues "New" and "Green", People's Daily Overseas Edition, January 25, 2025

101. Xinhua News Agency Reporters. The "Handshake" Between China and Africa's Largest Freshwater Lake, Xinhua Net

102. Chen Si. Fighting the Green Development Battle and Building a Beautiful Western Gateway to the Capital—Interview with Yu Huafeng, Secretary of Mentougou District Committee, Front, 2024 (11)

103. Wang Yuehua, Wang Linwel. Using Green as the Brush and Ecology as the Ink to Draw a Bright "Background Color", Huangpu News, December 27, 2024

104. Feng Xuan. With "Green" as the Foundation, Moving Towards "Beauty" —Interpreting the Keyword "Beautiful Ningbo", Ningbo Daily, October 28, 2024

105. Hui Yulan. "Beautiful Suzhou" Cultivates New Advantages of Lucid Waters and Lush Mountains, Suzhou Daily, December 22, 2024

106. Lu Zhijia. Comprehensive Treatment of Nanming River in Guiyang," Ecological Pain Points" Transform into Beautiful Changes, Xinhua Net

107. Jiang Shiliang, Li Jingcheng. Guiyang: Establishing the City on Ecology and Playing a Green and Beautiful Movement, Guizhou Pictorial, 2024 (9)

108. Gu Qianjiang, Wang Chunyu, Yang Siqi, Liu Heyao. Ice and Snow Are Also Invaluable Assets, Outlook, 2025 (12)

109. Li Zicheng. Observing How Ice and Snow Empower Green Development from the Harbin Asian Winter Games, China Environment Network

110. Guangming Daily Joint Research Group. Ice and Snow Economy with

"Hot" Unlimited Power—Research and Reflection Based on the Development Status of Heilongjiang Province's Ice and Snow Economy, Guangming Daily, February 6, 2025

111. Wu Shuai. Increasing Development's "Gold Content" through Ecological "Green Content" Qingdao Daily, April 8, 2025

112. Feng Manlou, Xiao Lingling. Qingdao High-tech Zone: Basically Completed "Carbon Peak" Goal and Advanced Planning for "Carbon Neutrality", qdcaijing. com

113. Liu Cheng. Qingdao Constructs Green Development System, Economic Daily, January 15, 2025

114. Jin Wenbing, Huang ShishI. Wuhan Explores New Paths for Ecological Priority and Green Development, Wuhan Evening News, November 4, 2024

115. Tao Lei, Yang Guangming, Liu Yang. Wuhan: Polishing the International Wetland City Brand through High-Quality Protection, China Green Times, November 1, 2024

116. Jin Wenbing. Turning "Green" into Gold: Wuhan Strives to Write a Beautiful Chapter of Harmony Between Humans and Nature, Changjiang Daily, January 5, 2025

Afterwords

Adhering to the path of ecological priority and green development is an inevitable requirement for establishing a new development stage, implementing new development concepts, and building a new development pattern. Under the guidance of Xi Jinping's Thought on Ecological Civilization, all regions are continuously expanding China's green territory through practical actions to expand, develop, and protect greenery. This not only builds an ecological barrier for the sustainable development of the Chinese nation but also allows billions of people to truly experience the happiness of bluer skies, greener mountains, and clearer waters.

The blueprint for green development has been drawn. The Outline of the 14th Five-Year Plan (2021-2025) for National Economic and Social Development and Vision 2035 of the People's Republic of China proposes that by 2035, China will basically realize socialist modernization. This includes broadly forming green production and lifestyle patterns, achieving a steady decline in carbon emissions after reaching peak carbon, fundamentally improving the ecological environment, and basically realizing the goal of building a Beautiful China. The "Opinions of the CPC Central Committee and the State Council on Accelerating the Comprehensive Green Transformation of Economic and Social Development" further clarifies the implementation path for green development. It firmly follows the path of ecological priority, economical and intensive use of resources, and high-quality green and low-carbon development. Using carbon peaking and carbon neutrality work as the lead, it coordinates efforts to reduce carbon, decrease pollution, expand greenery, and promote growth. It deepens ecological civilization system reform, improves green and low-carbon development mechanisms, accelerates the comprehensive green transformation of economic and social development, forms spatial patterns, industrial structures, production methods, and lifestyles that conserve resources and protect the environment, comprehensively advances the building of a Beautiful China, and accelerates the promotion of a modern society where humans and nature coexist harmoniously.

The power of thought knows no bounds, and the tree of truth remains evergreen. Xi Jinping's Thought on Ecological Civilization, with the concept that "lucid waters and lush mountains are invaluable assets" as an important component, has brought transformative practices to the eastern land and achieved breakthrough progress and landmark achievements that benefit the world. China respects, adapts to, and protects nature, working with the world to build a community of life on Earth through green development. In the new era and new journey of Chinese-style modernization, China unswervingly follows the path of green, low-carbon, and sustainable development. Chinese wisdom, responsibility, solutions, and actions promote a world moving toward green development modernization, which will make new and greater contributions to protecting our Earth home.

Also, the Silk Road International Think Tank is firmly fulfilling the mission and responsibility of a new type of think tank, maintaining a vigorous "progressive tense", continuously recording, researching, and disseminating China's good cases, experiences, and models of green development, providing more timely, targeted, and high-quality think tank outcomes for comprehensively promoting the construction of a Beautiful China and building a clean and beautiful world.

It should be noted that in the compilation process of this book, we have referenced and drawn on the research and practical achievements, materials, and data of some institutions and scholars. The Editorial Committee has noted these in the References and hereby expresses sincere gratitude. We invite copyright owners to contact the Editorial Committee of this book (email: 158950711 @ qq. com) so that we can express our thanks and provide modest remuneration. If there is any disputed content, relevant persons are encouraged to contact us promptly, and adjustments will be made in the next edition of the book. The cover photo was taken by Cao Zhen, Silk Road Interncotional Think Tank.

Due to time constraints and the limited knowledge of the compilers, errors and oversights in this book are inevitable. We hope readers will provide timely feedback. We are also very willing to engage in extensive and in-depth exchanges, discussions, and cooperation with readers on various topics of green development.

Refer to QR code

China's green development: regulatory and policy planing